DESIGN BEFORE DISASTER

I0103496

DESIGN BEFORE DISASTER

JAPAN'S CULTURE OF PREPAREDNESS

MIHO MAZEREEUW

University of Virginia Press
CHARLOTTESVILLE AND LONDON

The University of Virginia Press is situated on the traditional lands of the Monacan Nation, and the Commonwealth of Virginia was and is home to many other Indigenous people. We pay our respect to all of them, past and present. We also honor the enslaved African and African American people who built the University of Virginia, and we recognize their descendants. We commit to fostering voices from these communities through our publications and to deepening our collective understanding of their histories and contributions.

University of Virginia Press
© 2025 by the Rector and Visitors of the University of Virginia
All rights reserved
Printed in the United States of America on acid-free paper

First published 2025

9 8 7 6 5 4 3 2 1

LIBRARY OF CONGRESS CATALOGING-IN-PUBLICATION DATA
Names: Mazereeuw, Miho, author.
Title: Design before disaster : Japan's culture of preparedness / Miho Mazereeuw.
Description: Charlottesville : University of Virginia Press, 2024. | Includes bibliographical references and index.
Identifiers: LCCN 2023043111 (print) | LCCN 2023043112 (ebook) | ISBN 9780813950914 (hardcover) |
    ISBN 9780813950921 (paperback) | ISBN 9780813950938 (ebook)
Subjects: LCSH: Emergency management—Japan.
Classification: LCC HV551.5.J3 M39 2024 (print) | LCC HV551.5.J3 (ebook) | DDC 363.340952—dc23/eng/20240124
LC record available at https://lccn.loc.gov/2023043111
LC ebook record available at https://lccn.loc.gov/2023043112

Furthermore:
a program of the J.M. Kaplan Fund

Publication of this volume was assisted by a grant from Furthermore: a program of the J. M. Kaplan Fund.

サントリー文化財団 SUNTORY FOUNDATION

Publication of this volume was assisted by a grant from the Suntory Foundation.

Illustrations not otherwise credited are by Larisa Ovalles and Miho Mazereeuw with support from students listed in the preface.

Cover art: Kaze-no-Sato Park, designed with residents to include numerous embedded *bōsai* functions.
(Larisa Ovalles and Miho Mazereeuw)
Cover design: Cecilia Sorochin

TO MY FAMILY

CONTENTS

PREFACE

Near the end of 1994, my parents, Yoshiko Taki-Mazereeuw and Jacob Mazereeuw, moved to Kobe, Japan. By a stroke of luck, they were not in the city when the earthquake hit on January 17, 1995, but my father's workplace was destroyed, and they participated in the city's long recovery. This book stems from their knowledge, loving support, and everything they have taught me in life. Since 1995 they have continued to collect newspaper clippings for me. My mother has patiently helped me digest complex Japanese texts and visited many parks and reconstruction sites in Kobe. Her passion for history and habit of devouring nonfiction have been an inspiration. Both of my parents also traveled to the Tohoku region with me, providing encouragement and support. Their appreciation for Japanese antiques, including *ukiyo-e,* undoubtedly influenced the drawings in this book. My father, a marine engineer who sailed for several years, often noted that on a ship, you always prepare for the worst-case scenario. You make sure that every part of the ship is designed to classification rules and International Maritime Organization (IMO) regulations, so that equipment and infrastructure are in place, and that everyone (including the guests) is prepared—especially to respect the ocean and its power. In a similar manner, this book aims to share the design of space and infrastructure in Japan and to describe how communities prepare for catastrophic events and care for this planet. It reflects more than twenty-five years of research, fieldwork, and the stories and efforts of many survivors.

There are so many people whom I would like to thank, starting with my parents, as mentioned above. Pierre Belanger, who raises the bar on any project and encourages a steadfast commitment to research excellence, provided endless support. My daughter, Nina Mazereeuw, has traveled with me to Tohoku since she was three, bringing happiness to sorrow-filled surroundings. She encouraged me, teased me, and was by my side, especially during the last years of finishing this book during the height of the pandemic. I couldn't have completed this without her humor and love. I am inspired every day by her strength and tenacity as she tackles her own ambitious goals.

This book could not have been written without the tireless work of Saeko Nomura Baird, Larisa Ovalles, Lizzie Yarina, and Endo Kenya, who all traveled with me on several research trips. Saeko helped me find cases and meticulously researched the complex policy and funding structures of projects, contributing throughout all the years of the project. Her enthusiasm for the book kept me going and her research prowess continues to amaze me. Larisa led the beautiful artistry of all the drawings, most of which she drew herself, and guided student illustrations. Even the cover design stems from Larisa's Midas touch of aesthetic acuity. Lizzie furthered the fieldwork, the interviews, the early stages of writing, and the book's organization. Kenya was instrumental in finding landscape and recovery projects and conducting fieldwork and interviews. He also performed an exhaustive, comprehensive fact-check. Kenya and Saeko are now working on the Japanese edition of this book. Claudia Bode helped with an early review of the book. Taketani Maya led the research on many of the schools and conducted pivotal fieldwork and interviews. Aditya Barve provided the critical outside eye on both drawings and texts, while he, David Moses, Eakapob Huangthanapan, Pimpakarn Rattanathumawat, and Mayank Ojha kept advancing the Urban Risk Lab. I've been fortunate to work with numerous talented student researchers on the drawings and research: Jon Brearley, Chen Chu, Takahashi Ryosuke, Ichikura Ryuhei, Helena Hang Rong, Evellyn Tan, Lynced Torres, and Jie Zhang. This research contributes to the Urban Risk Lab and is also inspired by all its incredible members over the years.

I thank Hashim Sarkis and Gary Hildebrand, who taught me in my formative years, for believing in me and this topic back in 2002, when the design professions were still questioning the relevance of this subject. James Wescoat, to whom I owe much of the literature, is a true academic—and the person who advised me to write the book. Meejin Yoon is a role model and leader without whom I could not have survived my early years at MIT. Larry Vale and Anne Sprin supplied invaluable advice on navigating the tenure process and on writing and publishing. I am indebted to Hiraoka Yoshihiro, who led us through many years of the 2011 tsunami recovery. Starting in May 2011, following his red Volkswagen Golf through the debris transformed my life as he modeled generosity and care in all our exchanges with communities. I thank Murakami Akinobu for all of the discussions, sharing his depth of knowledge and connections to academics in Japan; Rajib Shaw, for guidance and valuable suggestions; and Robert Fenton, who provides us with wisdom and support in putting this research into practice within the United States. Rich Serino, the senior advisor to the Urban Risk Lab, teaches us everything from emergency management and ways to galvanize policy change to how to lead with modesty, kindness, and respect for every individual.

I am grateful for the support of Atsuko Fish, who inspired the Tohoku fieldwork and led the creation of the Fish Foundation and Japan Disaster Relief Fund in Boston (JDRFB) in 2011. Thanks to Richard Samuels for our long conversations, for advice on publishing in both the United States and Japan, and for Hayashi-ULVAC MISTI Japan support. The MIT HASS Grant, Harvard GSD Arthur W. Wheelwright Travelling Fellowship, the Furthermore Grant by the J. M. Kaplan Fund, and Suntory Foundation's Support for Overseas Publication Grant provided incredible financial support required for the research and publishing of this book.

I am indebted to Boyd Zenner for her encouragement and for accepting this project for the University of Virginia Press. I hold in my heart deepest sorrow for our collective loss in her passing and am so grateful to have had the opportunity to work with her. Thank you to Mark Mones and Ellen Satrom for their patience and for bringing the book to fruition! Lisa Sone Twaronite, thank you for your editorial advice on early drafts. Lucy McKeon, thank you for helping me shorten and edit the text. Thanks to Laura Reed-Morrisson for her fastidious care in the copyediting process and her warm, calm disposition during a stressful time.

And my immense gratitude to the residents of Kobe, Kumamoto, and the Tohoku region for their generosity in sharing their wisdom and experiences with us. Their resilience and perseverance inspired this book.

ABBREVIATIONS

JAPANESE ORGANIZATIONS

CAO   Cabinet Office, Government of Japan 内閣府 https://www.cao.go.jp
           /index-e.html

DMAT   Disaster Medical Assistance Team 災害派遣医療チーム https://www
           .dmat.jp/

FDMA   Fire and Disaster Management Agency 総務省消防庁 https://www.fdma
           .go.jp/en/post1.html

JMA   Japan Meteorological Agency 気象庁 https://www.jma.go.jp/jma/indexe
           .html

JPA   Japan Prefabricated Construction Suppliers and Manufacturers Associa-
           tion 一般社団法人プレハブ建築協会 https://www.purekyo.or.jp/

JR   Japan Railways 日本旅客鉄道株式会社 https://www.jreast.co.jp/multi
           /en/

MAFF   Ministry of Agriculture, Forestry and Fisheries 農林水産省 https://www
           .maff.go.jp/e/

MHLW   Ministry of Health, Labor and Welfare 厚生労働省 https://www.mhlw
           .go.jp/english/

MIC   Ministry of Internal Affairs and Communications 総務省 https://www
           .soumu.go.jp/english/index.html

MLIT   Ministry of Land, Infrastructure, Transport and Tourism 国土交通省
           https://www.mlit.go.jp/index_e.html

MOE   Ministry of the Environment 環境省 https://www.env.go.jp/en/

NHK   Japan Broadcasting Corporation https://www.nhk.or.jp/

NILIM   National Institute for Land and Infrastructure Management 国土交通省
国土技術政策総合研究所 http://www.nilim.go.jp/english/eindex.htm

SDF   Japan Self-Defense Force 自衛隊 https://www.mod.go.jp/gsdf/english
/index.html

TMG   Tokyo Metropolitan Government 東京都 https://www.metro.tokyo.lg.jp
/english/index.html

TECHNICAL TERMS

L1   Level 1 tsunami: a relatively common tsunami, caused by a magnitude 8.0
or lower earthquake

L2   Level 2 tsunami: a tsunami that occurs once every five hundred to one
thousand years, caused by a magnitude 9.0 or above earthquake

NGO   nongovernmental organization 非政府組織

NPO   nonprofit organization 非営利団体

TEB   tsunami evacuation buildings 津波避難ビル

TET   tsunami evacuation towers 津波避難タワー

TP   Tokyo Peil 東京湾中等潮位: a measurement that uses the median sea
level of Tokyo Bay as the zero-meter reference surface

Two-Two
Rule   method of defining high-risk zones by determining areas susceptible to
more than two meters of water from a L2 tsunami

DESIGN BEFORE DISASTER

INTRODUCTION

Every year, for a week or so in April in Japan, cherry trees bloom and people flock to parks to view the blossoms. Friends and families gather on blankets and benches for the iconic tradition of *hanami,* or cherry-blossom viewing, to eat, drink, and revel under the ephemeral pink canopies. However, this tradition is more than just a celebration of the changing seasons: it arose out of a need for disaster mitigation. During the winter, Japan's riverbanks soften through the freeze-thaw cycle, and they risk erosion from spring floods. But the weight of many bodies and footsteps can help compact a riverbank, so attracting people to the cherry trees planted along the riverside helps create a man-made solidity, supporting the bank's survival for another annual cycle.[1] This is but one example of many in which traditions were formed with potential natural disasters in mind. In Japan, even a spring picnic can be disaster reduction in disguise. Japanese society has developed in lockstep with the persistent risks posed by the earth, skies, rivers, and seas.

BŌSAI CULTURE

Japan's long history of negotiating and responding to disasters steeped its citizens in a culture of preparedness known as *bōsai* 防災, literally translated as "disaster prevention." Disaster researchers understand, of course, that it is impossible to entirely prevent a disaster from occurring, but the term *bōsai* refers to a host of mitigation, management, and preparedness activities and is commonly used in Japan.

A "culture of preparedness" is increasingly recognized as integral to disaster-related plans across the globe, as exemplified by the 2005 UN Hyogo Framework for Action, the 2015 UN Sendai Framework for Disaster Risk Reduction, and inclusion in the US Federal Emergency Management Agency's (FEMA) 2018–22 Strategic Goals, under the recommendation "Build a Culture of Preparedness." Similar language has begun to appear in state and local plans as well. Although the inclusion of such language is significant, directives remain generalized in their guidance. Japan's culture of preparedness, manifested in everyday spaces and traditions, predates any state-led programs—and yet experts such as Kawata Yoshiaki warn that it is waning and in need of revival.[2] This book adopts the term *bōsai culture* to describe the knowledge and techniques developed to reduce the impact of disasters, the structure of social and educational systems to pass them on, and ways of integrating them holistically into daily life. The goal is for individuals beyond Japan to espouse bōsai culture so that its practices become part of society's collective consciousness.

As early as 1212, the poet Kamo no Chōmei wrote in his "Tale of the Ten-Foot-Square Hut" that "the current of the flowing river does not cease, and yet the water is not the same water as before. The foam that floats on stagnant pools, now vanishing, now forming, never stays the same for long. So, too, it is with the people and dwellings of the world."[3] Buddhism teaches impermanence and the evanescence of all things. Embracing the temporal, adapting to constant change, bringing people together to move, to repair, to exist in symbiosis with nature: these ideas are at the core of bōsai culture.

THE *WAJŪ*

Villages living with water created a multiscalar system of "anticipatory design"—a framework named by and detailed in this book. A quintessential historical example is the *wajū* (meaning "inside the circle"). Built in the Edo era by farmers, a wajū is a ringed embankment surrounding settlements and agricultural land; it is based on vernacular knowledge of flood-prone areas. Eighty-two wajū stood in the Nōbi Plain around the basins of the Kiso Three Rivers. Today, only a few large wajū remain, owing to the advancement of modern flood controls introduced by Johannis de Rijke, a Dutch civil engineer, during the Meiji era. Farmers, who had neither political nor economic power, built wajū to protect their fields and houses.[4] As they shared and managed the temporal dynamics of the basin with neighbors and adjacent villages, collaboration and coordination were critical in protecting themselves from, and living with, water.[5]

Built in 1653 within the fertile lands of the river's dendritic drainage pattern, Takasu Wajū stands at zero meters above sea level within large rice fields.[6] Covering a 4,260-hectare area, it is one of the most famous remaining wajū in Ōgaki and has a nested system of small wajū within a large one. Many small wajū are connected to natural embankments to both protect the farmland and community and to release water back to the river through a *toimon* (drain gate), carefully mediated through topography and small channels.

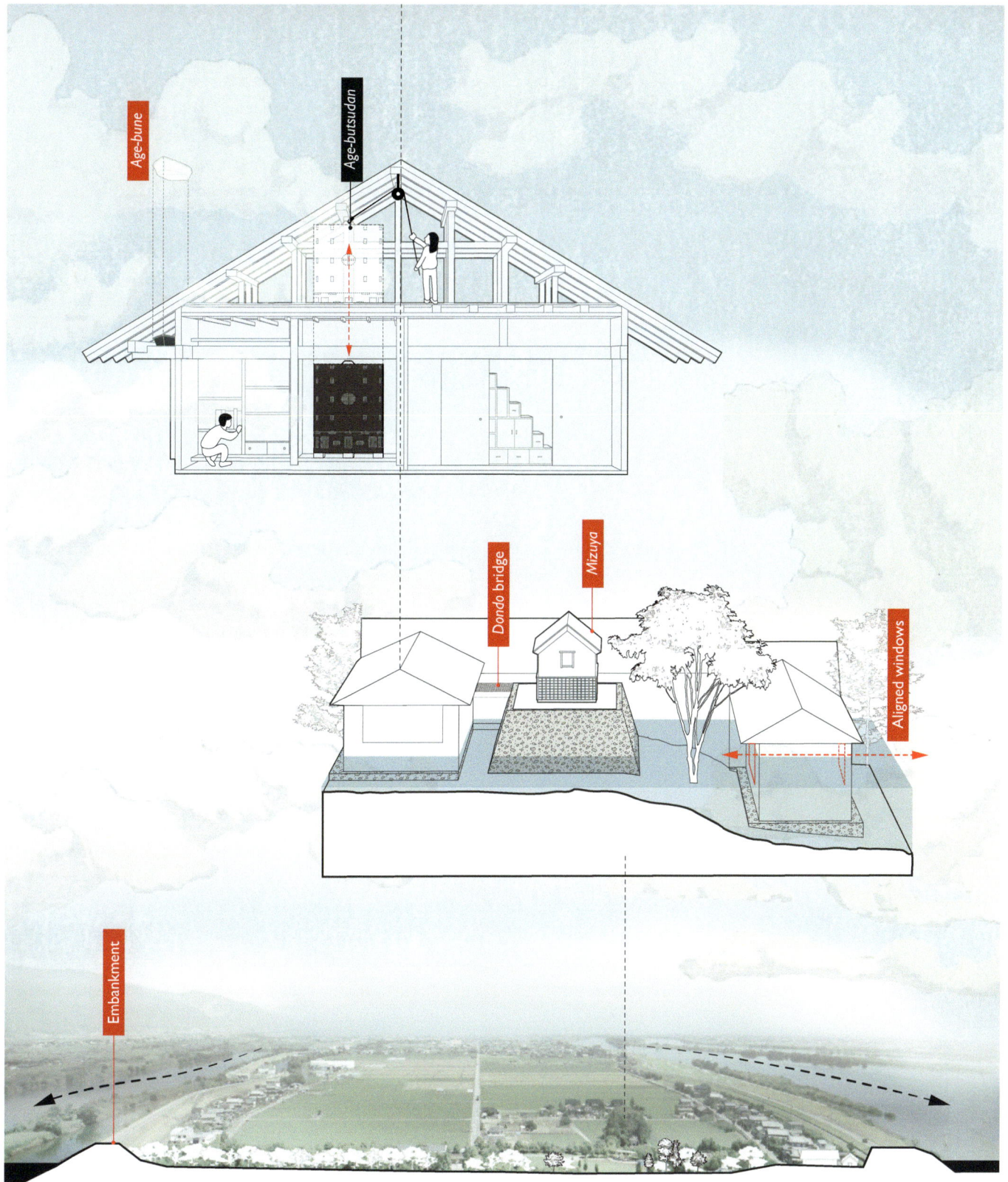

Figure 1. The *wajū:* multiscalar strategies for living with water.

The collective arrangement of buildings, all the way down to the scale of the furniture, amplified the effectiveness of this nested bōsai system. Homes were built on raised ground or on stone walls around fifty centimeters high. A centrally located *mizuya* (water house) was a grain warehouse on the same property, built up to eight meters above the ground, though more commonly about two to three meters.[7] Mizuya were built inside wajū to protect property and lives from flooding; they became evacuation shelters during floods. In them, residents stored emergency food, such as rice, miso, and soy sauce, as well as family treasures, and they lived temporarily in the structures until the water receded. Mizuya and the main houses were usually connected with a covered corridor—an evacuation path called a *dondo* bridge.[8] The cluster of houses was arranged so that the mizuya would not block daylight or ventilation to the main houses but would protect them from the cold, dry winter winds. Trees were planted as windbreaks, and their roots supported the structure of the embankments and broke the speed of the floodwaters.[9] Families who could not afford a mizuya climbed up to attics, nearby embankments, or community high grounds called *jomeidan* (life rescue platforms),[10] or they went to a *jomeiboku*—a large tree on the raised property of shrines—to be rescued.[11]

The main residences featured other anticipatory design elements at different scales. Large windows were arranged at the same location and same low height on both the north and south sides of the building so that a flood could pass through the house and then drain more quickly. A boat stored under the eaves or ceiling of the house, enabling quick access for rescuing people, was called *age-bune. Age-dana* were raised shelves under transom windows that allowed goods to be stored during the rainy season—from June to October. The most distinctive feature was the treatment of Buddhist family altars, which are normally located in the family room or main bedroom in order for Japanese families to offer incense and prayers to their ancestors. The *age-butsudan* had an elaborate pulley system for hoisting the family altar to the attic during floods.[12]

Wajū incorporated other aspects of religion and memorials in their numerous small stone monuments and miniature shrines. At points where embankments frequently collapsed, the wajū residents built small shrines to guardian deities, which served to warn future generations about hazardous locations. Even today, many stone monuments and bōsai storage elements remain on the embankments.[13] The constant presence of water reminded people that its movement could not always be controlled by human interventions, such as levees; instead of fighting nature, they lived with it, using precautionary warnings and contingency plans.

The wajū represented not only the circular shape of the embankment but also the people working together in the social structure of the flood management community. Villages and neighborhoods created systems among themselves for managing, mowing, and repairing the embankments and regularly clearing the channels of silt to reduce flooding. Contingency plans included frequent evacuation drills and communication strategies, as well as a coordinated system for recovery if a flood damaged a neighboring village. In this way, residents strengthened social and physical infrastructure within the whole watershed.[14] Japanese bōsai culture, expressed in the wajū, connects social infrastructures with the nested design of landscape, villages, housing clusters, homes, and even furniture.

DESIGN BEFORE DISASTER: ANTICIPATING HAZARDS AND BEING PROACTIVE

Through a study of disasters in Japan and their aftermath, this book introduces the importance of spatial design and aims to galvanize designers and others to anticipate and prepare for disasters, across time and across scales. By sharing methods, policies, and projects, this book suggests a framework for anticipatory design through considerations of social/spatial integration, top-down/bottom-up initiatives, everyday/disaster uses, ecology/engineering cohesion, and the disaster timeline. Although focused on Japan, the book is intended for the rest of the world—perhaps especially for countries with fewer resources or those that elect to apply public funds toward other objectives. The anticipatory design framework embodies a form of resilience that is not static but represents a process of change, empowering communities to prepare for calamity through their everyday activities and proposing ways forward, together, through uncertain futures.

The heart of *Design Before Disaster* is a series of case studies that draw out the role of space in elements of Japan's disaster-prepared built environments, articulating how the anticipatory design principle was foregrounded or could be improved upon. Each typology has been developed within a specific historical, social, cultural, and political context, illustrated by detailed contextual descriptions within the chapters. Analyses of the cases show not only what has been successful but also what has been less effective—or even detrimental. Japan's deep history of planning for disasters offers many examples of all of these.

The projects presented in this book are not intended as replicable prototypes that can simply be copied and pasted into other contexts. Even within Japan, attempts to impose cookie-cutter "solutions" have proved problematic: such top-down models can lack local engagement and specificity as well as spatial diversity in relation to the people and communities for which they are intended. Without engaging with designers and communities on the ground, progressive programs for disaster preparedness usually fall far short of their full potential. A Japanese proverb from the Kamakura era advises, "Gou ni itte wa gou ni shitagae" (When you go into the village, follow the villagers). Once one enters a place, one should adapt to its customs. This phrase is most commonly used to encourage respectful behavior, but it is an essential design principle to respect the genius loci of unique locations.

Figure 2 (*next page*). Map of projects explored in this book.

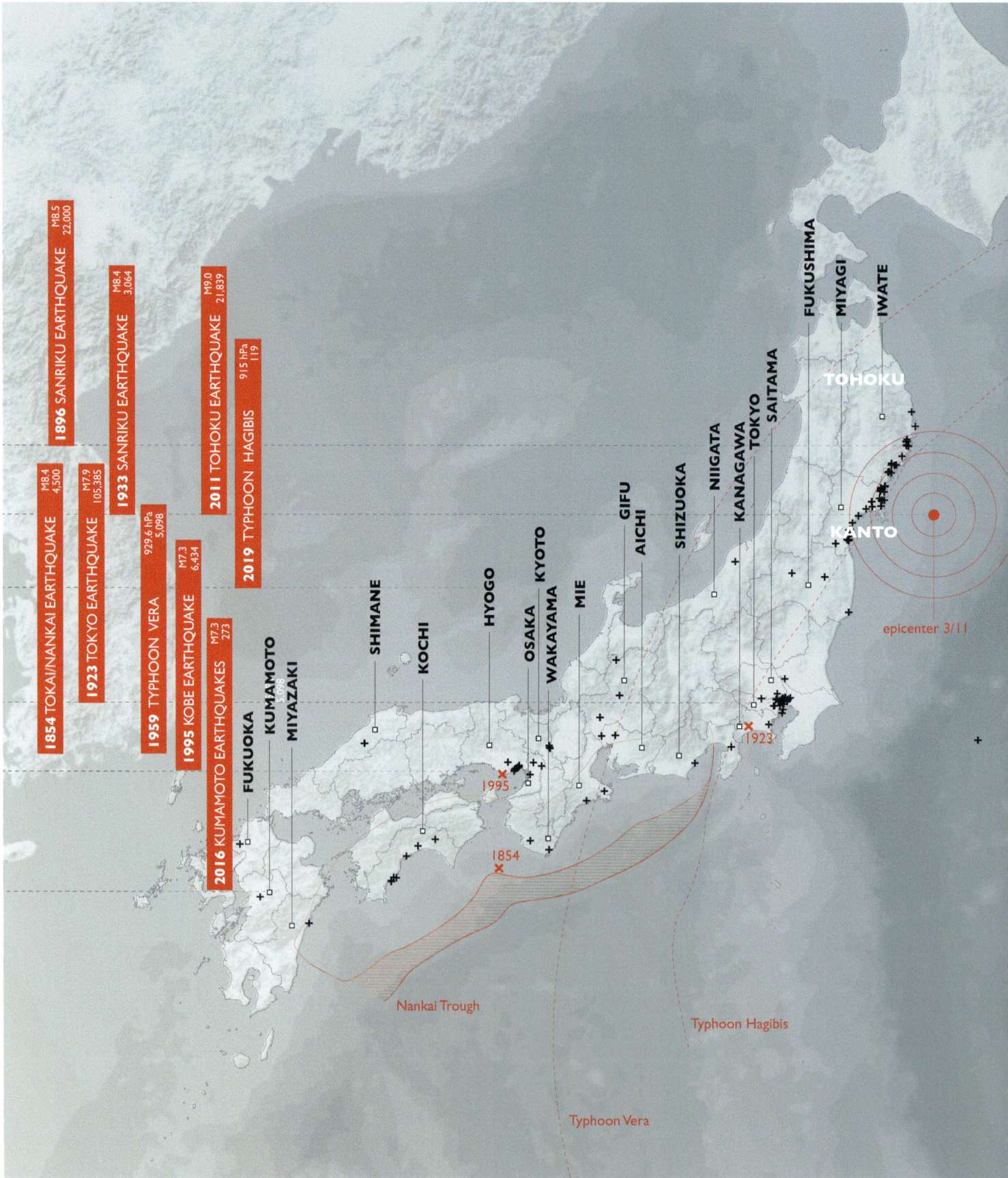

1896 SANRIKU EARTHQUAKE — M8.5 / 22,000

1933 SANRIKU EARTHQUAKE — M8.4 / 3,064

2011 TOHOKU EARTHQUAKE — M9.0 / 21,839

2019 TYPHOON HAGIBIS — 915 hPa / 119

1854 TOKAI/NANKAI EARTHQUAKE — M8.4 / 4,500

1923 TOKYO EARTHQUAKE — M7.9 / 105,385

1959 TYPHOON VERA — 929.6 hPa / 5,098

1995 KOBE EARTHQUAKE — M7.3 / 6,434

2016 KUMAMOTO EARTHQUAKES — M7.3 / 273

FUKUOKA

KUMAMOTO

MIYAZAKI

SHIMANE

KOCHI

HYOGO

OSAKA

KYOTO

WAKAYAMA

MIE

AICHI

GIFU

SHIZUOKA

NIIGATA

KANAGAWA

TOKYO

SAITAMA

FUKUSHIMA

MIYAGI

IWATE

TOHOKU

KANTO

epicenter 3/11

× 1923

× 1995

× 1854

Nankai Trough

Typhoon Hagibis

Typhoon Vera

IWATE	**Kamaishi**	Senjuin Temple • Kamaishi Tsunami Evacuation Network • Zenyuseki Project • Greenbelt Evacuation Path • Horaikan Hotel Kizuna no michi • Kamaishi Breakwater • Jorakuji Temple and Unosumai Shrine • Unosumai Elementary School and Kamaishi Higashi Middle School • Community-Care temporary housing • Unosumai Bosai Center	**Rikuzen-takata**	Rikuzentakata Reconstruction • NPO Riku Cafe • Shotokuji Temple • Tapic 45 and Takata Matsubara Museum/Park
			Miyako	Taro Seawall and Urban Planning • Aneyoshi Tablet
			Ofunato	Ibasho House • Okirai Elementary School
			Otsuchi	Collabo-School
MIYAGI	**Ishinomaki**	Okawa Elementary School • Ogatsu School Michi-no-eki Jobon-no-Sato • Ogatsu Reconstruction	**Sendai Iwanuma**	Kaigan Koen Boken Hiroba • Morino Project Millennium Hope Hills • Tamaura-nishi Housing
	Kesennuma	Inawashiro Hospital • Hotel Boyo • Naiwan Mukaeru Seawall • Moune Dai-ni Relocation • Minamimachi Murasaki Market • Shishiori School	**Shichiga-hama Onagawa Watari Yamamoto**	Shichigahama Reconstruction • Shobutahama Public Housing • Onagawa Reconstruction Watari Green Belt • Arahama Middle School Yamashita Middle School • Yamashita Dai-ni Elementary School • Yamamoto Reconstruction • Fumonji Temple
	Minami-sanriku	Kaminoyama Hachimangu Shrine • Hotel Kanyo • Nagashizuso Ryokan • Shizugawa Evacuation Network • Isuzu Shrine • Mishima Shrine • Yoriki Relocation • Utatsu Middle School		
FUKUSHIMA	**Aizu-Waka matsu**	Miharumachi Wooden Recovery Housing • Aizu-Matsunaga Danchi • Itakura Wooden Panel System		
	Iwaki	AEON Mall Iwaki Onahama		
SAITAMA	**Kasukabe**	The Metropolitan Discharge Channel		
TOKYO	**Bunkyo Chiyoda Chuo**	Tokyo Dome City Mitsubishi Estate and Daimaruyu • The Imperial Hotel • Dojunkai	**Minato Nakano Ota Setagaya**	Toranomon Hills Complex Nakano-Shiki-no-Mori Park Haneda Airport Futakotamagawa Park
	Edogawa	Super Levee • Tokyo Rinkai Park • Matsue Elementry School	**Shinagawa Suginami Sumida**	Shinagawa Pocket Park Network Suginami Dai-ju Elementary School Narihira Rain Water Tank, Rojison • Sumo Arena • Tokyo Skytree • Shirahige Higashi Apartment • Fujinoki-san-chi
	Itabashi Koto	Itabashi Evacuation Path • Kiyosumi Garden • Motomachi Park		
KANAGAWA	**Kawasaki Kamakura**	Higashi-ogishima Park Kamakura Central Park	**Takatsu**	Ecological Learning at the 16 Elementary Schools in Takatsu
SHIZUOKA	**Fukuroi**	Inochi Yama	**Yoshida**	Pedestrian Bridge Tsunami Platform
AICHI	**Nagoya**	Shikemichi Road and Dozou Zukuri		
GIFU	**Ono**	Palette Pier Ono	**Takasu Shirakawa**	Waju Shirakawa-go
MIE	**Taiki Minamiise**	Nishiki Towers Fire Station and Museum Minamiise Preemptive Public Facility Relocation		
KYOTO	**Kyoto**	Higashiyama Fire Fighting Project • Horikawa River • Kyoto Imperial Palace		
OSAKA	**Sakai Toyonaka**	Sakai Senboku National Logistics • Hattori Ryokuchi Park	**Daito**	Fukakita Ryokuchi Park
WAKAYAMA	**Kushimoto**	Kushimoto Preemptive Public Relocation • Wakayama East Fishermen's Association • Floating tsunami shelters		
HYOGO	**Chuo**	Rokkomichi North & South Park • Matsumoto Stream • Oji Zoo and Park • Minatogawa Park • Kamisawa Pocket Parks • Kaze-no-sato Park • HAT Kobe Fureai Public Housing	**Mano Nada Nagata Miki**	Mano Machizukuri Kinmokusei Street Joint Housing Project Mikura 5 Housing Miki Sogo Bosaikoen
KOCHI	**Suzaki Kochi**	Suzaki City Hall Tsunami Evacuation Stairs Kokatsu Project	**Kuroshio**	Saga District TET • Okata Akatsuki-Kan • Tosa Seinan Park Observation Deck • We Can Project
SHIMANE	**Misato**	Misato Preemptive Group Relocation Planning		
FUKUOKA	**Fukutsu**	Kamisaigo River Flood Management		
KUMAMOTO	**Kumamoto**	Parks in Kumamoto		
MIYAZAKI	**Hyuga**	Hyuga Tsunami Evacuation Stairs		
NATIONAL		Tsunami-hi • O-Jizo-san • Stramps• Bosai Living Zones • Mokumitsu Districts • NIGECHIZU • Cliff Relocation Project • Bosai Collective Relocation Project • Compact City Projects • Iza! Kaeru Caravan! • JPA • Minashikasetsu		

In this way, the lessons from these detailed cases model a spatial practice this book terms *anticipatory design.* The cases themselves are not intended as "ideal" designs that can be easily transplanted. Rather, their complexities, both positive and negative, underscore how deeply contextual such spaces, infrastructures, and practices need to be. Much work remains, even in Japan, to embed and integrate bōsai culture holistically into more projects. The systems under study are plans, projects, and typologies that Japan has developed in response to the volatility of its land. The goal is to share mechanisms of embedding anticipatory design through the inclusion of designers, planners, emergency managers, policymakers, nonprofit organizations, and local communities as an integral part of disaster preparation in all parts of the human-built world.

The intended audience for this book includes spatial designers (those working in architecture, landscape architecture, urban design, and planning) as well as emergency managers and policymakers. For designers in both academia and practice, these cases can form the basis of a conceptual framework for anticipatory design. For emergency managers, they illuminate the essential nature of socio-spatial design in creating disaster-prepared spaces and embedding awareness into the everyday environment. For policymakers, the book stresses the importance of design thinking and community impact in the development of disaster-related policies. Design experiments and post-occupancy reviews can also suggest changes to improve policies and funding mechanisms.

The original drawings included here harken back to Japanese *ukiyo-e,* not only in adopting similar color palettes and annotation methods but also in depicting people performing everyday activities. Some illustrations show how space is used both during "normal" days and in times of disaster; others aim to clarify policies and zoning requirements. The anticipatory design framework highlights the need to bring multiple disciplines together in order to create dynamic spaces—the social and the spatial, the top-down and the bottom-up, the everyday and the post-disaster, ecology and engineering—and to consider the whole disaster timeline as our inevitable future by including the input of citizens, emergency managers, policymakers, local governments, activists, nonprofit organizations (NPOs), designers, scientists, sociologists, environmentalists, hydrologists, ecologists, educators, businesses/the private sector, and engineers. Spaces of disaster mitigation are not just feats of technical engineering; they are also places in relation to specific communities that transform across the disaster timeline.

BOOK STRUCTURE

Design Before Disaster is divided into seven chapters. Following this introduction, chapter 1 provides a theoretical foundation for the book, introducing the five key considerations for anticipatory design. These principles, and the larger theoretical foundations for the book, are supported by a discussion of crucial concepts from international disaster literature.

Chapter 2 provides a geophysical and historical context for disasters in Japan. The countless catastrophic events within its history have forged policy, education, and the built environment. Although much of this history has been covered by other scholars, this book focuses on issues that affect spatial planning, and it is necessary to include this background to fully understand the context of the following chapters and to recognize how the resulting policies have shaped the urban environment.

Chapters 3, 4, and 5 detail a series of cases organized by scale and design discipline. Each section begins with the historical context, applicable policies, and uses during a disaster and then describes typologies to uncover new ideas and potentials. The projects are fundamentally interlinked across scales, and multiscalar thinking is reinforced by cross-referencing between chapters. After researching and selecting these cases from a multitude of options (such as fieldwork in more than fifty parks), I selected those that offer lessons for designers and planners and allow space for designers to bring creative approaches to similar projects in the future. Each chapter closes with a consideration of recent policies that encourage proactivity and may stimulate the invention of new typologies.

Chapter 3 examines how disaster concerns have shaped Japanese cities and planning. The examples include infrastructures and networks associated with mitigation and preparedness: evacuation routes and fireproofing systems. Other sections examine typologies derived from reconstruction: *machizukuri* community-planning processes, coastal strategies, and resettlement to high ground. In each case, the planning model is discussed relative to its unique social, spatial, and historical context. These transformations at the scale of the city inherently pose questions about the balance between top-down, government-led projects and more community-led interventions, how costs and trade-offs could be negotiated—and how planning for recovery can begin before a disaster.

Chapter 4 surveys the Japanese bōsai park system, a multiscalar network of landscapes for emergency evacuation and post-disaster logistics. The chapter is structured by typologies from the largest scale—bōsai hubs and networks—to city parks and community pocket-park networks. The chapter closes with a discussion of the role of outdoor learning in disaster preparedness, in part as a launching point for larger considerations of embedding natural systems education into environments. The park networks illustrate the potential of spaces to perform multiple functions around the disaster timeline, transforming from everyday recreation and education spaces, already at the heart of communities, to vital post-disaster resources.

Chapter 5 investigates the roles of everyday public architecture, such as schools and shrines, as dual-use evacuation spaces. It also includes a discussion of housing, particularly Japan's rigorous post-disaster temporary housing program. Distinguished architects such as Ban Shigeru and Ito Toyo have carved out prominent niches in the field of disaster recovery, but in addition to their work, *Design Before Disaster* features that of other designers, less well known outside of Japan, in order to strengthen the potential for many more architects to engage in these types of projects. The diverse typologies illustrate the importance of connecting physical design with existing sociocultural practices, such as neighborhood networks or religious traditions, and new social practices, such as educating or institutionalizing roles and responsibilities.

Chapter 6 discusses the new networks and players who have begun preparing for the Nankai Trough event, which is predicted to occur within the next thirty years. The efforts being made by both the city and prefecture present us with new typologies and ideas, and they stress the importance of all stakeholders sharing their ideas and participating in efforts to prepare for an uncertain future.

Chapter 7 calls for a larger disciplinary movement. Globally, a paradigm shift is increasingly necessary as our climate crisis intensifies and increases disaster risk. A coherent discipline that combines design and disaster preparedness does not yet exist, but in our rapidly urbanizing, climate-changed world, designers must increasingly consider disasters, and disaster managers must grapple with risks embedded in the ways cities are built. The cross-disciplinary focus of this book, which includes the allied spatial design disciplines as well as those linked to disaster planning, underscores how the phenomenon of disaster cannot be understood through isolated units or moments in time. Design that anticipates disasters is inherently multidisciplinary and multiscalar.

In the words of Bruno Latour, disasters are "matters of concern,"[15] interconnected across time and space in relation to concepts, knowledge, and human and nonhuman actors. When designing for disasters, spatial designers must think at multiple scales while working with other disciplines and professions. Trends toward urban resilience alongside groundswells of humanitarian projects in response to recent catastrophes have emerged across design disciplines, but with a commitment to research and collaborations, designers' contributions can be even more meaningful throughout the disaster timeline.

1

ANTICIPATORY DESIGN IN DISASTER PLANNING

Disaster management theory and social science provide principles and language that allow us to discuss disasters with increased specificity. The language of design is insufficient to address the nuances of disasters. Designers have adopted the word "resilience," but that word has become all-encompassing, including so many definitions that it cannot articulate particular goals, time frames, or populations. Appropriate vocabulary is essential to any consideration of such complex issues. The terms and concepts explained below are used throughout this book to add specificity to the descriptions and to position the anticipatory design framework within foundational, multidisciplinary work by notable academics.

DISASTER TERMINOLOGY

Most important is understanding the notion of a *disaster* itself. Though definitions vary, the most common describes a disaster as occurring when a hazard (hydrological, geological, or other) disrupts the normal operation of a social system.[1] In this sense, a tsunami on an uninhabited island is not considered a disaster unless it has some impact on human society. Although they do not fall within the purview of this book, there are disasters caused by humans that may not seem to directly affect society but require urgent attention. For example, in Australia, climate and environmental changes resulting from human actions have led to harrowing fires and the decimation of coral reefs. Disasters are not "natural."[2] This has been widely discussed since the 1970s. By way of where and how they live, humans participate in the creation of disasters—building and cultivating environments, altering ecosystems, and creating inequality.

The parallel concept of *risk* concerns the potential for disasters to occur. Risk is not easily defined, given that different individuals, cultures, and communities will experience and gauge risks differently. While risk as a technical metric measures the probability and magnitude of disasters, perceptions of risk can also be socially amplified or attenuated through cultural understanding, media, personal experience, and social exchange.[3] Ulrich Beck's notion of the *risk society* describes how risk is embedded in the fabric of our contemporary everyday lives, from microplastics in our water to climate change and rising sea levels. Beck defines risk as "a systematic way of dealing with hazards and insecurities induced and introduced by modernization itself,"[4] underscoring that our contemporary risks are invisible, interconnected, distributed, constructed, and pervasive. For spatial disciplines, the idea of a risk society calls for constant consideration, across all types of spatial projects, of how design can help mediate risks. Although most designers are less inclined to use the term "disaster risk reduction" (or DRR), the World Bank has championed the term and has accentuated the importance of "mainstreaming" it to find mechanisms that will bring disaster risk reduction into conventional urbanization.

To do this, designers would benefit from a clearer understanding of risk in addition to the disaster cycle. A useful rubric for this is detailed in Blaikie et al.'s *At Risk* and is updated in Wisner, Gaillard, and Kelman's "Framing Disaster":[5]

$$\text{Disaster Risk} = \text{Hazard} \times [(\text{Vulnerability}/\text{Capacity}) - \text{Mitigation}]$$

While this reads as a formula, the mnemonic is intended as a qualitative framework that illustrates relationships involved in risk: namely, that hazards and vulnerability amplify risk, but capacity and mitigation can reduce it. There are several definitions of risk,[6] but this book adopts this one because it incorporates the important roles of capacity and mitigation. Spatial design can potentially contribute to all of these factors: poorly conceived designs can increase vulnerability and even increase the magnitude of hazard impact, while thoughtful, holistic design can mitigate risk and, perhaps most essentially, increase the capacity of communities to cope and adapt. This disaster risk rubric is unpacked below in order to provide specificity in terms of the ways designers can reduce the impacts of hazards and increase the coping capacity of communities. By adopting specific language and concepts beyond "disaster" and "resilience," this book provides tools for designers to incorporate anticipatory design into practice.

Hazards

Although the term *natural hazard* is clearly incorrect in most contexts, it is used to differentiate earthquakes, tsunamis, typhoons, and the like from entirely human-caused terrorism, war, and political hazards. Despite significant scientific strides, it is often impossible to accurately predict the magnitude, time of occurrence, location/space/scale of impact, time/space of exposure, rate of recurrence, or the potential cascading effects of nature-based hazards—and now climate change has rendered prediction even more difficult. Hazards are often considered to be out of designers' purview, and for centuries they were considered to be "acts of God." But hazards can be caused or amplified by human actions, including—or even primarily—our designs for the built environment. For example, urbanizing floodplains with asphalt and concrete reduces space for water, increasing flood hazards, a phenomenon that contributed to the devastating floods in Houston during Hurricane Harvey in 2017.

Ironically, even infrastructure designed to mitigate hazards can increase them. For example, building a seawall or levee around one community tends to increase flood levels elsewhere, as the same quantity of water is displaced. Gilbert White, who pioneered natural-hazards research, has argued since 1945 that relying primarily on levees often increases flood damage.[7] The construction, and occupation, of the built environment is one of the largest contributors to global CO_2 emissions (currently at about 42 percent),[8] making unsustainable, inefficient designs complicit in intensified storms, heat waves, and other hazards caused by the change in climate. Furthermore, cascading hazards (landslides, cholera outbreaks, nuclear disasters) lead to multi-hazard events that can intensify effects such as "inflation and market instability, loss of livelihood, [and] land tenure problems."[9] Anticipatory design must consider these interdependent links and avoid hazard accentuation by considering downstream impacts, with the understanding that projects are inexorably entwined with the environment and the potential hazards that surround them.

Vulnerability

Risk varies based on the *vulnerability* of potentially impacted populations. Neil Adger defines vulnerability as "the state of susceptibility to harm from exposure to stresses associated with environmental and social change and from the absence of capacity to adapt," placing emphasis on how vulnerability is heightened by "inadvertent or deliberate human action that reinforces self-interest and the distribution of power."[10] Susan Cutter succinctly refers to it as "the potential for loss" due to social conditions, exposure to hazards, and their combination.[11] Many have identified factors that affect social vulnerability: resources (money, information, technology, language, knowledge); power (political, representational); age (children, elderly); physical/mental illnesses (health, mobility, and so on); beliefs (religion, customs); and social infrastructure (networks, connections, support).[12]

Vulnerability is often considered to be outside the purview of design. Most projects do not directly address the societal complexities of poverty, elderly populations, or politically, economically, and racially disenfranchised populations. But because poor designs can increase vulnerability, designers have a responsibility to consider the possible negative effects of their designs. Projects that disrupt social networks, economies, or traditions can also indirectly contribute to vulnerability. Infrastructure projects that displace populations, separating them from their livelihoods and their peers, can make communities more vulnerable even as they seek to protect others.[13] Spatial justice and equitable design call for considering how projects might increase hazards and vulnerabilities for groups beyond the projects' immediate clients. Through the lens of vulnerability and disaster risk, design can either reproduce or combat "unjust geographies."[14] Much of disaster management emphasizes vulnerable communities that are likely to experience disasters most acutely, yet these groups are often left out of power structures and decision-making processes.[15] In this way, planning and design activities often fail to serve those who need them most. Vulnerability is multiscalar and needs to be considered on individual, household, community, watershed, and regional levels.

Increasingly, our interviews have found that people are often uncomfortable with, or even resent, being labeled as vulnerable. It is necessary to create tools to give them more agency, amplify their voices to overturn injustices, and realign systems to produce more equitable outcomes for all. For these reasons, this book focuses on how to increase coping and adaptive capacity in neighborhoods.

Capacity: Coping and Adapting

Vulnerability stands in juxtaposition to *coping capacity,* the ability of individuals or groups to protect and meet their needs using available resources. Similarly, in discussions around climate change, *adaptive capacity* is used frequently and is defined by the Intergovernmental Panel on Climate Change (IPCC) as "the ability of systems, institutions, humans, and other organisms to adjust to potential damage, to take advantage of opportunities, or to respond to consequences."[16] One factor in a community's potential to cope is its social capital: the trust, relationships, and shared practices that knit people together. Frederick Cuny explains that "in every society there is a variety of internal social structures that help individuals and families through difficult periods."[17] In the Japanese context, Daniel Aldrich's book *Black Wave* demonstrates that in areas where "residents had strong ties to one another and to decision makers, people worked together to push past bureaucratic obstacles and support innovative leadership. Less connected communities with fewer such ties faced harder recovery processes and lower survival rates. Such communities also found themselves in the iron grip of top-down, standardized recovery plans."[18]

Traditional disaster-preparedness activities are mechanisms for increasing coping capacity. Developing emergency response plans, such as evacuation drills, neighborhood disaster-preparedness organizations, and evacuation route planning, falls into this category. Working with preexisting social organizations can help designers consider how the spaces they create can serve preparedness activities. Design can also make disaster-related information visible and embed preparedness knowledge into everyday lives, as several projects in this book will show. Capacity can be expanded indirectly, too: this book argues that design that is contextual, sustainable, and considers both direct and indirect stakeholders is generally conducive to increasing capacity. Most importantly, the design of neighborhoods and public spaces can improve coping capacity by increasing moments of interaction. This can start with involving residents in the decision-making process from the beginning.

This book takes as a foundational principle Eric Klinenberg's concept of "social infrastructure: the physical spaces and organizations that shape the way people interact." He differentiates this from social capital, which predominantly focuses on relationships and networks. Social infrastructure specifies that "local, face-to-face interactions—at the school, the playground, and the corner diner—are the building blocks of all public life."[19] He uses this term in both *Heat Wave* and *Palaces for the People,* and in the latter he goes on to describe how social infrastructures "affect people during ordinary times."[20] Designers are perhaps even better equipped to alter the disaster risk rubric by expanding the capacity of individuals and groups to prepare for, cope with, and adapt to disasters. In many cases, increasing capacity will leave people better prepared for multiple and diverse disasters, which is particularly important in an era when climate change is upending standard hazard models and projections.

Mitigation and Adaptation

When discussing climate change, the term *mitigation* most often refers to actions to reduce or eliminate greenhouse gas emissions. In the realm of architecture, landscape, and urbanism, this might mean reducing the use of carbon-intensive materials, retrofitting buildings instead of building new ones, implementing renewable energy systems, cultivating forests, designing parks and green roofs, or adopting pedestrian-friendly strategies to allow projects to reduce, rather than amplify, the effects of global warming. The use of the term can cause confusion when speaking of mitigation strategies for reducing impacts of disasters, in which direct forms of mitigation use the tools of "land-use planning, building codes, insurance, engineering and warning systems."[21] Designers can create defensive infrastructure, nature-based coastal strategies, swales, and retention parks for flood reduction, elevate homes out of flood zones, build outside of high-hazard areas, or retrofit homes for seismicity, floods, wind loads, heat, or cold. Cuny separates *passive* mitigation measures, such as building codes and zoning, from *active* mitigation, which includes programs for housing improvement or economic diversification, and he reminds us that in places where codes are unenforceable, active measures need to go hand in hand.[22] Many of these disaster mitigation strategies overlap with what people are more recently calling adaptation strategies, especially when it comes to elevating homes or moving entirely out of coastal zones or floodplains.

In Japan, widening roads for fire reduction, relocating flood- and tsunami-vulnerable villages to high ground, and creating coastal buffer forests are all examples of direct mitigation. However, mitigation can also be indirect.[23] Dennis Mileti outlines six vital components of sustainable hazard mitigation. These are: enhance environmental quality without reducing "the carrying capacity of the ecosystem" for any of its inhabitants; enhance people's quality of life; foster local resilience and recognition of local environmental hazards; increase economic vitality; plan for inter- and intragenerational equity; and create a participatory process by adopting "a consensus-building approach, starting at the local level."[24] He recommends that these criteria be included in all new developments.

Resilience

The term *resilience* holds increasing sway in design circles as well as in governmental, NGO, and multilateral agendas, but its definition often remains broad. Each discipline has defined it with slightly nuanced specificity. Ecologist C. S. Holling differentiates between two definitions of resilience: "engineering resilience" refers to a maintenance of equilibrium, or a "steady state," after a disruption, and "ecological resilience" refers to a system's capacity to bounce back after a disturbance without taking on a new structure.[25] Simin Davoudi prefers a third definition, "evolutionary resilience," which considers crises as opportunities to "bounce forward" within a dynamic, rather than static, context.[26] In Japan, where the word "resilience" is gaining popularity, Tatsuki Shigeo describes resilience as the power of disaster survivors to recover psychologically. His sociological research from 1995 and 2011 reveals seven important factors that enhance resilience, such as resolving housing issues, reconnecting with people, accepting the local government's support, and preparing for the next disaster.[27] This book uses the term *resilience* as a hybrid: it combines Davoudi's more forward-looking "evolutionary resilience" with the concept of social-ecological resilience described by Adger et al., which accentuates the ways in which human society and our environments are interconnected,[28] and Cutter's definition of community resilience, "the ability to prepare and plan for, absorb, recover from, and more successfully adapt to actual or potential adverse events."[29]

Discourse on resilience is increasing in spatial disciplines, particularly among urban planners and landscape architects. In the planning world, this work focuses on governance, systems, and processes, but its broad application has the potential to obscure the ways in which contemporary risk is constructed by the way we build our cities. Larry Vale outlines how translating the abstract concept of "resilience" into the real space of urban planning can also be problematic in that the depoliticization of planning activities may prioritize the resilience of some groups over others. He poses the question, "Resilience for whom and against what?"[30] Landscape architecture is increasingly embracing the concept, particularly in terms of the design of ecological landscapes as a counterpoint to hard infrastructures associated with flood prevention and climate-change adaptation. Anuradha Mathur and Dilip da Cunha were early explorers of living with environments in flux, particularly through their work on designing with/for water in Mississippi, Mumbai, and Bangalore. Catherine Seavitt, Guy Nordenson, and their colleagues' projects *On the Water, Rising Currents,* and *Structures of Coastal Resilience* were seminal works that examined how soft systems could act as buffers against storm surges and rising sea levels in New York City. Kate Orff's writing in *Toward an Urban Ecology* and projects by her firm, SCAPE, imagine "landscape as a zone of collective engagement" as they design "living breakwaters."[31] In Europe, the work of many Dutch designers, such as De Urbanisten, is at the forefront of a parallel conversation, epitomized by the now-pervasive concept of dual-function "water squares" that transform everyday public spaces into flood reservoirs when water levels rise. While much of this design research is focused on flood and climate change–related environmental risk, these approaches also hold value for broader explorations of built environments. Projects like water squares or living breakwaters illustrate how the effectiveness of these landscapes depends not only on their performance as infrastructures to buffer urban areas against excess water but also as social spaces (in the case of water squares) or ecological elements (in the case of living breakwaters).

"Resilience" is increasingly used in descriptions of projects, but it still primarily revolves around climate change and associated "slow risks," such as sea-level rise. The interdisciplinary popularity of the term has the potential, however, to open the possibility of an interface for the disaster management, social science, engineering, and design disciplines. The common use of "resilience" across these fields, particularly in relationship to environmental risks, suggests shared goals—of making places safer, better prepared, and better for living—as well as the potential for working across disciplinary lines to achieve these goals.

Disaster Timelines

Disaster researchers and emergency managers use the term *disaster cycle* as a way of understanding disasters: from pre-disaster mitigation and preparedness to post-disaster response and recovery. This frames disasters as part of a continuous cycle instead of a series of discrete, one-off occurrences. While disasters often enter the public eye only *after* they have occurred, the disaster cycle is a key concept for understanding how projects and typologies discussed in this book relate to anticipatory design. This book uses the standard four phases of emergency management, or the disaster cycle,[32] but it broadens the territory of each phase and adds adaptation.

Preparedness refers to actions that ready people for the impacts of disasters, including anticipating issues that may arise and creating plans associated with response and recovery. This is often interpreted to mean pre-positioning of supplies, evacuation

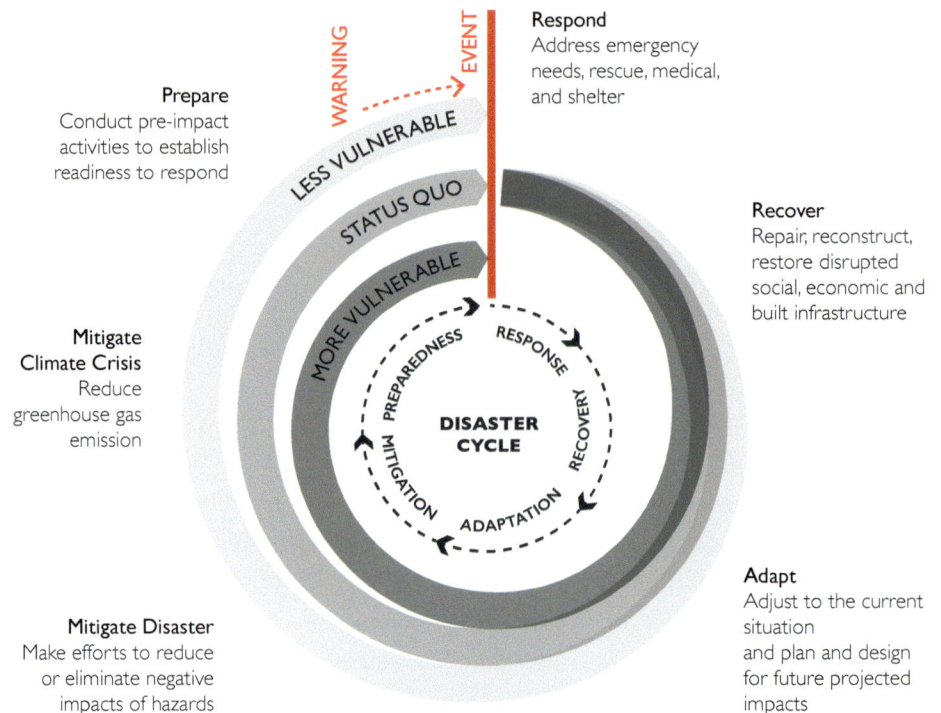

Respond
Address emergency
needs, rescue, medical,
and shelter

WARNING

EVENT

Prepare
Conduct pre-impact
activities to establish
readiness to respond

LESS VULNERABLE

STATUS QUO

MORE VULNERABLE

Recover
Repair, reconstruct,
restore disrupted
social, economic and
built infrastructure

**Mitigate
Climate Crisis**
Reduce
greenhouse gas
emission

PREPAREDNESS

RESPONSE

**DISASTER
CYCLE**

MITIGATION

RECOVERY

ADAPTATION

Mitigate Disaster
Make efforts to reduce
or eliminate negative
impacts of hazards

Adapt
Adjust to the current
situation
and plan and design
for future projected
impacts

Figure 3. Recurring phases of the disaster cycle. Enhanced adaptation, mitigation, and preparedness strategies can reduce vulnerabilities.

drills, and improving education and communication. *Mitigation* refers to actions taken to prevent or reduce the likelihood or impacts of hazards, often through physical interventions in the built environment. The most common association is with levees, seismic retrofits, and land-use control. *Response* actions are taken immediately after a disaster to aid survivors and protect lives and property; they include "attempts to contain and control the disaster and provide relief to victims."[33] *Recovery and reconstruction* are actions that help return people and cities to their daily lives and contribute to a new, disaster-resilient urban system by *building back better.* Donald Nelson, Neil Adger, and Katrina Brown define *adaptation* as "the decision-making process and the set of actions undertaken to maintain the capacity to deal with future change or perturbations to a social-ecological system without undergoing significant changes in function, structural identity, or feedbacks of that system while maintaining the option to develop."[34]

Not all projects fit neatly into these distinct phases, and many span several, but the categories serve as a framework for describing the role of projects in relation to the time surrounding disasters. Preparedness and mitigation are typically framed as occurring *before* a disaster, response and recovery coming *after,* and adaptation coming before or after, but all can be understood as part of a wheel, or cycle, which more accurately depicts the recurring nature of disasters and their associated actions over time. Especially in hazard-prone areas, each locality can develop mechanisms to reduce the impact of the next disaster by considering the cycle as the continuation of the timeline and broadening knowledge while widening the scope of each phase. For example, preparedness is mostly considered to encompass stockpiling supplies, warnings, and conducting drills, but Cuny argues that it should include "developing disaster assessment plans; establishing relief and reconstruction standards and policies; developing stand-by plans for economic assistance to victims; [and] developing crop salvage and marketing plans for economic assistance to victims."[35] Thinking within these cycles can help localities prepare specific longer-term ordinance changes and post-disaster permitting and put in place scenario-based planning mechanisms.

Phase Free

Similarly, academics in Japan such as Meguro Kimiro and Hada Yasunori have pushed back on the singular notion of disaster risk reduction and have championed the idea of disaster timelines without phases. Their concept of *phase free* promotes quality of life and focuses on five principles: "phase free use, everyday use, intuitive use, inspire people, and easy to spread."[36] This connects directly with the notion explored in this book of how the anticipatory design framework embeds dual-use thinking into all elements of our cities.

Post-disaster Timelines

Within the post-disaster phases, it can be helpful to define specific spatial typologies associated with response and recovery. The following terms and definitions— *evacuation spaces, temporary shelters, temporary housing,* and *permanent housing*—are adapted from Enrico Quarantelli[37] but are described below in the Japanese context.

Evacuation spaces, such as tsunami evacuation towers or evacuation parks, are used during disasters to escape danger. In Japan, parks are key evacuation spaces for many disaster types, with sirens or other alerts to signal their use. Depending on the type of disaster they are designed for, they might include facilities such as running water and toilets.

Temporary shelters are spaces such as school gyms, hotels, religious spaces, or friends' houses, where people spend the days and weeks following a disaster when they cannot return home. While these spaces meet basic needs, daily routines are disrupted. Often these are congregate shelters, which lack privacy and other comforts. Meals are often provided by volunteers, donations, or shelter staff using stored emergency supplies.

Temporary housing in Japan is intended to last up to two years while permanent housing can be planned and built. Temporary housing is often modular or prefabricated, but vacant existing housing stock (i.e., rental units) is also used. Japan has an extensive system for the provision of prefabricated temporary housing units.

Permanent housing refers to rebuilt or new permanent homes. In Japan, this may include both private homes and disaster public housing (which the government develops and for which it provides affordable rental subsidies). After major disasters in Japan, the reconstruction of permanent housing has often included *readjustment,* where lots are shifted to accommodate widened streets and parks for improved evacuation, or *relocation* to sites considered less exposed to natural hazards, such as hilltop sites less vulnerable to tsunamis.

Evacuation spaces and temporary shelters are more closely linked to the response phase, while temporary and permanent housing bridge into reconstruction and recovery, as people begin to reestablish their lives and routines. These terms, emerging from social science and disaster management literature, begin to illustrate how defining disaster phases can aid in creating designs to accommodate specific disaster-related needs.

ANTICIPATORY DESIGN

Inspired by and learning from countless authors, many named above, the anticipatory design framework detailed in this book is posed as a method for integrating disaster reduction and awareness into built environments and human societies, to visualize future scenarios, and to design for them before a disaster. This framework is based on the MIT Urban Risk Lab's (risk.mit.edu) research and practice as well as typologies and analyses encompassed in the following chapters. The framework illuminates five principles to consider in spatial design in disasters, including four coupled concepts— social and spatial, everyday and disaster, top-down and bottom-up, ecology and engineering—as well as the disaster timeline. The projects selected for this book are intended as a starting point for discourse on how to expand the role of design in disaster mitigation, preparedness, response, recovery, and adaptation. As Murao Osamu notes, "Although spatial design (architecture, urban design, and landscape design) is an essential component of disaster management, the relationships between spatial design and disaster management have rarely been discussed in the literature."[38] This book attempts to close that gap by introducing disaster management concepts and Japanese typologies to designers and planners—demonstrating the importance of carefully designed spaces for various moments throughout the disaster timeline.

Resilience suggests a condition, a state of being, though a dynamic one. Particularly for spatial design disciplines, the term *anticipatory design* suggests an action, and a process, rather than a state. This book advocates for anticipatory design as an optimistic and forward-looking term that recognizes broad participation (by designers, emergency managers, policymakers, and larger communities) in *creating* these safer, better-prepared, more livable places, which is particularly important in a world increasingly rocked by both slow and rapid disasters.

Social/Spatial Integration

For anyone who has been through a disaster, the relationship between society and space is obvious. Those fleeing a disaster not only need an evacuation space but also need advance knowledge of how to get there and how to engage in social support once they arrive. Disaster preparedness must link physical infrastructure/spaces with culture/social practice. As Kathleen Tierney argues, "disasters and their impacts are socially produced,"[39] and as such, strategies to reduce their impact must engage with or even transform social practices. Designing spaces for evacuation and sheltering, in particular, require consideration of how the physical space will help people cope in disaster situations. Spaces can support the ways in which communities come together after disasters, drawing on existing social patterns and relationships as well as traditional or cultural activities.

In Japan, disaster preparedness has long been understood through this pairing, as described in the *sakura*-viewing and wajū examples. However, a more recent technocratic emphasis on top-down, engineered solutions often disconnects communities from acknowledging the effects of their spaces and decisions. Although there are some positive examples, siloed reconstruction efforts "typically approach restoration of the built environment as separate from social intervention."[40] This is not to say that technology and culturally based solutions are always at odds: successful design can mediate between scientifically backed disaster infrastructure and the specificities of local communities. A "reflexive" approach to infrastructure can go "beyond single-operation functionality" to integrate local cultures, social practices, and physical urban fabrics.[41] For designers, this approach stresses that creating disaster-prepared environments requires consideration not only of physical resources but also of "social capital," the relationships and practices that hold communities together.[42]

Top-Down/Bottom-Up Placemaking

Planning for disasters is multiscalar, requiring a tricky balance of the top-down (policy, funding, zoning, codes, standards) and the bottom-up (community engagement, grassroots endeavors, local specificity, local placemaking). There is a collective approach to Japanese disaster preparedness, including broad participation in state-sponsored drills and, at times, a reliance on the state, but a truly successful disaster management strategy will require both. While "all disasters are local,"[43] they are also fundamentally intertwined with multiscalar policies, infrastructures, natural processes, and social norms. Local governments and communities need a guarantee of state support when disasters overrun local capacity, and national standards can guarantee a certain level of awareness across the board. However, to be embedded in the daily lives of citizens and to be specific to local contexts (demographic, geographic, political), regulations need to be translated to local sites. Communities on the ground can often identify response needs and visions of preparedness that are invisible at the national scale.

Everyday/Disaster Dual Use

Fundamental to the implementation and use of projects is the relationship between everyday uses of spaces and their functions in a disaster context. When the scope of disaster infrastructures becomes too narrow, they become disjointed from their users' everyday lives. In fact, spaces and infrastructure are most effective post-disaster if they are already integrated into people's everyday lives pre-disaster. As Richard Serino, former deputy administrator of FEMA, notes, "Having procedures embedded in everyday practice is essential, so that there isn't a steep learning curve when there is a disaster."[44] The moments during and immediately following a disaster are marked by chaos and uncertainty; preemptive familiarity with resources and services is crucial.

Many international precedents suggest creating multifunctional spaces that also take on a role during disasters, but the Urban Risk Lab's international fieldwork has shown that dual-function spaces generally work best. From a design perspective, multifunctionality offers a Swiss army knife of options, which often leads to generic, flexible spaces. But multifunctional spaces often end up lacking ownership and responsibility and can involve a complex cast of characters, which makes for less-than-ideal circumstances should a place need to be used in the stressful period immediately after a disaster. Advocating for dual functionality allows designers to be creative through the specificity of program, context, and culture. Buildings, landscapes, and infrastructure construction cost an exorbitant amount; therefore, anticipatory design encourages dual-function design from the beginning.

Ecology/Engineering Cohesion

Sensitivity to flora, fauna, and the seasons and respect for nature's forces—as reflected in Japanese arts and cuisine—play a large part in Japanese traditions and culture. In the push toward "modernization," structures to control these forces proliferated across Japanese coasts, rivers, and mountains, especially in response to disasters, but engineering is not necessarily at odds with ecology. The professions of ecological engineering, biotechnical stabilization, ecosystem restoration, and landscape architecture can design infrastructure that not only protects people but also enhances natural habitats. There are places where concrete infrastructure is needed and places where soft marshes, forests, and other flora do a better job of protecting all species, including humans—especially in the long run.

Shimatani Yukihiro, who creates river- and flood-control design (*kawazukuri*) projects through resident participation and environmental assessment, points out that because "Japan's flood control measures have been done only by the civil engineering experts, we need to consider it more comprehensively, including urban planning designers."[45] The Kamisaigō River project most clearly depicts a participatory process, holistically tying in habitat creation and education with flood mitigation and riverbed restoration. Especially with the onslaught of disaster events escalated by climate change, it is more important than ever to increase natural ecosystems where possible and design symbiotic relationships between ecology and engineering.

Consider the Disaster Cycle Holistically

Design practices in a disaster-related context often isolate their focus on one portion of the disaster timeline. For example, humanitarian practices such as Architecture for Humanity (now rebranded as Open Architecture Collaborative) or ArchiAid (which formed in Japan after the Tohoku tsunami) design and build projects in *response* to a catastrophe. Currently, popular resilience projects are focused on the *mitigation* of risk through swales, berms, and stilted or floating houses, often emphasizing sea-level rise. The *reconstruction* phase is typically managed by local governments and approached by the selected architects and developers as a standard design and construction project.

While each of these design practice typologies fills an important niche, anticipatory design argues for an approach that considers a broader disaster timeline. Disaster managers are trained to think about the disaster cycle over time: from mitigation, preparedness, disaster event, response, recovery, adaptation, and back to mitigation and preparedness. Owing to bureaucratic structures, however, governments, financial mechanisms, personnel, and responsibilities are often siloed into distinct groups. Anticipatory design empowers designers to not only think about the single moment of the disaster but rather consider systemically interrelated scenarios and timelines, featuring diverse scales and populations, for different types of disasters.

Our era of anthropogenic climate change has brought the need for anticipatory design to the fore. Often, the fields of disaster preparedness and climate change adaptation appear to be siloed; there is a "lack of scaled integration" between them.[46] Dennis Mileti, in his seminal book *Disasters by Design,* identifies Gilbert White, a geographer, and Eugene Hass, a sociologist, as the pioneers of an integrated approach to hazard research. The two paved the way for the fields of geography and sociology to work with "climatology, economics, engineering, geology, law, meteorology, planning, psychology, public policy and seismology."[47] This transdisciplinary approach must continue—and it must include designers. The holistic concept of anticipatory design is intended to better link slow and fast environmental hazards in concert with the everyday experience of space.

While some typologies in this book focus on seismically induced disasters and their associated cascading hazards (tsunami and fire, for instance), these lessons speak to much broader risk profiles. As climate change intensifies the effects of heat waves, typhoons, and flooding, Japan has begun to incorporate broader, climate-amplified considerations. Preparing for frequent events, such as heat waves, can magnify coping capacity and push forward the concept of anticipatory design to include more bottom-up approaches, site-specific design, local flexibility, and diversity. While Japan is a forerunner in disaster research, there is still significant space for its designers to become integral to creating urban policy. An agile approach to disaster preparedness and risk reduction, facilitated through anticipatory design, will help make Japan and the world better prepared for the hazards to come.

2

HAZARDS AND POLICIES

Enduring numerous disasters, adapting, and creating subsequent policies have shaped Japan's physical environments and human populations. Three seismically induced disasters in particular have played outsized roles in shaping Japanese design, planning, policy, and disaster management: the 1923 Tokyo earthquake, the 1995 Kobe earthquake, and the 2011 Tohoku triple disaster (in particular, the earthquake and tsunami). The volatile nature of the archipelago has shaped settlements, architecture, arts, and social organizations. The catastrophes described above—as well as countless other disasters—have created Japan's bōsai culture. This chapter traces Japan's major disaster history chronologically and demonstrates how key events and turning points shaped the policies and attributes of Japan's built environment.

EARLY HISTORY TO THE END OF EDO

684

Japan has a documented history of disasters that extends back well over a millennium. The earliest event on record is the 684 Hakuhō Nankai earthquake and tsunami (though the term *tsunami* did not emerge until nearly a thousand years later). This Nankai megathrust earthquake struck the Kochi area of Shikoku Island and is estimated to have had a magnitude of 8.3 or higher.[1] Around the same time, early accounts of Shintoism, Japan's Indigenous religion, were also recorded. Attunement to, and even worship of, nature is embedded in Shintoism. Before the development of modern disaster-resistant engineering, knowledge of one's environment was essential to surviving frequent hazards.

Figure 4 (*next page*). Timeline of hazards, subsequent policies, and projects that have shaped the Japanese built environment.

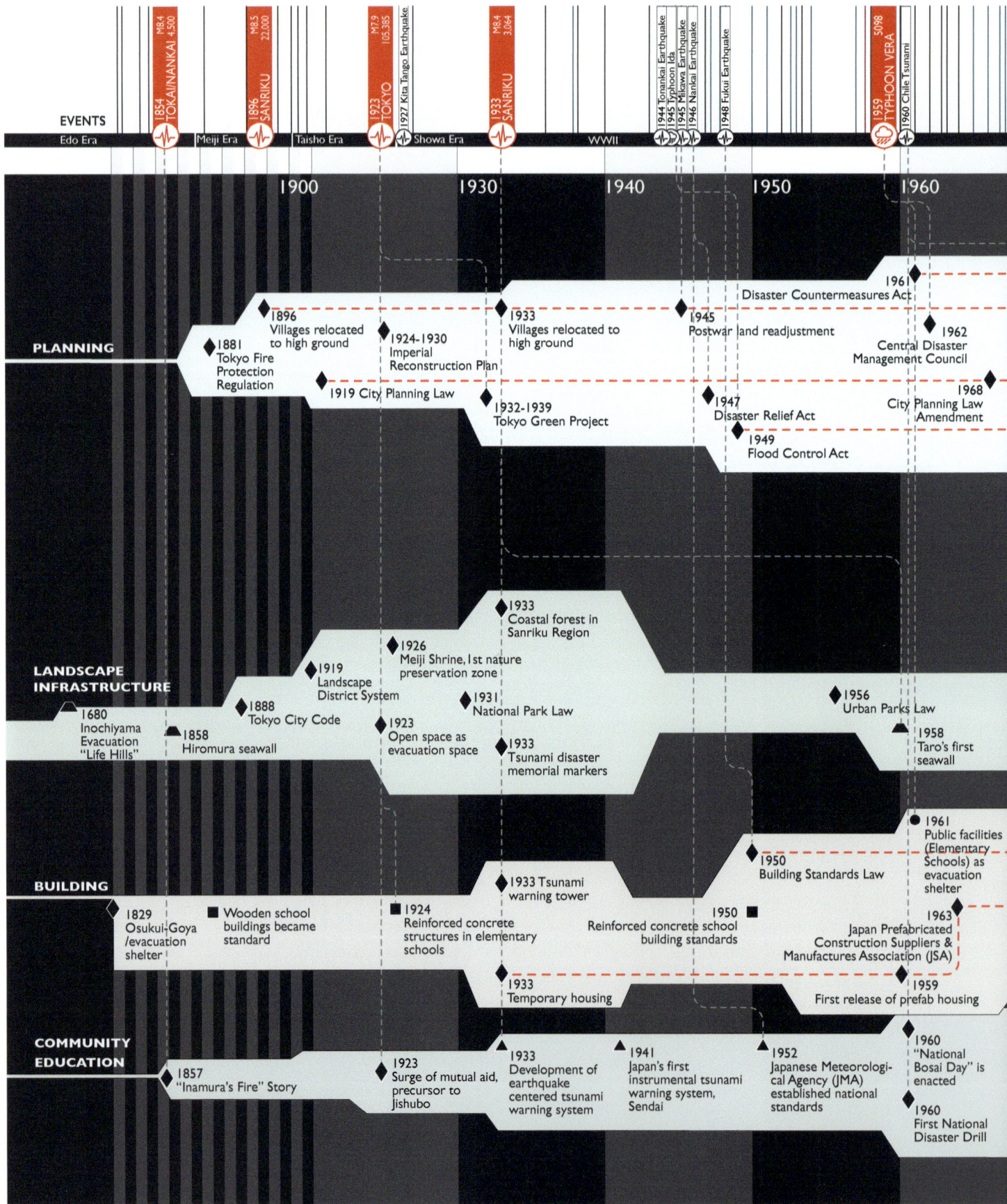

Edo Era | Meiji Era | Taisho Era | Showa Era | WWII

1854 TOKAI/NANKAI M8.4 4,500
1896 SANRIKU M8.5 22,000
1923 TOKYO M7.9 105,385
1927 Kita Tango Earthquake
1933 SANRIKU M8.4 3,064
1944 Tonankai Earthquake
1945 Typhoon Ida
1945 Mikawa Earthquake
1946 Nankai Earthquake
1948 Fukui Earthquake
1959 TYPHOON VERA 5098
1960 Chile Tsunami

1900 | 1930 | 1940 | 1950 | 1960

PLANNING

1881 Tokyo Fire Protection Regulation

1896 Villages relocated to high ground

1919 City Planning Law

1924-1930 Imperial Reconstruction Plan

1932-1939 Tokyo Green Project

1933 Villages relocated to high ground

1945 Postwar land readjustment

1947 Disaster Relief Act

1949 Flood Control Act

1961 Disaster Countermeasures Act

1962 Central Disaster Management Council

1968 City Planning Law Amendment

LANDSCAPE INFRASTRUCTURE

1680 Inochiyama Evacuation "Life Hills"

1858 Hiromura seawall

1888 Tokyo City Code

1919 Landscape District System

1923 Open space as evacuation space

1926 Meiji Shrine, 1st nature preservation zone

1931 National Park Law

1933 Coastal forest in Sanriku Region

1933 Tsunami disaster memorial markers

1956 Urban Parks Law

1958 Taro's first seawall

BUILDING

1829 Osukui-Goya /evacuation shelter

Wooden school buildings became standard

1924 Reinforced concrete structures in elementary schools

1933 Tsunami warning tower

1933 Temporary housing

1950 Reinforced concrete school building standards

1950 Building Standards Law

1959 First release of prefab housing

1961 Public facilities (Elementary Schools) as evacuation shelter

1963 Japan Prefabricated Construction Suppliers & Manufactures Association (JSA)

COMMUNITY EDUCATION

1857 "Inamura's Fire" Story

1923 Surge of mutual aid, precursor to Jishubo

1933 Development of earthquake centered tsunami warning system

1941 Japan's first instrumental tsunami warning system, Sendai

1952 Japanese Meteorological Agency (JMA) established national standards

1960 "National Bosai Day" is enacted

1960 First National Disaster Drill

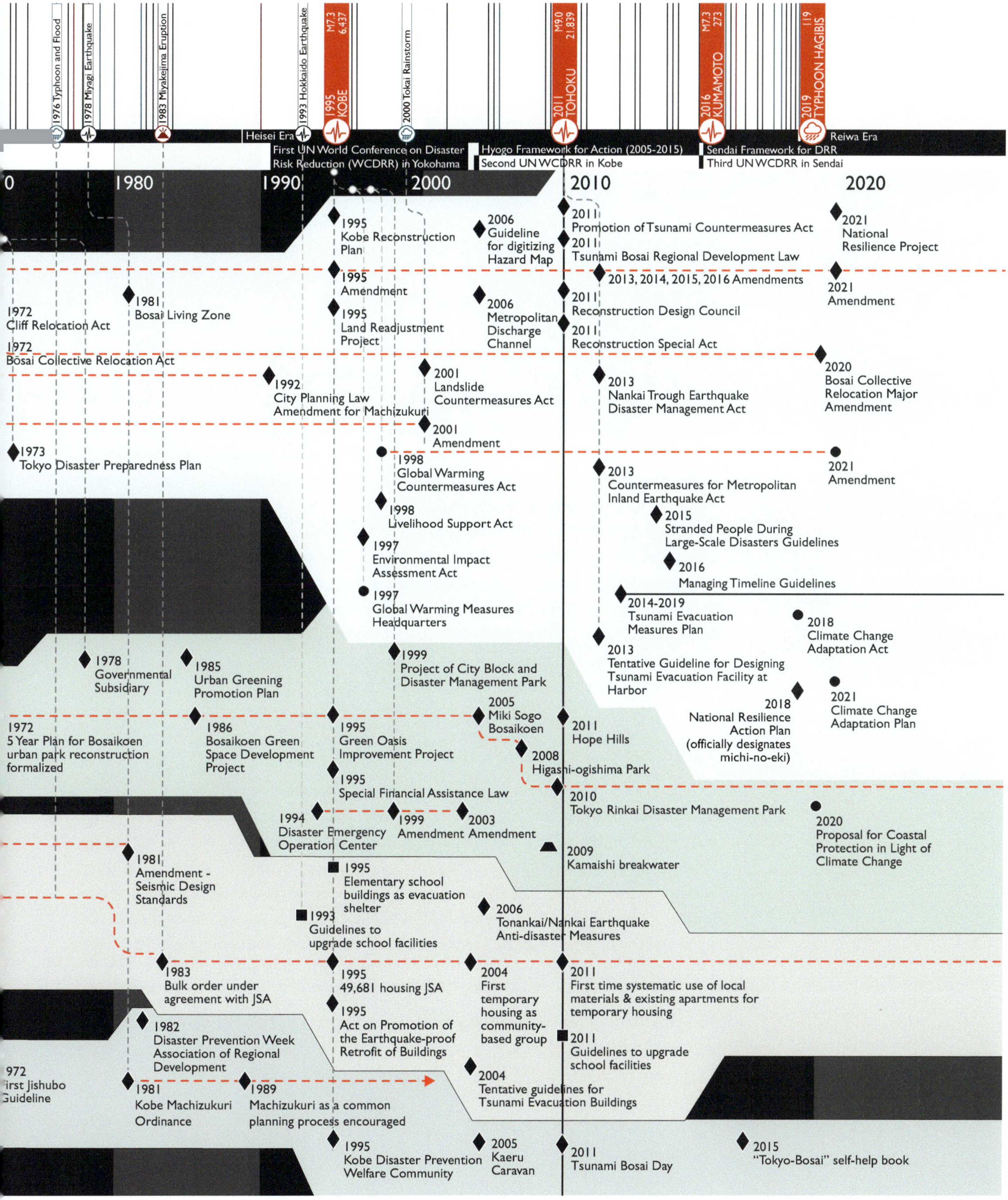

Top timeline markers:

1976 Typhoon and Flood
1978 Miyagi Earthquake
1983 Miyakejima Eruption
1993 Hokkaido Earthquake
1995 KOBE — M7.3 6,437
2000 Tokai Rainstorm
2011 TOHOKU — M9.0 21,839
2016 KUMAMOTO — M7.3 273
2019 TYPHOON HAGIBIS — 119

Heisei Era · Reiwa Era

First UN World Conference on Disaster Risk Reduction (WCDRR) in Yokohama
Hyogo Framework for Action (2005-2015)
Sendai Framework for DRR
Second UN WCDRR in Kobe
Third UN WCDRR in Sendai

Decade scale: 0 | 1980 | 1990 | 2000 | 2010 | 2020

Events:

1995 Kobe Reconstruction Plan

2006 Guideline for digitizing Hazard Map

2011 Promotion of Tsunami Countermeasures Act

2011 Tsunami Bosai Regional Development Law

2021 National Resilience Project

1995 Amendment

2013, 2014, 2015, 2016 Amendments

2021 Amendment

1995 Land Readjustment Project

2006 Metropolitan Discharge Channel

2011 Reconstruction Design Council

2011 Reconstruction Special Act

1972 Cliff Relocation Act

1981 Bosai Living Zone

1972 Bosai Collective Relocation Act

2001 Landslide Countermeasures Act

1992 City Planning Law Amendment for Machizukuri

2013 Nankai Trough Earthquake Disaster Management Act

2020 Bosai Collective Relocation Major Amendment

2001 Amendment

1973 Tokyo Disaster Preparedness Plan

1998 Global Warming Countermeasures Act

2013 Countermeasures for Metropolitan Inland Earthquake Act

2021 Amendment

1998 Livelihood Support Act

2015 Stranded People During Large-Scale Disasters Guidelines

1997 Environmental Impact Assessment Act

2016 Managing Timeline Guidelines

1997 Global Warming Measures Headquarters

2014-2019 Tsunami Evacuation Measures Plan

2018 Climate Change Adaptation Act

1978 Governmental Subsidiary

1985 Urban Greening Promotion Plan

1999 Project of City Block and Disaster Management Park

2013 Tentative Guideline for Designing Tsunami Evacuation Facility at Harbor

1972 5 Year Plan for Bosaikoen urban park reconstruction formalized

1986 Bosaikoen Green Space Development Project

1995 Green Oasis Improvement Project

2005 Miki Sogo Bosaikoen

2011 Hope Hills

2018 National Resilience Action Plan (officially designates michi-no-eki)

2021 Climate Change Adaptation Plan

1995 Special Financial Assistance Law

2008 Higashi-ogishima Park

1994 Disaster Emergency Operation Center

1999 Amendment

2003 Amendment

2010 Tokyo Rinkai Disaster Management Park

2020 Proposal for Coastal Protection in Light of Climate Change

2009 Kamaishi breakwater

1981 Amendment - Seismic Design Standards

1995 Elementary school buildings as evacuation shelter

1993 Guidelines to upgrade school facilities

2006 Tonankai/Nankai Earthquake Anti-disaster Measures

1983 Bulk order under agreement with JSA

1995 49,681 housing JSA

2004 First temporary housing as community-based group

2011 First time systematic use of local materials & existing apartments for temporary housing

1982 Disaster Prevention Week Association of Regional Development

1995 Act on Promotion of the Earthquake-proof Retrofit of Buildings

2011 Guidelines to upgrade school facilities

1972 First Jishubo Guideline

1981 Kobe Machizukuri Ordinance

1989 Machizukuri as a common planning process encouraged

2004 Tentative guidelines for Tsunami Evacuation Buildings

1995 Kobe Disaster Prevention Welfare Community

2005 Kaeru Caravan

2011 Tsunami Bosai Day

2015 "Tokyo-Bosai" self-help book

1603–1868

During the Edo era, the arts flourished in Japan, and *ukiyo-e* (drawings of the float-ing world) were born. These were printed with hand-carved woodblocks, and many depicted the hedonistic life of the merchant class, but landscapes by artists such as Katsushika Hokusai and Utagawa Hiroshige showed the human connection to the environment as a primary theme. Nature, hazards, and disaster imagery became central to Japanese visual culture. Hokusai's iconic *ukiyo-e* print *The Great Wave off Kanagawa* (ca. 1830) has become so ubiquitous that it is now a smartphone emoji. The print illus-trates the raw power of nature threatening man-made vessels and has become a highly visible symbol of respecting the ocean's strength.

Japan also has a long history of enacting disaster mitigation policies and creating community organizations in reaction to major disasters. As early as 1629, Edo (now Tokyo) introduced regulations and urban design strategies to reduce building loss from fires. These fires were so frequent that a common adage was "Fire and fight are the splendor of Edo," and they were treated as part of a natural cycle of life. During the Edo era, disaster assistance was provided through tax relief and the provision of crops from "charitable granaries," or *gisō*.[2] Disaster preparedness through community-level organizations also strengthened during this time with *suibōdan* (community-based flood-management groups), which formally began in the seventeenth century, and ci-vilian firefighting organizations in the eighteenth. The *machibikeshi* (town firefighters) were organized in the merchant and artisan districts of Edo in 1718. *Machibikeshi,* who mostly worked second jobs as steeplejacks, numbered over ten thousand in Edo, with thirty in each district. Each group had unique clothing and banners. Their government salaries were low, but the job came with privileges, such as free admission to plays, and *machibikeshi* were treated as local celebrities.[3]

1854

A legend of tsunami preparedness, *Inamura-no-hi,* describes the old man Gohei, who, upon feeling a long and slow earthquake, predicted that a tsunami was on its way. However, the rest of the village, preparing for a harvest festival, took no notice. Observing the sea pull back to reveal the rocky ocean bottom, he realized the wave was imminent. To catch the attention of his neighbors, he set a series of sheaves of rice ablaze on the hilltop, lighting up the sky as the sun began to set. The 400 villagers ran up the hill to help put out the fire and watched the massive tsunami ravage the village below. Gohei was celebrated for saving their lives. This story was widespread in Japa-nese fifth-grade textbooks from 1937 to 1946 and then revived in 2011.[4] The story was also published by the Asian Disaster Reduction Center (ADRC) in eight languages as a tsunami education tool.

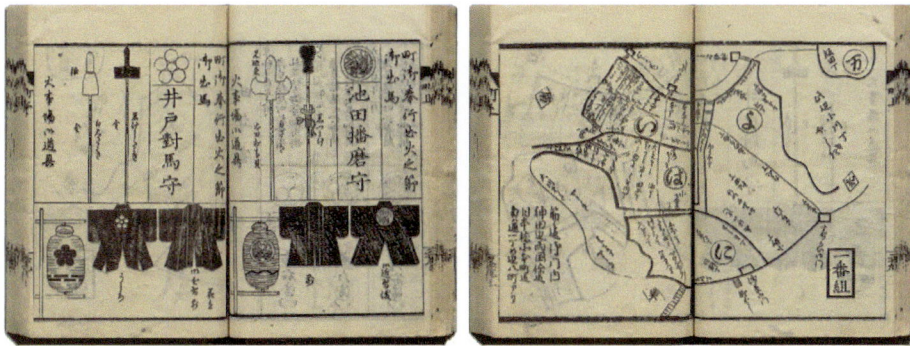

Figure 5. *Machibikeshi* uniforms and organization within Edo districts.

Figure 6. *Ukiyo-e* woodblock print of the Ansei flood event during the Edo era.

This parable was based on a true story from around the November 5, 1854, Ansei Nankai earthquake (magnitude 8.4) and resulting tsunami. Hamaguchi Goryō was actually a young man in the town of Hiro, whose residents had developed the practice of running to high ground after a tsunami caused by the 1707 Hōei earthquake had killed 300 people. Goryō, with a group of young men, lit the evacuation route with burning stacks of rice sheaves; out of approximately 1,300 residents, all but 36 survived, despite the total inundation of their village. Goryō then used his own funds to build a five-meter-high and six-hundred-meter-long seawall to protect the village and to employ those whose livelihoods were destroyed in the disaster.[5] The embankment protected houses and inhabitants in 1946 when the Showa Nankai earthquake and tsunami struck the town.[6]

Playwright, writer of fiction, comic book creator, and newspaper reporter Kanagaki Robun was almost buried alive in the Ansei earthquake. Soon after, he published the *Ansei-kenmon* magazine with Mikawaya Tetsugoro. It sold so well that after a typhoon hit Edo on August 25, 1856, Robun was commissioned to create another magazine. He interviewed survivors in the aftermath of the typhoon and storm surge that had worsened the damage from the previous year's earthquake.[7] Instead of depicting pure terror and suffering, these prints often showed signs of mutual cooperation, and their beauty transcended journalism as art.

MEIJI ERA TO TAISHŌ ERA (1869–1926)

The 1880 Provision and Saving Act for Natural Disaster marked the beginning of major national disaster-related legislation. That same year, British architects and scientists and their students from the Imperial College of Tokyo helped found the Seismological Society of Japan, indicating a shift toward Western disaster cultures.[8] The 1891 Nōbi earthquake, notable for damaging European-style brick and stone buildings, led to the establishment of the Council on Earthquake Disaster Prevention (CEDP), which created new legislation. In 1919 two laws were introduced: the City Planning Law and the Urban Building Law. These initially applied only to the nation's six major cities and introduced Japan's first zoning and land readjustment strategies and first building codes, respectively. While the codes included structural requirements, they initially did not include wind, snow, or earthquake loads. They were amended in 1924, after the 1923 Tokyo earthquake, to include seismic loading—the first codes in the world to do so. The amendment also banned brick buildings, introduced from the West, which collapsed catastrophically in the quake.[9]

Three tsunamis left their mark on Tohoku in the 115 years prior to the 2011 event, occurring in 1896, 1933, and 1960. The magnitude 8.5 Sanriku earthquake and tsunami in 1896, with run-up heights of thirty-eight meters, claimed more than twenty-two thousand lives. One reason for the high death toll was that the precipitating earthquake was felt only weakly on land, giving little warning to prompt coastal residents to evacuate.[10] The rise of popular journalism helped document response activities, as seen in Yumani Shobou's illustrated article about the 1896 Sanriku tsunami. Accompanying texts described a temple hermitage converted into a post-disaster headquarters, survivors wrapped in Buddhist flags to fend off the cold, and the distribution of rice rations.[11] Such images in popular culture show how altruism prevails during disaster response.

1923 Tokyo Earthquake

The Tokyo earthquake of September 1, 1923, also known as the Great Kanto Earth-quake, was a magnitude 7.9 temblor with an epicenter in Sagami Bay, ninety-eight kilometers southwest of the city center. The first tremor hit at 11:58 am, when many residents were cooking their lunchtime meals over open flames. The shaking knocked over cookstoves and ignited a conflagration that consumed 43.6 percent of the city.[12] Fires burned for nearly two days, overwhelming the city's firefighting infrastructure while a series of aftershocks struck—six greater than magnitude 7.0.[13] Broken water pipes and blocked roads added to the chaos, and the strong, shifting winds from a typhoon in the Sea of Japan spread the flames rapidly and unpredictably.

Over 105,385 people were killed in the disaster, mostly from fire. Sixty percent of the buildings in Tokyo were completely destroyed by the disaster, and the destruction of some neighborhoods was near total, with damages exceeding 90 percent in the Nihon-bashi, Asakusa, Fukagawa, and Honjo districts[14] as well as in the neighboring city of Yokohama, which was closer to the epicenter and built on alluvial soil that amplifies ground motion. In ten prefectures, 372,659 buildings in total were damaged, and electricity, water, rail, and other lifelines were severely impaired.[15] Tokyo's *shitamachi* (low city) working-class neighborhoods were located on softer ground, closer to sea level, and experienced twenty-five times more fatalities than the *yamanote* (high city), Tokyo's traditionally aristocratic districts located on more stable bedrock. Though buildings in the *yamanote* were also primarily wooden, they were of higher quality and spaced further apart, and grounds around wealthy homes and temples helped

→火に追われた避難民上野駅前に押し寄す　（大正十二年九月一日大震火災の光景）

Figure 7. Evacuees with their belongings jammed near Ueno Station in 1923.

stop the spread of fire. Open spaces such as the Yokojukken River, the Imperial Palace, and Hibiya Park, as well as shrines and parks around the *yamanote,* also served as firebreaks.[16]

As the flames closed in, citizens fled their neighborhoods for open spaces. Many brought their furniture, clothing, and other home goods on their backs or in carts, and their attempt to salvage belongings proved deadly, clogging streets and bringing evacuation to a standstill in some instances. Even open spaces were not entirely safe, as wood, paper, and fabric ignited, burning many of the evacuees to death. One such devastating site was the Clothing Depot property, where 38,000 people were killed in a firestorm.[17] Though rivers and other bodies of water saved some lives from fire, they took others: an estimated 5,300 disaster victims died by drowning. For example, Benten Pond in Shin-Yoshiwara Pleasure District was filled with almost 500 bodies of drowned sex workers.[18]

Response

Catastrophic damage to Tokyo's lifeline infrastructure, including water, road, rail, telephone, and telegraph lines, made emergency food supplies, potable water, and other forms of relief difficult to procure in the immediate aftermath. Although Tokyo's main water plant was not heavily impacted, the distribution network of water pipes and aquifers across the city was severely damaged at more than two hundred distinct locations. On September 3, the Relief Bureau directed all available personnel to transport water to the disaster zone from Yokosuka, Osaka, and Nagoya. The army then distributed around 250 barrels of clean water to each disaster-stricken ward, refilled daily until infrastructure was repaired. The Japanese Red Cross provided medical assistance, and the army, alongside other government groups, handled rescue, debris clearance, and lifeline restoration.[19] With transit networks damaged, nonimpacted prefectures used oceans and rivers to ship rice and other emergency goods to Tokyo. A complex system delivered food from across Japan, and Tokyo military officers oversaw its distribution at seven major ports and train stations.[20]

In addition to official mechanisms, mutual aid and self-help groups provided much of the relief, given the limited capacity of government and delays associated with broken infrastructure. Neighbors helped rescue the injured, shared *onigiri* rice balls, and crowded into surviving residences, including larger homes, temples, and intact neighborhoods.[21] Private businesses also responded quickly, with merchants using construction materials stockpiled outside the city to rapidly build emergency markets and food stalls in a matter of days.[22] This mutual assistance is a repeated theme in Japanese history, as communities manage resource issues locally, through neighborhood associations, when national programs fail to meet specific needs. It also underscores the importance of already existing strong social networks in response to large-scale disasters.

Around 528,000 refugees remained in Tokyo; an additional 250,000 fled the city.[23] Within a week, the city government launched plans to build temporary housing barracks in open spaces, including various parks, schoolyards, the outskirts of shrines, and even the Imperial Palace grounds.

Policy

In the Meiji era, popular art forms became ways to communicate disasters as national catastrophes. In her analysis of the visual culture associated with the 1923 Tokyo earthquake, Gennifer Weisenfeld notes how images were used both by the state, to construct a narrative that rationalized its large-scale reconstruction program, and by individuals, to "advocate their own visions for the future" in response to the disaster.[24]

The 1923 earthquake was momentous not only for the scale of its destruction but also for how it transformed the city, reshaping Tokyo as we know it today, with wider, "modernized" streets and park networks. Japanese metropolises had been shaped by Edo-era urban projects, and the disaster struck at a time when the administration was beginning to adopt modern Western forms of city planning, such as zoning. The earthquake led to the comprehensive Imperial Reconstruction Plan, which sought to transform Tokyo's urban fabric to reduce the impact of future earthquakes and fires by widening roads and introducing reinforced concrete school buildings and evacuation parks. The plan was partially implemented, resulting in disaster measurement policies and a surge in bōsai culture. Another significant change to Tokyo's urban form was a sudden increase of suburban housing models that led to extensive migration out of the city.[25]

National Bōsai Day

The 1923 earthquake brought not only a physical transformation of the city but also a social metamorphosis as self-government systems took shape in communities. In urban districts where neighborly relations had dwindled, mutual aid after the disaster evolved into neighborhood associations.[26] These were the predecessors of *jishubō,* an abbreviation for *jishu-bōsai-soshiki* (neighborhood disaster-preparedness organizations), officially defined by the central government in 1963. To commemorate the 1923 earthquake, the Disaster Countermeasures Act established September 1 as National Bōsai Day. Every year, an official Disaster Preparedness Week features disaster-reduction fairs and disaster-response drills across the country at national, municipality, and community levels.

1933 Sanriku Tsunami

A decade later, on March 3, 1933, at 2:30 am, another Sanriku earthquake struck. It had an estimated magnitude of 8.4. Fortunately, its death toll of around three thousand was relatively low, despite maximum tsunami run-ups as high as twenty-nine meters. While some settlements had been relocated after 1896, the 1933 disaster prompted a more comprehensive tsunami mitigation strategy, with ten countermeasures incorporated into reconstruction plans, including relocation to high ground, tsunami buffer forests, evacuation route planning, and seawalls (recommended for smaller tsunamis).[27] For these projects, 85 percent of civil engineering restoration and 65 percent of new infrastructures received national subsidies and low-interest loans.[28] The disaster also led to the nationally backed resettlement of nearly one hundred fishing villages to higher ground, but many of these settlements slowly shifted back to the coast over the course of eighty years, only to be destroyed again in 2011.[29]

SHOWA ERA TO PRESENT

Japan's next severe disaster would come not from nature but from the hands of fellow humans. During World War II, air raids decimated major Japanese cities and led to catastrophic civilian fatalities, both from conventional firebombing and from the atomic bombs dropped on Hiroshima and Nagasaki. Japan's disaster management laws proliferated in the postwar era. The 1946 Showa Nankai earthquake led to the creation of the Disaster Relief Act, and Typhoons Ida (1945) and Kathleen (1947) precipitated the Flood Control Act.[30] The 1948 Fukui earthquake led to the 1950 Building Standards Law, which replaced the Urban Building Law and established more modern earthquake engineering regulations.[31]

1959 Typhoon Vera

In 1959, a class 5 typhoon pummeled the Ise gulf coast.[32] Typhoon Vera landed at 6:00 pm on September 26 and took 5,098 lives in thirty-two prefectures, the highest death toll for a typhoon since the Meiji era. A center barometric pressure of 929.6 millibars upon landing made it the third biggest typhoon in Japanese history. In hard-hit Aichi Prefecture, 105,726 buildings were destroyed or washed out.[33] Typhoon Vera was the trigger for Japan's first comprehensive disaster measurement law, the Disaster Countermeasures Act enacted in 1961. This led to the construction of coastal flood defense infrastructure and the revision of design standards for seawalls, many of which had been completely destroyed. Government spending on defensive coastal infrastructures increased from ¥1.8 billion in 1958 to ¥13.8 billion after the 1959 typhoon—and to

¥31.1 billion in 1960, after the Chilean tsunami that year.[34] That tsunami also led to the creation of an international tsunami warning system.

The Disaster Countermeasures Act is the backbone of Japan's bōsai policy, as it established the central government's mechanisms for disaster prevention, including the creation of the Central Disaster Management Council headed by the prime minister. The council is tasked with creating the high-level Disaster Management Plan, upon which local-level plans are based. The act also defines the roles of prefectures, municipalities, public institutions, and citizens in disaster management, with a general emphasis on centralized decision-making.[35] It is frequently revised in the wake of major disasters. The term *jishubō* was officially recognized in the high-level Disaster Management Plan in 1963 to denote an organization working with local governments to enhance the efficiency of disaster relief. In the 1970s, the first "jishubō guidelines" defined the roles of jishubō as first responders to earthquakes in urban areas.[36] Jishubō proliferated across the country, including in rural regions, as disasters in the 1980s fueled interest and the government began to subsidize their activities.

Building codes were also frequently revised following severe disasters. For example, in 1981, regulations introduced in response to the 1978 Offshore Miyagi earthquake stipulated that buildings should be constructed so as not to be damaged by medium-scale hazards (snow, storm, or seismic) and should not collapse as a result of a large-scale hazard. The 1995 Kobe earthquake revealed the effectiveness of the 1981 building standards and seismic code revision of the Building Standards Law: 95 percent of the homes that collapsed were built before 1981, and only 5 percent of collapsed buildings were built according to the new regulations.[37]

1995 Kobe Earthquake

The magnitude 7.3 Kobe earthquake, commonly known as the Great Hanshin-Awaji Earthquake, struck just before sunrise on January 17, 1995. In contrast to the Tokyo earthquake, in which fire caused the most destruction, building collapse caused 80 percent of Kobe casualties, with most deaths resulting from crushing or suffocation rather than fire. In total, 6,434 people were killed and 43,792 injured; over half of the survivors were elderly. While 144,000 houses were partially destroyed, 105,000 houses were annihilated.[38]

The Kobe metropolitan area occupies a narrow band of dense urbanization, sandwiched between mountain and ocean. As before, correlation was strong between geography and vulnerability: lowland areas on softer soils prone to liquefaction, generally populated by lower-income households, suffered a higher rate of destruction. A twenty-by-two-kilometer strip containing the city's densest neighborhoods and 80 percent of its population was the most severely impacted, with more than 30 per-

Figure 8. Matsumoto district, collapsed and charred from the 1995 earthquake and subsequent fires.

cent of buildings damaged.[39] The design of the city, with lines of transportation and lifeline infrastructure primarily running parallel to the coastline, proved to be an obstacle itself, as debris blocked vital areas and delayed rescue; volunteers even resorted to bringing in supplies on foot. The collapse of the Hanshin Expressway elevated bridge, considered a major engineering feat of the time, became an iconic symbol of devastation. Two offshore reclaimed-ground islands that suffered liquefaction were completely severed from the mainland.

Despite better-reinforced buildings and improved disaster-preparedness policies, many of Kobe's neighborhoods remained labyrinths of tightly packed, old wooden buildings—particularly neighborhoods that had been spared during World War II and escaped postwar upgrading or land readjustment programs. Although timber construction is generally considered safer in earthquakes, large numbers of old and unrenovated wooden buildings collapsed, as their heavy tile roofs intensified the buildings' movement; in many cases, the second floor crushed the first. Most of the doomed structures were over thirty years old. About 40 percent of the destroyed homes were timber frame, 28 percent brick, 6 percent reinforced concrete, and 10 percent steel frame or other systems.[40] The older wood-construction neighborhoods were particularly vulnerable to fire fueled by gas leaks, including those in the Hyogo and Nagata wards. Eighty-three hectares burned to the ground, as debris blocked roads and broken pipes interfered with water supplies and firefighting.[41] The high rates of destruction in

DESIGN BEFORE DISASTER

these neighborhoods demonstrated "the futility of a sole reliance on technocratic fixes and the imperfections of their institutionalization" as well as "the vulnerability of socioeconomic groups unable to afford modern, earthquake-resistant accommodation."[42]

As one would expect, the number of elderly people who perished in Kobe was high, but there was also a surprising spike in the number of deaths among young adults in their early twenties.[43] This indicated that college students living in low-cost housing (such as rooming houses), where their lives were transient rather than embedded in the community, met their demise because neighbors who were not aware of them did not know to search for them in the rubble.[44] This points to how necessary it is to design housing and public areas to create more opportunities, through space, education, and events, for neighborly interactions that might eventually lead to friendships.

Response

Broken transportation and communication hindered relief operations and left many survivors feeling stranded. Some public facilities designated as emergency headquarters, including the city hall, ward offices, and police stations, also collapsed, slowing relief efforts. About 40 percent of city employees were survivors themselves,[45] and only 41 percent were able to report to their jobs that day.[46] The Self-Defense Force (SDF) was not mobilized until nearly twenty-four hours after the quake because of bureaucratic and logistical challenges as well as "attitudes about the role of the military in Japanese civil society"—for at that time, the use of the military was disconnected from local preparedness efforts.[47] With telecommunications exceeding capacity and power also cut in many places, affecting television and radio, the impacted areas became an informational "black hole."[48]

With the lack of government response, many owed their survival to self-reliance and their neighbors: approximately 34.9 percent of survivors self-rescued, 31.9 percent were rescued by family members, and 28.1 percent were rescued by friends or neighbors, in contrast with only 2.5 percent by police, firefighters, and the SDF.[49] These numbers affirm the strength of mutual support and social relationships.

As people struggled to find loved ones and reach evacuation sites, the skies filled with black smoke. Fearing aftershocks and gas leaks, or recognizing that their homes were destroyed, survivors evacuated to shelters such as public schools, communal facilities, parks, parking spaces, empty lots, public housing sites, hotels, and company housing, mostly within a five-hundred-meter radius.[50] Shelters provided emergency services such as food, water delivery, portable sanitation, and power generators. The majority of evacuees were middle-aged or elderly.

Narrow streets, damaged roads, and fallen debris impeded firefighters and emergency access: 70 percent of all damaged four-meter-wide roads were not even walkable because of the debris.[51] With the water supply disrupted, fire crews refilled their trucks from undamaged, privately owned water tanks, swimming pools, rivers, and even the sea.[52] Fires were finally extinguished after twenty-nine hours,[53] but the restoration of lifeline infrastructures took longer, with 1.3 million homes without water for up to three months. Another 2.6 million households temporarily lost power, which was restored after six days, while 860,000 lost gas supply (creating the secondary risk of gas leakage).[54]

The Kobe earthquake was a turning point, as it was the first urban center that had touted its modern seismic engineering standards only to be razed by an earthquake and subsequent fires. Before 1995, mitigation focused mostly on improving structural engineering, but Kobe's devastation clearly demonstrated that more holistic preparations were essential. An on-site emergency headquarters was established in the disaster area to ensure a prompt response at the local level. However, due to the disrupted communication channels between prefecture and municipality offices, the prefecture had to call more than ten thousand evacuation shelters directly to figure out which emergency resources each needed.[55] The lack of centralized coordination made food and water distribution chaotic; for example, rice (grain) arrived at shelters without any cooking utensils.[56] In response, a logistics network was established through bōsai parks and regional bōsai hubs via land-based, marine, and aviation-based transport methods.[57] Lessons learned about coordination issues and infrastructure failures led to the development of the Disaster Medical Assistance Team (DMAT), after even hospitals that had survived the quake faced utility outages.[58] In addition, a cooperative agreement was created between prefectures and an emergency communication network for municipalities.[59]

Policy

The 1995 earthquake was the first major seismic disaster to strike after the 1923 earthquake and the initiation of modern Japanese bōsai policy. After the earthquake, a series of legislative acts related to disaster mitigation and response addressed shortcomings observed during the catastrophe. The new Seismic Retrofitting of Buildings Act responded to the high destruction rate of older buildings by providing national and local subsidies to homeowners who opted to retrofit their homes. Recognizing the impact that losing their homes had on families, the Livelihood Support Act was put in place in 1998 to provide grants to those affected.[60] Another critical realization concerned overreliance on engineering—and technological hubris. Murakami Suminao, director of the Laboratory of Urban Safety Planning, warned that the notion that "a building can withstand every possible combination of conditions that exists in nature is simply irresponsible,"[61] and thus Japan began considering development much more holistically. Japan's Fifth Comprehensive National Development Plan (1998) made a point of learning from the Kobe earthquake, combining disaster-specific measures, such as the development of improved evacuation systems, with improving the seismic resilience of buildings and infrastructure, establishing regional bōsai hubs, improving disaster-related communications, and developing new bōsai technologies and other disaster research.[62]

Self-Help, Mutual Support, and Bōsai Education

Another inflection point was the outpouring of strong mutual aid among local residents as well as a spirit of volunteerism that had not been seen before in Japan. Nearly 1.5 million people from across the country assisted Kobe's survivors in the thirteen months following the earthquake.[63] As Alpaslan Ozerdem and Tim Jaco state, until the Kobe earthquake, "the overall assumption was that disaster management was a far too serious business for civil society to take an active role in. For the most part, it was considered from a technical and organizational perspective in which the main actors were state institutions and local authorities. The civil population at large were regarded as the victims of disasters (and certainly not a resource of skills and experience which might be mobilized to respond to a disaster) for whom the public sector were saviors."[64] As the post-disaster surge of volunteerism led to formalized groups supporting the reconstruction efforts for several years, the Nonprofit Organization Law was established in 1998 to assist these groups in acquiring legal status. This was, in part, reflected by the machizukuri movement, which burgeoned to help residents vocalize their opinions and design ideas during the reconstruction process.

The support of local governments to the jishubō also became more official under the amended Disaster Countermeasure Acts in 1995, which created a national subsidy system and put local governments in charge of fostering jishubō.[65] Members are expected to patrol their neighborhoods daily, stockpile supplies, and organize drills or provide bōsai education; during a disaster, they act as first responders and assist with evacuation in cooperation with firefighters. Each member has a specific role—president, vice president, firefighting crew, rescue crew, evacuation guidance crew, and meal and water service crew—allowing them all to jump into action quickly when a disaster strikes.[66] Participation has been steadily growing since the 1980s, and as of 2019, 84.1 percent of households are in a district covered by a jishubō. In 2022, there were more than 166,833 jishubō organizations nationwide.[67]

Lower participation by young people and apartment dwellers could threaten these groups in the future, particularly as current constituents age. In an effort to address this, after the Kobe earthquake, many jishubō reaffirmed the traditional custom of *mukō san gen ryōdonari* (three houses across the street and neighbors on either side of your house). The six homes would support each other daily, whether in acquiring supplies or in providing temporary care for the elderly or for children. Jishubō and neighborhood associations nationwide adopted this slogan and encouraged bringing a small gift, as a means of introduction, when moving into a new neighborhood.

The Kobe earthquake taught citizens the importance of self-help and mutual support among peers without waiting for government assistance. Since then, various forms of bōsai education have focused on teaching children to become self-reliant. One program, developed from 117 surveys and fifty survivor interviews from the earthquake, is Iza! Kaeru Caravan! (Let's Go! Frog Caravan!), run by the Kobe-based nonprofit +arts. Often held in parks, the program features activities through which children can accumulate points and acquire bōsai skills while having fun. Nagata Hirokazu, the president of +arts, expanded the work in partnership with artist Yorifuji Bunpei, publishing two books and creating customized business card–sized bōsai manuals for employees of big companies such as Tokyo Metro and Tokyo Gas. Pushing further into popular culture, +arts collaborated with Kanai Masaaki and Yano Naoko from the lifestyle brand MUJI to create Itsumo Moshimo (Always be prepared), a campaign that promotes preparedness through objects from everyday life.[68] Nagata and his team have also created BOU-LEAGUE, a bōsai Olympics-type event, which involves working with sports businesses and holding events in a variety of places, such as shopping centers and colleges. The BOU-LEAGUE games, designed using only black and white, focus mainly on teens and young adults competing through time trials and physical ability to increase their disaster reduction knowledge. These innovative collaborations have helped Nagata's initiatives spread nationally and globally.[69]

2011 Tohoku Triple Disaster

Japan met catastrophe again on March 11, 2011, when the triple disaster of a massive earthquake, tsunami, and nuclear accident wreaked death and destruction on coastal communities in the Tohoku region. The Great East Japan Earthquake (hereafter the 2011 Tohoku disaster) was one of the most devastating seismic, tsunami, and nuclear disasters to hit any nation. The magnitude 9.0 undersea megathrust earthquake struck at 2:46 pm on March 11, 2011. Eight prefectures experienced shaking greater than SI6.0 (Miyagi, Fukushima, Ibaraki, Tochigi, Iwate, Gunma, Saitama, and Chiba).[70] Within thirty minutes, the onslaught of water ravaged over 650 kilometers of coastline, inundating over 561 square kilometers, reaching run-up heights of nearly 40 meters, and pushing up to 49 kilometers inland via the Kitakami River. Fifteen Japanese prefectures were affected by both the earthquake and tsunami, from Aomori all the way to Chiba. As of March 1, 2020, an estimated 19,729 deaths were caused by the disaster, with an additional 2,559 people still missing.[71] In many towns, death rates neared or exceeded 10 percent, which was particularly traumatic in small, close-knit communi-

Figure 9. Evacuees huddling on roofs as the tsunami inundates Rikuzentakata on March 11, 2011.

ties. As in the Kobe earthquake, the elderly were the most severely hit: 65 percent of the dead were over sixty years old. While many of the impacted communities (and the region of Tohoku overall) are aging, the death rate of the elderly was twice their ratio in the population,[72] most likely reflecting the difficulty of evacuating long distances on foot and climbing steep hills.

The force and height of the tsunami were unfathomable. As it rushed the coast, it swept down everything in its path: forests, buildings, even seawalls. Water reached above the rooftops of multistory buildings and overturned concrete towers, leaving houses and cars floating across the landscape. Boats were pushed inland, sometimes left perched on top of buildings as the waves receded. Those structures that survived the first onslaught were often destroyed by the powerful force of the water pulling back out to sea—or by the second or third tsunami waves. In total, 1,271,687 buildings were severely damaged or destroyed, including two-thirds of local government buildings.[73] Fires also broke out, especially in areas with oil refineries and natural gas plants, and turned damaged houses into a floating, burning mass.

Destroyed infrastructure delayed relief operations, as many coastal towns faced the loss of the only supply lines connecting them to the outside world. Lifelines were disrupted for weeks or longer: 8.91 million households lost power, 480,000 lost their gas supply, and 2.2 million were without water. Over a million phone lines were downed,

Figure 10. Shizugawa coast photographed on June 11, 2011, from inside a home located twenty meters above sea level.

and sewage was also disrupted across thirteen prefectures.[74] However, infrastructure also helped in some unexpected ways; near Sendai, some elevated highways prevented water from reaching further inland.

Coastal Fukushima experienced a smaller tsunami than other prefectures, but it is still suffering from displacement caused by the Fukushima Daiichi nuclear plant disaster, the only one of the four nuclear plants in the tsunami-impacted region to have suffered a meltdown. The loss of safety equipment and power, as well as fumbled decision making, led to the crisis.[75] Without sufficient cooling, meltdowns occurred in three of the plant's reactors. The Fukushima disaster encapsulates the way modern societies create risks beyond those posed by nature alone. The scale of the meltdown can be attributed to a combination of the tsunami itself, insufficient planning for this type of hazard, and poor management following the initial destruction. The evacuation process was complicated by delayed information sharing, so residents lacked clarity about when they should evacuate or where they should go, potentially contributing to unnecessary radiation exposure.

Quick evacuation is crucial to surviving a tsunami, which can arrive only minutes following an earthquake. Although a tsunami warning sounded within three minutes of the March 11 earthquake, the first announcement underestimated the tsunami heights, prompting many residents to evacuate to insufficiently high areas or not at all.[76] The tsunami heights were corrected in later announcements, but for some, these came too late. Evacuees fled to a combination of designated and ad hoc sites. Many relied on training from frequent evacuation drills, particularly in schools, and ran to familiar spaces such as parks, schools, and shrines on high ground. In flat areas such as the Sendai plain, many fled to multistory buildings. However, the extreme run-up heights submerged some evacuation sites, including officially designated ones, contributing to the high death toll.

Compared to an earthquake alone, in which the aftermath is often a patchwork of collapsed buildings, the 2011 Tohoku tsunami annihilated the entire urban fabric, leaving a landscape stripped of all markers and left with only mangled steel, concrete, and wood as memories of what had once existed. Stagnant water pooled in what had been foundations of homes. Boats and buoys obstructed highways and broke roofs of three-story buildings. The immensity of the impacted area meant that survivors faced extensive and diverse catastrophes, differentiated by topography, by urban or rural density, and by whether damage was caused by the earthquake, tsunami, or nuclear contamination.

Response

The 2011 disaster struck on a very different scale from the preceding 1923 Tokyo and 1995 Kobe earthquakes, which were centered primarily in urban areas. This disaster impacted hundreds of kilometers of coastline, ranging from the midsize city of Sendai, with a population of 1.2 million, to scattered villages and fishing hamlets along narrow inlets of the rugged ria coastline. This geographic diversity and its broad scope made responding to an already devastating disaster even more challenging. This was one of many factors complicating the Tohoku response. Official post-disaster plans were typically tailored to specific hazards (earthquake, tsunami, technological disasters, flood, fire) and fell short of addressing this cascading, multi-hazard megadisaster.

The SDF played a large role in the immediate response, rescuing nineteen thousand survivors. Emergency firefighters and interprefectural emergency police also helped with rescue and response, while DMAT provided medical aid. Many civil society organizations also figured prominently in the response, including NGOs and volunteers, often aided by international resources.[77]

The scale of disaster required not only immediate evacuation but also long-term use of emergency shelters, as large areas of settlement had been wiped away entirely. The primary shelters were schools: 622 were used following the tsunami, often for periods of many months.[78] Other local sites that had not been designated as evacuation sites but accepted evacuees for long periods were shrines, temples, hotels, and *ryokan* (traditional inns). Survivors then moved to temporary housing, which was still in use in much of the impacted region in 2019, eight years after the disaster.

Regulations such as the 1961 Disaster Countermeasures Act stipulated that the central government play a major role in framing the reconstruction following the 2011 disaster. However, the reconstruction was also shaped by the nature of the disaster: with the majority of local government buildings destroyed, many local officials lost in the disaster, and the annihilation of the status quo across the Tohoku coast, locally led planning was difficult, particularly in the tsunami's immediate aftermath. Although some existing policies were applied, the government rushed to pass new regulations. Essentially, the national government provided funding and guidelines, the prefectures provided support for larger mitigation infrastructure, and municipalities eventually managed the implementation of the projects and navigated their various complexities.

In April 2011, one month after the disaster, the Reconstruction Design Council was established to create a high-level approach to reconstruction. The fifteen-member expert panel included architect Ando Tadao, regional planning expert Onishi Takashi, and disaster mitigation and reconstruction expert Kawata Yoshiaki. Their recommendations underscored a community-centered, locally led approach. In June, the Reconstruction Design Council announced seven principles, proposing a combination of hard infrastructure and soft strategies as well as a shift from the conventional "line" defense (seawalls) to "multiple layered defenses" (redesigning rivers and roads through land adjustment or machizukuri) for the reconstruction of Tohoku.[79]

The Tsunami Countermeasures Committee,[80] a subset of the Central Disaster Management Council, announced the preliminary seawall strategies on June 26 and published the final report on September 28, 2011.[81] Committee members defined Level 1 as the relatively frequent tsunami caused by a magnitude 8.0 or lower earthquake; for L1, coastal infrastructure such as seawalls should be built to protect lives and livelihoods. A Level 2 tsunami occurs once every five hundred to one thousand years, caused by a temblor with a magnitude of 9.0 or above; for L2, comprehensive tsunami measures are recommended for major infrastructure, including resettling to higher ground and updating hazard zoning and early warning systems.

On August 11, 2011, the Basic Policy for Reconstruction was released. It designated 277 municipalities as Special Reconstruction Areas to be supported with a wide range of subsidies and taxation measures.[82] In the policy, forty fundamental infrastructure-related reconstruction subsidy programs were administered through the five ministries, including seawall construction, collective relocation, land readjustment, and projects to raise the ground.[83] This funding structure encouraged municipalities to take on large-scale reconstruction strategies, with the central government covering 100 percent of approved construction projects.

In December 2011, the Tsunami Bōsai Regional Development Law was enacted, recommending disaster reduction with multilayered protection that combines hard and soft measures. The prefectures first determined the tsunami inundation levels, using current and historic data, and then considering the simulations provided by the central government, they established seawall heights. The amount of destruction in 2011 was correlated with the inundation depth, and researchers determined that the inflection point was at about two meters. With this data point, any area susceptible to more than two meters of water from a future L2 tsunami would be a high-risk zone.[84] This L2 rule of two meters became known as the Two-Two Rule. Based on this, the Tsunami Warning Zones (yellow) were created with enhanced evacuation plans and routes; Special Tsunami Warning Zones (orange and red) marked areas within the two-meter inundation zone, where casualties would be high. In both orange and red zones, building construction (e.g., housing, hospitals, welfare facilities) is regulated, and some municipalities completely restrict construction.[85]

Despite language surrounding "layered" systems of defenses, seawall construction constitutes the most visible response to the catastrophe, followed by ground elevation and relocation. Akimoto Fukuo notes that the "multiple defenses" concept, formulated by the national council, was not effectively translated to other government agencies.[86] Although some communities protested against seawall construction (especially around fishing ports), decrying the significant loss of landscape and the negative impact on the ecosystem, 66 percent of seawalls had been completed as of January 2020.[87] The total seawall length in Miyagi was extended from 155 kilometers before the tsunami to 239 kilometers after it.[88]

Not surprisingly, the three hardest-hit prefectures adopted varied approaches to reconstruction. Fukushima had to contend with complex radiation issues in order to establish exclusion zones. Miyagi employed Article 84 of the Building Standards Law (also used in Kobe) to impose a moratorium on building for eight months[89] and restricted construction in the designated zones in several municipalities: Kesennuma, Higashi Matsushima, Natori, Minamisanriku, Onagawa, and Yamamoto. All building activities, except for temporary structures, were banned. By law, the default maximum period of restriction was two months, but a special measure was enacted after the Tohoku disaster to extend the period up to eight months. Some municipalities created special exclusionary areas. For example, in Onagawa, the restriction was not applied in the commercial area, because property owners argued that the restriction would impede economic recovery.[90] Iwate, with its less dense urban areas and more numerous rural areas, chose Article 39, which designated disaster risk zones, asking residents to halt rebuilding in inundated areas because of the possibility that they would need to resettle to higher ground.[91] The prefecture had each municipality designate the disaster risk zones by enacting an ordinance according to its situation.[92]

The 2011 Tohoku disaster strained preexisting regulations due to its massive scale and multi-hazard attributes. It resulted in several revisions of the Disaster Countermeasures Act to improve regional and large-scale disaster management: to provide

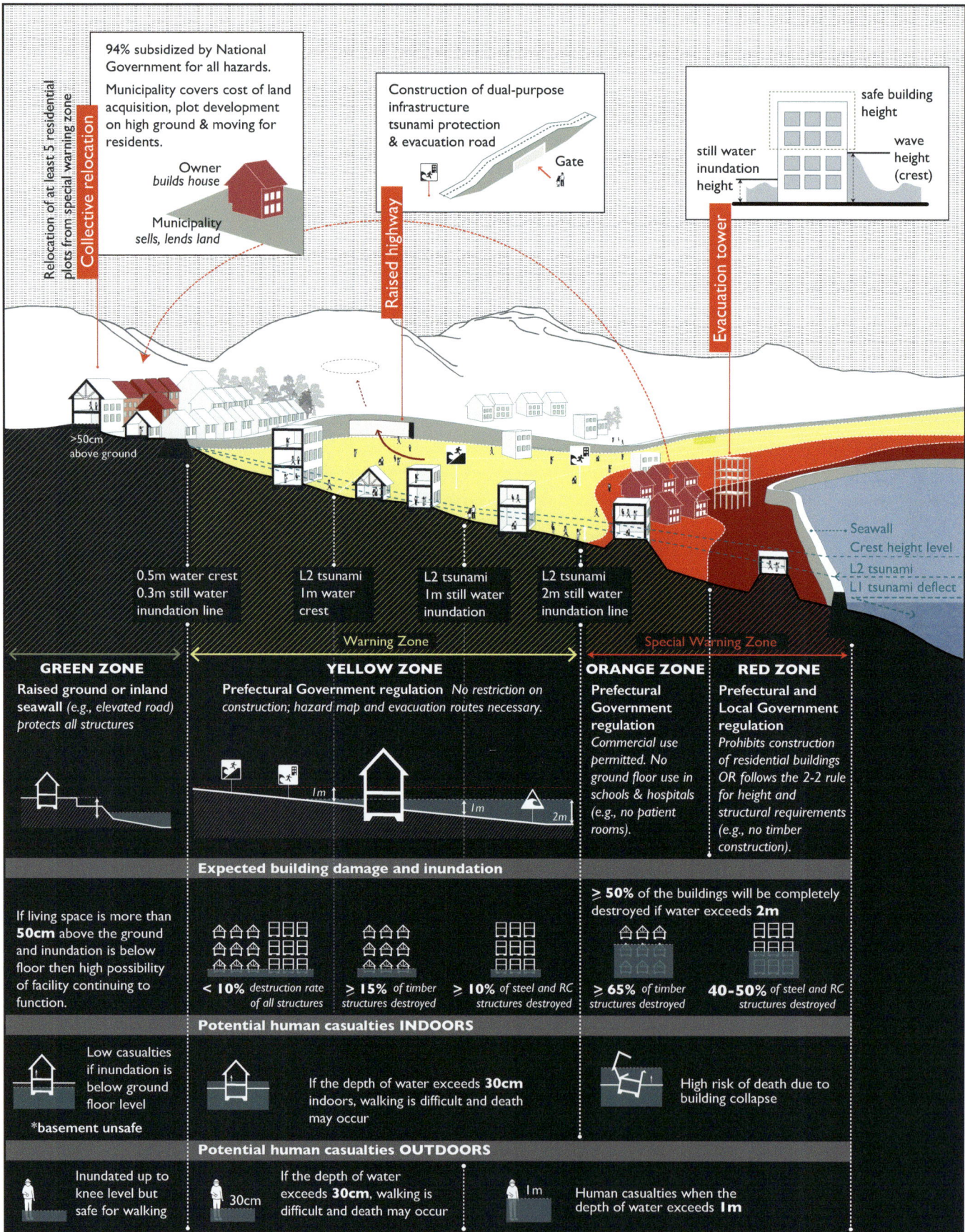

94% subsidized by National Government for all hazards.

Municipality covers cost of land acquisition, plot development on high ground & moving for residents.

Collective relocation

Relocation of at least 5 residential plots from special warning zone

Owner *builds house*

Municipality *sells, lends land*

Construction of dual-purpose infrastructure tsunami protection & evacuation road

Raised highway

Gate

Evacuation tower

safe building height

still water inundation height

wave height (crest)

>50cm above ground

0.5m water crest
0.3m still water inundation line

L2 tsunami
1m water crest

L2 tsunami
1m still water inundation

L2 tsunami
2m still water inundation line

Seawall
Crest height level
L2 tsunami
L1 tsunami deflect

Warning Zone

Special Warning Zone

GREEN ZONE

Raised ground or inland seawall (e.g., elevated road) protects all structures

YELLOW ZONE

Prefectural Government regulation *No restriction on construction; hazard map and evacuation routes necessary.*

1m

1m

2m

ORANGE ZONE

Prefectural Government regulation *Commercial use permitted. No ground floor use in schools & hospitals (e.g., no patient rooms).*

RED ZONE

Prefectural and Local Government regulation *Prohibits construction of residential buildings OR follows the 2-2 rule for height and structural requirements (e.g., no timber construction).*

Expected building damage and inundation

If living space is more than **50cm** above the ground and inundation is below floor then high possibility of facility continuing to function.

< 10% *destruction rate of all structures*

≥ 15% *of timber structures destroyed*

≥ 10% *of steel and RC structures destroyed*

≥ 50% of the buildings will be completely destroyed if water exceeds **2m**

≥ 65% *of timber structures destroyed*

40-50% *of steel and RC structures destroyed*

Potential human casualties INDOORS

Low casualties if inundation is below ground floor level

*basement unsafe

If the depth of water exceeds **30cm** indoors, walking is difficult and death may occur

High risk of death due to building collapse

Potential human casualties OUTDOORS

Inundated up to knee level but safe for walking

30cm

If the depth of water exceeds **30cm**, walking is difficult and death may occur

1m

Human casualties when the depth of water exceeds **1m**

better support to local government disaster response, including shelter designation; to improve evacuation planning and rapid response; to encourage local residents to propose their own disaster-preparedness plans, including hazard maps; and to improve incorporation of disaster prevention into people's everyday lives by having them participate in drills and knowledge-sharing activities.[93]

Following the disaster, the Cabinet Office (CAO) expanded a support system for community-level bōsai projects and dispatched expert advisors to districts that were establishing forward-looking community bōsai plans.[94] Community-led disaster management plans, such as those formed by jishubō, were also integrated into municipal plans.[95] In addition, the Act for Enhancing the Citizen Fire Corps was created to augment local disaster management capability.[96] At least 712 organizations participated in the Japan Civil Network for Disaster Relief in East Japan, a nationwide group supporting Tohoku disaster survivors.[97] This shift toward volunteerism, NGOs, and NPOs suggests the increasing role of civil society in Japanese disaster preparedness and response.

Tsunami Preparedness Day

Following the Tohoku disaster, November 5 (memorializing the 1854 Ansei Nankai tsunami date) was named "Tsunami Preparedness Day," with large drills, citizen evacuation workshops, first-aid education, and symposia held annually in tsunami-vulnerable coastal regions nationwide. In 2021, 10 national authorities, 118 local public bodies, and 28 private-sector organizations operated tsunami bōsai events.[98] At the local level, annual disaster drills take place in designated evacuation spaces in each school district and are hosted by the city fire department, jishubō, and *shōbōdan* (citizen fire corps). Most of the evacuation drills on November 5 prioritize *tsunami tendenko,* underscoring the importance of taking responsibility for one's own evacuation with the expectation that one's family and loved ones will do the same. The purpose of this practice is to prevent family members from wasting valuable evacuation time seeking one another. The *tsunami tendenko* maxim is credited with saving many lives during the 2011 Tohoku tsunami, particularly among children who evacuated on their own rather than waiting for instruction. November 5 was memorialized in 2015 by the UN General Assembly as World Tsunami Awareness Day.

2011 Wakayama Landslides

The Tohoku disaster was not the only calamity to hit Japan in 2011. Typhoon Talas made landfall in early September 2011, damaging the mountainous areas in Wakayama, Nara, and Mie Prefectures. Despite previous structural efforts in the region, such as "cutting hazardous cliffs, concrete-block pitching, slope frameworks, [and] retaining

Figure 11. Layered coastal tsunami protection policies and associated zones.

walls"[99] and planting vegetation, this disaster triggered 3,000 landslides.[100] The 2011 Great Kii Peninsula flood was designated an "Extreme Disaster" by the national government. In Wakayama, fourteen rivers exceeded the flood-risk level, and in Mie, several wajū collapsed into the Ainoya River. The typhoon was large and slow, prolonging heavy rainfall, which exceeded 2,400 millimeters in some areas. Nationwide casualties included 82 dead and 113 injured. In addition, 380 houses collapsed, 3,625 houses were damaged, and 5,499 houses were totally inundated.[101] Wakayama, where the damage was greatest, suffered 96 sediment disasters, including 58 mudslides, 4 landslides, and 34 avalanches. Water overtopped blocked areas in the river channels, forming mudslides that buried downstream villages. Some Japan Railways (JR) train lines were closed for up to three months as a result of collapsed bridges.[102] On September 4, when the emergency disaster headquarters of the central government was established, the number of evacuees in the three prefectures had reached 4,801. Even after that, landslides continued to destroy houses, and emergency sheltering in some areas lasted for two months. The Disaster Relief Act was enacted in Wakayama, Nara, Mie, and Okayama and applied to 160,000 affected residents. The Japan Society of Civil Engineers stated that this typhoon was another reminder that structural reinforcements alone cannot always prevent disasters.[103] They need to be combined with zoning, evacuation, and other soft measures.

The 2011 Great Kii Peninsula flood was a wake-up call, as only one out of the thirteen affected locations had been previously designated as a warning zone. It was the first flood event for which the Ministry of Land, Infrastructure, Transport and Tourism (MLIT) organized an emergency field investigation, based on the 2001 Landslide Countermeasures Act, to inform residents about the risk of landslides; to establish warning and evacuation systems; to control new housing construction according to zones; and to improve the safety and security of the designated areas. Municipalities are required to take appropriate measures based on the Disaster Countermeasures Act, such as formulating a local bōsai plan that includes evacuation instructions for residents.[104] In small mountainous municipalities, most settlements are in warning zones, as are their evacuation shelters. Based on the Landslide Countermeasures Act, measures to raise awareness to "protect oneself" encourage residents to monitor hazardous areas and provide information, such as precipitation rates, to inform their decision making. In defining hazard zones, it is not the technical aspects that take time but the building of consensus among residents who often oppose such designations because they tend to decrease land value and heighten concerns about depopulation in already shrinking villages. Real estate agents in Japan are required to explain hazard information and geotechnical aspects to buyers,[105] but challenges remain in how to respond through existing land-use policies and design measures. This other 2011 disaster likely prompted Tohoku resettlement plans for mountainous areas to include drastic measures against landslides.

FREQUENT TORRENTIAL EVENTS IN RECENT YEARS

As a result of climate change caused by global warming, severe typhoons and deadly torrential rainfalls unlike any seen before have become an annual occurrence between July and October. These events are also occurring in geographically unprecedented regions, extending even to Hokkaido. Torrential rains in 2018 led to widespread river flooding, urban inland floods, and mudslides, causing 237 deaths and destroying 21,460 houses. Lifelines were severely damaged, leaving 263,593 households without water.[106] The following year, Typhoon Hagibis wreaked havoc in more than twenty prefectures. Thirty-five thousand hectares of riverine flooding resulted from forty-seven broken levees at 142 locations. Urban flooding submerged underground stations and power supplies, disrupting electricity and water supply for over a week. More than 950 landslides occurred in mountainous regions. Over 100,000 houses were damaged, inundated, or completely destroyed. A concerning statistic from this event is that evacuation advisories were issued to 7.97 million people, but only 237,008 actually evacuated.[107] In both events, the elderly accounted for 60 to 80 percent of the dead and missing, reaffirming the need to focus on vulnerable populations.

After these events, the Disaster Countermeasures Act was revised to issue evacuation *orders,* rather than *advisories,* to clarify the message when the alert level is at four. If it reaches the highest, level five, the message is changed to "emergency safety assurance," meaning that if you are already in a safe location, such as the upper floor of a secure building, *stay* and do not evacuate. Since these instructions are still challenging, municipalities are obliged to create "individual evacuation plans" for each resident as a community support system. This effort is especially important for aiding vulnerable people living alone in hazard zones; based on an analysis by municipalities, 510,000 have been identified. The central government will pay ¥7,000 per person to municipalities in order to formulate plans for each person for the next five years.[108] These events are some of the many recent alarming examples of more intense and unpredictable rainstorms and typhoons unexpectedly striking regions with little experience in coping with disasters.

PREPARING FOR A TOKYO INLAND EARTHQUAKE

An M7 class (magnitude 7.3) earthquake directly below the Tokyo Metropolitan Area has a 70 percent probability of occurring in the next thirty years.[109] The worst damage prediction (as of October 2019) is 23,000 fatalities, 610,000 houses completely destroyed or burned, and damages of up to ¥95 trillion.[110] Fires in densely populated areas with timber-framed homes could last for two days. Since Tokyo is one of the most crowded urban areas in the world, such a disaster raises fears of an unstable power supply, information disruption, transportation paralysis, and millions of people stranded away from their homes.

The national government created the Act on Countermeasures for Metropolitan Inland Earthquake in 2013, which includes a law aimed at promoting bōsai for the predicted earthquake and an emergency action plan for maintaining central administrative functions. In March 2015, the CAO created the Plan for Emergency Countermeasures for the Inland Earthquake. This plan aims to improve seismic resistance of houses to 95 percent and reduce the estimated deaths and building damage by 50 percent.[111] To meet these ambitious goals, the plan sets timelines and targets actions in the areas of emergency transport routes, rescue, medical care, supplies, and fuel within the first seventy-two hours. As outreach to residents is also fundamental, in 2016, the Tokyo Metropolitan Government (TMG) worked with Dentsu and Nosigner to produce a disaster-preparation book for Tokyo, which included maps, diagrams, and comic strips. The books were distributed to 6.7 million households,[112] and the designers have documented on their website how the black-and-yellow graphics have been copied in several other products as the symbol for disaster awareness.

PREPARING FOR A NANKAI TROUGH EARTHQUAKE AND TSUNAMI

The devastation of the 2011 Tohoku disaster galvanized planning for a Nankai Trough megathrust earthquake. With a devastating temblor of magnitude 8.0 or 9.0, followed by a tsunami, such an earthquake has the potential to impact Japan's Pacific coast from Shizuoka Prefecture down to Kyushu at the archipelago's southern tip.

The Nankai Trough is the subduction zone where the Philippine Sea plate is sinking under the Eurasian plate at a rate of several centimeters per year. An earthquake occurs whenever the strain accumulates and the Eurasian plate suddenly releases. Nankai Trough earthquakes have occurred repeatedly in Japan, with a frequency of every 100 to 150 years. The last one was the Showa Nankai earthquake (1946), so in the next 30 years, there is a 70 to 80 percent chance of a similar quake.[113] According to damage estimates by the government, a massive megathrust earthquake could cause damage far beyond that of the 2011 Tohoku disaster—perhaps up to twenty times greater—across the thirteen prefectures on the Pacific coastline. The worst-case scenario could lead to 82,000 perishing in collapsed houses, 10,000 in fires, and 230,000 in the tsunami; approximately 2,386,000 homes could be destroyed.[114] There is some controversy around these estimates, but in general, the emphasis has been on preparing for the worst case.[115]

The Tsunami Evacuation Measures Plan was created in 2014 as part of the Act on Nankai Trough Earthquake Disaster Management. This five-year plan designated 139 municipalities along the Pacific coast as priority Tsunami Evacuation Regions, emphasizing mitigation infrastructure, preparedness activities, and preemptive action. Types of projects range from the development of welfare facilities, schools, and hospitals—which might be required to facilitate a group relocation project—to evacuation route and space planning.[116]

COMPREHENSIVE BŌSAI-SAFETY SUBSIDIES

To contend with such unprecedented massive disasters and frequent devastating floods, the government established comprehensive grants to support mitigation projects as well as citizens' grassroots bōsai activities. The bōsai-safety subsidies created in 2012 focus on building and repairing infrastructure to protect lives and livelihoods. Every year, over ¥1 trillion of subsidies are issued to municipalities.[117] Hazards range from earthquakes and tsunamis to frequently occurring typhoons, riverine floods, and landslide disasters, and projects include flood-control measures in mountainous regions, raised highways reinforced to seismic standards, development of tsunami-mitigation and flood-management facilities, tsunami evacuation facility construction, bōsai parks and hubs development, and fire reduction and seismic measures in dense urban areas.[118] Regional activities, such as creating hazard maps and risk assessments, developing bōsai education and drills, stockpiling emergency supplies, and building community councils, are included.[119] With this, the government aims to create a "disaster aware society," where every stakeholder in the nation is prepared for future disasters. It encourages a shift to a society in which governments, businesses, and residents all share knowledge of, and preparedness for, disaster risks.[120]

DISCUSSION

Hazards, policies, and cultures of disaster preparedness have shaped Japan's physical environments. This context is described above not only to provide background for the typologies discussed in the following chapters but also to show how they developed in very specific spatial and social contexts. While many lessons can be drawn from Japan's bōsai cultures and spaces, this background suggests that Japanese typologies cannot simply be dropped into other contexts. Rather, they provide lessons that can shape an anticipatory design process, which can in turn be used to tailor typologies for at-risk contexts across the globe.

At scales from seismic-resistant buildings to citywide infrastructure designed to stop the spread of fire or the arrival of tsunamis, bōsai ideas are embedded in all levels of Japanese daily life. How these spaces are used by people—from parks as sites for disaster-preparedness drills to community buildings as vertical tsunami evacuation spaces—has further shaped the development of a series of spatial typologies across Japan.

3

URBAN SYSTEMS

The places we inhabit—cities, towns, suburban and rural landscapes—are interconnected systems. This interconnectedness is both physical and social, and it is made particularly visible during a natural disaster. The capacity to respond effectively during a disaster has to do not only with individual knowledge and preparedness but also with a community's ability to work together, whether to help put out fires in dense neighborhoods (as in Kobe) or to encourage evacuation beyond designated sites based on the scale of the disaster (as in Tohoku). These examples affirm that urban systems must deal fundamentally with cross-scalar social and spatial negotiations between top-down, government-led projects and the impacted individuals and communities on the ground.

Some aspects of disaster preparedness or mitigation can—and should—be taken on at the scale of the individual, building, or household, but collective planning is essential in mediating the aspects of disasters that have to do with shared social fabrics. Japan's history of strong central planning has played a fundamental role in shaping disaster-preparedness planning across the nation, but this chapter will also explore the shift in recent decades toward engaging the public in community-based planning processes. The cases highlight the importance of the anticipatory design strategy of combining the top-down and the bottom-up, a tension present across the projects but epitomized by multilayered machizukuri community-planning projects.

Inevitably, different groups will have different visions of what an area's future will look like. Collaborating across scales is inherently a form of negotiation, embedded with cost-benefit trade-offs—and not only monetary trade-offs but often far more significant ones in terms of qualities of space and place. In order to make streets wider for evacuation routes following the 1923 Tokyo and 1995 Kobe earthquakes, households were asked to reduce their lot sizes, and they were restricted in the ways they

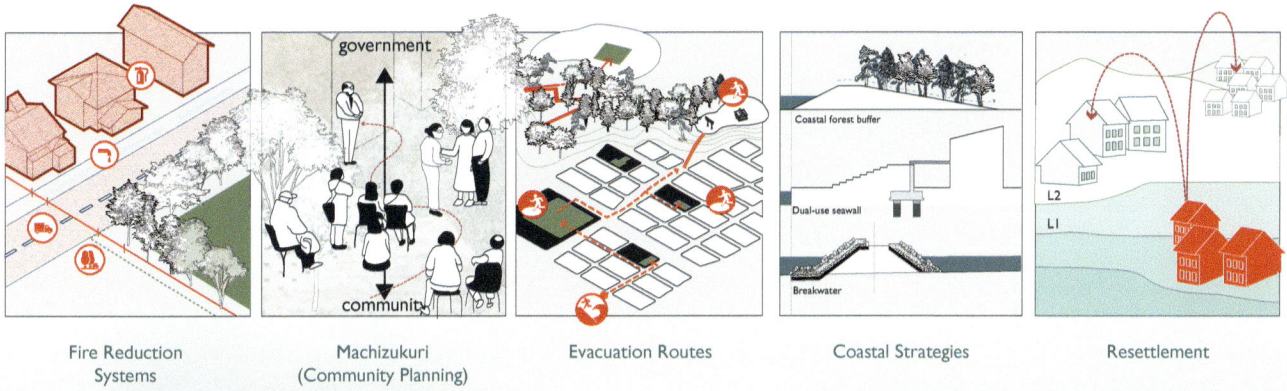

Fire Reduction
Systems

Machizukuri
(Community Planning)

Evacuation Routes

Coastal Strategies

Resettlement

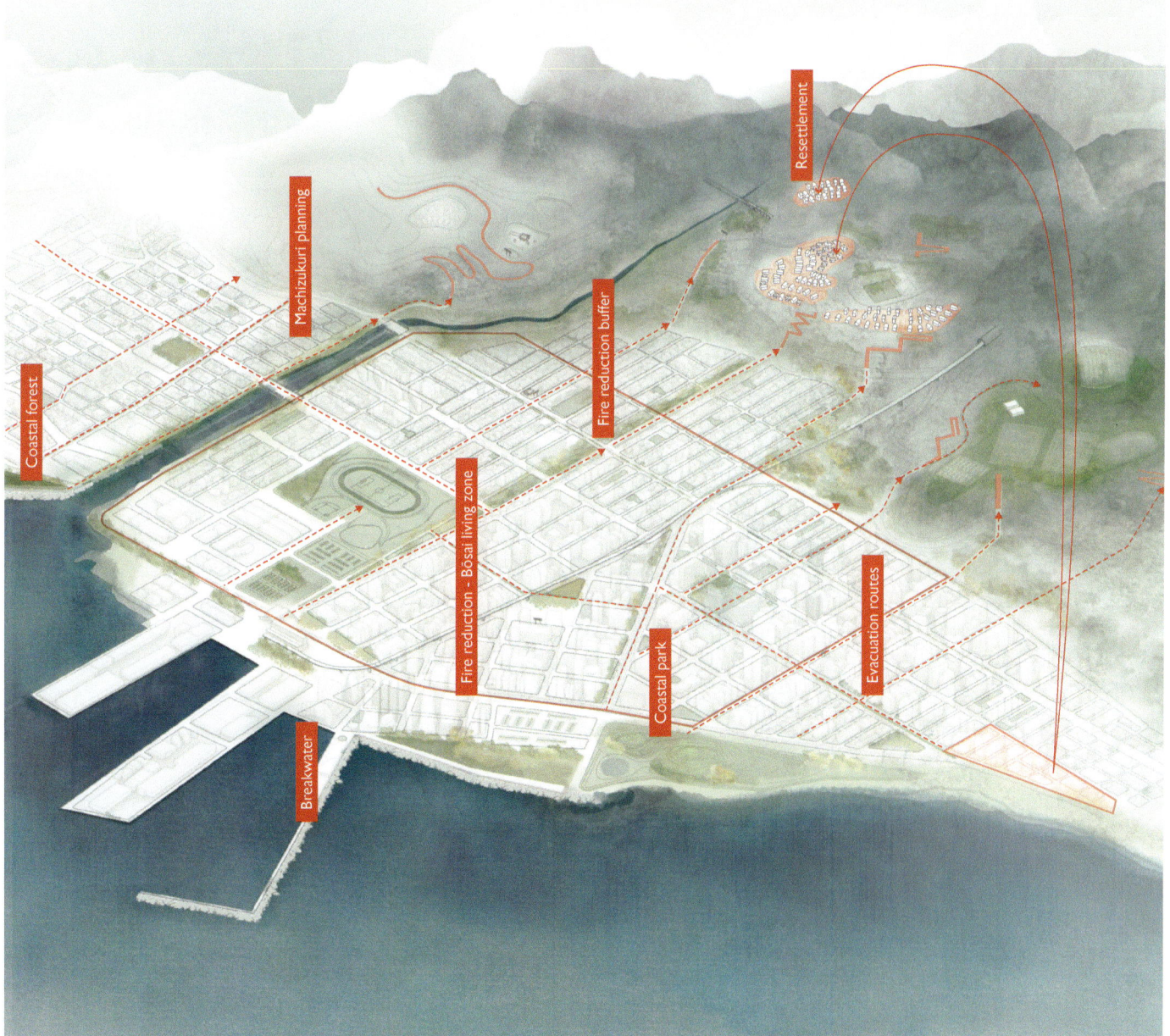

Figure 12. Urban systems for disaster preparedness and mitigation.

could rebuild. While this helped avoid future fires, it often placed a high burden on individual households. It also asked communities to trade their traditional character of narrow, winding streets and dense wooden housing, with their associated lively public streetscapes, for a more regular street grid. These issues are even more strikingly illustrated by the transformations in the Tohoku region, where reconstruction projects are fundamentally changing the nature of the area, separating fishing villages from the sea via massive seawalls and razing mountaintops to support elevated settlements despite shrinking populations. Framing these trade-offs as not only part of a technical cost-benefit analysis but also as a socio-spatial issue strengthens designers' roles in adapting cities to reduce disaster risks.

With climate change and rapid urbanization increasingly intensifying disasters across the globe, urban systems must carefully consider many different contexts. The programs and cases discussed in this chapter emphasize the book's anticipatory design framework of top-down/bottom-up, and in several cases, designers have played an important role mediating between top (e.g., government policies, centralized planning, municipal projects) and bottom (e.g., individuals, communities, local businesses, neighborhood associations, nonprofits). Making on-the-ground connections even as part of large-scale transformative projects can also help mitigate the equity issues often associated with these types of programs. These cases suggest that beyond providing new visions of disaster-prepared futures, designers can also be key to negotiating those transformations across time and space.

THE JAPANESE PLANNING CONTEXT

Japan's early city planning should be understood in the context of the dense, sprawling cities that burgeoned during the Meiji era. While city centers for the elite classes borrowed from Western planning models, housing for the masses was constructed entirely without regulation. This resulted in densely packed and poorly built wooden housing, sometimes without basic infrastructure. Labyrinthine neighborhoods were kindling when fires broke out, and poor construction made even wooden homes vulnerable to earthquakes. Dead-end and winding alleys made escape and response difficult when a disaster did strike. Farms, fields, and other open spaces were filled in, meaning that there was often nowhere for evacuees to go.

Japan has historically been ruled by a system of powerful central governance, with many urban planning parameters handed down through national policies and regulations. The Meiji period established a strong central bureaucracy, with local officials designated by the central government—thus making local governance beholden to national aims over local concerns.[1] While planning was controlled down to the local scale, it prioritized high-level urban infrastructure, efficiency, and growth. This included policies to prevent widespread destruction from environmental hazards, such as laws and reconstruction projects implemented after the 1923 Tokyo earthquake and the 1933 Sanriku tsunami. Meanwhile, communities were left to organize on their own for local management of streets, wells, and waste, contributing to strong social ties. Individuals and families took a personal stake in disaster preparedness; during the Edo period, working-class families "kept emergency baskets ready in conspicuous places."[2] Preparedness was foundational to Japanese life.

Recovery and Reconstruction

The Japanese language distinguishes between *fukkyū* (recovery, restoration) and *fukkō* (reconstruction). While *fukkyū* refers to returning infrastructures to their prior condition following a disaster, the more expansive *fukkō* includes incorporating long-term adaptation into the reconstruction process and considering the city as a whole, including households, businesses, and other spaces of citizens' daily lives.[3] In contemporary terms, *fukkō* is similar to the concept of "building back better": using disaster as an occasion to improve urban systems in order to strengthen them against future hazards. In this sense, disasters become an opportunity to rethink cities and spaces. Learning from the *fukkō* model of reconstruction can in some cases be an opportunity, though in cases such as in the Mano district in Kobe, *fukkyū* plays a more critical role. Urban designer and disaster recovery specialist Kobayashi Ikuo has noted the importance of understanding the specific context and people in order to employ the best mechanisms.[4]

Particular disasters have been key in shaping Japanese cities. The Imperial Reconstruction Plan after the 1923 Tokyo earthquake established modern, centralized Japanese city planning (*toshi-keikaku*) and played a large role in shaping Tokyo as we know it today. Following the disaster, the term *fukkō-keikaku* (reconstruction plan) also came into use. The 1923 earthquake was prefaced by the 1919 City Planning Law, which included the introduction of zoning, a centralized building code, and mechanisms for *tochi kukaku-seiri* (land readjustment), a process by which private land is pooled and parcel boundaries shifted. Owners give over a percentage of land to become part of a collective project, such as a widened road or a park, and in some cases private plots may be relocated entirely.[5] In Japan, land readjustment is often undertaken in the name of disaster mitigation. Due to increased property values, owners can end up with higher-valued assets with less land, but the process can be contentious. These tools allowed for the introduction of citywide plans to mitigate and prepare for disaster risks.

Toshi-keikaku

City planning shaped later reconstruction projects, notably following the 1933 Sanriku earthquake and tsunami and the annihilation caused by World War II's fire- and atomic bombs. Planning power was held primarily by the Home Ministry, which continued to be the case into the postwar years of rapid growth. City planning came down from the national government with minimal local involvement and basically no citizen participation.[6] The rapid economic growth that followed the postwar era pushed urban growth into new areas in the low coastal zones (and as a result, this relatively new development suffered severe damage during the Tohoku tsunami).[7]

Though there has been some shift away from centralized planning in Japan's postwar years, the central government continues to play a strong role, especially following large catastrophes. This was again made visible in the response and reconstruction following the 2011 Tohoku earthquake and tsunami, which was largely shaped by central government regulations that focused on heavy infrastructure and relocation-based responses, but within that framework, there are cases of successful integration of broader community goals.

Machizukuri

Centrally focused Japanese planning often prompted communities to take initiative in local planning. Neighborhood associations—the smallest unit of which is called *tonarigumi,* consisting of five to ten families in the same district—originated in 1597, but around the turn of the twentieth century, national legislation formalized groups in both urban and rural areas to strengthen community networks. An enactment from July 1900 created hygiene associations in which families would perform sanitation maintenance together.[8] During World War II, the neighborhood association was considered a subsidiary of the national government—to expedite top-down communication, distribute emergency supplies, and coordinate air-raid evacuation drills—and was made compulsory across Japan.[9] These groups, in which the majority of Japanese households still participate, address community-level issues "such as public safety, emergency management, welfare services for youths and senior citizens, and beautification"[10] and often collaborate with local governments.

Though abolished during the US occupation, neighborhood associations reemerged in the postwar years alongside a new type of community organization, the machizukuri council. The term *machi* translates as "town," but in *machizukuri,* it implies both the physical and social environment—and *zukuri* suggests a process of making with care. Though it lacks a consistent definition, and there isn't a succinct English translation, *machizukuri* can be generally understood as a community-led local planning system. In the words of Satoh Shigeru, professor emeritus of Waseda University and former director of the Research Institute of Urban and Regional Study, "*machizukuri* was born as an ideal philosophy grounded on local discussions about the improvement of the built environment, lifestyles, and the local community." He describes it as a social movement inviting participation for a "true democracy," which includes citizens whose voices might not be heard by the government.[11] The term was introduced in 1952 by

Masuda Shiro, and machizukuri developed as a direct counterpoint to top-down *toshi-keikaku*.[12] Machizukuri consisted of bottom-up, democratically organized groups often initially formed around specific local concerns, and in this way, the evolution of these groups outlines the process-based condition of making and remaking shared environments.[13] In the 1980s, as national law began to require community participation in planning, local governments formalized machizukuri groups and processes, allowing their recommendations to directly inform urban plans.

URBAN SYSTEMS: CHAPTER ORGANIZATION

This chapter discusses five urban systems that illustrate the negotiation of the top-down and the bottom-up in preparing for disasters—and the types of trade-offs that emerge. "Fire Reduction Systems" examines the role fire has played in reshaping Japanese cities and affirms a multi-hazard approach to anticipating cascading and interlinked events. "Machizukuri" builds upon those strategies through community workshops and residents' roles. "Evacuation Routes" looks at the retrofitting of the urban fabric to allow people to escape disasters more easily. "Coastal Strategies" analyzes the extensive seawall construction following the 2011 Tohoku disaster and its sociopolitical and ecological implications. "Resettlement" puts moving plots and rebuilding in the context of Japanese urban planning, with an emphasis on both pre- and post-tsunami high-ground resettlement processes.

Fire Reduction Systems

As in many cities in Europe and the United States, catastrophic fires in Japan cleared the way for projects to both modernize and fireproof cities, including widened streets, improved water infrastructure, and building codes focused on fire resistance.[1] Many of these plans remained unrealized in Europe and North America, where the era of major fires ended primarily as a result of increased wealth, leading to sturdier building materials and suburbanization.[2] By contrast, in Japan, the traditional urban fabric consists of dense wooden housing, which amplifies fire risk, and narrow alleys that allow flames to jump easily between structures. Japanese homes added further kindling, with sliding *shoji* doors made of paper as well as straw *tatami* mats. Mitigating these risks required a drastic transformation of Japanese cities and urban planning: the post-1923 reconstruction project gave birth to the role of modern disciplines (architecture, landscape design, engineering) and urban forms (land readjustment, streets with sidewalks, bridges, disaster-prepared parks) in Japan's disaster-conscious model of planning.

Fire reduction strategies in Japan can be divided into mitigation strategies, which seek to reduce flammable materials in the urban environment or create buffer zones to prevent a fire's spread, and preparedness strategies, which help citizens or professionals fight or escape from fires. Today, wide roads are still used as firebreaks between neighborhoods, and they are sometimes bordered with less flammable tree species. In some cases, buildings themselves, through the use of fire-resistant materials and fire-suppressant features, become firebreaks. Parks, often encircled by fire-resistant trees with sufficient width and density, can serve as both evacuation spaces and buffers. (A ten-meter-wide forest in two rows, with low foliage porosity, is recommended.) Preparedness includes informing residents of evacuation routes and providing water access for firefighting and post-disaster domestic use. Many of the projects described here prioritize ensuring water availability even when municipal services are disrupted. In addition to regulations to reduce fire risk, these projects accentuate how designing and planning for fire safety requires the consideration of government-level policies, subsidies, and neighborhood-level action. Because of the way fire travels, spreading across any flammable material, fire protection calls for a collective approach.

Owing to this cross-scalar connectivity, planning for fires also inherently involves considerations of individual concessions and equity. In Japanese history, property owners have often been asked to make sacrifices by rebuilding or by giving up land in order to increase fire resistance on a larger scale. In many of these cases, working together as a community has also built important social ties that will help the community be better prepared for the next disaster. The following projects share the ways in which grassroots initiatives and government programs can work together to help create fire-prepared cities. They thus illustrate the potential for design to serve as a bridge between top-down and bottom-up approaches to disaster preparedness.

HISTORY OF FIRE REDUCTION IN JAPANESE URBANISM

Japan's culture of preparedness and attention to environmental hazards has shaped the urban fabric from as far back as the Edo era. Dense Japanese cities were modified following and anticipating disasters, particularly fires, which roared through neighborhoods full of wooden structures with thatched roofs. Key fire prevention systems included *hirokōji,* widened streets intended to serve as firebreaks; *hiyokechi,* plazas designed to serve as evacuation spaces and to help stop fires from spreading;[3] *hiyoketsutsumi,* seven-meter-tall berms that also slowed spreading flames; and *uekidome,* a tree and plant nursery acting as an evacuation space. After the Great Fire of Meireki (1657), which leveled two-thirds of Edo and killed around 100,000 people, the government promoted construction with more fire-resistant materials, such as board or tile roofs (rather than thatch) and stone walls. The shogunate also encouraged fire reduction methods in reconstruction, such as widening roads and establishing open spaces. This was also the time *machibikeshi* firefighter organizations formed.

A severe fire in Edo in 1829 led to the creation of the *hinomiyagura* (fire lookout towers). Neighborhoods determined suitable locations for the towers depending on topography and social customs; locations included on top of a community center, beside a shrine or a busy intersection, or by the riverside in case of flooding. Such Edo measures showed recognition that fire reduction requires the physical infrastructure to connect with the social infrastructure. These innovative systems, from urban design to temporary post-disaster shelters, have continued to develop and evolve in Japan through the present day.

Meiji-era urban codes introduced seven-meter-wide fire-gap roads to help keep fires from spreading.[4] Fire prevention measures of the period also included the construction of brick neighborhoods in the early 1870s (such as the Ginza Brick Street) and the 1881 City of Tokyo Fire Protection Regulation, which called for the use of fireproof materials, including plaster and tile, along designated roads. Homes that violated the plan were forcibly demolished and residents were forced to pay removal costs.[5] These

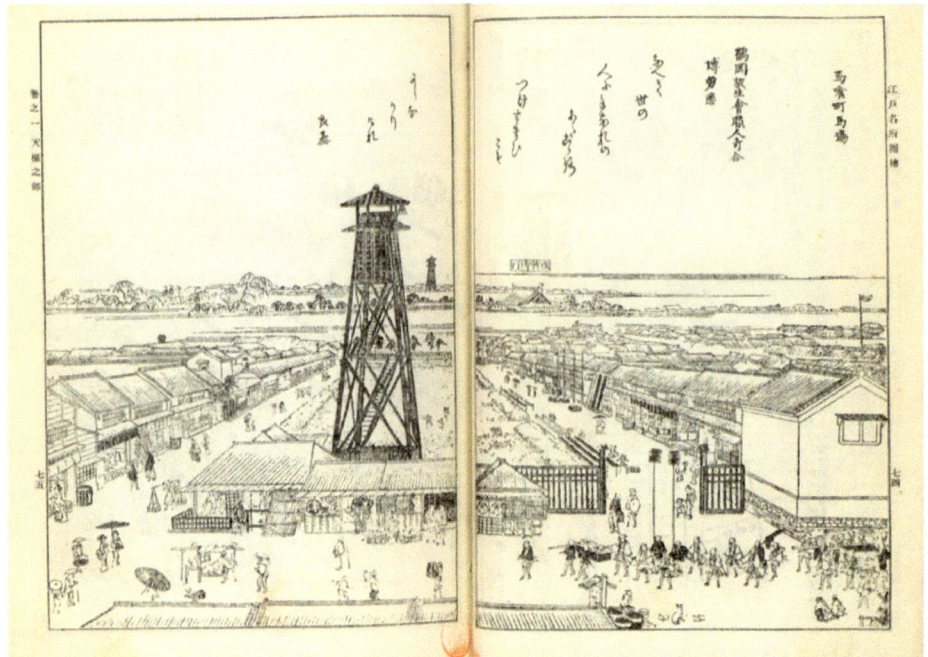

Figure 13. *Hinomiyagura* (fire lookout towers) stand above the skyline in Edo.

strategies, though unjust, are believed to have contributed to a nearly fourfold decrease in large fires between the Meiji and Taishō eras.[6]

Urban Design after the 1923 Tokyo Earthquake and Fire

The 1923 Tokyo earthquake occurred at lunchtime. Toppled cookstoves ignited conflagrations across the dense urban fabric, and 80 percent of the city's built-up area burned,[7] which amounted to 43.6 percent of the entire city.[8] Roughly 92,000 people were killed by fire, while 13,000 died from other causes (primarily collapsed buildings).[9]

The Imperial Reconstruction Plan, led by cabinet minister Gotō Shimpei, was Japan's first comprehensive city plan. Implemented between 1924 and 1930, the plan included not only the burned areas but also the undamaged ones, establishing a systematic approach to fireproofing.[10] Rather than simply rebuilding what was there before, the plan set out a visionary, top-down design to raise a fireproof Tokyo from the disaster's rubble. Gotō initially proposed to purchase all of the incinerated land at a rate of three billion yen, but ultimately the project was scaled down to 3,040 hectares, approximately 80 percent of the burned area.[11] The readjustment revolved around the creation of firebreaks, widened roads, and open spaces to stop the spread of conflagrations.

DESIGN BEFORE DISASTER

The reconstruction plan was Japan's first and largest city planning program, and it continues to shape contemporary approaches to disaster-resistant urban design today. Ten percent of the burned area became parks and boulevards designed as both evacuation routes and firebreaks,[12] a "park system" model that drew on Chicago's post-1871 reconstruction plan.[13] Approximately 260 kilometers of new roads, including the Meiji Ring Road, were created to serve evacuation and firebreak functions.[14] Over 600 kilometers of roads were widened through land readjustment and "modernized" with paving, sidewalks, and street trees.[15] Only 9 percent of Tokyo roads were paved in 1921; this number surged to 91 percent in 1935, after reconstruction was completed. Ultimately, Tokyo's post-1923 reconstruction shaped the city as we know it today.

The plan drew on Western cities as models: namely, London, Paris, Berlin, and Vienna. It also followed a broader European trend toward urban greenbelts, which were primarily intended to control sprawl and provide urban dwellers access to recreational green spaces. In post-quake reconstruction, land readjustment was used not only to widen roads for evacuation and fireproofing but also to introduce a network of parks across the city to serve as evacuation spaces during future catastrophes. After the reconstruction plan came the 1939 Tokyo Green Space Plan (or Tokyo Circular Greenbelt Project), which proposed a 143.8-square-kilometer greenbelt, formed of agricultural land, parks, cemeteries, and private gardens, as well as a park system for the city.[16] Interest in the fire buffer and evacuation potential of the greenbelt and other open spaces grew in the late 1930s owing to concerns about air defense during the Japan-China War.[17]

Shōbōdan Firefighting Associations and Community Action

Japanese fire preparedness relies not only on architectural and infrastructural solutions but also on people power: firefighting and disaster-prevention teams. Municipal firefighters were established in Japan as early as 1873, led by local police chiefs.[18] In addition to formal, full-time firefighters, Japan also maintains a network of *shōbōdan* (citizen fire corps, descendants of Edo-era *machibikeshi*). Under the Fire Organization Act, there were 818,478 shōbōdan firefighters across Japan as of April 2020,[19] but the numbers have been steadily declining. Members typically have other full-time jobs and are paid a small stipend by the government. Considered part-time civil servants, their preparedness work focuses on organizing first-aid classes; visiting homes for fire-prevention instruction and installation of fire alarms; patrolling the community for fire-safety measures; maintaining fire-reduction equipment; supporting the vulnerable and elderly in fire preparedness; and providing disaster drills. They are also trained as first responders to help extinguish fires before the arrival of fire trucks by using portable, locally stored water pumps as well as to provide evacuation guidance and rescue assistance and to clear obstacles from fire truck routes.[20]

During the 1923 Tokyo earthquake, Tokyo had 824 full-time firefighters, 61 vehicles, and two pumps. In addition, 1,402 shōbōdan firefighters helped with 120 hand-towed water pipe vehicles as well as a thorough network of fire hydrants.[21] However, they were unprepared for the scale of the event or for the earthquake damage to the water infrastructure. Firefighters were able to extinguish less than 30 percent of the fires, and 22 of the firefighters perished.[22] Many citizens took it upon themselves to help hold back the fires, with such actions as pouring buckets of water on not-yet-ignited buildings to help keep the fire from spreading; in some cases, local pumps were used to help put out fires that were already burning. In the towns of Kanda-izumi and Sakuma, residents used a combination of bucket brigades and intentionally collapsed buildings near the fire (an Edo-era practice) to stop the fire from spreading. After more than thirty hours, they were able to protect many of their neighborhoods, even as the areas all around them burned to the ground.[23] This level of coordination and cooperation requires social capital. Ironically, the same dense urban environment that fostered the spread of fires also created the close-knit communities best able to fight them. The challenge is creating these intimate areas for social gathering without jeopardizing safety.

Fire and Planning after World War II

Following the destruction caused in World War II, much of which stemmed from fires ignited during American bombing raids, the government launched a second 1943 Fire-proofing and Greenbelt Plan. It was replaced in 1946 with a plan emphasizing circular greenways and radial corridors. In July 1948, the Ministry of Construction, currently under MLIT, designated 180,000 hectares of green space inherited from the fireproof-ing greenbelt as the "Tokyo City Planning Green Space." Ultimately, this greenbelt system was only partially realized, owing to the difficulty of gaining local consensus and acquiring land; it was subsequently used as a tool to reduce sprawl.[24]

FIRE REDUCTION IN PLANNING PROCESSES TODAY

Fire awareness is so prominent in Japan that it has become essential to city planning. Under the bōsai-safety rolling subsidies covering all hazards, the MLIT subsidizes one-third of fees to assess the municipality's disaster risk, considering building collapse, fire hazards, and the difficulties of extinguishing fires and evacuating.[25] The project also covers the development of evacuation routes and evacuation sites, the fire protection of roadside buildings, the removal of old wooden buildings, and support for residents' disaster-preparedness activities.

As noted above, Tokyo is preparing for a magnitude 7.0 inland earthquake, for which the spread of fire is a primary concern: two thousand fires would be expected to spread to more than 412,000 buildings, with a maximum death toll of 23,000 lives.[26] This alarming forecast has made planning more urgent and instigated a number of proactive projects.

Bōsai Living Zones

As municipalities are required to conduct a city planning survey every five years, they are highly attuned to the locations of fire-vulnerable neighborhoods. Tokyo developed bōsai living zones in 1981 as a model for fire protection. This concept separates neighborhoods, which are approximately sixty-five hectares in size (the size of a public school district based on a daily walking range), via firebreaks in order to keep fires from spreading across the city; it also calls for expanding evacuation spaces and removing or renovating dilapidated buildings.[27] This model is also meant to strengthen activities in the community, with a conceptual shift to creating a city or neighborhood from which you will not have to evacuate because it has been designed to be safe for sheltering in place.

Bōsai living zones are designated throughout all cities in Greater Tokyo. Firebreaks are noncombustible spaces—such as roads, rivers, rail corridors, parks lined with fire-resistant buildings—meant to limit the spread of urban fires. They are distributed in a gridded system, with three levels of hierarchy to make all bōsai living zones similarly sized. The largest grid consists of the skeletal bōsai axis located every three to four kilometers (major highways and wide rivers), major firebreak belts every two kilometers (highways and wide roads), and general firebreak bands every kilometer. Rivers and lakes are identified as firefighting water supplies if there is sufficient water availability and space for firefighting vehicles to park. If the width is twenty-four to twenty-seven meters, the flanking urban fabric must be built out of at least 40 percent noncombustible materials. When the width is sixteen to twenty-four meters, the noncombustibility rate needs to be 60 percent or more, and when the width is eleven to sixteen meters, it needs to be over 80 percent.[28] In urban areas, firebreak bands require at least six meters for emergency vehicle access. The bōsai living zones project differs from earlier top-down models, as it supports local participation through the machizukuri community planning process, thus creating integrated social and spatial fire-reduction efforts.

Mokumitsu Districts

Within these zones, structures that are particularly flammable are a priority, and through a lot of effort in consensus building, *mokumitsu* (dense timber housing) districts nationwide have been reduced in area from 5,745 hectares in 2012 to 2,982 hectares in 2019. Tokyo has been proactively applying both bottom-up and top-down approaches—providing subsidies as well as property-tax exemptions to both individual homeowners and large private corporations—that have allowed the city to address

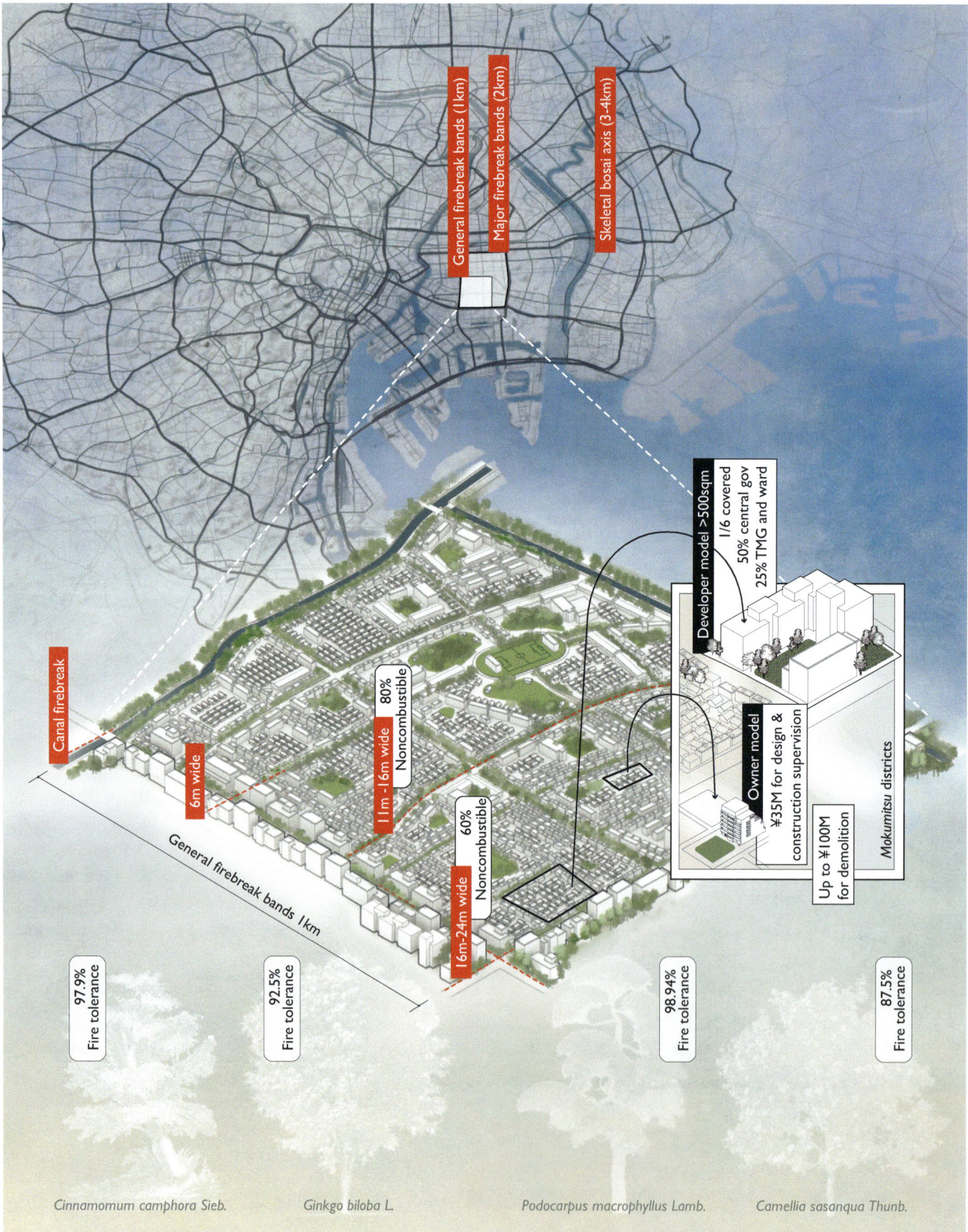

General firebreak bands (1km)

Major firebreak bands (2km)

Skeletal bosai axis (3-4km)

Canal firebreak

6m wide

80% Noncombustible

11m - 16m wide

60% Noncombustible

16m-24m wide

General firebreak bands 1km

Developer model >500sqm
1/6 covered
50% central gov
25% TMG and ward

Owner model
¥35M for design & construction supervision

Up to ¥100M for demolition

Mokumitsu districts

97.9% Fire tolerance

92.5% Fire tolerance

98.94% Fire tolerance

87.5% Fire tolerance

Cinnamomum camphora Sieb.   *Ginkgo biloba* L.   *Podocarpus macrophyllus* Lamb.   *Camellia sasanqua* Thunb.

84 percent of such areas.[29] For plans led by developers with plots larger than five hundred square meters, the Residential Revitalization Project provides subsidies for those projects that have access roads wider than six meters and that create fire-resistant residential structures with four or more stories and ten or more units. Although the specific amount depends on each ward, a subsidy generally covers one-sixth of demolition, survey and design, and construction of shared facilities. Of that amount, the central government bears 50 percent, and the TMG (with the ward) covers 25 percent.[30] More interesting perhaps are the 10-Year Fireproofing Project subsidies for individual homeowners and collective housing in *mokumitsu* districts.[31] The collective project is often facilitated through a bōsai machizukuri process and/or with the support of an NPO to help neighborhood residents actively engage and lead. In general, the TMG and a ward government will pay up to ¥10–15 million to demolish a house and about ¥35 million to design and supervise construction of a new house. They also provide property and urban planning tax exemptions for five years.[32] Although not commensurate with the cost and effort of rebuilding a home, the program jump-starts individual and collective conversations about rebuilding neighborhoods, at a variety of scales, while there is still time to discuss preferences and designs during blue-sky days.[33]

FIREFIGHTING TO PROTECT HERITAGE

Higashiyama

Shōbōdan and jishubō are closely related and important to larger preparedness projects. Kyoto's historic city center contains many traditional wooden houses and narrow streets, which allow fires to spread quickly and make evacuation difficult. Kyoto had the most fires per capita among large Japanese cities after World War II. To counter this, the city encourages households and facilities with wells to register them for emergency use. As of July 2020, 382 households, 94 businesses, 47 schools, 46 public baths, 48 public facilities, and 17 temples/shrines have registered wells with the city and are included on a regularly updated map online.[34] As a result of strengthening such disaster management activities with the cooperation of citizens, the city now has one of the lowest fire rates in Japan.

Kyoto served as the Japanese capital for more than a thousand years, and it is endowed with a large number of historic cultural sites, many of which are designated as national treasures or World Heritage Sites. To protect these Higashiyama-area assets (many of which are wooden structures) from fire, a coalition came together in 2011 that included the city fire department, the local shōbōdan, and the jishubō as well as temples, shrines, and businesses, with national funding of ¥800 million.[35] The center of the project is a firefighting rainwater-supply system, which features two 1,500-square-meter earthquake-resistant water tanks, over two kilometers of poly-

Figure 14. Bōsai living zone and *mokumitsu* district urban design guidelines, highlighting fire-tolerant tree species.

ethylene water pipes, and a water pump at Kōdaiji Park, next to the temple, that can operate for six hours following a power outage.

The project also includes handheld fire hoses installed in sixty-three sites along the water pipes. Twenty powerful units are allocated to firefighters, and forty-three can be used by regular citizens or even visitors. Mounted in wooden boxes designed to blend in with the neighborhood's aesthetics, each unit includes a thirty-meter hose and easy-to-follow instructions.

The Kyoto Fire Department encourages people to use the hoses for everyday activities, such as watering plants or washing cars, which underscores the importance of familiarity with disaster-related infrastructure.[36] This freely available water supply has contributed to the greening of the neighborhood and is supported by the local community. The Kiyomizu and Yasaka bōsai network hosts an annual bōsai drill, which typically draws around five thousand people. It serves not only to increase familiarity with post-disaster procedures, including the firefighting water-supply system, but also strengthens community ties. More residents participate in drills now than before the project, which has contributed to an overall increase in bōsai knowledge.[37]

Shirakawa-gō

A similar community-engaged preservation project can be found in the historic village of Shirakawa-gō in Gifu Prefecture. It became a UNESCO World Heritage Site in 1995 and has sixteen hundred residents. An association was established in 1971 to protect the village's 114 gasshō-style thatched-roof houses, collaborative lifestyle, and agricultural waterways from urbanization and natural disasters. The most significant project implemented by the association was the water drencher system, which took over a decade to build (1977–88). The system starts with a six-hundred-ton water tank, installed on the hill, which is connected to the agricultural irrigation canals. Gravity pulls the water down the eighty-meter height difference between the tank and the village. In an everyday context, it is used for rice cultivation. Fifty-nine water cannons and sixty-two fire hydrants were installed through the village: two cannons that can be rotated 360 degrees are set diagonally for each gasshō-style house, with the aim of creating a thirty-meter-high film of water to prevent the house from burning. The cannons are installed in gasshō-shaped storage boxes to blend into the historic landscape.[38]

Once a year, residents practice operating the water cannons as they test and inspect the infrastructure. They are organized in groups of one-hour fireguard circuits, four times daily: at 10:00 am and 6:00 pm by a pair of women, and at 8:00 pm and midnight by a pair of men. This routine strengthens the existing bonds among residents, who also help each other with farming and repairing the thatched roofs.[39] On November 4, 2019, a fire burned down two gasshō-style huts four hundred meters from the

Figure 15. Annual community-based firefighting drill in the historic village of Shirakawa-gō.

village. Residents had just completed their annual drill on October 27, so upon hearing the siren, they immediately used the water cannons to douse flying sparks and saved their village.[40]

FIREFIGHTING WITH RIVERS AND CANALS

Horikawa River

In 1985, twenty-five river-adjacent communities established an association to regenerate the Horikawa River in central Kyoto. Residents and the city government held a series of workshops; an on-site walk helped participants identify issues and brainstorm project themes such as "rich in nature," "historic preservation," "symbol of community renovation," and "bōsai function."[41] These were incorporated into the design of the new Horikawa River. In the year 2000, more than a thousand people attended eighty-two workshops. The completed project includes the extension of the river, an integrated underground sewage tunnel independent from the stream, walking paths, and riverside parks.[42] This project was incorporated into the Kyoto Water Coexistence Plan established in 2004, and it encouraged residents, NPOs, local businesses, and the city to work together to improve the riverbed environment. Especially around the Ichijō Street Modoribashi Park, greening activities have been thriving and efforts have been made to return fireflies to the inner-city stream, inaugurating the Kyoto Horikawa Firefly Project.[43] With direct access to the stream, the Modoribashi Park is popular among families with young children throughout the year.

The disaster-preparedness features of the project have an emphasis on fire response. The profile of the river is designed with basins on either side, which fill when the river flows. If the flow is blocked or dammed, water will remain in these channels, which can be used for firefighting or for post-disaster domestic uses. Where the river reaches the center of the city, near Nijō Castle, a manual dam system is designed to capture water during emergencies. Wooden boards, which are usually stored underneath the bridges, can be inserted into the riverbed to retain the water, and city firefighters and local shōbōdan can use a pumper-truck hose in order to extinguish fires in the area.[44] In addition, the lushly vegetated Horikawa parks along the river are emergency evacuation spaces from the fire—a local jishubō manages the public toilets and the emergency supply storage.[45] These are examples of anticipatory design, with top-down and bottom-up cooperation reviving the riverine ecology.

MULTI-HAZARD PLANNING

Sumida Ward

Urban firewalls are not a new concept in Japan, where houses are lined with fifteen- to thirty-centimeter-thick mudbrick (a technique called *dozou-zukuri*) and thick plaster storage houses, called *kura,* help prevent fires from spreading.[46] The *kura* design, which developed in iconic styles with white plaster, became popular as the main typology of fire-protective architecture in the Edo era, especially in dense castle towns.[47] In many places, the *kura* would also have a roof, which was separated from the rest of the construction by being mounted on timber. When a fire broke out close by, the "easily detachable roof would be dragged off, meaning that no combustible material would be in direct contact with the plastered surfaces."[48] *Kura* were often arranged to block the main home from winter winds—protecting the home from any gusts that could spread fire as well as from the harsh cold.

This concept of fire-resistant architecture that serves as a buffer was employed to a new degree in Tokyo. Sumida Ward is a dense historic neighborhood in a flood-prone area of eastern Tokyo, and it still has large areas of wooden housing and lacks open spaces for evacuation. To help lessen Sumida's fire and flood risk, a combination of top-down and bottom-up projects has emerged in recent decades, stemming from the work of academics such as Uchida Yoshikazu (1885–1972). Exploring these projects shows not only how government, private sector, and community projects can be mutually reinforcing but also how the relationship between spatial and social preparedness infrastructure can encompass a combination of everyday and post-disaster functions.

Figure 16. Designed with a small manual dam system, the Horikawa River basin collects water for firefighters.

Spurred by Takayama Eika's 1965 estimate that an earthquake similar to the one in 1923 could result in 410,000 deaths in Kōtō Ward, the TMG formed the Kōtō Redevelopment Plan in 1969.[49] The Shirahige Higashi public apartments were built as part of this larger disaster-preparedness endeavor in the low-lying Shirahige neighborhood, a former factory district on the western edge of Sumida Ward in the sixth district of the Kōtō Redevelopment project. Both Takayama and Murakami Suminao were involved with the design, which assigned everyone in the Kōtō Delta a designated place to evacuate within thirty minutes of their homes and allocated one square meter per person and at least fifty hectares overall to protect evacuees from radiant heat.[50]

Figure 17 (*next page*). Multiscalar projects reflect top-down and bottom-up efforts in Sumida Ward.

Evacuation route

15m

4m

6m

9m
8m
6m

30m   30m

Fire-resistant barrier

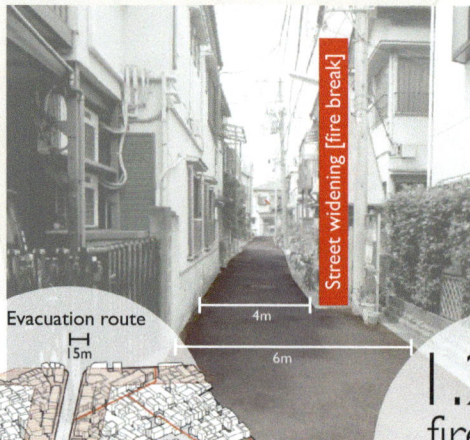

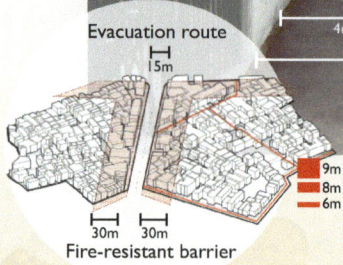

Street widening [fire break]

Fire shutters

1.2km firewall

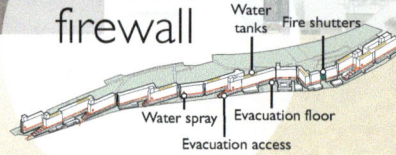

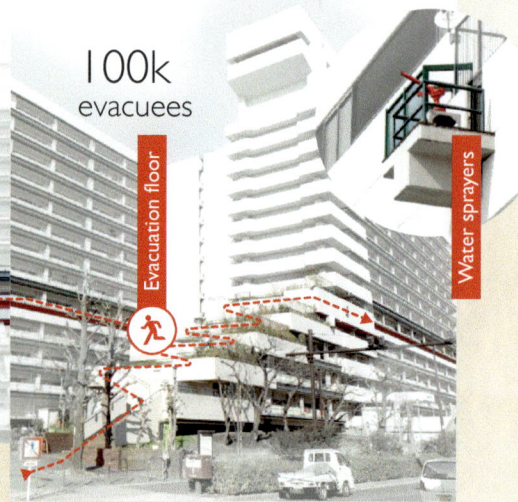

Water tanks   Fire shutters

Water spray   Evacuation floor

Evacuation access

100k evacuees

Evacuation floor

Water sprayers

1969
Basic Disaster Prevention Plan for the Renewal of the Koto Delta

Structural improvement and protection of the area. Six large disaster management bases (*bosai kyokuten*) were to be created for evacuation.

1978
Sumida Fireproof Promotion Project

Increasing the number of fire-resistant buildings in the ward to stop the spread of fire.

1983
Disaster-Prepared Land Readjustment Plan

Ward divided into 25 districts separated by major roads lined with fire-resistant buildings. Widening streets within the districts.

1986
Shirahige Higashi Disaster Management Base

1.2km of 40m high-rise apartment blocks serve as a firewall protecting a 10.3 hectare open space along the Sumida River to accommodate 100,000 evacuees.

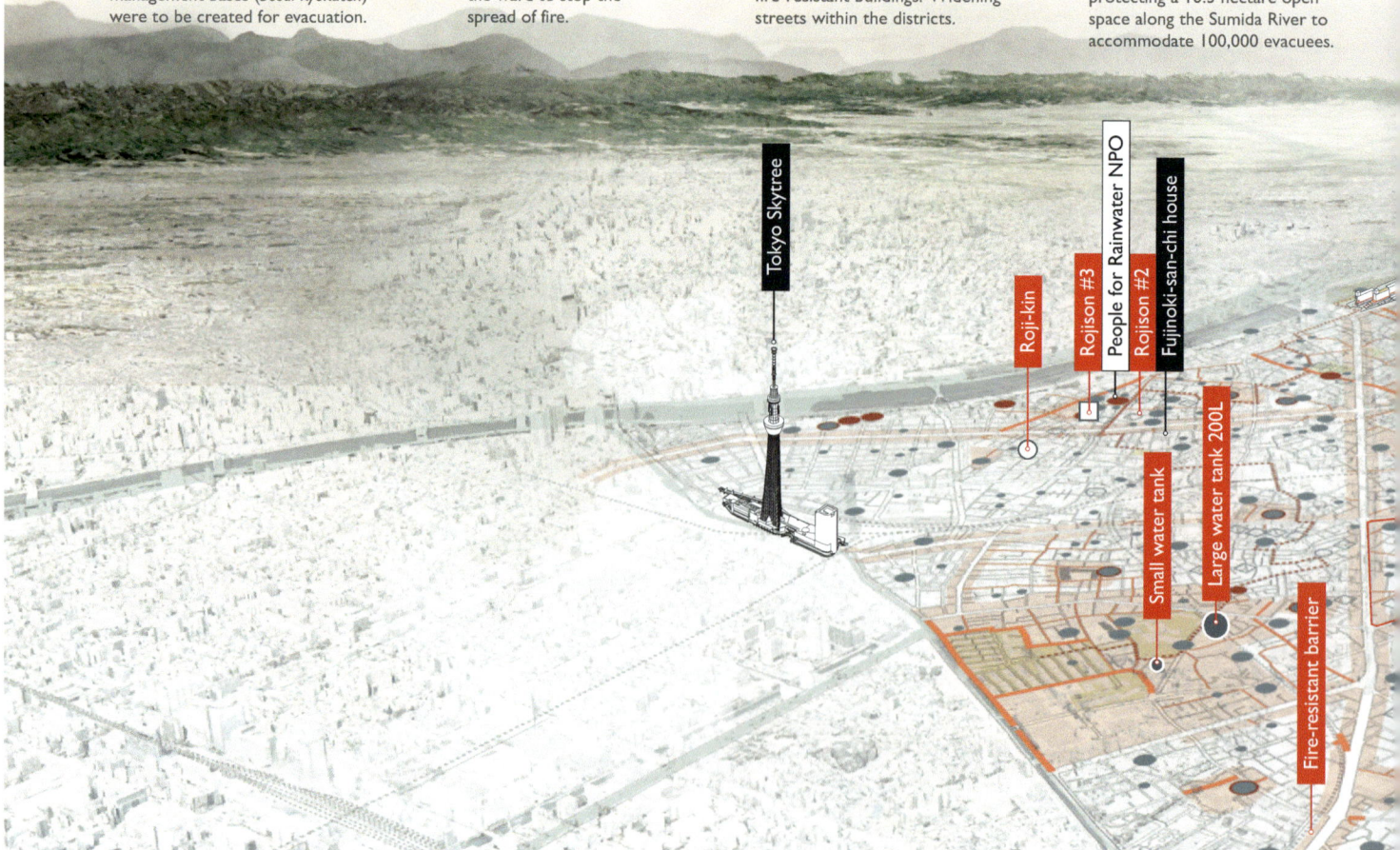

Tokyo Skytree

Roji-kin

Rojison #3

People for Rainwater NPO

Rojison #2

Fujinoki-san-chi house

Small water tank

Large water tank 200L

Fire-resistant barrier

Sedimentation tank

Manual pump

Water tank 3tons

$10k
underground tanks 5t

$3k
large tanks >1t

$400
small tanks <1t

Large water tank - 200L

$130k
subsidy

Roof & exterior walls:
fire protection materials

Column, beam reinforcement

Reinforced plasterboard walls
Meshed glass windows
Fire protection shutter
Earthquake-resistant frame
Water storage & sprinkler
Seismic reinforcement panel

Sujikai (seismic reinforcement)

Sumida Shien-tai - NPO

2,635t
Tokyo
Skytree

underground
water tank

21
rojison
3-20 tons

1987	1st Rojison completed		
1995	Hanshin-Awaji Earthquake Rainwater Utilization Guidelines		
2012	Ten-Year Fireproofing Project		

"Protect our own local community through maintaining alleys which are daily community spaces turning into the evacuation paths in a time of disaster."

Private sector incentives.
Rainwater storage tank installation subsidy.

New subsidies for rebuilding individual residences or groups of homes.

Shirahige public housing

Firebreak band >6m

Fire containment district

"Sumida's strength is through human connection... fostered by living, working and belonging to the community."

SHIGEMOTO SAHARA
SUMIDA WARD COMMUNITY LEADER

When the city planning decision was made in 1972, the population at the site was 2,396 people in 867 households. These included 183 homeowners, 101 owners of homes on lease-hold land, and 403 renters. After the readjustment process and temporary relocation, 102 of the 183 original property owners returned on reserved floors through their rightful acquisition agreement. For previous renters and new families, the TMG built 1,295 affordable public units. In addition, the Tokyo Housing Company developed 187 units.[51] The apartments opened in 1982, and 5,300 people moved in. Although the project is sometimes critiqued as "slum clearance,"[52] the involvement of the eight Shirahige East Residential Associations led to a high rate of returning residents, who continued to conduct many community activities.

The associations take pride in caring for the vulnerable. Since the apartments were built about forty years ago, the age of the residents has risen; 47.4 percent of the residents were aged sixty-five and over in 2020.[53] The apartment complex consists primarily of public housing, which is prioritized for the elderly, young families, and people with access and functional needs, so protecting these households is even more important. Teams help maintain the homes by installing equipment to prevent furniture from falling during earthquakes. They also help evacuation during emergencies. After the 2011 Tohoku earthquake shook Tokyo, core members of the association carried the elderly up the stairs back to their rooms, since they could not use the elevators. During the annual bōsai drills, the association trains for first aid, lifesaving, initial firefighting, emergency toilet installation, and emergency food preparation. This way they are also prepared to accept evacuees from areas outside of the complex, such as from the dense wooden housing area to the east.[54] Bōsai awareness among residents is high, with a 74.9 percent participation rate of residents in disaster drills.[55] The association also cooperates with local Sumida NPOs, showing its facilities to the attendees of bōsai excursions.

Completed in 1982, the twelve apartment blocks, all 40 meters high, are designed to resist forces equivalent to the 1923 Tokyo earthquake with piles that reach bedrock to mitigate the effects of liquefaction. They also serve as a 1.2-kilometer-long firewall, protecting a 10.3-hectare open space for one hundred thousand evacuees.[56] On a regular day, this open space serves as a playground for the schools that occupy the complex. The basement stores water tanks and one week of emergency rations for eighty thousand people.[57] Open entryways between the buildings are equipped with fire shutters and sprinklers, which deploy automatically. A water tank with drenchers at the top of the building will open to create a water screen covering all windows and doors. Exterior water sprayers can also be aimed to protect people trying to escape the fire.

The twelve blocks are staggered with large entries to the park along the river, allowing the 1.2-kilometer-long wall to appear less obtrusive than one would imagine. Shared porches on the fifth floor of each building are used for growing plants, airing futons, and providing quick evacuation access to the ground. The street facing the ground floor is lined with stores, workshops, small factories, and public facilities. At the time of this writing, many of the stores were vacant, but some small upgrades could quickly revive the spaces. The innovative design was costly to build and maintain, making the system difficult to replicate,[58] but it stands as an influential precedent for designers.

On a smaller scale in Sumida Ward, the Narihira district association recognized a need for both firefighting and potable water after a disaster. They worked together to install twenty large two-hundred-liter stainless steel water tanks around their neighborhood, locating the tanks under the eaves of residential houses, in parks, and on school grounds. The ward published rainwater utilization guidelines and provides subsidies to residents of up to 50 percent of the material and installation fees, with a cap of ¥50,000.[59] As of 2019, 310 subsidies have been provided, and the tanks have twice been used to successfully extinguish fires.[60]

Shortly after the water tanks project, the *rojison* project was established in 1987 in the Mukōjima district as a more sustainable collaboration between the municipality and community organizations. *Rojison* are small gathering spaces with underground rainwater storage tanks in alleys to provide clean water and also serve disaster-preparedness functions for the community. Historically, the neighborhood lacked a clean water supply, as both the river and wells were contaminated by industry. Rainwater collected through gutters on adjacent houses is funneled through a sedimentation filter into tanks in these micro-parks. The water is accessed via a manual pump, meaning that it can still be used even if the power goes out. Some *rojison* include fishbowls under the water pumps to demonstrate water quality. Maintained by the local community, the *rojison* often include street furniture that stores emergency supplies, play equipment, community bulletin boards, or potted plants watered with the pump systems. At one *rojison,* the rainwater is used to irrigate a community vegetable garden, which becomes the site of a harvest party each fall.[61] These everyday functions, along with the community's role in developing and maintaining the project, integrate the *rojison* into daily life. When a disaster does strike, residents are already familiar with the response systems. *Rojison* became a symbol of multi-hazard neighborhood safety: protecting residents from flash floods, acting as a water source if a fire ignites, and providing water for post-earthquake use if municipal water mains break.

As of 2019, there are currently twenty-one *rojison.*[62] The project was also supported by the development of a local "disaster management community-building newspaper." Originally a ward project, the newspaper was taken over by the local jishubō, which also supports ways of maintaining access through narrow alleys so that residents can escape during disasters. Jishubō affirm that mutual support is crucial, so they facilitate community-building activities to share bōsai knowledge among neighbors. Such coordination would be impossible without the residents' participation and commitment. A community leader explained that many small businesses, factories, and workshops dot the mixed-use area; the coexistence of many generations, all living and working in this pedestrian-friendly environment, creates a place where neighbors know one another and exchange daily greetings.

Sumida's bottom-up programs are complemented by local government policies to mitigate and prepare for fire-related disasters. In 1979, it launched the Sumida Fireproof Promotion Project, which was designed to increase the number of noncombustible buildings by providing subsidies. The first of its kind in Japan,[63] the project works with the more holistic 1983 Disaster-Prepared Land Readjustment Plan, which subdivides the ward into twenty-five districts separated by major evacuation roads lined with fire-resistant buildings. Individuals, businesses, and nonprofits can receive subsidies to rebuild using fire-resistant materials, such as reinforced concrete.[64] So far, the southern part of the ward has reduced wooden housing to 30 percent, and new subsidies—such as those from the 10-Year Fireproofing Project for rebuilding individual residences or groups of homes—are helping the northern neighborhoods.[65]

NPOs

Civil society groups also play a large role in helping households access subsidies. The project is shifting to add support for new or renovated semi-fire-resistant wooden buildings, which are more affordable than fully fire-resistant structures. With an adjustment from the original goal of fireproofing to one of fire reduction, the think tank NPO Sumida Shien-tai (previously called Sumida Kaigi) gives workshops and lectures to share information on new regulations and strategies. The Fujinoki-san-chi building itself is a showcase of combined multi-hazard fire and seismic retrofit strategies to show residents (and visitors) the efficacy of partial renovations, which include lightweight fire-retardant roofing, fire-retardant timber used to widen a wooden column, and post-disaster potable water storage with a combined sprinkler system. Waseda University's Hasemi Laboratory advised the retrofits and the Sumida Ward Seismic Reinforcement Council approved the seismic performance. It received a ¥13 million subsidy and many donations, which also support the neighborhood's elderly as well as a community kitchen for children's meals and activities. For example, in order to embed bōsai knowledge into everyday life, NPO Sumida Shien-tai created *furoshiki* (rugged Japanese cloth, traditionally used for wrapping and transporting goods) with bōsai maps of the neighborhood using the motif of Hokusai manga. One *furoshiki* fire map is made from fire-retardant material to shield the wearer's head from flying embers. A *furoshiki* water map is made with waterproof material and can be folded into a container to transport water.[66] When it is not holding classes or activities, the NPO runs a small lunch restaurant.

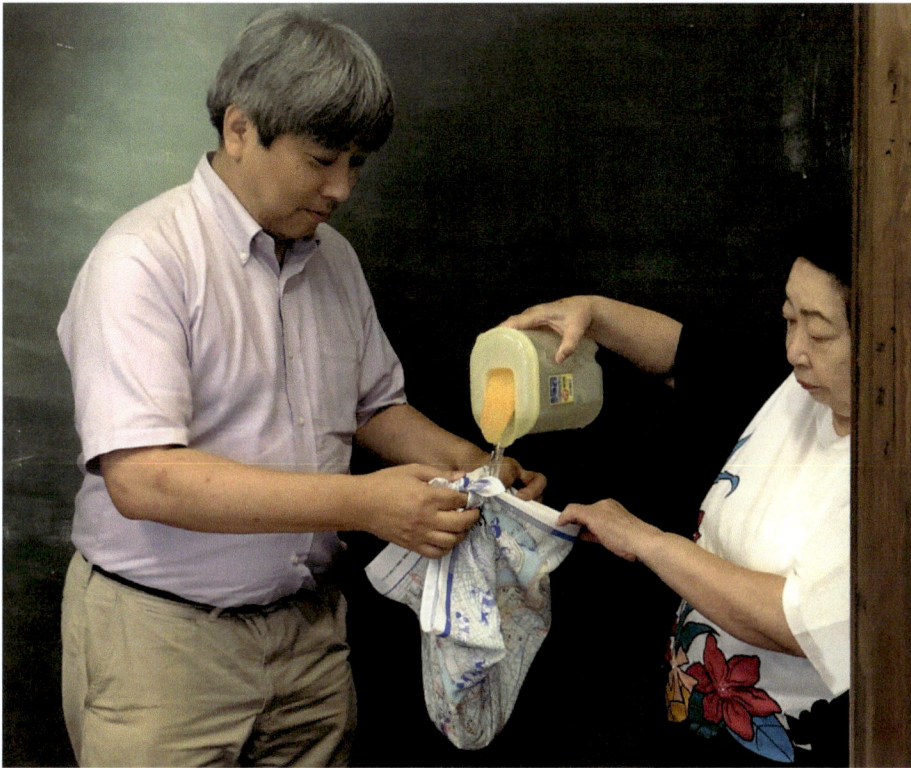

Figure 18. Leaders of the Sumida Shien-tai nonprofit organization demonstrate how the water *furoshiki* can be used to map all the water collection points—and can carry water during an emergency.

Government and Private Sector Projects

Sumida's low-lying nature—much of the ward was built on infill and has subsided over time—and its rapid development of impervious areas mean that many governmental efforts have focused on rainwater storage for flood prevention. According to the projected flood inundation map of Sumida, much of the ward's eastern side is projected to be flooded to a depth of over five meters and could be inundated for over two weeks.[67] The Sumida city hall and its iconic sumo arena both have large rainwater catchment systems. The sumo arena, built in 1984, has a 1,000-ton rainwater tank in the basement that meets an impressive 70 percent of the arena's water usage needs.[68] The 2012 Skytree broadcasting tower, boasting the highest point on the Tokyo skyline, incorporates multiple rooftop catchments, which drain to an 800-cubic-meter rainwater harvesting tank, as well as Sumida Ward's largest underground water detention system, which holds 1,835 cubic meters to prevent flooding in the surrounding community. Anticipating the effects of climate change, the system can collect 50 millimeters of rain per hour.[69] The private developer, Tobu Railway Company, decided not to apply for the Sumida Ward subsidies; rather, the company installed the system as part of its

Corporate Social Responsibility activities. In combination with maintaining rooftop gardens and recycling water to cool the building and flush toilets, the system saves 3,000 to 4,500 cubic meters of water consumption annually.[70] To raise awareness for the whole area, the public restrooms across the street from the Skytree tower use rainwater from the terraced, landscaped bike storage building. This new addition to Sumida demonstrates how top-down infrastructure can symbiotically mix with private entities and community partnerships. As of March 2018, within Sumida Ward, 645 facilities can store or reuse 24,010 cubic meters of rainwater—about 90 liters of water per resident.[71]

DISCUSSION

Systematic transformations to the urban fabric can be made through processes that combine grassroots planning with more comprehensive policy—and, sometimes, with the goals of private entities, like those in the decades-long and ongoing Sumida Ward projects. Each case in this section was selected to highlight symbiotic top-down and bottom-up efforts and intersecting combinations of social and spatial efforts via urban, landscape, and architectural strategies. Each of the strategies—organizing to protect heritage, or increasing access to water through rivers and canals, or using architecture and urban regulations to reduce the spread of fire—is vital. In particular, the success of the large-scale Shirahige public housing would not have been achieved without the residential association, which reminded people how to use the embedded infrastructure and to care for the most vulnerable. The ongoing Sumida Ward projects exemplify how the residents mobilized and successfully linked with urban-scale financing and policy to reduce both fire and flood risk with hyper-local knowledge. This allowed communities to invent their own anticipatory design interventions ahead of an impending earthquake.

In rapidly developing cities, fires remain a major concern. For example, in the first half of 2018, Manila had already experienced 2,200 blazes, primarily in dense, informal neighborhoods.[72] And fires are disastrous around the world in peri-urban and rural areas as well, as seen in the devastating fires in California, which were exacerbated by climate change–induced droughts and the expansion of urban sprawl into more rural districts. Often, reducing fire risk requires systematic changes to the urban fabric. Such changes, if imposed solely from the top, can be disruptive or even violent for communities on the ground. The cases above show how fire resistance can be reduced not only by mega-scale projects, which reshape the urban fabric, but also through networked interventions such as wells, water tanks, rivers, and fire hoses combined with community training and response, all of which engage local communities directly in fighting fires. The approaches described above suggest how fire resistance must be managed as a collective project. They also show the ways in which it can become a part of everyday life.

Machizukuri

Japan's history of catastrophic disasters led to several major urban reconstructions, which were leveraged as opportunities for bōsai transformations. While historically much of this reconstruction was conducted through top-down projects, the second half of the twentieth century brought a shift toward more bottom-up processes, including machizukuri, which was made prominent following the 1995 Kobe earthquake and the 2011 Tohoku disaster. In a country known for strong, centrally planned disaster preparedness and response, bōsai machizukuri projects are significant for their connection of bottom-up processes to policies and programs. However, tension can occur between these two mechanisms, such as when a top-down approach immediately after the Kobe earthquake ultimately gave way to machizukuri processes only after many major decisions had already been made. Given the role of designers as mediators between communities on the ground and government policies and programs, the machizukuri system also provides a framework for how designers might operate in the context of post-disaster reconstruction—and, more broadly, in creating a vision for safe urbanization.

HISTORIC CONTEXT

The 1924 Imperial Reconstruction Plan was Japan's first foray into the *fukkō* model of reconstruction. It specified building an improved city with modern park networks designed as evacuation spaces and widened, tree-lined roads that improved circulation and served as firebreaks. Because it was implemented through a top-down approach that lacked public participation, many protested the required 10 percent property contribution to land readjustment, and some were entirely displaced from their communities in the process.[1]

Japan's postwar years saw a partial transition away from such centralized planning. After the City Planning Law was amended in 1968, planning power shifted somewhat to prefectures and municipalities, with the governor having primary authority. While the 1968 law paid lip service to public consultation, it was not a requirement, and bureaucrats retained decision-making power. This changed in 1980 with the next amendment, which created the District Planning System (requiring citizen participation in making plans) and passed machizukuri ordinances, which themselves provided an organizational framework for bottom-up planning. The first of these was the Kobe Machizukuri Ordinance, enacted in 1981.[2] The 1992 amendment of the City Planning Law required that all cities include community engagement, through public hearings and clear diagrams, in the creation of master plans.[3]

This community-driven trend was also evident in the immediate aftermath of the 1995 Kobe earthquake. In the midst of the catastrophe that paralyzed the local government, neighborhood residents helped each other and saved lives. This ability to recover through self-help and mutual support among communities inspired the amendment of the Disaster Countermeasures Act in order to urge both national and local governments to increase risk reduction and preparedness activities in the public realm.[4] This law naturally facilitated a bōsai machizukuri movement among residents in the context of earthquake reconstruction.

The First Machizukuri Groups in Japan

Urban sprawl in the mid-twentieth century not only increased Kobe's disaster vulnerability through the expansion of poorly regulated, dense neighborhoods but also reduced environmental quality as these neighborhoods encroached upon polluted factory districts (or vice versa).[5] Machizukuri citizen groups emerged in Kobe in response to these impacts on the lives of urban residents. In an early example, a 1963 community group from the Maruyama district protested the intrusion of construction trucks' repeated trips through their neighborhood for a land reclamation project.[6] Calling their group *machizukuri,* their strong and vocal organization was able to reform city policy on other local environmental issues as well.[7]

The Mano machizukuri group also formed in the 1960s in response to concerns about air pollution from nearby factories in their working-class Kobe neighborhood. In the 1960s and 1970s, Japan was at the peak of its torrid economic growth, which brought oil refineries, highways, and serious air pollution to cities. Instead of filing legal actions to gain compensation from companies, the Mano district's approach was led by strong resident leaders, who solved the problem through discussion. By the mid-1960s, this movement spread throughout Kobe, and forty-three companies, including large ones such as Kobe Steel, signed a pollution-prevention agreement. While the group's work first focused on protesting against the city, in the late 1970s, it shifted to a system of collaboration with local government.[8]

By 1980, the Mano machizukuri deliberation council had produced an alternative plan to the city's industrial zoning for the district, seeking to improve the quality of urban space for residents by lobbying for street plantings, playgrounds, parks, nurseries, and eldercare facilities. Portions of this plan were incorporated into Kobe's District Plan via regulations enacted the same year.[9] Mano's community participation was extensive, and it included the creation of a "machizukuri school" in 1970 that engaged wide audiences through expert-led lectures and workshops on local planning issues.[10] As a result of this successful combination of top-down and bottom-up planning with residents and experts, the Mano machizukuri movement is considered a paradigm in community-led planning.

When the post-earthquake fires broke out, the tight-knit community was able to organize bucket brigades to extinguish some of the flames. This level of social cohesion is often attributed to the great leadership of Mouri Yoshizō, a resident who had led by example since the 1960s through inclusion and trust. After the 1995 Kobe earthquake destroyed the *nagaya* (tenement housing), Mano district residents wanted to keep the *nagaya* parcels and narrow streets. "For us, it is more comfortable to live in a familiar community rather than to have sudden change by *fukkō* city readjustment. The most important thing is that the people who live in the town can handle the town and thrive in it."[11] After taking on the *fukkyū* restoration method, the town looked very similar to the parcel structure before the earthquake, and 80 percent of residents returned. The machizukuri school also continued to issue weekly *Mano News* for more than three years to help new residents and new schoolteachers (who often get transferred into new regions) understand their community.

This history paved the way for the Kobe Machizukuri Ordinance, giving formal standing to the bottom-up planning of machizukuri groups. The Mano machizukuri group in particular played a role in shaping the policy, including the emphasis on combining local knowledge with technical expertise.[12] The ordinance established (1) machizukuri councils; (2) the Expert Dispatch System, which provides city funds for consultants such as architects and urban designers to support machizukuri councils; and (3) a partnership agreement with the city, which creates a process for implementation. Mayors are required to review machizukuri proposals for both hard (physical) and soft (regulatory) changes to their districts and to make efforts to execute the citizens' plans.[13] This formalization of machizukuri creates an interface between communities and government.

The groundwork for the Kobe machizukuri movement was laid by architect Mizutani Eisuke, who theorized the concept of *machi-jūku,* which strengthens the argument that cities are composed not only of physical infrastructure but also of people and communities. In addition to shaping city policy, many of the architects and landscape architects who went on to become consultants through the Expert Dispatch System were educated by Mizutani.[14]

Top-Down and Bottom-Up Design in the Kobe Reconstruction

Reconstructing urban Kobe to its pre-disaster state would have perpetuated underlying conditions that contributed to the scale of the disaster, which particularly impacted vulnerable populations, including elderly people and people in low-income, working-class neighborhoods. Kobe's urban development lagged behind the more modernized Tokyo: less than half of the households in the areas affected by the Kobe earthquake had flush toilets as of 1993.[15] Narrow roadways blocked by debris and neighborhoods filled with flammable wooden buildings complicated the response. Accordingly, the city made decisions that would reshape Kobe, widening streets, expanding evacuation routes, and embedding evacuation spaces into the reconstruction design.

The first phase of the city's response was largely top-down and prioritized physical recovery: the repair and redevelopment of major infrastructure, including large roads and parks.[16] While the national government largely funded the reconstruction, planning occurred primarily through city and prefectural governments.[17] On February 1, 1995, Article 84 of the Building Standards Law imposed a moratorium on rebuilding in order to give the city time to evaluate land readjustment areas and "avoid disordered urban rebuilding,"[18] because part of what had hindered the 1923 vision of reconstruction was the speed with which individuals had independently undertaken their own rebuilding efforts. On March 17, two months after the disaster, the Disaster Reconstruction Project Urban Plan was adopted, requiring streets facing homes to be a minimum of six meters wide, with each of those streets connected to a twelve-meter-wide street with sidewalks.[19] These regulations were designed to ensure that evacuation routes would remain clear in future disasters, improving emergency vehicle access and preventing the spread of fire. The plan, developed by the one-hundred-member Earthquake Restoration Council, also included a network of seventeen-meter-wide evacuation roads and an evacuation park in each neighborhood.

Kobe designated city-managed reconstruction in areas where damage rates exceeded 65 percent.[20] In Kobe's dense inner city, 125 hectares were designated for land readjustment and 26 hectares for urban redevelopment.[21] The earthquake had once again spotlighted the importance of open space during and after disasters, and 30 percent of the land was to be designated as public space in the readjustment plans, including a network of one-hectare bōsai open areas.[22] The most heavily damaged districts were those that had been spared during World War II and, as such, had not been readjusted in postwar rebuilding. Reconstruction initially relied on preexisting plans: redevelopment projects had been identified in Kobe's preexisting master plans as early as 1965. The plans, which are updated every five years, had just been revised at the time of the earthquake. The redevelopment projects were framed as new, modern urban centers accommodating increased density and improved disaster resilience.[23]

This rapid planning did allow quick construction of temporary homes and shops and also helped ensure that rebuilding was done safely. However, residents complained that their voices and experiences had not been taken into account. They felt that decisions had been made while they were seeking shelter with friends or family outside their neighborhoods, and many had never been notified. The public comment period for the plan had lasted only two weeks, and it occurred in a chaotic post-disaster period when many survivors were still trying to meet their basic needs.[24] Many were specifically concerned about decreased lot sizes, or even displacement to other parts of the city, as a result of readjustment and redevelopment.[25] Moreover, faith in the central government had been shaken by its slow response and the failure of supposedly seismic-resistant infrastructure, including the dramatic collapse of the Hanshin elevated expressway.[26] The city received a flood of letters objecting to the initial plan, and two hundred people protested at the city hall in March 1995. While these protests may seem conservative by Western standards, they were radical in Japan at that time. This public response led to a mayoral announcement, on the evening following the city hall protests, that the second phase of more detailed planning would be conducted through machizukuri processes.

This second phase emphasized more specific neighborhood design, and reconstruction shifted toward a more participatory process. Machizukuri reconstruction councils, which included an architect or urban planner, were designated for each area, and citizens could become a part of their local reconstruction planning. Five hundred machizukuri experts (architects, landscape architects, and planners from the Expert Dispatch System) were appointed, upon request, across the city in addition to their roles on the councils.[27] Ward staff sought out residents who had been moved to temporary housing around the city, and participation was based on citizens' interest and willingness, with no special background required. However, by the time machizukuri were organized, high-level planning decisions had already been fixed: the decisions communities could shape were in the design details.

Kobe's background of active citizen participation created structures that could help realize bottom-up response and recovery planning. For example, in the Mano district, citizens proactively moved elderly residents to the 104 temporary housing units built in the district's two parks so that they could remain within their social network and familiar surroundings.[28] This allowed easier facilitation of meetings and decision making, compared to districts where residents were spread across disparate temporary housing sites.

Machizukuri participation was required in land readjustment planning.[29] While major roads and parks had been set, a consensus building process was used to determine the specific locations of neighborhood streets and pocket parks. Beyond their capacity to act quickly, leveraging social relationships and local knowledge in the crisis, machizukuri groups played a formative role in the new Kobe, rebuilt from the earthquake's rubble, especially because land readjustment required a lot of negotiation. Landowners needed to donate part of their property to create new, wider streets or pocket parks. In order to support reconstruction and redevelopment planning, new machizukuri councils were formed in addition to those that already existed, and by the second phase of reconstruction planning, the government supported the creation of these groups. The roughly twelve recognized machizukuri councils that had existed before the earthquake bloomed to more than one hundred in the years following the disaster.[30]

MACHIZUKURI RECONSTRUCTION PROJECTS

Rokkōmichi North and South: Readjustment and Redevelopment

The Rokkōmichi area provides an example of how readjustment and redevelopment programs were carried out in Kobe. Rokkōmichi North and West were designated for land readjustment in response to a packed residential district, while Rokkōmichi South was designated as an urban redevelopment district.

Prior to the earthquake, the Rokkōmichi North district had a population of around 4,182. Most of the neighborhood consisted of prewar *nagaya* housing, similar to that in Mano. The earthquake devastated the neighborhood, damaging 70 percent of buildings and killing 60 people. More than half the population was displaced, many to temporary housing placed in other neighborhoods or outside the city.[31] In protest of the government's top-down reconstruction proposal, residents in Rokkōmichi North collected citizens' opinions to share with the city and formed a joint machizukuri council composed of eight neighborhood-based councils. In the process of creating a proposal for the city, the council established five study groups to examine the areas of housing, bōsai, living environment, roads, and parks.[32] On a rotating basis, three consultants supported the neighborhood councils through the Expert Dispatch System.[33]

One of the group's major contributions to the proposal was shaping the design of Rokkō Kaze-no-sato Park. A nearby school was also a designated evacuation space. The road study group designed the official evacuation roads to both spaces with distinctive green sidewalk pavers to embed awareness of this route in residents' everyday lives,[34] since in a disaster, panic makes it difficult for people to get oriented. Although property adjustments were required to accommodate wider roads and parks, residents were able to design their process, and the area remained a low-rise, primarily residential neighborhood.

Rokkōmichi South district, where 58 percent of the buildings collapsed, was chosen as a post-earthquake redevelopment area. Actually, pre-disaster plans had already slated Rokkōmichi South as a new city center, as the area was considered an emerging hub and in need of improved multimodal transit.[35] Against this backdrop, when the redevelopment areas were announced on March 17, residents' confidence in the government was at its nadir. After the machizukuri process was instated, 20 leaders of each block met almost every week with a few consultants and government officials. The small size of the meetings helped make the participants' sincerity and earnestness evident, and trust was eventually reestablished.[36] Some 489 displaced families in

Green evacuation path

Community center

Rokkōmichi South were able to stay in temporary housing within the district, resulting in the residents' active participation in the machizukuri council.[37]

A one-hectare park was planned for the center of the district. Residents initially protested the large park, which they feared would increase the density and height of the surrounding development, irrevocably transforming their traditional street-based

Figure 19. Rokkōmichi North community center and green evacuation path.

communities. In spite of vocal protests and counterproposals for a distributed park network, low-rise housing, and a community hub, six alternative designs, and six months of discussion,[38] the large park remained in the city's plan—perhaps because of a national government grant attached to an evacuation park of at least one hectare. Eventually, the detailed design was informed by the four machizukuri councils, each representing one block in the district.[39] The councils were responsible for collecting opinions, building consensus, and producing the proposal. Ultimately, they conducted a survey in which 56 to 85 percent of residents (depending on the block) agreed that a one-hectare park was indeed necessary for disaster safety.

The Rokkōmichi South Park design was created following thirteen workshop sessions of the park planning committee, with guidance from the Urban Environment Design Coordination Council.[40] The park would be surrounded by redevelopment project towers and the station, and a second disaster-prepared open space, Rokkōmichi South Station Plaza (0.4 hectares), would also be built. Although modifications were made based on local opinions collected during the machizukuri process and through mail-in voting, the scale and density of the development were controversial.[41] Dwelling units were increased by 130 percent and ample retail and parking areas were added, changing the atmosphere of the neighborhood to a concrete high-rise metropolis, primarily in the name of "safety" (but the floor/area ratio was determined by the developer's floor price).[42] The conciliatory approach created some compromises, but even in a developer-influenced project, pre-targeted by the city for urban densification, the machizukuri process resulted in some positive decisions: the shape of the park was changed to allow for more south-facing apartments for residents in blocks two and three,[43] and a design competition was held for a memorial sculpture.

1995 Matsumoto Stream Project

The Matsumoto neighborhood in Kobe was relatively undamaged during World War II, meaning that the original, fire-vulnerable fabric of narrow alleys and dense wooden houses remained intact. The neighborhood also had a high proportion of elderly people. When the earthquake struck, homes collapsed and the lifeline infrastructure was severely damaged, including sewage, water, gas, electricity, and telephone. Debris blocked the narrow roads, preventing fire trucks from entering, and fire subsequently destroyed 80 percent of the neighborhood's wooden homes.[44]

As part of larger readjustment projects following the earthquake, the city proposed to widen the roads between Matsumoto and the adjacent district from 7 meters to 17 meters to prevent the spread of fire. The machizukuri council was established on May 19, and the reconstruction was to be planned through the machizukuri process, alongside consultants hired by the city to help residents with the design. The community thought that a 17-meter road was excessively wide and eventually came up with a proposal to maintain the 7-meter road but line it with an activated pedestrian path of 3.5 meters on one side and 6.5 meters on the other.

During community meetings, which began not long after the disaster, the conversation often returned to individuals' experiences as survivors. The phrase "If there was water, then . . ." was frequently heard.[45] The destruction of water infrastructure made it impossible to stop the spread of the flames, despite the firefighters' efforts. Responding to this collective experience, an urban planner, Yamaguchi Kenji, sought outside precedents for bringing water into the neighborhood. He drew upon the Bächle (literally "little river"), a thirteenth-century water-supply system that runs through the city of Freiburg, Germany, using water from an adjacent river. The Bächle provided water for firefighting and other everyday uses, and it also served as a stormwater drainage system. Inspired by this precedent, the Kobe City Planning Department successfully convinced the sewage treatment facility and the Kobe City Sewage Department to divert the cleaned water from the nearby Suzurandai treatment facility and resurface the purified water, allowing residents to interact with it and get to know the treatment process before returning it to the sea.

Around two thousand tons of water flow from the treatment facility every day, turning a waste product into an urban amenity. The Matsumoto stream enlivens the streetscape: residents plant flowers along its perimeter, and children and the elderly raise brightly colored carp. If the neighborhood catches fire, the water will provide an essential firefighting supply.

Machizukuri consultant Tsuji Nobukazu, who stayed with the project for eight years, stressed the importance of collaboration. This project required the participation of the sewage company, the machizukuri and landscape consulting team, and the residents. Within the machizukuri council, resident leaders spoke to all the property owners to request their contribution of land to the project. Consensus was finally reached after 160 meetings and workshops over six months.[46]

Once the project was completed, management of the stream shifted to local residents. A resident caretaker contributes goldfish each January; others also donate goldfish, but some are stolen or eaten by birds. The caretaker spends a few hours cleaning the stream three times a month and prunes the plants to maintain their health, keep the environment beautiful, and prevent kids from slipping on moss. The design process for the stream specifically considered issues that could arise from shared responsibility, so each block has its own water entry point and drainage according to the sloped design.[47] This places responsibility on the residents to clean the block in front of their homes.

2011 Onagawa Reconstruction

The 2011 Tohoku disaster brought its own set of particular complications. Unlike in post-earthquake Kobe, people could not return until the water receded back to the

Figure 20 (*next page*). The Matsumoto stream is an everyday respite for urban dwellers and an additional source of water in emergencies.

2hrs
cleaning the stream

3x
a month

Bench supply storage

Water source

Original building facade line

6.5m

7.0m

Suzurandai sewage
treatment plant

Small-scale hydro
power equipment

ocean

ocean

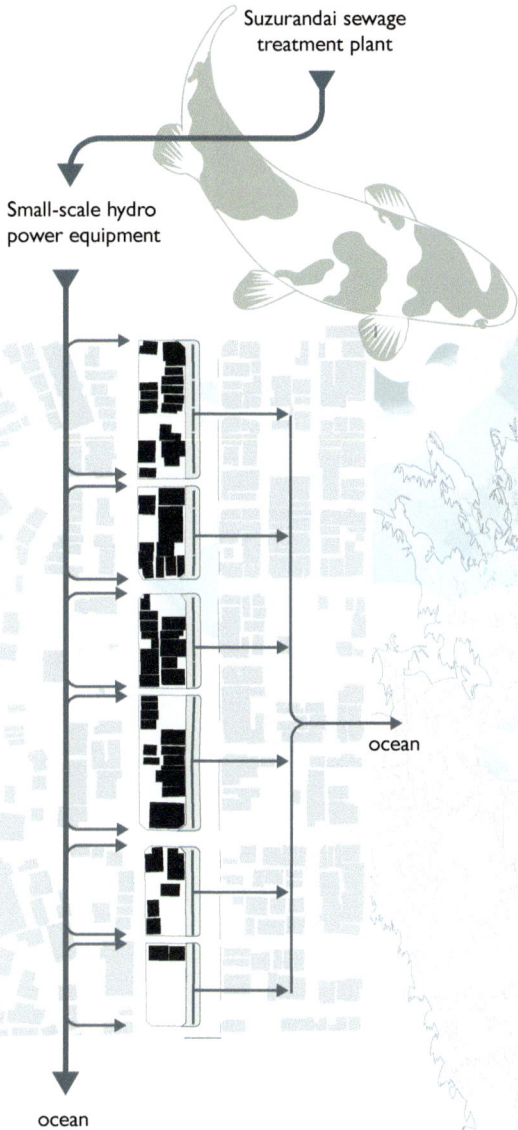

Sunday community cleaning days are officially held twice a month along this stream. The neighborhood culture has its strengths and weaknesses; it is important to take this into account when improving bosai infrastructure. Working together also helped reconnect a community fragmented by the disaster. At the time of writing, 20 years after the project was initiated, residents and neighborhood children are still raising carp in the clean and well-maintained stream. This project highlights the anticipatory design principle of creating dual-use projects to address everyday needs as well as emergency needs, while carefully considering neighborhood interactions.

Resident interview by author, July 2001
Fieldwork 2015 & 2019

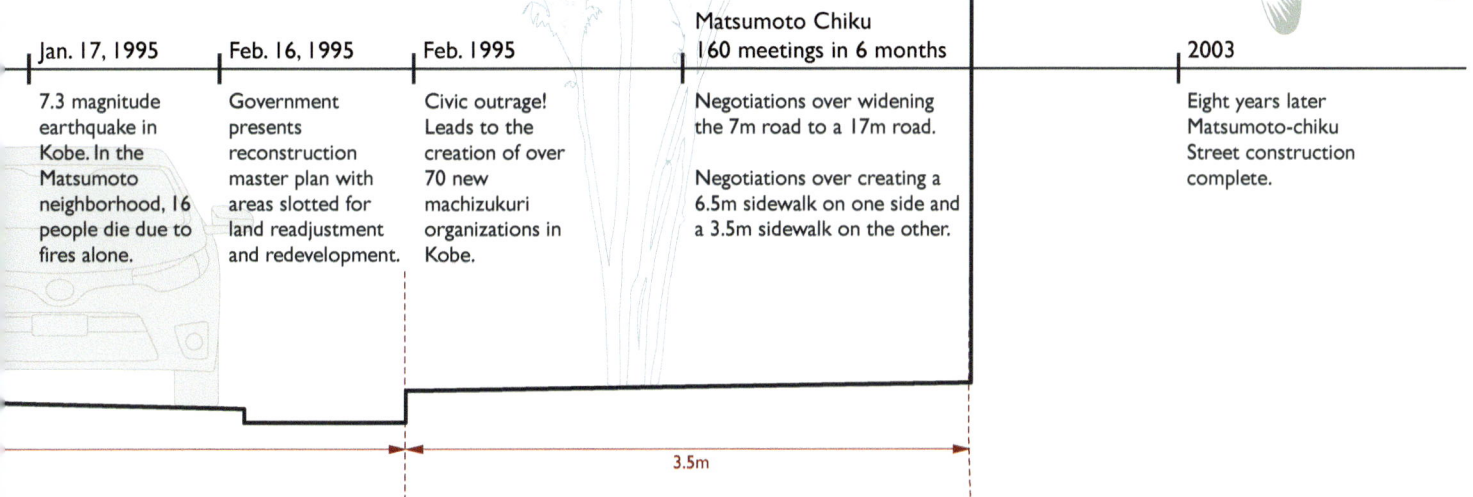

Jan. 17, 1995	Feb. 16, 1995	Feb. 1995	Matsumoto Chiku 160 meetings in 6 months	2003
7.3 magnitude earthquake in Kobe. In the Matsumoto neighborhood, 16 people die due to fires alone.	Government presents reconstruction master plan with areas slotted for land readjustment and redevelopment.	Civic outrage! Leads to the creation of over 70 new machizukuri organizations in Kobe.	Negotiations over widening the 7m road to a 17m road. Negotiations over creating a 6.5m sidewalk on one side and a 3.5m sidewalk on the other.	Eight years later Matsumoto-chiku Street construction complete.

3.5m

ocean or drained, and many areas were completely annihilated, erased of any markers. Although the government set a moratorium for rebuilding, a number of large zoning decisions after the tsunami were determined by policies described in chapter 2. Despite all this, some machizukuri projects were able to carve out unique solutions.

Onagawa is close to one of the world's three largest fishing grounds, the Kinkazan shore. Blessed with an excellent bay shape, the port is home to Japan's fish-processing industry. Comprising fifteen hamlets, forests, and a town center with the train station, a library, and shopping districts, Onagawa was devastated by an 18.5-meter inundation height and 34.7-meter maximum run-up—the highest in Miyagi Prefecture. About 320 hectares of the densely populated area were inundated; out of a population of 10,051 people, 831 lost their lives; and 2,924 residential houses and 1,394 nonresidential buildings were completely destroyed or washed away, including the town hall and the fire station.[48]

Onagawa rapidly formed a reconstruction planning committee with local business owners, industry, academics, residents, and town administrators. With the newly elected and enterprising mayor, Suda Yoshiaki—who also had a keen eye for design—the machizukuri council insisted on the importance of the quality of space. Sue Yusuke, an urban designer, was selected as the reconstruction coordinator. They adopted a fast-track system, wherein construction could start immediately after the budget, consensus, and design plans were secured. By bringing all the stakeholders together, they could conclude each meeting with agreements and shorten the bureaucratic process. Through more than two hundred workshops, all of the stakeholders had a sense of ownership and value from their shared machizukuri vision.[49]

Rather than returning to its pre-earthquake form, Onagawa embraced the challenge of designing a sustainable city with a shrinking population, an ambition shared among decision makers in both the public and private sectors. The complete destruction of the town created an opportunity to develop a new place, program, and identity for the youth. Some elderly residents nostalgically preferred to rebuild what had been there before, but others convinced them to prioritize the future. Mayor Suda emphasized creating a town that could "remain vibrant under a declining population" and would balance safety with a lively and sustainable environment. Many neighboring towns ignored the latter and sacrificed quality of life.[50]

Onagawa's highest priority was to encourage the community to return—safely and as soon as possible—and the first step was to avoid building a seawall. Records of the seawall blocking the view of the ocean's pullback, thus delaying evacuation, concerned the residents, as did potential flooding of the lowlands between surrounding mountains and a future seawall. They wanted to create "a town where the sea can be seen from everywhere," but to raise the entire town center would take eight years, and there was a desire to start recovery measures immediately.[51] Therefore, they developed a

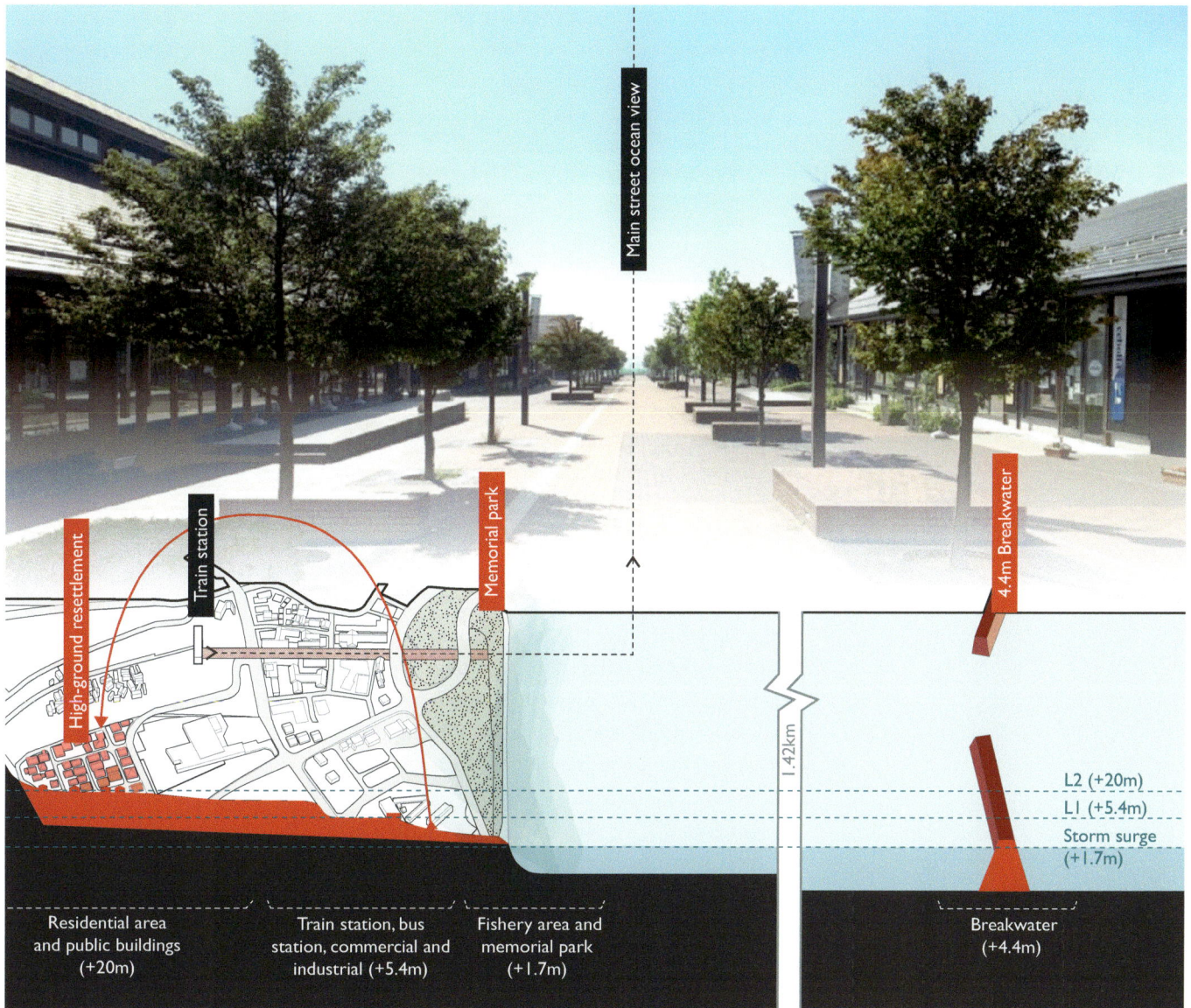

Figure 21. Onagawa's recovery and resettlement efforts create a new main street, perpendicular to the ocean, flanked by local shops.

three-stage plan: creating an elevated evacuation; moving the residential area to the Tokyo Peil (TP)+20 meter high ground (safe from Level 2 tsunamis); and raising an area to TP+5.4 meters (above Level 1) for train and bus stations as well as commercial and industrial areas.[52] Other fishery-related facilities and parks, including a memorial park, were rebuilt along the coast (TP+1.7 meters).[53] The plan also called for a 4.4-meter breakwater to protect against storm surges and smaller tsunamis. This plan allowed Onagawa to quickly restore the port and revive the fishery businesses and supply chains—critical economic drivers for recovery.[54] It also started raising the ground to support the new town reconstruction sooner than neighboring regions.

One of the pinnacles of the machizukuri design meeting's accomplishments was the town center. It was envisioned as a lively hub, and to ensure that it would thrive even if Onagawa continued to shrink, the mayor banned commercial development outside this district. Even before the tsunami, the mayor had been researching how to connect the town to the ocean. He selected Onodera Yasushi as the urban designer; Onodera created a 15-by-300-meter pedestrian promenade connecting the center of the commercial area to the sea. This new axis for downtown Onagawa, showcasing its exceptional views, is lined with small individual tenant-type shops made of local cedar. Businesses that had lost their stores in the tsunami and new local entrepreneurs who started businesses afterward were given priority, encouraging such trendy ventures as cocktail bars, artisanal coffee, Spanish tileworks, and a workshop making guitars.[55] The town also increased the number of young workers by offering internships and trial migration programs. From this central commercial area, multiple evacuation routes lead straight up to the hills. The routes are wide, three-lane roads, so that people can even abandon their cars during an evacuation and run the rest of the way if necessary.

At the terminus of the promenade is the JR Onagawa station building, called Yupo'po, designed by Ban Shigeru, which opened in December 2015. One of the first buildings completed, the airy new station building is also home to an *onsen* (hot spring bath) on the second floor. This rare combination was afforded by the geothermal tap that survived the earthquake and tsunami. Residents who were part of the machizukuri process painted tiles for murals in the *onsen*. The signature wood lattice visible through the building and the roofline symbolizes the wings of a black-tailed gull "soaring towards a bright future"[56] of recovery. Ban became part of the Onagawa recovery early on, also designing a container-based temporary housing system, which prioritized public space with a market in the center.[57] The machizukuri design meetings are continuing, at the time of this writing, to facilitate discussions about the park at the edge of the bay, and an Onagawa Miraizukuri (Future-Creating) Public Corporation has been established. This group, comprising town government (24 percent) and private enterprises (76 percent, most of them run by local residents), curates events in the city center and programs to support the commercial ecosystem for the region. The machizukuri council—transformed into the *miraizukuri* council—continues to engage with the public in the hope that the true essence of machizukuri will remain, not simply as a process for gathering public opinion but one that actively cares for and transforms the city over time. The case of Onagawa asserts the importance of a locally driven reconstruction process, which led to the necessary minimum ground elevation, eliminated the shoreline seawall, and ultimately sped up reconstruction.

DISCUSSION

Community leaders like those in the Mano district, designers like those involved in the Matsumoto stream project, and machizukuri coordinators like those in Onagawa can help negotiate between top-down and bottom-up needs, analyzing the policies while synthesizing and advocating for residents. They might also be considered "localizers," translating big-picture goals and international precedents into strategies that fit neighborhood needs and add to the overall quality of life. Machizukuri processes can certainly take a long time and require the investment of residents to discuss options and gain consensus, but such efforts will result in positive, lasting impact and a durable social network.

Regardless of who facilitated the development, an iterative design process was at the core of successful projects, especially when machizukuri prevailed as a movement beyond simply soliciting input from citizens after a disaster. Kobayashi Ikuo defines "machizukuri" as "a continuous effort to improve community by self-governing people."[58] Year-round bōsai planning, embedded in the social practices of a community, not only ensures that proper physical infrastructure for disasters is in place but also helps establish the strong coping capacity that is vital in disaster response and recovery. By considering the whole disaster timeline, this machizukuri process can continue into "normal" times by envisioning, creating, and caring for a town loved by its residents. In the case of Kobe's response, preexisting centralized plans and development projects, although initially contentious, set a foundation from which to launch reconstruction quickly; community-based bōsai plans already in place could be similarly leveraged. Creating plans before calamity strikes will improve the effectiveness of bottom-up planning and design when a disaster does occur, and preestablishing a vision for the community can help speed up recovery. This is the true meaning of machizukuri: not simply a planning tool but a way to increase social capacity.

Evacuation Routes

Evacuation routes are designated paths and roads that help people navigate from their current location to a safe location—an evacuation space—after a disaster warning. The warning might be an official announcement or might be inferred based on knowledge and experience—such as running to high ground in anticipation of a tsunami after experiencing a long, strong earthquake on the coast. Evacuation routes are often labeled through signage or other marking systems, and evacuation drills or personal preparedness planning can familiarize nearby residents with them. The creation of evacuation routes may seem like a relatively straightforward endeavor for cities built in the modern era, but in many cities, most roads run parallel to coastlines, offering fewer direct routes to higher ground. Similarly, in dense, labyrinthine Japanese cities and in the rugged, undulating countryside, creating a sufficiently direct and spacious route to safety can be significantly more complex.

Depending on the type of disaster, evacuation routes and evacuation modes may vary. After a tsunami warning, evacuation on foot to high ground is typically recommended, whereas a fire calls for evacuation on foot to open spaces; a typhoon warning, which is usually issued several days before the storm hits, frequently recommends that the vulnerable population should evacuate to official shelters in advance. But when a disaster is urgent, as with a fire or tsunami, evacuation by car can lead to deadly traffic jams. Making clear which evacuation route pertains to which hazard type is one challenge for evacuation route planning, and in this way the physical infrastructure also requires education around evacuation practices.

In Japan, *hinanro* (evacuation roads) are designated by municipalities based on guidelines and dimensions regulated by the CAO,[1] whereas residents decide on other *hinankeiro* (evacuation routes) based on their understanding of the neighborhood. The evacuation road, path, or greenway must be wide enough to accommodate those fleeing the hazard (i.e., tsunami, flood, or fire), and buildings and trees along the road should be earthquake- and fire-resistant so that the disaster does not cause the route to become dangerous or inaccessible.[2] Evacuation routes in Japanese cities are often part of a multistage process, from primary to secondary evacuation sites.

Like many structures for disaster preparedness in Japan, evacuation routes are planned through a combination of local initiatives and top-down policies. Policies regulate elements like evacuation road widths or signage, while community-scale projects often deal with a finer grain of evacuation—how residents navigate or find shelter within their neighborhood. This section brings to the fore how integrating community evacuation route planning into social networks links to larger comprehensive plans. Within urban bōsai strategies, evacuation route planning as a preparedness measure can be a counterbalance to larger infrastructural strategies, such as seawalls. In Tohoku and other tsunami-vulnerable regions, a key decision involves balancing the level of protection and cost of seawall projects with evacuation routes, which don't guarantee property protection but are relatively low cost and can be very effective in increasing preparedness plans and protecting human lives.

TOHOKU EVACUATION

After the Tohoku earthquake struck in 2011, knowledge of and access to evacuation routes meant the difference between life and death. In some cases, delayed evacuation may have been caused by low initial estimates of tsunami height: the first warning, three minutes after the earthquake began, estimated a three- to six-meter tsunami; after twenty-eight minutes, that was revised upward to ten meters. By that point, the wave had already reached some parts of the coastline. Because of the tsunami's unprecedented size, many of those impacted were not in areas identified on local hazard maps. Residents may have believed that they were outside the tsunami's reach, or they may have trusted that the seawall would hold the water back.[3] Some did not evacuate because the 2010 tsunami warnings from the earthquake in Chile did not result in a great deal of damage, leading them to consider the 2011 warning a false alarm.[4] A number of evacuation spaces were not high enough and were flooded by the tsunami. Despite overarching general recommendations to evacuate from tsunamis on foot, many attempted to evacuate by car (especially on flat plains[5]), and some became trapped in traffic jams that proved fatal.

Despite these cases, evacuation knowledge in Tohoku was very strong, given the educational efforts through all sectors of society and the area's long history of earthquakes and tsunamis. Schools and neighborhood associations in the region regularly sponsor evacuation drills. These sorts of preparedness programs condition most people to immediately evacuate independently when a tsunami does strike, with the regional refrain of *tsunami tendenko* reminding people to save themselves first.

COMMUNITY-BASED EVACUATION ROUTES

Itabashi Ward, Tokyo: Fire

One example of an evacuation route planning process that joined local government and private property owners is the Emergency Evacuation Path Development on the

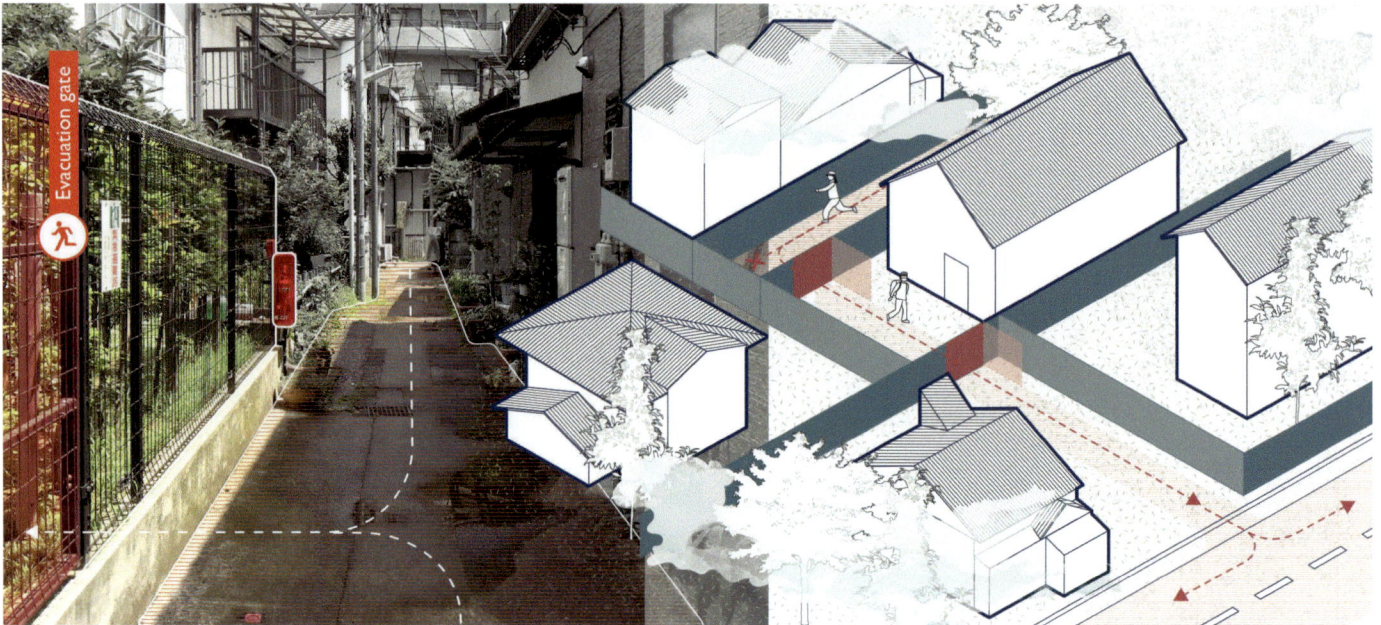

Figure 22. To help people escape to wider main streets during a fire, Itabashi Ward officials negotiated with landowners to build shortcuts through private property.

Dead-End Streets Project in Itabashi Ward, designed in response to lessons from the 1995 Kobe earthquake and fire. Initiated in 1996, this local-level project sought to ensure that occupants would be able to safely escape Itabashi Ward's maze of narrow streets and dead-end blocks after an earthquake, in anticipation of an inferno. Residents conducted field analysis to map roads that might be blocked by debris, have a high probability of fire, and contain dead-end alleys. After this process was completed, six ward officials spoke with property owners in the dead-end zones and reached agreements to use private land for disaster evacuation routes. In 1997, Itabashi Ward funded the remodeling of walls and fences with operable gates that would allow for evacuees to pass through private property to wide main streets.[6] To spread knowledge about the new evacuation routes, community information programs created signage on fire extinguisher boxes along the paths. This was the first time in Japan that new evacuation routes were created without the acquisition of buildings or land, increasing evacuation capacity at a minimal cost (less than ¥210,000 per project). The project has continued since then with a modest annual budget, and as of July 2020, eighty-one evacuation routes are available for the neighboring 962 households.[7] With 2,571 dead-end paths identified in the ward, these efforts will continue. Despite the challenges of negotiating with property owners and tenants, abating their fears of crime and the infringement of privacy, and inventing solutions to modify fences and walls, several other cities, such as Kyoto, Kobe, and Yokohama, have followed suit. This impressive level of community-based initiative in the creation of redundant evacuation infrastructures won the Bōsai Machizukuri Award in 2009.

Kamaishi, Iwate Prefecture: Tsunami

Kamaishi offers a case of neighborhood collaborative tsunami evacuation plans similar to the fire evacuation path project in Itabashi Ward. Residents living in the hills near Ozaki Athletic Park agreed to allow evacuees to run through their properties to reach the park as quickly as possible. The main entrance of the park has 227 steps from the port level, and in the middle is a path from the Hamakko children's park, which is an initial evacuation space. Right after the 2011 tsunami hit, about one hundred residents initially gathered in the children's park. Once the tsunami reached two meters below the park, the shōbōdan led people to Ozaki Athletic Park, about three hundred meters higher. In this neighborhood, residents regularly held tsunami evacuation drills and fostered close relationships. On the day of the disaster, people encouraged each other, and many evacuees carried the elderly on their backs.[8]

EMBEDDING SIGNS INTO THE LANDSCAPE

Public Projects: Guidelines and Street Signs

In the chaos of a large-scale disaster, local residents—not to mention visitors—can have difficulty making immediate and accurate evacuation decisions. Therefore, the design of evacuation paths and guidance signs can be crucial to survival. Evacuation paths can be designated for fire, landslide, flood, or tsunami. For tsunamis, evacuation distance is calculated by the first wave's arrival time minus evacuation initiation time multiplied by walking speed. Average walking speed is considered one meter per second, using the average pace of an elderly person, a large crowd, or a person unfamiliar with the geography. When considering vulnerable populations, such as people with physical challenges, infants, and those who are ill, the average speed decreases to half a meter per second. Designating the shortest and safest route to the evacuation target point is vital, so these guidelines are important to consider.

Evacuation planning needs to pay attention to the following points. Evacuation routes should be as wide as possible, and detour routes should be secure in case debris hinders the route. Plans should avoid designating roads parallel to coasts or along rivers, as the tsunami might arrive earlier than predicted and might move up rivers. Plans need to designate roads to evacuate in the same direction as the tsunami movement and avoid evacuation toward the coast, even if there are high elevation spots on the coast. The range (feasible evacuation distance) should be reachable to the evacuation target point through the evacuation route within the tsunami arrival time, and areas outside this range should be considered evacuation difficulty zones. The designation of evacuation difficulty zones should be used not only to make assumptions on a map but also to carry out evacuation drills and determine whether evacuation would be possible for all within the expected tsunami arrival time.

According to the Fire and Disaster Management Agency (FDMA), there are four elements that a sign should have: visibility (recognizable at a glance); comprehensibility (effortlessly understandable); memorability (readily recallable); and harmony (embedded into the landscape).[9] Nighttime illumination is also critical for visibility. One example is a sign triggered by a solar panel light system with motion sensors. Another is light-storing luminescent panels, such as the tsunami signs installed in Yonaguni, Okinawa Prefecture. In consideration of evacuation guidance for visitors from foreign countries, the signs are displayed in five languages (Japanese, English, Korean, traditional Chinese, and simplified Chinese), and the pictograms and locations and heights of signs are standardized within the Japan Industrial Standards (JIS) Z 9098 Disaster Prevention Sign Guidebook. As of March 2018, there was deliberation as to whether it was possible to create an international standard through the International Organization for Standardization (ISO).

Other Types of Signs: Tsunami Stones

Tsunami-hi (tsunami stones) are markers placed following tsunamis at the level of the inundation line in coastal regions across Japan, from Hokkaido to Okinawa.[10] Up to three meters high and sometimes many centuries old, the markers bear messages that remind viewers of past disasters. The roles of *tsunami-hi* have transformed over time. The earliest stones were typically marked with Buddhist sutras reflecting the belief that disasters, including tsunamis, resulted from a failure to abide by Buddhist tenets.[11] During Japan's Edo period, as literacy increased, tsunami stone inscriptions shifted from religious messages to ones that provided factual information about tsunamis (e.g., date, time, tsunami characteristics, buildings and people lost). As scientific understanding grew about how and why earthquakes occurred, the stones played an increasingly instructive role regarding safe building practices and evacuation zones after the severe Tohoku earthquakes and tsunamis of 1896 and 1933. For example, one inscription says, "Run to the highest place. Do not run only to a far place because you will be caught up by the tsunami."[12] Relief money distributed by the *Asahi Shimbun* after 1933 created a network of *tsunami-hi,* and although individual stones reflected the identity of each community and municipality, prefectures issued written guidelines that required the stones to include lessons from the 1933 tsunami.

The village of Murohama, Miyagi, is similarly famous for the role its tsunami marker played in retaining collective memory. The stone reminds villagers of an event from over a thousand years ago (likely the Jogan earthquake of 869 AD). Murohama's occupants had evacuated to the nearest hill following a strong earthquake. From its summit, they saw the tsunami wash in from the coast, but a second wave had traveled up an inlet and loomed toward them from the opposite direction. The waves crashed together at the hill where the evacuees stood, drowning them all. The place name, Futatsu-bashi (two bridges), is believed to refer to this phenomenon.[13] In 2011, villagers heeded the warning and fled to a further hill after the earthquake, even though their alarm tower had collapsed in the quake. Nearly all the residents survived. However, coverage of Japan's tsunami stones often notes the many cases in which citizens failed to heed the stones' warnings, often as a result of excessive faith in the technical protections of seawalls and early warning systems. The case of Murohama may be an outlier, in which the relevance of the markers survived because of the oral narratives maintained by close-knit communities.[14]

Stones were less effective in places with newer populations who were less connected to traditional narratives.[15] But the failure of tsunami stones in such locations serves as a valuable reminder of the importance of maintaining the combined physical and social infrastructure of disaster preparedness. In many places, newer residents who lacked generational knowledge of historic tsunamis were more affected than those with deeper ties to the region and community. Tsunami stones, or any other danger zone marker, must remain integrated into the culture and living memory of a place in order to remain effective.

Following the 2011 tsunami, the creation of new tsunami stones or other disaster memorial markers has sometimes faced opposition due to their perceived ineffectiveness in informing action. Yet new tsunami stones are being constructed, as are other types of markers. The National General Association of Stone Shops in Japan has organized the construction of new tsunami stones, outfitted with QR codes that allow visitors to see what the site looked like in the past as well as footage from the last tsunami.[16] This mixed-media approach speaks to a call for intergenerational markers to include more graphic and universal images that provoke a visceral response, although whether these digital systems can remain accessible over long periods of time is questionable.

Some tsunami stones are being created through collaborative processes, such as the Zenyuseki project in Kamaishi. This black granite memorial marker is carved with lessons from schoolchildren who experienced the catastrophe. Their messages to the future include, "If a tsunami comes, let's run away"; "If a tsunami comes, each person must protect one's life"; and "If there is an earthquake, go to high ground."[17] By bringing the community into the construction, perhaps this project will be more successful than other *tsunami-hi* in maintaining a living narrative around the object.

Other Types of Signs: O-Jizô-san

In parallel to the creation of new *tsunami-hi,* the O-Jizô-san Project creates stone monuments that employ the commemorative role of memorials to both pay tribute and educate the public about past disasters. Jizô is a Japanese bodhisattva who watches

The stones should be placed on the submergence lines and show the date of the disaster, fatality, and number of inundated houses. This marks the tsunami submergence line and warns descendants that areas lower than the line could be easily submerged by future tsunamis.

- Ishiguro Hidehiko

"After a big earthquake, there will be a big tsunami. Come to this location and wait. If a tsunami arrives, go higher than this location. The tsunami will catch you if you go far, rather than going high. Always keep a place prepared where you will escape to high ground"

Taro, 1933

"If there is an earthquake, beware of tsunami. If a tsunami comes, go to a higher place"

Kamaishi, 1933

O-Jizô-san

O-Jizô-san

O-Jizô-san

O-Jizô-san

Ishiguro Hidehiko, "Iwate Prefecture Shōwa Earthquake Disaster Memorandum" [in Japanese], Tsunami Digital Library, March 5, 1933, http://tsunami-dl.jp/document/036.

over living children and travelers as well as the souls of the deceased. His statue is often placed to mark deaths from unnatural causes and to ease transitions to the afterlife. The O-Jizô-san Project is working to construct fifty Jizô statues across the tsunami-affected area of eastern Japan.[18] For each event memorializing those who perished, the surrounding community shares a meal or rice cakes together, reinforcing the connection between religion, traditions, and bōsai cultural markers within the landscape.

ACCESSIBILITY: PUBLIC PROJECTS

Although a lot of emphasis is placed on accessible, universal design in emergency shelters and temporary houses, accessibility is still an issue in evacuation routes, especially with sites such as shrines and forest paths, which often have numerous stairs or feature uneven terrain. In some parts of Tohoku, evacuation routes have been outfitted with "stramps"—stairs straddled by steep ramps on either side—to help small vehicles such as Japanese micro-vans, bikes, and wheelchairs reach high ground.

The "greenbelt" evacuation path in the Tōbu district of Kamaishi is a 750-meter-long embankment with an elevation of 8 to 12 meters, enabling visitors and workers in the shopping center, hotel employees, sightseers, and workers around Kamaishi Bay to quickly access high ground.[19] In addition to stairs, there are five ramps from municipal roads for wheelchair and bicycle access. The bottom entrance at the harbor is a gentle, wide slope, which allows easy access to evacuees on wheels. The red pavement color was chosen to be noticeable even from a distance. This embankment evacuation path also works as one of the multilayered tsunami defenses, with the Kamaishi Bay breakwater, the seawall, and the raised National Highway 45 that runs next to it.[20]

In contrast with areas such as Iwate and northern Miyagi, where the ria geography means that a hill is always nearby, the flat expanse of floodplain means that high ground might be far away. Such situations require an alternative way to evacuate vertically, above the level of the incoming tsunami. As far back as the Edo period, Fukuroi (in Shizuoka Prefecture) has been building *inochi-yama* ("life hills") as vertical evacuation spaces for residents. Two of the Edo-period structures remain today.[21] More recently, Fukuroi created an additional four *inochi-yama* to prepare for the possible Nankai Trough earthquake. These spaces can accommodate up to 1,300 evacuees. The gentle 8 percent slope of the ramp makes it easier for disaster-vulnerable populations to evacuate. The tops of *inochi-yama* are developed as parks, viewpoints, and walkways.[22]

ACCESSIBILITY: PRIVATE (CITIZEN-BASED) PROJECTS

In addition to the local government-based projects described above, strong local leaders can also play a significant role in evacuation planning. Iwasaki Akiko, owner of Horaikan, a hotel in the Unosumai district of Kamaishi, built her establishment as

Figure 23. Tsunami stones and O-Jizô-san memorialize past events while educating the public about them.

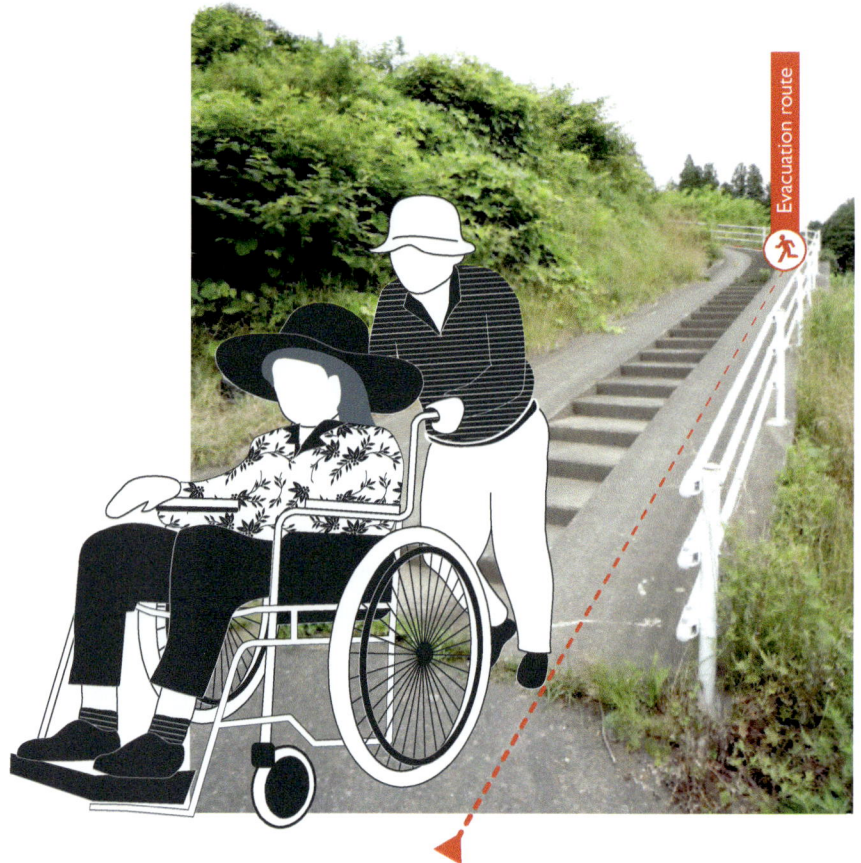

Figure 24. Stramps—part ramp, part stair—are constructed across mountainous regions to provide universal access to high-ground evacuation spaces.

a four-story steel building after seeing how vertical evacuation buildings were used during the 2004 Indian Ocean tsunami and observing the destruction associated with the Kobe earthquake.[23] She intended her hotel to be an alternative to seawalls or other structural measures that would have reduced the area's value as a scenic destination, and the building was designated as an official vertical evacuation site. However, given the intensity of the earthquake, those nearby chose to evacuate up a forest trail behind the Horaikan during the 2011 disaster.

From her hotel lobby, converted into a makeshift presentation space with chairs and a projection screen, Iwasaki shared her tsunami experience. After the earthquake began to shake the ground, 30 people (hotel staff, guests, and neighbors) evacuated to the hotel, initially arriving at the parking lot. A shaky cell-phone video shows Iwasaki helping guide people to the path when the tsunami reaches the hotel, and she runs and then swims to escape the rushing waters as onlookers watch in horror from the hill. The water reached the second floor of the building. Kamaishi harbor had been protected by a seawall, which had blocked the view of the incoming wave; the force of the tsunami broke it. After the waves receded, Horaikan was used as a shelter, housing up to 120 people over fifteen days.

In 2014, Iwasaki completed her project of widening her forest trail and making it wheelchair accessible. The "kizuna no michi" ("path of bonding") draws upon lessons learned from the experiences of the elderly and disabled on March 11, 2011, as they struggled up the narrow forest path. Iwasaki was inspired by her grandmother's mantra: "If you have a tsunami, go to the mountain." The path is built on land owned by the hotel, though part of the area is an ecological preserve, so trees cannot be removed and the path cannot be wider than ninety centimeters. The path was built with volunteer labor and donated materials, and Iwasaki collaborated with the Kamaishi Forest Cooperative Association so that the route could plug into existing forest paths.

Iwasaki uses her story to raise awareness as well. At the time of this writing, she was hosting several guests every week to share her experience of living through and responding to the disaster. Local leaders like her are often key to demonstrating that more private landowners could consider making their land accessible for evacuation, as government-owned land is often limited.

COMMUNITY EVACUATION PLANNING

The 2011 Tohoku disaster underscored the importance of frequently discussing evacuation routes with families and neighbors in order to evacuate to a safe place quickly in the event of a disaster. The NIGECHIZU (evacuation map) workshop created by Nikken Sekkei's volunteer department is a method for remembering, measuring, visualizing, and planning the shortest path for tsunami evacuation.[24] The workshop assumes an elderly person's walking speed to be forty-three meters per minute, and participants use string to measure the sinuous roads in three-minute intervals. The path is then colored based on these three-minute increments, starting with green and ending with black, for over twenty-one minutes. Areas inundated by past tsunamis are layered onto the map, landslide hazard areas are marked as obstacles, and arrows are drawn for the safest, fastest ways to reach evacuation spaces.

The NIGECHIZU workshop was first held in collaboration with the Kinoshita Isami laboratory at Chiba University and the Yamamoto Toshiya laboratory at Meiji

Horaikan Hotel

Evacuation route

津波が来たら山に行って

"IF A TSUNAMI COMES, RUN TO THE MOUNTAIN"

Ms. Iwasaki

University. It started in Tohoku and expanded nationally to include places vulnerable to future tsunamis, riverine flooding, and landslide disasters, and many universities across the country have been conducting the workshop.[25] The first one was held with junior-high students in Rikuzentakata. The NIGECHIZU created by the students were reviewed and edited by the neighborhood firefighters in the next workshop, and then among female members of the Fisheries Cooperative Association. Local women discussed the map to incorporate their perspectives; in this way, the evacuation plan was prepared with the local knowledge of each community member. In other municipalities, a series of NIGECHIZU workshops ended up developing a district-wide bōsai plan. NIGECHIZU has also been applied to landslides, fires, and multi-hazard disasters, and it features an online repository of ideas from additional people who could not attend the workshops. The software simulates the feasibility and cost effectiveness of an evacuation design created through each NIGECHIZU workshop.[26] This community workshop increases communication across all ages and can help share preparedness tasks within neighborhoods. It raises bōsai awareness and helps build a system of cooperation in the event of an emergency.

In one workshop held in Yoriki, Miyagi Prefecture, and facilitated by Hiraoka Yoshihiro from Miyagi University and the MIT Urban Risk Lab, the first step—along with measuring with string—was to record the stories and challenges associated with evacuating on March 11, 2011. This revealed that steep areas should have a shorter string measurement, as it takes people longer to ascend them. The completed map led to deliberation over the seawall height and location; through the discussion, it emerged that the residents' first priority was to invest in better evacuation routes, since their bay has ample high ground but only ad hoc paths to reach it. Residents also recollected the need for redundancies and multiple options in case certain routes were blocked by debris, water, or fire. Some 67 percent of the participants (of the 80 percent of the households that responded) preferred lower seawalls to protect against storm surge. The entire town resettled on higher ground and does not have a seawall.

BUILDING IN REDUNDANCY

Path networks can play an important role when normal circulation networks are disrupted. In the Shizugawa district of Minamisanriku, a forest ridgeline path network allowed children and families who had evacuated to the elementary and high school to move between evacuation sites in order to find siblings and other family members. When main roads are inundated and impassable, this type of redundant circulation network in the hills can be essential for moving people and resources after a disaster, ensuring that secondary options exist even if one route is disrupted. Many buildings, such as Inawashiro Hospital and Hotel Bōyō in Kesennuma, also connect to path

Figure 25. The Horaikan hotel and forest trail were instrumental in evacuation and shelter during the 2011 Tohoku disaster.

Figure 26. Community-based evacuation map workshop.

Figure 27. The Inawashiro Hospital evacuation route, directly connected to the hilltop behind the site.

networks in the hills via roof bridges—a redundancy plan in case lower streets are inundated. Another striking example is Okirai Elementary School in Ōfunato, where a city councilor worked tirelessly to create an evacuation bridge from the second floor of the school to the higher road. The bridge was completed just four months before the tsunami came, and all the students at school that day survived.

DISCUSSION

As the above cases demonstrate, for evacuation routes to be effective, their intended users must be familiar with them. In the words of Suppasri et al., evacuation routes require "hard" as well as "soft measures," including "experience and awareness" and an effective "communication system."[27] In other words, evacuation routes require both social and spatial approaches. Without these soft measures, people may fail to evacuate or may become disoriented if a sign is missing or damaged, and they might even evacuate to a more dangerous location. Through education and signage—or better yet, by creating the routes and physical design together as a community—occupants of an area should know which evacuation routes to use in the event of different disaster types. People need either preexisting knowledge or access to clear and effective information during the event in order to use evacuation routes properly.

Much of the existing research surrounding evacuation route planning centers on algorithmic approaches to modeling evacuation traffic flows. While this research is helpful in considering how to manage movements of large volumes of people and vehicles, it should be tempered with community-centered approaches, embedded in engagement and participation (such as NIGECHIZU). The top-down should be combined with the bottom-up. Through education, people's behavior patterns can be shifted—as demonstrated by the strong emphasis on long-term community engagement in many of these cases.

Inscribing knowledge into the physical environment can help reinforce knowledge gained in a drill or on a map. Walking daily past tsunami stones, seeing O-Jizô-san, or noting the evacuation direction embedded into the sidewalk supports subliminal, rote learning. This type of design and planning can also incorporate backup and redundancy plans throughout neighborhoods in case some routes become inaccessible during a disaster.

Coastal Strategies

Residents of Japan's Pacific coast traditionally survived tsunamis through observation and evacuation. Coastal villagers recognized the ocean's pullback as a sign of a coming tsunami and took refuge on higher ground. However, the increase of technical and national planning capacity since the 1930s has led to a desire to create structures that can deflect tsunamis' destructive force.[1] While coastal Japan has built seawalls to prevent storm surges and inundation as well as an extensive network of levees to prevent riverine flooding, this section focuses in particular on the seawalls, breakwaters, coastal forests, floodgates, and new typologies intended for tsunami protection (but many of these examples can be used to protect the coast from storm surges as well). It identifies opportunities through positive examples of what an anticipatory design framework might offer. The top-down/bottom-up concept asks how affected local communities might play a larger role in deciding what trade-offs and risks are desirable for their particular context. Dual-use projects can help reframe large urban infrastructure beyond technical engineering projects and, instead, interface with local planning and the daily lives of coastal dwellers to create better solutions.

HISTORIC CONTEXT

As with other sorts of catastrophes, tsunamis in Japan led to the creation of urban plans and infrastructures designed to mitigate them. Although some seawalls were built soon after the 1854 tsunami, the 1933 Sanriku tsunami marked the first systematic, regional approach to tsunami-mitigating urbanism.[2] After the disaster, the Earthquake Disaster Prevention Council (a group of experts and academics supporting the government) proposed extensive mitigation and preparedness recommendations, which the national government incorporated into its reconstruction plan.[3] Pacific coastal cities were rebuilt, surrounded by seawalls and buffer zones, and many fishing villages were relocated to high ground. The ten-point reconstruction strategy also included mechanisms such as evacuation routes, tsunami watches, and the construction of memorials to help keep alive the memory of tsunamis.[4] Following Typhoon Vera in 1959, the government built more coastal defense structures, typically three to four meters high, designed for typhoons and storm surges.[5] The 1960 Chilean tsunami, which impacted

Japan's entire Pacific coast and especially the Tohoku region, led to further concrete seawall and coastal dike construction as well as the world's first tsunami breakwater, located across the thirty-eight-meter-deep Ōfunato Bay. Eight years later, these new structures were effective against the 1968 Tokachi-oki tsunami; however, they also gave coastal dwellers a false sense of security as memories of past tsunamis faded.[6]

Seawalls and Breakwaters

The 2011 tsunami surpassed both social expectations and technical estimates for tsunami height, exceeding even those of the 1896 tsunami, which took more than twenty-two thousand lives. A large number of Tohoku residents trusted that tsunami prevention structures would protect them, but many of these structures were broken or overtopped, as they had been designed based on the smaller 1896 tsunami. The MLIT estimates that of 300 kilometers of seawalls from Iwate to Fukushima, more than 190 kilometers were damaged.[7]

Breakwaters, also severely damaged, differ from seawalls in that they are located offshore and are typically discontinuous, allowing ships to pass through a gap between two walls. The Kamaishi breakwater, nearly 2 kilometers long and 63 meters deep, held the Guinness World Record for the world's deepest breakwater and was designed specifically to defend against tsunamis of up to 5 to 6 meters high. The walls cost ¥120 billion, took thirty years to construct, and were completed in 2009, only two years before the Tohoku tsunami. The walls' seventy-seven support caissons weighed 16,000 tons each,[8] but half of them toppled as water rose 10 meters on the seaward side and scoured their bases.[9] The Tohoku tsunami exceeded design heights: a GPS station located about 20 kilometers off the port of Kamaishi measured the tsunami at 6.6 meters, and others closer to shore measured heights between 7 and 9 meters. While the breakwater fell short of complete protection, the simulation calculated that without it, the tsunami would have hit the coast at a run-up height of 13 meters.[10] The breakwater also delayed the arrival of the tsunami by an estimated six minutes,[11] providing precious time for people trying to evacuate.

Taro Seawalls

Taro, a northern district in Miyako, Iwate Prefecture, illustrates the importance of connecting mitigation infrastructure with natural topographies and social systems. The small settlement has suffered several catastrophic tsunamis in recorded history, and residents carried the knowledge between generations in order to remain prepared, adapt, and evacuate as much as possible. The 1896 tsunami was particularly catastrophic, rising 15 meters above sea level. Out of 2,248 Taro residents, 83 percent lost their lives.[12] Many of the survivors were fishermen who avoided the tsunami's destructive path while out fishing in deep waters.[13] These seafarers returned to find all 335 homes washed away—their entire village erased. In 1933, a 10-meter tsunami again struck the village, killing 972.[14]

In the wake of the 1923 Tokyo earthquake, this era also saw the emergence of scientific analysis of natural disasters, which allowed for more targeted interventions. Engineers from the University of Tokyo proposed to relocate the town to high ground and construct a seawall or a buffer forest zone; however, the relocation plan was too expensive, and studies found that there was not sufficient land available on the high-ground site to hold Taro's 500 households. As a result, only the seawall moved forward, a 10-meter-high curved wall designed to deflect water away from the village using the adjacent river's hydrology to its advantage. The force of the tsunami would be diverted upriver, protecting the town from its primary force. Land to the east and southwest was preserved as a buffer zone. In combination with the seawall, a land readjustment proposal placed new city blocks adjacent to the hillside with a radiating street layout perpendicular to the wall, allowing residents to easily evacuate outward and upward into the surrounding hills.[15] Evacuation was considered down to the scale of the intersections, which were designed with chamfered corners so that evacuees running from a tsunami would not have to slow down to look both ways.[16] Evacuation systems and city design thus went hand in hand.

Initially, Taro was not granted funding for the curved-wall proposal, and eventually residents took matters into their own hands, unable to reconcile with the idea of leaving their ancestral homes. The majority of Taro residents decided to move forward with the proposal, funding construction from their own pockets and governmental loans. Construction began, and in the project's second year, it was converted into a public project funded by prefectural and national revenues. After several years of work, construction was halted during shortages associated with the Japan-China War in 1940. Following a fourteen-year hiatus, a small-scale tsunami in 1952 provided an impetus to reinitiate construction in 1954. When completed in 1958, the seawall was the world's largest: 1,350 meters long, with a base of 25 meters and a height of 10 meters above sea level.[17] Importantly, this initial seawall was designed not to stop the tsunami but rather to redirect it in order to provide more time for evacuation and minimize the force of the tsunami on buildings, preventing some physical losses. However, this intention was not properly communicated to the community, and over time, many saw the wall as a protective measure that eliminated the need to evacuate.

Taro remained undamaged in the 1960 Chilean tsunami, though the town built two additional seawalls as part of a nationwide seawall construction program that followed the disaster. As opposed to the first wall's deflective design, these walls were designed as barriers to block the tsunami. All three were built at a height of 10 meters, equivalent to the reach of the 1933 tsunami. The resulting web of defenses reached 2,433 meters, one of the world's largest feats of tsunami mitigation engineering.[18] By then, memories had faded—and in fact, the eastern tsunami buffer zone from the first seawall project was rapidly built up by new residents in the 1960s.[19] To protect this new district and maximize financial support from the Japanese government, Taro undertook these hefty infrastructural projects, which apparently were not tailored to their site with the sensitivity of the first seawall's plan.

The 2011 tsunami surged through the town, overtopping all three seawalls by more than 7 meters. The force of the wave as it pulled back out to sea destroyed the two more recent walls and everything in front of and behind them—84 percent of the entire housing stock.[20] The 1933 wall withstood the force of the wave, owing to its more hydrodynamic design, and some homes behind it remained standing; a few residents who had climbed onto these roofs survived. This older wall was also thicker: 25 meters, instead of 15, at the base.

The death toll in Taro was over 200, and the primary cause of death was drowning.[21] When the earthquake struck, many residents believed that the seawalls would protect them; those in their sixties who remembered only the 1960 Chilean tsunami (and had forgotten the town's deeper history) thought that it was not necessary to flee. Elders in their nineties, who remembered the 1933 disaster, urged everyone to evacuate.[22]

Taro's infrastructure was rebuilt as part of the national plan for reconstruction. The town resettled residential areas to high ground, constructed a 14.7-meter seawall outfitted with an automated gate closure system following the original curved wall, completed a 10-meter raised road, and raised ground in urban areas. Commercial zones remain at lower elevations, and the harbor will stay an industrial site outside of the new seawall. Taro's experience reinforced the importance of social infrastructure, so it prioritized community connection in its recovery process, making sure that existing neighborhoods were grouped together in temporary housing to facilitate discussion and quick decision making. Some citizens decided to resettle to Otobe Hill (40 to 60 meters above sea level) to the northeast of Taro in the same area proposed in the 1933 plan; new civil engineering technologies have made development on this site possible.[23] Through surveys and four residents' meetings, the group came to a decision about relocation, seawall and land use plans, and evacuation facilities. By law, the government only requires one hearing in which the public can comment. However, Taro's process, similar to machizukuri, engages the residents in all the decision making and ensures that vulnerable populations, especially, have a voice.[24] Original lessons on holistically designing urban streets in accordance with seawall shape, rivers, and topography have been physically lost as a result of the vast destruction during 2011, but hopefully, increased community involvement in decision making and ownership of the new design layout will broaden awareness and social capacity for generations to come.

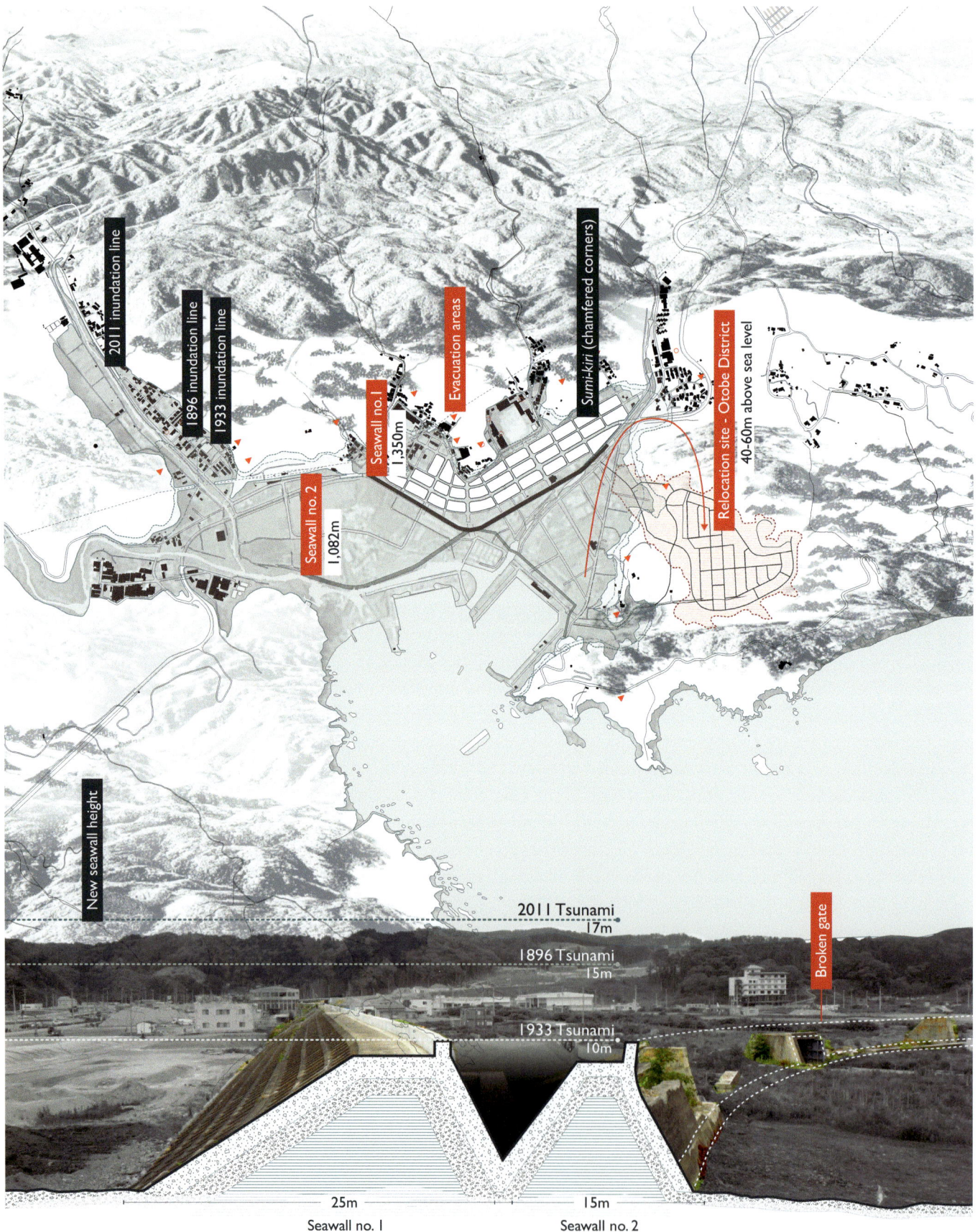

2011 inundation line

1896 inundation line

1933 inundation line

Seawall no. 1
1,350m

Evacuation areas

Sumi-kiri (chamfered corners)

Relocation site - Otobe District
40-60m above sea level

Seawall no. 2
1,082m

New seawall height

2011 Tsunami
17m

1896 Tsunami
15m

Broken gate

1933 Tsunami
10m

25m
Seawall no. 1

15m
Seawall no. 2

2011 TSUNAMI HEIGHTS, COASTAL INFRASTRUCTURE, AND COMPETING VIEWPOINTS

Seawall construction in the Tohoku recovery garnered a lot of contentious attention, especially seawalls built like those in Taro, with heights such as 14.7 meters. On April 28, 2011, members from MLIT and the Ministry of Agriculture, Forestry and Fisheries (MAFF), academics, and representatives from Iwate, Miyagi, and Fukushima Prefectures discussed high-level decisions such as the seawalls' civil engineering standards. On June 27, the second committee specified types of structures and heights of seawalls for protection against an L1 tsunami. In the three prefectures, 1,700 kilometers of coastline were divided into sixty "regional coasts" categorized by the shape of the bay, surrounding hills, and historic tsunami records.[25] But this regional coast idea did not take into account the nuances of individual coasts and bays, such as bathymetry, mouth of the bay versus inner bay, direction of wave, topography, the presence of a river near the coast, density of settlement, and local needs across these diverse sites; instead, the expected L1 tsunami height of each regional coast was set at the same level across that section of coastline.[26] To determine the height, prefectures were first asked to field-survey the most recent tsunami run-up measurements as well as historical records from the 1933 tsunami and the 1960 Chilean tsunami. If the historical records were unavailable or insufficient, then the Central Disaster Management Council simulated L1 tsunami heights (based on data from the 1896 Sanriku tsunami) in some regional coasts and then used those heights.[27] Some regions performed the simulations recommended by the Central Disaster Management Council on their own.

The Tsunami Countermeasures Committee emphasized the need for localization. Kawata Yoshiaki, the chairman of the committee, stated, "The risk can be reduced by building evacuation routes and other measures, not necessarily the tsunami wall for L1. We've left room to create a plan that works for each locality."[28] In some regions with a complex mix of bays and beaches (which have a distinctly different wave height than bays) and where local leadership was strong, the regional coast was divided into individual coasts, and seawall heights were designed accordingly. But in general, the prefectural administration did not want to prolong the seawall design period for fear that projects would not be able to secure their full reconstruction budgets. All subsequent reconstruction decisions depended on the established height of the seawall, and initially, the funding timeline was set with a five-year limit.[29]

Municipalities then established their Two-Two boundaries, checking where a tsunami of this height would hit the specific topography in their town, to define their land-use zoning. Since simulation results are enmeshed with subsequent design decisions (such as breakwater and embankment heights), testing designs should have required several iterations. Onoda Yasuaki lamented that "unfortunately, only a few municipalities took this multi-cycle approach in their planning"[30] to rerun the simu-

Figure 28. The complex history of the Taro district's seawalls and urban design.

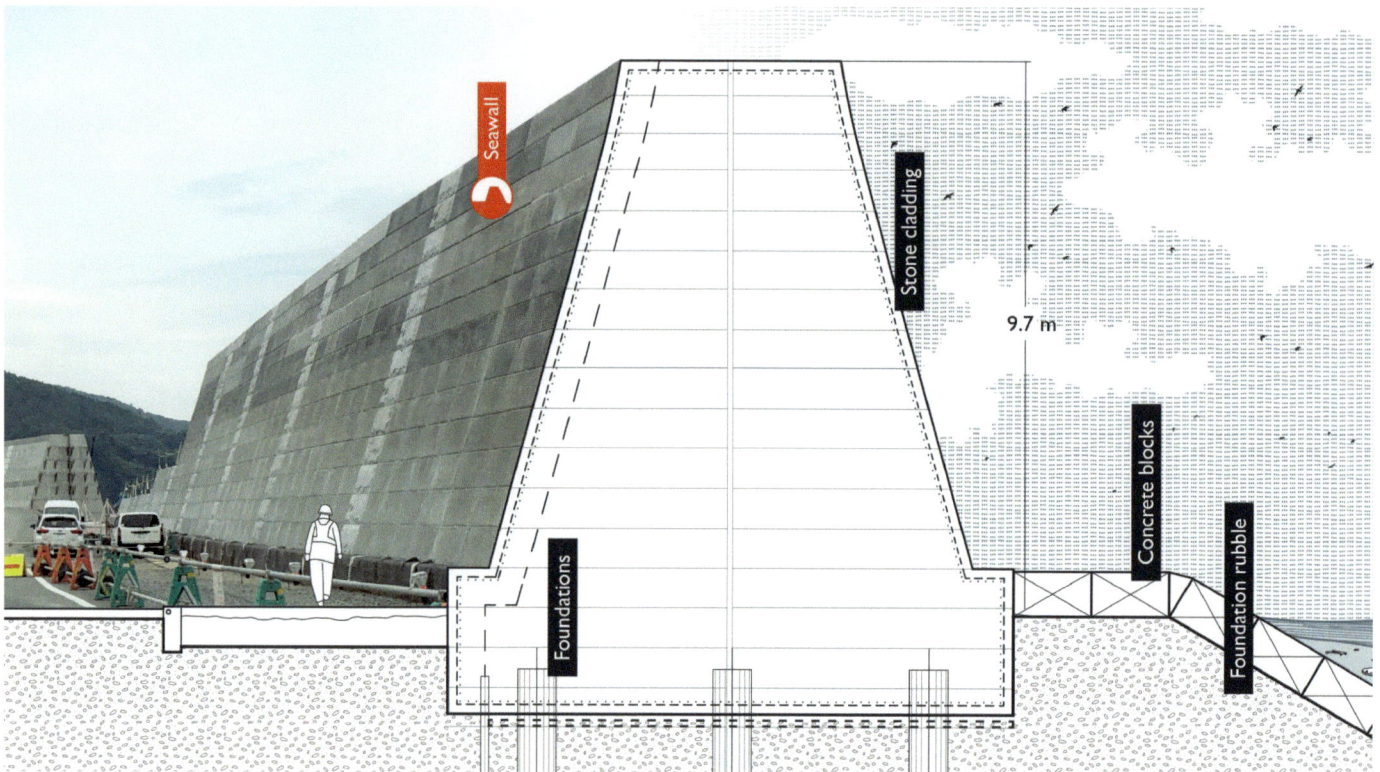

The labels in the figure: Seawall, Stone cladding, 9.7 m, Concrete blocks, Foundation rubble, Foundations

Figure 29. Seawall construction in Ishinomaki. At 9.7 meters high, the seawall blocks ocean views and impedes ecological processes.

lations based on various design approaches, as this would have required support from both the prefectural and national governments. The aspiration to rebuild as quickly as possible was dominant in the region, and another round of simulations would have taken more time, so, regrettably, that was not realistic.[31]

Each prefectural and municipal authority had the right to determine the exact seawall height based on the approximation provided by the simulation, taking into account the topography, safety, environmental protection, landscape, secondary dikes (such as raised ground and highways), the heights of high-ground residential areas, and machizukuri processes, if they chose to incorporate them. This process was conducted by only a couple of large consulting firms and was loosely controlled by the central government. In fact, the Tsunami Countermeasures Committee stated that "after sufficient coordination with coastal managers, the final height of the seawall should be set, taking into account the cost of facility development and the structural durability for the regional coast."[32] However, many processes did not provide much of an opportunity for residents to discuss the plans, most likely as a result of the initial five-year time limit to fund infrastructure reconstruction projects nationally. As expected, small local governments, already strained from the lives lost, felt pressured to adhere to national and prefectural guidelines quickly to avoid being saddled with all the reconstruction costs. Ubaura Michio argues that the organizational structure of local governments, operating under siloed conditions and constrained by limited timelines, prevented sufficient consensus building around seawalls.[33]

The MLIT issued guidelines for landscape consideration in the restoration of the river and coastal structures in November 2011. This provided advice on landscape, ecosystem, sustainability, and long-term maintenance as well as costs in the restoration of the coastal facilities, assuming that urgent reconstruction would be carried out on a large scale.[34] And yet concerns emerged in the September 2012 committee meeting that "construction work without environmental assessment has already been underway in many areas, and rare species are suffering great damage from them."[35] Since disaster recovery seawall projects were not subject to environmental assessment, some municipalities only conducted simplified assessments.[36] In addition, the committee included academics but not fishery professionals, who know more about ocean ecosystems and coastal conditions for fishermen. These alarms did not, however, slow down reconstruction.

In many cases, high seawalls ended up being built even where entire settlements had relocated to high ground. This incongruity illustrates how the government prioritizes certain actions. Seawall reconstruction was considered a disaster recovery project, allowing for fast-tracked timelines. The Act for Reconstruction of Disaster Stricken Public Facilities does not require cost-benefit analyses, environmental impact assessments, or local buy-in for such projects. Seawalls were planned before decisions about where and how to rebuild were made at the community planning level.[37] Even in some areas where environmental impact assessments were applied, it was often just for preserving the scenery.[38]

Eventually, the government extended the timeline of the reconstruction subsidy to a full ten years. In December 2013, responding to residents' concerns about the height of the seawalls and the delayed construction in certain regions, the Reconstruction Agency stated that the development of seawalls could be reviewed to consider local needs because social consensus building with the residents was important. In response to this, Iwate and Miyagi began to reconsider the heights of seawalls and responded with more flexibility. Toru Doi, the parliamentary secretary as of 2014, asserted that "the national government should deeply regret the fact that we initially set the period of reconstruction projects as five years, or until 2015. Due to time constraints, municipalities have lost the opportunity to address the seawall issue in a deliberate manner. As a result, the residents felt that the government was proceeding with the reconstruction project unilaterally."[39] As of the end of June 2020, 197 of the 621 seawalls had been revised to a lower height (below L1 tsunami height) or relocated, but a tremendous amount of seawall construction was moving forward.[40] Along the Pacific coastline from Fukushima to Iwate, 432 kilometers (20 percent) were committed to seawall construction. For Iwate, the total coastal length with seawalls was extended to 85 kilometers from 68 kilometers, and in Miyagi, the total length of seawalls was extended to 239 kilometers from 155 kilometers before the tsunami.[41]

The cost of the Tohoku seawall construction reached ¥1,350 billion as of 2018, and the project is far from over.[42] A number of critiques of seawall construction emerged in response to these top-down infrastructure schemes. A major concern is how much they actually add to human safety, especially when they fail.

Defensive infrastructure can provide a false sense of security, so that residents evacuate too slowly or not at all. This theory is supported by statistical research that shows that the existence of a seawall at, or higher than, a tsunami's projected height delayed evacuation by nearly 30 percent in Tohoku. Regardless of tsunami height, walls delayed evacuation in the range of 11 to 15 percent.[43] Walls also block the view of the incoming tsunami and the ocean pullback, both of which serve as indicators that a tsunami is imminent. A false sense of security might lead to eventual rebuilding in the hazard zone, which occurred in Taro. In addition, the latest research shows that tsunami waters that overtop a 10-meter seawall create a destructive current and reach speeds of 8 meters per second (30 kilometers per hour), which can sweep humans away even at depths of only 15 centimeters.[44] Immediate and informed evacuation is key to survival.

While prefectural governments have mostly supported construction of these seawalls, some nearly 15 meters high, many residents, especially those whose livelihoods in tourism and fishing rely on relationships with the sea, were increasingly unhappy with these fortifications dividing land from ocean, particularly in communities that were not initially consulted regarding seawall heights and placements. Tourists who find themselves gazing out over masses of concrete rather than deep blue horizons may decide to book their next vacation elsewhere. For people involved in fishing, being unable to see the ocean affects their ability to determine plans for the day based on their reading of wave turbidity. The land-water interface is also critical for bringing in their catch, and in many cases, fixing and drying equipment.[45]

ECOLOGICAL IMPACT—MOUNTAIN TO OCEAN

Furthermore, seawalls can disrupt local ecosystems extensively, with impacts on nearshore fisheries and the dense webs of oyster and seaweed cultivation that crisscross the bays of northern Tohoku. Seawalls up to 45 meters wide at the base can obliterate the entire coastal zone habitat. Tidal flats, marshes, sea turtles, Manila clams, and endangered plant habitats are all impacted (if not eliminated), especially where the wall is built right at the shoreline rather than further inland. Though prefectures are consulting experts, small-scale coastal construction—including hazard-mitigation projects such as seawalls—does not require ecological impact assessments.[46] Between 1998 and 2016, the Ministry of the Environment recorded a decrease of 86.3 kilometers

Figure 30. A Tohoku resident in July 2012. He uses bamboo to demonstrate how high the 8.5-meter wall would be and explains how fishermen need to see the ocean to determine their daily plans.

of natural coastline and an increase of approximately 145 kilometers of artificially altered coastline, primarily due to coastal reconstruction work after the tsunami.[47]

The most acclaimed and influential critique, from long before the 2011 tsunami, is "mori wa umi no koibito" (the forest is the ocean's love), a phrase made popular by a Kesennuma-based oyster farmer, Hatakeyama Shigeatsu, in the 1990s. Kesennuma Bay has a long history as a major landing port for deep-ocean fishing, but it is also an excellent, nutritious environment for farming oysters, scallops, and seaweed. In the late 1960s, pollution and severe red tides led to the deterioration of Kesennuma Bay's environment, causing great suffering for ocean livelihoods. Hatakeyama recognized pollution originating from red soil flowing in from eroding coniferous forests as well as from factories along the Ōkawa River.[48] He recruited farmers to plant trees in the forest upstream of the Ōkawa River and protested the impounding dam 8 kilometers upstream to protect the nutrient flow to the sea. Through forest planting and environmental education, Hatakeyama increased awareness among all the residents about how the ocean relies on nutrients from a healthy, mountainous forest. The separation of forest nutrients from the ocean by seawall construction and the degradation and eradication of forests to develop flat hilltop residential areas have prompted a revival of Hatakeyama's narrative. As a result of his efforts, the 10-meter levee of the Nishi-Moune River was finally removed in 2020 — reviving the river, ocean, marsh, and marine life.[49]

As of 2021, the method of seawall height specification has changed. Local communities will now be able to choose their seawall construction from a number of options that take into account other tsunami bōsai countermeasures. The multiple options provided will be based on a holistic risk assessment that takes into account more than five thousand simulations, the probability of a tsunami occurring in each region, the projected human risks (given future population decline), and other tsunami mitigation measures, such as relocating to higher ground.[50]

DUAL-USE SEAWALLS AND LEVEES

Naiwan District—Seawall Integrated with Waterfront Tourism

The Naiwan district in Kesennuma was famous as a regional center of the fishing industry. Renowned for seafood, the picturesque port town with unconstrained ocean views attracted many tourists, but the 2011 tsunami destroyed much of the district—336 out of 401 residences. To recover from the devastation, Kesennuma deemed it essential for the Naiwan district to regain its business prosperity and worked to align bōsai and community redevelopment.

In the hometown of author and oysterman Hatakeyama, many residents opposed seawalls and preferred construction of more evacuation routes to nearby hills. "Live with the Ocean" became Kesennuma's reconstruction slogan and goal.[51] Alas, Miyagi Prefecture had committed to constructing a seawall to prevent an L1 tsunami at a height of 6.2 meters above sea level in this location. One proposal called for raising the ground by 1.8 meters so that the actual wall would only be 4.4 meters, but that would still have blocked the ocean view.

The Naiwan district reconstruction machizukuri council was established in June 2012. Abe Toshihiko, architect and co-founder of the firm SMDW, was designated as coordinator, and he structured the council with three subcommittees: one focused on residential housing as well as commercial and public facilities; a seawall study group; and a group of experts in the fields of engineering, architecture, landscape, and illumination to consider the feasibility of the proposals. Finally, in October 2012, the Miyagi Prefectural Assembly agreed that "the shape, height, and position of the seawall should be determined according to the topography, landform, contexts of urban areas and fishing villages, and residents' opinions."[52]

After a year and a half of deliberations and several rejected proposals, the machizukuri council finally decided in March 2014 to create the seawall, and residents thought the plans for the district were finalized. In order to make the most out of the seawall construction, they decided to develop a waterfront commercial facility called Mukaeru (Welcome) on the north, consisting of a café, a bar, and stores, and a public

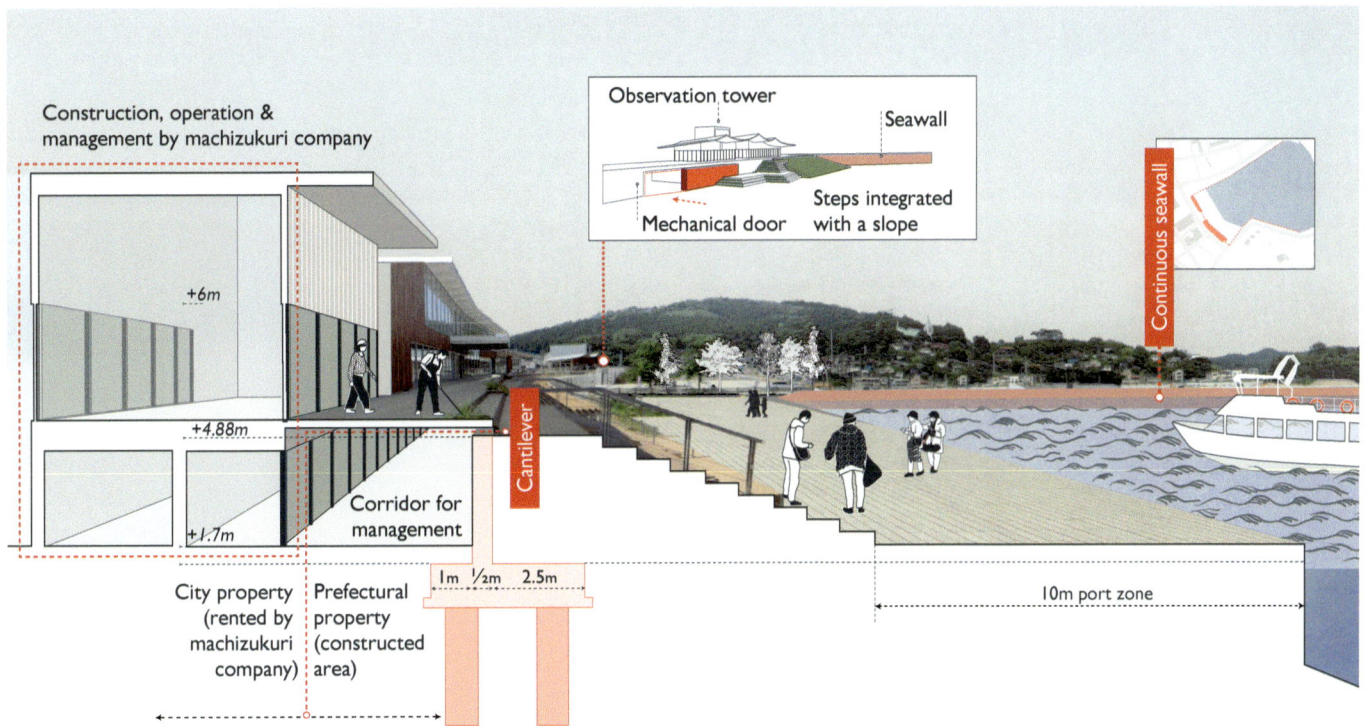

Figure 31. The Naiwan seawall's complex ownership and management structures are reflected in its separate parts, which are designed to operate as a unified system.

facility, Umareru (Birth), on the south, with a youth support center, co-working space, and a tourism center. They also proposed a grassy landscaped slope and stairs, which would offer a smooth transition space where visitors could relax, and an amphitheater for events. At this point, Miyagi Prefecture rejected the proposal, claiming that the seawall proposed by the council did not restore Kesennuma to pre-tsunami condition and so funds could not be allocated.

The machizukuri council argued that redesigning the waterfront space to connect the sea and the town would reflect the importance of the residents' vision and encourage an economic rebound by attracting future tourists. The council's perseverance and the design iterations led to solutions that were finally able to satisfy all parties. The commercial facility, public facility, and seawall were designed to look like an integrated project. A large opening between the two facilities connects the ocean to the town, but a tsunami gate would close if needed. The sloped landscape and stairs are justified as a mode of necessary evacuation infrastructure to allow people to quickly get over the seawall, especially once the tsunami gate is closed, and the stairs are officially designated as an evacuation facility/path.[53] Finally, the prefecture agreed to install infrastructure that differed from pre-earthquake conditions. The completed seawall was TP+4.87 meters and constructed on TP+1.8-meter raised ground, in anticipation of an L1 tsunami.[54]

Creating an integrated waterfront landscape required coordination between the council, the residents, the prefecture, and the city to design the facility and plan its long-term operation after development. Since all of the property from the seawall to the ocean belonged to the prefecture, and inland was owned by the city, the machizukuri council decided to transform into a machizukuri company, a new business entity called the Kesennuma Regional Development Company, Ltd., so that they could lease the land and have input into the final design decisions.

Under the guise of one continuous landscape and building, careful design allows the complex jurisdictional structure to exist. Although the machizukuri company leases the land from the city, the company owns and manages the Mukaeru building. Umareru, the public facility adjacent to it, is also managed by the company. The two buildings are connected by a corridor covered by a three-meter-wide wooden boardwalk, which carefully cantilevers over the seawall but does not touch it.[55] By hovering over the seawall, it does not interfere with the structural integrity of the wall, nor does it disturb the jurisdictional silo. The quayside waterfront and seawall belong to the prefecture, but the terraced green slope is maintained by the machizukuri company.

Local restaurants boast fresh seafood and "slow food" by promoting traditional regional cuisine. (The slow food concept, originally from Italy, encourages planting, farming, and feasting within the local ecosystem.) The redesigned waterfront embraces the history of the town's fishing industry and is an ideal place for tourists and residents to interact. Other designers and groups, including the MIT Urban Risk Lab, designed similar types of dual-use seawall projects during the Tohoku reconstruction, but complex administrative issues and funding silos prohibited their further exploration. Hopefully, this successful case in Kesennuma will pave the way for new projects.

SUPER LEVEES

The ria topography and river corridors propelled tsunami waters several kilometers inland, wreaking devastation along their path and causing deaths far from the coast in areas hydrologically connected to the sea. This provided even more impetus for the Tohoku reconstruction to build up levees around river corridors. Even before 2011, riverine flooding had been a major hazard in Japan, and as a result of climate change, more intense storms are expected to increase flood risk.

Five rivers around Tokyo and Osaka are planning or have built super levees, which are designed for two-hundred-year-flood levels. They are wider than traditional concrete levees: typically, they are thirty times as wide as they are tall and resist earthquakes.[56] Site selection is based on areas where a levee break would have high human

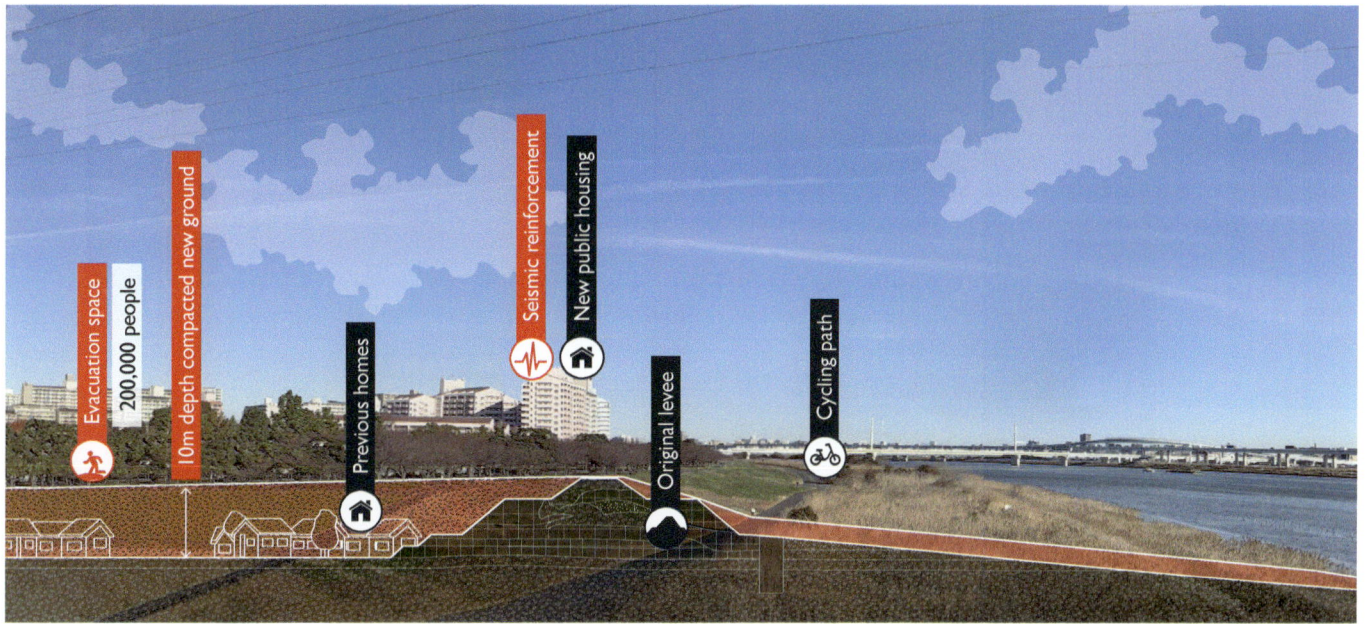

Figure 32. Super levee along the Arakawa River.

costs. With their increased width and gentle slopes, super levees are less vulnerable to destruction from an earthquake or overtopping, and they create spaces for other activities on top. As climate-related flood disasters increase, with more frequent cloudbursts of over 100 millimeters per hour and an escalation in storm intensity, there is renewed interest in these projects.

While super levees are designed with an emphasis on pluvial and fluvial flooding, they can also prevent inundation from tsunamis that are funneled up river channels. Tokyo, too, faces tsunami risk along rivers due to its proximity to the Sagami Trough: in 1703, a magnitude 7.9 to 8.2 tremor triggered a 2-meter tsunami in what was then Edo, contributing to the disaster's death toll.[57] A Nankai Trough earthquake has a projected tsunami height of up to 2.5 meters in the Tokyo area.[58] While Tokyo has focused on earthquake preparedness over tsunamis, the 2011 Tohoku tsunami and Nankai Trough simulations have led to increased tsunami planning along Tokyo's rivers, including seismic retrofits to levees and safeguards so that structures do not collapse even if tsunami heights exceed the anticipated limits.[59]

Super levees are built at such a scale that they require significant transformations to the urban fabric, raising questions about who benefits and who is harmed in their creation. There are also questions as to what level of risk should be tolerated and along what return periods.[60] Increased construction costs are often justified through the development opportunities they create.[61] Existing super levee projects in Tokyo, such as the Ōjima-Komatsu River super levee at Higashi-ōjima on the west bank of the Arakawa River, include public housing programs, parks, and cycling paths. The Ōjima-

Komatsu River super levee project was created by the MLIT at a cost of ¥48.8 billion. Between 1987 and 2007, zones of dense, small homes below sea level (as a result of annual subsidence) were replaced with high-rise apartments and large parks, including Ōjima-Komatsu Park, which doubles as an evacuation space for up to two hundred thousand people in case of disaster.[62]

TMG, the Urban Renaissance agency (a semi-governmental organization), and the MLIT (as river administrator) worked on the rezoning and land readjustment; Edogawa Ward representatives explained the necessity of the embankment to residents, created a method for building consensus, and helped residents relocate permanently or move temporarily with the guarantee that they could return after construction was complete.[63] During the twenty-four years of construction, residents were displaced from their neighborhoods for three or more years, which resulted in some litigation, but in many cases Edogawa Ward helped residents find temporary housing in the vicinity and set up temporary spaces for factories to remain operational.[64] It was still especially difficult for the elderly population to move twice, but overall, steady communication helped collective decision making and many tight-knit social networks remained intact, an important component of disaster preparedness.

The super levees, which have the potential to generate huge profits for those organizations winning construction and development contracts, led to some speculation that their construction was driven more by profit than by disaster mitigation needs.[65] On the other hand, large-scale projects that require careful consensus building have such long timelines that it is difficult to incentivize the private sector to partner with the government.[66] The exorbitant costs involved mean that private-public partnerships are key to scaling such initiatives. Although controversial, this project is an opportunity to learn what complexities climate change resettlement (and in this case, land raising) can bring. It foreshadows the future in Japan and beyond.

COASTAL BUFFER FORESTS

While seawalls and super levees are relatively new additions to Japan's dossier of disaster risk reduction tools, Japanese coastal regions have a much longer history of using forests as a way to mitigate coastal inundations. For over four hundred years, coastal pine forests have been used as buffers against tsunamis as well as typhoons, storm surges, wind, and waves. They double as the iconic landscapes—white sandy beaches contrasted with black pine trees—that served as a major tourism draw in Tohoku before the disaster. Also related are *igune,* smaller forest groves typically composed of Japanese cedar, that are grown to protect houses and settlements.

The feudal lord Date Masamune is credited with ordering the cultivation of large swaths of coastal black pine forests in the area of Sendai, which served to protect residents from sandstorms and inundations in the early 1600s.[67] In exchange for the use of forest products, such as firewood, local villagers were tasked with maintaining the forest. This system became official in 1948, when Miyagi created the first community-led coastal forest conservation organization, which monitored the health of trees and the maintenance of space. More than twenty-eight such groups were created. After these coastal forests proved effective as buffers against tsunamis in 1933 and again in 1960, greenbelt buffer planting continued across the region in the service of tsunami mitigation. Its use has declined since the 1970s, however, with the increased use of concrete and the growing prominence of electricity and gas as energy sources. By 2010, the forest conservation organizations were dissolved, owing to residents' lack of interest and younger generations' forgetting the importance of forests.

The 2011 tsunami affected some 3,660 hectares of coastal forest along the Tohoku coastline—in some cases eradicating it entirely.[68] In Rikuzentakata, the coastal forest dating from the seventeenth century was obliterated, perhaps because lowland trees had not rooted to a sufficient depth.[69] Surviving coastal forests were often associated with other coastal infrastructure such as embankments, which helped protect them from destruction. Even where the wave did not destroy them, many of these forests have died since the tsunami as a result of saltwater intrusion.

Based on the recent disaster in Tohoku, the MAFF has updated its coastal disaster mitigation forest recommendations: for tsunami mitigation, buffer forests are at least thirty meters wide, and for large tsunamis, at least seventy meters wide. The MAFF recommends the use of embankments two to three meters above the water table to allow trees to root more deeply. It also prescribes appropriate tree species: on the ocean side, Japanese black pine (*Pinus thunbergia*), red pine (*Pinus resinosa*), Japanese emperor oak (*Quercus dentata*), and Japanese cheesewood (*Pittosporum tobira*); on the landward side, Japanese barberry (*Berberis thunbergia*), white oak (*Quercus alba*), and painted maple (*Acer pictum*) can also be used. Mixing pine and broadleaf trees with different canopy heights can help buffer water flow further, establish an interdependent, stronger root network, and foster greater ecological diversity.[70] Spacing of no more than five thousand black pines per hectare is recommended to allow trunks to develop larger diameters. Historical data suggest that coastal forests can be effective buffers for tsunamis up to five meters if the trees' height is double that.[71] For higher tsunamis, researchers recommend combining the forest buffers with other, harder systems, such as seawalls, embankments, and elevated roads.[72]

Morino Project

The Morino Project uses indigenous, deep-rooting trees in combination with low seawalls, created out of debris, as a disaster mitigation measure. This project stems from the research of Miyawaki Akira, who promotes the "potential of natural vegetation" (PNV)[73] method for creating disaster mitigation forests on berms, behind dikes, in or-

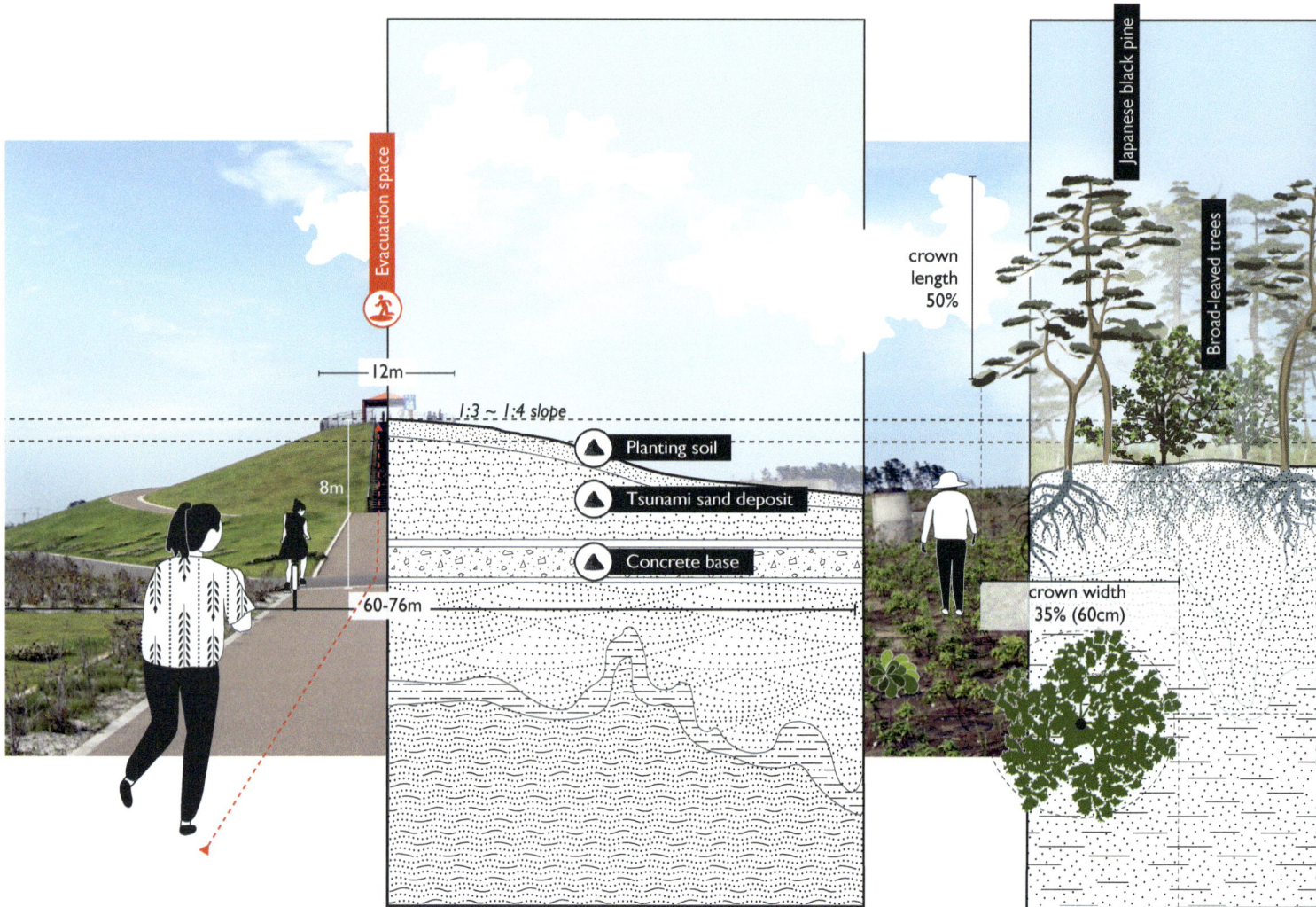

Figure 33. Diagram of multilayered coastal protection, featuring low seawalls, evacuation hills, and a buffer forest planted and cared for by residents.

der to reinforce the structural stability of the seawall.[74] The primary strategy included creating thirty- to one-hundred-meter-wide forested berms, five to ten meters high. Including the height of the trees, the overall protection would reach a height of around thirty meters.[75] Recommendations call for a mixture of more than a dozen types of evergreen broadleaf trees that are native to the region, planted with a density of three trees per square meter.[76] The trees would mature in fifteen to twenty years. The Morino Project picks up seeds (e.g., acorns) that grow wild near the site in order to prepare seedlings, and it works with volunteers to raise the seedlings for the first three years. Over 90 percent of saplings successfully establish roots. The Morino Project outlines

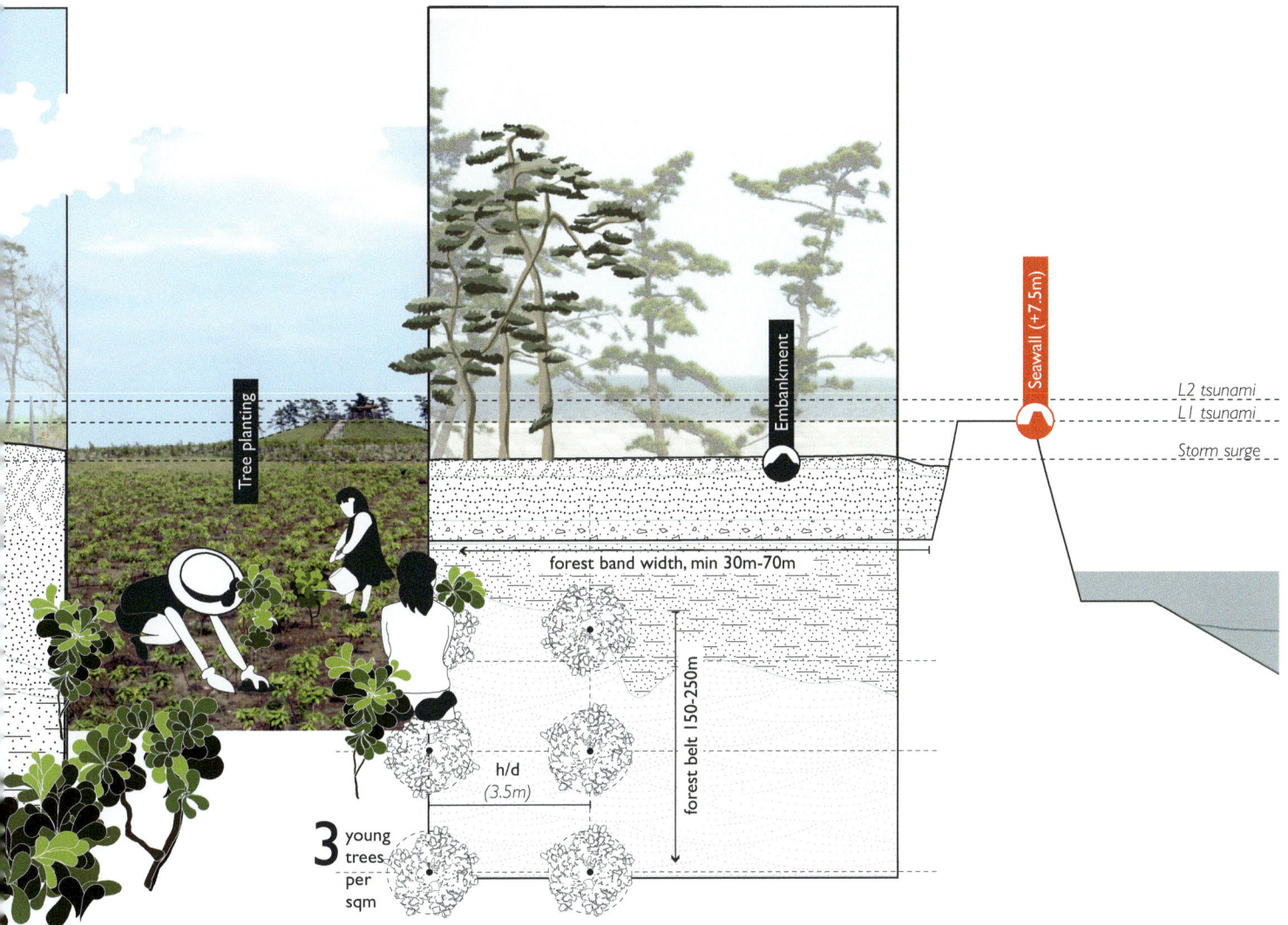

Tree planting

Embankment

Seawall (+7.5m)

L2 tsunami

L1 tsunami

Storm surge

forest band width, min 30m-70m

forest belt 150-250m

h/d
(3.5m)

3 young
trees
per
sqm

several advantages to this approach, such as reducing a tsunami's force, hindering objects from being pulled to sea by the undertow, requiring limited maintenance, and having ecological benefits. Though not widely adopted by the central government in its original form, the PNV method has a large following in prefectures from Aomori to Fukushima, especially in the Sendai plain.

A greenbelt buffer as part of a layered system is being applied in Sendai, drawing on its historical use of pine forest buffers. Along the coast, "disaster-reduction forests" are being restored, intermingled with recreational infrastructure along the Teizan Canal, which was built for delivering cargo in the Edo era but also had a tsunami-reduction effect in 2011.[77] Evacuation hills, like those at the Millennium Hope Hills Park, will provide high ground for visitors in this area when a tsunami strikes. Coastal breakwaters in some areas will further protect this zone. The combination of the breakwater and buffer forests can defend against an L1 tsunami, and the elevated highway will be restored between the coast and the main residential areas, serving as an additional defense against an L2 tsunami. In zones that remain vulnerable, new construction is prohibited and relocation is encouraged. These multiple redundancies of protection depict the "layered approach" to tsunami mitigation.[78]

Now that forests are being replanted along several coastlines, questions about maintenance have arisen. In January 2014, Miyagi Prefecture started a program to plant and maintain coastal disaster-reduction forests with the participation of citizens and companies. A coalition of private sector businesses, NPOs, and community members will care for the forest, weeding and monitoring the health of the trees for five to ten years.[79]

Perceptions of the effectiveness of coastal forests are still mixed. In some cases, coastal forests appear to have slowed the force of the wave, stopped debris as large as ships from traveling inland, and protected homes behind them. However, in other cases, uprooted trees became projectiles themselves, causing further destruction as they pummeled inland.[80] Some neighborhoods suffered more casualties because pine trees blocked residents' view of the ocean, and they could not see the water receding. A study analyzing historic tsunamis as well as that of 2011 found an inverse relationship between coastal forest area and damages, suggesting that either they were effective in reducing the wave's force or that they displaced coastal construction, causing people to build in higher zones;[81] similar results have been observed in statistical simulations.[82] Research on various species must continue; meanwhile, scientists are also creating statistical models of combining forests with hard systems and topographic undulations, as tsunami parks are more ecological than concrete seawalls. Significant research is still necessary, since the actual design of each forest or park and the relationship to its urban or geographic context can reduce risk but can also potentially increase it, especially in the case of large tsunamis.[83]

DISCUSSION

There are no straightforward solutions for living with tsunami risk. The construction of and response to seawalls in post-Tohoku Japan illustrate the ways in which disaster mitigation infrastructure is not just a technical issue but also a social, political, and ecological one. While there are clear benefits to seawalls, particularly if they are successful in holding back or slowing down a destructive tsunami, saving lives, homes, and local economies, they also can have complicated downsides. Recalling Gilbert White's cautionary words that flood fortifications are often "the signal for accelerated movement into the floodplain,"[84] planners of seawalls and levees need to consider their cascading impacts, which might create more harm by speeding up the flow of water or pushing it into neighboring contexts.

The construction of coastal fortifications in post-2011 Tohoku poses complicated questions about how to design for events that might occur only once a century or even once a millennium. What kinds of sacrifices should people be asked to make in their everyday lives and experiences of space for an event that even their great-grandchildren might never experience? If measures are deemed to be necessary, then how can they make a positive contribution to people's daily lives rather than having a negative impact? If they are designed to have dual uses, how can management and funding silos be simplified to more readily accommodate those proposals? Projects that treat communities as active agents and consider dual-use strategies (such as Naiwan) or increase ecological diversity (such as Morino) offer alternatives. But they also require time, residents' commitment, and careful planning, which are not always possible when memories of loss reverberate and policies prescribe quick decision making.

Resettlement

Reconstruction poses many challenges, but resettlement is among the most daunting. Resettlement, or "managed retreat," as it is now sometimes called, is growing more popular as a climate resilience strategy as awareness of rising sea levels increases. But this tactic has a longer history in the realm of post-disaster reconstruction. Japan's history shows both the potential of this model and its risks, particularly when rapidly implemented in the context of urgent post-disaster reconstruction and on the massive scale of an entire region. Forced relocation is always complicated, as memories and relationships are tied to place. When governments involve local citizens in discussions and decision making, some potentially better approaches emerge to ease the resettlement process.

FROM THE 1933 TSUNAMI TO THE 2011 RECONSTRUCTION

As described in the previous chapter, Japan's central government took a heavy-handed approach to the 2011 Tohoku reconstruction. In addition to constructing seawalls, reconstruction has also included leveling mountains and moving whole communities to new higher-ground sites. Although many of the schemes seem radical, the approach resembles those that followed the 1933 tsunami, in which the central government enacted a large-scale and centralized reconstruction plan with comprehensive hazard mitigation measures, based on recommendations from the Council on Earthquake Disaster Prevention.[1] Though some settlements were relocated to high ground after the 1896 tsunami (which was nearly as severe as the 2011 event), many residents eventually returned to the coast, where their houses were again destroyed by a tsunami in 1933.[2] The post-1933 reconstruction reshaped the Tohoku coast, as it prioritized relocating urban residential areas to high ground and building protective infrastructure, such as seawalls. Smaller fishing villages were prioritized for relocation, while larger, more urbanized settlements emphasized moving only residential areas to high ground; coastal industry and commercial sites remained on low-lying areas linked with wide direct evacuation routes.[3] At the end of a nationally funded process that took only one year, ninety-eight villages in Miyagi and Iwate Prefectures were relocated to high ground.[4] Most of the 1933 hilltop relocation communities safely survived the 2011 tsunami, although a handful of these resettlement sites were destroyed as a result of the wave's unprecedented scale.

In some settlements, the messages carried through time on the tsunami stones sometimes made the difference between life and death. The six-hundred-year-old "Aneyoshi Tablet," in particular, became famous for the role it played in its small village in Miyako in Iwate. Though commercial and fishery buildings were built along the coast, Aneyoshi villagers continued to heed the stone's warning to build their houses above the tsunami line (sixty meters above sea level): "Living on higher ground will make the lives of our descendants more peaceful. Remember the catastrophic tsunami. Never build houses below this point. The tsunamis of 1896 and 1933 reached this point, and the villages were completely destroyed, leaving only 2 and 4 survivors. Be careful now, even after many years."

Aneyoshi's residents moved all their dwellings to high ground after the 1896 and 1933 tsunamis. As a result, Aneyoshi was one of the small coastal hamlets that remained safe in 2011, even though the tsunami reached up to nearly thirty-nine meters there. Forty residents (in twelve households) survived the inundation because they all safely evacuated above the stone; the water stopped just fifty meters away.

However, the majority of communities impacted by the more recent disaster had sprawled back to the coast between 1933 and 2011. The memory of the tsunamis had faded: those whose livelihoods depended on the sea sought to be closer to their work, and they again built homes in vulnerable locations, especially if they still owned land by the coast. The new seawalls gave them a false sense of security, too, and many were uncomfortable living in mountainous forested areas, fearing landslides.[5] In order to prevent a similar return to coastal zones, the 2011 reconstruction process provided a multitude of new programs. The central government's argument for the radical nature of the 2011 reconstruction planning is that people forget: thus, "planning needs to build in long-term memory."[6]

2011 TOHOKU RESETTLEMENT POLICIES AND PROGRAMS

The August 2011 Basic Policy for Reconstruction outlined forty grant programs that were supervised by the Reconstruction Agency. These projects were directly funded by the national government—which typically covered 50 to 75 percent of the cost, depending on the program—and municipalities were reimbursed through taxes for the remaining amount incurred locally, so that the total coverage was 100 percent. The four methods most frequently used in the reconstruction of neighborhoods were land readjustment, relocation to high ground (individual and collective relocation), public housing, and bōsai infrastructure for fishing villages. Specifics of each municipality were shaped by the Tsunami Bōsai Regional Development Law—post-tsunami national legislation that applied to the Tohoku reconstruction as well as future tsunami disasters. The L1/L2 tsunami predictions and the Two-Two Rule specify hazard zones within each municipality. Once the hazard zones were established, the municipalities engaged in the lengthy process of discussing options with residents and putting plans in motion. Depending on the results of the Two-Two Rule and the severity of the inundation, residents were provided options and subsidies through the programs detailed below.

Environmental assessments are required by developers, general contractors, and civic engineering firms for large-scale public works that are likely to have a significant impact on the environment, according to the 1997 Act on the Assessment of Environmental Impacts. This process requires year-round or at least seasonal field surveys for at least one year. However, to speed up the recovery from the Tohoku earthquake, the Great East Japan Earthquake Reconstruction Special Area law was enacted with specific, simplified methods for land readjustment projects with areas of 75 hectares or more and railway projects of 7.5 kilometers or more.[7] This special act shortens the process to just a few months: it designates the relevant municipality to perform the assessment with the advice of experts, summarize the investigation, prepare a prediction, and submit it to the prefecture and the central government. The assessment is revised based on the feedback from these entities and, after a public viewing, the Ministry of the Environment (MOE) approves it and the project is implemented. On the other hand, because of the simplified procedures of the preliminary assessment, the inspection requirements after construction are broader than those under the procedures of the environmental impact assessment method.[8]

However, except for large-scale land readjustment projects such as in Rikuzentakata, most of the reconstruction projects covered fewer than 75 hectares. Legally, the municipalities were not required to conduct environmental impact assessments.[9] In Miyagi and Iwate, there were no explicit methods of environmental impact assessment for the smaller projects. The governor of each prefecture was required to give environmental considerations to the development companies and suggest operators to implement the necessary measures.[10] These measures are not based on field surveys of ecosystems throughout a year in all seasons, as usual environmental impact assessments require, but are instead based on the methods developed by companies themselves or in conjunction with the opinions of experts. In August 2013, Miyagi initiated an environmental advisor system with twelve academics in environmental education and agriculture as well as ornithological experts and botanists who met regularly,[11] but by then many high-level decisions had already been made. No doubt the pressure to rebuild people's lives as quickly as possible makes it difficult to justify lengthy environmental impact assessments, but, given the transformative effects that even the small-scale projects had on the landscape in the Tohoku region, it is harrowing to imagine the long-term consequences of all the resettlement projects along the coast.

Land Readjustment Program

Land readjustment, used in Kobe after the 1995 earthquake, was also operationalized by the MLIT, but in Tohoku there was an added complication of raising land. The program was used to increase the topographical height in zones of L2 tsunami inundation, allowing for commercial, industrial, and residential mixed uses. Residential projects required an even higher evacuation area, such as an upper floor. If former landowners wanted to rebuild on the same lots after they were raised and land-adjusted, then they would be required to donate part of the property to create a new, wider street (as in Kobe). The land readjustment and infrastructure construction, implemented by the municipality, would be subsidized by the central government. Although each landowner would have less land after the readjustment, the price of the land would increase in light of the wider street and the safer neighborhood on raised ground.[12] If the former residential zone was changed to mixed-use after the land was adjusted, the city would buy the land from the property owner based on the adjusted land price, after taking into account factors such as the location of the land, street conditions, and public transportation access.[13]

Relocation of Homes to High Ground Program

Residents owning property, either residential or farmland, in tsunami-inundated areas that were being rezoned as high-risk were encouraged to sell the land to the municipality and relocate.[14] At the owner's request, the municipality purchased the inundated plots (in areas now designated as a hazard zone) from residents at 60 to 80 percent of the pre-tsunami value (except for areas designated as coastal forest, which were purchased at 40 percent).[15] The fees and sales prices were calculated by the municipality. Most of the inundated plots remaining within the special tsunami hazard (Red/Orange) areas were zoned for industrial, aquaculture-related use, community agriculture gardens, commercial space, or park space.[16]

After selling their land to the municipality, residents could then choose to move to public housing or rebuild individually or as a collective. Individually, they could rebuild on other plots they owned outside of the hazard zone at their own expense, or they could move to another city. The individual relocation option was partially subsidized using the Relocation of Unsafe Housing in Proximity to Cliffs and Other Hazard Zones Project (hereafter called the Cliff Relocation Project).[17] The option of collectively moving to a site provided additional subsidies through the Bōsai Collective Relocation Project. In this case, groups of five or more lots would move to new plots in high ground developed by the municipality. Those plots would be leased or sold to the residents.

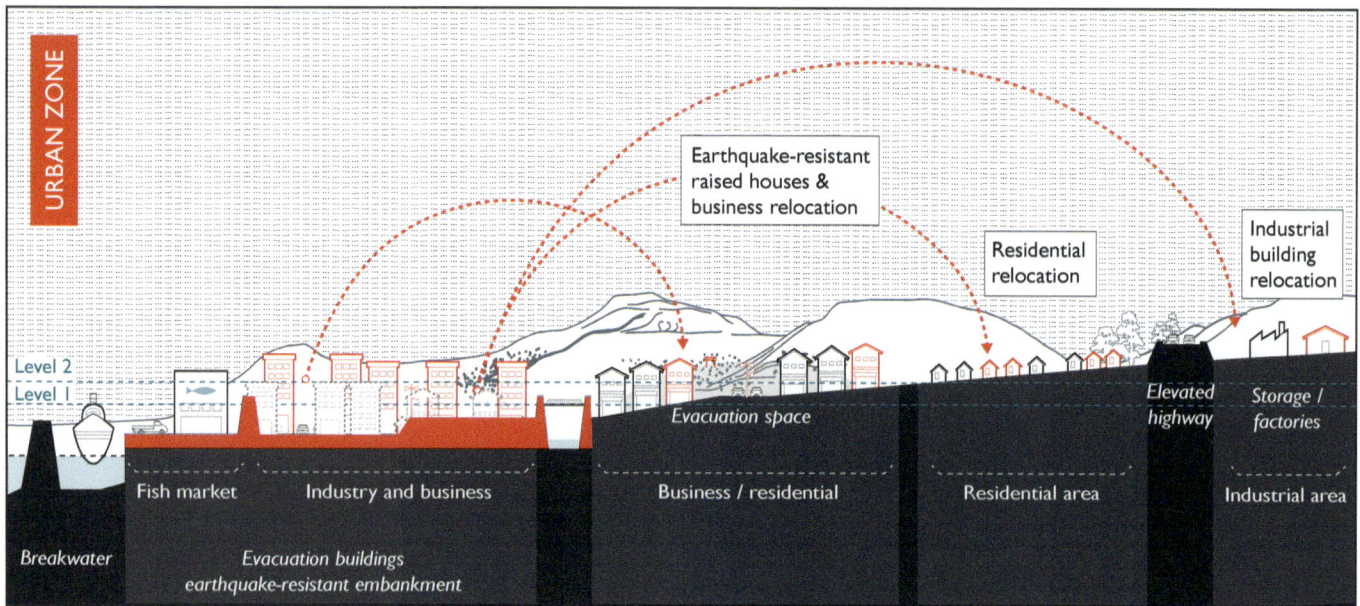

URBAN ZONE

Earthquake-resistant raised houses & business relocation

Residential relocation

Industrial building relocation

Level 2
Level 1

Evacuation space

Elevated highway

Storage / factories

Fish market

Industry and business

Business / residential

Residential area

Industrial area

Breakwater

Evacuation buildings earthquake-resistant embankment

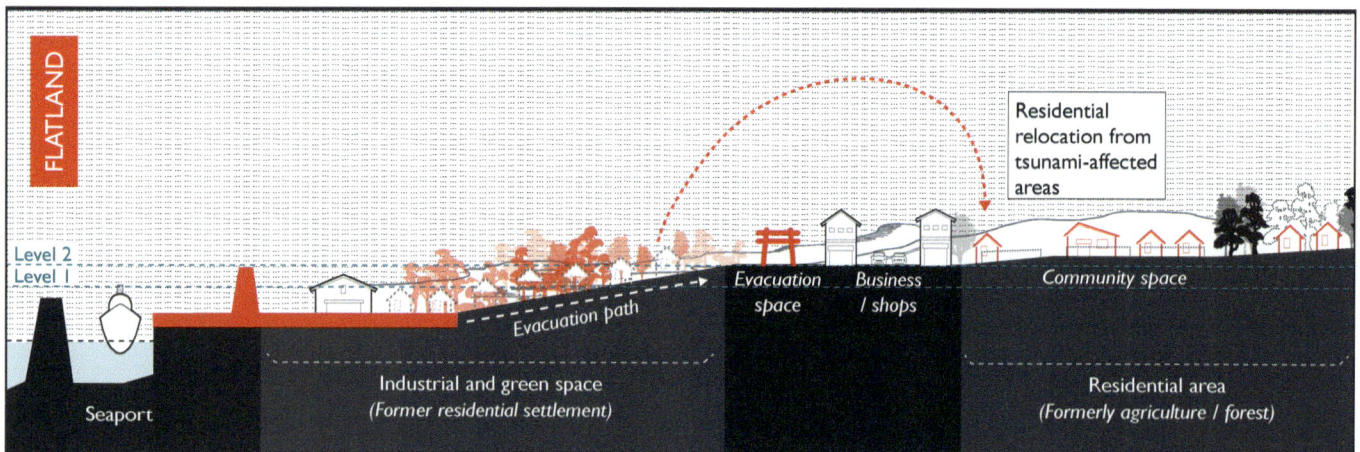

FLATLAND

Residential relocation from tsunami-affected areas

Level 2
Level 1

Evacuation path

Evacuation space

Business / shops

Community space

Seaport

Industrial and green space
(Former residential settlement)

Residential area
(Formerly agriculture / forest)

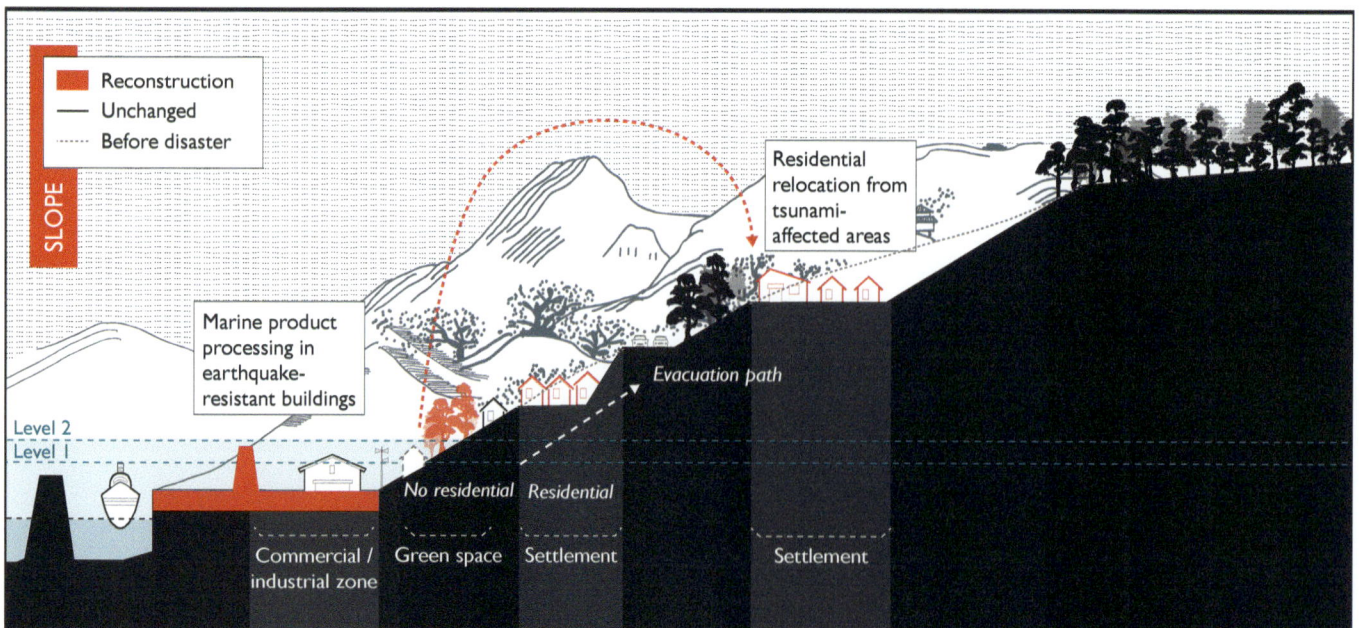

SLOPE

■ Reconstruction
— Unchanged
┈ Before disaster

Residential relocation from tsunami-affected areas

Marine product processing in earthquake-resistant buildings

Evacuation path

Level 2
Level 1

No residential

Residential

Commercial / industrial zone

Green space

Settlement

Settlement

Cliff Relocation Project

After a devastating typhoon in 1971, the Cliff Relocation Project was established in 1972 to relocate houses from hazard zones before a disaster, especially where landslide prevention work would not be enough to mitigate future disasters. The subsidies for removing a house and groundwork for the vacant site (up to ¥975,000) and the interest on mortgage loans for purchasing land and building a house (up to ¥4.21 million) are provided to those who relocate. Half of the subsidies are paid by the central government and half by the local government.[18]

Although it started as a mitigation project to avoid landslide damage, when the Great East Japan Earthquake Reconstruction Special Area Act was enacted in December 2011, the central government decided to apply it to damaged housing, as long as some portion of the damaged house remained (even if just the foundation) and was located in a hazard zone. Upon requests from municipalities, in January 2012, it was modified to include damaged houses that had already been removed, and those who had already rebuilt a house on their own could receive subsidies from the project.[19]

Bōsai Collective Relocation Project

The Bōsai Collective Relocation Project was also developed in 1972 and was intended for both pre-disaster and post-disaster measures. The subsidies cover relocation from multiple hazard types. Between 1972 and 2006, this program was used for the post-disaster relocation of 1,854 households after landslide, flood, earthquake, tsunami, and volcano disasters. After the Tohoku disaster, the government used this method to designate 37,001 houses with the option to move away from high-risk areas and create 12,439 new parcels and public housing units in high-ground relocation areas.[20] The project originally required a minimum of ten plots to move together to the newly created residential site, but as a result of difficulties in consensus building, this was adjusted to a minimum of five plots. With this change came a shift in focus to using existing residential complexes and vacant land scattered throughout the existing settlements rather than creating new sites.[21] Since the reconstruction grants cover the reconstruction of roads, this grant could also be used for road maintenance and repair.[22] Most municipalities offered a public plot selection process from the allotted options, and most groups picked sites close to their existing homes or to new facilities. This emphasis on collective relocation is particularly important, as it reduces the shock of moving and helps communities maintain strong social ties, which are fundamental for recovery.

While relocation to high ground was a key reconstruction strategy for Tohoku, finding sites was not always easy: the Sendai plain presented difficulties in establishing relocation sites due to the area's large, flat expanse. The rugged ria topography lacked flat

Figure 34. Resettlement strategies defined the reconstruction of Tohoku's coastal regions after 2011.

high-ground sites, necessitating large-scale earthworks to either raise ground or flatten hilltops; just preparing the sites cost a tremendous amount. Preparing plots along the ria coast was estimated by Inamura Hajime to be 1.4 times more costly than in the flat plains.[23] For example, for a mountainous Ishinomaki site, the process of flattening the hilltops, building roads and bridges, and creating lifeline infrastructure cost over ¥62.7 million per plot for each of the fifty-three residents.[24]

Once the high-ground plot is established, residents have the option of purchasing or renting the lot, which is administered by the municipality. In Kesennuma, 20 percent of residents applied to buy the land; the rest are renting.[25] Although numerous subsidies and tax breaks were offered, especially for the Bōsai Collective Relocation Project, property owners still needed to fund most of the construction of their new homes. For many households, the cost of taking on new loans to (re)build an entire house was too high, causing some families to choose public housing or to leave town entirely. At of the end of May 2020, 30,234 public housing units had been completed,[26] and government subsidies keep the rents low.[27]

These policies led to big projects with long timelines. In some areas, people finally moved into their new homes in 2019. In Miyagi, it took ¥560 billion and eight years. Out of the 83,000 homes destroyed in Miyagi Prefecture, 40 percent of owners did not participate in these government programs, often moving away from the coastal municipality.[28] By the time the plots were finally ready, some had passed away; others had suffered declining health and could no longer live on their own, or their finances had changed and they could no longer shoulder a full mortgage. Still others grew roots in new locations. Many dropped out of the program, leaving municipalities with the new complications of vacant lots.[29] For example, Momonoura, in Ishinomaki, started with twenty-four households planning to relocate, but only five households eventually moved, making the average cost over ¥186.4 million per plot.[30] Similar narratives were heard all across Tohoku. Researchers also question whether those large-scale projects are appropriate for areas where populations were shrinking even before the tsunami. In the three main affected prefectures, 12,439 private plots were created; of these, 8,336 units were created by the Bōsai Collective Relocation Project.[31] Some of the plots remain empty for reasons described in the following case studies.

2011 TOHOKU RECONSTRUCTION CASE STUDIES

Rikuzentakata: Large-Scale Relocation

One of the most dramatic collective relocation projects was in Rikuzentakata, home to 24,246 people prior to the disaster. The southern part of the city was devastated by the 1896 and 1933 tsunamis. An embankment was built after the 1933 event, and a seawall was built after the 1960 Chilean tsunami. In 2011, that wall was overtopped; the wave broke the seawall gates and inundated the city. The narrow river valley amplified the tsunami run-up to twenty meters, with water traveling up to three kilometers inland.[32] Thirteen square kilometers and 42.9 percent of buildings were flooded; 3,805 buildings were destroyed, including the city hall, schools, and fishery buildings. The death toll, which reached 1,550 with 207 missing, was amplified by large populations of elderly people who were unable to quickly evacuate. One-fourth of municipal employees were killed.[33] Given the expanse of the city, there were startling differences between those who lost everything—homes, family members, livelihoods—and those whose lives remained relatively intact.

Immediately after the tsunami, there was citywide pressure to rebuild Rikuzentakata as quickly as possible, and most residents agreed with the proposal to use land readjustment to raise ground and rebuild neighborhoods in the city center. In the meantime, the Reconstruction Agency was established in February 2012, and it informed the city that developing the lowlands would need to become a national government project. The city had to obtain consent from all the landowners before starting construction, which substantially delayed the start. Numerous complications arose. For example, if an entire household had perished in the tsunami, the city needed to seek out relatives living elsewhere for approval of land redevelopment. The initial delay in reconstruction in Rikuzentakata was a result not of residents' opposition but of the time taken to find landowners. Given that it was an emergency reconstruction, the city made numerous requests to streamline the procedure, but the national process remained, as officials feared infringing on property rights. With these complex delays, in order to complete the reconstruction, the city decided to prioritize speed no matter the cost.[34]

The 300-hectare reconstruction project of rebuilding seawalls, raising ground, and terracing hills for new residential areas exceeded ¥189 billion.[35] The preexisting seawalls were 3 meters and 5.5 meters high: the 3-meter wall (intended to prevent erosion) was rebuilt to the same height, and the higher one was replaced by a 12.5-meter wall, designed to deflect a L1 tsunami (projected at 11 meters). It is 2 kilometers long and was completed in 2017 at a cost of nearly ¥37 billion.[36] Soil was added between the two walls to regenerate the black-pine forest tidal embankment for which Rikuzentakata had been renowned. The ground was raised 10 to 12 meters for the housing and commercial buildings in the city center (the Takada district). Material excavated from surrounding mountains was used to raise a large area of the town. One adjacent hill was cut down from 120 meters to 50 meters in the excavation process, and yet no environmental assessment of this process was done.[37] During a 2015 visit, dynamite blasts and heavy machinery were actively removing hilltops and delivering fill via three kilometers of conveyor belt to speed up delivery to the lowlands. The system cost ¥12 billion and was intended to shorten the reconstruction phase from 9 to 2.5 years.[38] The conveyor system was dismantled in 2015 after moving 5 million cubic meters of earth. The massive earthworks then needed compaction, so land readjustment was ongoing

Imazumi district - 560 houses

Mountain detonation area

Soil conveyor belt - 3km

Temporary soil storage sites

Takata district - 1650 houses

Compacted and raised ground

¥12billion

5 million m³ of earth

at the time of this writing. This case addresses the poignant complexity of resettlement during reconstruction and how access to large amounts of funding may increase the scope of projects, delaying their outcomes and creating detrimental effects for the survivors and the environment.

Despite the challenges of the project and extended timelines in the central district, some smaller constituencies within Rikuzentakata, such as the Naruishi and Ōishi districts, had easier communication processes. The key was that their residents were able to move to the same temporary housing unit together and meet frequently to make resettlement plans. Depending on their tsunami experiences and their finances, some chose to focus on moving with their community, while some chose to wait for the plots on the high ground so they could be very high up and far from the ocean; some had the resources to rebuild on their own, and some moved to public housing, which was completed quickly and already occupied in 2015. The public housing also focused on community cohesion through public rooftop decks and small shops on the ground floor.

Kesennuma: Local Leadership and Action

Many researchers, activists, local governments, and residents were critical of the national budget covering 100 percent of the reconstruction, claiming that the spending was unnecessary, was fiscally irresponsible, and encouraged extraordinarily large plans. Residents of Moune Dai-ni District, home to oyster farmer and activist Hatakeyama Shigeatsu, balked at the first relocation plan proposed by Kesennuma, which had a development cost of more than ¥100 million per plot. Even though residents knew the national government was backing the full amount, the city's plan for relocation stalled.

Hatakeyama Takanori, a local leader, countered with a plan prepared with the help of an NPO, The Forest Is the Ocean's Love, and Yokoyama Katsuhide from Tokyo Metropolitan University. They planned the community reconstruction holistically, including environmental assessments and considering effects on future fisheries. By reducing the cut ground and reusing soil for embankments, the proposal aimed to reduce the construction cost to ¥35 million per plot. The plan was adopted, and while the final cost was ¥50 million per plot (resulting from increases in the cost of labor and materials), that was still half of the city's originally proposed amount.[39] Since all the residents originally living in the hazard zone relocated to high ground, residents decided not to construct the 9.9-meter seawall projected for the district. Instead, they focused on using the remaining tsunami-inundated land for strengthening the fisheries,[40] and coastal wetlands were restored after seventy years.

In a moment of such devastation, it is difficult to imagine the strength and clarity of thought needed to turn down available government funds, take a stand against the region's status quo, and advocate for an alternative solution. Such leadership and

Figure 35. The complexity of large-scale reconstruction in Rikuzentakata.

consensus-building skills are not always available, especially within post-disaster time constraints, but the communities of Kesennuma have been steeped for decades in Hatakeyama Shigeatsu's philosophy and conversations about the ecology of the region.

Ogatsu: *Keiyakukou* versus Political Mergers

Each small beach hamlet or village along the ria coastline in Tohoku has a unique history of culture and governance. In the face of population decline, these small settlements are now managed as part of a larger municipality (after a forced merger). Sociopolitical and economic differences, as well as geographic distances, complicated decision making and the reconstruction process. One such example is the town of Ogatsu in Ishinomaki.

Historically, Ogatsu consisted of fifteen small beach villages. More recently, the town was divided into two main settlements: the Ogatsu district town center, with the town hall, hospital, elementary school, and homes, and the rest of the *hama* (beach districts), scattered hamlets engaged in the fishing and inkstone industries. Each district has different characteristics in terms of population size and autonomy, and each has its own *keiyakukou,* a community mutual support association traditionally located in each hamlet throughout the Tohoku region. The association helps families with rituals and other events, such as weddings and funerals, and it provides mutual support for resource management (e.g., in fishing or farming).[41] In 2005, all of Ogatsu was merged into the peripheral area of Ishinomaki, which adopted the one-city, one-electoral-district system. The number of councilors from Ogatsu was reduced to zero, making it difficult for local voices to be heard in the reconstruction process.[42]

The 2011 tsunami devastated Ogatsu, leaving 80 percent of its houses destroyed, 173 people dead, and 70 people still missing. Business and public facilities were ravaged, along with 612 out of 646 houses in the town center.[43] Given the extent of the damage, most people moved outside the town limits for both initial shelter and temporary housing. In particular, Ishinomaki created a policy of constructing large temporary housing complexes far inland and allocating them to survivors through a lottery system. This resulted in only 161 temporary units being built within the Ogatsu line, accommodating only 12 percent of households from the destroyed homes. Residents scattered across the region to rental units, relatives' houses, or inland temporary housing.

At the end of April 2011, Ishinomaki enacted the Basic Policy for Reconstruction for the entire Ogatsu region, categorizing it as a fishing village surrounded by high ground, despite the complex topographical and socioeconomic variations between hamlets and town center residents. Amid concerns of a potential delay, a reconstruction machizukuri council was quickly formed to discuss the project with the residents, but it proved difficult to reach consensus among 3,000 people scattered across several temporary housing clusters built outside Ogatsu.[44] According to a questionnaire conducted by the machizukuri council, 58.1 percent of the respondents in the former town center wanted to rebuild on their original (pre-tsunami) property, even with future tsunami risk.[45] However, Ishinomaki's categorization designated all land inundated by the tsunami as a "special disaster hazard zone (red/orange zone)," and Ishinomaki banned the construction of new houses, requiring collective relocation to higher ground (TP+20 meters) to ensure safety. Only facilities related to fishing—including work areas, fishing gear storage areas, and boatyards—could be rebuilt in the hazard zone, in order to protect people's livelihoods.

Unlike those in the town center, residents of the more fortunate hamlets, some of them relatively undamaged, were able to remain in the district. They began clearing debris without support from the municipal government; some even resumed fishing in late July. Noting the strong local ties, the administration decided that each hamlet would move just above the vicinity of the affected area (to eighteen high-ground areas)[46] rather than engage in a large-scale relocation that would consolidate the settlements. In many cases, the *keiyakukou* of each hamlet collectively owned land in the mountains, and thus relocating as a group was comparatively simple. This is similar to the commons, in which jointly owned forest, bamboo, or mountainous land is managed cooperatively. The *keiyakukou* also formed a base for consensus building, with a variety of leaders and modes of communication. Of course, the relatively small number of households made both decision making and infrastructure building much easier.

On the other hand, for the town center, Miyagi instructed Ishinomaki in 2013 to construct a seawall of 9.7 meters along the Ogatsu Bay. Despite clear opposition from the town center's former residents, the council accepted the construction of the seawall in order to avoid delays in other projects. Even after the administration officially finalized its reconstruction plan for Ogatsu, the lack of flat land within the ria topography meant that site preparation would be needed before development could begin. As a result, many residents who had planned to return to the town after temporarily living elsewhere decided not to return and moved even farther away. The high-ground residential plots were not completed until 2018. Only 50 of the original 620 households from the old town center have returned to the high ground.[47]

As of April 2020, Ogatsu was still constructing a 9.7-meter-high, 1.8-kilometer-long seawall.[48] Workers needed to transport and compact fill to raise the ground, and so it took nine years to complete the commercial facilities near the seawall.[49] Out of twelve shops in the temporary mall, only five will relocate to the new facility. Ogatsu's population has fallen from 4,300 people before the disaster to 1,189 people as of the end of March 2020. The area has no railway station, and it is thirty minutes from the nearest interchange on the Sanriku Expressway.

The politics of government mergers, which instigated mistrust, reverberated throughout many parts of Tohoku, and such tensions were heightened by time constraints and rushed decision making, not to mention the inherent complexities of reconstruction projects more generally. Ogatsu offers a cautionary tale as populations age, towns continue to shrink in rural Japan, and mergers become more common across the world.

Yoriki: *Keiyakukou* versus Spatial Mergers

The importance of a community's social ties for collective relocation is underscored by the case of Yoriki hamlet, which has a long history of a *keiyakukou.* The tsunami washed away thirty-three of the forty-five houses in the quiet fishing bay,[50] but due to the hamlet's small size, all of the households were able to move to the same temporary housing site, which sped up the process of building consensus. It also helped that the *keiyakukou* owned shared land two kilometers away on high ground. The active engagement of community leaders, who asked all community members for their opinions, helped them come to a decision by June 2011.[51] In the reconstruction period, eight houses were rebuilt by individual households and twenty-two were rebuilt under the Bōsai Collective Relocation program.[52]

The Yoriki fishing port is also one of the rare communities that does not have a soaring seawall along with the port. This is partially because Yoriki made the decision to move to high ground earlier than most hamlets. Community members worried about a high seawall affecting their daily fishing activities in terms of the marine environment and the ocean's visibility. These concerns—in combination with the lack of residential properties along the coast as well as comprehensive coastal evacuation plans—allowed residents to reduce the seawall's height to a short storm-surge protection wall.

The Yoriki relocation site could accommodate forty houses. The town of Minamisanriku suggested including Niranohama, a neighboring district that had been struggling to select a relocation site, since there was surplus land and the site was located between the two hamlets. All the residents agreed. The arrangement of individual houses at the relocation site was designed through close communication with the residents. In the end, a single community center was constructed at the new site, with a partition installed that could be opened in order to promote interaction and respect between the districts.[53]

According to one resident very familiar with the neighborhood, the relocation site is rife with challenges. The houses are closer together than they were before the tsunami, necessitating a more "urban" lifestyle, which compels people to become concerned with privacy and security.[54] The standardized subdivision design for relocated housing aims to create unilateral equity, but it lacks sensitivity to specificity, which further design iterations could have negotiated. Since Yoriki's *keiyakukou* owned the land, more flexibility and creativity in design could have resulted in residences nestled into the topography with more privacy and greater adherence to former spaces and routines.

Figure 36. Rapid resettlement in the hamlet of Yoriki.

The dynamics of their previously socially close-knit but spatially independent community also changed with the merger with Niranohama. New relationships like this take time to develop. Despite these challenges, the relocation project was completed on October 30, 2014,[55] years before many other projects in the region, and residents were able to move out of temporary housing into their new homes much sooner.

COMPACT CITY PROJECTS

Some municipalities took the reconstruction as a chance to transform their region into a compact city to tackle depopulation and social issues related to the elderly. The compact city project aims to help towns with shrinking populations consolidate districts according to their functions—for example, residential areas with grocery stores and medical, welfare, and childcare facilities—through a location optimization plan created by the municipality. Theoretically, this is not only economically and environmentally efficient but also reduces elderly isolation and public works administrative costs, and it can be used to move residents out of hazard zones.

In order to encourage residents to move out of these disaster-prone areas, MLIT recommends that municipalities ask residents to relocate voluntarily or use the compact city planning subsidies to plan for larger collective action. Municipalities with a population of fewer than one hundred thousand with a declining population rate of 20 percent or more can receive up to ¥5.5 million in subsidies for their location optimization planning processes and an additional ¥5 million for the residential relocation planning.[56] With the optimization program, the residents living on the outskirts of the city, in hazard zones, are encouraged to move into the city or to existing nodes connected by transportation so that open units and idle plots in safe areas can be used more effectively. Additional significant measures are expected to support these voluntary relocations.[57] If the compact city planning process results in actionable projects, then subsidies from the Bōsai Collective Relocation Project would apply and vacated plots would be deemed a hazard zone.

Especially after the 2011 disaster, it seemed ideal to build compact cities in low-risk areas by aggregating functions and maintaining the surrounding agricultural land use and lifestyles.[58] However, some municipalities have been criticized for rather forcefully gathering survivors into limited districts without thorough consultation. One top-down reconstruction compact city project was Yamamoto in Miyagi.

Yamamoto

Yamamoto, known for its rice paddies, strawberry fields, and clamming, had thriving agricultural and fishery industries. But as with many municipalities in Tohoku, Yamamoto has a high number of elderly people (30.8 percent) and has been rapidly depopulating since 1995, when residents began migrating to municipalities closer to Sendai.[59] Sprawl was also a major issue, as Yamamoto did not establish zoned districts.[60]

Six coastal settlements in Yamamoto were destroyed in the 2011 tsunami: 50 percent of houses[61] and 90 percent of the strawberry farms were submerged in saline tsunami waters. About 9,000 people were affected, and 636 lost their lives.[62] After the disaster, the Yamamoto government feared an accelerated outflow of residents—especially due to delayed reconstruction—and wanted to resettle survivors to safe districts as quickly as possible. In light of its worsening financial situation, the town hoped to implement cost-effective new settlements by integrating reconstruction strategies using subsidies from the Tsunami Reconstruction Hub Development, Land Readjustment, and Bōsai Collective Relocation Projects.[63]

In August 2011, the town announced three types of tsunami hazard zones along the coast: zone one, where reconstruction was prohibited as inundation had exceeded 3 meters; zone two, where reconstruction was permitted with the foundation raised by 1.5 meters; and zone three, where reconstruction was permitted with the foundation raised by 0.5 meter.[64] People owning lots in zones one and two could sell their properties to the town and relocate outside the tsunami hazard zones.[65] This zoning was forcibly adopted without sufficient agreement even within the town hall, and despite petitions, it moved forward as planned.[66]

Mayor Saito Toshio announced the reconstruction plans in December 2011, transforming the town into a compact city and completing the transition before 2018. The new town consolidated the residences into three new areas around the new

JR Jōban Line stations, which had been moved one kilometer inland as a result of the extensive tsunami damage. Coordinating with the central government, prefecture, and surrounding municipalities, Yamamoto planned multiple tsunami defenses: the 7.2-meter seawall (MLIT); the 3-meter tsunami forest (Forestry Agency); the 9-meter evacuation *inochi-yama* hills (local government); and the raising of both the former JR Jōban Line and prefectural highway 4 to 5 meters.[67] They believed this quick, transformative plan would appeal to current residents as well as attract young families (commuters to Sendai) even from outside of the town.

The three selected areas were bundled with housing and amenities. The site north of JR Shin-Yamashita Station reclaimed 37.4 hectares of rice fields and prepared 201 regular residential plots (to rent or buy) and 246 public housing units, a supermarket, a bōsai community center, a nursery school, an elementary school (Yamashita Dai-ni), a childcare support center, and a park. The 9.3-hectare middle site, close to the existing Miyagi Hospital, was made into a medical and eldercare hub by adding welfare facilities for the elderly, a park, 10 individual housing plots, and 72 public housing units. The 9.3-hectare south site was developed adjacent to the existing settlement and JR Shin-Sakamoto Station, with 40 housing lots and 72 public housing units, a convenience store, a post office, a bōsai community center, a park, and the Japan Agricultural Cooperatives office.[68]

The six coastal settlements were designated to move into these three new districts, but residents' opinions were not included in the selection of sites or in the reconstruction plan. Thirty-seven households in the Kasano district and seventeen households in the Iso district asked to move to an inland district close to strawberry fields as their own collective relocation project,[69] but the town did not accept any proposals other than those prepared by the city and even set the minimum collective relocation size to fifty households, whereas the national standard was five.[70] Residents from hazard zones one and two were moved into the newly developed sites with up to ¥4 million in subsidies using the Bōsai Collective Relocation Project, but residents in zone three were left behind, without any financial support or options for moving. At the time of this writing, residents remaining in zones two and three who are eligible for the Livelihood Support Act (stipulating substantial damage to the home) can qualify for a subsidy of up to ¥1 million for rebuilding the foundation, constructing a retaining wall, or raising the land on the site to meet each zone's construction regulations.[71] Even if the residents can rebuild, challenges remain: residing in a "hazard zone" will likely encumber future property values. Their additional separation from other residents might also seem unjust.

Despite many protests, Mayor Saito was firm in the top-down compact city approach, and quick, decisive acts meant fast results. Public housing occupancy began in April 2013, which was the fastest in Miyagi. Although the resettlement process was quick, conflicts arose in the relocation sites among the residents from different settlements. In one location it was necessary to create two neighborhood associations due to the differences in cultures, customs, and even languages.[72] The fact of rushed relocation, with no incorporation of residents' input, possibly aggravated matters. Residents in zone three are rebuilding in place at the time of this writing, and the consequences of separating them from the relocated community are yet to be seen. Hazard zones rarely align with political boundaries and community networks, so the separate strategies for zones may be viewed as arbitrary and yet often have long-lasting effects.

The population of Yamamoto has declined since the disaster, with about 1,700 fewer people than estimated in the town's earthquake recovery plan.[73] Despite the swift reconstruction, many people moved to urban areas—including those who evacuated to other municipalities and never came back.[74] Quick construction is often equated with quick recovery, but in the case of Yamamoto, caught between contradictions of speedy, cost-effective town planning and preserving residents' lifestyles and preferences, further research is necessary.

PRE-DISASTER RESETTLEMENT POLICIES AND SUBSIDIES

The Tohoku disaster highlighted how complex reconstruction processes can be for communities grieving lost lives (and livelihoods), with residents scattered in temporary homes across the region and time pressures both from funding streams and from individuals desiring a return to normalcy. Lessons learned were incorporated into amendments to existing programs so that local governments and residents could plan more prudently for anticipated disasters.

COLLECTIVE RELOCATION—PREEMPTIVE ACTION

The Bōsai Collective Relocation Project, applied preemptively, calls for similar measures to those carried out after the Tohoku earthquake. The municipality reviews the predicted coastal hazard zones and encourages the relocation of communities in those zones. In anticipation of the Nankai Trough earthquake and tsunami, 139 municipalities were designated as Tsunami Evacuation Regions, stressing the importance of preemptive relocation. In these areas, national subsidies increased for collective relocation projects from the original 75 percent to 94 percent coverage,[75] with the municipality paying the balance. If residents adopt the plan, the municipality will acquire the residential land in the hazard area, develop new plots on high ground, and provide moving costs to residents, using national government subsidies. The municipality sells or leases the new plots to residents, and the residents build their own houses.

Although the subsidies were generous, the need to self-finance new house construction made consensus building among neighbors difficult. Given this challenge, no residential projects were implemented from the program's inception in 1972 through to 2020.[76] In order to make it more accessible and useful, significant amendments were made in April 2020. For example, the required plot minimum was lowered from ten to five (the interim test of this during the Tohoku reconstruction proved to be helpful).[77] In addition to residential plots, any attached agricultural land can be sold to the municipality. Renters are also eligible for moving fees when relocating to existing housing on high ground and can choose among the newly developed or existing vacant homes or existing public housing. In the original program, it was necessary for the whole district to reach consensus in order to purchase the original land in the hazard zone. There still needs to be a consensus among neighbors within the group, but if an affected owner is unreachable, the group may still proceed. The entirety of the remaining land does get deemed a complete hazard zone, and future construction could be restricted by the municipality.

What remains the same is that the municipality sells or leases the new plot to the resident and the onus of building the new house is solely on the resident. If the resident takes out a mortgage to acquire a plot or construct a house at the relocation site, the municipality subsidizes the equivalent amount of interest and pays for moving costs. Most importantly, in this revised subsidy, the national government pays municipalities half of the expenses for the planning; this includes decision making with residents, selecting relocation sites, and formulating the project plan. There is no limit to the planning period, as it is expected to take time to reach consensus, and relocation could in some cases take decades.[78]

The national government now bears 94 percent of the cost of the collective relocation in advance (which is the same measure as for the Nankai Trough tsunami), and it applies to all hazards.[79] This is especially important as the recent increase in the number of severe typhoons and localized torrential rain damage has renewed attention to the dangers facing residential areas along rivers and in mountainous regions. Among 269 surveyed municipalities, 89 percent have residential areas in potential flood zones and 32 percent within landslide warning areas.[80] This is attributed to recent residential construction in such zones, which failed to take into account (or deliberately ignored) the risk of flooding and landslides to pursue short-term profits.[81] Discussions of pre-disaster relocation for landslides and floods have increased substantially.

Floodplain Relocation: Misato

In light of the major amendment of the Bōsai Collective Relocation Project in 2020, rural municipalities prone to floods have begun considering their pre-disaster relocation plan. For example, the Gōno River, treasured for its scenic beauty, is also infamous for inundating the surrounding areas of Misato in Shimane Prefecture. In the 2018 West Japan flood event, 270 houses over 340 hectares were flooded, and during the July 2020 flood event, forty-five locations of the Gōno River overflowed, inundating 265 hectares and 104 houses.[82] While most areas are demanding the prompt completion of levees, a district of Misato suffering from annual flooding is taking another approach: five households are applying for Bōsai Collective Relocation Project funds. As of early 2021, the town's subsidy cap of ¥10 million per house was insufficient to develop plots on high ground in the same district, which increased the costs for individuals—who contemplated moving to other districts.[83] Fortunately, they were able to lower the project cost by combining it with government subsidies for road maintenance, thus reducing the burden on residents, and by March 2023, a 6,100-square-meter residential high-ground development site was completed (by leveling a mountain) within the district. The site is 7 meters above the flood area. The five households (twelve people) requesting resettlement are expected to be relocated by the end of 2024.[84] The biggest challenge in carrying out the Bōsai Collective Relocation Project, especially in aging rural communities, is the 6 percent financial burden on residents. This case clearly demonstrates the importance of a holistic approach to projects, finding ways to overcome financial blocks though regional considerations in maintenance and infrastructure planning. These types of conversations, planning, and construction, albeit slow, open new methods of preparation. Should a disaster occur tomorrow, the families already have a working relationship and have their recovery process planned.

PREEMPTIVELY RELOCATING PUBLIC FACILITIES

During the Tohoku tsunami, twenty-eight city halls were damaged and lost important administrative data. This resulted in serious delays in rescuing affected residents and initiating recovery. As of January 2021, 184 municipalities nationwide have their city halls in tsunami hazard zones. Of those, 78 do not have a backup office, or their backup office is also in a hazard zone.[85] The national government strongly encourages municipalities, especially in the Nankai Trough Special Tsunami Evacuation Regions, to relocate public facilities that will function as emergency and recovery hubs as well as those that are used daily by vulnerable populations. As of December 2020, 62 municipalities out of the 139 Nankai Trough Special Tsunami Evacuation Regions have already relocated their main facilities or are in the process of doing so. As of this writing, there are 191 public facilities in total: fire stations, childcare facilities, city halls, elementary and middle schools, and disaster hub hospitals.[86] Although many municipalities along the coast have difficulties in securing land on high ground, public facility relocation projects have accelerated.

Relocation to Attract Young Families: Minamiise

Minamiise, at the eastern end of the Kii Peninsula in Mie Prefecture, is planning for an estimated twenty-two-meter-high tsunami, expected to arrive within eight minutes of an earthquake and submerge 80 percent of the settlement.[87] In addition to designating 242 tsunami evacuation facilities and evacuation routes, the town is relocating the fire department, two senior nursing facilities, two elementary schools, a daycare facility, and the town hospital to high ground.[88] The senior nursing facilities will serve as a special shelter prioritizing seniors and other vulnerable populations. The hospital is embedded with bōsai infrastructure and designed to be fail-safe in order to operate as an additional evacuation shelter for those who cannot evacuate to the senior nursing facility. Next to the hospital, a part of the town hall is designated as the Minamiise regional coordination center and is used for meeting and staff training space during blue-sky days; it will transform into its disaster response headquarters when needed.[89] The town is also investigating potential sites for temporary housing after a disaster as part of its preemptive disaster reconstruction plan.

Minamiise is planning to relocate a low-lying fishing hamlet with an especially high number of elderly people to higher ground, using the Bōsai Collective Relocation Project,[90] in conjunction with the New Kizuna Project to increase the population by providing tsunami-safe housing and property on high ground to incoming young families.[91] It is granting housing acquisition subsidies to individuals between the ages of eighteen and forty-five who move to the town and settle for at least ten years.[92] Families who purchase or build a new house are eligible to receive up to ¥2 million, and families who purchase an existing house will receive up to ¥500,000 to refurbish it. As of July 2020, the town has developed four new residential plots and is building a two-story apartment complex, where it intends to relocate houses and public housing.[93] The municipality is also building an apartment complex in another district and seeking to purchase private land to develop additional plots and apartments. The town aims to attract ninety-four new young households before 2025[94] to the tsunami-safe high grounds, which will be further protected by a raised national highway designed to function as a seawall.

DISCUSSION

Post-2011 Tohoku demographic trends are different from those following the 1896 and 1933 tsunamis, when the population was drawn to the region's rich fishing grounds. With overall populations and local fisheries both in decline, similar post-disaster growth is highly unlikely (unless there is a major shift to launch new economic generators in the region). Many scholars lament that reconstruction planning ought to have given greater priority to the specific needs of shrinking and aging communities. Across the region, declining populations pose the question of whether undertaking such extensive infrastructure construction was the best course of action and how the maintenance of those infrastructures will be managed. Maki Norio and Laurie Johnson recommend that "a future recovery organization structure needs the ability to flexibly address an array of unforeseen circumstances and . . . implement the new measures that are required."[95]

Reconstruction is difficult, and decisions surrounding resettlement are the most challenging. People are attached to their land, their histories, generations of hard work and memories, their sense of place, and their social networks. Complex trade-offs exist between speed and consensus (in the case of Yamamoto) or cost and time (in the case of Rikuzentakata). Although globally we are increasingly seeing calls for post-disaster resettlement, under frameworks such as buyouts and managed retreat, approaching resettlement before a disaster has significant potential for reducing losses. To plan around an if/when framework may seem preposterous to some, but relocating before rather than after a disaster helps avoid not only the immediate consequences of the disaster and loss of lives in the first place but also many of the costs described here: rushed decision making, fracturing of communities, and long reconstruction timelines, leaving residents living in cramped temporary housing for extended periods. If resettlement strategies could be considered for city planning in hazard-prone regions as part of a longer-term vision for the future, then citizen involvement, environmental assessments, planning, and design could all lead to better, more distinctive scenarios for each community, culture, and place.

Urban Systems Discussion

Japan's strong centralized system has helped it thrive in spite of constant earthquakes, blazes, and floods. A central approach is important for broad coordination, such as ensuring evacuation routes and emergency vehicle access across cities or creating warning systems that can effectively communicate across large areas. But it is equally important for residents to play a role in shaping their environments and for planning systems to have the flexibility to accommodate local participation. Japan has offered examples of this as well, namely, through bōsai machizukuri movements, which integrate the bottom-up into larger planning projects as well as more informal approaches, such as evacuation routes. Including local voices ensures that spaces meet the needs of their occupants, and participation in bōsai spatial planning strengthens social networks and improves community coping capacity more generally.

INTERNATIONAL CONNECTIONS

Urban theory is steeped in arguments over whether cities (towns, regions, landscapes) are best planned from the top down or from the bottom up. Jane Jacobs and Robert Moses are classic figures in this debate—a journalist and a public official, respectively, who, in the mid-twentieth century, battled over whether the future of New York was best planned from the bottom or the top. This tension continues to play a significant role in the discourse around planning and urbanism, including in the growing dialogue around urban informality. Urban scholar Ananya Roy argues for working with informality and "confronting how the apparatus of planning produces the unplanned and unplannable."[1] Anne Spirn, through her work in West Philadelphia, argues for grassroots "landscape literacy" to combat the ways in which existing maps and plans may encourage false assumptions, particularly in marginalized neighborhoods.[2] Scholars like Gavin Shatkin stress how, in an increasingly neoliberal world, the top-down approach may have as much to do with private corporations as it does governments, as privatization plays a growing role in shaping urban development.[3]

TOP-DOWN/BOTTOM-UP

Although unanimity is difficult to achieve, in several cases designers (architects, landscape architects, and planners) have played a critical intermediary role negotiating between top (e.g., government policies, centralized planning, municipal projects) and bottom (e.g., individuals, communities, local businesses, neighborhood associations, and nonprofits). Making on-the-ground connections can also help mitigate issues of inequity often associated with these types of transformative large-scale projects. Beyond the potential to provide new visions of disaster-prepared futures, designers can also be integral to those transformations across time and space, and among the more successful examples are those that make connections between the top and the bottom. The Matsumoto stream project is one notable example, where the community group was able to take an innovative approach to a fire-prepared roadway by bringing together Kobe's Planning Department and Sewage Department. Importantly, designers served as the liaisons who helped envision the proposal but also mediated between local needs and municipal policies. In Onagawa, the mayor took the lead in formulating a reconstruction plan, in collaboration with a designer and residents, and conducted more than two hundred workshops with the aim of attracting a younger generation to settle there.

However, these processes take time, and tensions among cost, speed, quality, and consensus often demand compromises. The collection of cases in this chapter, which scale from micro-local networks to large-scale infrastructures, pose questions about the costs (social, economic, environmental) of projects, specifically as they are balanced against the risks of rare catastrophic disasters. Larger infrastructures like seawalls may save lives, but they can also increase wave heights in other areas, and they are expensive and disruptive to ecosystems and to everyday life. Shortcuts that undermine environmental assessments to prioritize speedy reconstruction never benefit the ecology and habitats in the surrounding area, and they endanger all in the long run. In contrast to heavy infrastructure, evacuation route projects are less likely to disrupt livelihoods and ecosystems and in many cases are more fail-safe than infrastructural solutions, but they often require the permission of property owners and thus time for consensus building.

Especially after the 2011 tsunami, the speed of recovery became a central issue. The initial five-year cap on national funding rushed decision making and may have compromised localization and design processes in many of the municipalities. At the time of the disaster, five years certainly seemed too long to be in temporary housing; that cap, originally intended to benefit survivors, ended up jeopardizing the process in many areas. Lamentably, municipalities that pushed for speed ended up with projects that were larger in scale and often took longer to complete. Opportunities for ample top-down funding brought on an overwhelming sense that without these programs, recovery would be impossible, which pressured decision making during critical times. In addition, consistent population decline in the region meant that local governments faced uncertainty about the financial burden of maintaining these large infrastructures in the future.

Several critics pay particular attention to the quality of the consensus-building process, questioning how much consideration was given to include uncertainty and alternative design options in light of accelerating population decline. Nagamatsu Shingo's research identifies a paradox: towns with larger-scale reconstruction programs typically have higher rates of out-migration and associated population decline.[4] The Yamamoto and Rikuzentakata cases also remind us that more funding doesn't necessarily equate to a better recovery, and in both cases consensus building was difficult, owing either to political will or to the scale (and distribution) of the population.

Ultimately, it should be up to the impacted communities to make these kinds of decisions about how their lives will be transformed. This was not always the case in the aftermath of the 2011 Tohoku tsunami or earlier disasters, often because the dispersion of survivors to scattered temporary housing sites made it difficult for communities to organize a collective response. Such a response depends on benevolent local leaders to not only survive the disaster but to put their own grief aside to listen to all voices. It also requires an egalitarian relationship between residents and local government.

Reconstruction and resettlement are always complicated, and an ideal, inclusive, equitable process is difficult to achieve when people are grieving, livelihoods are lost, communities are scattered in temporary homes, speed is necessary, resources are limited, and residents want their lives to return to a sense of normalcy. Although some machizukuri processes have succeeded, as shared in previous sections, many others took years before residents felt themselves to be on the path to recovery. For rural municipalities, delayed reconstruction exacerbates population outflow, which further jeopardizes recovery. Post-disaster, amid bereavement, is a particularly difficult time to engage various stakeholders in complex problems that need creative solutions.

What if we could start these conversations now?

Some disaster reduction projects have already been introduced: mitigation and preparedness projects in fire protection, bōsai living zones, and, in a few prefectures, pre-disaster resettlement projects. The most recent type of subsidy is for thinking through a reconstruction process based on an urgent scenario. Emergency managers regularly undergo scenarios and exercises to prepare for disasters, but they tend to remain within the immediate response phase and not delve into problem solving for issues during recovery and reconstruction phases. The new collaborative reconstruction zone subsidies now encourage such workshops to take place.

NEW POLICIES: COLLABORATIVE RECONSTRUCTION ZONE

In the wake of the 1995 Kobe earthquake, Tokyo established a set of guidelines to prepare for reconstruction and livelihood recovery in case of a Tokyo inland earthquake. In particular, the Tokyo Metropolitan Earthquake Countermeasures Ordinance of 2001 makes a point of cooperation between the government and the residents in a reconstruction process. Within this plan are several frameworks outlining reconstruction goals, land use, and urban infrastructure development policies to be formulated within two months of the disaster.[5] The necessity of such planning was further emphasized by challenges during the Tohoku reconstruction process, demonstrating that government-led reconstruction alone could not fully accommodate specific community needs. The TMG made efforts to include citizens' opinions in fundamental policies through surveys,[6] and in 2017 it issued a more detailed pre-reconstruction process.

The TMG created two sets of reconstruction guidelines, one for municipal government officials and one for residents, from which each is expected to create manuals appropriate for their specific locale and demographics.[7] The latter includes the "Handbook for Pre-Reconstruction of Urban Areas," which encourages the formation of a neighborhood reconstruction council (with *jichikai* [neighborhood associations], jishubō, machizukuri councils, condo management associations, and local businesses)[8] in each elementary school district, and defines the parameters of a Collaborative Reconstruction Zone.[9] The TMG aids this citizen-centered reconstruction by pairing mechanisms of self-help and community support with public assistance through advisors such as machizukuri leaders, NPOs, volunteers, and companies. Then the council works with the municipality to create reconstruction plans, establishing rules for environmental conservation and rebuilding. The programs include lectures by experts, walking and map making, discussions about issues, and visions of reconstruction.[10] These community collaborative reconstruction plans are reviewed and subsidized by the TMG up to ¥5,000,000 per program.[11]

The other major emphasis of this effort is to secure locations for post-disaster temporary housing and businesses—key to helping residents maintain their social networks and remain in their original district. In each Collaborative Reconstruction Zone, the council is expected to plan temporary building construction policies, establish a communication system with shelter sites, confirm with survivors their intent to remain on-site, sign agreements for emergency temporary housing, and provide construction support for *jiriki* (self-help) temporary housing. Whereas designated temporary housing sites are usually on public land, if insufficient, the TMG supports municipalities to clear debris and secure private land providing a no-renewal-within-five-years land loan, which has greatly increased the potential of temporarily borrowing private land.

Although theoretically ideal, a bottom-up approach alone will slow consensus building among various stakeholders and create constant reconstruction across the city. Therefore, the reconstruction timeline is outlined by the TMG. Each municipality will conduct a housing damage survey within a week after the disaster, and then, within two weeks after the disaster, the TMG will define a construction moratorium in areas where 80 percent of houses were burned or collapsed. Within a month, each municipality will designate districts where reconstruction will take place, and temporary housing sites should be set up within three months.[12] Since this is a relatively new program at the time of this writing, concrete examples could not be found, but these actions are all set in motion to encourage municipalities to proactively address community issues with residents in normal times so that reconstruction can go more quickly, smoothly, and equitably.

By preparing in advance during blue-sky days, the government and residents can take time to discuss how to proceed with mitigation efforts now and plan reconstruction while specifically designing plans for their local conditions. Most municipalities and emergency managers train for emergency responses, but few prepare for the recovery process. More voices participating in this process also builds social capacity. With ample time, ecological and environmental assessments can be conducted with due process; the consideration and inclusion of natural systems should be viewed as an asset. By starting this process now, decisions do not need to be made immediately; creative solutions and possibilities can guide discussions and potentially even lead to improved visions of the imagined future of each place. Reframing reconstruction planning as a process informed by anticipatory design—one that engages the wider citizenry and considers a wider time frame, including well before a disaster strikes—could help alleviate many of the shortcomings faced in disaster reconstruction.

This, too, is easier said than done. It requires increasing awareness, so that people understand the urgency of the situation, and inviting all relevant people to the table, incentivizing participation, and listening with care and persistence. Today in Japan, neighborhood associations and machizukuri remain strong, but younger generations may feel less tied to specific places or communities and may lack interest in these traditional models of community-based planning. The tradition of delivering a *kairanban* (community clipboard) from one neighbor to another and sitting in the *engawa* (living room porch) to chat has all but disappeared in many urban areas. This potential shift away from traditional community organizing in Japan suggests that new types of networks might be leveraged by younger generations to facilitate bottom-up planning, perhaps through social media or other digital tools. As Japan ages and changes, it will be important to reconsider what bōsai urbanism looks like in the context of a large elderly population and a workforce infamous for working 24/7. It's clear that new innovations will be necessary to have these continued conversations.[13]

4

PARK NETWORKS

Open spaces play important roles after a disaster, offering safe havens from aftershocks, spreading fires, falling debris, rising waters (if on high ground), or floodwater basins (if on low ground), and yet they are rarely designed specifically for sheltering evacuees. Japan is unique in developing an extensive network of open spaces designed to play a role during disasters. These *bōsaikōen* (disaster-prevention parks) operate as part of a multiscalar evacuation and logistics network and are key in preemptively designing for evacuation in Japanese cities. They also provide moments of respite in dense urban contexts. Embedding these spaces in people's everyday lives increases their post-disaster accessibility.

Municipalities may use different terminologies, but most follow a similar nested system of actors, networks, and spaces. There are exceptions to the rule, but as a high-level overview, the seven national logistics hubs are each the center of a network involving multiple prefectural logistics hubs, regional logistics hubs, municipal mixed bōsai hubs, primary evacuation spaces, and initial evacuation spaces. By engaging multiple spheres of government and scales of spaces, the network effectively leverages the anticipatory design principle of integrating top-down planning with dynamic situations on the ground. While residents' needs can be best identified locally, central and prefectural governments have greater resources and capacity to provide assistance (especially from places not directly affected by the disaster).

HISTORY OF EVACUATION PARKS IN JAPAN

Japan has a long history of preserving open spaces for bōsai roles. During the Edo period, some public open spaces were preserved as *hiyokechi,* evacuation spaces from

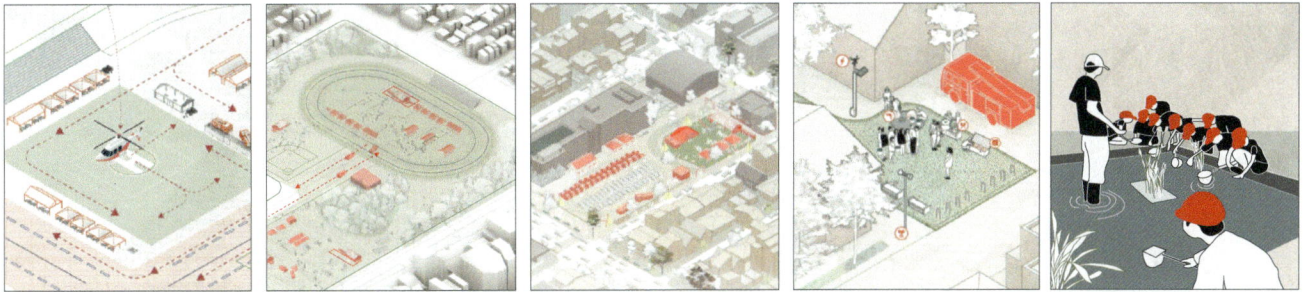

Logistics Hubs   Mixed Bosai Hubs   Primary Evacuation Spaces   Initial Evacuation Parks   Education in Parks

National hub

Logistics hub

Initial pocket park

Initial neighborhood park

Mixed municipal bosai hub
> 10ha

Pocket park
r = 250m

Initial neighborhood park
r = 500m

Municipal bosai hub
r = 1,000m

Municipal bosai hub
r = 1,000m

Figure 37. Park networks and their roles in disasters.

fire. However, prior to the Meiji era, public parks as we now know them did not exist in Japan. Rather, most open spaces existed as part of the grounds of castles, temples, and shrines, as officially designated cherry-blossom viewing sites, in elite household compounds, or as productive farming or wilderness and forest landscapes. Most public life occurred in the streets, home to a proliferation of performers, fairs, and festivals.[1] Higashi Yūenchi Park in Kobe, which first opened in 1868, is one of the oldest parks in Japan and was intended exclusively for foreigners.[2]

The 1888 Tokyo City Code is considered the start of Japan's modern city planning. The Ministry of the Interior created the Tokyo Revision Committee with a vision of upgrading Tokyo's sanitary, fire-protection, and transportation infrastructures.[3] Parks were included as key urban facilities that contribute to the "beauty" of future cities. Imperial advisors sent to Europe to study urban design deemed London, Paris, Berlin, and Vienna model cities. With these as a reference, the committee aimed to create one park per 1.2 square kilometers (or per 20,000 people).[4] The Tokyo Code Ordinance, enacted in 1888, provided a legal and financial framework, and in the following year it created a comprehensive master plan on urban facilities, including roads, rivers, bridges, rails, and markets.[5] The ordinance and master plan conceived of forty-nine parks in Tokyo, but most of them ended up being just officially appointed and re-purposed existing open spaces, such as grounds of temples, shrines, and *hiyokechi*— familiar public spaces from the Edo period.[6]

Hibiya Park, the first fully public designed park, was the exception. It opened in 1903, marking the beginning of a new era of park design and planning in Japan. Its designer, Honda Seiroku, was heavily influenced by German landscape architecture. In 1919, the Landscape District Guideline was established in the City Planning Law to allow prefectures to preserve open spaces within their cities. Later, in 1931, the National Park Law was created for conservation.[7] Despite all this, rapid industrialization initially eliminated remaining urban open spaces as cities swelled with growing populations and industrial landscapes; by 1923, Tokyo was densely built up, with only about 1.7 percent of land remaining open as parks.[8]

1923 Tokyo Earthquake

The 1923 Tokyo earthquake and fire shaped the Japanese conception of parks not only as spaces of leisure, like the European parks on which they had been modeled, but also as bōsai spaces. During the catastrophic earthquake and the fires that consumed the city, many survivors escaped the flames by fleeing to open spaces within the urban fabric. Ueno and Hibiya Parks provided evacuee camping areas for a recorded total of 1,570,000 people two days after the earthquake.[9] The Outer Garden of the Imperial Palace was one of the largest temporary shelters, holding 5,000 survivors, and was also used by the Japanese Red Cross to treat 3,913 injured and 6,682 sick people for 132 days.[10]

A private garden owned by Iwasaki Yataro, the founder of the Mitsubishi group, safely accommodated over 20,000 evacuees. The 40,000-square-meter Kiyosumi Garden was redesigned in 1878 with ponds and constructed topography as a traditional Japanese garden. The park was protected by a brick wall, moat, and less flammable trees, such as those from the *Schima* genus.[11] (The park was donated to Tokyo after 1923.) On the other hand, open spaces where people evacuated into dense clusters with their (flammable) belongings provided fuel for the flames: 40,000 people fled to the 25,000-square-meter open space at the Military Clothing Depot, and 38,000 perished as their possessions ignited.[12] These experiences illustrate that open spaces are not inherently safe during a disaster, but large parks, if properly designed and managed, can contribute to fire preparedness. In comparison to Kiyosumi Garden, the Military Clothing Depot's lack of a fire-resistant perimeter, lack of topographical modifications and fire-retardant trees to block winds, and lack of a water supply made evacuees vulnerable to the spreading flames. Some researchers advocate for bōsaikōen designs to consider such topographical and water elements.[13]

Parks also prevented flames from spreading to some districts of the city. Tokyo's twenty-seven preexisting parks played an important role in the immediate response and long-term aftermath, serving as evacuation spaces, fire buffers, and sites for shelter construction.[14] The Marunouchi area was largely protected by the Imperial Palace moat and Hibiya Park, which acted as buffer zones; similarly, parks, shrines, and other open spaces helped protect areas to the north of the city.[15]

Recognizing this role, the Imperial Reconstruction Plan allotted for the construction of three new large parks (Sumida, Kinshi, and Hamachō) and fifty-two smaller parks, surrounded by a perimeter of less flammable trees, with both everyday and disaster functions in mind.[16] The smaller parks were built adjacent to new, reinforced concrete elementary schools and became key nodes of the rebuilt, fire-resistant Tokyo while memorializing the catastrophe. The construction of these parks adjacent to elementary schools helped embed them in the community—a necessity for evacuation spaces.[17] Following World War II, this model spread throughout Japan.[18]

Motomachi Park was one of these fifty-two small parks and is thought to be the only one surviving in near-original condition. Opened in 1930 along the Kanda River, the park was planned with the adjacent elementary school as an extension of its playfield, and it serves as both a memorial site and a place for everyday recreation.[19] The art deco–style memorial hall houses mass graves from the earthquake and quickly became a site of pilgrimage.[20] During disasters, the park serves as an evacuation site, and it is surrounded by a buffer forest of less flammable trees. Low-oil-content tree species such as Japanese chinquapin (*Castanopsis*), Japanese zelkova (*Zelkova serrata*), ginkgo

(*Ginkgo biloba*), Chinese parasol tree (*Firmiana simplex*), and plane trees (*Platanus*) are much less flammable[21] than high-oil trees or wooden houses and help keep fires from spreading into the park. In a 2006 case that aimed to repurpose the site for a high-rise development, a group of academics, school alumni, parents, and citizen activists won the case to preserve the park,[22] a rare victory in central Tokyo.

In the following years, Japanese cities escalated their efforts to set aside open spaces as "landscape districts." The first was set up in Tokyo's Meiji Shrine in 1926, when ownership of 11,800 square meters was transferred from the Imperial Household Agency to the Foundation Bureau for the Meiji Shrine (held by the Home Ministry) and the area was designated as a *hiyokechi*.[23] For everyday use, a botanical garden opened in the space. Although the initial purpose was to incorporate the scenic landscape and approach to the shrine for the great number of worshipers of Emperor Meiji,[24] both the shrine and the outer garden are currently designated as evacuation areas. Tokyo's first open space plan in 1939 modeled a system of greenbelt, boulevards, and scenic parks based on Western precedents. During World War II, despite the pressures of the conflict, many of these spaces were preserved as evacuation sites as firebombing raids led to devastating fires across Japanese cities. However, postwar development infilled 63 percent of former evacuation parks.[25]

In 1956, Japan passed the Urban Parks Law, which included disaster functions among its provisions (although it was decades before their implementation became widespread). The 1972 Five-Year Plan for Urban Park Construction formalized planning procedures for bōsaikōen,[26] and the park project budget became a significant allocation from the national treasury. In order to design and build bōsaikōen, the Bōsai Green Space Development Project was established in 1986 so that MLIT urban development funds could be used to acquire land and construct the minimum required bōsai facilities.[27] Kobe's green space network, using riverside parks for disaster preparedness, originated in lessons learned from the 1938 Great Hanshin flood, which killed six hundred people.[28] Later plans, such as the 1985 Kobe Master Plan for Parks and Open Spaces, foregrounds the need for fire buffers and evacuation spaces,[29] but the 1995 Kobe earthquake was a striking reminder of the paramount importance of open spaces during an earthquake.

1995 Kobe Earthquake

During the 1995 earthquake, 176 city parks were used, many with overlapping functions: 117 as evacuation spaces (with tents); 125 as first aid, relief supply logistics, heliports, and material distribution spaces; and 15 for recovery activities such as debris storage and SDF hubs.[30] These spaces were also outfitted with ad hoc temporary toilets, baths made out of used oil drums, and water distribution. Several of the tent villages in parks stood for over two years and became sites of shower houses, communal kitchens, temporary stores and restaurants, aid stations, volunteer coordination locations, and village headquarters. In these contexts, the design of parks shaped their post-disaster functionality: long and narrow parks had fewer temporary shops and other community services because they did not easily fit into the temporary housing layout. It was also difficult for evacuees who were not acquainted with each other before the earthquake to develop a sense of community in these narrow parks that did not have a centralized common space.[31]

Some of the tent villages also provided assistance for the rehabilitation and reconstruction of surrounding areas, including lodging facilities for volunteers, emergency operations centers of local governments, first aid spaces, emergency supply distribution spaces, and bases for the SDF.[32] While these parks were used for those purposes, most were not designated as evacuation sites in the Regional Disaster Management Plan,[33] primarily because the fault below Kobe had not been previously identified and so the earthquake was unexpected.[34] They were thus created on an ad hoc basis.

The use of parks during and after the Kobe earthquake led to a renewed investment in bōsai planning and bōsaikōen. In March 1995, the Special Financial Assistance Law provided affected local governments with central government subsidies for 80 percent of the costs to rehabilitate damaged parks.[35] Land readjustment subsidies were also used during reconstruction to introduce bōsaikōen into otherwise dense neighborhoods, which was significant for the inclusion of machizukuri processes in park design. Existing and new parks were outfitted with decentralized lifeline infrastructure, such as water tanks and solar panels.

In the same year, the Greening Priority Districts Project was established to prevent fire spread, reduce heat-island effects, and improve urban landscape through greening. The central government subsidized up to one-third of land acquisition costs and half of facility development costs.[36] Kobe used this national program to develop its Green Kobe 21 Plan and created four types of green axes for disaster prevention: the river axis, the foothills axis, the street-tree axis, and the seaside axis.[37] Other than the foothills axis, which created forest biotopes between mountains and the city to reduce destruction from landslides and prevent uncontrolled urban growth,[38] these operate as evacuation paths, emergency vehicle routes, and fire buffers during a disaster. The axes form a one-kilometer grid, with routes running parallel to the waterfront and perpendicularly from the sea to the mountains, creating the bōsai living zones. They also link critical bases, such as city hall (including the emergency operations center), ward offices (including community emergency hubs), and bōsaikōen.[39] Within ten years, the Green Kobe 21 Plan revived three rivers, widened the mountain foothills greenbelt by 327 hectares, created twenty-two new parks along the street-tree axis, and established the Kobe earthquake memorial park.[40] Revisions in 2011 to the Green Kobe 21 Plan placed added emphasis on urban heat island and air pollution mitigation, linking the plan to larger climate-change and environmental risks.[41]

2011 Tohoku Triple Disaster

Although urban parks did not play as significant a role in the 2011 Tohoku event, many smaller hilltop parks and hilltop shrine grounds were used as evacuation spaces, some officially designated and some not. Learning from this experience, reconstruction efforts to create new high ground have included parks within new residential areas, and in the low-lying plains, new hills have been constructed as evacuation parks.

NATIONAL POLICIES AND SUBSIDIES FOR PARKS

Recognizing the important role parks played in recent earthquakes, the central government quickly amended existing acts and institutionalized ways to increase green spaces in dense Japanese cities. The 1956 Urban Park Law was amended to add bōsai facilities to existing urban parks using national subsidies.[42] Such facilities included food and medicine storage, earthquake-resistant water tanks, emergency communication systems, and heliports. The 1995 Green Oasis Improvement Project helped densely populated urban areas acquire idle or unused land to create small green initial evacuation spaces. Cities with a population of over one hundred thousand were eligible for the MLIT urban development loans to create primary evacuation and initial evacuation spaces, which are larger than one hectare (including surrounding streets), in dense urban districts. In 1999, the Bōsaikōen Block Development Project was created to integrate the development of bōsaikōen and improvements of surrounding vulnerable areas.[43] In this project, the Urban Renaissance agency manages everything from land acquisition, design, and development to financing (with a national subsidy) upon the municipality's request. For municipalities, such projects become more efficient by reducing administrative procedures, but putting a single agency in charge of everything, including the design, could help explain some of the more formulaic results seen around Japan.

PARK NETWORKS: CHAPTER ORGANIZATION

This chapter takes a deep dive into the complex and multiscalar nature of the bōsaikōen network, a phenomenon largely unique to Japan (though newly emergent in China as well). During the Kobe earthquake, open spaces were used not only as evacuation sites but also for the logistics associated with relief efforts and for longer-term temporary housing. People fled to city parks, fearing fire and aftershocks, while the SDF used larger parks and Itami Airport for logistics and supply distribution. The lack of a coherent system posed numerous coordination challenges and underscored the need for a comprehensive bōsaikōen network. To accomplish this, the government expanded the types of bōsaikōen in 1996 to include a multiscalar network of bōsai

Figure 38. A bōsaikōen network ranging from national hubs to local parks, all with designated roles in logistics and evacuation.

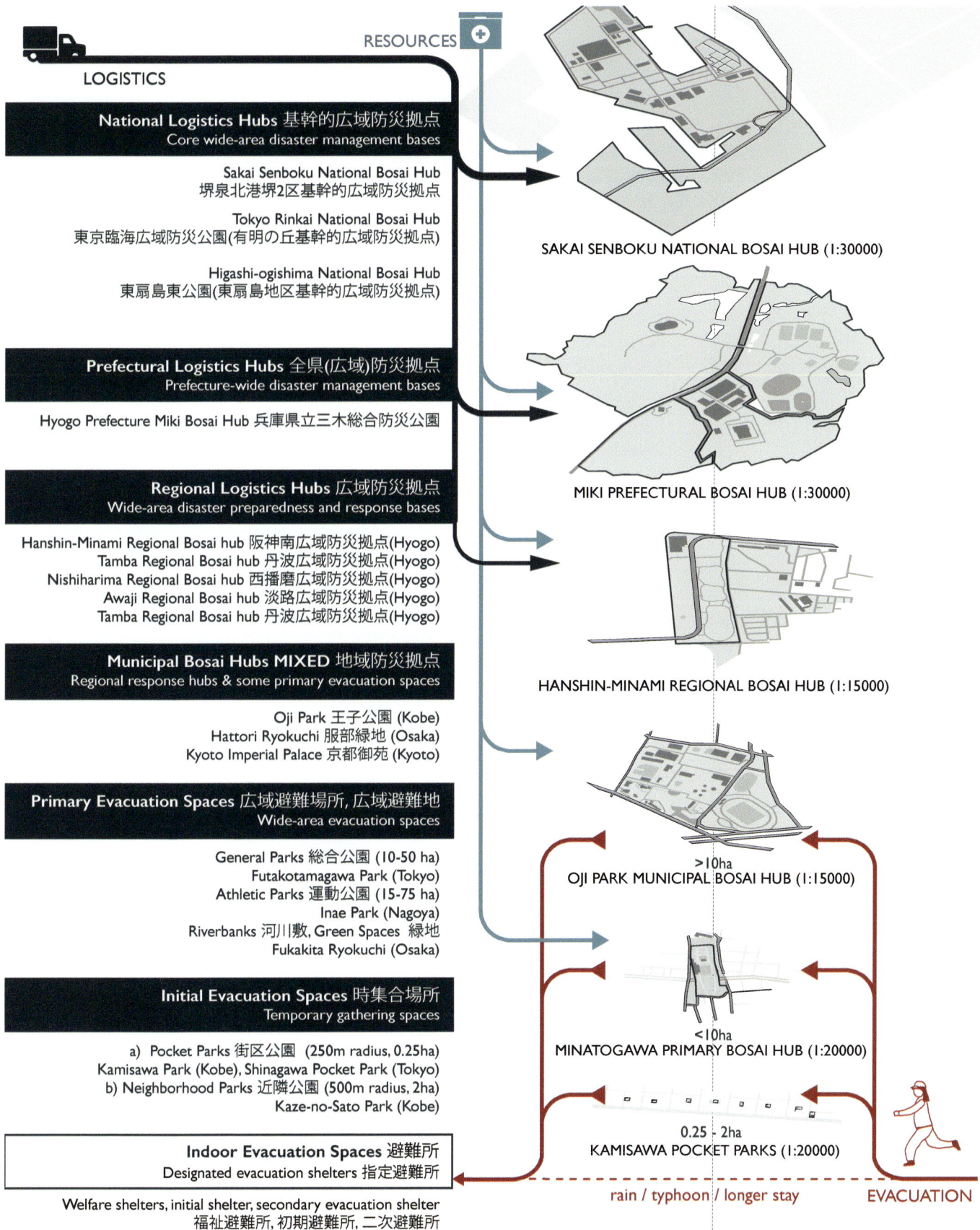

RESOURCES ⊕

LOGISTICS

National Logistics Hubs 基幹的広域防災拠点
Core wide-area disaster management bases

Sakai Senboku National Bosai Hub
堺泉北港堺2区基幹的広域防災拠点

Tokyo Rinkai National Bosai Hub
東京臨海広域防災公園(有明の丘基幹的広域防災拠点)

Higashi-ogishima National Bosai Hub
東扇島東公園(東扇島地区基幹的広域防災拠点)

SAKAI SENBOKU NATIONAL BOSAI HUB (1:30000)

Prefectural Logistics Hubs 全県(広域)防災拠点
Prefecture-wide disaster management bases

Hyogo Prefecture Miki Bosai Hub 兵庫県立三木総合防災公園

MIKI PREFECTURAL BOSAI HUB (1:30000)

Regional Logistics Hubs 広域防災拠点
Wide-area disaster preparedness and response bases

Hanshin-Minami Regional Bosai hub 阪神南広域防災拠点(Hyogo)
Tamba Regional Bosai hub 丹波広域防災拠点(Hyogo)
Nishiharima Regional Bosai hub 西播磨広域防災拠点(Hyogo)
Awaji Regional Bosai hub 淡路広域防災拠点(Hyogo)
Tamba Regional Bosai hub 丹波広域防災拠点(Hyogo)

HANSHIN-MINAMI REGIONAL BOSAI HUB (1:15000)

Municipal Bosai Hubs MIXED 地域防災拠点
Regional response hubs & some primary evacuation spaces

Oji Park 王子公園 (Kobe)
Hattori Ryokuchi 服部緑地 (Osaka)
Kyoto Imperial Palace 京都御苑 (Kyoto)

>10ha
OJI PARK MUNICIPAL BOSAI HUB (1:15000)

Primary Evacuation Spaces 広域避難場所, 広域避難地
Wide-area evacuation spaces

General Parks 総合公園 (10-50 ha)
Futakotamagawa Park (Tokyo)
Athletic Parks 運動公園 (15-75 ha)
Inae Park (Nagoya)
Riverbanks 河川敷, Green Spaces 緑地
Fukakita Ryokuchi (Osaka)

<10ha
MINATOGAWA PRIMARY BOSAI HUB (1:20000)

Initial Evacuation Spaces 時集合場所
Temporary gathering spaces

a) Pocket Parks 街区公園 (250m radius, 0.25ha)
Kamisawa Park (Kobe), Shinagawa Pocket Park (Tokyo)
b) Neighborhood Parks 近隣公園 (500m radius, 2ha)
Kaze-no-Sato Park (Kobe)

0.25 - 2ha
KAMISAWA POCKET PARKS (1:20000)

Indoor Evacuation Spaces 避難所
Designated evacuation shelters 指定避難所

Welfare shelters, initial shelter, secondary evacuation shelter
福祉避難所, 初期避難所, 二次避難所

rain / typhoon / longer stay   EVACUATION

spaces, thus creating the following interconnected hubs and parks (and the sections of this chapter are organized accordingly).

Logistics Hubs: Logistics hubs of varying kinds allow for spaces to be predetermined as sites for planning supply coordination in the event of a disaster. National hubs are established as the national disaster headquarters in collaboration with multiple prefectures when a catastrophic event occurs.[44] They administer high-level coordination and logistical support, such as accepting, sorting, and distributing emergency relief supplies from domestic and overseas sources. They also provide a base camp for the SDF, FDMA, Police Agency, and disaster medical support. Prefectural hubs allow for emergency management cooperation between prefectures and cross-jurisdictional relay bases for supplies. Regional hubs are parks that are fifty hectares or larger. During non-disaster times, national, prefectural, and regional bōsai hubs collect data and prepare plans that allow them to respond efficiently to a range of hazard types.

Mixed Bōsai Hubs: These are always ten hectares or larger and should provide two square meters of space for each potential evacuee. Many of the hubs operate primarily to coordinate emergency supply logistics, but some support a mixture of logistics operations and public evacuation to certain allocated zones.

Primary Evacuation Spaces: These are typically city parks that operate as the main gathering spaces for surrounding neighborhoods and have embedded infrastructure.

Initial Evacuation Spaces: These are neighborhood parks, typically a minimum of one hectare (including the streets surrounding the park) and pocket parks, that are identified as the first official point for evacuation.

The chapter includes a discussion of education in parks and environmental education, which provides a launching point for exploring how bōsaikōen might further embrace their bōsai roles on an everyday basis, improving awareness and action.

Logistics Hubs

After a catastrophic event, the disaster response resources of prefectures and local governments might be overwhelmed. Furthermore, hazards frequently impact multiple jurisdictions. Disasters do not respect political boundaries, and logistics hubs function not only at the urban scale but also at cross-prefectural and national scales, servicing wide rural areas and large urban agglomerations struck by seismic disasters, flooding, or other catastrophes. Transportation networks are also important for allowing goods and people to move smoothly between these hubs and communities after a disaster, especially if that disaster disrupts some typical circulation routes. While this large-scale logistical coordination may appear to be within the realm of emergency management professionals, the design of these networks—or more specifically, the spaces within these networks—is critical.

Hubs must be sited in locations least susceptible to hazards, avoiding liquefaction and floods, or must take substantial mitigation measures. National logistics hubs are sited with consideration of transport connections by land, sea, and sky so that the national government and local governments can seamlessly cooperate to carry out emergency responses. The geographical distance between the hubs must be carefully considered, too; if one of them is affected by the disaster and unable to function, others must be able to back it up. Of the seven national hubs currently in existence, coastal Higashi-ōgishima Park (Kawasaki, Kanagawa Prefecture) and Sakai Senboku Port (Sakai, Osaka Prefecture) are designed to accept and distribute supplies by sea or river, while the centrally located Tokyo Rinkai Park (Kōtō, Tokyo) is easily accessible to downtown Tokyo via road and helicopter.

As noted above, national, prefectural, and regional logistics hubs collect data and plan responses to a range of hazard types. These spaces also have everyday leisure and recreation functions for the broader public, ranging from park and sports facilities to spaces for bōsai training, but during a disaster they are never used for public evacuation. From the immediate moments after an alert, these large hubs operate as the coordination and camping areas for the SDF as well as distribution of domestic and international supplies. The design decisions for these spaces prioritize movements of helicopters and trucks. These large-scale facilities are carefully sited in locations with multiple points of access: air, sea, and highway. They also all work as a network of redundancy plans—with multiple forms of protection in tandem to support the nation.[1]

The 1995 Kobe earthquake brought true devastation, but it also provided a learning opportunity. When the tremor hit, real-time communication about the stricken area was difficult to receive, and there was no centralized place for relief efforts, including human and material resources, to use as a logistical hub. Standard municipal bōsaikōen (typically ten hectares) did not have sufficient space for these sorts of operations. Even those that were designated for logistical activities with landing pads were so full of people that helicopters could not land, making time-sensitive medical transport impossible.[2] While perhaps a less glamorous aspect of disaster preparedness and response, logistical arrangements are essential to saving lives and meeting emergency needs. In Kobe, these factors were further complicated by the scale of the event: response logistics were required for the Kobe municipality and the larger region in parallel. The disaster impacted multiple prefectures, necessitating multiscalar coordination of response by national, prefectural, and regional hubs.

Ultimately, large parks outside the center of Kobe as well as in other regions in Hyogo Prefecture were used to meet some of these logistical needs: Village of Happiness Kobe and Kobe Sports Park were used as the headquarters for the SDF operations, the emergency heliport, and the relief goods collection point. Miki Forest Park and Greenpia Miki Park became hubs for collecting and distributing emergency goods and, later, for reconstruction efforts. These sites, which are slightly outside of Kobe's city center, were selected because they were better suited to accepting large amounts of goods from elsewhere in Japan and had large, clear areas available for sorting materials and coordinating volunteers. Located on stable ground in inland sites, they were unaffected by the earthquake.

The operation of the large parks outside of Kobe as SDF logistics sites provided a precedent for the formal establishment of national and prefectural logistics hubs, the first of which was a prefectural logistics hub established in Miki. In response to the need for cross-prefectural coordination for large disasters, in June 2001 the central government created the policy for national logistics hubs to function as urban- or regional-scale coordination sites. The first created under this program was the two-part Tokyo Bay national logistics hub at Higashi-ōgishima Park (2008) and Tokyo Rinkai Park (2010).

NATIONAL LOGISTICS HUBS

Higashi-ōgishima Park and Tokyo Rinkai Park

Before the Kobe earthquake, the suburbs of Tokyo had three logistics bases, but since they were operated by different jurisdictions of the central government, they were siloed in their functions. None could operate as a comprehensive national logistics hub. They now all work in a network with the new Tokyo Rinkai Park and Higashi-ōgishima Park at the center. The three previously existing logistics bases (Tachikawa, Saitama, and Yokohama) operate in tandem with the new central hub, each with a role in the redundancy plan.

In 2001 the Metropolitan Bōsai Base Improvement Council, which is the institutional infrastructure consisting of prefectures and municipalities within the greater Tokyo region, specified that in order to protect the city, multiple hubs needed to be sited twenty to thirty kilometers apart to ensure that they were not simultaneously damaged in the event of a disaster. The council establishes regional plans and management policies outlining what each government agency or prefecture would be responsible for if disaster should strike.[3] Each site should be accessible by various transportation networks, including land, sea, and air, because the hub oversees the larger metropolitan agglomeration including Saitama, Chiba, and Kanagawa Prefectures.[4] For those reasons the Tokyo Bay waterfront was selected as the main site, taking advantage of the redundant transportation networks: highway connections, major rivers for transporting rations inlands, and several ports to receive overseas relief supplies, as well as Haneda International Airport, Tokyo Heliport, and Yokohama Heliport to secure air routes.

The Tokyo Bay national logistics hubs are the central command and distribution center, but given spatial constraints, they are sited in two parts: a communication and personnel headquarters near the city center at Tokyo Rinkai and a coastal hub for receiving and distributing goods by water at Higashi-ōgishima. These bōsai hubs not only function during disasters but also serve the public every day, as leisure spaces and/ or spaces for disaster-related education and training. As such, Tokyo Rinkai provides a jogging track and disaster education facility, and Higashi-ōgishima serves as a waterfront recreation park.

Located in Kawasaki just to the south of Tokyo and on the waterfront built from reclaimed land in 1990, the 15.8-hectare Higashi-ōgishima Park serves as a hub for emergency goods distribution.[5] With its proximity to the Kawasaki port, it can receive and coordinate supplies arriving from abroad, transitioning resources from maritime to local road and river delivery. In collaboration with local agencies, it functions as the center of an aquatic delivery network, with reinforced docks and roads along Tokyo's rivers. Following a disaster, the park will process, sort, and dispatch relief supplies. This park also contains a helipad and serves as a site for first responders.[6] Normally, the park at Higashi-ōgishima can be used by the general public to swim and sunbathe at the artificial beach and grassy recreation areas. The area's plan was based on a simulation of the 1605 Keichō Earthquake. After an anticipated 8.5-magnitude earthquake, Higashi-ōgishima expects a tsunami of between 2 and 3.71 meters (depending on the tide height).[7] In the event of a tsunami, visitors can use one of the five evacuation buildings on the island.

Tokyo Rinkai Park works in collaboration with the Higashi-ōgishima distribution center to dispatch necessary goods and services to disaster-impacted sites. The

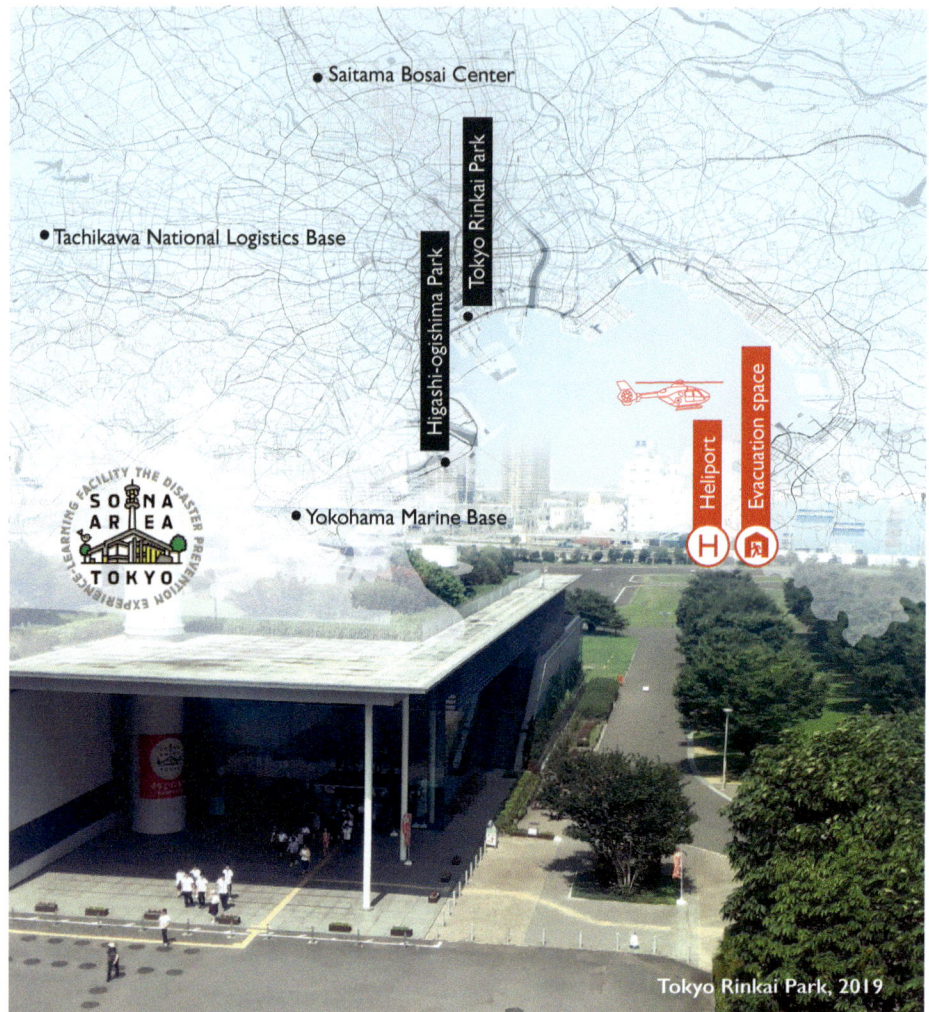

Figure 39. Tokyo Rinkai Park working in tandem with Higashi-ōgishima Park and three additional logistics bases.

13.2-hectare Tokyo Rinkai opened to the public in July 2010. Although it features emergency facilities (such as manhole toilets, cooking benches, pergola shelters, lamp-post power stations, and LAN communications) used for drills and educational activities on regular days, Tokyo Rinkai is not an evacuation space: any visitors will be asked to leave the park following a disaster to make way for essential operational functions.[8] Evacuees will move to the Ariake Forest Park nearby, or, during inclement weather, to the Tokyo Big Sight exhibition center, which is a designated evacuation shelter.[9] The SDF and other relief teams will enter after the park is cleared of civilians.

The park is centrally located and easily accessible by helicopters; it lies five hundred meters from the coast and around seven kilometers from Tokyo Station, which is close to the seat of the national government. Drills are conducted to facilitate these connections, and the heliport has undergone ground-stabilization liquefaction countermeasures. When a large-scale disaster occurs in the metropolitan area, the Tokyo metropolitan local emergency headquarters will activate in the building and operate a base camp for emergency response, including a medical relief site serving local and national service organizations, the SDF, and firefighters and police. Gridded tree plantings provide shade and help create a zoning system for medical relief.[10] Roads within the park are paved to allow for ambulance and emergency vehicle access. The headquarters building is outfitted with emergency generators, seven days' worth of food and water supplies, and a disaster-prepared communications network (including landlines and satellite) to communicate with the ministry and prefectural and local governments. The building is a seismically isolated structure, and surrounding paved areas are designed to resist liquefaction through the use of the "cement deep mixing" method.[11]

The park tends to be quiet, with occasional picnickers or elderly walkers on the exercise circuit, but the indoor educational facility is always buzzing with visitors, from tourists to school groups. Tokyo Rinkai Park's emergency headquarters building is equipped with an experiential learning facility with programs emphasizing disaster-preparedness information for both international and local visitors. The main attraction is an earthquake simulation tour operated by MLIT. Participants use a tablet for an interactive experience, answering questions as they walk through a mock-up of a large-scale metropolitan earthquake. Visitors begin the tour by entering an elevator, where they are jolted by a startling earthquake simulation. Eerie emergency lights and cacophonous sounds guide their passage through the darkness until they arrive outside and see the disaster-stricken neighborhood. Walking through debris and answering questions on the tablet, visitors arrive at the evacuation area, where displays demonstrate emergency paraphernalia and examine the importance of mutual-assistance principles. The whole experience can be jarring—and thus memorable. The upper floor includes an exhibit showcasing the various data concerning what a large-scale metropolitan earthquake might look like; projection mapping and multilingual infographics explain evacuation procedures and how to register as a disaster victim. An exhibit of self-help techniques requiring only simple craft skills instructs visitors how to make a sling out of a plastic bag or a tent out of clothes-drying posts, a tarp, and plant pots. At the end of the trip, visitors can peer into the Emergency Operation Center.

Sakai Senboku Port and the Floating Dock in Osaka Bay

Similar to the network around Tokyo, the western urban agglomeration, which includes the Kyoto, Kobe, and Osaka metropolitan areas, has established a regional network of bōsaikōen and logistics hubs linked by durable transportation routes. This is called the Keihanshin Metropolitan Area Extensive Logistics Hub. Coordination between multiple spaces and government bodies is particularly important in this sprawling, urbanized area, where dense urban districts can cross multiple prefectural boundaries.

The Keihanshin Region contains the national logistics hub called Sakai Senboku Port in Osaka, which was created in 2012 at a cost of ¥26.4 billion. This hub was set up to deal with large-scale disasters, especially those involving the Tōnankai and Nankai Trough earthquakes and Keihanshin inland earthquakes.[12] The site serves as a 27.9-hectare waterfront green recreation space,[13] and in the event of a major disaster, the same site will be used for the base camp and staging areas for regional support units, domestic and foreign NGOs, the heliport, emergency vehicles, emergency equipment storage, and coordination of emergency supplies. For coastal access, the earthquake-resistant quay wall (130 meters long and 7.5 meters deep) is supposed to be used for easy acceptance and distribution of goods by water.[14]

The hub also features a unique floating bōsai base.[15] Typically, this 80-by-40-meter floating dock is located in the Osaka Port at Universal Studios Japan (USJ), serving as "Universal City Port," a docking station for the Captain Line shuttle cruiser between Universal City and the aquarium on the opposite side of the port. In the event of a disaster, the dock is towed to the Sakai Senboku Logistics Hub (15 kilometers away).[16] The 4-meter-high floating structure includes storage areas for 200,000 water bottles, helipad spaces, and a detachable roof, which can be removed during a disaster. Senboku Port was dredged to better accommodate the floating dock and relief ships with up to 1,000 tons of cargo, and it was outfitted with cranes to unload supplies and a secure warehouse for storing relief goods.[17]

As uniquely interesting as the combination of USJ and national logistics hubs is, the designs of the actual park and the floating dock are wanting. The program and description of the design evoke potential in such partnerships and are better left to the imagination of the reader. Unfortunately, the floating base was designed and built only for calmer waters in the inner bay, so it could not be used to respond to 2011's triple disaster because it could not travel in the choppy open waters of the Pacific Ocean. In comparison, the 80-by-24-meter float from Hokkaido was built to transport goods and was thus outfitted with a thick steel frame; it transported relief supplies to Fukushima Prefecture ports and was used as a mooring facility in Sōma until October 2011.[18]

PREFECTURAL LOGISTICS HUB

Miki Sōgō Bōsaikōen in Hyogo

The Miki Sōgō Bōsaikōen is the first prefectural logistics hub in Japan and is designed to serve the entire Hyogo Prefecture. The siting drew upon lessons learned from the

1995 earthquake, where peri-urban parks were more easily able to accept resources from outside the city and deliver them to local nodes. The 202.5-hectare facility is connected to Kobe by highways perpendicular to the more densely populated urban coastline, and it avoids the Nojima fault that runs down Kobe's spine as well as the Yamazaki fault. To ensure that the hub does not become damaged during future earthquakes, officials sited it on more stable ground outside the city, and its distance from the coast makes it less vulnerable to typhoons.[19]

Miki Sōgō Bōsaikōen is unique in its emphasis not only on everyday recreation and the preparedness functions associated with post-disaster, prefecture-scale resource distribution but also on disaster training in non-disaster times. It hosts the Hyogo Prefectural Emergency Management Training Center along with the Hyogo Earthquake Engineering Research Center (and is the only such site to include research).[20] Through this diverse programming, the park operates throughout the disaster timeline—from immediate response and early recovery roles, to research and other programs that increase overall mitigation capacity, to education programming that helps improve community preparedness.

The Hyogo Earthquake Engineering Research Center includes a three-dimensional, full-scale earthquake testing facility (also known as "E-Defense"), one of the world's largest shaking tables for testing structural seismic resistance. During the Kobe earthquake, many buildings and infrastructures that were thought to be earthquake resistant collapsed. The 3-D shaking table more accurately simulates the possible ways a temblor could shake and can reproduce the patterns of past earthquakes. This allows the system to be used to design and test improved earthquake-resilient structures, including buildings of up to six stories, which are able to simulate an earthquake's effect on twenty-story buildings by using spring foundations.[21] However, the facility is quite expensive to operate, with annual maintenance costs of around ¥2.4 billion (as of 2013).[22]

On regular days, the park serves as a major regional sports and recreation center. Facilities include baseball and soccer fields as well as indoor spaces such as a stadium and a gymnasium. These large indoor and outdoor spaces also fulfill post-disaster needs, accommodating large numbers of personnel. Switching between everyday and emergency functions is facilitated by the architecture. For example, the stadium, designed by the firm AXS SATOW, is configured to be efficiently dual-purpose: connected by large garage doors giving trucks access for accepting supplies, it can be used for sorting, packing, and redistributing supplies in the field during a disaster. The 5,000-square-meter area underneath the stadium seats holds 53,300 alpha rice packets, 68,000 blankets, 3,640 blue tarps, 45,700 diapers, 790 temporary toilets, and 397 tents (as of September 1, 2014).[23] The "Beans Dome" tennis facility, designed by Endo Shuhei, is a vast, bean-shaped dome clad in vegetation. A continuous interior space is made possible by a steel space-frame structure, and the central tennis court is sunk into the earth to create separation between the courts. Large glass panels at the base of the

Figure 40 (*next page*). The Miki Sōgō Bōsaikōen is the first prefectural logistics hub in Japan with multiple dual-use spaces.

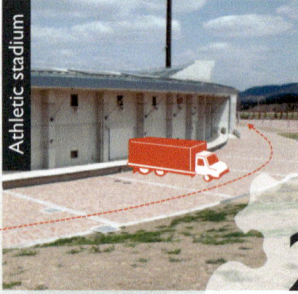

Athletic stadium

Running track
Supply distribution
Loading dock

20k evacuees

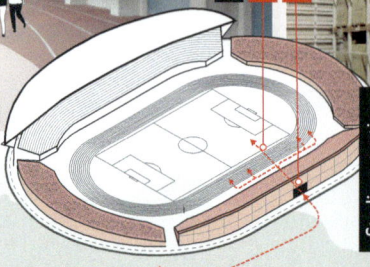

Stadium seating

5,000sqm supply storage

68k blankets

45.7k diapers

3.64k blue tarps

53.3k packs of alfa rice

397 tents

790 temporary toilets

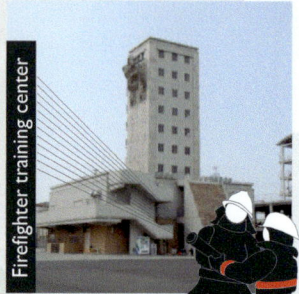

Firefighter training center

Kobe city center

Highway access to Kobe

National Self-Defense Force
Earthquake testing facility

Emergency info dispersal & monitoring center
Firefighting academy

Supply storage & distribution
Athletic stadium

Accommodation for relief workers
Tennis court

Heliport
Soccer field

Accommodation for relief workers
Soccer fields

Heliport
Baseball field

202.5ha
Miki Disaster Management Park
and Research Center

Figure 41. Miki "E-Defense," March 29, 2007. The facility is testing the effect of a magnitude 8.0 earthquake on the top two stories of a six-story building (using a rubber base isolation system to simulate the sway).

building can be removed following a disaster to allow relief vehicles to drive directly inside.[24] Roof louvers can open to bring in fresh air if people are sheltering inside, and ovaloid skylights above each court provide natural lighting if electricity is disrupted. The green walls also help regulate the building's climate, limiting the need for heating and cooling.[25]

Besides daily use for major sports and recreation, Miki Sōgō Bōsaikōen serves as a space for citizens to learn about disaster preparedness, engaging the broader public with the park's bōsai functions. Features include a Disaster Preparedness Library and education space where people can learn from simulated disasters such as earthquakes. The site also puts on the annual Hyogo bōsai leadership course, which trains 120 bōsai leaders for emergency relief and response efforts as well as evacuation procedures.[26] The park celebrates National Bōsai Day with annual drills focusing on response activities for residents and with experiences that involve rescuing survivors, performing first aid, and setting up shelter operations. In cooperation with the fire department, families can also enjoy games related to extinguishing fires and tightrope walking, bōsai quizzes, emergency calls, and the SI 7 earthquake experience.[27] Every year, over 2,000 participants gather for the event and receive hands-on bōsai education. Adjacent spaces offer additional disaster-preparedness programming, including a series of events to simulate realistic disaster scenarios. In a truck set up to depict the inside of a kitchen, for example, participants must crawl under the table and turn off the gas once

Figure 42. Earthquake drills for the public at Miki Sōgō Bōsaikōen.

the shaking stops. They learn preparedness strategies by rehearsing evacuation protocols, such as crawling with their noses and mouths covered to escape from a building on fire (reproduced by plumes of dry ice), as well as firefighting techniques.[28]

DISCUSSION

Bōsaikōen networks in Japanese cities facilitate the movement of resources from large, centrally planned logistics hubs to local bodies and communities in need. Spatial designers have a role to play in terms of how these networks and associated spaces interface with the public and with post-disaster operational systems. Miki Park illustrates how architectural features like dynamic stadiums can facilitate switching between disaster and everyday functions. Siting is also a design consideration, with complex and interrelated factors; for example, while coastal sites facilitate water-based resource distribution, they are also more vulnerable to inundation via storm surge, sea level rise, or tsunami. Similarly, while urban sites are central, they may be difficult for deliveries to reach post-disaster and they may be spatially constrained, such as the hub in Tokyo (which is split into two sites). On the other hand, larger rural sites might lack everyday interconnection with the public. Parks like Miki combat this with extensive public programs, research and training facilities, and the construction of regional stadiums.

Despite the mandate from the central government for public use of the space, these programs must be more broadly considered, not treated as a checklist item or an obligation. Dual-use design principles encourage more creative, bottom-up design approaches, which explore mutually beneficial uses for sites. Discussions began in 2012 for additional national logistic hub locations in Kyushu[29] and, more recently, in central Japan near Nagoya in 2020.[30] Hopefully these will incorporate better dual-use strategies, especially in light of Japan's high land prices and the sizable investments these large hubs require.

Mixed Bōsai Hubs

Logistically oriented bōsai hubs and evacuation-oriented bōsaikōen typically occupy separate spaces in order to keep evacuees from disrupting logistical functions (and vice versa). Mixed bōsai hubs are parks where both logistics and evacuation-oriented functions are co-located, though they still occupy different areas to avoid disruption and collision. Managed mostly at the municipal or prefectural level, part of the park is allocated for the general public's primary evacuation space; most of it is used as a supply distribution site and as rescue and relief headquarters, allowing firefighters, police, and the SDF to coordinate with national and prefectural hubs. Embedded within communities, these mixed hubs can best identify local needs and then make requests to larger logistics hubs for supplies or services, directing the right materials and personnel to local schools and parks and eventually to communities. They are sited with direct transportation routes to other logistics hubs and evacuation spaces, thus taking into consideration post-disaster accessibility when some routes are blocked.

These multifunctional spaces illustrate the potential of both an everyday and post-disaster framework for anticipatory design along with the coordination of top-down logistics networks and the bottom-up design of pocket parks. Since catastrophic disasters are rare events, these hubs are typically dual-function; spatial design is particularly significant when considering the effectiveness of bōsai hubs as everyday spaces. Some of the cases studied here have been more effective than others in this respect.

BŌSAIKŌEN INFRASTRUCTURE

Bōsaikōen are embedded with infrastructure that provides resilient duplicates for lifelines often disrupted during a disaster: water, power, sanitation, food services, and communications. Many of these components also have everyday recreation and leisure uses within the park. For example, some benches house cookstoves to be activated when an emergency requires feeding large groups of people. Other benches serve as storage for emergency supplies. Pavilions can be turned into enclosed tents for medical or organizational uses, through unrolling tarps stored in the eaves or adding side or roof panels. In some cases, swing sets or play structures can also provide frames for installing larger tents. Though ponds or streams cannot provide drinking water, they can be used in other ways, such as in fighting fires. Some park structures transform in use

Figure 43. Dual-use furniture and types of infrastructure for bōsaikōen.

Bench — Kamado cooking bench
USD$3,000
Cooking equipment
Furnace

Bench — Supply storage
USD$3,000
operable top

Manhole cover — Emergency toilet
USD$2,000
Portable enclosure
Toilet stool
Manhole cover

Lamp — Off-grid power
USD$18,000
Solar panel

Speaker — Information
USD$3,000

Gate — Fire shower barrier

Water pump — Water supply
USD$3,000

Pool pond — Water supply storage

Open space — Underground water tank

Pavilion — Emergency shelter
USD$50,000

Play structure — Evacuation shelter

Play structure — Evacuation space

but not in form: a baseball diamond or running track might double as a helipad. Loud-speakers can be used for event music and everyday announcements and can broadcast emergency messages after a disaster.[1] The use of park infrastructure is often practiced during annual drills or "bōsai events" organized by city governments.

Some embedded infrastructures remain hidden unless a disaster strikes, such as below-grade, earthquake-resistant water tanks or emergency generators. Manhole toilets, marked on a normal day by rows of steel plates flush with the grass, can be outfitted with seats and tents and serve as emergency toilets. Both the potable water systems and toilets are most often linked to a municipal pipe with a system that closes it off should an earthquake occur. Other attributes that simply make these parks appealing also contribute to their post-disaster role, such as having good connections to multiple transportation routes or being accessible to those with special needs. Solar-powered lights keep parks safely lit at night and can continue to serve as post-disaster emergency lighting, since they do not rely on the electrical grid. To help protect these spaces from fire, the parks are often landscaped with fire-resistant trees and shrubs around the perimeter; parks in a flood or tsunami zone might include evacuation hills. These features, when designed with care, also contribute to the overall landscape design and everyday performance of the parks.

REGIONAL BŌSAI HUBS

Oji Zoo and Park, Kobe

Oji Park comprises the Oji Zoo and the Oji Sports Center (a football stadium and track, tennis courts, swimming pool, indoor sumo wrestling ground, and gymnasiums). The park is located 3 kilometers away from the Kobe city center and on a major railway line. Because of its easily accessible location, the park is very popular; annual visitors to the zoo and the sports center top 1.5 million and 400,000, respectively.[2]

In the immediate aftermath of the 1995 earthquake, Oji Park was used in numerous ways. The park became an emergency evacuation site; the gymnasium was used as a shelter; and the 68,000-square-meter zoo housed the SDF tents. The helipad was used for medical and emergency relief supply coordination. The 15,000-square-meter football stadium served as a temporary morgue, and the 6,000-square-meter field was used for temporary housing.[3] Some residents complained about the noise of the helicopter, but given the park's prime location and the rarity of disasters, the park is now officially designated as the emergency evacuation space for earthquake, tsunami, and fire events. The indoor facility of the Oji Sports Center is designated as an evacuation shelter for landslide, flood, and tsunami events,[4] the Oji Zoo is the logistics hub for land transportation, and the football stadium is the helipad for the SDF.[5]

Kyoto Imperial Palace

The Kyoto Imperial Palace, originally built in 794, was the home of the Japanese imperial family until the Meiji Restoration shifted the capital to Tokyo in 1869. It remains an active palace. The surrounding Imperial Park is a public oasis that, as of 2014, doubles as a prefectural operation bōsai hub. Sited at the center of Kyoto's dense fabric, this hub is unique for its immensely touristic, historic, and sacred location. During a disaster, the 65-hectare park, which typically draws tourists visiting the Imperial Palace and serves as a site for general urban recreation, becomes a logistical hub and post-disaster headquarters for relief and recovery. In addition to storing supplies and hosting rescue workers, this prefectural hub will distribute food and other supplies to local hubs as requested.[6]

Portions of the park are adapted for specific post-disaster functions. For example, the Tominokōji sports ground serves as the heliport; an adjacent open space is designated as the FDMA hub.[7] Embedded infrastructure includes wells in the palace area and a supply of water via an underground tank and Demizu-no-ogawa stream; the eastern parking lot is punctuated with one manhole toilet per parking space. Gates are designed to accommodate emergency vehicles. The palace VIP guesthouse becomes the on-site post-disaster headquarters. The palace is outfitted with radio equipment via the Kyoto Disaster Defense Information System. If the entire palace is used only as an extended evacuation space (and not a logistics hub), then it can accommodate up to 173,500 evacuees. If it is also serving logistics functions, evacuees are directed to two smaller zones at the northern end of the palace.[8] The palace also plays a role in preparedness and training events for both disaster logistics teams and the general public.

MUNICIPAL BŌSAI HUBS

Hattori Ryokuchi Park

Another example of the combination of a logistical and evacuation-ready hub is Hattori Ryokuchi Park in the northern part of Osaka. This 126.3-hectare green space opened as one of the four air defense green spaces in 1941 in Osaka during World War II. The park is designated as a landscape district, lush with more than ten ponds and wetlands, forests and hills, and a large round flower bed. It is hydrologically connected to two rivers, originally as an overflow area to prevent flooding of the Taka River. It also has attractions such as a museum of old Japanese farmhouses, an amphitheater, a horse-riding center, several playgrounds, a barbecue area, and various sports fields. The park is popular throughout the year with residents living in the neighborhood, who visit regularly to see cherry blossoms, exercise, picnic, and play with their

Figure 44 (*next page*). Kyoto Imperial Palace evacuation sites, showing their planned use during the hours and days after a disaster and their embedded dual-use infrastructure.

Kyoto Imperial Palace

Facilities and wells

National Emergency Operations HQ

Omiya Palace

Facilities and wells

Helipad

Kan-in-no-miya Museum

Site evacuation map

Days/ weeks

Immediately after

Few hours/days after

children. In addition, numerous volunteer groups create events in which children interact and learn about preserving wetlands and caring for woodlands through adventure playgroups, agriculture, and nature schools.[9]

However, Hattori Ryokuchi Park can quickly transform into a bōsai hub in the event of an earthquake or fire. The logistics support is under the jurisdiction of the Osaka prefectural emergency response headquarters, the SDF Osaka Northeast district unit, and the Osaka Prefecture Fire Department's north branch, while the evacuation site for citizens is coordinated by the cities of Toyonaka and Suita. Five power generators in the park can provide electricity for the entire park for seventy-two hours, and recently renovated bathrooms in the evacuation site are equipped with manhole toilets on the exterior, tripling their capacity. All of the speakers in the park are earthquake resistant, and vending machines provide free beverages in the event of a disaster.

Good BBQ, a popular outdoor restaurant filled with customers in nice weather, is a cornerstone of the park. Iconic roofs cover the shared sinks, while long tables have embedded stone-lined barbecue pits or grills to the side. Users can purchase barbecue meats and drinks at the entrance to combine with other delicacies brought from home. According to an agreement with Osaka, in the event of a disaster, the whole facility will become an emergency kitchen that will provide meals and lend BBQ equipment to evacuated citizens. Shigeyuki Masuda, who is in charge of the BBQ plaza, has a ham radio license and has volunteered to inform the local government about evacuation shelter capacity in times of disaster.[10] Osaka has been holding "bōsai hiking" events since 2012, in which participating families locate disaster toilets and emergency generators in the park and experience a simulated flood using virtual reality, a demonstration of how to use an automated external defibrillator, a firefighting challenge for children introduced by the fire brigade, a no-matches fire building exercise in the BBQ plaza, and a disaster-preparedness quiz.[11] Those who participate collect stamps (very popular among children) at each location and are offered miso soup made in the BBQ plaza. The event is a unique example of popular daily use that is directly applicable to post-disaster use—and includes a commercial restaurant.

While Hattori Ryokuchi Park thus offers a good example of building bōsai culture, which Osaka tries to encourage through linking daily activities and bōsai knowledge, many of the residents are unaware that the park is a primary evacuation site. Interviews with various park visitors who live in the neighborhood and go to the park on a daily basis showed, unfortunately, that most of them thought that they would evacuate to the neighborhood elementary school in case of an earthquake or fire; they did not consider Hattori Ryokuchi Park as an evacuation site. One interviewee took a photo of the park evacuation area map to remember the evacuation areas. Many signs in the neighborhood state that Hattori Ryokuchi Park is an evacuation site, but within the park, none of the signs indicate where to go. Although about one hundred residents

Figure 45 (*next page*). Hattori Ryokuchi Park, with public education programs and dual-use evacuation sites.

Emergency power
Police dept area
Fire dept area
Evacuation spaces
Emergency bathroom
Logistics/supply storage
Heliport
Emergency power
SDF/JDF
Logistics
Evacuation shelter

Water supply station

BBQ table cooking

Public bathroom
Emergency manhole toilet

Water reservoir
Emergency water supply

Good BBQ food stand

Good
BBQ

Light along evacuation path

Emergency pavilion

Solar powered speaker

Vending machine, free during emergency

Bosai drills/training

take part in the annual "bōsai hike" in February, local governments must increase effective communication about disaster-preparedness efforts with the citizens.

This lack of awareness is not unique to Hattori Ryokuchi Park. For example, a large-scale survey in Kyoto, involving 2,267 interviews with the city's residents, showed similar results: 53 percent of the residents could not identify any of the seventy-six primary evacuation spaces in the city.[12]

Kumamoto Parks

A similar study was conducted after the 2016 Kumamoto earthquake, when only a few locals knew how to operate the park infrastructure during the evacuation. The 2016 earthquake was the first time that multiple earthquakes had hit a metropolitan city with a well-developed bōsaikōen network. The series of quakes had a mainshock magnitude of 7.3 and killed 273 people.[13] Immediately after each earthquake, the urban parks were used as emergency evacuation sites. A report by the Organization for Landscape and Urban Green Infrastructure analyzed the use of thirty-three parks based on interviews with local leaders and residents involved in park management. Most parks had recently conducted evacuation drills, and the study found that while local residents who had participated in evacuation drills evacuated smoothly, others from outside the neighborhood were not aware of designated evacuation spaces. Many evacuees who feared that an aftershock would cause their homes to collapse at night came to the park to sleep.[14]

Kumamoto experienced water supply disruptions for up to four days after the earthquake. Five of the parks studied had one-hundred-ton seismic water tanks, and all were used; four parks used water supply trucks and distribution tanks; nineteen distributed bottled water. Sanitation was provided using existing temporary toilets, portable toilets, and, in two parks, temporary toilets dug by hand. Two parks had manhole toilets, but only one was used—owing perhaps to older manhole covers having become rusty and stuck or to a lack of knowledge on how to operate the system. While four of the parks had *kamado* (cooking) benches, only one was used,[15] most likely because people did not know about them or know how to use them, or because most perishable foods had rotted by the time the organized relief meals ended. In other parks, local residents and volunteer organizations brought food and cooking materials to serve the community, but they did not use the *kamado* benches, either.[16]

The biggest change in behavior after the Kumamoto earthquake, compared to previous earthquakes, was the evacuation and sheltering in personal vehicles in parks. Residents worried about the possibility that aftershocks would cause further damage and did not feel safe remaining in their homes. Of the parks surveyed above, twenty-nine accepted vehicles.[17] The park gates were opened either by the community leader or by city officials. One difficulty the parks faced was that many evacuated in their cars so that they could bring belongings and have a place to sleep; however, the cars took up more room than the planned evacuation area of two square meters per person.[18] In some cases, adjacent facilities such as community halls, schools, and hospitals were also used by evacuees. Having the majority of people residing in cars created new complications around nighttime security, bathroom access, and communication with evacuees about resources and access to supplies.[19] Kumamoto currently has 24 primary emergency supply hubs and 147 local evacuation parks with emergency supply storage and other embedded lifeline infrastructures.[20]

NEW TYPOLOGIES

Given the scale and overwhelming devastation of 2011's triple disaster, many nontraditionally assigned locations had to serve as evacuation spaces in the immediate aftermath of the tsunami. One type of local facility that supported evacuees was the roadside rest areas, *michi-no-eki.* Typically, these government-sponsored rest areas offer local crafts, local produce, and delicacies for sale to tourists and the surrounding community. Most are located inland near highway interchanges and possess large parking lots.

Michi-no-eki Jōbon-no-Sato

After the 2011 Tohoku disaster, the *michi-no-eki* Jōbon-no-Sato in Ishinomaki provided food to affected neighbors. Since the power was out, they used emergency generators, flashlights, and calculators. After the water supply returned on March 24, the hot spring bath reopened to serve more than a thousand people daily—disaster survivors, construction workers, and volunteers.[21] Designed by Seki Kukan Sekkei, the baths, some of them outdoors, provided respite during the long and arduous days. The *michi-no-eki* also supported the recovery of livelihoods, allowing people to sell local products. In October 2013, Jōbon-no-Sato countersigned with Ishinomaki to cooperate officially in the event of a disaster.[22] This was the first time in Japan that a local government and a *michi-no-eki* signed a disaster agreement.

Since numerous *michi-no-eki* were used to support survivors, both after 2011 and after the 2016 Kumamoto earthquake, the national government officially designated *michi-no-eki* as temporary evacuation sites in the 2018 National Resilience Action Plan. This subsidized the installation of bōsai infrastructure such as emergency power generators, seismic water tanks, emergency storage, manhole toilets, and emergency communication systems.[23] As of February 2020, out of 1,160 *michi-no-eki* across the country, 500 were equipped with bōsai infrastructure.[24] In addition, during the fall of 2020, MLIT let prefectures designate 1 or 2 bōsai *michi-no-eki* as mixed bōsai hubs— functioning as initial evacuation destinations for residents as well as the regional

Figure 46. The Jōbon-no-Sato roadside rest area (*michi-no-eki*) functions as a new typology of evacuation space.

logistics base of recovery and reconstruction in the event of large-scale disasters. By August 2021, there were 39 officially designated bōsai hub *michi-no-eki* across thirty-six prefectures.[25]

Palette Pier Ōno

One such example is Palette Pier Ōno, in Gifu Prefecture, which originally opened in July 2018. Normally, this *michi-no-eki* is a public transportation hub; it includes a child-support facility (with play structures built from local timber) and a very popular restaurant with seasonal local goods and a bakery.[26] The parking lot of Palette Pier Ōno, which is equipped with a large potable water tank, can be used as an evacuation space for the first twenty-four hours; after that, evacuees are sent to the nearby school, and it serves the fire department, police, and heliport.[27] The iconic circular lawn, sixty meters in diameter—designed by Daiken Sekkei and representing the O for the town of Ōno—becomes the activity base for the SDF. For Gifu Prefecture, Palette Pier Ōno is one of the sixteen bōsai hubs for logistics support connected by the Tokai Ring Highway.[28]

DISCUSSION

With bōsai hubs taking on many shapes and programs—ranging from a zoo to the Imperial Palace grounds, from a regional park to *michi-no-eki*—and transitioning from

Figure 47. Palette Pier Ōno, an iconic bōsai hub that includes a child-support facility and a restaurant with seasonal local goods.

fully public resources to spaces shared between the SDF and the public, signage and other forms of communication with residents become especially important. As noted in the Hattori Ryokuchi Park example, public events and core programmatic locations such as the BBQ designed for both everyday and emergency use can help, but they are in themselves not enough. Better communication strategies are needed for targeting more mobile, younger generations as well as transient populations such as tourists or foreign workers. Anticipatory design research has great potential to help make infrastructures readily identifiable, from typological studies to the iconography of elements. More user testing and analysis are needed. Both spatial design and persistent, effective communication efforts are vital for ensuring that the components of these mixed spaces work optimally together.

Primary Evacuation Spaces

Compared to other aspects of Japanese disaster preparedness or mitigation, little has been written in English on bōsaikōen, particularly in terms of how national and urban policies manifest in communities. The term *bōsaikōen* can refer to nationally subsidized evacuation spaces of ten or more hectares (such as the two types of hubs previously discussed) or more generally to disaster preparedness parks, which are typically a minimum of one hectare. The diversity of bōsaikōen, which could be even further expanded to adapt to local cultures and ecologies, shows how bōsai spaces can come in many forms, especially in combination with educational programs. Primary evacuation spaces are typically located within a maximum walking radius of two kilometers from the population they are intended to serve, forming a network of parks across Japanese cities.[1] Ideally, they are accessed via evacuation routes that are at least ten meters wide,[2] and designs often include many possible entrance points. Although parks smaller than one hectare cannot receive national funding, municipalities can fund them. Some parks were even created by the surrounding communities themselves, and many are maintained by local residents, particularly retirees.

On most days, bōsaikōen simply serve as public spaces for the surrounding community—oases from extremely dense and chaotic Japanese cities. They are part of the daily lives of neighborhood residents, and this familiarity makes them even more effective during disasters. In order to help the public become increasingly familiar with the bōsai infrastructure in the parks, municipalities host multiple events. For example, drills are held annually on the anniversary of major disasters, such as January 17 in Kobe, March 11 in the Tohoku region, and September 1 throughout Japan. Some parks have additional bōsai events to engage children or use signage or media to further publicize their bōsai roles, which is critical for raising awareness. The large spatial and infrastructural investments in bōsaikōen are more easily justified when they serve their cities not only during disasters but also on an everyday basis.

TYPOLOGIES OF BŌSAIKŌEN

Rooftop

The Kobe Minatogawa Park is a large 2.3-hectare neighborhood park 7 meters above the ground at its highest point, and it is designated as a tsunami, earthquake, and fire evacuation space. It negotiates the topography of the site by resting on top of the Minatogawa Park station, clothing stores, restaurants, bars, a department store, a movie theater, and a large parking lot; a major arterial road passes under it.[3] Families and children fill the park on weekends, and the site is also a popular venue for events, such as music festivals and the Minatogawa Park Handicraft Market held every month.[4]

To make the park and the neighboring Hyogo Ward general office easily accessible to the elderly and those in wheelchairs, a new slope was installed at the northern park entrance. This improvement in 2019 also included a renovation of the building to create a 120-square-meter multipurpose area, with digital signage on the first floor and a Minatogawa citizens' hall on the second floor, as an indoor space for evacuees during a disaster.[5] This new interior space was allocated based on the experiences of the 1995 earthquake, after which the volunteer headquarters of Hyogo Ward were located in the park—the first official volunteer center in Kobe.[6] The park was also used for sheltering in informal tents for several years after the earthquake.

Memorial

The integration of both memorials and evacuation functions is also a component of parks built following the 2011 Tohoku disaster. The Millennium Hope Hills memorial park on the Sendai plain is operated by Iwanuma City in Miyagi.[7] It is sited atop land that was home to a village historically known for salt making. The village was destroyed by the tsunami, and signage details the story of this loss for visitors.

As of fieldwork in 2019, a total of six small parks and fifteen hills had been constructed from tsunami rubble covered with topsoil spread along ten kilometers of the coast. These hills and the series of parks are connected by a three-meter-high garden pathway. About 350,000 trees consisting of more than seventeen kinds of broad-leaved saplings were planted in the parks; in fifteen to twenty years, they will become a forest and will help mitigate tsunamis.[8] The project is led by the Tohoku Life-Saving Green Embankment Promotion Council, and tree planting was conducted by thousands of volunteers. The fifteen conical evacuation hills, ranging from eight to eleven meters high and sixty to one hundred meters in diameter, stand out in the otherwise flat expanse of floodplain surrounding Sendai.[9] Wheelchair-accessible ramps spiral around the perimeters of each hill, while steep evacuation stairs allow for a quick sprint to the top. The topography also creates space for play, where children roll and tumble down the grassy surfaces. Primary evacuation elements are provided on top of the hills, such as benches containing emergency goods, solar light charging stations, and a pavilion. The extended field can also be used as a heliport.

The six parks are designed to pass on the memories and lessons learned from the 2011 disaster to the next generation. Ainokama Park is a base for environmental conservation activities such as tree planting and nurturing as well as for the bōsai education days, when tsunami survivors share their memories with visitors. Ninokura Park has

Figure 48 (*next page*). The various stages and roles of bōsaikōen defined by the Ministry of Land, Infrastructure, Transport and Tourism (MLIT).

0 PREPARATION

Before a disaster

Training, education and drills

1 LIFE SAFETY

Hours after a disaster

Used for evacuation, first aid, securing life, and preventing the spread of fire

2 SHELTER

Days after a disaster

Emergency relief site to secure water, food, energy, clothing, and a place for temporary evacuation

3 RECOVERY

Weeks after a disaster

Used as disaster headquarters with information for occupants to return home, shelter, or start reconstruction

4 RESTORATION AND RECONSTRUCTION

Parks serve as a base for reconstruction activities and some host temporary housing units

On the park

Playground

Sports

Omatsuri

Public restroom

Monument of the old Minatogawa ruins

Kobe City Hyogo Ward Office

Evacuation shelter

Helicopter landing

Fire department

ゆうあげ

たこやき

バルシネマ

湊川駅

Cinema

Eyeglasses shop

Barbershop

Karaoke

Bubble tea

Izakaya

Parking

Subway station

Underpass

Under the park

a sheep farm and vegetable farms run by Iwanuma and the Japan Youth Overseas Co-operation Association.

Public-Private Partnerships

Nakano-Shiki-no-Mori Park in Tokyo is a 1.5-hectare bōsaikōen developed in a public-private partnership urban-redevelopment district, allowing for different parts of the development to be financed and managed by multiple partners in a coordinated manner. The roads and Nakano-Shiki-no-Mori Park were acquired by the ward and developed using a machizukuri grant administered by MLIT.[10] The Park Avenue, a Wi-Fi-embedded twenty-four-meter-wide pedestrian space active with food trucks and events that bridges Nakano-Shiki-no-Mori Park and the business complex, was developed by Tokyo Tatemono Corporation.[11] These two open spaces were developed as an integrated cohesive area that can be used seamlessly in normal times as well as during a disaster.

This park is positioned as a part of the 110-hectare Nakano Station Area project, initiated by the Machizukuri Study Committee, the ward, and Tokyo Tatemono to create new businesses and a public facilities cluster, including a hospital and universities with a community bōsai focus.[12] As of this writing, the Nakano Ward office was to move to this site by fiscal year 2024. The whole area is located on a hilltop supported by the solid bedrock of the Musashino Plateau, reducing earthquake vulnerability and eliminating the possibility of liquefaction. The park is an official evacuation site for the ward and is further outfitted with an emergency generator, manhole toilets, battery charging stations, and wireless internet.[13] Water features in the park—a pond with interactive fountains and a playful stream channel—serve as a supplemental emergency water supply. Located near the JR line and new office buildings, the site bustles with families, students, and office workers, who flock to the popular food trucks that park along the southern edge of the site at lunchtime. During one springtime visit in 2018, the trees were in full bloom and people had spread tents and blankets across the lawn under falling cherry petals, with families picnicking and children playing in the grass.

The recent trend toward public-private partnerships for bōsaikōen helps offset the economic burden these large spatial infrastructures place on cities.[14] This allows for private interests to help support the redevelopment and management of public open spaces, though private companies want evidence of return on investment before committing. As private companies might be more focused on profit than preparedness, such partnerships risk ignoring high-vulnerability, low-income communities in favor of wealthier locales. Private developers may be more motivated by short-term revenue instead of long-term resilience, meaning that careful management and oversight will be required on the part of the government if these kinds of relationships are deemed useful.[15] The Nakano-Shiki-no-Mori Park example involved the machizukuri study

Figure 49. With dual-use programs above and below, Kobe Minatogawa Park negotiates the terrain to make this large public evacuation space accessible.

Cherry trees
Evacuation
Administration building
Emergency water supply
Emergency toilets
Water supply
Pond

Figure 50. Nakano-Shiki-no-Mori Park, developed in a public-private partnership.

committee, so it thoroughly considered both the everyday uses of the site and included businesses in the endeavor to strengthen the response to a potential disaster. But it is important to keep in mind that some public-private projects may end up with conflicting priorities.

Ecology

As rare green respites from the density of Japanese cities, some bōsaikōen have explored ecological roles. Connecting risk-mitigation functions (such as reducing flooding) and ecological functions (increasing groundwater infiltration as well as diversity of flora and fauna) contributes to larger resilience goals. Sound ecological systems able to absorb shocks are sustainable, good both for supporting the environment and for reducing disaster risk.

Futakotamagawa Park is a 6.3-hectare bōsaikōen that has received attention, including the best (AAA) rating of the Japanese Habitat Evaluation and Certification Program (JHEP) for biodiversity and ecosystem functions.[16] The park was planned alongside Futakotamagawa Rise, a commercial, office, and residential area, as part of an 11.2-hectare redevelopment project with the TMG, Setagaya Ward, and a consortium of private-sector players to reduce hazards in the region. The park's foliage includes native species; some species, like Kurogane holly (*Ilex rotunda*) and Chinese bayberry (*Myrica rubra*), are planted adjacent to residential areas to help stop the spread of fires. Built in conjunction with the Tama River embankment, a recreational path along the levee links to the park via a bridge over the adjacent road. Cherry and pine trees planted on the levee and riverbanks help prevent erosion. These trees also connect to local landscape heritage: the riverside is among the one hundred most beautiful Setagaya Ward landscapes noted by residents.[17] Included in this list is Kokubunji-Gaisen, a geological linear cliff landscape that runs parallel to the river on the other side of the park. Parts of Kokubunji-Gaisen remain undeveloped, as ecologically rich forest strips are home to freshwater springs and aquatic habitats for saw crabs, fireflies, and dragonflies.[18] The design of Futakotamagawa Park incorporates this and aims to restore the *satoyama* landscape (the communal zones between mountains and rice paddies). The park has approximately 7,000 square meters of forest with mixed broadleaf deciduous tree species that reflect the local *satoyama* environment.[19]

Completed in 2015, the redevelopment area including Futakotamagawa Park received a Gold Certification for LEED (Leadership in Energy and Environmental Design) Neighborhood Development. The ¥1.75 billion park also includes a Japanese garden, a bike path along the Tama River, a Mount Fuji viewing point, a children's area (including a book corner), and cafés and shops. Fifteen solar and wind-powered LED lights are located near the park entrances, along with evacuation routes and embedded infrastructures (for instance, sixty manhole toilets). Emergency wells around the park are used in non-disaster times to supply ponds and children's play areas. Systems to increase rainwater infiltration, such as permeable pavement (over 13,700 square meters), retention ponds and tanks (with the capacity of 5,500 cubic meters), and a sloped topography, lessen flood risk inside the park while reducing runoff and increasing groundwater absorption. The park can manage about 7,450 cubic meters of stormwater runoff, which exceeds the 1,000-cubic-meter-per-hectare management guideline set by Setagaya. Typhoon Hagibis in 2019 did not affect this park, but the surrounding area was flooded.

In addition to its ecological role, Futakotamagawa Park is also notable for the machizukuri planning process that brought together neighborhood associations, the

Figure 51 (*next page*). Futakotamagawa Park plays an important ecological role while functioning as a neighborhood evacuation space; the design considers multiple timelines.

3. Emergency temporary housing
4th week and onward

Temporary housing

2. Resource loading, water supply and cooking
4 days - 3 weeks

Water supply vehicle

Resource base

Kamado bench (12)

Bosai storage (2)

Chinese bayberry
(Myrica rubra)

I. Evacuation / gathering
up to 3 days after disaster

Manhole toilets (60)

Fire-resistant forest belt

Evac space (10,000ppl)

Water well (3)

Renewable power lights

Main evacuation route

Cherry & pine trees

Tama River

Water resource (160m³)

7,450m³ of stormwater runoff

*Kurogane holly
(Ilex rotunda)*

shōbōdan, and the Japanese Red Cross. Involving these stakeholders allowed for locally specific consideration of how the site would function in three stages after a seismic disaster. The group identified how the park could be used as an evacuation space for ten thousand people (days 1–3); as a resource and logistics base, including a soup kitchen with six cooking benches; for water and supply distribution (day 4 through week 3); and, if needed, as a site for temporary housing for one hundred families and thirty-two single people (from the fourth week onward).[20]

A multiphase community engagement process also ensured that Futakotamagawa Park's design for everyday use aligned with local needs and desires.[21] In 2009–10, the twenty-six-member Park Investigation Committee, formed by representatives of local organizations and community volunteers, used surveys, open houses, workshops, review meetings, and newsletters to involve local residents in the project and receive input. From 2010 to 2012, community workshops engaged themes surrounding park design and management; events included assisting with flower planting and sharing emergency-food meals. These efforts culminated with the creation of a Park Support Association, which focused on ecology, children, and safety.[22]

Flood Mitigation

Fukakita Ryokuchi Park in Osaka combines evacuation with flood mitigation. The 50.3-hectare park, sited on the Neya River, serves as a flood basin after heavy rains, helping accommodate expanded river volumes. A levee at the height of the river's embankment encircles the park, and the inside of the park is subdivided into three floodable zones based on rainfall intensity (according to flooding probabilities of once in three years, ten years, and thirty years). As each zone reaches its capacity, it overflows into the next zone. The park can accommodate a total of 1,460,000 cubic meters of water.[23] Since the opening of the park in 1982, the Neya River has flooded about twenty times,[24] with the worst events in 1999, 2013, 2018, and 2021, when all three zones were submerged. The park prevented the inundation of the surrounding neighborhoods in all of these events.[25] All of the park amenities were inaccessible to the public until the water level receded to its normal height. In the 2021 event, once the river subsided around midnight, the water gate in Zone A was opened to release water back into the Neya River slowly, to avoid downstream flooding, and Zones B and C were opened the next morning. Zone A, the wetland zone, was closed to the public for the next ten days.[26]

The park also serves as a primary evacuation site to protect residents in case of a fire. However, this raises a concern shared by many: a lack of clarity about when to evacuate there. If residents mistakenly come to Fukakita Ryokuchi Park during a flood, they risk being caught in the waters themselves—running toward the danger rather than away from it. (For example, the heliport is located in a zone floodable once every ten years.)[27]

Figure 52. Fukakita Ryokuchi water retention park, with three zones designed for everyday activities, evacuation, and inundation.

50.3ha
Fukakita Ryokuchi Park

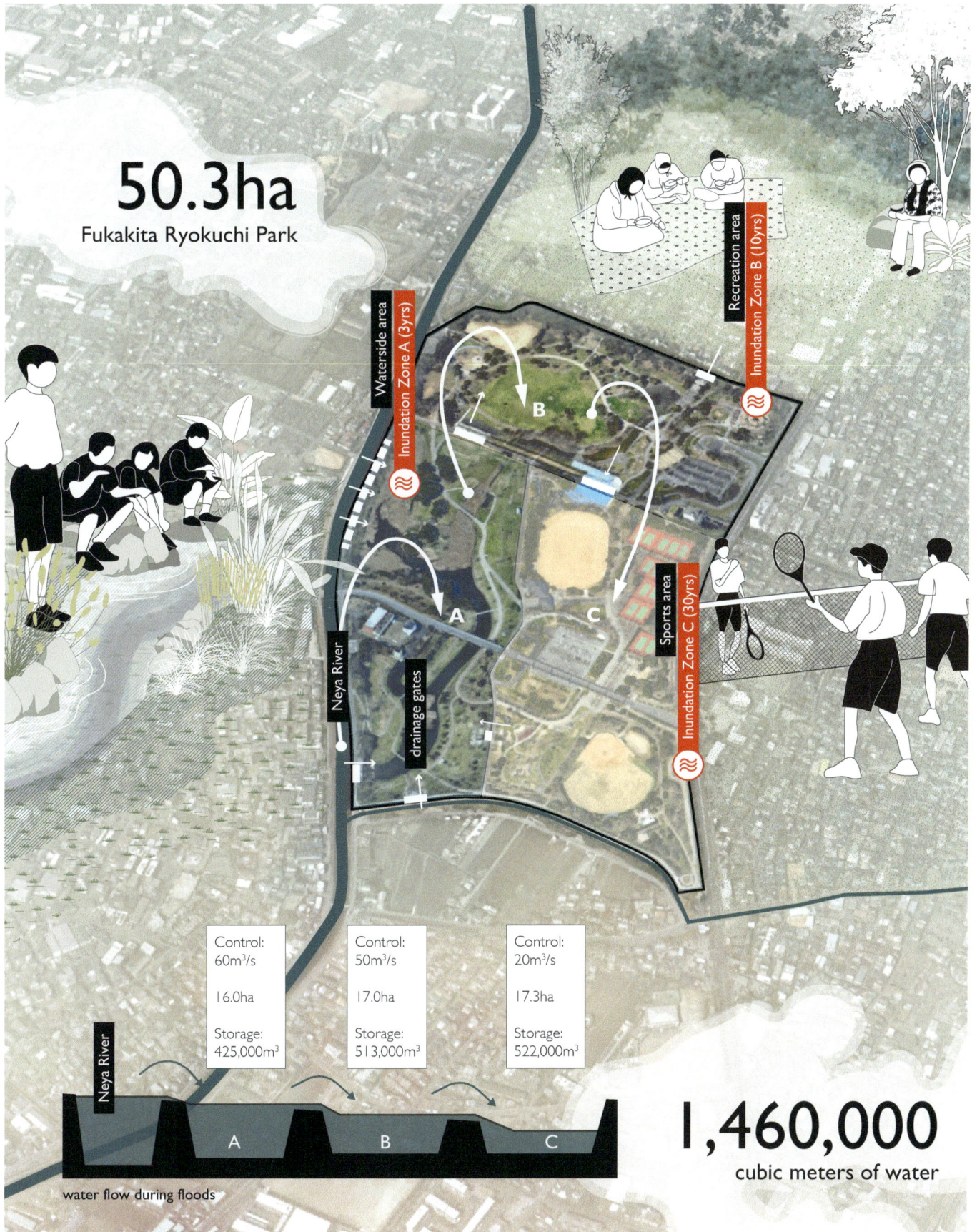

Waterside area
Inundation Zone A (3yrs)

Recreation area
Inundation Zone B (10yrs)

Sports area
Inundation Zone C (30yrs)

Neya River

B

A

C

drainage gates

Control: 60m³/s	Control: 50m³/s	Control: 20m³/s
16.0ha	17.0ha	17.3ha
Storage: 425,000m³	Storage: 513,000m³	Storage: 522,000m³

Neya River

A   B   C

water flow during floods

1,460,000
cubic meters of water

For the most part, during typhoons and riverine floods, people are instructed to go directly to the nearest (flood-safe) designated indoor shelter, which is usually a local public school gymnasium or a civic sports hall, not outdoor evacuation spaces. But for parks like this, which are a safe haven for one type of disaster but dangerous during another, communication surrounding safe emergency action is of particular importance.

DISCUSSION

In June 2013, the Disaster Countermeasures Act was revised so that the municipality would designate each park or facility according to the type of disaster and develop signs based on the Hazard Specific Evacuation Guidance Sign System.[28] Ideally, bōsai-kōen and associated shelters would be safe from all of the hazards an area faces, so that evacuees do not need to select the appropriate park to which to flee dependent on the type of disaster. But this is challenging in a country faced with so many disparate hazards; in the meantime, proper education and communication are essential.

The diversity of the bōsaikōen discussed above suggests a range of possibilities in scale, development processes, park emphasis, and design details. There is no single formula for embedding disaster preparedness into landscapes. While top-down policies can limit the adaptability of bōsaikōen design, distinct features of each park respond to its context, from flood prevention in Fukakita Ryokuchi Park to the elevated evacuation spaces of Minatogawa Park. Public-private collaborations, as in Nakano-Shiki-no-Mori Park, can respond to criticism that bōsai infrastructure is unjustifiably expensive,[29] though it is important that private collaborations are regulated to ensure that they continue to meet local needs.

The parks in this section, in particular, were selected for their unique features, illustrating the variety and potential of this model. However, fieldwork documenting more than fifty bōsaikōen revealed that for the majority, the potential to adapt to their physical and social contexts might be limited by standards and requirements. To receive national subsidies, bōsaikōen must meet nationally set checklists for specific infrastructures (e.g., manhole toilets, cooking benches), which might impede creativity. The examples introduced here highlight some of the few cases that attempt to vigorously strengthen the bōsai mindset through integrated processes, including approaches to stakeholders, functions, structured/nonstructured measures, and nature-based solutions. Imbuing parks with ecological functions for increased resilience over the long term, establishing them in collaboration with communities or private partners, and bringing landscape designers into the process are all measures that can expand the potential of these dual-function open spaces in Japanese cities.

Initial Evacuation Parks and Pocket Parks

Primary evacuation parks are typically city parks that can accommodate large groups of evacuees; however, they may be placed as far as two kilometers away from the areas they are evacuating. Micro-scale open spaces in dense Japanese neighborhoods can also play an important role. Initial evacuation parks cannot function as municipality-designated primary evacuation spaces, since they would not provide sufficient protection from spreading fire and falling objects. But many serve as spaces to which people run immediately after a disaster. Initial evacuation spaces typically support a five-hundred-meter radius,[1] meaning that more of these spaces are located closer to homes than primary evacuation spaces are; they are thus especially helpful for the elderly, young children, or others with limited mobility. Tokyo alone has 221 primary evacuation spaces (parks, campuses, cemeteries) for its twenty-three wards,[2] approximately 2,500 official initial evacuation spaces (small parks, plazas, playgrounds, parking lots, temples, and shrines), and even more spaces that unofficially perform related roles in communities.

These small parks are an important part of bōsai infrastructure owing to the close relationships they have with the communities that surround them in everyday life — as well as after a disaster. These are spaces in which children can play or neighbors can chat or read the newspaper. While they lack the grand scale of larger bōsaikōen, the parks described here contribute to neighborhood preparedness through small-scale devices like hand-operated water pumps, pavilions, *kamado* benches, and sometimes even manhole toilets. Such dual-function bōsai infrastructures are particularly important when residents are able to shelter in their homes after a disaster but lifeline infrastructures remain disrupted. Off-grid utilities and services can allow residents to remain in their homes, traveling only a short distance to their neighborhood pocket park to access necessities like water and sanitation.

MACHIZUKURI PLANNING

Kamisawa, Kobe

The Kamisawa neighborhood was spared during the World War II firebombing, leaving the densely packed apartments and *nagaya* houses intact. The district lacked open space and had many winding alleys and dead-end streets that inhibited emergency vehicle access, so creating safe and comfortable living environments became central to Kobe's urban renovation project in the 1970s.[3] As part of the land readjustment regulation, districts under redevelopment require 3 percent of their area to be green space.[4] For a district of this size, typically two large parks (2,000 square meters each) would be created; however, an experimental workshop held in 1994 and a later series of dialogues with the local neighborhood association after the Kobe earthquake identified residents' preference for more numerous, smaller parks. The city decided to create a series of eight smaller pocket parks totaling 4,150 square meters, connected by an improved residential road that was widened to 4 meters.[5] Each park of approximately 20 by 20 meters was placed at the center of a group of houses, spaced 100 meters apart along the road. Completed in May 2001, the parks include simple play structures and water pumps for everyday and disaster use; three of the parks also include large water tanks for firefighting purposes.[6] These small parks are mostly used by surrounding neighbors, so it is easy to feel safe in them—children can play freely, supervised by the community.

The Kamisawa parks are among the first examples of bottom-up planning models influencing bōsaikōen design. A consultant was brought in from Tokyo to guide the process, designing the parks with surrounding residents to give each a distinct community identity.[7] For each park, between one and five workshops were held, involving residents, construction companies, and local officials. The process began with brainstorming, establishing a theme, and then creating a sketch. Based on the mockup, more detailed designs were developed.[8] The process applied in the park called Kamisawa 2, in particular, employed machizukuri workshops' small-group debate and creative exercises. For many, this interactive process was an eye-opening experience, given the typical top-down decision-making process of Japanese planning. Kamisawa 2 became a valuable precedent for machizukuri planning, attracting publicity to Kobe's post-earthquake readjustment and reconstruction process.[9] The final workshop in the series continued after the Kobe earthquake in tandem with the land readjustment process, so parks 2, 4, and 8 added one-hundred-ton earthquake-resistant water tanks. The process established in the Kamisawa district influenced the reconstruction process for the larger city.[10]

While the collaborative process for creating Kamisawa pocket parks was successful, the planning lacked a model for comprehensive and ongoing maintenance. In the beginning, enthusiasm surrounding the parks rolled over into widespread contribution to their maintenance. However, interviews twelve years after the parks' completion revealed that a single elderly woman was caring for them. She will not be able to take on this role forever, and it is unclear how maintenance will continue in her absence.

Figure 53. Kamisawa pocket parks, developed through one of the first bottom-up planning processes, are equipped with emergency infrastructure and are easily accessible by residents.

Water tank

Evacuation route

Park maintenance

Evacuation space

1979	1994	Jan. 17, 1995	Feb. 16, 1995		May 2001
City land readjustment. Land Readjustment Regulation: 3% of district area to be green space.	Start of experimental workshops and community meetings.	7.3 magnitude earthquake in Kobe. Several people die due to fires alone.	Government presents reconstruction master plan with areas slotted for land readjustment and redevelopment.		Construction complete

Community meeting for park design

Kaze-no-Sato Park

Another park that was created through an extensive machizukuri process was the Rokkōmichi Kaze-no-Sato bōsaikōen. As mentioned above, the joint machizukuri council created a park study group, which focused on the design and culture of the space and implemented them as part of the land readjustment strategy. The park study group researched the legal parameters and restrictions of park design in Japan, toured existing parks, and solicited feedback from schoolchildren.[11] They organized a total of eleven workshops led by the Environmental Landscape Design Office. This team stayed with the Community Development Council throughout the entire eight-year process. Community participants reported that the presence of the expert consultants was essential in mediating an effective relationship between the community and Kobe.[12]

The collaborative design process for Rokkō Kaze-no-Sato led to the incorporation of several unique components. The site was divided into two parts: one side is for sports and the other side is for smaller children and the elderly, to ensure that people of all ages can use it. A jogging circuit was designed around the four-hundred-meter perimeter to help elderly residents stay fit. Organized groups walk at 5:00 am, 6:00 am, and 7:00 am and are accountable for each other's health. Plants nurtured in the nursery and sunflower garden are transplanted around the district.[13] The lawn is mowed only twice a year, so that long grasses become a habitat for grasshoppers and small animals and an adventure play space for children. Children were invited to participate in the design workshop for play areas and decided to make a crawfish habitat in a pond in the shape of a fish. The small biotope still thrives fifteen years later and is a staple for ecosystem education.

Residents strongly advocated for creating a community meetinghouse, especially since they struggled to find a place to gather after the earthquake. Park regulations stipulated that meetinghouses could only be built in larger parks, but the meetinghouse was approved as a reconstruction project. The construction costs were fully covered by the Safe Community Plaza Project,[14] one of the disaster-reconstruction subsidies offered by the Great Hanshin-Awaji Earthquake Reconstruction Foundation. A competition entry from young designer Watanabe Kenshi called House of Wind was chosen for its natural ventilation system and wooden construction.[15] The meeting center houses daily functions for the elderly, welfare support, and community activities while serving as a base for collecting and transmitting information during disasters.[16]

Bōsai functions include a one-hundred-ton earthquake-proof water tank, portable toilets, and a storage space for emergency goods.[17] The north side of the site has a steep slope, and the 3.5-meter difference in elevation was used to create an underground storage space, which helped avoid conflicts with the park regulation that limits the area covered by roof structures to no more than 2 percent.[18] This solution came out of a joint workshop with the Housing Study Group. Landscaping included fruit trees, which could provide a source of food in an emergency.[19] The park finally opened in March 2006, eleven years after the post-earthquake land readjustment process had started.[20]

As with the Kamisawa project, park maintenance is a ubiquitous challenge. In Kaze-no-Sato Park, the House of Wind Club was established as a management committee to maintain and operate the meetinghouse. The club is a group of counselors, elected from each block in the Rokkōmichi North area, who manage the park by themselves without government subsidy. In order to maintain the facility in good condition, they introduced a membership system with an annual fee of ¥1,000 per person. As of September 2020, the House of Wind is still actively used for social dancing, group exercises, flower arrangement, craft activities, and martial arts classes.[21]

POCKET BŌSAI OPEN SPACE SUBSIDY

Since July 2019, Kobe has been promoting the development of spaces used as parks, initial evacuation spaces, firefighting sites, and emergency vehicle rotation sites, with similar aims as the Kamisawa parks project—to prevent the spread of fires in dense urban areas. This series of projects is called "small bōsai open spaces in dense urban areas" and starts with an agreement between the owner of a dilapidated house, the machizukuri council, and Kobe. The city borrows the land at no cost for three to five years, exempts landowners from property tax, and provides a subsidy for the demolition of the derelict house. The city also subsidizes the machizukuri council to develop, maintain, and manage the land as a bōsai open space. The development subsidy is ¥300,000 plus ¥9,000 per square meter of land, up to a maximum of ¥1.5 million.[22]

Shinagawa Pocket Park Network

Some of Tokyo's most populous, dense urban areas are also undertaking various initiatives to establish small community-level bōsai open spaces. Parts of Shinagawa Ward are still sinuous neighborhoods with extensive wood-frame construction and narrow streets, which exacerbate fire risk. To mitigate and prepare for disasters, the ward is working to widen streets and reduce the amount of wood construction. Shinagawa enacted bōsaikōen regulations as early as 1979, and as of 2014, it established a multiscalar park network—including the creation of thirty-seven pocket parks across the ward that serve as local bōsai bases.[23]

Figure 54. Kaze-no-Sato Park was designed with residents to include numerous embedded bōsai functions.

Labels on figure: Fruit trees · Amphitheater · Underground storage space · Community garden · Emergency food · Soccer field · Evacuation space · Community center · Community center · Jogging circuit

"What do you want to do at the park?"

The pocket parks are play areas maintained with government subsidies via the Shinagawa Children's Parks Ordinance, and they help children learn about disaster preparedness from a young age. For example, Honsan Kujira Plaza opened in 2010 after local community volunteers held five study meetings and petitioned for a pocket park, needed for both everyday and post-disaster functions in their community.[24] The

100 ton water tank

Water pump

Evacuation path

Small biotope

" What does this park need? "

plaza is only 182 square meters, yet it contains a forty-ton water tank, a whale-shaped cooking bench, storage, ten manhole toilets with lids illustrated with sea animal mosaics designed by local children, and ten pillars that can support a tent, all created by the community.[25] Another example in the network is Kame-san park, which is just 151 square meters but is located near Bunko-no-mori Park, which serves as a larger evacu-

Emergency supply storage

Turtle cooking bench

Water fountain & washing station

Emergency toilet

Figure 55. Kame-san, one of the smallest bōsai pocket parks, has benches that help children learn about disaster preparedness.

ation area. In Kame-san park, cooking *kamado* benches in the form of *kame* (turtles) give bōsai infrastructure an identity easily remembered by all, including children.

DISCUSSION

While the networks these pocket parks form are essential for disaster preparedness, the spaces themselves are often lackluster—composed of dirt, concrete, a few plants or pieces of furniture, and not much else. This perhaps stems from the limited budgets for parks in Japan. The concept of a multiscalar network of bōsai open spaces can be fundamental during a disaster, as the history of parks in the Kobe earthquake shows; giving more attention to these spaces could make them not only more useful but also more appealing, endearing them to their communities. Emphasizing the anticipatory design framework for these sorts of projects can help expand the potential of these spaces, offering additional possibilities, precedents, and opportunities for creative design.

Anticipatory design does not have to be monumental. These networks of pocket parks show how even the introduction of very small but linked open spaces, which offer both everyday and post-disaster functions, can contribute to the character of a neighborhood as well as its disaster preparedness. Their very integration into the community (and their proximity to households) is what makes these pocket parks significant as bōsai spaces. Connection to everyday routines increases familiarity, so that users are likely to be aware of evacuation spaces and their resources after a disaster. Community-driven processes to create and manage bōsai pocket parks also strengthen a community's social capital.

Education in Parks

Traditional Japanese culture has a strong relationship to the environment, with many gardens, festivals, and arts revolving around observations of seasons and subtle shifts in the natural world. This familiarity with the environment is often critical to survival: the ocean clearly shows that a tsunami is coming when the tide pulls sharply out to sea, and awareness of topography can help one stay clear of floodwaters. Following a disaster, knowledge of edible plants, dominant wind directions, or sources of potable water can be essential. In today's technology-obsessed Japan, this connection to nature is mostly disappearing. Programs and parks that reconnect people to environment-based education, both general and bōsai-specific, contribute to a culture of preparedness.[1] Parks as spaces of education illustrate how the design of physical spaces can influence how we learn about, understand, interact with, and navigate natural and built environments.

As discussed above, it is common for city parks to serve as evacuation spaces equipped with bōsai furniture. Whether local residents know of the existence and use of such parks, however, is another matter. Larger bōsaikōen thus engage and educate surrounding communities through permanent facilities, drills, and other events. Although logistics hubs such as Tokyo Rinkai Park and Miki Sōgō Bōsaikōen do not accept evacuees during a disaster, these parks invite the general public for disaster preparedness education during normal times. Both of these parks meet pedagogical objectives through structured, hands-on activities and training drills.

Bōsai education in parks can take the form of explicit training and drills on how to use open spaces post-disaster, or they can foster designs that encourage stewardship of natural ecologies or more open-ended adventure play that develops skills around solving problems, navigating risk, and cultivating self-reliance. These enhance abilities to negotiate the inevitable chaos and uncertainty following a disaster.

Playful Learning: Kaeru Caravan

Iza! Kaeru Caravan! (Let's Go! Frog Caravan!), briefly mentioned in chapter 2, is a program that uses parks, school grounds, and other open spaces to provide dynamic, interactive bōsai education for families. Disaster education drills can be boring or even distressing, which may lead to reduced participation rates and less retention of infor-

Figure 56. Iza! Kaeru Caravan! is a popular bōsai education program for families.

mation. During Kaeru Caravan events, children learn how to cope with fire, floods, and other natural disasters through bōsai drills combined with games, which vary based on the needs of the communities where they are held. By participating in the drills, children can earn points to use in a toy exchange. The *kaeru,* or frog, serves as the program's mascot and is a homonym for "exchange."[2] The artist Hiroshi Fuji, who often uses toys in his art and engages local communities, already operated a nation-wide toy exchange program, so this became the hook to gain popularity among children.

For example, a target game teaches children how to use a fire extinguisher as they spray water at frog-shaped targets. Groups work together in a race where a frog-shaped mannequin is carried in a blanket stretcher; in the process, they learn teamwork in evacuating an injured person. While the frog characters and the competitive nature make these games easy and engaging, the skills they teach were vetted by the Kobe Fire Department and could become essential in a disaster.

The president of +*arts,* Nagata Hirokazu, shares his philosophy through a soil, seed, wind, and water analogy. Soil is the local context and the local people: some places are fertile, some less so. For example, Japanese communities used to traditionally come together to organize festivals, but now many places simply hire festival operators. In some places only the elderly attend bōsai drills, and no one says hello to their neighbors. Nagata's team had to create a seed that could grow in any kind of soil. An ideal seed is a customizable program and method that is incomplete and has space to grow. It is made to be altered and localized—as people customize the program for their own context, they come to own it. The seed also needs to be creative, fun, and inspirational to draw people in and get them to invest their time and energy. As the person who shares the seed, Nagata is the wind. He makes it clear that he can't stay, and he won't come every year to host Kaeru Caravan. Each city needs to gather a team to be the water—people to adopt, adapt, and carry it forward for many years to come (often the local parent-teacher association or jishubō). As they create their own Kaeru Caravan, participants are building up their social capital in the process. Ultimately, Nagata's goal is to recover local *kizuna* (bonding) and societal wealth, lost in the race to increase development and economic activity, and channel it toward the common good.[3]

The program was based on interviews with survivors of the Kobe earthquake and launched there on the disaster's tenth anniversary in 2005. It was further improved by consultation with survivors of the 2011 Tohoku tsunami.

Over time, Kaeru Caravan has spread to more than thirty-four prefectures in Japan and across nineteen countries. There are spin-offs, such as the Red Bear Survival Camp, which teaches the skills and creativity needed to survive at least seventy-two hours after a disaster, both outdoors and within a shelter.[4] By encouraging a do-it-yourself-the-next-time philosophy, where groups make the program their own, not only do the children learn but the organizers do too. This develops social capital in the anticipatory design framework: the *+arts* programs are equivalent to top-down education, and the modifications made by each locality are the bottom-up adoption of that knowledge, which strengthens the program and the community.

Agricultural Learning: Kamakura Central Park

Kamakura Central Park is a 23.7-hectare general public park located adjacent to a large-scale residential area in Kamakura City. The park was designated as a primary evacuation site in 2004, and every year, in the fall, a bōsai festival takes place, giving a celebratory spin to the typical drills.[5] Local residents and community firefighters gather to participate in emergency preparedness activities, often leveraging dual-function bōsai infrastructures already integrated into the park's design, such as cooking rice using a *kamado* bench.[6] The event also includes drills for emergency education, such as how to use an automated external defibrillator (AED).[7] Children play a simulated firefighting game, and all ages are welcome to try using a fire extinguisher and experience a vehicle that shakes to simulates a seismic experience. A *kamishibai* (picture-story) storyteller provides a visual narration of bōsai stories. The goal of both festivals is to spread awareness throughout the community. Making these response activities visible in a festive atmosphere before a disaster occurs increases knowledge and familiarity with them for their post-disaster use.

In addition to publicly sponsored drills, nonprofit organizations also use Kamakura Central Park for bōsai and environmental education. For example, Yamazaki's Yato

Association uses the central zone, cleared of trees, for agriculture.[8] Children plant vegetables and rice, remove weeds, harvest produce, and make miso and pickles. This improves children's ability to be self-reliant both pre- and post-disaster while teaching them about plant growth, maintenance, and the park's balanced ecosystem.

Another unique educational aspect is the botanical garden inside the park. It displays more than twenty types of hedges and trees for visitors to appreciate, such as evergreen shrubs like Japanese holly, red tip photinia, and euonymus. This exhibit connects to the city's initiative to subsidize homeowners' efforts to green their property boundary in order to improve the historic city and prevent fire from spreading in case of earthquakes.[9] The subsidy is for half of the standard cost of such plantings, with a maximum of ¥150,000, unless it is combined with the Kamakura Block Wall Countermeasure Project Subsidy, in which case it increases to two-thirds of the cost. It stipulates that the plantings need to be at least three meters long and must be in place for at least five years.[10] The project acts as a bōsai vegetation showroom while demonstrating and encouraging residents to apply for the subsidy to increase plantings within the city.

Coastal Learning: Forest Projects

Participating in the creation of mitigation landscapes also contributes to disaster-related learning. For example, several associations have educational and volunteer events to plant saplings along the coast. The Miyagi Coastal Forest Regeneration Project, the Watari Green Belt Project, the Mori-no-Bōchōtei Association, and the Morino Project are regenerating forest belts along the Pacific coast as buffers against tsunamis. Students in classes on disaster preparedness and regional studies learn about caring for saplings and eventually plant the trees as part of the buffer forest. In this way, they gain knowledge not only about the ecology of the planting system but also about their role in storm surge and tsunami mitigation. In Miyagi Prefecture's project, tree planting festivals drew support from an even wider group of collaborators; 9,000 black pine seedlings were planted during a 2018 festival held by a Tokyo-based public benefit corporation.[11] The Mori-no-Bōchōtei Association had a total of 325,698 trees planted by more than 40,000 volunteers in 2019,[12] and the Morino Project had 570,514 trees planted by 62,279 participants as of the end of 2022.[13] In Watari, the residents worked with the local government, small businesses, and university students. They incorporated boardwalks and agriculture in the design and are proud to imagine the children of the future using and loving their "handmade" forest.[14] Participating directly in their community's disaster preparedness gives students a more comprehensive and hands-on understanding of natural disasters and response.[15] The tree planting projects on the Miyagi coast concluded in 2022, and all the young trees are being maintained by these associations.

Ecological Learning: Sixteen Elementary Schools in Takatsu

The landscape itself can educate, providing lessons about natural systems and their connections to mitigation and preparedness. Sixteen elementary schools in Takatsu, Kawasaki City, adopted projects to teach students about local ecosystems and their schools as local emergency shelters through bōsai education. Students grasp the importance of flood control through local topography and water circulation, along with how to use rainwater tanks that are connected to groundwater-fed disaster-preparedness wells operated by manual hand pumps. Each grade learns about the ecosystem of living things: healthy water circulation; larger watersheds and small watersheds, including the school retention pond, through the creation of biotopes; and rainwater reuse on school grounds.[16] For example, students plant native grasses (for butterflies and grasshoppers) and deciduous trees to learn about composting leaves and soil water retention. The goal is for future bōsai machizukuri to create a low-carbon, resource-conserving society that respects local biodiversity and ecological systems.[17] The Japanese model of "integrated learning," in which students work collaboratively around a theme of their choosing, often has a landscape focus. Many disasters result from extreme variations in natural processes, so improved understanding of landscape systems can be key to helping youth not only comprehend and navigate disasters but learn the causes and effects of their actions as well. This is especially crucial considering the adverse weather effects of our climate crisis.

Heuristic Learning: Kamisaigō River Flood Management

During Japan's rapid economic growth, many riverbanks were encased in concrete or fully culverted and developed without environmental assessments, paving the way for rapid urbanization. Even as they controlled floods, these projects diminished the role of rivers as fire buffer zones, worsened urban heat-island effects, decreased the variety of species in and around rivers, and reduced recreation spaces for neighboring communities.

More recent flood-control projects have started emphasizing the importance of biodiversity and protecting the whole riverine environment. New projects promote a "natural reclamation method" as a way to improve the environment through a participatory design process among neighboring residents and with a relatively low cost to the local government.[18] One is the *kawazukuri* (river-planning) method used for small and midsize rivers, which prioritizes allowing the river to flow autonomously. Human intervention is limited to diversifying the velocity of the water by creating micro-topographies, changes in depth, and building groynes (spur dikes) with natural materials.

One important participatory case is the Kamisaigō River *kawazukuri* project. Flowing through Fukutsu in Fukuoka Prefecture, the riverbank was lower on one side, frequently inundating the neighboring residential areas. Because the concrete revetments created fast flows, resulting in a dearth of wildlife and making it difficult for residents to access the river, they requested that the city culvert it.

To address these issues, the *kawazukuri* project launched in 2007 along a one-kilometer stretch of the river. The early workshops were challenging. The new design created by the residents doubled the width, but concrete revetments were still planned. Shimatani Yukihiro's team from Kyushu University was invited by the city to introduce landscape strategies, but residents, frustrated with the recurrent flooding, opposed the ideas, and early workshops were unsuccessful. After a year of discussions using models created by Shimatani's team, the stakeholders finally reached a consensus to start *kawazukuri*. In December 2009, the local residents, Fukutsu officials, and Kyushu University established the "association to promote Kamisaigō River as the Number One River in Japan"[19] to facilitate their collaboration. Residents participated in more than eighty workshops from 2007 to 2016, surveying the river and discussing improvement plans, monitoring and maintenance systems, and desired usage.

Ultimately, the width of the river was doubled by aligning the project with an ongoing residential redevelopment project by the Urban Renaissance agency. This slowed the river's flow, also reducing the risk of flooding further downstream where a storm reservoir was constructed as part of a park. With the added width given to the river, one bank was built as a gentle vegetated slope to facilitate access to the waterfront from the residential area. Native trees were planted along the river, which attract a variety of birds and prevent pests. The wall on the other side was redesigned using large stone blocks, increasing crevices for small creatures.

Efforts to increase biodiversity included slowing the water flow with logs and large stones. These groynes create pools and new habitats and encourage the river to meander. As a result, three years after the restoration, the average number of fish species had tripled and the overall fish population increased twelvefold.[20] Researchers confirmed that endangered fish such as Japanese eel (*Cobitis matsubarae*), species of weather loach, and Japanese rice fish now live in Kamisaigō River.[21]

Residents, students from Kyushu University, and schoolchildren collaborated to build the groynes. Fourth graders of the local elementary school studied the Kamisaigō River as part of their curriculum and learned about the functions of the river water and living organisms; they then helped install the logs and large stones.[22] This participation, from the design through to the construction, has created shared ownership, which has a lasting sense of stewardship. Maintenance, management, river cleaning, biodiversity monitoring, and mowing of the grass are all led by the neighborhood association. Beyond the environmental classes still frequently held in the river, children can be seen playing, searching for and interacting with river creatures, and organically learning from the natural environment. This has also enhanced the children's concerns

Flood reduction project

Open space

Stakeholder cooperation

Groynes with local material

Place for environmental education

Endangered fish
now living
in Kamisaigo River

Oryzias latipes

Anguilla japonica

Silurus asotus

Cobitis matsubarae

12	600
10	500
8	400
6	300
4	200
2	100
0	2009

2011   2012   2013

Before   After restoration

Average species   Average population   Population   Density
per 50m   per 50m

for the flora and fauna and led them to pick up litter in the area.[23] The Kamisaigō River project is featured in the Ministry of Education's fifth-grade science textbook as part of its Building Sustainable Society Unit, addressing four hundred thousand children in elementary schools across Japan.[24]

The project mitigated floods by reducing the velocity of the water with native vegetation and meanders, but its success had an even broader impact: property prices have increased in the area, and residents feel connected to the river and its natural processes through education and a social commitment. Shimatani regards the Kamisaigō River Project as the creation of a social contract by local residents.[25] A long-despised, problematic river was rebuilt by the hands of the local people as the new core of the neighborhood, fostering community belonging and care.

Adventure Learning: Kaigan Kōen Bōken Hiroba

While explicit bōsai education is certainly important, forms of learning that encourage knowledge of the environment and adaptive thinking can also help people act quickly in the chaos and uncertainty following a disaster. An expanded notion of anticipatory design would include projects that help cultivate increased environmental awareness, resourcefulness, and self-reliance. One middle school principal interviewed during 2011 used his knowledge of streams in the mountain behind the school to help students and people sheltering in his school identify safe drinking water.[26] Another man, Hatakeyama Makoto, who had been swept out to sea used his knowledge of currents to navigate the water flows back to shore. He now advocates for nature exploration to be embedded in bōsai education in school, stating that in everyday life, there are many opportunities to learn and put this knowledge to the test so that it becomes ingrained.[27] An understanding of nature, the surrounding environment, and physics helped these individuals survive. Outdoor spaces provide an important setting for this sort of learning, and some types of parks are even transforming from manicured lawns into wilder environments to encourage what has been called "adventure learning."

As play becomes more and more focused on technology and structured environments in our modern world, a movement is growing to reintroduce unstructured "adventure play" spaces. One of adventure play's most famous advocates, Japanese American sculptor Isamu Noguchi, designed Japan's first adventure playground, Kodomo-no-Kuni (Land of Children), in Yokohama in 1965.[28] Adventure play has been shown to improve creativity, social interaction, flexible thinking, and problem-solving skills, all abilities that could be key in surviving a disaster and its aftermath.[29] In addition to knowledge of evacuation or response procedures, these sorts of intangible skills prepare young people to deal with the contingent circumstances associated with emergencies—creating spaces where children are able to construct, experience, and

Figure 57. The Kamisaigō River project reduces flooding and increases fish species in the region through community and school participation.

Figure 58. Kaigan Kōen saved lives during the 2011 Tohoku tsunami and now features programs to teach children lifesaving skills.

navigate risk. It has even been suggested that adventure play can help children cope with the emotional trauma associated with surviving a disaster.[30]

Kaigan Kōen Bōken Hiroba (Coastal Park Adventure Plaza) is another adventure playpark that not only has a role in adventure/bōsai learning but also served as an evacuation site during the 2011 tsunami. Established in 2005 in Wakabayashi, Sendai, the park is located eight hundred meters inland from the coast. The playground and park were originally constructed on a reclaimed landfill sited in a wetland, forming a small hill in an otherwise flat landscape. The top of the play structure has an expansive view of the Sendai plain and Pacific Ocean. Managed by a local NPO, Bōken Asobiba (Adventure Playspace), children learn problem-solving skills through play that are useful in disasters. The Bōken Asobiba's motto is "Giving children survival ability through play."[31] There are no restrictions on play at Kaigan Kōen: children can dig holes and make tunnels anywhere in the park and even learn how to make fire (with adult supervision). A full-time "play leader" keeps an eye on children but generally facilitates rather than restricts their activities. By providing the environment and tools, Bōken Asobiba encourages children to be creative and bold. They learn to solve problems using the available resources—a crucial skill during a disaster.

On March 11, owing to the 5-meter-seawall along Sendai's coast, only one tsunami hit this area—the second and third waves did not surpass the seawall. The playpark was not designated as an evacuation space, but five people (two park staff and three neighboring residents, plus one dog) evacuated here when they heard the pine trees breaking and saw the black wall of water rushing across the plain. They spent one night on the top of the highest play structure, 15.9 meters above sea level. A park staff member used the kinds of resourcefulness he teaches in the park, helping the evacuees make a tent and cover themselves with a large vinyl sheet for warmth.[32] The tsunami was strong enough to wash away the 15- to 20-meter-wide pine forest belt densely planted along the coast, which had grown since the seventeenth century. The shape of the hill, an oblong oval perpendicular to the coast, minimized damage to the top of the park: it allowed the water to go around the park when it was struck by a tsunami over 7 meters high.

The park was closed after the tsunami and reopened on July 8, 2018, with the addition of new memorial features and with the hill redesignated as the "Hill of Evacuation." While many components of the park (various play equipment, the play leader's office) were restored to their pre-disaster form, modifications include space for a helicopter to land adjacent to the hill in case a secondary evacuation is necessary. To further mitigation efforts, areas surrounding the park were raised 6 meters, and pine trees are being planted for wind and wave protection on the higher ground.

DISCUSSION

For bōsaikōen to be effective, they need not only good spatial design but also social engagement: surrounding populations must be aware of their role. And as previously discussed, this is not always the case, particularly among foreign visitors and younger populations. Park-based education, be it conventional drills like those held in Tokyo Rinkai Park or more playful events like Iza! Kaeru Caravan, help people learn where they should go after a disaster and what they can expect once they arrive.

While conventional disaster drills are standard fare in Japan, more experimental forms of nature-based bōsai education, such as those related to Kamisaigō River, are rarer. This is reflected not only by the types of activities and engagement but also in the forms of the parks themselves. Connecting the design of parks to people's everyday learning and experience as well as to adventure play, which teaches about risk and resourcefulness, can allow the design itself to contribute to education. In this way, parks can increase awareness and knowledge about their specific disaster-related functions or can contribute more general problem-solving abilities.

Beyond parks with specifically bōsai functions, landscapes designed to foster creative thinking can generate new relationships to our environments in ways that can improve people's abilities to navigate the uncertainty, chaos, and resource constraints of disasters. Open-ended adventure play, such as that offered in places like Kaigan Kōen, teaches creative problem solving and self-reliance. Adventure parks help children of all ages understand the risks and potentials of their landscapes and can improve their resourcefulness and ability to understand and cope with risk during a disaster. Together, these different typologies of landscapes and better understanding of nature can instill important response and survival skills.

Park Networks Discussion

Japan's bōsaikōen networks are perhaps the most coherent and systematic example of the anticipatory design concept of linking the everyday to post-disaster needs. They are inherently dual-function, serving their communities as recreational, educational, and social spaces under blue skies and as evacuation spaces or logistical hubs after a disaster. Notably, the infrastructure and furniture that allow them to perform these dual functions during the disaster are designed, planned, and even practiced pre-disaster. The examples from previous sections illustrate the importance of open space operating around the disaster timeline and the need to integrate this dual-use knowledge into people's everyday lives—to emblazon a cognitive map of such uses and spaces into each individual's mind.

INTERNATIONAL CONNECTIONS

Parks and open space have also been important to disaster response and recovery in other parts of the world, but rarely are they specifically designed for evacuation, and none are as systemically considered as Japan's. During the 1906 San Francisco earthquake, private life flooded into public space: communities came together to cook meals in streets or parks, and makeshift tent cities eventually gave way to formal temporary housing in places like Golden Gate Park.[1] More recently, three architecture firms were invited to create designs for the park, ranging from dry-composting restrooms to art installations.[2] Similarly, after Hurricane Katrina in New Orleans, FEMA used city parks as sites for temporary housing units.[3] FEMA also assigns open spaces as points of distribution for post-disaster supplies, but it mostly relies on large parking lots and vehicle-based pickup and prioritizes logistical efficiency.

Japan is the first country to systematically designate open-space networks that integrate everyday and emergency functions. Based on actual or projected seismic events, other nations have begun to follow suit. In particular, China constructed its first "disaster-prevention park" in Beijing in 2008. The Yuandadu Wall Relics Park embeds emergency infrastructure, including evacuation spaces, water supply, toilets, helipad, and communications. Yuandadu Park has precipitated a spree of disaster-prevention park construction, further spurred by China's 2006 five-year-plan on disaster prevention, which set a minimum of one-fifth of the nation's urban parks to be designated as disaster-prevention parks. As a new model for China, general awareness about disaster-prevention parks as well as broader networks and evacuation routes are still being improved upon.[4] Portland, Oregon, has established fifty Basic Earthquake Emergency Communication Nodes (BEECN), open spaces where people can go after a disaster to establish emergency services, including medical care and communications. However, permanent relief infrastructures are not yet installed as of this writing, and the parks are not specifically designed for this use.

CONNECTING SOCIAL AND SPATIAL

The majority of bōsaikōen documented in this book are well used as community and recreation spaces, but in most cases, residents may not know that the spaces are designed to transform into resource hubs following a disaster. While the invisibility of bōsai functions may be appealing for everyday use, it could be problematic in a post-disaster context. Informal interviews with visitors to major parks in different cities revealed that while some elderly neighborhood residents were aware of the park's bōsai functions, many local residents—such as young mothers with small children who visit every day, or nearby office employees who commute through the area—were not aware that the parks are evacuation spaces. Although the national government standardized signage in front of parks and on surrounding streets in 2016, signs alone are clearly not enough.

Emphasizing the creation of bōsaikōen as a design process rather than an infrastructural installation can help adapt them more specifically to their contexts (both everyday and post-disaster) while more clearly communicating their role within the city. The layering of everyday and post-disaster functions into park components has the potential to meet emergency needs and to make public spaces and infrastructure better and more interesting. Bōsaikōen with unique local identities and events will feature more prominently in people's cognitive maps of the city, even for occasional visitors. Design features that illuminate emergency infrastructure by making them more playful, interactive, or useful on an everyday basis will help visitors retain the fact that such places are for post-disaster evacuation and relief as well as everyday respite and recreation.[5]

CONNECTING ECOLOGY AND ENGINEERING

Currently, most bōsaikōen are designed as evacuation spaces for seismic emergencies, but as climate change brings unexpected fluvial and pluvial floods, they will likely need to function in multiple roles. The concept of embedded multiuse infrastructures has a long lineage in landscape architecture, as Frederick Law Olmsted famously integrated urban flood prevention infrastructure and ecological systems into his park designs. For example, Olmsted's park network design for the city of Boston, the Emerald Necklace, replaced polluted marshes with a system of stormwater retention and wastewater management integrated into leafy oases: he imagined the parks to have not only an infrastructural but also a social role, providing public health benefits as urban sanctuaries away from the chaos of surrounding streets and buildings. Such perspectives on landscapes and infrastructure, which would reframe public parks and bōsaikōen as productive spaces more than solely leafy respites, are particularly essential today: when designed as such, landscapes can make our cities safer from disaster risks and climate change.

Flora and fauna in Japanese parks will be even more important in the coming decades. As previously discussed, heuristic learning through outdoor nature play is fundamental to childhood education and can counteract the notion of climate complacency. Learning in, playing in, and loving greener spaces will hopefully convince future generations to find more ways to protect, care for, and create ecologically sustainable futures.

PARK NETWORKS AROUND THE DISASTER TIMELINE

Before a disaster, the morphology or ecology of landscapes and parks can serve as a tool to mitigate floods and other hazards. For example, open spaces can stop the spread of fires by interrupting a fabric of built kindling, especially when surrounded by less flammable tree species. Forests have long served as buffers against winds and waves in Japan, including coastal tsunami forests as well as the more recent development of landslide buffer forests. Trees also play a critical role in carbon sequestration; on average, one mature tree absorbs about twenty-two kilograms of carbon per year.[6] Vegetated landscapes increase permeable surfaces so that water can percolate back into the ground, recharging the water table, while also reducing floods downstream. Careful topographical design of such softscapes can collect or store floodwaters to limit their impact on neighboring sites while creating natural habitats, which in turn increases opportunities for ecological education. Shaded parks, especially those with fountains, provide a respite during heat waves and help combat urban heat-island effects as their shade cools surfaces. Unfortunately, many smaller municipal parks in Japan have limited maintenance budgets and resort to fewer shrubs and deciduous trees. But incorporating mitigation measures into parks, plazas, playgrounds, and other landscapes has the potential not only to reduce a community's disaster risk but also to improve the quality of these spaces.

Many bōsaikōen are used for preparedness, annual drills, and festivals; to brush up emergency response skills and rehearse disaster scenarios with city employees, firefighters, and local jishubō; and to educate the public on the importance of self-help and mutual support through fun games and cookouts. Adventure playparks teach similar skills in a more heuristic manner through creative play, but they also intend to teach disaster navigation skills and improve children's abilities to cope with risk and uncertainty. Continuous bōsai education contributes to the maintenance of bōsai culture in existing family networks and future generations.

In much of the world, people are taught to move outdoors immediately after earthquakes to seek safety from collapsing buildings and debris. In this disaster-response phase, open space plays a key role in evacuation. Disasters can turn the architecture we create into hazards of flames or falling debris, especially in areas without a strong history of earthquake-resistant codes and construction. In Japan, open spaces have long been considered safe havens from conflagrations in dense neighborhoods. They are also important spaces for connecting with friends and neighbors and accessing essential post-disaster resources. Each ward in Japan has a map of all the evacuation spaces, encouraging families and friends to make plans for where to meet and how to get there in case of an evacuation. Though many of the relief and response roles of open spaces are unplanned and undesigned across much of the world, Japan's bōsaikōen system illustrates the potential of making such roles integral to the design of parks. High-ground parks, shrine grounds, and forest trails can provide space to escape tsunamis. In low-lying districts, some parks are built on elevated ground as evacuation sites from flash floods and storm surges. As climate change places these neighborhoods increasingly under threat of rising tides, creating high-ground parks will become even more essential.

NEW POLICIES: STRANDED COMMUTERS

Evidence that parks operate as collective spaces throughout the disaster timeline has prompted new policies allowing parks to play an even larger role as coordination hubs with storage units for distributing supplies to surrounding buildings.

If the Tokyo inland earthquake occurs during a weekday at noon, it is expected to suspend public transportation, leaving about 3.9 million commuters within Tokyo stranded in the city.[7] Even if an earthquake occurs elsewhere in the country, trains in the impacted area will be halted, stranding people at many stations across a wide area. Parks near prime stations frequented by more than 300,000 commuters daily are now being adapted to accept stranded commuters and visitors before they are relocated to nearby overnight accommodations. Installation of emergency supply storage, earthquake-resistant water tanks, and emergency power generators is permitted in these parks. The supply stockpile in the park is distributed in coordination with the buildings surrounding the park, which have agreed to provide indoor overnight accommodations.[8] These designated parks also form a network of rest areas, which will provide water and toilets for people walking long distances home. A minimum group of five parks sized five hundred square meters or larger, located within five hundred meters of roads identified in the Regional Disaster Management Plan as safe for those

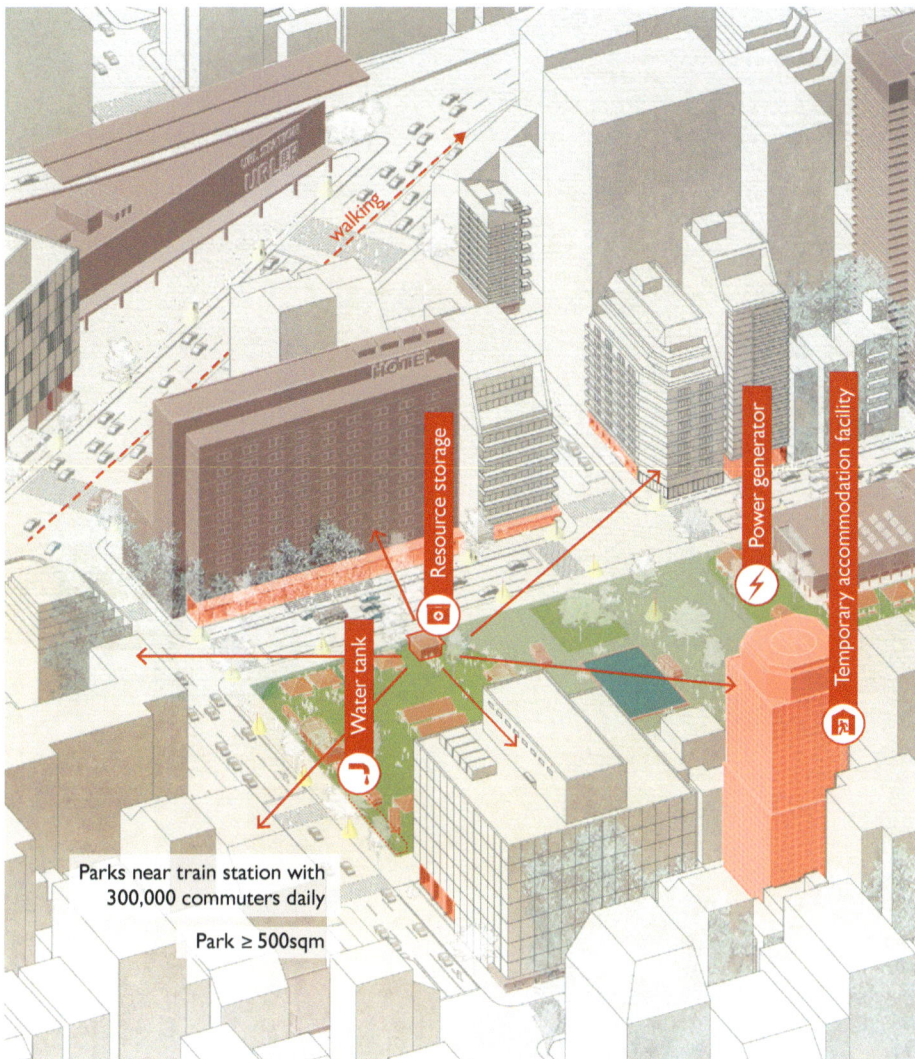

Parks near train station with
300,000 commuters daily

Park ≥ 500sqm

Water tank

Resource storage

Power generator

Temporary accommodation facility

walking

Figure 59. Parks are central nodes for hosting stranded commuters.

walking home, can apply for subsidies. Municipalities (and some private entities) can apply for one-third of the land acquisition cost for a park and half of the installation cost for storage and a water tank. The financial support for these projects is covered by the Bōsai Safety Subsidy, which also applies to toilets, drinking fountains, lights, and planting vegetation.[9]

Tourist destination cities have been quick to implement this program. In Kyoto, along with parks, station plazas and the outdoor spaces of temples, shrines, and museums are designated as emergency gathering spaces. Visitors are guided to a nearby designated space by the city's emergency messaging service on their phones; if public transportation is halted overnight, they are transferred to a temporary accommodation space.[10] The emergency gathering guidebook is published in six languages, and tourist agencies are encouraged to hand out copies within each location, local jishubō, and local businesses to aid the evacuees.[11] As the currently linear process of evacuation becomes more decentralized, clear communication will become even more important.

5

ARCHITECTURAL TRANSFORMATIONS

LIVING WITH HAZARDS

Japan is renowned for its traditional wooden architecture, constructed with such a high level of technical skill that entire buildings, even multistory pagodas, can be built without nails or screws. Like vernacular architectures around the globe, Japanese architecture developed in tune with its environment—including environmental risks. Along with Buddhism, the pagoda was transported from China to Japan around 1,500 years ago. While Chinese pagodas were often built from stone, in Japan the typology was translated into wood, taking advantage of the vast forests of Japan's mountainous interior and making the structures more resistant to tremors. As a flexible material, wood can absorb vibrations, while more brittle materials such as stone or brick often collapse when shaken. The oldest-known five-story pagoda at Hōryūji further accommodates shaking through what we now refer to as base isolation. Rather than affixing directly to a foundation, the wooden elements connect to a central column, or *shinbashira*, which is only lightly connected to the stone base and can slide laterally to accommodate movement. This technique is also incorporated in the individual stories of the pagoda, which can each move independently as a result of the flexibility and specific shape of each timber joint. Deep, heavy eaves help the structure remain balanced, which allows the *shinbashira* to serve as a damping pendulum, absorbing vibration and minimizing movement. Many of these structural logics, from base isolation and flexibility to damping pendulums, have been incorporated into Japan's— and the world's—skyscrapers, which are designed to move with rather than resist a trembling earth. Japan excels at this earthquake engineering, learning from traditional knowledge and pursuing new challenges in tandem with architects. Most universities

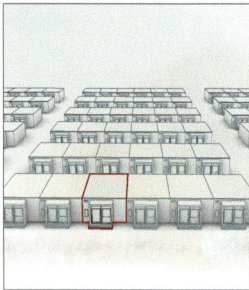

Housing
Temporary to
Permanent

Shrines and Temples

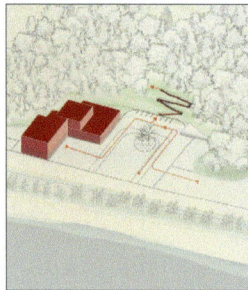

Hotels

Schools

Tsunami Evacuation
Structures

Amusement park

Community center

Fire department

Shrines & temples

Housing

Mall

Michi-no-eki

Train station

Pedestrian bridge

Tsunami evacuation structures

Parking

Hotels

Schools

Fish market

Convenience store

Museum

Floating tsunami shelter

Airport

in Japan educate architects and engineers together, helping build decades-long partnerships and bringing both fields to their world-renowned status. It is now time to more deeply connect the social and spatial aspects of disasters and to work with anthropologists, sociologists, ethnographers, and psychologists to better understand how to design for dual uses that meet everyday needs as well as those that arise during or after disasters.

SOCIAL AND SPATIAL

Human beings have an overwhelming natural impulse to help during and after a disaster. Architects quickly assemble to help design and build temporary social structures and temporary housing. For example, in 1923, Endo Arata built several barracks; Kon Wajiro's group focused its efforts on heavily damaged working-class neighborhoods and learned from documenting temporary shelter construction and the life of survivors through drawings.[1] Other temporary forms of public facilities, such as clinics, libraries, daycare centers, and employment agencies, were established over the course of about one month,[2] and public baths were established within three months of the disaster.[3]

Following a catastrophic disaster, shelter alone is insufficient to sustain a population. Successful temporary post-disaster housing must meet not only physical needs through shelter and logistics but also sociocultural needs, such as maintaining community ties. Providing post-disaster social spaces helps meet these needs: the creation of temporary spaces to gather, carry out everyday activities, and relaunch livelihoods is fundamental to recovery. By allowing communities to come together, these spaces are crucial in rebuilding social infrastructure, which in turn plays an important role in rebuilding place.[4]

After the 1995 Kobe earthquake, Ban Shigeru's paper-tube housing and paper-tube chapel reignited architects' focus on post-disaster conditions, and his contributions to the field since have been celebrated through numerous books and prizes. Similarly, after the 2011 Tohoku earthquake, architects sprang into action to create a range of temporary community spaces to help meet needs beyond shelter. Municipalities and prefectures organized some of these efforts, while other bottom-up projects arose with outside organizations, universities, or architects, including such figures as Ban, Takeuchi Yasushi, Hiraoka Yoshihiro, Kuma Kengo, Kobayashi Hiroto, and Ito Toyo. Ito curated his Home-for-All community center with several architects and in collaboration with the community; the project took home the Golden Lion at the 2012 Venice Biennale. Architecture nonprofits also figured prominently, such as Architecture for Humanity and ArchiAid, a network of Japanese architects that formed following the 2011 disaster and built a number of community projects along the Tohoku coastline. Others, such as Naruse-Inokuma Architects, prioritized the long-term recovery of

Figure 60. Architectural transformations.

the community by designing NPO Riku Cafe in Rikuzentakata. The temporary café managed by women transitioned to a permanent enterprise emphasizing senior health. Local timber was used in both structures; wooden interiors with high rafter ceilings, clerestory windows in the gables, and cushioned floor seating give the space a communal feel. Similarly, Ibasho House in Ōfunato, founded by Kiyota Emi, an environmental gerontologist and architect, venerated the role of elders in the region. The local NPO grew beyond a café/library to include a vegetable garden, farmer's market, ramen shop, and children's daycare.

Some architects, like Kajima Momoyo, conducted field surveys, talking to residents about their "ways of life and the landscapes" prior to the tsunami, to consider reconstruction plans linking the past, present, and future of coastal Ishinomaki. From this she created a way of working called "Architectural Ethnography," exhibited in the 2018 Venice Biennale.[5] These methods harken back to Kon's surveys in post-earthquake Tokyo, in which he sought to find "social ethos in everyday space."[6] While Kon's work went on to improve rural and urban housing, fashion, and ornament, his methods for an ethnographic process—recognizing traditional values and understanding architectural space empirically—have influenced many since.[7]

Some structures, such as shrines and temples, inherently manifest the importance of connecting the social and spatial dimensions of design. But particularly when conceptualizing new buildings for use during dire times, the profession needs to commit to learning from people in a thoughtful and just manner[8] and learn from or work with academics who comprehensively survey people's needs. While not all challenges can be resolved through design, spaces can certainly relieve or heighten post-disaster stresses as well as residents' ability to confer and inspire a spirit of recovery.

TEMPORAL TRANSFORMATIONS

Vernacular Japanese architecture is aligned with notions of modularity, flexibility, change, the ephemeral moment, and being one with nature. Timber structural frames, largely built through interlocking joints without nails, could be dismantled, relocated, and rebuilt. The most notable is the Hakogi house, considered the oldest standing farmhouse in Japan, built in the Muromachi era (1336–1573) and used as a residence until 1977, when construction of the Donto dam flooded the original site and the home was moved to higher ground.[9] The poet Kamo no Chōmei wrote during a time when Kyoto was often ravaged by disasters and is known to have lived in a movable mountain home he designed himself, embodying the Buddhist notion of transience and the acceptance of impermanence.[10] Although moving an entire home was less common in Japan than in Southeast Asia, the structural clarity allowed such options to be available. One can imagine that aspects of relocation, especially emotional ties to spaces, can be easier to cope with when a home can move with you.

The main timber structural members, especially the columns and beams, were all made clearly visible as part of the architectural identity and for education. This structural clarity is celebrated, as it expresses how gravitational forces are carried from the roof to the ground, and any alterations to the home must respect those core elements. Many of the interior walls then are free to subdivide spaces, with varied programs using *fusuma* (sliding doors) and *shoji* (screens).

The other essential element of Japanese architecture is the tatami mat. These flooring pads, with a standard 2:1 dimension, are traditionally woven from *igusa* (rush grass) with a rice straw core. Originally developed as cushions and bedding in the Nara era, tatami became common as flooring material in noblemen's houses by the Kamakura era and were adopted by common people as well after the 1868 Meiji Restoration. The tatami is used as a standard increment of measurement and construction metric called *tsubo* (equivalent to two tatami, approximately 3.3 square meters). The standardized construction, combined with the sliding doors, creates a flexible ground plane within the house. As part of Japan's "shoes-off floor culture," a tatami room can be used for just about anything. The mats are firm enough to support furniture items yet soft enough to sleep on with the addition of futons, which are stored in special deep closets during the day to make room for other uses. Throughout the cycle of the day, with foldable and portable furniture, the tatami room transforms: bedroom, living room, study, dining room. In public buildings, this is amplified, as tatami rooms can accommodate multiple events and activities, growing and shrinking in size accordingly.

As architect Maki Fumihiko notes, "We've taken Westernization as almost synonymous with progress. It's been our national ethos these last 150 years. Yet objectively speaking, we always feel . . . not pressure necessarily, but an urgency from tradition. Although we, myself included, tend to create buildings in modernist language, tradition somehow unconsciously comes out in the scale, proportions or treatment of space."[11] It is the hope that this "urgency from tradition" persists—not only in the manners described by Maki but also in the care, connection, and process of creating bōsai culture.

The typologies described in this section are imbued with flexibility to varying degrees and allow for transformations between everyday and disaster functions over time. Some draw their lineage from the vernacular described above; others fall short of their potential. It is hoped that by sharing these projects, more architects will engage in methods of social inquiry and design while keeping the imminence of disasters in mind.

ARCHITECTURAL TRANSFORMATIONS: CHAPTER ORGANIZATION

"Housing: Temporary to Permanent" discusses various types of reconstruction housing to emphasize the need for a greater continuity between temporary and permanent housing options. Other typologies in this section are all public or communal spaces, which play a role in a series of phases around the disaster timeline. "Shrines and Temples" argues that cultural spaces, notably those that support societal needs, are fundamental for communities both in the immediate aftermath of a disaster and for recovery. Hotels are significant for their role as temporary shelters, especially for the vulnerable, and the community leadership of their owners. Schools play a major role throughout the entire disaster timeline and clearly connect social and spatial functions. Tsunami evacuation buildings and towers are buildings or open-air structures that allow people to evacuate above the level of tsunami waters when there is no high ground nearby.

Housing: Temporary to Permanent

The reconstruction of homes following a disaster can take years. Before permanent housing can be completed, temporary housing fills the gap. The provision of this interim housing for disaster survivors has a long history in Japan. During the Edo era, the shogunate government provided post-disaster housing in the form of the *osukui-goya* (rescue shed). Built in the *hiyokechi* and *hirokōji* open spaces, these were rapidly deployable after a disaster; they were primarily made of wooden walls, floors, columns, and partitions that were stored in nearby warehouses and could be assembled in half a day by skilled carpenters. The structures were approximately 3,300 square meters, and after the 1829 Great Fire, each of ten *osukui-goya* accommodated between two hundred and five hundred people.

Japan's 1947 Disaster Relief Act specifies that temporary housing be provided for up to two years and three months after a disaster, although some housing was used for more than nine years (in Kobe and Tohoku).[1] In residential areas that need to be rezoned or relocated, or where plot sizes are too small to hold temporary houses, the housing sites are located far away from the original locations. Once relocation sites or properties have been cleared of debris or stagnant water (or pollutants, especially after floods or fires), the repair or construction of permanent housing commences. Social networks are almost always disrupted as people are moved into various temporary housing locations—and then again as people move from their temporary housing into permanent housing.

This section addresses the history and organization of temporary housing as well as radical post-disaster permanent housing experiments acknowledging the major social issues of each era: new construction methods and typologies for addressing the lack of affordable housing in Tokyo after 1923; new land readjustment and joint housing typologies in Kobe after 1995; and new designs for aging populations in Tohoku after 2011. These all embody the fundamental notion of the collective: community members sharing with and supporting one another through the creation of semipublic spaces. This chapter consciously combines temporary and permanent housing so as to imagine the potential for a more seamless process between the two. Cases are organized chronologically, toggling between temporary housing and permanent housing.

For permanent housing typologies, a selection of collective housing projects demonstrates the prospect of increasing social coping capacity. The notion of collectivity is

Figure 61. *Osukui-goya,* rapidly deployable rescue sheds.

not new to Japan; in fact, it is ingrained in the social and spatial structure of many working-class neighborhoods. For example, *roji* (narrow alleys) within densely packed *nagaya* housing proliferated across Japan. The common space at the end of *roji* often contained toilets, bathhouses, small shrines, shops, and a well, acting as a semiprivate space.[2] Evelyn Schulz refers to the phrase *idobata kaigi* (gossiping at the well during chores) as these social and community assembly spaces. She argues that rapid reconstruction after the 1923 earthquake and World War II led to the loss of relationships and social environments embedded in the *nagaya* neighborhoods.[3] Shared maintenance activities, such as sweeping, shoveling snow, watering plants, or spraying water to dampen the summer heat, are what historian Jinnai Hidenobu suggests led to the formation of social bonds: "It was in such micro-spaces in which a certain degree of self-government took shape."[4] These are precisely the types of organizational conversations and structures that lead to social capital before a disaster strikes. It is important to find ways for cities to evolve while spatial and social structures remain intact. In the disaster timeline, while transitioning from the original neighborhood to temporary housing and then from temporary to permanent housing, the fostering of social networks is critical. Designing more integrated typologies and policies will facilitate the recovery process, making it smoother and less disruptive to the social networks that are vital for residents' physical and mental health.

1923 TEMPORARY HOUSING

Within days of the 1923 temblor, the city government launched plans to build temporary housing barracks in open spaces, including Shiba Park, Hibiya Park, Ueno Park, Yasukuni Shrine, and Meiji Shrine. Given the massive housing need, barrack construction expanded into the smaller open spaces of neighborhood parks, shrine and temple grounds, and the sites of sixty-eight schools. By November 15, two months after the earthquake, the Tokyo government and its municipalities were managing 101 barracks complexes for 21,367 households, sheltering a total of 86,581 people.[5]

Built with tin roofs and wood or rush interior walls, each barrack ranged between 10 and 30 square meters, with at least one tatami room, a toilet, and a *doma* (earthen entryway). The noisy and crowded barracks complexes included communal toilets and laundry facilities, communal cooking facilities, and hot-water bathhouses. The larger ones had a temporary housing management office, clinic, daycare center, barbershop, stores, and a city library. The counseling facility in Hibiya Park was run by the Salvation Army, Honganji temple, the YMCA, and other private institutions, and it received between 20 and 250 legal consultations a day.[6]

By the end of February 1924, 170,639 barracks had been constructed. Considering the spike, this figure most likely includes informal barracks constructed by individuals who did not have access to units operated by the Tokyo government.[7] This figure grew to 230,000 barracks at its peak. Many complexes were created in the vicinity of the seriously affected areas and helped maintain existing social networks, giving residents the energy to rebuild in their familiar neighborhoods. However, in *shitamachi* locations such as Honjō, Fukagawa, and Asakusa, the government could not control the rapid expansion; the barracks soon became overcrowded and unsanitary, rapidly deteriorating to squalid conditions. In October 1925, the Tokyo government designated these areas as special nonsanitary zones. The government expedited the elimination of barracks and moved to secure alternative housing for the displaced. Donations collected by the Home Ministry were used to build 2,000 small houses (six *tsubo* per house) in the periphery of Tokyo—Tsukishima, Minowa, Sarue, and a former clothing depot. In 1926, these small houses were designated as municipal public housing.[8]

At the same time, measures were put in place to help residents who were able to rebuild on their own by avoiding immediate removal of their barracks. The Home Ministry had initially intended to use the 1919 Urban Building Law for temporary housing to raze these sites and dismantle such housing by the end of August 1928, but instead, the ministry created a special ordinance to largely suspend the law. After March 1924, building new barracks was prohibited, but existing barracks could be grandfathered in to remain on-site. In order to remain, they needed to be a maximum of two stories and had to have access to proper sanitation and airflow.[9] These decisions were designed to prevent uprooting the population and to allow the self-initiated recovery process to continue.

1924–1941 PERMANENT HOUSING

Dōjunkai Foundation

The Home Ministry realized the need for a more long-term solution, so on May 23, 1924, its Social Bureau used part of the earthquake relief donations ¥10 million (approximately ¥25 billion as of 2023) to establish the Dōjunkai Foundation. People not only lost their homes in the disaster, but many became disabled or lost their jobs as a result of serious injuries. The Dōjunkai Foundation's role was to provide such people with safe housing and security, including jobs. Its mission was to implement social policies, provide housing, and support survivor recovery—including livelihood projects for the injured, those with special needs, and unemployed evacuees as well as workshops for retraining survivors for the job market.[10]

In 1924, Dōjunkai constructed 2,160 temporary housing units to replace the barracks; these were rented at a rate of five yen for an eight-tatami-mat unit. The residents of these temporary units were given the benefit of priority transition into permanent housing, which the Dōjunkai was building at the same time.[11] However, one year after the earthquake, more than 13,713 households, totaling more than 51,000 people, continued to live in barracks provided by the Tokyo government, according to a survey by the Tokyo City Social Affairs Bureau.[12] The city was expected to remove all the residents from the complexes by the end of October 1924, so the Bureau for Social Affairs tried to match refugees with housing options, some of which were as far away as Hokkaido—over 1,200 kilometers away. As expected, such moves were unpopular and met with resistance.[13]

Immediately after the temporary housing was built, the construction of permanent housing began. A total of 3,494 units were built in eight suburban areas of Tokyo and four locations in Yokohama. The architects were influenced by British garden city planning and the German *Siedlungen* model[14] but also aspired to include *bunka seikatsu* (cultural lifestyle) while trying to widen the middle class and provide housing to the broader public.[15]

For example, in the Matsue development in Edogawa Ward, each block was made up of about thirty units of single and duplex residences and attached to shops, with a courtyard containing a communal well at the center. Mothers worked on the porch facing the courtyard as their children played there. The tree-lined main street had shops, and the perpendicular street had the neighborhood hall, a restaurant, and a vocational training center, which formed the center of the community. Adjacent to this, a celluloid factory was built to try to integrate opportunities for employment. However, not all locations could build workplaces near the community, so many of the suburban housing locations ended up being unexpectedly unpopular.[16] Though they were built for the low-income working class, many of the potential residents could not afford the housing association fee and the cost of commuting to their workplaces.

Learning from those challenges, the Dōjunkai built reinforced-concrete apartment buildings in disaster-affected areas and adjacent areas within the city limits, both in working-class factory districts and uptown districts. Fourteen were located within Tokyo and two in Yokohama. However, only the Sarue apartments in Fukagawa could accommodate the same residents who were on-site prior to construction. This project was commissioned by the Home Ministry to serve as a model for the 1927 Troubled Residential District Reformation/Revision Law to clear the so-called slums. Barracks residents were moved to temporary housing and then to these three-story reinforced-concrete apartments.[17]

For other Dōjunkai apartments, residents were selected by lottery, and the rent was set according to the size of each unit. These apartments gained great popularity for their locations and their projection of a modern lifestyle. For example, the mid-rise Aoyama apartments on Omotesandō Street had one thousand applicants for 137 units. The complex was advertised as new and modern, with "earthquake-proof" reinforced-concrete construction, fire-door protection, anti-burglary security, a choice between Japanese or Western-style built-in furniture, running water, electricity, gas heater and oven, flush toilets, shared access space for drying clothes on the roof, and small self-contained kitchens with trash chutes.[18] Although individual units were small, to conform to social housing, shared amenities were plentiful: they included landscaped gardens, communal rooftops, well-water access with hand pump, restaurants for residents, and large shared kitchens. Units for big families had larger courtyard-facing balconies to hint at the traditional *engawa*. The cement stucco detailing and delicate ironwork in the communal stairs and entrance areas expressed a Western flair, while inside apartments, tatami and *fusuma* interiors provided material familiarity and a traditional, flexible use of space. Similarly, modern horizontal clerestory fenestration, circular windows, and protruding rectangular bays and lintels were carefully mixed with vernacular sliding windows.[19]

Despite being low-budget, post-disaster public housing, each of the sixteen housing complexes was designed to suit the character, scale, and topography of each location, resulting in diverse building forms even within each site. This was made possible by enlisting both young architects[20] and influential ones as well as structural engineers and professors; most prominently, Uchida Yoshikazu was a board member of the Dōjunkai committee and chief architect.[21] All the projects featured a variety of public and semipublic pedestrian outdoor spaces through U-shaped buildings or the arrangement of blocks and recessed entrances that created small courtyards. Underscoring the importance of outdoor and indoor community spaces, several locations even had

Figure 62 (*next page*). Dōjunkai post-earthquake permanent housing, a new typology for Tokyo.

3,494 units

Uguisudani
Minowa
Otsuka Joshi
Edogawa
Uenoshita
Yanagishima
Nakanogo
Kiyosunadori
Sumitoshi
Higashi-cho
Toranomon
Aoyama
Mita
Daikanyama

Yamashita-cho
Hiranuma-cho

Cafeteria

Aoyama Apartments

Edogawa Apartments

Children's playroom, bathhouse, barbershop, social room, cafeteria

Original color photo credit: Kanehira Youki, purchased from /http://www.apartment-photo.gr.jp/text201.html
Original map title: Damage distribution map of wooden buildings near Tokyo during the September 1, 1920 earthquake
Metropolitan Police Department Security Department Building Division publication (public domain at archive.library.metro.tokyo.lg.jp)
Original black and white photo credit: Stewart, David B. *The Making of a Modern Japanese Architecture*. New York: Kodansha America, 2002.

Cafeteria

Laundry room

Music room & sunroom

bathhouse

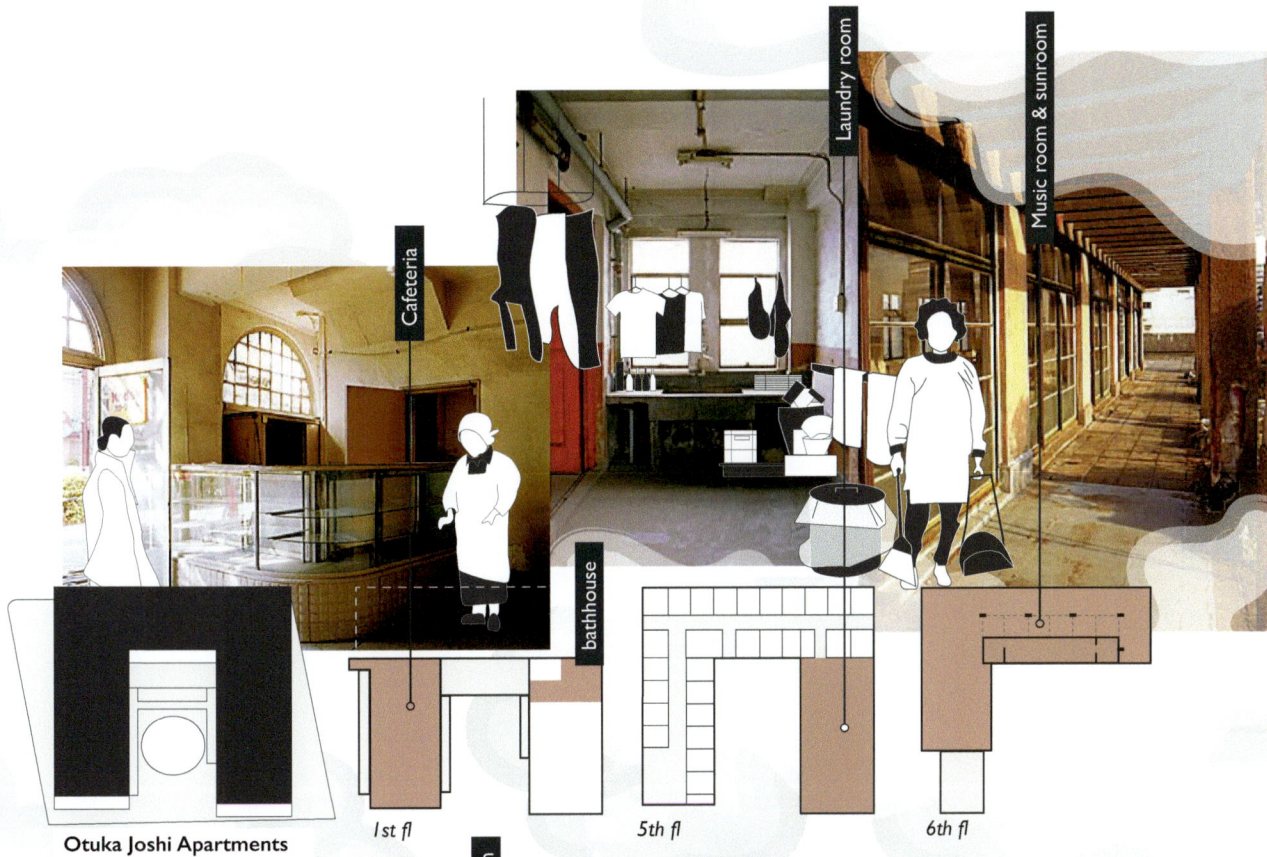

Otuka Joshi Apartments

1st fl

5th fl

6th fl

Bathhouse

Stores

Dining room, social room

Toukoen Apartments

Daikanyama Apartments

bathhouses and children's playrooms. One location had an outdoor courtyard used as a lobby, connected to the reception area. That building, the Otsuka women's apartment, made safety a priority, as it was specifically for professional women such as journalists, teachers, and doctors. The community laundry room was paired with the music and sunlight rooms on the top floor, and unlike other apartments, the bathhouse and dining room were for residents only. The café on the first floor, which supported women's entrepreneurship, was operated by the residents. The project was founded to support female empowerment and became an icon of the movement.[22]

Some scholars, like Imaizumi Yoshiko, are critical of the Dōjunkai housing, claiming that it segregated residents despite the original intent of trying to "widen the middle class." Others, like Satoh Shigeru, attribute part of the eventual recovery from the 1923 earthquake to the Dōjunkai apartment typology, allowing for more residential density in the city and a new type of collective urban housing.[23] As one of the first reinforced-concrete housing projects with embedded bōsai concepts, Dōjunkai transformed the predominantly unplanned urban fabric of low-rise *nagaya* into carefully designed multistory collective housing. It introduced a new lifestyle in a time of despair. The foundation was the main housing authority until 1941, and it revolutionized urban living in Japan by creating 12,076 temporary and permanent dwelling units.[24]

1945 ONWARD: THE SURGE OF PREFABRICATED HOUSING

In the aftermath of World War II, Japan faced a shortage of 4.2 million homes. To quickly rehouse its war-torn population, the nation embarked on a program of prefabricated (prefab) housing. By 1963, the Japan Prefabricated Construction Suppliers and Manufacturers Association (JPA) was formed to promote forward-looking prefab construction models. Because the factory environment is highly controlled and can replicate units at high volumes, prefab homes can often be built at a reduced cost and with a great degree of quality control. These qualities—speed, cost, ease of construction, and the ability to pre-build—make prefab units particularly useful for post-disaster applications. The majority of Japan's post-disaster temporary housing is constructed using prefab methods, which are also widely used for conventional housing: 15 percent of new housing is prefab,[25] including many high-end homes. Japan's long history of post-disaster housing and prefab applications has made the nation an expert in these technologies.

Japan Prefabricated Construction Suppliers and Manufacturers Association

The Japanese use of prefabrication for housing has a unique factor: in addition to the pervasiveness of the model even in normal times, all Japanese prefectures made pre-disaster agreements with the JPA by 1997. After 2011, most prefectures made additional agreements with other prefab associations.[26] This ensures that when a disaster does strike, the process of establishing disaster housing can begin quickly and efficiently. Following the 1947 Disaster Relief Act, the JPA provided specifications as to the size, structure, and cost of each house. Individual municipalities further prepare construction manuals attuned to the specific characteristics of their community (climate, geography, disaster vulnerability, demographics). The selected company has flexibility on some specifications, such as exterior cladding material. Fourteen JPA companies have standby resources in place in case of a disaster, including 176 factories and storage sites for prefabricated houses. Each JPA member can have up to two hundred temporary units pre-stocked.[27]

At the prefectural level, preparations also include estimating housing unit quantities that would be needed after a disaster (85 percent of prefectures have this in place) and determining in advance possible sites for installing temporary units (93 percent of prefectures have done this).[28] Individual JPA companies have predetermined agreements with material suppliers to help ensure that parts are available after a disaster. These pre-disaster agreements also help combat building material price inflation, a common post-disaster problem.[29] Importantly, these pre-disaster agreements at multiple levels reiterate the Japanese commitment to preemptively strategize, putting post-disaster plans into place prior to a catastrophe. This process is put to the test in annual drills and table-top exercises, organized by the JPA, to ensure that plans and communication strategies run effectively.[30] Each construction company also conducts its own annual exercises.

Until April 1, 2017, the standard JPA unit was nine *tsubo* (29.7 square meters). Smaller units were sized at six *tsubo* (19.8 square meters) for single people, and twelve-*tsubo* (39.7-square-meter) units were planned for large families. Based on the lessons learned from the 2011 disaster, prefectures are now able to decide on the size and layout within the fixed amount of ¥6,775,000.[31] Over time, the standard unit size has grown to accommodate increased expectations for living space. The predefined structure is a lightweight steel frame infilled with floor, wall, and ceiling panels. The foundation is wooden piles. Up to six units can be combined into a single linear building, typically organized in rows with entrances facing north and living rooms facing south to maximize daylight. Complexes with more than fifty units include facilities for community gatherings.[32]

1995 TEMPORARY HOUSING

During the 1995 Kobe earthquake, nearly 639,686 houses and 42,496 nonresidential buildings were damaged or destroyed.[33] Many government-sponsored reconstruction and readjustment projects were not completed until 2003, and some neighborhoods were still rebuilding in 2005. The earthquake necessitated nearly 48,300 temporary

Figure 63 (*next page*). The JPA housing network across Japan, with predetermined agreements to provide temporary housing after a disaster.

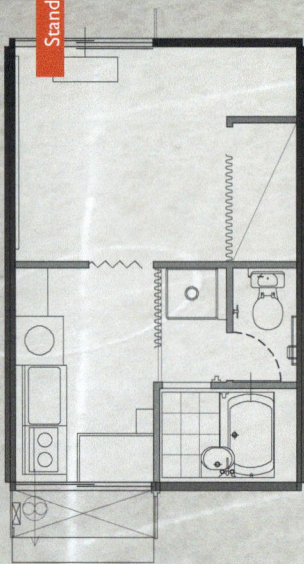

Standard 1DK

1800	1800
3600	

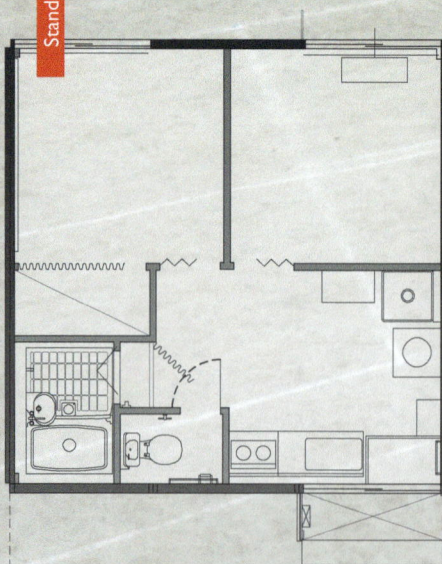

Standard 2DK

1350	1350	2700
5400		

contract

MEMBER COMPANY

JPA · president

↕

PREFECTURE · governor

MUNICIPALITY

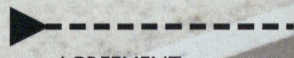

AGREEMENT

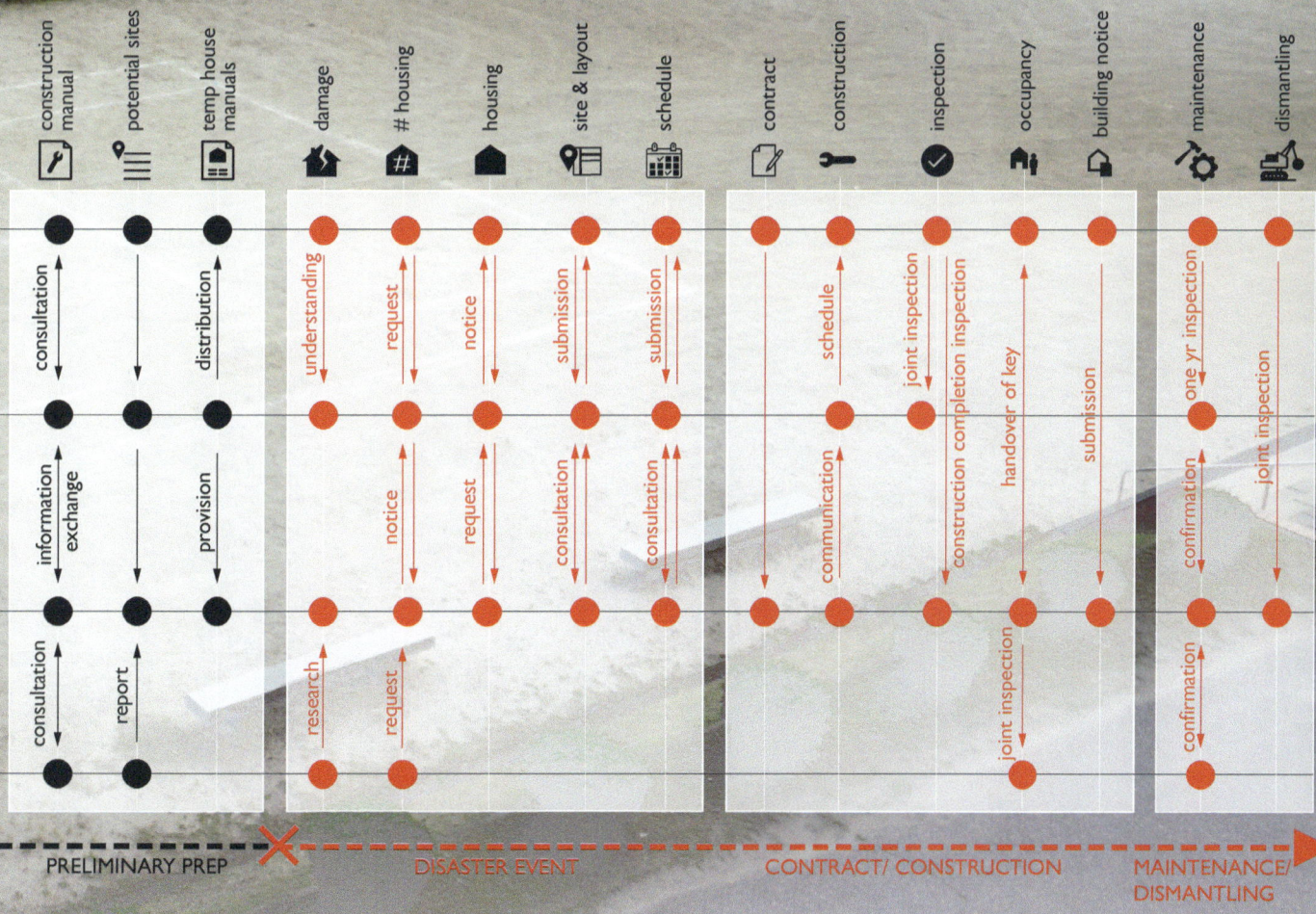

construction manual	potential sites	temp house manuals	damage	# housing	housing	site & layout	schedule	contract	construction	inspection	occupancy	building notice	maintenance	dismantling

PRELIMINARY PREP ✕ **DISASTER EVENT** **CONTRACT/ CONSTRUCTION** **MAINTENANCE/ DISMANTLING**

consultation — information exchange — consultation
distribution — provision — report

understanding — research
request — notice — request
notice — request
submission — consultation
submission — consultation

schedule — communication
joint inspection — joint inspection
construction completion inspection
handover of key
submission

one yr inspection — confirmation — confirmation
joint inspection

houses in 634 complexes,[34] of which 40,906 units were primarily JPA-supplied one-story and two-room steel structures of approximately 30 square meters.[35] The majority were completed within about three months of the disaster, and all were completed within seven months.[36]

Responding to residents' appeals to be housed near their former homes, the Higashi-nada and Chuo wards in Kobe used open spaces, such as parks alongside large tracts on Rokkō Island and Port Island, for temporary housing. Both islands, built as reclaimed land, were comparatively less dense, but they lacked amenities and easy access. For the most part, school grounds were not considered for housing, so children could return to school as soon as possible to restore a sense of normalcy. Many other wards lacked open spaces and therefore had to build their temporary housing on their outskirts, often two hours away by train and bus. Although these sites were distributed along rail lines, some were located a few kilometers away from the stations.[37] The housing construction manager of the Urban Housing Department of Hyogo Prefecture lamented, "We ought to have made a list of suitable sites before the disaster so that, when the disaster struck, we could fix the sites based on the number of units required. Then, at the state of creating the list, we could have gotten community consensus on problems that caused us headaches later, such as whether to use school premises and small private lots."[38]

To avoid relocation to distant sites and separation from their communities, schools, and livelihoods, many people remained instead in tents or privately rented prefabricated units in parks or playgrounds near their destroyed homes, in spite of government attempts to move everyone into shelters and temporary housing.[39] This led to construction of more than five thousand *jiriki* (self-built/initiated) temporary housing units. These units were an average of sixty-five square meters and were built at an average cost of ¥9 million. Eight hundred units were still in use nine years later and had been expanded and renovated for more comfortable use.[40]

Government-sponsored temporary housing was not available to everyone. Shortages arose in areas where fires severely damaged dense wooden tenement houses. The government had also established a "single-track" approach: to receive temporary housing, one had to remain in communal shelters (e.g., gymnasiums) until such housing became available. For some, that was up to seven months. Similarly, in order to receive access to permanent public housing units, survivors would have to remain in temporary housing units until public housing was completed. This was the only form of housing assistance offered, so those who sought to rebuild on their own received no support. Those who attempted to stay closer to their homes and jobs, through self-construction or by staying with friends and family, were similarly disadvantaged.[41] A quarter of the people who moved into public housing were previously homeowners and could have built on their own with the right advice and support from the municipality. Moreover, as the deadline loomed for publicly funded demolition under this single-track reconstruction approach, many survivors chose to demolish their houses even though many of the homes could have been repaired.[42]

Life in temporary housing was difficult. Occupants had just survived a horrific catastrophe, having lost their homes, their possessions, and in many cases their family members and friends. A lottery-based allocation system placed the elderly or people with special needs into housing first, which, in theory, seemed like a good decision. But this led to the fragmentation of communities across distant sites, making these residents even more reliant on public assistance.[43] Most of the occupants were elderly and/or low-income, since the government provides temporary housing assistance only to those who cannot otherwise afford post-disaster shelter.[44] Many sites lacked amenities such as shopping centers and medical services, and public transportation access was insufficient. This was particularly hard on the elderly, some of whom had limited mobility and more often lived alone. The tragic result was social isolation and up to one thousand cases of *kodokushi* (solitary deaths), in which people died alone and their bodies remained undiscovered for long periods of time. Alcoholism became a major problem: 40 percent of *kodokushi* victims (primarily men) had died from liver failure as a result of alcohol abuse.[45] Elderly women reportedly suffered from malnutrition in the temporary units.[46] Suicide rates rose as well.

These shortcomings can be linked to disconnection between the social and spatial: specifically, how the spatial design and planning for housing prioritized the physical needs of shelter without consideration of equally important social needs. The process lacked dialogue: occupants reported little to no participation in the post-disaster housing process, having no say in the type of housing they received or in types of amenities. Large families found themselves in overcrowded conditions in the small standard units. Bathroom designs with an elevated floor and high step into the bathtub were difficult, or impossible, for the elderly or for those in wheelchairs to use. Poor thermal design resulted in units that were too hot in summer and too cold in winter. Other problems were linked to the timeline of habitation: temporary housing was only designated for two years' occupancy, based on the Disaster Relief Act, but with reconstruction in many cases taking much longer, occupants faced uncertainty about their tenure. Further, the structures experienced leaks, mold, and rotting wooden foundations.[47]

In order to address the deficit of social amenities, temporary businesses opened in public spaces. For example, eighteen bars, restaurants, and shops whose premises had been destroyed on a shopping street near the Hanshin Ōishi train station operated in Togagawa Park.[48] These temporary enterprises allowed small business owners and their employees to retain their livelihoods, and their quick reopening meant that they could provide important amenities to citizens, maintaining their roles in the community. However, these interventions were limited and the lack of access to shopping was pervasive.[49] While some temporary social spaces—most notably Ban Shigeru's Paper Church—were created in the city, these types of amenities were especially lacking in temporary housing sites outside the city. This was particularly problematic given the disconnection of these sites from social networks and activities related to residents' livelihoods.

1995 PERMANENT HOUSING: NEW COLLECTIVE HOUSING TYPOLOGIES

Individual reconstruction following the Kobe earthquake was arduous because of the 1950 Building Standards Law, a national policy requiring that new construction be set back enough to accommodate a four-meter-wide road. However, Kobe venerated the cultural and social values of the traditional *roji,* and the city crafted a provision that if main roads were located every hundred meters, the *roji* could remain, as long as consensus among residents could be secured for engaging in fire-protection efforts.[50] But many original homes covered over 90 percent of their sites, and the standards prescribed that no more than 60 percent of the lots could be covered.[51] This was further complicated by Japan's complex land-ownership system, in which land and building could be owned and rented separately. While district planning in some cases was able to accommodate small alterations to the Building Standards Law, many households on small "nonconforming" lots required new building typologies to accommodate these regulations.[52]

New city regulations, such as the Bōsai Blocks Act for Dense Urban Areas, were enacted in May 1997 and promoted safer urban forms, especially self-initiated efforts by landowners.[53] This initiative produced positive results in Kobe, as it was easier to build public consensus than apply regulations to the land readjustment project. Under this system, Japanese government subsidized (1) one-third to one-half of the cost of land and construction for repairing housing and the improvement of facilities such as roads, parks, and meeting places; (2) one-third to two-thirds of the cost of acquisition and removal of damaged housing, relocating safe housing, and site and construction fees of public community housing to guarantee the residents' return; and (3) one-third of the construction costs of collective housing projects' common areas.[54]

The result was a number of experiments in collective *kyōdō tatekae* (joint rebuilding projects). Groups of adjacent owners in dense urban areas collectively financed the construction of apartment buildings or joint housing, sometimes adding floors or units that could be sold or rented to others as a way to help finance the project. Like machizukuri councils, joint housing groups received assistance from professional consultants through the Expert Dispatch Systems of Kobe and Hyogo Prefecture and were considered part of the land readjustment process. This new joint housing process allowed landowners and new participants to be joint owners; in some cases, original owners could choose to become tenants. Although site conditions, economic disparities between residents, and complex financing strategies made these plans challenging to implement, they offered the benefits of long-term development profits and ideal living conditions.[55] By 1998, a total of 4,318 units participated in joint housing reconstruction with great success.[56]

Kinmokusei Street Joint Housing Project

The first successful project was the Kinmokusei Street joint housing project in Nada Ward, led by CO-PLAN (Cooperative Planners Associates), which had been the tenant of a collapsed wooden apartment.[57] Under the Temporary Measures Act, when a rental unit was destroyed, the tenant was given the right to live there if the landlord rebuilt the housing. If the landlord chose not to rebuild, the tenant was given the right to rebuild and rent the unit. Combining government subsidies from the Bōsai Blocks Act, a housing loan system for self-initiated recovery, disaster recovery housing loans at below-market rates, and the joint housing project (a ten-year interest-free subsidy for projects constructing a single building on two or more plots of over two hundred square meters),[58] the Kinmokusei Street joint housing project was born. The three-story reinforced concrete structure was designed on two single-family home plots. In order to receive the subsidies, the plan required the creation of open space to prevent the spread of fire in the neighborhood; with this in mind, a parking space covered by a pergola was added along the street. On the ground floor, CO-PLAN operated a coffee shop, and another tenant ran a printing shop. CO-PLAN's office and two private rooms were on the second floor, and the third floor had two rental apartments. Although this project presented various problems and disagreements among tenants throughout the various stages, machizukuri consultant (and resident) Kobayashi Ikuo and Miyawaki Dan Architects' design managed to satisfy all parties.

Mikura 5

The Mikura 5 apartment in Nagata Ward was another experimental collective housing project coordinated by a local machizukuri NPO. Before the earthquake, the Mikura district consisted of 314 small timber-frame houses along narrow two-meter-wide streets.[59] Eighty percent of the district burned to the ground, and most households lost their homes and/or workplaces.[60]

The NPO, Machi-Communication, was founded by a local businessman, Tanaka Yasuzo, and a volunteer from Tokyo, Ono Koichiro. Soon after the earthquake, Ono brought a printing press from Tokyo and started distributing a newspaper called *Daily Needs* to provide survivors with supply distribution schedules, public bath locations, and other valuable information. Together, Machi-Communication helped organize traditional festivals, rice-cake making, and flower planting to encourage residents to return from the distant temporary housing sites. It also established the Mikura machizukuri association, with Tanaka as the chairperson.[61] After Kobe designated the

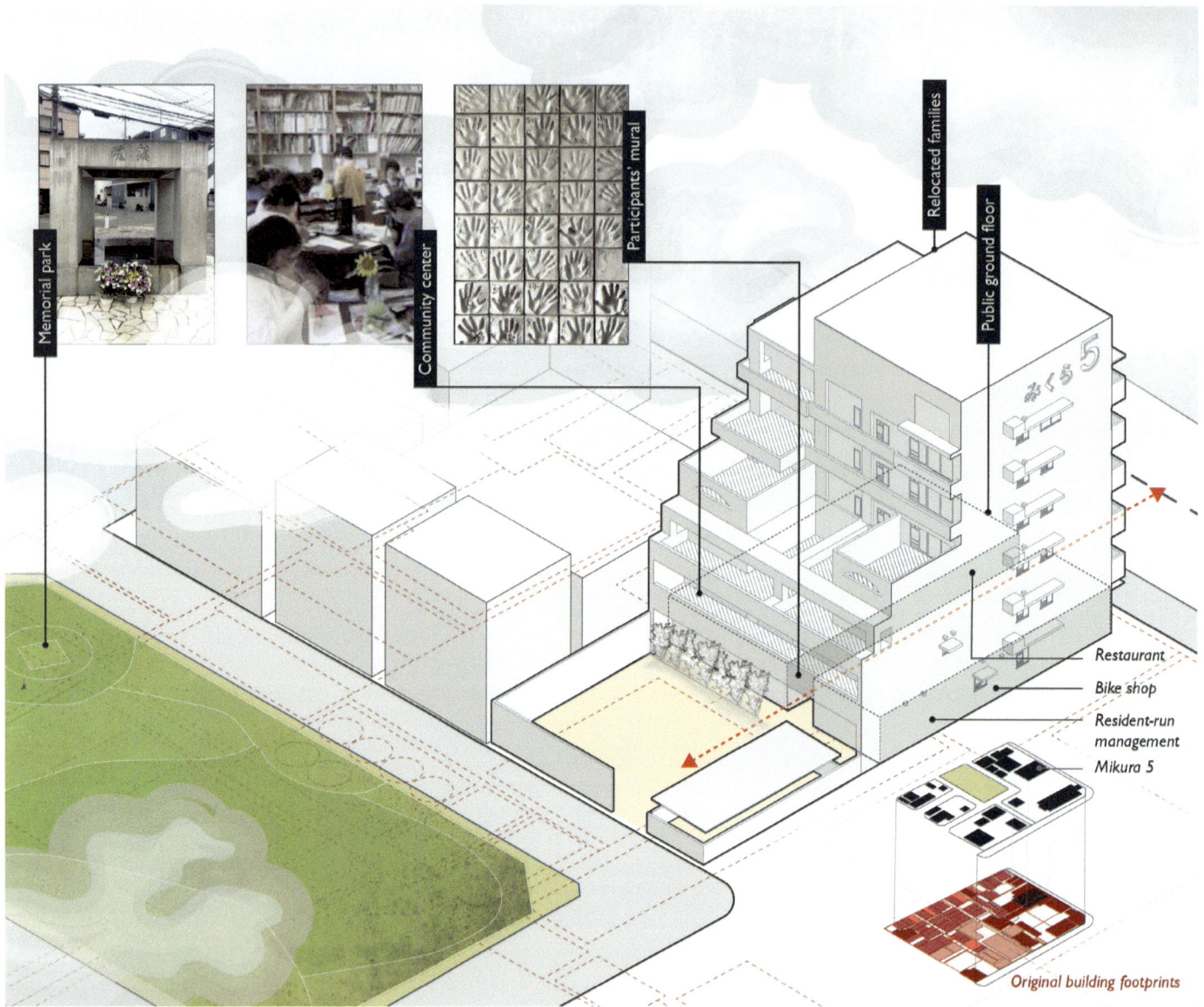

Figure 64. Mikura 5 collective housing created through land readjustment, with neighbors sharing a vision of recovery.

Labels on figure: Memorial park · Community center · Participants' mural · Relocated families · Public ground floor · Restaurant · Bike shop · Resident-run management · Mikura 5 · Original building footprints

Mikura district as a rezoning area, the association and Machi-Communication began discussions with architects, academics, and lawyers specializing in residents' rights; the goal was to aggregate small properties in the course of land readjustment.[62] In May 1997, they invited Endo Yasuhiro from Meijo University to hold a workshop on joint reconstruction, where residents expressed both individual needs and cooperative goals. Machi-Communication helped clarify objectives during the consensus-building process. The residents didn't always select the easiest solutions, but they agreed to endure challenges for their shared vision of recovery—an attitude rooted in their shared history, helping each other, as neighbors.[63]

DESIGN BEFORE DISASTER

Ten households and two shops joined the Mikura 5 project and created twelve units, differing in size and layout according to the situation of each household. Their original idea was to create additional rental units to offset construction costs, but they ended up having enough financial support within the original group.[64] Designed by Takeda Noriaki from Takeda Architecture & Design, the south-facing rooms feature generous balconies, and the façade steps down to allow ample light for all. A bicycle shop and a restaurant occupy the ground floor facing the main street. A public passage through the building connects the main street to the playground behind the building, open to everyone. Facing the playground on the ground floor is a community space called Plaza 5, run by the residents' organization and volunteers, which coordinates shared knowledge computer classes and daycare services for children and the elderly. Bringing together young volunteers and senior citizens was one of Machi-Communication's goals. Across the public passage, on the other side of Plaza 5, a tatami room is used for apartment management, social gatherings, and a guest room for residents' visiting relatives. Volunteers also use the room as an affordable accommodation. Displayed on the entry wall are concrete tiles with the handprints of Mikura 5 residents, construction workers, and members of Machi-Communication, showcasing their cooperation. Owing to its complexity, the project wasn't completed until 2001. Still, this project not only rehoused the residents but also became an important hub for the district through a land readjustment process of building trust and community.[65]

HAT Kobe *Fureai* Public Housing

The two projects above leveraged private property and citizens' cooperation, while the prefecture tested its public collective housing typology in the HAT Kobe reconstruction area. Happy Active Town (HAT) is an expansive mixed development with commercial spaces, offices, public facilities, and 3,542 units of public housing, built and operated by three separate entities: prefecture, city, and Urban Renaissance. Within the Waki-no-hama area of HAT Kobe are 1,656 disaster recovery housing units, of which 253 were constructed and are operated by the prefecture.[66]

One of these is the experimental Fureai apartment building, completed in April 1999. It has 32 one-bedroom units and 12 two-bedroom units designed for elderly people aged sixty and over. *Fureai* means "strong rapport" between diverse people. Here, the residents' association makes sure to include caretakers in the community. Dinner parties facilitate discussions with all residents and caretakers twice a month. Designed by Urban Renaissance agency + Ichiura Housing & Planning, the building has six floors, with every two floors grouped as a collective unit. Odd-numbered floors have a large, double-story communal room, including a shared laundry room, bathroom, and storage. Even-numbered floors have a small communal space with laundry and a place for chatting. Residents and neighbors can use the garden's five raised flower beds, which are seventy centimeters tall so that even people in wheelchairs can enjoy and easily maintain them.

Although intriguing as a typology, the design presents some challenges. The high-ceilinged communal rooms tend to be inefficiently heated in winter, and residents are not able to change light bulbs themselves. The stairs connecting two floors are too wide and dangerous for the elderly and were designed to connect only units sharing a communal room, so accessing other floors requires residents to use the elevator. The communal space does not include tatami rooms, and the office space on the first floor is never used. Moreover, the shared rooftop space is inaccessible because its door is always locked. Many post-disaster housing developments have such open spaces on the rooftop or middle floor, but few are actually used and most are locked. This demonstrates the failure of housing design to carefully consider how the residents would live there as a community. Designers need to plan how these communal spaces will be accessed, managed, and maintained.[67]

2011 TEMPORARY HOUSING

The Tohoku disaster left 450,000 homeless,[68] and within four months many had moved from shelters into temporary housing. In most regions, vulnerable populations (elderly, families with small children, and residents with special needs) were prioritized for the transition from evacuation shelters to temporary housing, which resulted in another splitting apart of social networks. For those who moved into temporary housing later, efforts were made to help communities relocate together,[69] but attempts by municipalities to recruit neighbors as a group were also complicated. For example, Sendai initially recruited groups of ten or more households to relocate to temporary housing, but only five groups applied for this program because many neighbors were unreachable, and housing sites offered were far inland. The city reduced the group size to a minimum of five households, and 302 applications were submitted—still far fewer than the number of units offered.[70] Group relocations were further complicated by the nature of Tohoku's geography, the scarcity of flat land, and the scale of the devastation. By 2019 the *kodokushi* toll at temporary housing in Tohoku had reached 243.[71] While this rate was much lower than that following the Kobe earthquake, it still reveals how temporary housing programs need to prioritize social infrastructure.

A Test of the JPA Network

The 2011 Tohoku disasters provided an even broader test of JPA's framework, including adaptations made in response to Kobe's shortcomings. After a disaster strikes, prefectures solicit the JPA to build a set number of temporary houses. Based on previously assessed capacities, the JPA then requests that individual companies within the association proceed with selected projects. This top-down process allows construction to be rapidly initiated. The JPA served as the primary coordinator for temporary housing construction following the Tohoku disaster.

By March 14, Iwate, Miyagi, and Fukushima Prefectures had requested 32,800 units from the JPA.[72] Preemptive arrangements enabled temporary housing construction to begin as soon as eight days after the earthquake, with completion of some homes after just three weeks.[73] However, in many cases, sites that had been identified for temporary housing had been inundated, and the amount of housing requested exceeded the JPA's capacity. While the Disaster Relief Act states that construction needs to start within twenty days after a disaster, the 2011 event's massive scale meant that some housing took six months to complete. A few cases took even longer, particularly in Fukushima, where uncertainty surrounding the radiation zone and a lack of uncontaminated sites limited the prefecture's ability to act.[74] JPA prefab housing accounted for 80 percent of the 53,077 units built.[75] Although the standard limit for temporary housing is up to two years, the CAO extended the term, and as of June 2023, about one thousand people still lived in temporary housing.[76]

The JPA modified its standards in response to shortcomings documented in Kobe's aftermath, and in many respects the units performed better. Even so, temporary housing occupants in Tohoku faced difficulties, particularly in light of the prolonged habitation of the "temporary" units and the average age of the residents. The JPA allows individual prefectures to make tailored specifications based on local characteristics. Given the large proportion of elderly people, prefectures requested accessible designs—including ramps and railings—to accommodate those with limited mobility. They also called for additional weatherproofing, increased insulation, heated toilet seats, bath reheating systems, and measures to prevent pipes from freezing. Cold-climate retrofits were completed at the end of December 2011, and the barrier-free alterations were finished by March 31, 2012.[77] But even with the additional thermal retrofits, the units remained cold. These modifications and the structures' prolonged occupation caused them to deteriorate over time. Rotting wood pilings led to tilting, and mold formed in the ceiling cavities. The additions also added to the cost per house, which was ¥6.17 million in Iwate, ¥7.3 million in Miyagi, and ¥6.89 million in Fukushima—all exceeding the ¥2.38 million Disaster Relief Act standard at the time.[78]

Locally Designed and Built

Japan's Disaster Relief Act has prioritized the use of prefab units for temporary housing, but the statute also allows for units to be constructed out of wood. The supply of prefab units on hand was insufficient to house survivors owing to the unprecedented scale of the damage, so prefectures permitted local construction companies with certain qualifications to bid on additional temporary housing projects. Of all the units, approximately 13 percent (6,829 units) were built by local construction companies using local wood.[79] Forestry forms a significant portion of Tohoku's economy, and the region is famous for products such as Kesen cedar, which is produced in coastal Iwate and processed at a Rikuzentakata factory.[80] The wooden temporary units drew upon local materials and knowledge, and they had the added benefit of helping restart local economies (for example, in the hiring of local carpenters).

Much of the sourcing and pre-cutting was done in Fukushima, because the bidding requirements included using prefectural timber. Some JPA member companies also constructed units using wood; however, these companies only had a 10 to 20 percent rate of local timber use.[81] In total, 13,335 temporary houses (about 25.6 percent) were built with wooden construction.[82]

Even though local timber construction took ten days longer than prefab,[83] many survivors preferred living in wooden housing after the disaster. Therefore, a new foundation was established to ensure the immediate supply of wooden temporary housing for future disasters. The All-Japan Society of Wooden Construction, established in September 2011, was a consortium of the Japan Builders Network (JBN) and the National Federation of Construction Workers Unions. Similar to the JPA, the All-Japan Society of Wooden Construction has established set standard plans (two bedrooms + dining room and kitchen, nine *tsubo*) for emergency temporary housing, and its specifications are based on conventional wooden construction methods, using 105-millimeter square timber for the posts and foundations, with 18-millimeter planks mainly used for rough floors, exterior wall finishes, framing, and flooring.[84]

In Fukushima, twelve developers were selected to build 4,000 additional units. One was Miharumachi Recovery Housing Construction Society, which built 19 apartments in Miharumachi at a cost of ¥5.4 million per apartment, including disassembly. Local construction knowledge made building on sloped sites possible, which was essential given the shortage of land. Using JPA standards, the units were built using a post-and-beam system common in the area. A combination of local cedar and polystyrene insulation kept out the cold. Slab concrete foundations also served to stabilize temperature and prevent pipes from freezing. Fukushima is home to one of the largest sawmill companies in the country, and the cedar was sourced by a local forest owner's cooperative association. Evacuees assisted in construction. Occupants reported that the use of cedar improved their quality of life in the temporary units, as the scent and warm appearance of the wood created a calming environment.[85]

TIMBER TEMPORARY HOUSING TRANSFORMATION INTO PERMANENT HOUSING

Aizu-Matsunaga Danchi

The Aizu-Matsunaga Danchi transitional housing in Aizu-Wakamatsu resulted from an additional round of bidding, with several units built on the grounds of a hospital. Because the scale of the project was too large for an individual design and construction team, four teams were assembled and four housing variations were built. A team headed by Haryū Wood Studio built 40 single-story units at a cost of ¥5,628,000 each.[86] These houses were constructed from 114-millimeter-thick local cedar to provide thermal insulation and moisture control. While the other three teams used a stick-built model, Haryū Wood Studio's pre-cut "log house" method also allowed simple on-site assembly, and survivors were hired to assist with construction. Two people could easily lift one log into place, and a crane was only required to place the roof.[87] The design was based on the construction method used for a 100-unit temporary housing complex in the nearby city of Kōriyama, with small modifications to incorporate lessons learned from the earlier iteration; for example, in Aizu-Wakamatsu the homes were designed with flatter roofs that could withstand heavy snow loads so that the elderly would not have to shovel as much. An airy, open-plan design partitioned with curtains and sliding walls exhibited the qualities of the wood, which was also used for the floors and ceilings. A member of the design team explained that an additional benefit of the wooden homes is that people can easily make their own modifications. On the homes they designed, occupants had added small roofs over the stairs to keep off snow. Breezeways had been closed off or porch areas had been added or enclosed in other units on the site. By modifying their homes in these small ways, families could transform them to better suit their needs and retain a sense of agency over their accommodations.

The timber construction method also allows for the wood to be disassembled and reused, and timber pilings leave little trace once the building is removed. By the spring of 2018, the majority of Haryū Wood Studio's units at Aizu-Matsunaga had been disassembled, and paved walking paths and service grates were the only clues that houses had ever stood on the site. Disassembled housing materials were transferred to be used in other locations to build mid- to longer-term housing. One example is the recovery accommodation facility for residents of Namie, where part of the town is designated as a hazard zone owing to the Fukushima Daiichi nuclear power plant accident. This facility, constructed from Haryū wood, welcomes short temporary stays of residents who are hoping to return home. Another example is Iitate village, where 12 wooden temporary housing units were relocated from Nihonmatsu and Minamisōma after six years. The timber was reused for permanent housing with the addition of 100-millimeter glass wool insulation.[88]

Itakura Wooden Panel System

Several other wooden temporary housing projects in Fukushima were constructed using the "Itakura wooden panel system," in which pre-assembled wooden panels reinforced with galvanized steel sheets can be lifted into place inside a timber frame. With this system, eighty carpenters built 198 houses (162 in Iwaki and 36 in Aizu-Wakamatsu) within three months, at a cost of approximately ¥6 million for each house. The temporary homes were designed with the intention of reuse; every 2 temporary homes would become 1 unit of public housing. In July 2015, the 36 houses in Aizu-Wakamatsu were disassembled and rebuilt into 20 new units. Dismantling each house took a team of five carpenters only two days, and the rebuilt public housing included 65.6 percent reused materials. The reassembled homes cost 18.6 percent less than newly built homes, even including the storage and transportation of materials.[89] Reassembled homes, built on a lot close to the Aizu-Wakamatsu train station, are part of a complex with permanent one-, two-, and three-bedroom units for displaced Fukushima residents.[90] A more permanent concrete foundation elevated the units a few feet above ground level. Open rafters created lofts and high ceilings to open up the space. Traditional Japanese architectural elements were included, such as *fusuma* and an *engawa*. More conventional concrete front porches were used for flower planters and seating. Despite its small footprint, even the one-bedroom unit feels spacious with the incorporation of these features. Occupants report that these more permanent homes are more thermally comfortable than the transitional units: during the summer, the front door and *engawa* can be opened up for cross ventilation, and during the winter, the smaller and lower-ceiling bedroom space can easily be kept warm. The loft spaces are especially useful for Fukushima residents who are storing belongings for their eventual return to hometowns in the radiation zone.[91]

These cases of locally designed and built temporary housing are significant not only for the way they leveraged regional resources but also for the aesthetics of their designs. The wooden homes are warm and inviting, and they smell of cedar. Constructed by local companies from local materials, they bring back jobs, are better attuned to the climate and geography, and allow community members to participate in their own rehousing. The Itakura houses were intended to feel like normal homes, even if temporary, and they are designed with a loft under the roof, which opens up the space and creates extra room for sleeping or storage. The wood's tactile, thermal, and noise-insulating properties add to the positive experience of this housing, and this added comfort is especially important given the trauma recently faced by the homes' inhabitants. Temporary housing is not just about the basics of sheltering and utilities; these cases show how the architecture can also help support physical and emotional comfort in a difficult time without added cost. A space for residents to take off their shoes, a place to chat with a neighbor in the doorway: these and other small details help recreate cultural and social contexts and improve residents' experiences. These personal qualities and their impacts on the mental health and well-being of survivors become increasingly important in times of crisis.

COMMUNITY-CARE TEMPORARY HOUSING COMPLEXES

Kobe's social isolation problems affirmed that community building in temporary housing is one of the most important factors behind survivors' long-term recovery from the disaster. Community-based occupancy, introduced after the 2004 Chūetsu earthquake, aimed to maintain neighborhood ties and enhance social interaction in temporary housing complexes by securing sites close to each neighborhood before a disaster, so that communities can move together into the same complex. In addition to the survivor allocation process and the physical design of units, the configuration of temporary housing on-site in relationship to the other units can impact occupants' experiences.

In some projects, design efforts were also made to create relationships. The typical array of identical, monodirectional temporary housing rows lacks shared social spaces for informal meeting and is not conducive to building social networks. Public space is often neglected in temporary housing installations. Recognizing the problems of more technocratic approaches to housing, a team from the University of Tokyo (led by Otsuki Toshio and Tomiyasu Ryōsuke) and Iwate Prefectural University (led by Kano Toru) designed and built two "Community-Care" temporary housing complexes in the Iwate cities of Kamaishi and Tōno, with an eye to people with special needs and the elderly.[92] Beyond the daycare, clinic, and shops, the complexes included a mix of floor plans to help promote diverse family types, with facing entrances and open interior plans. In some zones, sheltered wooden decking in the alley created a shared semipublic space. The deck also eliminated the need for a step between the alley and the entrance to the home, improving accessibility. A preliminary study by the design team found that the semipublic space in the deck zone quickly filled with personal items like ornaments and flowerpots, as well as chairs and tables that created shared spaces for socializing. A laundry area designed with intimate seating similarly cultivated social interaction; it was particularly successful in engaging elderly men, who were otherwise less represented in shared spaces.[93] Occupants reported that this spatial configuration, which is a simple manipulation of the existing prefab model, enabled community building. Understanding that even short-term homes and the common areas around them are a community, rather than discrete units, can help counter the isolation that temporary housing can create.

TEMPORARY HOUSING *MINASHIKASETSU*

In addition to prefab housing, empty rental apartments helped meet the unprecedented need. Japan has a high vacancy rate—13.65 percent[94]—and rural areas like Tohoku in particular suffer from depopulation. In this national subsidy program of *minashikasetsu* (emergency rental housing), prefectures rent out vacant apartments as temporary housing, usually through contracts between the prefecture, the landlord, and the tenant. The monthly rent, fire insurance premiums, and brokerage fees are paid by the prefecture for up to two years, and the tenants can extend the contract annually.[95] Alternatively, the subsidy can be applied to apartment rental units that disaster survivors find on their own. The government's financial burden is much lower than it would be for constructing, maintaining, and demolishing prefab housing. Eighty thousand rental housing units, located across forty-six prefectures, supplemented the fifty-three thousand prefab units in seven prefectures.[96] Many were centrally located, and more than 40 percent of survivors preferred them over prefab housing because they could choose locations and move in sooner.[97] In January 2012, MLIT and the Ministry of Health, Labor and Welfare (MHLW) changed their policy to prioritize securing emergency rental housing and provided prefectures with guidelines on rental procedures.[98] They also encouraged pre-disaster coordination with local real estate companies, similar to the JPA agreements.[99]

Urban areas like Sendai faced challenges with this system because of high rental costs. According to the Disaster Relief Act, survivors were meant to receive housing within the same value bracket as the property they had lost. This resulted in the national government permitting survivors to move out of their original municipality. Over half of the tenants in Sendai wanted to continue living in the same apartment even after the subsidy period expired. However, only 9.8 percent of them could afford the full monthly rental fee.[100] This was also problematic for elderly people who then wished to move back to their original municipalities but had difficulty accessing up-to-date information online.[101] Isolation was an issue. Many prefab housing complexes emphasized support for social, physical, and mental health, monitoring, and community amenities, but individual rentals had few (or none) of these perks. Despite these challenges, the program remains one of the most useful tools for quickly rehousing people after disasters.

2011 TEMPORARY TO PERMANENT (HOUSING AND COMMERCE)

Some of the most ubiquitous temporary social spaces in the Tohoku post-disaster context are shopping complexes: supermarkets, barbers, laundromats, wholesalers, restaurants, cafés, bars, souvenir shops, disaster memorial booths, and community centers. Seventy temporary shopping centers were created after the earthquake, and three were still operating as of September 2020.[102] The city can acquire land and recruit shops (as in Rikuzentakata); local businesses may acquire their own land (as in Kamaishi); in some cases, temporary shopping centers are formed as a public-private collaboration. The businesses inside are typically operated by pre-disaster local business owners, allowing them to continue their trades. Others may be new operations initiated by disaster survivors looking for an alternative way to earn income. These spaces also serve as important gathering places for communities shattered by the disaster.

Minamimachi Murasaki Market

Naiwan district in Kesennuma is a central port with fisheries and tourism, and it was severely affected by the tsunami. Out of its 410 houses, 344 were partially or completely destroyed.[103] Most of the businesses were rental tenants, so they could not rebuild themselves. Local leaders spurred the creation of a temporary marketplace; a croquet shop owner, for instance, started offering goods out of his lightweight truck. Soon, several businesses gathered to form the Kesennuma Minamimachi Murasaki Market, which operated from December 2011 to April 2017. The market got its name because local residents evacuated to the Murasaki Shrine behind the shopping district. During a 2015 visit, the shopping street consisted of two rows of double-stacked container units, opening to a narrow alley with balcony access to second-level shops and restaurants. Shops sold local products, including items emblazoned with the town mascot, Hoya Bōya, a cartoon boy in the likeness of a local seafood product, the hoya. The block of units occupied a low-lying zone that had been inundated by the tsunami, and its exterior walls had been painted with colorful murals. The mini-district bustled with visitors sampling the many small businesses. The shopping street helped businesses bridge the gap before they could find more permanent quarters at the newly built Minamimachi Murasaki Shrine shopping center, attached to a public housing complex.

Since part of the district was designated as a hazard zone after the tsunami, property owners had difficulty securing land for housing. The thirty-five-person machizukuri council was established in 2012, and through discussions among experts, residents, and Kesennuma officials, it proposed a joint strategy that included business reconstruction and public housing development. Through land readjustment, former residential and business sites now within designated hazard zones were united to create a mixed-use project of housing, commercial, and community facilities. The upper-floor residential units were purchased by the city as public housing, and the ground floor was occupied by stores and other businesses, in line with regulations for development in hazard zones.[104]

After the Tohoku earthquake, large-scale reconstruction projects in many regions resulted in the fragmentation of communities and the loss of local culture. The Naiwan district avoided this by encouraging residents and the local government to interact frequently. The machizukuri council took responsibility for the consensus-building process with the city to address problems with constructing housing in the hazard zone. The residents were thus able to design their own unique mixed-use building (personal, public housing, and commercial) that fit their current and future needs. As a result, residents remained in the original district and created profitable communal facilities, with businesses maintaining their local identities. Rather than letting bōsai regulations restrict reconstruction activities, the machizukuri process helped both the city and the residents benefit from the project.[105]

Minamimachi Murasaki Shrine shopping center & public housing complex creatively applied reconstruction programs & subsidies

PUBLIC HOUSING
Purchased by the city

PROPERTY OWNER RESIDENCES

≤ ¥2 million subsidy provided through *disaster victims' relief subsidy & reconstruction housing loans* [ii] and

≤ 80% of the feasibility study, planning, design fees for the project, & construction of common areas for landlords were covered by the *disaster-safe building development project subsidies* [ii]

GROUND FLOOR BUSINESSES

≤ 25% of construction was covered using *small-medium business restoration subsidy* [i]

< 75% of construction was covered using *small-medium business restoration subsidy* [i]

Hoya Boya

Shopping center

2017 - present

Minamimachi Murasaki Shrine shopping center & public housing complex

City-owned land

2011-2017 Kesennuma Minamimachi Temporary Murasaki Market

Until 2011 Pre-tsunami buildings

Homeowners' land

[i] Kesennuma, "Reconstruction / Recovery Project Efforts and Issues," [in Japanese] (March 2018), 41, http://www.kesennuma.miyagi.jp/sec/s019/21suishinkaigi_shiryou2.pdf.
[ii] Kesennuma, "Progress of the Naiwan District Joint Housing Project for Post-Disaster Public Housing," [in Japanese] March 19, 2015, https://www.kesennuma.miyagi.jp/sec/s019/010/010/020/026/270319/26002703l9iinkai_01.pdf.

2011 PERMANENT HOUSING: COMMUNITY-BASED TYPOLOGIES

After long periods in temporary housing, new bonds form between residents—bonds that have the potential to be severed through transitions to permanent housing. In Kobe, when residents moved to permanent housing after five years in their temporary homes, they reported again feeling disconnected from the social networks that they had created while living in the temporary communities.[106] Many of the public housing sites were also distant from the residents' original neighborhoods, and people had little say about the units in which they were placed.[107] As of 2020, twenty-five years after the earthquake, solitary deaths still occur in permanent housing in Kobe; 75 people passed away this way in 2019, bringing the total number to 1,172. In Tohoku in 2019, the number of solitary deaths in permanent public housing surpassed the number in temporary housing, reaching 251. In Miyagi, the duration of time between the occurrence of death and discovery was also reported to be more than two days in 59.9 percent of cases.[108] This illustrates the isolation faced by residents in public housing and underscores that transitions out of temporary housing to permanent housing require equally careful strategies to help protect social ties, which are fundamental to recovery. This section introduces cases in which municipalities made efforts to maintain pre-disaster communities, from sheltering to temporary housing to permanent housing.

Shōbutahama Public Housing

Shichigahama was the smallest 2011 tsunami-affected municipality, with a population of 20,855 before the tsunami.[109] Situated on a peninsula surrounded by the ocean, 36.4 percent of the town was inundated, and 99 residents perished; 1,324 houses were severely damaged or completely destroyed. The most affected district, called Shōbutahama, endured a 12.1-meter-high tsunami two kilometers inland, and a fire broke out at the petroleum refinery. At the peak, thirty-six shelters were set up in the town, and up to 6,143 people evacuated.[110]

The town's thirteen districts had many generations of fisheries with tight-knit communities, each proud of its own unique culture. In the immediate aftermath of the disaster, the most common request from residents was that they would like to resettle with neighbors to the high ground within their original district. In the reconstruction process, the town established a vision with the residents at an early stage, encouraging them to remain and rebuild together through clear, transparent, bidirectional communication. For example, the town provided information about public subsidies and published the estimated price of inundated private property early, allowing residents to consider the sale price in their recovery plans.[111]

The district, which accepted a few people from other districts, made extra efforts to create a welcoming culture. In the Matsugahama district, four workshops were held

Figure 65. The Murasaki Market machizukuri process created a vibrant mixed-use project creatively using a variety of reconstruction programs and subsidies.

over the course of a year in which future residents gathered to discuss how to allocate residential units to satisfy all of their needs and what the community would be like after resettlement. Workshops included the district mayor, town officials, residents, the NPO in charge of community support at the temporary housing, and architect Onoda Yasuaki of Tohoku University, who helped draft the public housing guidelines to include strategies to increase communication between neighbors.[112]

Prior to the tsunami, each district of Shichigahama had its own assembly hall at the center of the community; the quick restoration of those assembly spaces was recognized as the key to community regeneration. Eight halls now operate as lifelong-learning facilities with disaster-preparedness functions on high ground near the resettlement housing. These typically function as a central gathering place for the community and, in the event of a disaster, as an emergency shelter for one hundred people.[113] The new local evacuation plan and the hazard map indicate routes from the coast to these emergency evacuation spaces. The width and number of evacuation roads were carefully planned according to the topography of the shore, the size of the flood hazard zones around it, and the number of evacuees who could be accommodated in the emergency shelters.[114] Onoda explains that "the municipality communicated carefully with residents and encouraged many survivors to remain. This enabled officials to put together a more accurate reconstruction plan for public housing."[115]

In addition to the community space, design of the public housing was carefully considered, especially in settlements with many single occupants and aging households. As a social measure, Onoda stressed the importance of building a guardianship system using existing organizations and networks, such as social welfare councils and nursing-care facilities.[116] He also proposed the "living (room) access" housing typology,[117] which enhances residents' awareness of each other and supports their ability to care for each other. In the living access typology, the living room and the entrance of the dwelling unit face the common spaces—such as the hallway and courtyard.

Many of the government housing apartments built after the Kobe earthquake were designed in accordance with conventional Japanese public housing—a single shared corridor with the unit's entry to a hall flanked by two bedrooms (most often with their curtains closed). Once the resident enters and closes the door, it is hard for neighbors to perceive what is happening inside. This allows for privacy, but it was also one of the largest causes of the *kodokushi* in the Kobe earthquake. With the living access design, there is a higher possibility that neighbors will notice at an early stage if any residents deviate from their usual daily activities or become inactive.[118] The planners chose the architects who submitted community-oriented proposals through a design competition conducted in cooperation with Tohoku University, Japan Institute of Architects, and ArchiAid.[119]

With Onoda's guidance, the public housing in all of Shichigahama had the goal of averting *kodokushi* and deterring suicide. For example, the Shōbutahama district

Figure 66. Shōbutahama public housing explored the living access housing typology within the Shichigahama relocation process.

Projects facilitating group relocation

Disaster recovery public housing construction projects

Devastated area reconstruction land distributions

Evacuation shelters, public facilities, misc. projects

Inundation zones

Conventional public housing

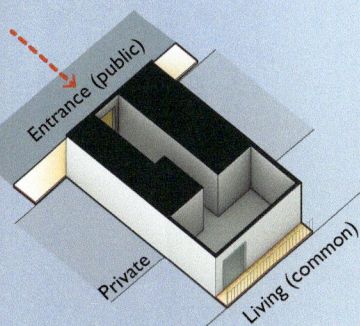

Entrance (public)

Private

Private

Living (common)

Living access housing

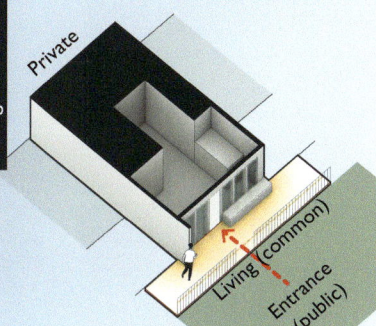

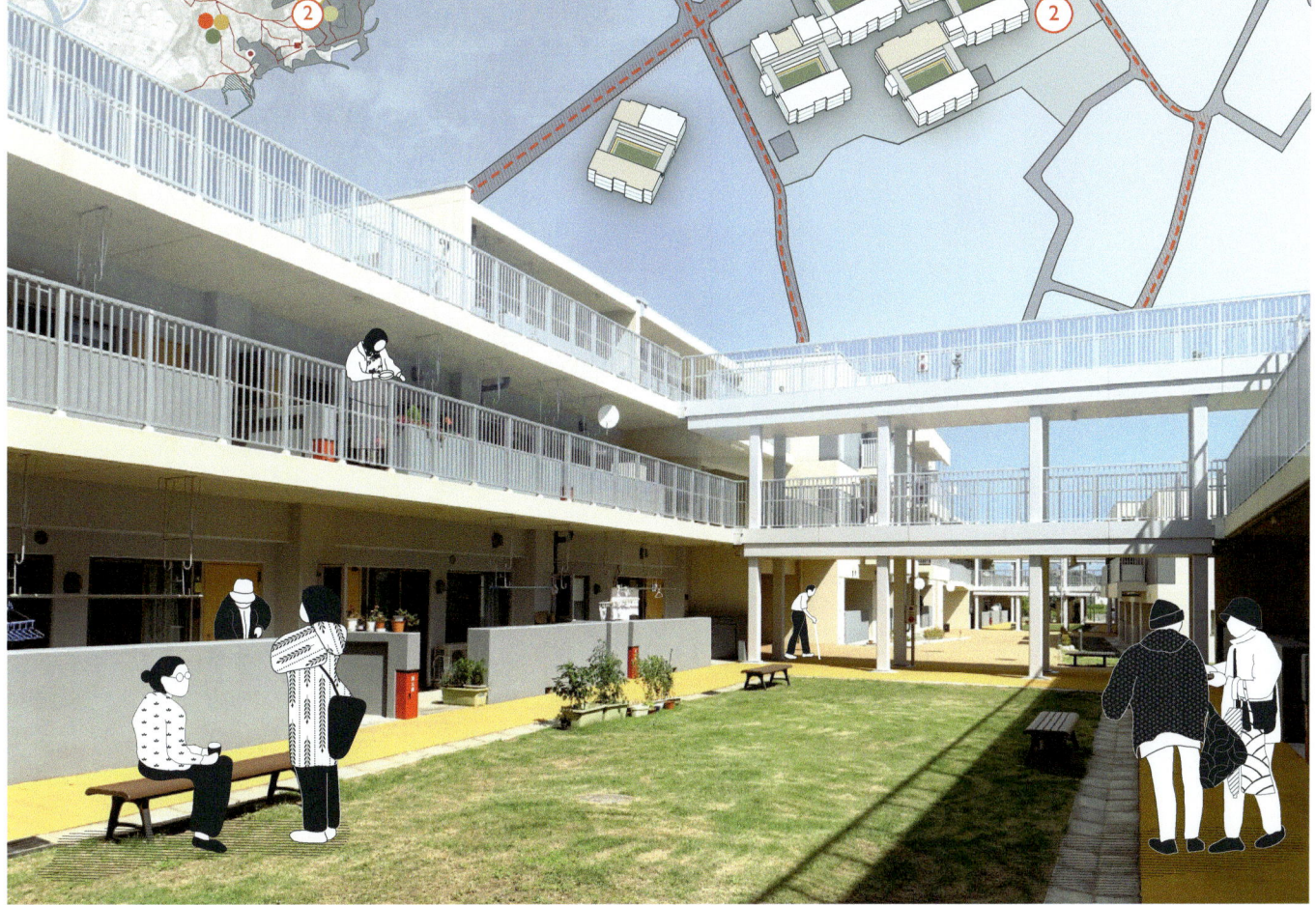

Private

Living (common)

Entrance (public)

Evacuation center

Shobutahama public housing

selected Atelier Hitoshi Abe's proposal, which divided one hundred units into five separate blocks in accordance with the pre-disaster neighborhoods. Each block has paired three-story wings, connected by a community deck, and the living rooms of twenty households face a shared courtyard. The courtyard not only serves as a place for the community but also provides an appropriate distance between the units facing one another, ensuring some privacy as well as increasing awareness of other residents. With this design, one can watch over the children playing in the courtyard from the community deck that connects the two buildings.[120] Openings facing the community garden are floor-to-ceiling sliding doors to allow for maximal light. In addition, a setback of units on the upper floors ensures sufficient sunlight to the living room of the first-floor apartment in the north wing.[121] The original design had community gardens and communal kitchens to increase the potential for social activities, but Abe laments that these were cut due to questions of maintenance and management.

Tamaura-nishi Public Housing

Living access was not the only housing typology aimed at preventing isolation and fostering neighborly interactions. The Tamaura-nishi relocation housing site, designed through the machizukuri process with the city and representatives from the six former coastal settlements, also aimed to encourage community building.

On the flat plains south of Sendai, Iwanuma City consisted of six settlements along the coast. The tsunami flooded 48 percent of the city and destroyed 1,245 houses. Soon after the disaster, representatives of each settlement and city officials started discussing plans, and in November they agreed on a twenty-hectare bōsai relocation site prepared by city officials in the Tamaura district. A machizukuri council was established with representatives from each settlement, the city, and academics. Through twenty-eight meetings between June 2012 and December 2013, the council determined the land use and layout of residential lots and public facilities, such as parks and assembly halls.[122] Residents in Iwanuma evacuated to shelters and then moved into temporary housing together, district by district, with their original neighbors, so each settlement could discuss their reconstruction plan from an early stage.[123]

The bōsai relocation site was divided into four public housing blocks (111 units), five self-build plots (158 plots), four parks, four community assembly spaces, and a shopping center. Each block is connected by the Teizan greenway pedestrian path, which crosses the entire relocation site to encourage socializing among residents in different blocks.[124] Four local architects were selected through a competition for each public housing block. Although the designs vary, all of them consist of one- or two-story housing that blends in with the surrounding landscape of single-family houses.[125]

Teshima Hiroyuki of the Urban Architectural Design Group/UAPP connected forty-four wooden houses via a universally accessible common deck, arranged in

Figure 67. Tamaura-nishi public housing. Residents moved to shelters and temporary housing together to plan their reconstruction.

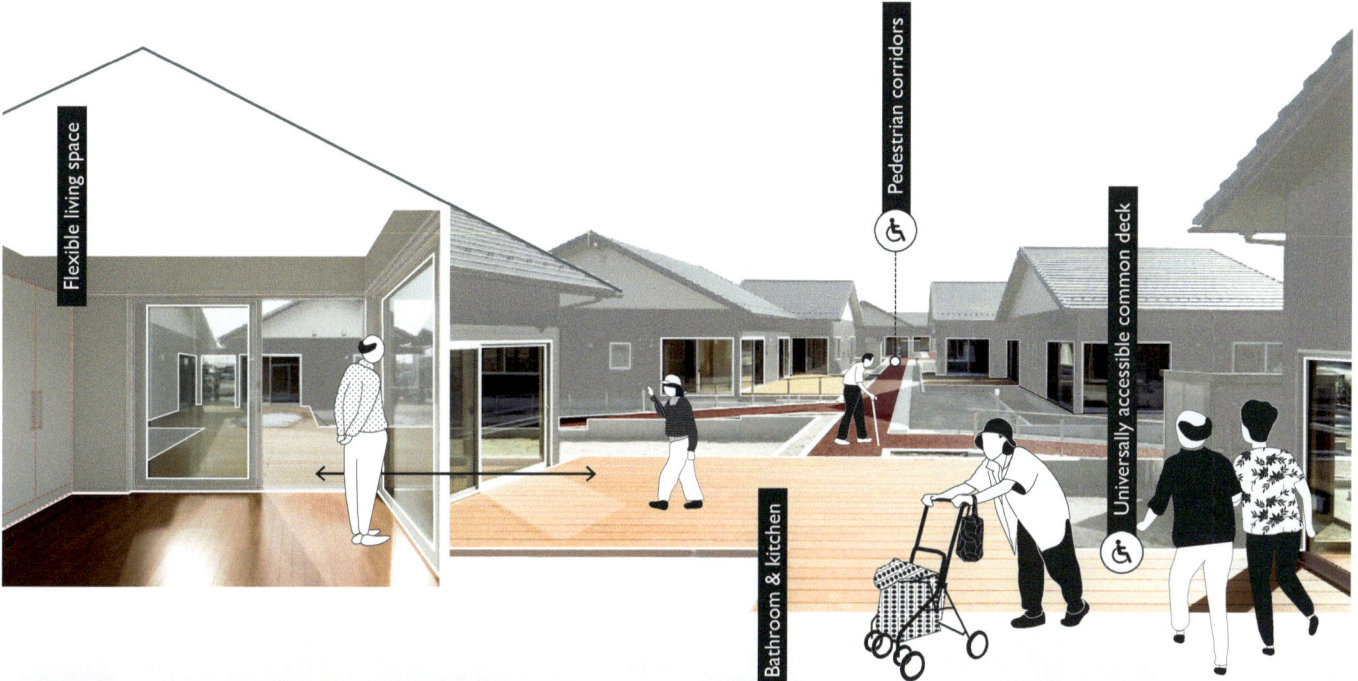

Flexible living space

Pedestrian corridors

Universally accessible common deck

Bathroom & kitchen

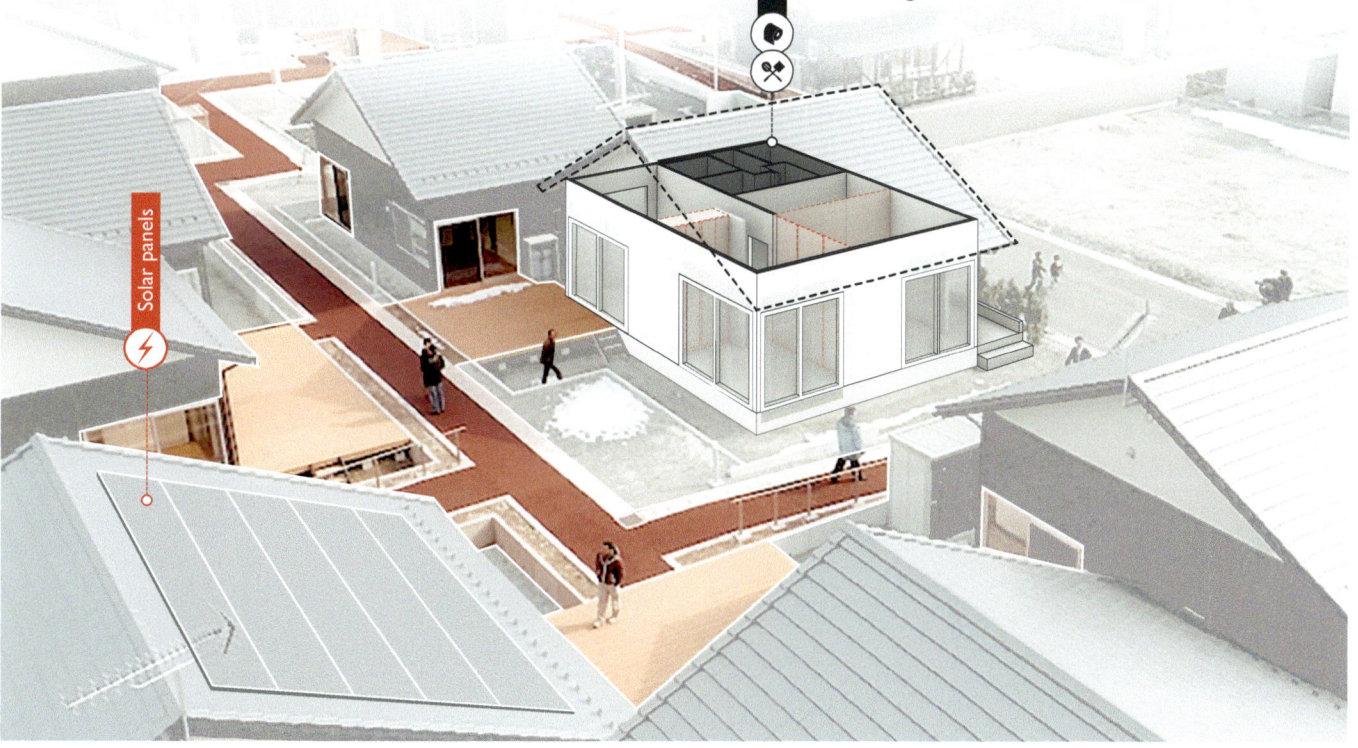

Solar panels

a rotating manner according to the site conditions of the Tamaura-nishi B-1 block. Clusters of three or four units are linked, but to complement the surroundings, they are made to look like single-family houses. Each unit is laid out with the bathroom and kitchen in one corner and the remaining 75 percent of the floor area as living space that can be partitioned by sliding doors. Bathrooms have two entrances, so the elderly can have quick access from any room; the built-in furniture, which is fixed to the walls for seismic safety, can be moved to meet a resident's spatial needs by unclipping the brackets.[126] In order to avoid the dull uniformity in most reconstruction public housing, the units are oriented and staggered around pathway intersections. The universal-access common decks have embedded wood fibers and seem like an extension of each living area; they are connected to the pedestrian corridors by a slope. This connection enables elderly residents to build community by easily visiting each other; it also connects to the Teizan greenway pedestrian path, which leads to the other residential blocks, parks, community assembly spaces in the parks, and the grocery store and pharmacy.[127]

2016 AND BEYOND

After the 2016 Kumamoto earthquakes, the *minashikasetsu* became even more popular. The rental allowance was up to ¥60,000 per month for individuals and up to ¥90,000 for households with five or more members. As of August 2018, 70 percent of survivors had moved into *minashikasetsu*.[128] This brought with it a range of issues: some people had much longer commutes and school transfers; the physical and mental health of the elderly worsened, owing to the lack of regional medical and monitoring services; and people felt isolated, detached from neighborhood ties. In the town of Mashiki, which was the most severely affected by the earthquake, 75 percent of survivors moved out of the municipality to live in *minashikasetsu,* leaving their communities. Of the twenty-eight people who died of *kodokushi* after the earthquakes, twenty-two were living in *minashikasetsu.*[129]

Despite these challenges, urban centers with limited space may need to employ the *minashikasetsu* process. For example, Tokyo is planning preemptive reconstruction scenarios, including how to best use *minashikasetsu* as a tool. A Japan Broadcasting Corporation (NHK) simulation estimates that if a magnitude 7.3 earthquake hits Tokyo, at least 570,000 temporary housing units will be needed—but according to its estimates of land availability, only 80,000 can be built. On the other hand, as of 2017, there were 490,000 vacant apartments in the city and surrounding districts.[130] Beyond the loss of social ties, high rent prices are a major hurdle in Tokyo. The rental subsidy after Typhoon Habibis was ¥95,000 a month for a one- to two-person household and ¥150,000 a month for a family of five, which is substantially lower than rental rates in Tokyo. The TMG has committed to support the high rental costs by signing agreements with five of the largest property management associations,[131] but allowance and rental price discrepancies between different regions in the country are a looming concern.

DISCUSSION

Much can be learned from Japan's approaches to temporary and reconstruction housing, which continue to evolve with the experience of major disasters. Its use of prefab homes, with an emphasis on preestablished agreements, shows the importance of blue-sky planning in order to allow temporary housing to be rapidly deployed (especially if suitable locations are also determined in advance). This shows the potential of a centralized, top-down approach to establish a baseline of housing quality, performance, and speed of deployment.

However, there are some limitations to prefabricated units. Not only is the construction fee high, but so is the cost of demolishing temporary housing, not to mention the cost to the environment (in life-cycle analysis). Per-house construction and demolition costs were ¥3.26 million after the 1995 earthquake, and although 11,858 prefab units were donated to other countries suffering from disasters, the disassembly or disposal of the rest remains unknown.[132] After the Tohoku earthquake, the construction and demolition fees for a house averaged ¥8.51 million. On the other hand, in the case of leased temporary housing, the average three-year rental was ¥2.16 million per apartment, which is about a quarter of the cost of construction and demolition of prefab temporary housing.[133] Projects like the Itakura wooden panel system house suggest how temporary housing parts might be reused in the creation of permanent homes.

Considering the transition from temporary to permanent housing as part of the disaster timeline underscores the challenges of moving in and out of temporary housing, particularly in locations where reconstruction will be a long and difficult process. Being near community members is important for residents to engage in discussions and make informed collective decisions. Perhaps a new typology can transfer a home from temporary to permanent,[134] or perhaps a process like Mikura 5 can start even before a disaster, as proactive reconstruction planning. Planning for post-disaster housing that accommodates existing social networks and keeps survivors close to home can leave communities stronger and better able to cope with the impacts of a calamity. The sooner residents can move into permanent housing and begin to rebuild their lives, the better prepared they will be for subsequent risks.

Shrines and Temples

Shrines and temples are major hubs of culture and community in Japan, particularly in rural villages and towns, and in *shitamachi,* low-lying and dense urban areas. Shrines are the sacred spaces of Shintoism—an Indigenous, polytheistic, and animist religion formalized in the eighth century. Especially in rural agricultural areas, Shinto shrines are the visceral cores of society. Members of the community have a sense of belonging to the shrine as one of *ujiko* (shrine parishioners, or children of the guardian god), which fosters the tight-knit relationships among them. Historically, in many shrines, ceremonies were held to support agricultural production and community life, and residents were involved in shrine management and care. Shrines are also used as spaces where older residents educate young residents through cooperatively managing festivals.[1] Buddhist temples are places of worship and ritual tradition and often hold monasteries. One of the meanings of the Chinese character for temple 寺 is "government office," and temples in the Edo era often served as public offices. Until the end of the 1800s, temples were also the center of intellectual activities in local communities. Buildings in the temple complex were used for *terakoya,* a type of school or training center for local children (which was the origin of Japanese elementary schools), and for *kou,* which provided adults a place to learn Buddhism and exchange information.

Shrines and temples are part of the everyday lives and practices of the residents of Tohoku. They are public and community spaces, visited frequently, especially for important life events—births, weddings, deaths—and at moments of major decisions. This centrality of shrines and temples as social, cultural, educational, and even administrative hubs of communities, in addition to spatial factors such as their high-ground positioning and flexible architecture, made them crucial for disaster preparedness and response, particularly in rural Japan. As vernacular everyday gathering spaces and post-disaster spaces, they have served as key sites for evacuation, sheltering, and disaster response, both historically and during recent disasters. In the context of anticipatory design, shrines and temples are important for illustrating how existing culturally embedded public spaces can perform—and are necessary hosts for—essential activities throughout the disaster timeline: education and creating community before disaster strikes, evacuation and sheltering during a disaster, and post-disaster recovery of society and faith.

SHRINES AS HIGH-GROUND EVACUATION SPACES

Shintoism foregrounds relationships to nature. Shrines were often built on ridgelines, hilltops, and slopes, with reverence for the natural environment, as it is believed that the hearts of mountains are the homes of Shinto gods. Buddhist temples, by contrast, are more commonly positioned on flat ground closer to residential areas.[2] Before the Edo era, in the Tohoku region, shrines were commonly built on or near fortress sites that had been constructed on hilltops to allow for panoramic views of the lands below.[3] Researchers found that the majority of shrines in the Sanriku region remained outside the inundation zone during the 2011 tsunami.[4] Running up to a shrine following a strong earthquake is part of the vernacular disaster-preparedness knowledge of the area, a lesson passed down by community elders. Iconic red *torii* gates marking the entrances to shrines dot coastal landscapes to easily identify evacuation paths.

Mishima Shrine

The spatial relationship between a shrine and the rest of the town can help facilitate this evacuation function. European towns often have an agora at the center, but Japanese settlements in mountainous geographies developed along roads. In such linear villages, shrines were located at the periphery of the village, interfacing with the forested mountain where the spirits live.[5] For example, Mishima Shrine in the Utatsu district of Minamisanriku is sited on top of a thirty-meter hill near the town's coastal edge. Founded in 1337, the shrine is dedicated to the god of the sea and of business. The entrance *torii* gate marks a stairway leading to the shrine, and both align with the town's main street. The continuity between the urban fabric and the sacred space of the shrine facilitates cultural festivals and events that traverse the area between town and shrine, while providing a clear evacuation route up the hill. During the 2011 tsunami, which reached nearly fifteen meters in Utatsu, sixteen survivors evacuated to the shrine. Fearing that the tsunami would eventually wrap the whole hill from both sides, they soon continued their evacuation to reach the Utatsu Middle School through the small road at the back of the hill.[6] This redundant system of shortcuts and back roads through high ground saved many lives across Tohoku.

This shrine's cultural and physical connection to the town also helped energize people's resolve. Utatsu traditionally held a *matsuri* (festival) every four years, with residents chanting in unison and carrying the *mikoshi* (religious palanquin) from the shrine down through the main street and back up to pay homage to the shrine, while the youth would play *taiko* (drums). Despite the obliteration of the buildings in the urban center, the town held a *matsuri* in 2012 to revive the spirit and rebuild the community. One resident exclaimed that a spirit seemed to roar perseverance in rebuilding

Annual festival

2011 inundation line

the city and that the festival was beautiful and powerful.[7] From organizing the procession to coordinating the lockstep solidarity needed to carry the *mikoshi,* holding such festivals is both symbolic and socially unifying.

Isuzu Shrine

Shrines are sites of varied local practices, such as in Minamisanriku, where children are tasked every year with clearing the steps to the shrines.[8] Isuzu Shrine in the Shizugawa district of Minamisanriku, dedicated to the sun goddess, functioned effectively as an evacuation space in part because of its established relationship to the nearby Togura Elementary School, which had designated it as a cold-weather tsunami evacuation space just three months prior. During the 2011 tsunami, 190 students and teachers, realizing that the previously designated site of the school rooftop would be inundated, evacuated first to Utsuno hilltop and then, following increased tsunami height warnings, to the shrine. Students from the adjacent preschool also evacuated to the shrine, even though their evacuation plan, too, had been to gather on the school rooftop. One child who did not make it up the hill quickly enough was lost, as was a teacher who left to warn her husband at home. Twenty evacuees stayed overnight in the shrine.[9] Social familiarity with these public, high-ground spaces makes them effective as both designated and impromptu evacuation sites.

IMPORTANCE OF ACCESS AND COMMUNICATION

Despite the numerous success stories linked to high-ground evacuation sites, stair-stepped routes are challenging for those with mobility impairments. In the Unosumai district of Kamaishi, this had deadly consequences. Jōrakuji Temple and Unosumai Shrine, located on high ground near the mountains, are two of the three designated evacuation spaces in this district.[10] Not many residents participated in evacuation drills, and among those who did, the elderly had difficulty evacuating up the steep hills. In an effort to increase the number of participants, the neighborhood association began holding the events at the District Bōsai Center, built in the low, flat urbanized area. The second-floor hall of this center was used as an evacuation shelter, equipped with a kitchen and emergency storage, after the tsunami caused by the Chilean earthquake on February 28, 2010. On May 23, 2010, and March 3, 2011 (days before the 2011 Tohoku tsunami), evacuation drills were held there, too. Kamaishi officially authorized conducting evacuation drills at the center, under the condition that in the event of an actual tsunami, the evacuees would use the back hill of Jōrakuji Temple and Unosumai Shrine. Unfortunately, this was not communicated well, and the name "Bōsai Center" was also misleading. At least 128 people who evacuated to the center lost their lives, while the 60 residents who evacuated to Jōrakuji Temple were all safe.[11] This case con-

Figure 68. Aligned with the town's main street, Mishima Shrine became an evacuation space and later helped with recovery.

veys how important clarity and communication are to survival; it also illustrates how efforts need to be made to provide access for everyone to the designated evacuation spaces.

TEMPORARY SHELTER

Unosumai's case was unfortunately not unique; a large number of public buildings officially designated as shelters were inundated during the Tohoku tsunami. More than one hundred religious facilities consequently became temporary shelters in the days and weeks following the disaster.[12] Japan has a long history of shrines and temples being used as shelters; records from the 1896 Sanriku tsunami mention people residing in a temple, borrowing the Buddhist flags for warmth,[13] and the grounds of religious facilities were used to construct refugee barracks after the 1923 earthquake.[14] In Tohoku, many shrines and temples predate the 1896 and 1933 tsunamis, meaning they are likely at elevations above inundation lines. Historical accounts show that these religious facilities held stockpiles of emergency supplies and were traditionally used as coordination and evacuation sites following disasters. They had water sources, such as lakes and wells, since they were originally not connected to a public water system; many also had traditional non-flushing toilets or septic tanks and could continue to operate off the grid.[15] The flexible Japanese architecture of shrines and temples is conducive to their use as evacuation spaces. Many used after the tsunami had tatami spaces for sleeping as well as toilets and meal preparation facilities (some later had outdoor toilet facilities constructed for the evacuees). Some temples had monks' quarters, meaning that futons were available, but even where there were none, floor seating cushions could be used for sleeping. Tatami were comfortable for seating and sleeping, and *fusuma* provided flexibility and privacy.

Shōtokuji Temple

Shōtokuji Temple in Rikuzentakata, which housed 150 evacuees for 140 days, illustrates many of the strengths of temples as temporary shelters. Prior to the disaster, the temple was used monthly for lectures, discussions, and warm meals. It had a spacious kitchen, where dozens of people could cook together using propane gas stoves, with rice, sweets, and tea in storage. The monks' quarters had large tatami rooms, two interior eight-person bathrooms, and two outdoor vault toilets. Halogen oil heaters were stockpiled for unexpected emergencies; these heaters were crucial for keeping evacuees warm in the cold nights following the disaster. Water was available from the hill behind the temple. Although power outages lasted over a month and a half, special large candles for Buddhist sermons lit the rooms. Large open spaces around the temple allowed children to play freely. Schoolteachers visited the temple to teach students there, returning the temple to its traditional function of *terakoya*. The chief priest managed the shelter, providing clear leadership and resolving problems. For many, it was natural for religious residents to shelter at a big temple, even if they were not followers there.[16]

RECOVERY AND RECONSTRUCTION PLANNING

Shrines and temples have traditionally been created and protected for the collective benefit of the community. They were, and many still are, places for local residents to gather and celebrate shared cultures and practices, which in turn strengthens social ties, making communities better prepared for disaster. Often local *matsuri* are organized by the shrine, and a community group would form through mutual support, especially in connection with the land (historically these groups helped residents handle difficult milestones, such as deaths, illnesses, or poor harvests). These sorts of repeated social events, which occur annually across Japan, are a means of drawing people together, establishing shared identities, forming relationships, and nurturing the involvement of younger generations. Temple and shrine priests have traditionally been leaders of the local community, and in many cases, priests have taken a leading role in rebuilding. In turn, the strong social capital they create contributes to a community's capacity to recover following a disaster.

Kaminoyama Hachimangū Shrine

In 2005, before the tsunami, the towns of Shizugawa and Utatsu merged to become Minamisanriku. In order to unite the communities, which had been independent municipalities with their own unique cultures, senior priest Kudō Mayumi of Kaminoyama Hachimangū Shrine established the new Minamisanriku Town Charter to foster a sense of unity.

Since the tsunami, Kudō has been working even more passionately to rebuild the community through bōsai education and bōsai machizukuri. On March 11, 2011, the tsunami arrived just below the *torii* gate of her shrine. As she fled to the evacuation shelter, she experienced the trauma of the tsunami ravaging the town. In order to relay her terrifying experience to children, she created a *kamishibai* (picture-story) show and later published it as a picture book.[17]

Shrines, temples, and other religious institutions also became headquarters for aid, in many cases working with volunteers from outside the religion, as the response of religious communities was largely practical and secular.[18] Because religious hubs are embedded in their communities, they transitioned seamlessly from response and relief efforts to long-term recovery planning, including assisting communities with the creation of spatial and community plans. For example, Kudō is also a committee member of Shizugawa Machizukuri Reconstruction Council, and she convened a study group called Seagulls Rainbow Conference to advocate for a natural wetland shoreline, without residences, for the western coast.

Fumonji Temple

In Yamamoto, Fumonji Temple became the hub to help rebuild the local community. Fumonji Temple is located only five hundred meters from the coast, in a residential area, and the tsunami destroyed the temple's main hall and cemetery.[19] Despite a dire financial situation and talk of merging with a nearby temple, the priest, Sakano Bunshun, cleaned the main hall and repaired the cemetery by himself. In May 2011, Fujimoto Kazutoshi, who runs a livelihood support NPO for people with special needs, offered to help. He gradually expanded his activities to assist in the reconstruction of the neighborhood and eventually established the Teracen (Otera Volunteer Center) at the Fumonji Temple.[20]

Teracen holds a monthly earthquake reconstruction meeting at Fumonji Temple called Saturday Meeting, when residents and volunteers review and discuss topics such as reconstruction, local festival planning, disaster relief museum planning, and renewable energy.[21] The Saturday Meeting also publishes a monthly newspaper, with forty-six issues as of May 2020. Sakano is one of the meeting members, but he participates as a resident, not a religious leader. Academics and journalists from other regions frequently participate in the meeting, which plays an important role as a center of town revitalization and a place for cultural and intellectual exchange inside and outside the town.

Teracen organizers say that using the Fumonji Temple as a base has helped the volunteer center, organized by people who are not from Yamamoto, gain the trust of the local neighborhood. The temple has high social credibility and lends its status to the organization. Since the temple was the center of the community as a place of learning and welfare before the tsunami, it was an ideal base for reconnecting and reconstructing the community.

Collabo-School

Temples and shrines have provided study spaces for children who lost their homes in the tsunami. Collabo-School is operated by NPO KATARiBA, supporting teenagers in disaster-affected regions by providing equal educational opportunities to foster creativity and motivation for the future.[22] Ōtsuchi Ringakusha was established on December 13, 2011, as the second Collabo-School in Tohoku. Its mission is to raise future local leaders by teaching students from the third through the twelfth grade. About 90 percent of buildings in the Ōtsuchi town center were destroyed, so safe and spacious facilities for 200 students were found at Kozuchi Shrine, Dainenji Temple, Kichijōji Temple, the Fureai community center, and three prefab buildings.[23]

After the disaster, the educational environment was poor, especially for children living in temporary housing. Many had to study in the living room, where other family members were watching television. Most could no longer attend their pre-tsunami tutoring schools. In addition to academic problems, requests for mental health support increased. In response, the Ōtsuchi Ringakusha started after-school instruction, opened self-study rooms, and provided young volunteers to listen to children's concerns. The school worked with the local government, board of education, public schools, and universities to design the curriculum. Classes are taught by former tutors who had lost their jobs as a result of the disaster. With the local residents, the school has been working on intergenerational exchanges on topics like disaster reconstruction learning, bōsai education, traditional culture, and performing arts. As of March 2020, 143 students were attending Ōtsuchi Ringakusha.[24]

OFFICIAL ROLE FOR FUTURE DISASTERS

The Japanese constitution establishes the separation of religion and state to guard against the return of state Shintoism, which prevailed from the Meiji Restoration until World War II. Until recently, this context has prevented the widespread formalization of evacuation and sheltering agreements between government and religious institutions. Without state support, long-term sheltering in particular put a disproportionate burden on managers of shrines and temples and their associated communities.[25] Evacuation spaces and shelters with a preexisting relationship to the communities they serve are more likely to be effective, and shrines and temples are central to the Japanese cultural landscape. It is worth noting that while 80 percent of Japanese people participate in Shinto practices, only a small percentage officially identify as Shinto;[26] for many, religious spaces and practices may be more cultural than religious. This suggests the potential to more fully integrate these spaces into evacuation plans.

The important role alternative sites played during the 2011 disaster has led to the gradual reassessment of this relationship.[27] For example, the chief priest of Senjuin Temple established a cross-denominational association with sixteen other temples in Kamaishi and Ōtsuchi in March 2011. In 2013, the association and the Kamaishi government agreed to designate temples as official evacuation shelters with emergency supplies to house evacuees. Similarly, in Miyagi, two shrines signed an agreement with the Shiogama government in 2014. The city installed emergency storage in order to accommodate 168 people for three days in the shrine's kendo hall. In Kyoto, where many temples had been already designated evacuation spaces, a new program was created, involving thirty-two temples and shrines, to help tourists stranded by a disaster's disruption of train lines.[28] And in May 2020, the Kyoto Police signed an agreement with Jōnangū Shrine, allowing the police to relocate its functions and make the shrine a logistics headquarters if the police building were damaged in a disaster.[29]

This progression accelerated after 2019 Typhoon Hagibis wreaked extensive damage. As of February 2020, there were 2,065 religious facilities designated as evacuation spaces.[30] According to Nikkei, 27 percent of existing designated shelters (mostly public schools and public halls) are in areas at risk of flooding and landslides,[31] and more in safe locations are necessary.

DISCUSSION

Leveraging shrines and temples for evacuation and sheltering stands in stark contrast to purpose-built tsunami evacuation towers, many of which go unused outside of drills and possible disasters. In learning from shrines and temples, it is important to examine how places and practices that already exist, and have strong connections to the communities, can be supported and leveraged to improve their bōsai potential. A shrine or temple's capacity for evacuation roles depends on both its spatial characteristics in terms of site (hilltops) and architecture (tatami rooms, cooking facilities); its social position as a community hub (through religious and cultural uses); and the trust and authority its revered leadership figures can offer during stressful conditions.

Embeddedness in existing social and cultural practices ensures factors like awareness, access, and maintenance are incorporated in projects. While Japan has started improving its support of religious institutions as disaster evacuation, response, and recovery sites, such institutions could have been even more effective if their role had been acknowledged and supported sooner. That is a lesson other countries can apply in their religious centers before disaster strikes. Small adaptations—such as increasing emergency storage, integrating off-grid energy, or providing emergency training and support for shrine and temple managers—could add to their post-disaster functionality. Although shrines and temples were carefully built with vernacular earthquake resistance, most are centuries old, and not all can afford seismic reinforcement. Temples and shrines that are certified as cultural heritage can receive subsidies from the Agency for Cultural Affairs to cover 50 percent of retrofit costs, but other individually owned spaces are not eligible.[32] The religious federation is creating a database to share the seismic resistance status of such buildings.[33] Hopefully such an analysis will lead to additional subsidies for structural retrofits in the near future.

Hotels

The aesthetic and cultural characteristics of traditional Japanese hotels, as with temples and shrines, make such spaces more comfortable as evacuation sites than cold, impersonal public buildings. Already designed to house people, hotels and inns are logical sites for evacuation, shelter, and (in some cases) longer stays. The success of hotels and inns as evacuation sites is linked to a combination of physical design and social contexts.

HOTELS DURING EVACUATION

Hotels are designed to accommodate large numbers of people and offer privacy and comfort that might not be available in evacuation sites like gymnasiums or multi-purpose halls. Traditional Japanese hotels are particularly flexible: tatami mat rooms can accommodate larger numbers of people with the simple addition of more futons, rather than being limited by the number of beds. Large, shared tatami rooms called *enkai-jō* are typically used for gatherings or parties and can be made available for additional sleeping spaces or other uses. Futons are put away in the morning so that throughout the day, rooms can be used for different functions, such as meetings or meals. Even small *ryokan* (traditional inns) have communal gathering and dining facilities, accommodating the wide needs associated with long-term evacuation stays. Most *ryokan* serve dinner and breakfast, so kitchens are already stocked with foods like rice and bottled water. Large shared baths, which many traditional hotels have in lieu of private bathrooms in each room, offer reserves of non-potable water for cleaning, bathing, and flushing toilets.

In addition to their physical space, the hotel cases examined in this section are also noteworthy for their locations and the preexisting social infrastructure that facilitated their post-disaster operations. Hotel staff are trained in helping accommodate guests, so they are often able to make people comfortable even in the face of hardship. In the small fishing and tourism-oriented towns and villages along the Tohoku coast, hotels and their owners may also play a central role in their communities, preparing them for leadership roles in the post-disaster context. Hotels have a responsibility to inform their guests about essential disaster-related information and help ensure their safety in case a disaster does strike. "Transient" populations, including tourists, are particularly vulnerable during disasters because they are less likely to be familiar with hazard risks and protocols, and they lack the social network that might advise them.[1] They may also be unfamiliar with the local language. After the 2011 disaster, many coastal Tohoku hotels took on the role of informing and supporting residents and transient populations, even where they were not officially designated evacuation sites (as very few were). Some hotels in the region had unsuccessfully attempted to receive official evacuation site designation prior to the disaster.[2] Understanding how hotels can serve their communities highlights the potential for them to play a larger role in emergencies.

Imperial Hotel, Tokyo

On September 1, 1923, the staff of Tokyo's Imperial Hotel was busily preparing a feast for the opening-day ceremony for their new building, designed by Frank Lloyd Wright. The brick-and-concrete low-rise complex, Wright's most famous building in Japan, was built surrounding a courtyard and reflecting pool. The earthquake, which struck at 11:58 am, only superficially damaged the building, which had been engineered with innovative seismic strategies. These included seismic separation joints, tapered walls that were thicker at the base, suspended utilities, and a reflecting pool that provided a (non-potable) reserve water supply for firefighting and other post-disaster functions. A cantilevered floor system placed the slabs on tops of walls and allowed them to move independently, like a waiter's tray, and the structure was designed to be flexible overall. Wright referred to it as a "jointed monolith."[3] Even the pipes were intended to be flexible, dangling inside the wall cavity.[4] To address concerns about fire, the hotel pioneered an electric kitchen, which could be easily turned off during tremors.[5] However, some of Wright's seismic innovations did not perform exactly as intended, such as the "floating" foundation on the site's alluvial soil (instead of deep pylons affixed to the bedrock below). This led to subsidence—and, some argue, to the ultimate demolition of Wright's building in 1968.[6]

Apart from minor damage, the building remained usable following the earthquake. Manager Inumaru Tetsuzō immediately took charge of the safety of both the hotel and its occupants. He asked the hotel chefs to begin to prepare a sweet potato soup, traditionally eaten during emergencies; when surrounding structures caught fire, he organized a bucket brigade using water from the courtyard pool. To gather provisions in the following days, he dispatched staff to the countryside (in the Cadillac that Wright had left behind) to collect several days' worth of food.[7]

In addition to sheltering the hotel's guests, who represented the most distinguished foreign visitors to Japan at the time and included dignitaries and ambassadors, at Inumaru's invitation the hotel also sheltered the staff of embassies that had been damaged or destroyed in the disaster. The United Kingdom was sited in the lobby balcony, and the United States was in the north wing. He also invited news agencies, which used

Figure 69. The Tokyo Imperial Hotel left a legacy of design to support evacuees after earthquakes.

DESIGN BEFORE DISASTER

POOL

SUNK GARDEN   LADIES LOUNGE   GENT'S LOUNGE   SUNK GARDEN

POOL

POOL

Hollow masonry shade
Alluvial mud
Shaft for flexible pipe
Tapered masonry walls
Top soil
Waffle slab

Supply storage
Public space
Shelter
Water source
Aid distribution

the banquet room and surrounding hallways, and welcomed public utilities into the south wing. The kitchen staff fed the hotel guests, and others prepared their meals in the parking lot outside.[8]

Disaster preparedness remains part of the Imperial Hotel's identity, even after the demolition of Wright's iconic structure and its rebuilding in 1970 as a modern seventeen-story, 772-room hotel. In 2005, hotel managers interviewed several prominent Kobe hotels to understand their experiences following the 1995 earthquake and consulted researchers at Kobe's Disaster Reduction and Human Renovation Institution to develop their business continuity plan, which lists actions for disaster preparedness. The plan specifically outlines what is to be done following different types of disasters and whose responsibility it is to do it. The Imperial Hotel conducts disaster drills twice a year and holds employee training up to six times per year to enact the plan.[9]

This planning allowed the Imperial Hotel to shelter over 2,000 commuters stranded in Tokyo after the Tohoku earthquake. Although Tokyo was relatively unscathed by the earthquake compared with other areas, the closure of transit systems stranded about 3.52 million commuters.[10] Many walked long distances to their homes but others lived too far away, and the Imperial Hotel opened its doors to anyone who needed a place to stay. Resources had been stockpiled as a part of their plan, and the stranded people were provided with blankets, water, and food at no cost. Loudspeakers provided emergency information, announcing the resumption of train services at 7:00 am the following day. In a thank-you note, one guest wrote, "At a nearby foreign-owned hotel, I was refused entry, but the Imperial Hotel lent me a blanket, and when the number of blankets became insufficient, they brought out large-sized bath towels." Since 2013, the TMG has subsidized the Imperial Hotel's emergency supplies for stranded commuters through the Emergency Accommodation Subsidy.[11]

Hotel Kanyō

In the Tohoku region in 2011, hotels played even larger roles as areas of refuge. Hotel Kanyō in Minamisanriku is a 244-room waterfront resort that can accommodate up to 1,300 guests; it is famous for its open-air *onsen* (hot-spring baths) in the rocky landscape, with views looking out over the Pacific Ocean. On March 11, after the earthquake struck, staff evacuated the guests to the hotel's nursery facility on a hill above the rest of the complex. It was not a designated evacuation space, but because the hotel stood on high-ground bedrock, neighbors evacuated there as well. The water reached up to the second level. Once it receded, the 350 guests, staff, and neighbors returned to the hotel and the staff prepared a meal. The hotel's owner, Abe Noriko, asked the staff to plan a menu for one week with supplies on hand for the evacuees.[12]

In neighboring Kesennuma, Abe's father's three-story house was designed with exterior stairs to the top of its roof for both family members and neighbors to evacuate.

Her father added the stairs because he lost his business during the 1960 Chilean tsunami. On the day of the 2011 tsunami, around 30 people, including a pregnant woman and several elderly residents, were saved. Abe's husband attempted to flee to an evacuation center but got caught in traffic, so he turned his car around and also took refuge at the house.[13]

In the following weeks, the hotel began to receive water deliveries and an electric generator. Volunteer and first-aid organizations used the building as a headquarters; 100 employees who had lost their homes continued to live there, and 600 neighbors[14] were permitted to lodge and eat there as an alternative to the designated shelter for a small fee (¥5,000/night).[15] On May 5, the hotel began to operate officially as a temporary shelter, initially accommodating 600 people from the Minamisanriku area (prioritizing businesspeople and households with students) and eventually hosting up to 1,000 people.[16] It served as a second evacuation space for the elderly and people with special needs who faced particular difficulties in the mass shelters. Because the hotel became an official shelter, the government subsidized the costs of housing and feeding evacuees.[17]

The region was without water for nearly four months, making simple daily tasks very difficult. After Abe observed an elderly woman attempting to wash her clothes in a frozen river, the hotel established a laundry service and amenities for the evacuees and the surrounding community. To help with management, occupants established a self-governing association, with leaders representing each floor. The town library had been destroyed, so a nonprofit called O.G.A. for Aid established a book corner with donated books and held events there.

At the end of August, occupants transitioned from the hotel to temporary housing. Recognizing that the social amenities provided by the hotel were particularly important for elderly citizens, the following day Hotel Kanyō established a shuttle between the temporary housing site and the hotel so that evacuees could return for *onsen* and tea.[18] This allowed community members to maintain routine social activities essential to their well-being. Abe was also actively involved in trying to revive the town's economy. She set up a guided tour bus and hired 13 local women to share their understanding of the area and the tsunami with tourists. To this end, the Abe Group (founded by her father) intends to leave in place the damaged Takano Kaikan building, with an inundation marker above the third floor, as a reminder of the tremendous height and power of the tsunami.

Nagashizusō Family *Ryokan*

A network of modest *ryokan* dots the region. While smaller than the grand hotels, their collective contribution to disaster relief was no less impactful when it came to accommodating people whose homes had been washed away. The small inn of

Nagashizusō in Togura is owned by the Endo family, who are in the fishing industry. With a small number of tatami rooms, shared baths, and home cooking, the inn was essential in the community's evacuation. The village in front of Nagashizusō was engulfed by the tsunami and the inn was one of the only places left standing, owing to its hillside location (although the tsunami reached halfway up its ground floor). To escape the violent waters, the family that operated the inn, as well as their guests, evacuated up through farmland behind their home. In spite of damage to its baths and parts of its ground floor, the *ryokan* was used as a shelter for about 100 people for two months. Without any utilities, electricity was provided via a generator donated by the owner's son.[19] These inns were not officially designated evacuation sites or planned shelters; rather, their roles in the evacuation emerged from their positions in small, closely connected communities.

Hotel Bōyō

Hotel Bōyō in Kesennuma also played an important role in the community following the tsunami, which destroyed nearly a quarter of this fishing town. The hotel was sited on a high waterfront ridge, and while the tsunami reached the facing road, it left the structure unscathed. The owner, Kato Eiichi, and his family and staff saw a black wall of water approaching and realized that the tsunami would be unprecedented, so they evacuated up a steep hill behind the building. A small outdoor stair connects the third floor of the hotel to the hilltop road behind, allowing direct access to high ground.

In the immediate aftermath, neighboring people began to arrive at the hotel in search of shelter. While it was not a designated evacuation site, Kato opened the hotel's doors to anyone in need. The ground-floor lobby and second-floor tatami rooms were used as evacuation spaces. The lifeline infrastructures of electricity, gas, and water were broken, so Kato brought out oil heaters, futons, and blankets to keep evacuees warm. The hotel had a stock of water, food, emergency flashlights, and large candles from wedding ceremonies. The following day, the hotel accommodated the injured, elderly, and disabled, who were unable to evacuate further. Ultimately, 250 evacuees sheltered there during the first few days following the tsunami, and 150 people lived in the hotel for seventy days. They were without water and electricity for the majority of that time.[20]

Twelve staff were at the hotel when the tsunami struck and were able to help distribute resources, while an on-site chef was able to coordinate cooking. Kato provided a strong leadership role, assigning rules and duties to the occupants. However, the position also put a large burden on him and his resources; his house had also been destroyed, and he and his family were sheltering at the hotel as well. Kato spent several days unsure about the fate of his sons and his mother, who were not at home when the

Inundation line

Evacuation route

Kato Eiichi

Isuzu Shrine

Port

Hotel Boyo

Emergency shelter

250 evacuees
70 days
12 staff

Figure 70. Hotel Bōyō, exemplifying the important role hotels play in sheltering victims after a tsunami.

earthquake struck, yet like many local leaders he took charge of others' needs during this time in spite of his own concerns.[21]

The city provided some compensation to Hotel Bōyō, but the costs associated with running the shelter ultimately put it into debt. It reopened on May 10 at the request of the mayor as a center for workers for the reconstruction project. By the summer of 2015, the hotel was operating at 60 percent capacity, and the majority of its guests were still construction workers. The city requested that the hotel become an official evacuation shelter, recognizing the success of the space and staff following the 2011 tsunami. Unfortunately, the combination of debts and a decline in tourism after the tsunami led Hotel Bōyō to declare bankruptcy in 2018.[22] This case clearly indicates the need for government subsidies to help facilities with repair costs after they are used for sheltering.

RECENT POLICIES AND SUBSIDIES

More recently, Japan developed clear policies that help facilitate the use of hotels in response to disasters. Hotels in Japan are required by the National Fire Services Act to conduct evacuation drills twice a year.[23] The Disaster Relief Act provides support for hotels and inns to shelter disaster survivors, particularly the vulnerable elderly and people with special needs. This is sometimes as part of a "second evacuation," in which those who might face life-threatening issues from long-term occupation of congregate sheltering are relocated to more comfortable facilities while temporary housing is being built.[24] An official system was created to preregister vulnerable residents (identified via the municipality) with the local All Japan Ryokan-Hotel Association so that they can be matched with vacant rooms.[25] When disaster strikes, the association sends requests to hotels to accommodate preregistered residents. Depending on the scale of the disaster, expenses are covered by national, prefectural, or municipal budgets. Prefectures also provide subsidies for hotels to improve their infrastructure. For example, in 2020, Tokushima Prefecture provided up to ¥20 million to hotels cooperating as shelters for the vulnerable. Funds were used for construction or renovation of guest rooms and bathing facilities as well as installation of slopes and handrails.[26] These subsidies and policies are part of a growing effort to move vulnerable populations to safer and more comfortable evacuation facilities.

DISCUSSION

Japan is beginning to institutionalize systems for supporting the roles that private hotels and *ryokan* had taken on—previously of their own volition, often at significant personal cost. Preplanned agreements with the Ryokan-Hotel Association allow shelters to be identified quickly and hotels to be reimbursed for their services during and following disasters.

For designers of hotels and other new typologies, the bōsai principle of dual use can play an important role in creating designs that are also effective after a disaster. In Japanese hotels, this multifunctionality is characteristic of traditional architecture, but there are other potential ways of embedding dual uses in large private buildings: through flexible materials or lightweight, movable components. To effectively integrate these projects into the anticipatory design framework, they should also be integrated with local planning systems, considering the availability of fresh water, evacuation routes, urban signage, and other factors. Designers can take an active role in this development. Even in Japan, where hotels are starting to serve as official evacuation buildings, they often lack signage, in part because they do not want the forewarning of a disaster to upset their guests.[27] One major challenge is how to make anticipatory design part of a space's architectural identity in an integrated and non-alarmist manner. Reflecting on the original Imperial Hotel and lessons learned from Tohoku, future hotels can be designed with a much larger support role in the disaster timeline in mind.

Schools

As familiar, well-built structures in the community, schools are fundamental throughout the disaster cycle because of the connection between their physical architecture and social practices and education. Pre-disaster education instills skills in students through science modules or disaster education exercises, which in some cases involve infrastructure embedded into the school's design. They also provide drills that include the wider community and strengthen social capacity. The siting of the school, on higher ground or outside of a floodplain, also increases awareness of the physical surroundings and location within the larger ecosystem. In the immediate moments after the disaster, the school grounds are often used as an evacuation space. In the hours and days following, existing school leadership can be important to the building's sheltering role, and schools are often retrofitted (and more recently designed) with components that help support sheltering functions. Longer-term, temporary housing is often established on school grounds as survivors wait for permanent housing to be repaired or (re)constructed. A school's physical design, its placement in a community, and its human resources all contribute to these multiple, critical roles.

SCHOOLS, DESIGN CODES, AND REGULATIONS

Public schools were first established in Japan in 1872. They were initially constructed of wood, but following the 1923 Tokyo earthquake (when 111 of the 195 schools burned to the ground),[1] 117 schools were rebuilt using reinforced concrete.[2] Architectural engineer Sano Toshikata, who was instrumental in promoting the use of reinforced concrete in seismic-resistant architecture, developed a school model with flush toilets, heating systems, and modern science classrooms (rather than tatami rooms).[3] By 1950, a shift to ferroconcrete was formalized in four standard school designs issued by the Architectural Institute of Japan.[4] During the same year, the Building Standards Law designated schools as "special buildings" requiring fire-resistant structures, which would allow occupants to evacuate before the structure was compromised. Evacuation standards, such as multiple stairways and exits, were also mandated.[5]

In 1992, the Ministry of Education, Culture, Sports, Science and Technology

(MEXT) established its guidelines for upgrading schools, clarifying that schools should be able not only to withstand large seismic events but also to remain safe and operable as evacuation shelters even after a major earthquake.[6] Following the 1995 Kobe earthquake, seismic retrofitting costs became eligible for national subsidies for earthquake bōsai projects, especially to improve schools built before the 1979 New Seismic Design Act. The allowable budget ranged from ¥4 million to ¥200 million, with a 33 percent subsidy.[7] The guidelines were upgraded several times, and "structural design" was added to the 2003 edition as an independent chapter.[8] Intended to make schools safer and more effective as evacuation shelters, these funds increased the national percentage of seismically resistant schools from 44 percent in 2002 to 98.8 percent by 2017.[9]

In addition to seismic retrofits, other projects have increased the disaster preparedness of schools and are eligible for additional subsidies, such as the installation of water-supply tanks, manhole toilets, renewable energy infrastructure (including solar and wind generation equipment), hand-pump wells, emergency storage, pools, and cooking benches.[10] During the Tohoku disaster, many evacuation shelters lacked heat due to large-scale power outages, and only a few places (such as medical facilities) had solar heating systems to maintain room temperature. This further affirmed the benefits of off-grid energy infrastructure during disasters. The guidelines for upgrading schools, amended in 2014, added tsunami design parameters, such as ensuring that buildings are structurally resistant to the force of a predicted tsunami if the rooftop is planned as a temporary evacuation space.[11] The regulations specify that in order for the school itself to be a tool for disaster education, elevation markers on each floor should inform children of the risk of tsunamis on a daily basis.[12] These kinds of small-scale design retrofits connect evacuation actions with the physical school building.

Beyond evacuation concerns, as a response to global warming and other environmental issues, MEXT announced the "Development of Environmentally Conscious Schools (Eco-Schools)," and in 1998, in cooperation with MLIT and MAFF, it started to promote eco-school construction. In June 2011, it added an amendment to require the use of school facilities as teaching materials for environmental education and to consider the maintenance of schools to reduce the burden on the environment. The 2016 Global Warming Countermeasures Plan stated that construction of new public buildings, including schools, has to show net-zero energy usage. Following this, MEXT created the eco-school implementation guidelines, which include environmental conservation activities and environmental education.[13] Many retrofits, such as installing renewable energy systems, rainwater collection, passive heating and cooling systems, and rooftop pools, are beneficial for both bōsai and sustainable futures, so the MEXT national treasury subsidizes eco-school upgrading and maintenance in addition to bōsai renovations.[14]

USE OF SCHOOLS AROUND THE DISASTER CYCLE

National-level regulations succeeded in incrementally upgrading the structural disaster resistance of schools, and now they are often some of the safest buildings in communities. But these types of guidelines, which can be highly specific and are sometimes seen as a checklist, can limit potential for innovative local adaptations. Compendiums of school building drawings were issued as early as 1895, standardizing school design.[15] Interestingly, the Ministry of Education abolished facility standards for elementary schools in 1904 over concerns about excessive standardization, and at the end of the 1970s, the standard school designs were relaxed to allow alternative arrangements of classrooms and open space.[16] However, the compendium continued to be widely used and, until more recent efforts, many schools across Japan were identical.

SCHOOLS DURING EVACUATION

Schools are already familiar spaces to the wider community, making them ideal sites for emergency evacuation. Since the 1923 reconstruction, evacuation spaces and schools have had a close relationship in Japan. A survey conducted by the Japanese Architects Association following the 1995 Kobe earthquake showed that people reported evacuating to familiar facilities, such as elementary and middle schools, because of their perceived safety, their proximity to home, their designation as known evacuation sites, and the fact that neighbors had evacuated there, among other reasons.[17] After the 2011 Tohoku earthquake struck, many residents evacuated to nearby schools.

Ōkawa Elementary School

Although many schools were designated evacuation sites, on the day of the 2011 earthquake some teachers and principals decided to evacuate still farther uphill, sensing that the long and powerful earthquake might trigger a very large tsunami. In rugged Iwate Prefecture, nine out of nineteen schools surveyed diverged from their initial evacuation plan and went to an alternative, higher evacuation space.[18]

One of the most devastating tragedies emerging from the failure of an alternate plan is the case of Ōkawa Elementary School in Ishinomaki, in which seventy-four students and ten teachers were killed. Ōkawa School was located out of the tsunami hazard zone, and the school itself was designated as an evacuation site. When the teachers realized that the tsunami would arrive at the school, they decided to evacuate higher and began to lead the students toward a nearby elevated bridge over the Kitakami River to reach another evacuation space—but they were enveloped by the tsunami.

The careful deliberation to maintain the Ōkawa School building as a tsunami memorial took six years. In a community meeting leading up to the decision, residents raised concerns about the difficult memories it prompted and expressed disgust at disaster tourists taking selfies at the site of their most traumatic loss. One father, who lost his daughter, called for the ruin to be preserved so that such mistakes by teachers would not be repeated.[19] In one survey, 54.4 percent of the residents living near the school wanted to demolish the whole building.[20] The mayor and residents' council reached a compromise after five meetings. Planting cherry trees in a memorial park around the school would visually buffer it so that those whose memories were triggered would have some peace.[21] At the time of this writing, the site had been turned into a memorial; even in the pouring rain, one encountered community members grieving and praying. Ishinomaki's mayor, Kameyama Hiroshi, stated, "It's an important place to remember and mourn the victims as well as educate people about disaster preparedness and pass on what transpired."[22] The events that occurred at Ōkawa School illustrate the necessity of school site planning and advanced scenario planning (including redundancy plans in case the scale of the event is greater than anticipated), as well as the importance of strong leadership in both faculty and students, including the ability to negotiate the uncertainty inherent to disasters.

The 2011 Tohoku disaster damaged or destroyed 7,693 school buildings in Iwate, Miyagi, and Fukushima Prefectures, and 728 students lost their lives.[23] As tragic as these accounts are, one must keep in mind that they are far outnumbered by success stories.

Unosumai Elementary School and Kamaishi Higashi Middle School

Kamaishi, in Iwate Prefecture, lost over one thousand people. However, all but five students (who were not at school) survived. The high survival rate can be attributed to successful education. In Unosumai Elementary School and Kamaishi Higashi Middle School, students practiced joint emergency drills annually, both with and without teachers, in case an adult was not nearby to help. Katada Toshitaka of Gunma University had been working with schools in Kamaishi since 2003, aiming for zero tsunami victims by teaching three principles. The first was "don't make any assumptions." Avoid fully relying on hazard maps, as the next tsunami could be worse, and it is necessary to remain cautious even if you are seemingly outside the tsunami inundation zone. The second principle was "do your best under the current circumstances." Even at the designated evacuation site, circumstances may require evacuating to an even higher location. The third was "be the leading evacuee." After a warning, don't hesitate to run immediately; if someone initiates evacuation, others will follow. Katada's principles were neither the conventional "threat-based education," which tells horror stories of past disasters, nor the most common "knowledge-based education," often equated to learning about hazard maps. Instead, he strengthened "behavior-based education,"

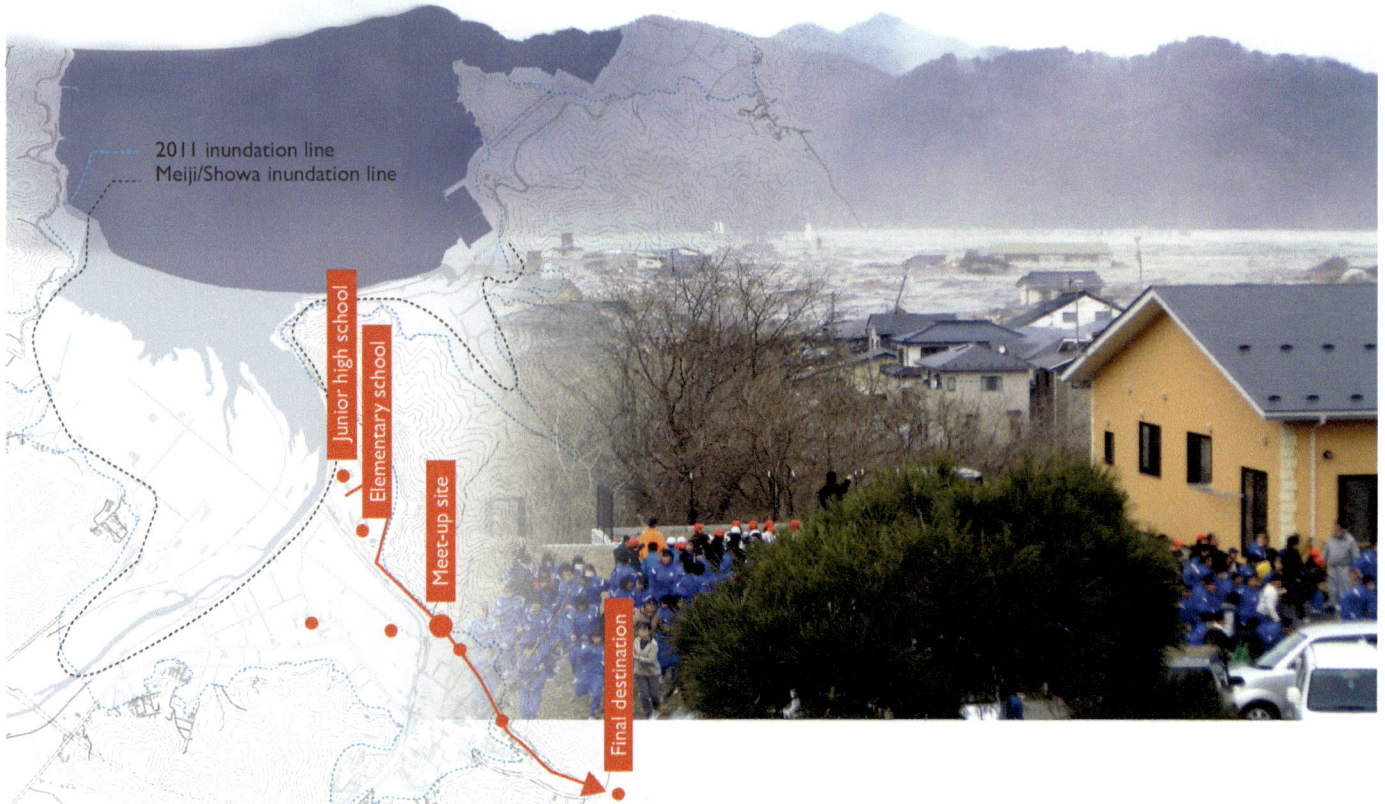

2011 inundation line
Meiji/Showa inundation line

Junior high school
Elementary school
Meet-up site
Final destination

Figure 71. Unosumai Elementary School and Kamaishi Higashi Middle School evacuation.

which fosters a proactive attitude toward protecting one's own life in the event of a disaster.[24] Katada's goal was to cultivate bōsai culture through children to their extended families and across the region.

Despite being located fewer than 500 meters from the ocean, 570 students from the two schools evacuated immediately after the earthquake and survived the tsunami. The principal of the middle school led them farther up nearby hills after arriving at the designated evacuation site, which was soon enveloped by the tsunami.[25] Middle school students held hands with elementary and daycare students and encouraged them. In addition, students who were already at home were able to help family and neighbors with proper evacuation procedures. Building preparedness behavior is a transferable skill; as more people know how to prepare, they can help and teach others.

Okirai Elementary School

Even a simple modification of a school building can make a significant difference. Okirai Elementary School in Ōfunato, located 250 meters from Okirai Bay (and

つなぐ手で
地域を守る
自主防災

ちいき
て
まも
じしゅぼうさい

"Holding hands
we protect the
neighborhood.
Self-reliant
Bosai."

Figure 72. Tsunami *karuta* game based on haiku.
Sharing memories will educate future generations.

0 meters above sea level), was completely destroyed when the tsunami swallowed the
three-story school building. All of its staff and 73 students were saved by an emergency bridge built between the upper level of the school and the back road on a hill,
which allowed the students to evacuate directly from the third floor. The vice principal
started the evacuation during the earthquake, and thanks to twice-annual drills, students kept moving uphill beyond the designated evacuation site.[26]

Following the 2011 tsunami, sixth graders at Okirai Elementary developed a version
of the traditional Japanese *karuta* game, which uses illustrated cards based on haiku

poems. The students created haiku and illustrations based on their own experiences during the tsunami. As a way of commemorating loss, students play the game annually on March 11 and use this time to talk about their disaster experiences. The emotional game provides an opportunity to learn and remember in a way that is meaningful for students.[27]

Since the tsunami, the school increased its number of evacuation drills to four times a year and expanded disaster education programs in collaboration with the city. The city firefighters held workshops with students using very large maps on the floor to help identify evacuation sites and routes, allowing them to visualize the evacuation process. Students then traveled to the evacuation points to determine how well the routes would work and adjusted the map accordingly. Their recommendations were brought to city hall to incorporate into the municipal evacuation plan. Students, professional consultants, and jishubō developed local hazard maps, helping everyone, including their parents, to think spatially about evacuation. This process not only allowed students to engage in real and meaningful municipal evacuation planning but also taught them to think about disaster preparedness spatially, moving between map-based representations and the physical world.

SCHOOLS AS EMERGENCY SHELTERS

In addition to serving as an immediate evacuation site to escape hazards, Japanese schools are primary sites for longer-term sheltering, providing lodging for residents whose homes have been lost or damaged by a disaster. Depending on the disaster, schools may be occupied as shelters for weeks or months as homes are repaired or temporary housing is built. In Japan, 91.5 percent of public schools are designated as evacuation shelters.[28] Their facilities have been gradually updated through the 2013 implementation of the Bōsai Facilities Improvement Project, and as of 2022, 82 percent of schools were equipped with emergency storage, 80.8 percent with drinking water, 73.2 percent with generators and an off-grid energy source, 82.9 percent with emergency communication systems, and 73.6 percent with portable toilets.[29]

1995 Kobe Earthquake

After the 1995 earthquake, at the peak, 181 schools sheltered 149,246 evacuees in Kobe.[30] School grounds offered versatile spaces for setting up sheltering infrastructure, including meal ration tents, storage tents, bathtubs, and portable toilets. In many schools, beyond the safety of the building as shelter, the leadership of teachers and principals was key. At one school, the principal arrived in the morning to find 2,000 scared survivors fearing aftershocks and had to calm people down. The delay of official information and external relief supplies aggravated tensions at evacuation sites. For example, supplies arrived in the middle of the night, but with only three hundred bread rolls for 2,000 people to share. The school principal played a vital role in recovering order. Water also had to be rationed to one-third of a cup per person until the SDF water tankers could supply it more regularly, several days after the earthquake. Due to the broken water mains, many accounts describe teachers and principals removing feces from toilets with plastic bags over their hands. Pressure and stress reached an apex as "seriously injured victims came to schools in search of assistance and corpses started to be carried to schools" even though doctors were not available on-site.[31] Although not trained for such events, teachers and principals had to rise to the challenge of managing such chaos and find methods to establish peace.

After the trauma of the first few days, new management systems were needed as people lived together in tight, uncomfortable conditions for months. Noise, light, temperature, privacy, water rationing, and toilet management all became issues. In some schools, teachers managed the shelter, while in others, teachers organized survivors into groups of 20 to 30 people. Each group elected a representative and then created a roster for chores, such as water and food distribution, supply management, toilet cleaning, and many other critical tasks.[32]

In other schools, the evacuees motivated themselves to self-organize. Kobe High School sheltered 800 evacuees in its gym and kendō and jūdō rooms for seven months. Spaces without partitions resulted in serious privacy issues and nighttime light nuisances. They also shared limited temporary toilets and washing machines, which drew water from the swimming pool. After two weeks, the evacuees formed a self-governing organization and divided tasks among themselves. Around that time, the city water supply was restored and temporary baths were set up outside the gym. Schools reopened on February 1, two weeks after the earthquake, but most evacuees remained on the premises. Many of them started leaving in the beginning of March, and on August 20, when the Disaster Relief Period ended, shelters were closed and the last three households moved out.[33]

After the Kobe earthquake, when water shortages were a major problem, MEXT subsidies for schools were amended again to incentivize retrofitting buildings with rooftop pools.[34] While the rooftop location is ideal for physical education classes and for thermal insulation, it also creates water pressure that allows distribution without electricity to toilets or for other uses. Many newly renovated or designed public schools now have swimming pools on their rooftops, providing a new design opportunity.

2011 Tohoku Tsunami

Following the Tohoku tsunami, 622 schools were used as shelters, and each hosted more than 400 evacuees. The most extreme case was Rikuzentakata Dai-ichi Middle School, which provided space for more than 1,000 people on the day after the disaster.[35] In some municipalities, such as Ishinomaki, damage was so extensive that even schools that had been inundated were used as shelters.[36] Evacuees faced several problems, particularly those resulting from the long duration of sheltering and the disruption of basic infrastructure, such as water to flush toilets. In many places it was snowing when the 2011 tsunami struck, and the cold became a fatal problem as disrupted gas and electricity lines meant that most heating systems did not function. At several shelters, including Shishiori Middle School (where electricity was not restored for a full month), some elderly people died within the first few days because of the cold.[37]

Utatsu Middle School

The case of Utatsu Middle School in Minamisanriku shows the challenges of long-term sheltering. Sited above the Utatsu district, the school played a central role as an evacuation shelter; it was the only public institution that was not inundated by the seventeen-meter tsunami. Utilities were disrupted, so occupants initially had to keep warm using distributed blankets as well as found items such as newspapers, curtains, athletic mats, cushions, and thermal insulation. A handheld power generator from an eighth-grade technology class was used to charge cell phones.[38] Non-potable water for daily use was collected from a nearby stream until the municipal system was restored in mid-May, two months after the disaster. After that, an NPO installed a temporary communal bath heated by wood pellets on the school grounds and initiated bathing days, alternating by gender.[39] Programs were developed to improve the quality of life for evacuees, especially physical activities to reduce the risk of blood clots caused by occupying cramped quarters. The school created play areas, a flu quarantine area, dressing rooms for privacy, and a meeting space for neighborhood associations and volunteers. Because of the level of devastation, school did not restart until May 10, the latest start date in the prefecture, and the building was occupied as a shelter for nearly six months, through the end of August.[40]

Resuming school activities quickly after a catastrophe is important to help children return to a state of normalcy and ensure that education is not disrupted. This issue was particularly crucial after the Tohoku disaster, when the scale of the destruction and time in shelters and temporary housing were unprecedented. However, recommencing a normal school schedule can be understandably difficult when a large number of neighborhood residents are calling the school home (temporarily), and friction can emerge between the needs of students and survivors. The amended guidelines for upgrading schools underlined that because schools serve as regional evacuation shelters, they need to plan for the potential of various disaster types and associated numbers of evacuees. The school principal and the municipality's disaster management division should work together to clarify the roles of each agency and prepare evacuation spaces for evacuees of all types, including those who are pregnant, the elderly, and people with special needs. In addition to reframing social roles, this might also be seen as a spatial design opportunity to find architectural strategies that will effectively meet the needs of everyone sheltering.

Yamashita Middle School

Yamashita Middle School in Yamamoto, built with the eco-school subsidies, illustrates how designing with attention to social space and sustainability can improve a school's capacity as an evacuation and shelter site. Compared to Japan's typical, standardized school construction, this school was intentionally designed to operate beyond its academic functions as a shared space for the community. According to the architect, Shioiri Takeshi, the school was created not only for students but also for residents to use as a "community education center" and space for "life-long education."[41] The school was designed with broad entries, indoor/outdoor gathering spaces, and large glazed surfaces in order to welcome the public, revitalizing local connections and especially supporting women through education.

When the tsunami struck, the entire Yamamoto plain was submerged, and 40 percent of its houses were destroyed. The earthquake occurred after the school day, so most students were at home, and four drowned. The town had the third-highest loss of life in Miyagi. Its death toll was high, most likely because the 1978 Miyagi Shore tsunami did not impact this region (unlike cities further north), and so residents did not anticipate a tsunami after the 2011 earthquake. The area did not have a seawall, so the shoaling beach was entirely destroyed and the JR rail line was severely damaged.[42]

Yamashita Middle School served the town as an immediate evacuation space and a long-term shelter. About 450 people sheltered inside the building itself, and the total was closer to 1,000, counting residents who slept in their cars in the parking lot. The building had been designed to be earthquake-resilient and was largely undamaged from the tremor. The entire school was used for evacuation except for the gym, which was structurally damaged (this loss forced people to invent a new process, which will be described below). People continued to arrive over the course of the day and night—between tsunami waves, and after the tsunami finally receded—and each person was registered. The school used existing supplies, blankets, and food from the cafeteria and from local farmers to care for evacuees. Petroleum gas stoves were set up so that volunteers could cook soup for survivors. Although the heating system was damaged, the passive solar design, including large floor-to-ceiling windows and well-insulated wooden surfaces, allowed the school to remain warm without power, even in winter.

After a few days, the town provided an electric generator and solar-powered heat-

Figure 73 (*next page*). The design and clear management structure of Yamashita Middle School helped residents shelter with dignity during the region's long-term recovery.

> **EACH CLASSROOM BECAME A NEIGHBORHOOD**
>
> **EVERYONE HAD A SPECIFIC TASK AND RESPONSIBILITY**

> **EVERYONE GATHERED IN THE COURTYARD TO HEAR STUDENTS PERFORM**

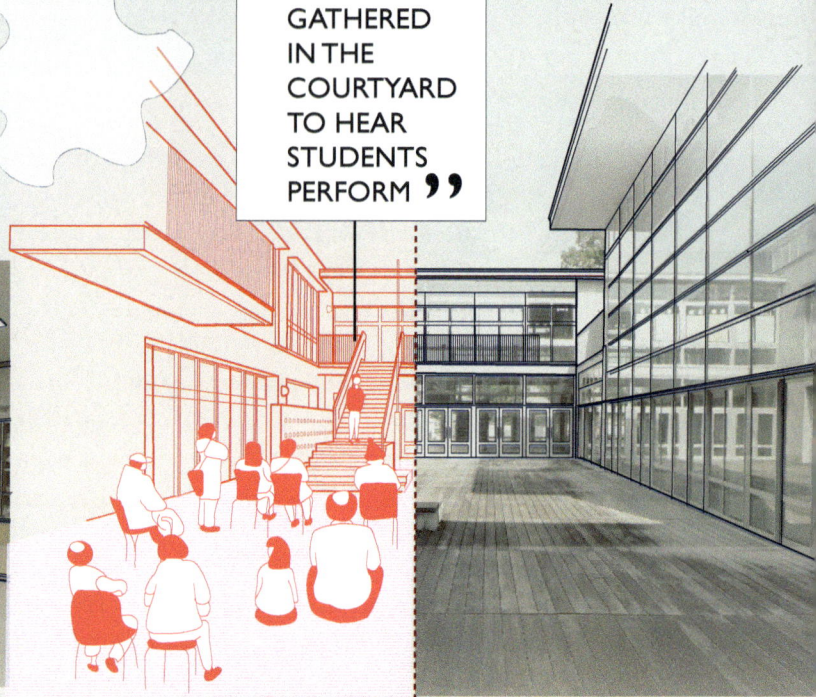

FLEXIBLE DESIGN

COURTYARD & CIRCULATION

Wide hallways and open public spaces for social activity, eating and gathering

CLASSROOM STRUCTURE

NEIGHBORHOODS

Every classroom is a neighborhood

Each neighborhood has **2** representatives

TASKS

- Cooking
- Cleaning
- Distributing supplies
- Trash
- Entertainment
- Coordination

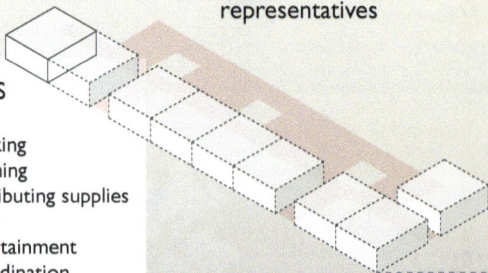

SUPPLY STORAGE & DISTRIBUTION

GYM

Gym acted as the main supply storage and distribution center.

1,000 Blankets

3,000 Water bottles

3,000 Food containers

" WATER FROM THE POOL LASTED US A MONTH! "

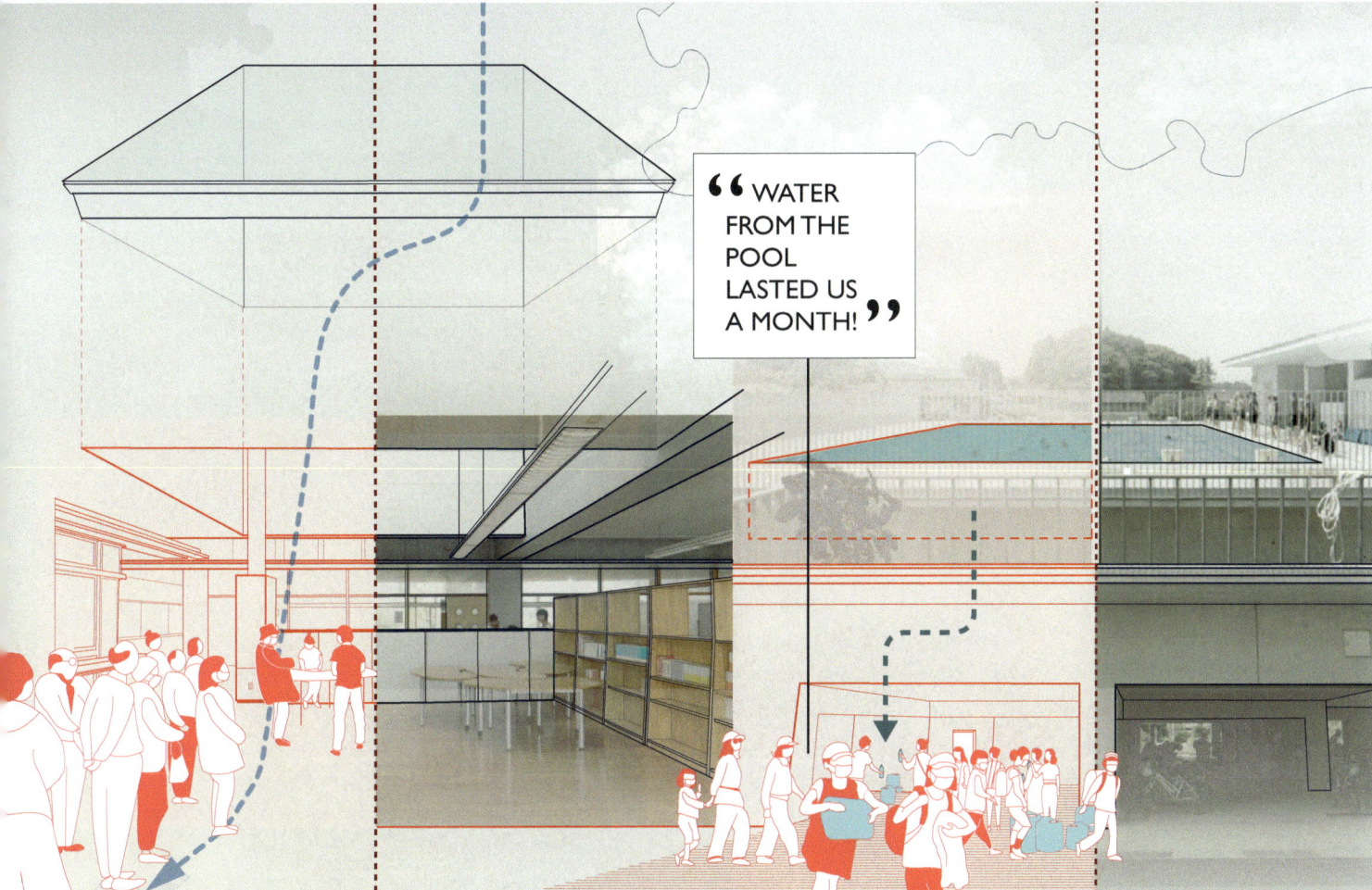

PASSIVE DESIGN
SKYLIGHTS
Natural light, heat and ventilation through skylights and large windows

WATER STORAGE SYSTEM
POOL
Rooftop pool acts as water storage that can be used for laundry and for the bathrooms/showers underneath it

Evacuation space

Classroom structure

Courtyard

Skylights

Flexible common spaces

Pool

Water storage

Gym

Supply storage

Parking lot

Evacuation shelter

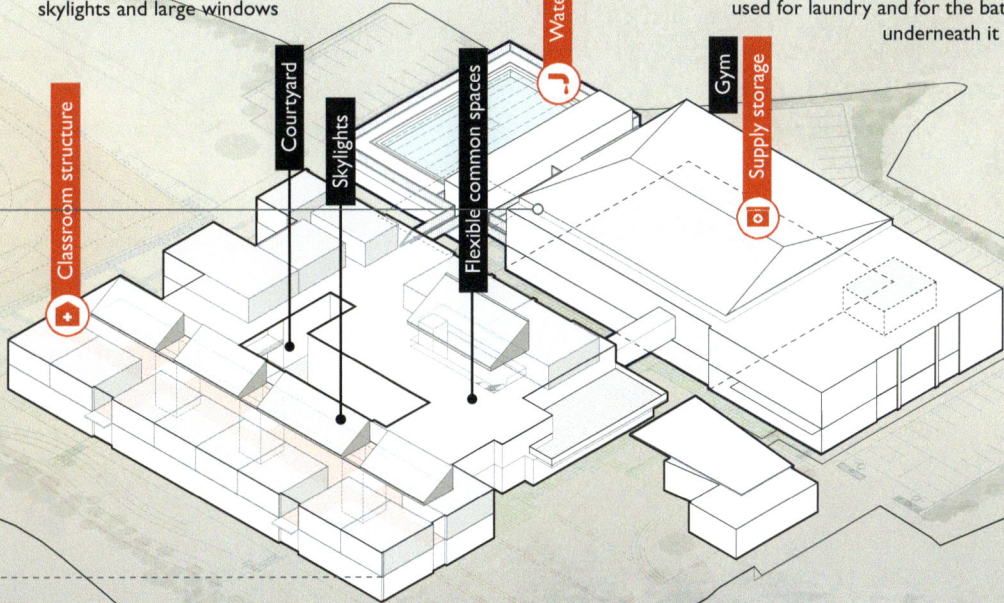

ing system, which maintained the school facilities at a comfortable temperature until electricity was restored on the sixth day.[43] City water returned after twelve days, on March 23. The biggest problem evacuees faced was sewage; the school lacked a system to deal with waste without consistent water and power supplies, but students brought water down from the rooftop pool to help flush toilets. The rooftop pool and surroundings were used as laundry spaces, as days in the shelter stretched into weeks and months.[44]

The firm, Tohoku Design and Planning Research Institute Inc., had designed the school with generous central gallery spaces, broad hallways, and stairs and classrooms exceeding standard dimensions, which provided extra spaces for interaction. The wide and inviting entrance lobby served multiple functions, such as a phone center and emergency headquarters. It also created space for a missing-persons bulletin board, which people used to post names and find loved ones. The indoor gathering spaces lit by skylights and outdoor courtyards were used for performances to uplift the survivors' spirits. The flexible open spaces for various types of learning made the Yamashita Middle School particularly effective as a long-term evacuation space.

Unlike in other schools serving as shelters, few conflicts arose between the school and evacuees. According to Takahashi Kenichi, a veteran teacher and director of disaster-preparedness education, the school was able to manage both the evacuation influx and the needs of the students through adaptive coordination. Rooms were assigned to each neighborhood, reflecting the urban organization within the school layout and ensuring that people knew each other. People were never housed in the hallways or courtyards, so these open spaces remained flexible for eating and socializing. This was important to the evacuees' quality of life.

The school principal was well-loved in the community and helped structure the management plan. Evacuees were treated not as guests but as autonomous residents. Teachers and the principal then provided support for their self-directed system. For example, each room where evacuees slept had two representatives to make decisions and mediate disagreements. These representatives met every day at 6:30 am to discuss emerging issues. Each temporary resident played an active role in tasks such as cooking, cleaning, distributing supplies, or removing trash.[45]

Teachers and students also assisted in managing the shelter. Middle school students returned to help after the disaster and continued to help even when school began again in late April. They provided entertainment through performances and concerts and made thank-you artwork for donors. Although many teachers were not from the area, and four had lost their homes, almost all stayed to help. One of these four was the principal, who slept in his office for the month following the tsunami. The school was managed as an evacuation site through joint efforts and did not require any additional volunteers except for occasional visiting entertainers.

It was important to the teachers that the school return to operation quickly so that the students could regain a sense of normalcy. Classrooms were used to house evacuees until April 22, at which point the remaining 70 evacuees were relocated to the repaired gym and outdoor tents provided by UNICEF. Classes began again on April 27, six weeks after the disaster.

Yamashita Middle School used the tsunami response as an opportunity to further improve disaster preparedness and has now collected supplies to accommodate 1,000 evacuees for a period of twenty-four hours. It is also expanding its bōsai education. First-year students make their own evacuation maps, second-year students undergo training in first aid and CPR, and third-year students learn how to set up tents.

SCHOOL SITES FOR TEMPORARY HOUSING

Temporary housing is another post-disaster function that school grounds can perform. School sports fields are often among the largest open spaces in a community, so in many cases they become sites for temporary housing. While disaster survivors occupy the interiors of schools as shelters for a period of months, they may occupy temporary housing on school grounds for years. Following the 1923 Tokyo earthquake, as of November that year, 43,529 people were sheltered in emergency barracks constructed on the grounds of sixty-eight destroyed primary schools.[46] For the most part, after the 1995 Kobe earthquake, school grounds were not used for temporary housing, due to the concern for students' education. In places where temporary housing was built, some activities were hampered, but in most situations, students tried to cheer up the elderly and help clean up around their houses. Teachers made efforts to "foster a spirit of compassion," and there were even cases of shared activities, such as growing vegetables.[47] In Tohoku, where it was difficult to find level ground equipped with lifeline infrastructure at higher elevations away from the tsunami-inundated areas, municipalities worried about losing their populations and had no choice but to use school grounds. Similar to experiences in Kobe, the more successful installations found ways to effectively engage with the school populations.

Shishiori Middle School

The Shishiori area of Kesennuma was most affected by the fires. Although it is difficult to imagine, debris floating on water, contaminated by leaking oil tankers, ignited. Despite the work of numerous fire trucks from as far away as Tokyo, it took over a month to control the blaze.[48] Shishiori Middle School was first used as an evacuation shelter, then slowly transitioned to temporary housing. During the sheltering phase, relationships became tense when almost 1,000 evacuees crammed into the gymnasium for the first few days. Three hundred people remained in the gym until September 2011. Luckily, the gym had small operable windows with mosquito screens, which allowed them to bring in fresh air and daylight, an unusual feature for a gym, which helped ease the stressful situation significantly.

As people moved into the temporary housing phase, housing units were placed opposite the entrance of the school, leaving an open space in between for recreation. This space served as an effective buffer and mixing zone, where temporary housing residents could cheer on students during sports practices and field-day events.[49] This case suggests the potential for spatial organization and design details to mitigate the social tensions that can arise in the aftermath of disasters.

SCHOOLS AND PREPAREDNESS EDUCATION

Schools connect their physical role for evacuation and sheltering to social knowledge through education. MLIT's bōsai education portal provides teachers with educational material based on disaster types, student grade, focus, and location,[50] making it easy to adapt the material to a specific place or event. NHK, Japan's public broadcasting service, creates television programs on preparedness and the science behind disasters. Public schools use these programs in social studies and science modules.[51] District-wide school drills are held annually by local jishubō and shōbōdan at designated evacuation spaces. Research has found that children are effective in communicating disaster-related knowledge to parents and other caregivers,[52] and the following projects facilitate the social and spatial aspects of such knowledge sharing.

Suginami Dai-ju Elementary School

Since the 1923 earthquake reconstruction, schools have often been built in conjunction with neighborhood parks. Sanshinomori Park and Suginami Dai-ju Elementary School stand in a lush landscape, with grand trees, a waterfall, streams, and a jungle gym slide built around a water tank. Both the park and school share water pump infrastructure with tree sprinklers, fire shower gates at the entrances, and water sprayers on the roof, with the capacity to extinguish fires in any direction. The five tanks store 1,710 tons of water,[53] and the local disaster-preparedness department comes every month to maintain it. Most schools in Japan are constructed with their open grounds on the south side of the building, but in this case, the park is on the west side, so that surrounding trees can protect evacuees who flee to the large open space. No fence separates the spaces, so the community can feel joint ownership of the park. The school district is considered a "unified bōsai community," and the roads surrounding the school purposely wind to slow down traffic and to give pedestrians the right of way.

Inside, big sliding doors separate classrooms, which are already assigned to neighborhoods. The rooms are designed to receive evacuees with cubbies and large furniture on wheels, and tracks in the ceiling allow floor-to-ceiling partitions to divide the rooms in variable ways. The building is designed to be barrier-free, both for children and for the many elderly people of the neighborhood. Recent renovations created a separate entrance and elevator for public access in the evenings, and the school further opened to the community by lending out its auditorium. Community members can also use the indoor gym, the heated pool, and specific classrooms outside of school hours.

There is a 1,500-ton potable water tank under the school grounds as well as storage areas for food, blankets, medicine, and cooking supplies, with estimated sustenance for around 2,000 evacuees for two to three days. The school and adjoining park are firmly embedded in the local neighborhood, with an annual cookout to use up the food in storage (located next to the school for easy community access) and to celebrate another year without a disaster. The school organizes this community-wide evacuation drill with the help of students and parents, who prepare food for about 900 people.[54] The community divides into groups responsible for different tasks in running an evacuation shelter, such as cooking, setting up temporary bathrooms, and medical relief as well as emergency communication. The local fire department participates in the drill; it demonstrates how to escape smoke-filled spaces and how to use fire hydrants.

During the 2011 earthquake, which also shook Tokyo, around 500 people evacuated to this school and took refuge. Several children stayed late when their parents could not pick them up. At that time, stored food and blankets were distributed. No doubt the design of the park and school, along with the annual feast and drill, contributed to the fact that operations ran smoothly during this daunting event.

Matsue Elementary School

Matsue Elementary School in Tokyo is designated as a neighborhood evacuation space for earthquake and flood events and creatively raises awareness by connecting curriculum and building design. Historically, the district suffered from several water-related disasters, and so all new school gymnasiums are now on the second floor. The school is located 1.25 meters below sea level, and according to the hazard map, the Arakawa River is only 800 meters away and could inundate the school with 3.38 meters of water.[55] The school was fully renovated in 2014 as the first eco-school in Edogawa: it features a green roof, rainwater reuse, a solar power generation system to operate off-grid as a shelter, and a courtyard for ventilation and natural light. The pool on the roof is efficient in cooling the building and for flushing manhole toilets using gravity. Water is kept in the pool even during the winter for emergency water use. Next to the pool are two long trough-like sinks, one of which is under a roofed area for post-disaster washing and cleaning uses. A one-hundred-ton rainwater catchment tank lies under-

Figure 74 (*next page*). Suginami Dai-ju Elementary School, paired with an evacuation park, is designed to play a number of roles for the neighborhood before and during disasters.

Water storage tank 1500 ton

Evacuation staircases

Water sprayers 460L/min (5)
35–50m radius

Supplies (Taki Dashi)

Tree sprinklers 70L/min (25)

Water storage tank 1710 ton (5)

Fire shower gates 30L/min (7)

Water storage

Suginami Elementary School

"The spirit of creating a school and park as a set was inherited from the 1923 reconstruction, and has since evolved and stands as a good example of enhancing community-wide preparedness."

Yoshii Keiko (Suginami Elementary School principal),
interview by Miho Mazereeuw and Maya Taketani, August 22, 2015

Movable track partitions

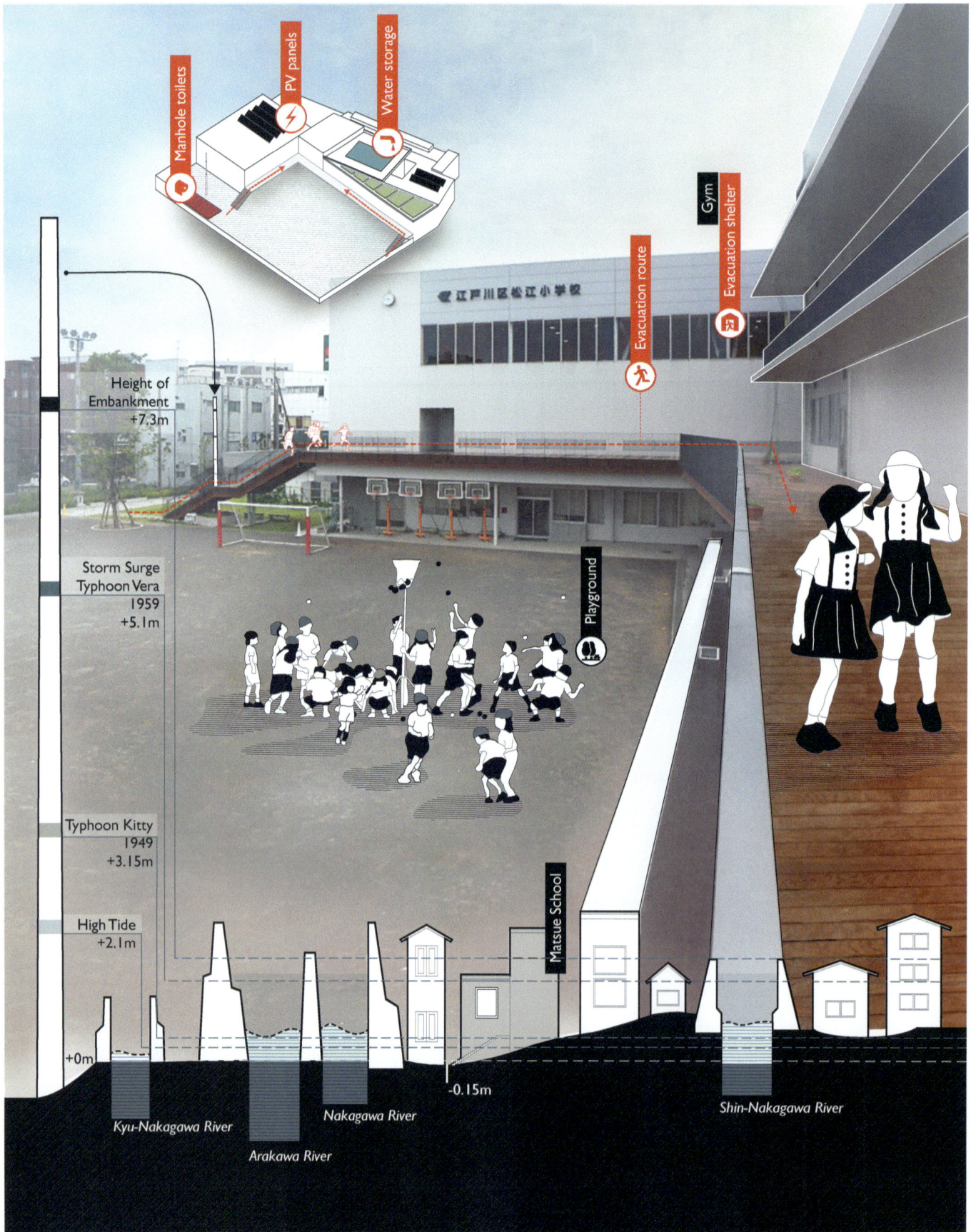

Manhole toilets

PV panels

Water storage

Gym

Evacuation shelter

Evacuation route

江戸川区松江小学校

Height of
Embankment
+7.3m

Storm Surge
Typhoon Vera
1959
+5.1m

Playground

Typhoon Kitty
1949
+3.15m

High Tide
+2.1m

Matsue School

+0m

-0.15m

Kyu-Nakagawa River

Arakawa River

Nakagawa River

Shin-Nakagawa River

neath one of the meeting rooms. During normal times, the school uses rainwater to flush all its toilets and to water the plants on the roof. Solar panels installed on the roof of the gymnasium provide energy for daily use and can allow evacuees to charge their cell phones.[56] The school, designed by the firm Ishimoto Architectural & Engineering, has exterior stairs leading to a large wooden balcony wrapping the sports field. This not only helps students evacuate to the second floor during floods but also provides a platform for cheering on schoolmates during athletic events. Large sliding doors frame each of the classrooms, but they can be completely opened up to create extra-wide hallways for a more open community feeling. The science and home economics classrooms have special desks with hidden faucets and gas burners under a hinged desktop. Each of these features can be especially helpful during post-disaster sheltering.

In addition to the basics of evacuation drills and bōsai videos, Matsue Elementary School embeds disaster preparedness in its curriculum. By engaging with the design of the building itself, the fifth graders learn about sustainability and the sixth graders learn about disaster preparedness for a full year. Fifth graders study sustainability through the school's various environmental systems, including the air conditioning and the heat-exchange system, the solar panels, and the green roof, and through the natural ecosystems of the Arakawa and Shin-Naka Rivers and the school's relationship to them. The goal of this class is for students to become interested in larger issues, such as global warming, by learning about something familiar to them. The sixth-grade curriculum is more directly connected to bōsai learning: how to set up a manhole toilet and install a tent structure over it. Their goal is to learn about the importance of preparedness skills more broadly.[57] These efforts to connect the school's design and education with furthering knowledge and understanding of the surrounding ecosystem and its hazards are fundamental in responding to the effects of climate change and to future disasters.

POST-2011 SCHOOL DESIGN

Yamashita Dai-ni Elementary School

In Yamamoto, two out of three elementary schools were inundated by the tsunami. Yamashita Dai-ni Elementary School, located 400 meters from the coast, was behind the 6.2-meter-high seawall, but the waters reached up to the ceiling of the first floor. All 200 students and teachers safely evacuated to the town hall on top of a hill. After the tsunami, the location of the original school was designated as a tsunami hazard zone, so the school was transferred to a new residential area near the newly raised JR Jōban Line Shin-Yamashita Station (which was also relocated 1 kilometer inland as part of the town's compact city reconstruction plan). The school is now designated as one of the core bōsai hubs in the new district, along with the bōsai center by the station and

Figure 75. Matsue Elementary School embeds bōsai education into the building's design.

Evacuation shelter
Gymnasium

Natural light

Ventilation and air circulation

Rainwater collection

Solar heat collection

Open classroom structure

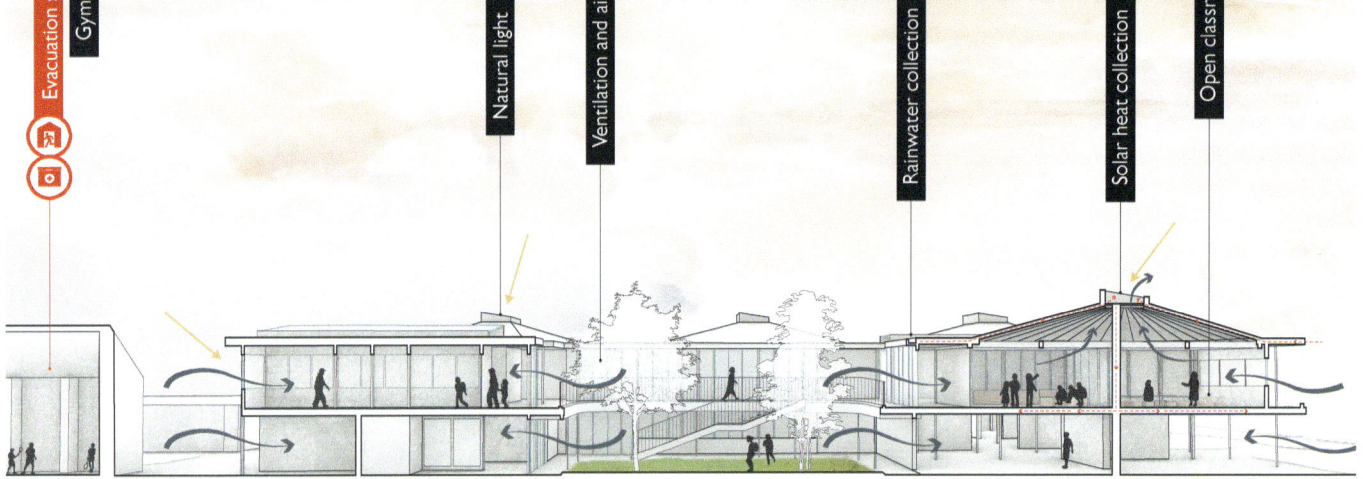

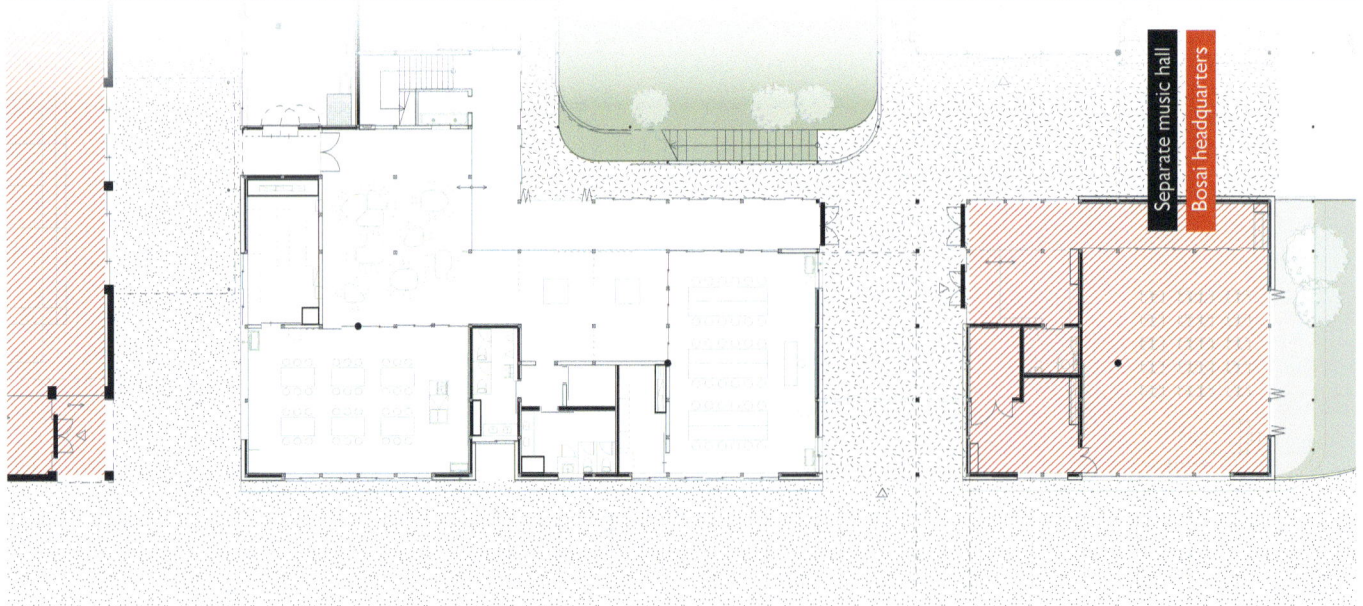

Separate music hall
Bosai headquarters

the town hall. The entire district is raised 2 meters. With the multilayered tsunami defense system, the school is considered safe, but as a precaution, it holds annual evacuation drills, sending residents farther up to the town hall on the hill.

Yamashita Dai-ni Elementary, co-designed by AXS SATOW Inc. and SUEP., makes efforts to open up to the local community.[58] Unlike a typical Japanese school, its central building faces the town's main street, which connects Shin-Yamashita Station to the town hall. Without fences, the school welcomes the community into its two-story wooden structure surrounding a courtyard. The music hall is made independent from the main building by large glass patio doors, and it is designed to be used for community festivals as well as bōsai headquarters.[59] The gym's entrance is directly accessible from the parking lot, making it easier to bring in emergency supplies. It is equipped with a low-energy floor heating system: the southern exterior wall is painted black to heat the air in the pipes that pass through the columns. If the sheltering period is prolonged, these two buildings can be disconnected from the main school so that education can resume.

The main school building has two exterior stairs in the courtyard by which residents can evacuate directly to the second-floor balcony. The entire first floor can be used for sheltering; the library, multipurpose hall, home economics classroom (kitchen), and carpeted computer classroom are reserved for vulnerable populations. All of the main classrooms are located on the second floor.[60] Each classroom in Yamashita Dai-ni Elementary—which was designed as an eco-school—features a skylight installed in the center with radiating wooden beams. Solar panels on the roof, the skylights, and the solar heat collection and circulation system control the temperature in the school building, and students use the rainwater collection system for watering plants.

Arahama Middle School

Watari City in Miyagi was entirely submerged 2.4 meters in 2011, and 450 residents evacuated and spent three days in the Arahama Middle School.[61] To return to a sense of normalcy, residents quickly agreed to rebuild the school on the same site, aiming for rapid reconstruction in order to bring survivors back to the town. Watari decided to build a lower seawall, so the ground floor of the school needed to be raised 2 meters. Families were concerned about how raising the ground would affect their traditional landscape, and they selected pilotis—a quicker to build, less expensive option—to mitigate tsunami damage.

The school's emergency features include more common items, such as the twenty-kilowatt solar panels with batteries, a power supply panel that can accept external power, restrooms that function even without water, and a food and blanket supply cache. For emergency drinking water, a faucet was installed in the water tank on the second floor. A special toilet system pulls water from the one-cubic-meter auxiliary

Figure 76. Yamashita Dai-ni Elementary School highlights sustainable design strategies, including a unique solar heat collection system, and is a core bōsai hub for the newly constructed neighborhood.

Figure 77. Arahama Middle School was designed to operate as a tsunami evacuation building for the neighborhood.

tank on the roof for two hundred flushes. This toilet usually drains to the municipal sewer system, but during an emergency it switches to a three-cubic-meter sewage tank installed on the ground within the piloti space.[62]

Seki Kukan Sekkei joined early in the process and worked with the school committee members to design the new Arahama Middle School as an evacuation center. The company made a 1,000-square-meter flat roof to accommodate evacuees; the roof is accessible to the surrounding community by two large exterior stairs on either side of the building. For ambulance access and supply delivery, the north side of the building has a ramp to the gym on the second floor. The gym is filled with light, easy to operate sliding doors that open to the second-floor balcony, which surrounds the building and can be accessed from all directions. If there is a need to evacuate, residents will be in this new type of gym, full of sunlight and air. In order to illuminate the piloti ground level, the architects made an atrium with stairs, and students use the space for bike parking and sports when it is raining.[63] Long, slim windows line the walls separating classrooms from the hallways to improve cross ventilation. Classrooms on the third floor have large, wide windows at a lowered height, so that seated students can see their town as it rebuilds and recovers. The architects thoughtfully considered the psychology of students in the recovery phase, incorporating features of everyday sustainability and everyday beauty into classroom and gym design.

Ogatsu School

Many districts are now combining nearby schools to address their shrinking populations. The Ogatsu School in Ishinomaki merged five schools into one joint elementary and middle school. As both the population of the towns and the number of students are shrinking, this school is designed to share space with the community: the concert hall (with an amazing view of the bay), the community tatami room, and the gym are all easily accessible from the exterior balcony. The third floor is aligned with the prefectural road for easy access and is used as a social welfare continuing-education hub. Inviting residents to use the facilities on a regular basis also helps form relationships among residents, students, and teachers, especially since public school teachers are on a rotation system and are not necessarily from the town. If the school needs to be used as a shelter, people will already know each other and be familiar with sharing spaces.[64] The circulation and programmatic use of the spaces are carefully considered in both regular timelines as well as post-disaster timelines, and the sectionally split double-height atrium workspace attached to the library has an extra-wide stair for evacuation. The linear design of the school and location of the gym are also directly tied to considerations of how the school may need to accommodate evacuees while classes restart. The cafeteria is designed to be next to the home economics classroom so the cooking facilities can be doubled during a disaster. The shared public facility and the school program were developed through a committee created in 2013, which included parent-teacher association representatives, residents, eight principals and vice principals, and academics. The lowest floor of the facility is 20 meters above sea level, and all the evacuation spaces are on the third floor, with multiple evacuation paths to the prefectural road. All necessary lifeline infrastructures go beyond the now-standard solar panels: the portable power generator can supply 50 percent of the gym power outlets, and with the installation of a receiving water tank along the road at the high point of the site, water can be supplied to all necessary parts of the building during a power outage, so that even septic tanks can be operated. The heaters are a special movable FF (Forced Draught Balanced Flue) type, so that in an emergency they can all be moved to the gym, which serves as the main evacuation space.[65]

Learning from and connecting to nature has been an important aspect of the school's success. Seki Kukan Sekkei was selected for this project not through a competition but through a proposal partnering with engineers, landscape architects, and residents throughout the design and construction process. The architects also ran workshops with both current and future students. This was especially important because the school was combining five geographically scattered schools. Their concept focused on "creating a rich learning space" by being "in harmony" with the local com-

School reopens

Day 1 to a few months after

Immediately after

Daily use

Fukko ring taiko | Ogatsu tire drum

Ogatsu's *"Date no Kurofune Taiko"* is a historical drumming art popular at the school, but the tsunami took their *taikos* (drums). To inspire students and community, the school staff created a *"fukkō ring taiko"* out of discarded tires and packing tape, which the students used throughout the recovery period. As a symbol of their strength, a *"fukkō ring taiko"* is displayed in the new school.

Community space
Special needs shelter

Auditorium
Offices/shelter

Ogatsu-ishi | Ogatsu stone tile

Kitchen
Evacuation shelter

Evacuation route to gym

Biotope

Irrigation system

munity and the natural environment. All the shared spaces and most classrooms over-look Ogatsu Bay to encourage students to develop activities while feeling a connection with the natural environment. The architects tried to minimize the cutting of trees and enhanced the natural spring on the site to create a future biotope—habitat for local flora and fauna—sliding through the pilotis of the open ground floor.[66] After the 2011 Tohoku disaster, many cities in the region were without water for over two months. Water conservation and knowledge of streams and fresh springs in the mountains for daily water needs were therefore critical. This school connects such bōsai knowledge with nature and environmental education through the design of the landscape and the building.

The rebuilding of the schools is necessary not just for education but for the spirit of the place. Including residents' opinions in the design process can instill hope during the construction timeline and is ultimately key to bringing residents back to the area. The shared spaces of Ogatsu School are visible from the prefectural road at night when those spaces are lit up and used for community activities, and this sight radiates the positive energy of *kizuna* (strength and bonding between people). In the ocean-view concert hall, children practice *taiko* (drum) and *kagura* (ceremonial dance) to revive their cultural heritage. The pride of the school is expressed in its façade, tiled with Ogatsu stone—a local slate that was used on the roof of Tokyo Station—which also supports the region's economic revival. All of these qualities add up in subtle ways to foster recovery.

DISCUSSION

Whether schools should be used as evacuation shelters is the subject of international debate because of students' need to quickly return to a sense of normalcy. The cases discussed here demonstrate the fundamental role played by Japanese schools through-out the entire disaster cycle: from their physical siting and location within the urban context as sites of pre-disaster education (in the Kamaishi case), to the school building's functions during evacuation (in the Yamashita case), to the inclusion of community spaces and programs within a school's very structure. Both the physical design of schools and their social infrastructure are key in disaster preparedness and response. They also help create a cumulative educational effect. Several studies have found that children who learn about disaster preparedness in schools are able to share their knowledge with their families at home; disaster education programs may thus also lead to families creating post-disaster plans.[67]

Because designers are trained in multifactorial decision making, they can help plan for beneficial design-related overlaps, such as closely linking bōsai and sustainability or leveraging temporal cycles of space usage throughout the disaster timeline. Architects

Figure 78. The Ogatsu elementary and middle school is specifically designed for multiple phases of emergency and recovery.

can also help schools think about how buildings themselves might contribute to education about disaster preparedness and climate change. Environmentally sustainable design, wide hallways, organization of classrooms, and leadership of the principals and teachers all come together to allow for an easier transition from school to sheltering the community in its time of greatest need. Open spaces designed to encourage interactions among students proved to be equally important during post-disaster sheltering: courtyards and solariums were used for eating, socializing, playing games, providing medical care, and distributing supplies. Each space is born out of a unique set of conditions, environment, and population. Such design processes and adaptations aim to inspire children and imbue them with life-saving knowledge and stewardship for the environment and their community. This can shift the paradigm, and it is exactly where our efforts should be placed as climate change promises more uncertainty in the future—and as our children become our new leaders. As Lori Peek states, "children, often identified as vulnerable, passive, and even helpless, have demonstrated that participation from all members of a community is invaluable to disaster risk reduction and individual and collective resilience."[68]

Tsunami Evacuation Buildings and Towers

When seeking safety from a tsunami, high ground remains the most secure location. Traditional reminders tell residents to "run to the hills," but reaching the hills in the time between an earthquake and the arrival of the water is not always possible: if the earthquake is close to the shore, a five-meter-high tsunami can arrive in as little as three minutes. Even with a longer warning, people with limited mobility may find some evacuation routes difficult. In many parts of Iwate and Miyagi Prefectures, the ria geography means that a hill is always nearby, but in the flat expanses of floodplains around Sendai, high ground may be a great distance away. Such spaces require an alternative way to evacuate vertically, above the level of the incoming tsunami.

The creation of dedicated structures for evacuation, as opposed to more costly infrastructural transformations such as seawalls and ground raising, are acupunctural strategies for saving lives in a tsunami or severe storm surge. As these projects involve significant investment, they can also meet everyday social needs, such as for recreation or gathering, thus supporting and amplifying collective community practices. They can play a larger symbolic role, too, by connecting the social and the spatial—namely, through education or engagement programs within the building, through warning systems that make it clear when and how these structures can be used in a disaster, and by fostering greater disaster awareness.

The 2011 disaster underscored the urgency of tsunami evacuation structure construction, particularly in the Nankai Trough region. Recently built tsunami emergency evacuation facilities come in several types: artificial high ground, the Tsunami Evacuation Building (TEB), and the Tsunami Evacuation Tower (TET). The classification of a structure as a building or a tower is based on the Building Standards Law's definition of a building, but owing to the complex nuances of the definition, TEBs are here defined as existing and newly built spaces that are frequently inhabited, and TETs are standardized, manufactured, primarily escape-only towers. Japan's growing network of tsunami evacuation structure typologies suggests opportunities for productively leveraging tsunami evacuation structures as dual-function spaces as they attract growing interest in Japan and around the world.

Figure 79 (*next page*). Tsunami evacuation building typologies.

1-2m inundation height

>9m building depth
perpendicular to coastline

>3m inundation height

>15m building depth
perpendicular to coastline

>1 sqm per evacuee
1-2 days' worth of food, water,
medical supplies, toilet & blankets;
generator; communication devices

>4 stories

3 stories

h

evacuation floor

aluminum railings

I-beam

column support

open lowel levels allow
water to flow through

ramp & stair
access (>2)

>3m

1-2m

inundation height

h x 2

fine sand & silt

sand & gravel

foundation pillars

reinforced concrete (RC)
or steel structure

till

impermeable bedrock

The number of required floors and the
depth of the building depend on the
assumed inundation height and the tsunami
direction, based on data from both prior
historic events and predictive modeling.
CAO, "Tsunami Evacuation Building 2005," 2.

16.58m

8.1m

Kochi Tower

Maehama Tower

Yoshida pedestrian bridge

Nakano Tower

760 people

11m
200 people

16m

Tsuzumigaura Elementary School

Wakayama Fishermen's Association

Shimizu Corp Frame

Suzaki Stairs

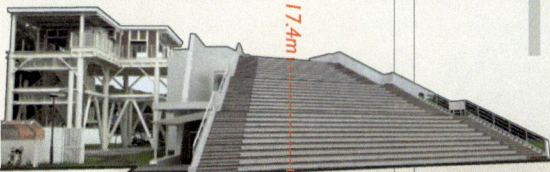
17.4m

400 people

+13m
20m
+6m

Okata Akatsuki-Kan

Nakatosa-cho Tower

AEON Mall

9m

14.75m
5.4m

13.2m

Tosa Seinan Great Park Observatory

Ya-shi Park Tower

Okada Port

230 people

22m
500 people

22m

13.71m

9m

Saga Tower

Nishiki Tower

Kushimoto Tower
(floating unit)

Tapic 45 Station

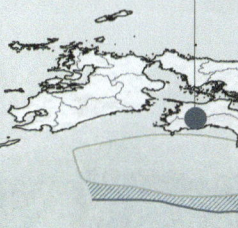

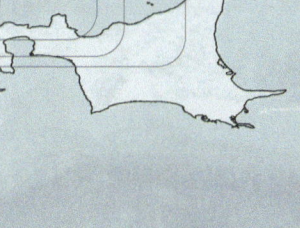

Nankai Trough

PRE-2011 DESIGNATION OF THE TSUNAMI EMERGENCY EVACUATION BUILDINGS

The Nankai Trough plate boundary has historically generated massive trench-type earthquakes every 100 to 150 years, and yet there has been little seismic activity since the 1854 Ansei-Tokai earthquake. Seismologists worry that this seismic gap means that a massive earthquake (and tsunami) is imminent on the Pacific coast, potentially stretching from Shizuoka Prefecture to Shikoku Island. In response to these predictions, the CAO created the Tōnankai/Nankai Earthquake Countermeasures Charter in 2003[1] and Guidelines for Tsunami Evacuation Buildings (TEBs) in 2005. A TEB is defined as "an existing or a new facility, in the expected inundation area, where local residents urgently and temporarily evacuate." The local government and the owner of a building agree on its designation as an emergency evacuation site. The building is required to be a reinforced concrete or a steel structure, built after the establishment of the Seismic Design Standards (1981), with confirmed seismic safety.

The number of required floors and the depth of the building depend on the assumed inundation height and the tsunami direction, based on data from prior historic events as well as predictive modeling. For example, for a tsunami of one or two meters, vertical structures must be at least three stories, and the depth of the building (perpendicular to the waterfront) needs to be at least nine meters. If the inundation is predicted to be greater than three meters, then the building should be at least four stories, and the depth of the building needs to be at least fifteen meters. These guidelines are intended to encourage the designation and maintenance of TEBs by municipalities along the Pacific coastline to increase options for evacuees, but they are not intended to guarantee survival.[2]

The 2011 Tohoku tsunami revealed that the TEB designation process was flawed and was not always properly conducted. The 2011 survey by the CAO of the tsunami-affected municipalities found 364 designated tsunami evacuation spaces, but few conformed to all the TEB guidelines, and some municipalities had underestimated the breadth of the tsunami hazard zone. Only 87 of the buildings were intended for urgent evacuation, with the rest for longer-term sheltering. Of the 87 buildings, only 35 TEBs were located inside the expected inundation areas, a crucial factor to allow quick escape to higher levels.[3] Given the unprecedented scale of the 2011 tsunami in both height and inundation area, a number of designated and ad hoc evacuation sites were overtopped, contributing to the large loss of lives.

POST-2011 DESIGNATION OF THE TSUNAMI EMERGENCY EVACUATION BUILDINGS

In response, a new article was added in the 2013 revision of the Disaster Countermeasures Act to ensure the smooth and safe evacuation of residents. The mayor of each municipality must designate, in advance, emergency evacuation facilities that meet safety standards; these must be independent from other, longer-term shelters, such as schools.[4]

In light of the projected risk of a Nankai Trough earthquake and the lessons from 2011, special disaster-preparedness regions were established along Japan's southern coast through the 2013 Act on Nankai Trough Earthquake Disaster Management. There are 139 municipalities expecting more than thirty centimeters of inundation within thirty minutes of the earthquake, and these were designated as Special Tsunami Evacuation Regions.[5] These regulatory zones have to meet certain targets. Local and regional governments are tasked with creating disaster-preparedness and post-disaster management plans. These include the designation or creation of evacuation spaces and evacuation routes as well as the identification of facilities that require relocation. Associated projects can receive up to two-thirds subsidy from the national government.[6] This combination of regulation and funding has led to a profusion of new projects designed to improve preparedness for a Nankai tsunami.

GUIDELINES AND SUBSIDIES

In order to increase emergency evacuation spaces, a plethora of government subsidies has become available. Most of the subsidies come as rolling grants under the heading of the Comprehensive Urban Disaster Management Project.[7] This includes many types of projects for all disasters. The Tsunami Bōsai Community Development Promotion guideline is prepared by MLIT for each municipality to plan and implement specific tsunami bōsai strategies.[8] Subsidies are available for projects for reconstruction, as well as new mitigation, that address multilayered protection (following L1/L2 and the Two-Two Rule) outlined in the Tsunami Bōsai Regional Development Law, including evacuation routes, TEBs, and TETs, with one-half to two-thirds of the costs subsidized by MLIT.

The evacuation space must be an additional two stories higher than the expected tsunami height and have more than two means of access, preferably at least one from the side away from the coast. If higher than twenty meters, it should include a lightning protection rod and durable, strong aluminum or steel railings. The required space per evacuee in a tsunami emergency evacuation facility is one square meter. However, depending on the constraints of the site and the predicted duration of sheltering (e.g., if there is another shelter nearby), the size can vary. If it is also a shelter (and not only a platform), it should contain one to two days' worth of food and water, medical supplies, blankets, a portable toilet, a generator, and communication devices. The site should be surrounded by multilingual signage for clear wayfinding as well as illumination for safe nighttime evacuation.[9] As of April 2021, Japan has 15,304 TEBs and 502 TETs.[10] Most—12,981—are in the Nankai Trough special disaster-preparedness areas expecting a tsunami height of at least three meters.

MANUFACTURED TSUNAMI EVACUATION TOWERS

Tsunami evacuation towers have various basic specifications and designs, such as steel structure or reinforced concrete structure, depending on their manufacturers. Although no national standards exist for tsunami evacuation towers, MLIT provides technical details for structural safety against tsunamis, and the ultimate decisions are entrusted to municipalities. The tsunami tower installation site should be an open space, a park or parking lot in a hazard zone where evacuation is difficult, or a port where there are no hills or designated tsunami evacuation buildings. The companies developing TETs are from steel and civil engineering industries.

In the flat stretches of plains, vertical evacuation structures can be even more essential because distances to high ground are so great. While the 2011 tsunami reached much lower heights (a maximum of around ten meters) in the Sendai plain compared to the more rugged ria coastline, fatalities and damages were similar in the two areas.[11] The tsunami reached up to five kilometers inland, and without high ground, a comprehensive system of evacuation towers, or sufficient evacuation knowledge, residents of the Sendai plain could not evacuate effectively. These experiences from the 2011 tsunami prompted the city to initiate a campaign to build thirteen new tsunami evacuation structures by 2017: six dedicated towers, five new fire stations with incorporated evacuation spaces, and two sets of exterior stairs added to existing schools.[12] Sendai's tsunami evacuation towers were designed through town walks and workshops among residents of each district. To familiarize the community with the evacuation sites, they are frequently used for evacuation drills and preparedness classes. Students conduct evacuation drills on the actual slopes with wheelchair users and the elderly in order to practice navigating the challenging routes and to increase awareness among aging residents. While these sites are architecturally less innovative than projects like Tapic 45 (described below), the approach of creating a network of universal-access evacuation spaces as requested by the community is particularly important in this low-lying region.

Pedestrian Bridges and Platforms

The only hill in the town of Yoshida, Shizuoka Prefecture, is home to the castle, originally built in 1505. According to simulations, if an 8.6-meter tsunami hits the flat coastal plain, 40 percent of the town would be submerged. In preparation, Yoshida built fifteen tsunami evacuation towers in 2013. The largest tower has a capacity of 1,200 people on a 628-square-meter platform and cost about ¥450 million; half the construction cost was subsidized by the national government.[13] The tsunami emergency evacuation sites are part of a town-wide project that seeks to ensure that all residents can reach a safe area within four minutes—the anticipated tsunami arrival time.[14] Yoshida was the first town to assemble a panel of researchers and technicians following the 2011 Tohoku tsunami in order to establish guidelines for safe vertical evacuation spaces.[15]

The broad concrete and steel open-air tsunami towers (4 to 8.1 meters high) occupy vacant sites in the low-density town, where nearly all buildings are one or two stories. The towers use a steel moment-frame construction with 30- to 40-meter-deep piles to help cope with possible liquefaction during an earthquake. As preliminary evacuation sites, these structures have no facilities other than basic solar lighting; they are simply places to escape the waves. However, they are linked to a larger evacuation and preparedness plan. Once waters recede, evacuees can proceed to secondary evacuation spaces such as the North Oasis Evacuation Park, a newly built bōsaikōen with embedded facilities including manhole toilets, cooking benches, a water tank, and shelter pavilions.[16] These evacuation towers attempt to serve an everyday function as well, with some doubling as extra-wide pedestrian bridges. They are the first of their type, built over roads and used during non-disaster times as pedestrian crossings. This function attempts to integrate the structures into the everyday fabric of the city, although one can argue that the roads they cross are not particularly heavily trafficked.[17] Open year-round, the evacuation structures can also serve informally as picnic sites and observation decks, offering striking views over the town and coast. The town also made a walking map and guides a walking "tour of the 15 evacuation towers,"[18] aiming to build community, promote exercise and health, and bolster successful evacuation—embedding the TETs into everyday activities.

RETROFITS TO EXISTING BUILDINGS

In the framework of the Tsunami Evacuation Facility Subsidy Program, the national government covers retrofits to existing buildings to prepare them for tsunami evacuation. The subsidies for retrofitting apply to the installation of external stairs, rooftop fences, rooftop decks, guide lighting, and other features defined by a municipality. The subsidy amount varies among municipalities, depending on location, but generally ranges between 50 and 66 percent of the costs.[19] External evacuation stairs are constructed by a range of companies, from small steel stair specialists to major general construction companies.

A large-scale example is the Frame Shelter by Shimizu Corporation, wherein a structural reinforcement frame creates a roofed evacuation space on the top of the building. Foundation piles and concrete slabs prevent the frame from tipping or sliding, and an evacuation staircase, surrounded by the steel frame, ensures the safety of evacuees. The detailed components are determined by the wave force and maximum tsunami inundation depth simulations. For a four-story building, the cost of using this system would be about half the cost of constructing a new tsunami-resistant building.[20]

Other examples are small-scale tsunami towers attached to existing buildings to make the building a designated tsunami evacuation space. Construction is usually combined with installing rooftop fences and a storage area for stockpiling supplies. External steel evacuation staircase costs vary greatly, depending on the project. For example, a staircase to the five-story Suzaki city hall (Kochi Prefecture) costs about ¥19 million,[21] whereas the one to the 378-square-meter rooftop in Hyūga (Miyazaki Prefecture), with solar lighting, an emergency power supply, and a stockpile storage bench, costs over ¥102 million.[22]

Fish Market

The Wakayama East Fishermen's Association constructed an evacuation tower on top of its fish market at the Kushimoto port in 2014, complete with a wind- and solar-powered desalination system. As a retrofit of the existing two-story building, the structure includes an open-frame steel staircase, which is attached to the side of the existing market and extends two additional stories above the existing roof. The rooftop of the tower reaches higher than the largest expected tsunami in this area (ten meters)[23] and accommodates approximately two hundred evacuees sixteen meters above the ground in an enclosed area. The desalination system, powered by renewables, provides water for prolonged evacuation, and the tower also stores emergency food and life jackets.[24] There are few tall buildings or hills that can serve as tsunami evacuation sites in the vicinity of the Kushimoto fishing port, and the fishermen's cooperative sought to create a secure evacuation site for their members and surrounding residents.

This project is part of Kushimoto's larger vision for establishing thorough evacuation networks, preparedness, and bōsai education, since much of the coastal town is in a tsunami inundation zone. Other components of the plan include the establishment of ninety-eight new evacuation paths; designation of 215 tsunami evacuation spaces on high ground; creation of thirteen TEBs in flat, low-lying areas and forty-eight longer-term shelters; formation of disaster management hubs such as the Uenoyama bōsai open space; and relocation of public buildings. The town has established a traveling lecture series, hazard mapping workshops, and disaster evacuation communication drills supporting the work of jishubō.[25] This connection of the physical infrastructure for evacuation with social programs, which help people understand when and how they should evacuate, is essential for creating safe and effective evacuation systems.

Floating Tsunami Shelters

One way to reduce the cost of tall tsunami evacuation towers is to install floating tsunami shelters. Kushimoto had built four evacuation towers in 2007, but the revised simulations in March 2013 revealed that the town was at risk for a seventeen-meter tsunami arriving in two minutes, and half a meter of water could cover the top of the evacuation structures in the Tanami district. While town officials considered building taller evacuation towers, they decided that the cost and space requirements were too high. Instead, able-bodied residents are encouraged to run to the surrounding hills, and the town invested in evacuation routes to facilitate this.[26] Kushimoto installed floating tsunami shelters on top of the existing towers in the Tanami district in February 2015 for elderly residents or others who might have difficulty reaching a hilltop evacuation space. The units, which resemble truncated subway cars, are constructed of reinforced plastic and weigh 1.3 tons each. As opposed to typical open-air evacuation structures, the enclosed shelters also provide a place to store food, water, and emergency goods and a space to stay warm and dry if the evacuation is prolonged. If water levels exceed the base of the platform, the units will begin to float and will remain upright even if rocked by water movement. Each unit can accommodate up to thirty people and is lit by solar energy. Occupants can be rescued by boat or helicopter. The project cost around ¥5.8 million, including installation, per shelter. The shelters remain unlocked, so they can be easily accessed in case of an emergency and can also be used by the community on an everyday basis. The units are produced by Tajima Motor Corporation, which notes that during non-disaster times, "secondary uses could be as diverse as a first aid station or even a karaoke booth."[27] However, according to interviews in 2018, they were not being used regularly.[28] Still, this case shares a creative solution that helped avoid rebuilding the newly completed towers.

DUAL-USE EVACUATION BUILDINGS

Tapic 45

As described above, prior to the 2011 triple disaster, most tsunami emergency evacuation facilities in Tohoku were preexisting reinforced concrete buildings. Based on a survey of five low-lying cities in Miyagi Prefecture, after 2011, more than 9,700 people evacuated to reinforced concrete buildings and survived.[29] One of Tohoku's successful pre-designated TEBs was the *michi-no-eki* (a rest area with a local produce market) in Rikuzentakata. The well-loved structure called Tapic 45 was triangular in section, with stadium-style seating on the building's sea-facing exterior that allowed visitors to watch the ocean like a stage. During the tsunami, this stepped surface made for easy evacuation. Since it was not a designated evacuation building, the employees inside feared a large tsunami and fled for higher ground. However, construction workers from the coast evacuated to the building and were able to climb up the stepped exterior and survive the inundation.[30] The tsunami reached 13.7 meters up the 19-meter-high building.[31]

Rikuzentakata's Tapic 45 is an example of a dual-function tsunami evacuation building, where the unique form allowed it to accommodate evacuation as well as its everyday use as a roadside visitor center and gathering place to enjoy the ocean view. In contrast with other concrete buildings that double as evacuation sites, such as schools or hospitals, its shape clearly indicates its potential as a space for emergency evacuation, and its exterior access eliminates possible barriers to entry, such as locked doors. In the chaos of an incoming tsunami, this formal iconography made the difference for those quickly searching for a safe space above the waters.

During the recovery phase, a small shrine was built as a secular space for visitors to offer prayers for the community, and now Tapic 45 itself stands as a memorial in the Takata Matsubara Tsunami Reconstruction Park, which opened on September 22, 2019. The memorial area consists of five parts: the Iwate Tsunami Memorial Museum, which includes a large retail component of local produce and crafts (the *michi-no-eki*); an axial path connecting the museum to the prayer table by the ocean; and a place to offer flowers on the seawall, which also provides a view to the regrowing coastal forest and the city. The memorialized Tapic 45 is connected to the museum by a promenade. Although the museum is not intended to be a tsunami evacuation space, the Symbol Road, a 25-meter-wide evacuation street, connects the tsunami reconstruction park to the Takata district evacuation area and, farther up, to the new hilltop residential district.[32]

Nishiki Towers Fire Station and Museum

Nishiki Tower I, in the small and remote fishing town of Taiki, Mie Prefecture, integrates everyday use into a purpose-built tsunami and typhoon evacuation building. The five-story, 22-meter spiral tower house has a fire station with a small fire truck and equipment, public toilets, a meeting room, and a museum of local disaster history on lower floors, with the fourth floor hosting a temporary shelter and the open-air fifth floor a covered evacuation space. The interior rooms are locked, and local community members as well as municipal staff hold keys; the top evacuation space remains open at all times and doubles as an observation space, providing a view out to the scenic harbor. During a tsunami, it would also afford observation of the incoming inundation. Up to 500 evacuees can be accommodated between the second through fifth floors, and the space is also outfitted with emergency generators and other supplies for people seeking refuge.[33] Stairs wrapping the exterior of the building allow for quick

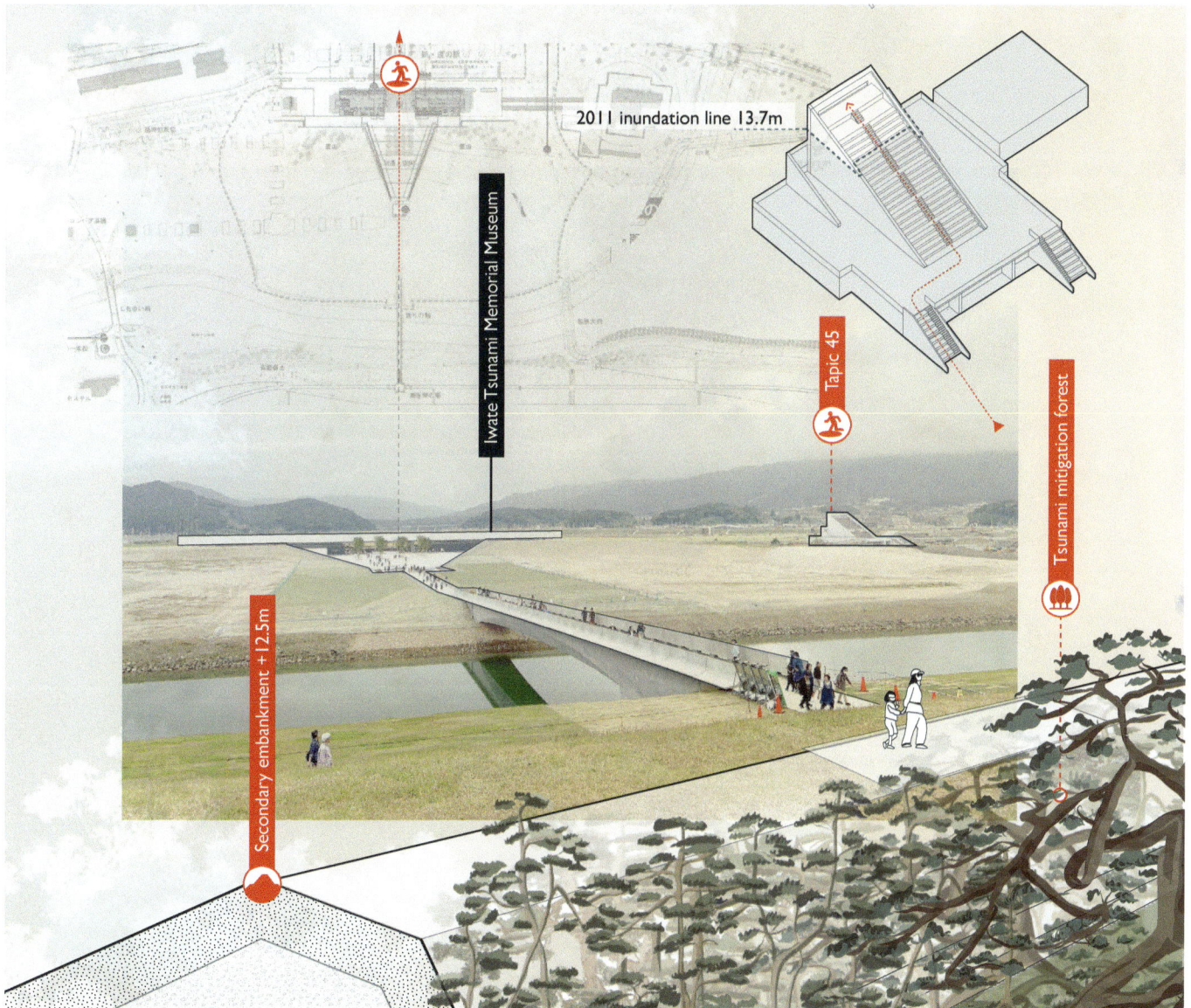

Figure 80. The Tapic 45 evacuation building and Takata Matsubara Tsunami Reconstruction Park.

2011 inundation line 13.7m

Iwate Tsunami Memorial Museum

Tapic 45

Tsunami mitigation forest

Secondary embankment + 12.5m

access to the upper levels, and its iconic form illustrates its potential for quick vertical escape. The tower was built by local initiative in 1997–98, in response to the area's long history of typhoons and tsunamis, to ensure that all residents could evacuate within five minutes of an earthquake or warning.[34] Designed to withstand a 7.0-magnitude earthquake with 6-meter-high inundation, the tower is built in the alluvial plain of the town center, where hilltop evacuation sites might be too distant but the particle

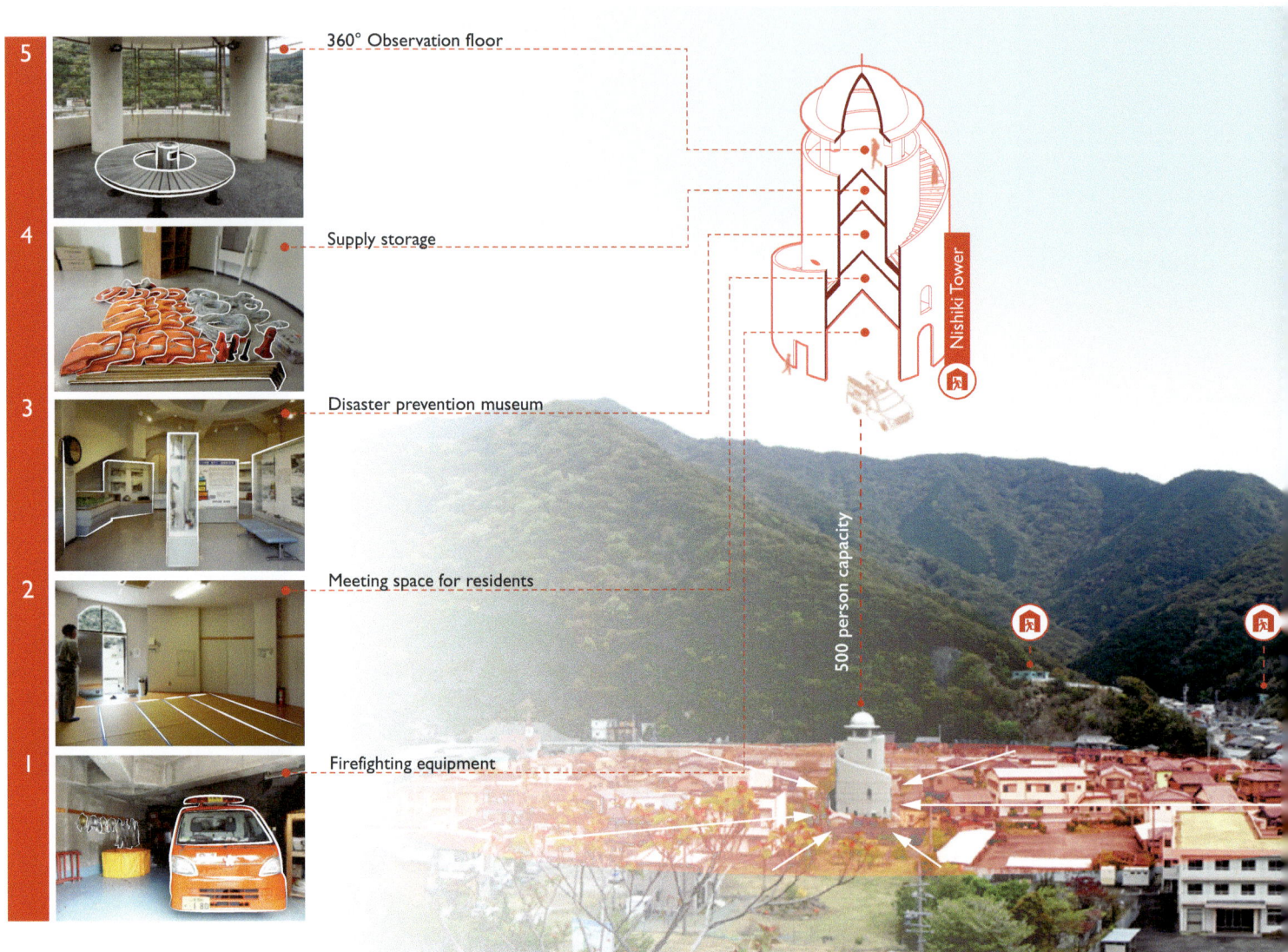

5 — 360° Observation floor

4 — Supply storage

3 — Disaster prevention museum

2 — Meeting space for residents

1 — Firefighting equipment

Nishiki Tower

500 person capacity

Figure 81. Nishiki Tower, designed as a fire station and museum, can host five hundred evacuees during typhoons and tsunamis.

sizes of the sand and gravel layer make liquefaction unlikely. The concrete piles reach 6 meters below grade (2 meters below the alluvial soil) to help the building withstand a ten-ton ship hitting it with a velocity of 10 meters per second.[35]

The town has thirty tsunami shelters in total, some nestled into the surrounding mountains. A new, modern town hall was also built in the surrounding hills to help ensure that municipal facilities are not damaged in a tsunami. The Nishiki area was seriously damaged by the 6.5-meter-high 1944 Tōnankai Tsunami, which killed 64 citizens and destroyed 88 percent of residential buildings and 92.8 percent of non-residential buildings.[36] While the town was still picking up the pieces from the destruction of the

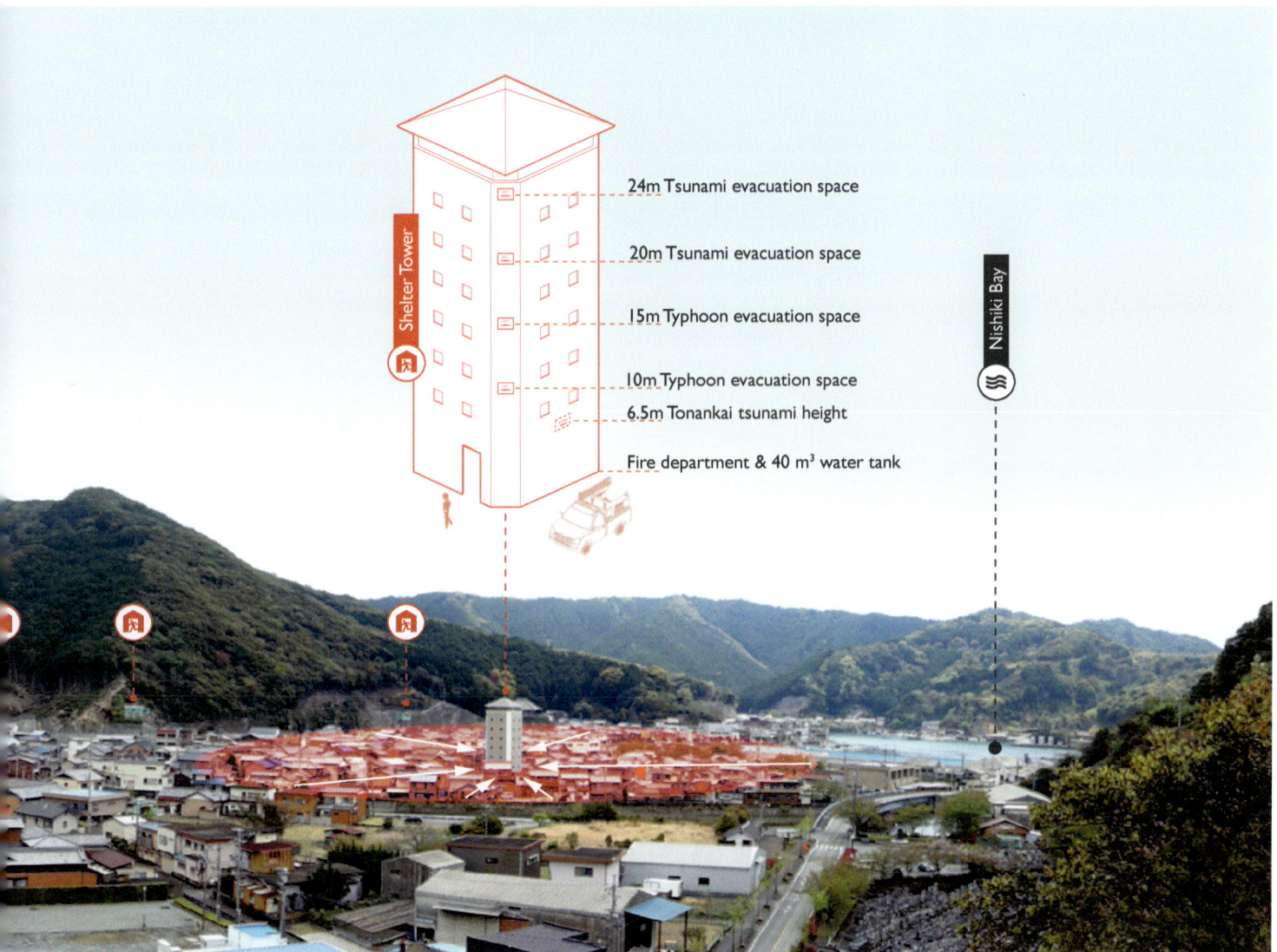

24m Tsunami evacuation space

20m Tsunami evacuation space

15m Typhoon evacuation space

10m Typhoon evacuation space

6.5m Tonankai tsunami height

Fire department & 40 m³ water tank

Shelter Tower

Nishiki Bay

1944 tsunami, it was again pummeled in 1959 by Typhoon Vera, which caused over 3,000 deaths in coastal Japan. Residents consider the tower a symbol of the area's deep history of living with disasters.[37]

To accommodate residents who live on the other side of the town's river and closer to the coast, a second tower, Nishiki II, was built in 2012. Each tower displays a placard indicating the height of the 1944 tsunami, and Nishiki II has an oversized ruler running up the side wall, indicating height above sea level. Inside, each floor also shows the height above sea level, allowing evacuees to understand their elevation relative to tsunami projections. Nishiki II, with a more conservative square floor plan and protected interior stairs, houses a typhoon evacuation room on the second floor in addition to tsunami evacuation rooms on the sixth and seventh floors and roof. The building also contains a 40-cubic-meter seismic water storage tank for firefighting in the densely built surrounding neighborhood.[38]

Taiki's evacuation plan considers how physical structures interface with local warning and evacuation practices. The town boasts a local tsunami warning system: after an earthquake with twenty seconds or more of shaking, any town employee can activate the warning. Rather than commemorating national disaster days such as those marking the Tohoku and Tokyo earthquakes, Taiki holds a town-wide evacuation drill every December 7, the anniversary of the 1944 tsunami. It also conducts nighttime evacuation drills with a high participation rate (30 to 40 percent of the residents).[39] One out of ten Taiki residents is a member of the local jishubō. In combination with these more formal structures, the town has a deep oral history of past disasters and preparedness advice, including folk songs town elders learned as children. The earthquakes off the coast of the Kii Peninsula in 2004 affirmed the town's combination of physical and cultural preparedness; although evacuation rates were very low in other parts of Mie Prefecture, 80 percent of Taiki residents evacuated. The town historically had 3.5-meter-high sea defenses, so its preparedness strategy had relied on evacuation rather than structural protection measures.[40] Town officials had two additional evacuation structures built, but more recently they added three seawalls (two 8 meters high and one 7.3 meters high) at the entrance of Nishiki Bay[41] to deflect the initial forces. Their city continues to promote its combined strategies, prioritizing evacuation.

NEW TYPOLOGIES

While the previously mentioned initiatives are projects led by municipal governments (supported by national subsidies), the following section describes a privately led tsunami bōsai retrofit project, incentivized by municipalities and funded by national subsidies.

AEON

AEON is a major Japanese distribution group consisting of more than three hundred domestic and overseas companies in various businesses with a primary focus on grocery stores. In 2012, it was the first retailer to sign the "agreement on supplies for large-scale disasters" with the SDF. According to the Disaster Countermeasures Act, on July 1, 2017, the company was designated by the prime minister as a "lifeline" during a disaster through supplying goods and logistical functions and serving as a temporary evacuation space in local communities.[42] AEON signed an agreement with Japan's ten electric power companies for mutual cooperation during times of disaster, and it will provide

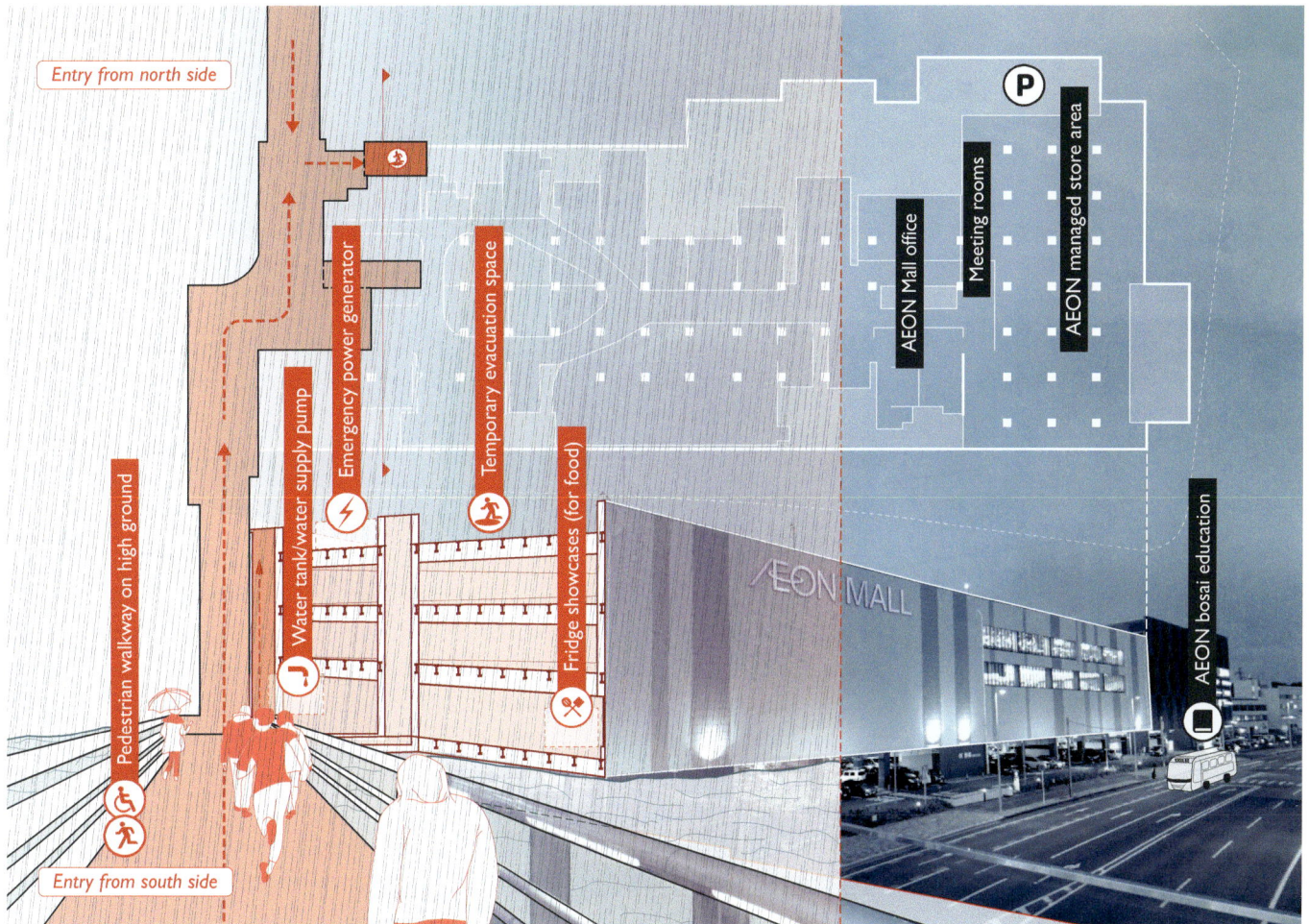

Entry from north side

P

AEON Mall office

Meeting rooms

AEON managed store area

Pedestrian walkway on high ground

Water tank/water supply pump

Emergency power generator

Temporary evacuation space

Fridge showcases (for food)

AEON bosai education

ÆON MALL

Entry from south side

Figure 82. AEON Mall was also designed as a tsunami evacuation space.

these companies with space to set up electricity recovery centers. In the 2018 July heavy rain event, AEON Mall Kurashiki opened up its multistory parking lot and its bathrooms to the public and accepted 2,300 vehicles.[43] When 2019 Typhoon Faxai hit Chiba Prefecture, AEON made its parking lots available to electric power companies to support early power restoration in the region. Since 2012, AEON has established fifty-three regional bōsai centers nationwide to serve as temporary evacuation space, offering relief and rescue space, food distribution, potable water, toilets, and mobile phone charging stations.[44]

In May 2018, AEON Mall Iwaki Onahama, in Ibaraki Prefecture, opened as Japan's first bōsai shopping mall, officially designated as an evacuation space.[45] Since the Onahama area was inundated up to TP+6.3 meters by the 2011 tsunami, the Raised Frame (RF)–steel construction five-story building has been designed with pedestrian bridges 6 meters aboveground. The bridges connect to both the city-side and ocean-side evacuation routes and emergency stairs, leading evacuees to the 13,390-square-meter rooftop. The 220-ton water tank on the second floor, the power generator (500 kilo-volt-amperes [KVA]), and a 200-liter oil tank on the rooftop make drinking water and electricity available for seventy-two hours during a power or water outage. Ten man-hole toilets are available on the first-floor parking lot, and emergency faucets supply water to flush toilets and wash hands. A large meeting hall on the fourth floor is ready to be used as a temporary shelter with emergency power outlets and water supply. The grocery section on the second floor will be an emergency rescue space.[46] They are planning to hold a large-scale public evacuation drill annually on June 5. Since 2019, AEON has created a network with more than 850 partners in governmental organizations and private companies. It also makes strong efforts to share bōsai education. For example, in collaboration with the Scout Association of Japan, it has conducted annual bōsai caravans for elementary-school kids in seventy places nationwide.[47]

DISCUSSION

The approach to tsunami evacuation facilities in Japan is still primarily a technical one. The opportunities afforded by significant investment in tsunami evacuation structures across Japan, and particularly in the Nankai region, are not always successfully lever-aged as opportunities to invest in public space. Endō Shūhei and his colleagues argue that, for the most part, the TETs were constructed without considering the surround-ing environment and that carbon copies of previous examples were rapidly constructed without necessarily reflecting residents' opinions in the design.[48] Nonetheless, it is important to remember that these coastal communities face an urgent and imminent danger. When evaluating cost and speed, it is understandable that it is not always pos-sible for each district to take the longer, more ideal community-engaged route for a uniquely designed TEB.

From Chile to the United States, countries are starting to invest in such structures. At the time of this writing, Washington State has the first tsunami evacuation plat-form in the United States, located on the roof of Ocosta Elementary School.[49] The second one is being constructed in the town of Tokeland, where the Shoalwater Bay Tribe is working with FEMA to build a space for more than 400 residents. The project received a $2.2 million grant from FEMA, and the 70-member tribe is generously con-tributing $1 million.[50]

Given the cost of these projects and their permanent position in their communities, it is important for them to take on the anticipatory design principle of integrating into existing everyday social activities. In cases such as Taiki, Tapic 45, and AEON, where the TEB is not just part of a city's evacuation planning but is designed as part of the city itself, these units can become productive everyday public spaces, enrich-ing the daily lives of local residents. In the best cases, these new evacuation spaces do just this — adapt to the needs of their particular geographies and populations. With community groups participating in the decision-making process, these structures can be built as public spaces in their own right for education, exercise, gatherings, and celebrations. Mechanisms to create such partnerships could be introduced so that spaces can be adopted by local groups, increasing the possibility for stewardship and care of these structures within the community. Considering that this type of structure is relatively new in our architectural vocabulary, even the retrofits and standard manufactured structures provide new fodder for future design typologies, partnerships, and collaborations. They may even inspire new urban imaginaries for how we occupy the sky during everyday activities and escape the waters when necessary.

Architectural Transformations Discussion

Temporality, agility, and transformation are prevailing tenets of traditional Japanese architecture, and some argue that this is due to its relationship with frequent disasters. As philosopher Michael Lazarin observes, "Rather than building for the ages, the Japanese view has always been that it is better to be able to reconstruct quickly after a fire, earthquake or typhoon. Even today, some shopkeepers store a supply of pre-cut, pre-mortised timbers in another part of town, so they can be 'back in business in three days' if disaster strikes. And they are fairly certain that it will, since ultimate reality is transiency and permanence is benighted illusion."[1] This notion is analogous to the *osukui-goya,* and some post-disaster temporary housing, such as Haryū Wood Studio, has no doubt been influenced by this ability to connect construction techniques to various timelines of building, dismantling, repairing, and rebuilding.

Tangentially, many architects have also developed tools for thinking about how buildings transform through time—physically or through inhabitation—drawing inspiration from notions of temporality like the passing of time in tune with the sun's movements and the changing of seasons, as well as how the flow of visitors affects spaces. A classic example of the latter is OMA's Yokohama Masterplan, which recognizes that various programs have their peak hours; its iconic drawing shows diverse ways in which bustling spaces, such as a wholesale market, can be occupied throughout the day.

Similarly, anticipatory design considers how to best integrate a building's many uses throughout the disaster timeline into the architectural design. Through temporal design, buildings can transform to support different people with diverse needs and safely shelter them with dignity during the most traumatic times of their lives.

Partnering with social scientists and ethnographers, or learning their methods of studying survivor experiences after each disaster, has improved how spaces perform during disasters, both structurally and socially. Even small revelations—such as the benefits of eye-level windows for ventilation, sunlight, and a view to the exterior for evacuees—have changed the way school gyms are designed: dark boxes have become layered spaces with sliding doors, windows, and balconies, carefully designed for both passive heating and cooling to remain habitable even without electricity. These features also make gyms, which often double as auditoriums, more environmentally friendly in their everyday uses.

The most successful case studies have had a committed architect or community leader to integrate cultural and programmatic needs over time, assimilating both disaster and everyday uses. Using the anticipatory design principles of dual use and consideration of the full disaster timeline, and with careful analysis of each locality, architects can reinvent many of these building types to fully address constituents' everyday needs and to transform, when necessary, to comfortably support people during the most difficult times.

EVERYDAY/DISASTER: NEW CONSIDERATIONS FOR TOKYO

Spaces are most effective after a disaster if they have already been integrated into everyday lives and routines before a catastrophe strikes. Considering how a building or space will be used throughout the disaster cycle is perhaps the most straightforward and effective way designers can integrate the anticipatory design framework into existing projects and practices. In many cases, the performance of a building during a disaster will be governed by codes designating seismic performance or floodplain elevation. Projects should go beyond these regulations and consider a project's social and spatial performance relative to preparedness, mitigation, response, and recovery. Spaces designed for dual use are not only more effective during emergencies to accommodate distraught populations but also make better everyday spaces. Beyond the parks, religious institutions, hotels, and public institutions described above, many other building types are now starting to be assigned a critical role during disasters—meaning the potential for designers to invent new dual-use typologies is enormous.

Tokyo was 373 kilometers away from the epicenter of the 2011 earthquake, which rattled the capital to its core. Chaos ensued: more than 400 buildings were damaged and all of the trains stopped, stranding more than 5 million commuters and visitors. Many people walked long distances to their homes or spent the night in their offices, in train stations, or in the lobbies of public facilities. According to the TMG, a total of 1,030 public facilities provided shelter for 94,001 stranded people,[2] and some were accommodated by a limited number of businesses, such as hotels and department stores.

Since 2011, many companies located in Tokyo whose buildings adhere to seismic standards encourage employees to stay in the office overnight after a disaster to reduce panic and chaos in the city. TMG encourages companies to stock supplies for all employees, plus an additional 10 percent for stranded people (about 100 people) for three days. Most residents living in central Tokyo are also aware of evacuation procedures near their work and home. However, the large number of tourists and other transient populations require clear information dissemination and large-scale planning, as they will be unfamiliar with local risks and evacuation routes and spaces.

A vast and growing network offers temporary overnight facilities for reducing chaos and securing the safety of visitors and residents during their walks home or back to their hotels. Preparing for the predicted Tokyo inland earthquake has increased the urgency of creating temporary rest spaces throughout the city. Beyond reducing the spread of fire, a great concern is the expected 3.9 million commuters who will have difficulty returning home. People who commute more than 20 kilometers from their homes are in this category.[3] The issue led to a policy framework for encouraging more private sector leadership to help maintain safety in the city.

In 2012, the TMG created policies to ensure that temporary stay facilities are available. It developed mechanisms to confirm commuter safety and support, allowing people to gradually return home rather than all at once. All private operators surrounding major stations carrying more than 300,000 passengers per day can sign an agreement with the local ward to accept stranded commuters, and the TMG provides three main subsidies.

(1) For spaces, two-thirds of the infrastructure construction and installation costs are covered by the central government and one-third by TMG.[4] Projects include renovating temporary rest spaces, such as lobbies and large halls, and stockpiling storage space, power generators, earthquake-resistant water tanks, disaster wells, and communication systems. New buildings must have space to accommodate over 100 people to qualify for the funds. Existing building retrofits must have room for at least 20 people. Space is calculated as at least 3.3 square meters for 2 people.[5]

(2) Emergency stockpiles are subsidized by the TMG with a budget of up to ¥7,500 per person (five-sixths of the cost) for seventy-two hours of stay: nine liters of water, nine meals, and one blanket per person. First aid, mattresses, diapers, formulas, sanitary items, baby food, and portable toilets are also eligible.

(3) To support communication, TMG covers five-sixths of the cost, with a cap of ¥2,500 per person, to purchase charging equipment.[6] Private entities must be equipped with emergency generators for seventy-two hours of electricity.

As of July 2023, over 1,239 public and private facilities in Tokyo have signed agreements to accept 470,430 people,[7] and other cities are following suit, although with slightly less urgency.[8] The types of facilities include Toyosu Market, Ryōgoku Sumo Hall, temples, department stores, universities, and several others detailed below.

Shimizu Corporation Office Building

Some businesses have combined the subsidy with grants to support post-disaster business continuity for greater impact. For example, the headquarters of the Shimizu Corporation acts as a regional bōsai center of the Kyobashi District and can accommodate 4,000 stranded people: 2,000 employees and 2,000 visitors. Employees are expected to stay in their office spaces on upper floors, and stranded commuters will be welcomed in common spaces on the first to third floors. The second-floor lobby has high ceilings, movable furniture, and the atmosphere of a contemporary lounge.

Figure 83. Recommended supplies for emergency stockpiles.

MINIMUM EMERGENCY STOCKPILE: 40 people (10 families) for 3 days
based on Shibuya Ward regulations for mid-rise and high rise buildings

BASIC SUPPLIES

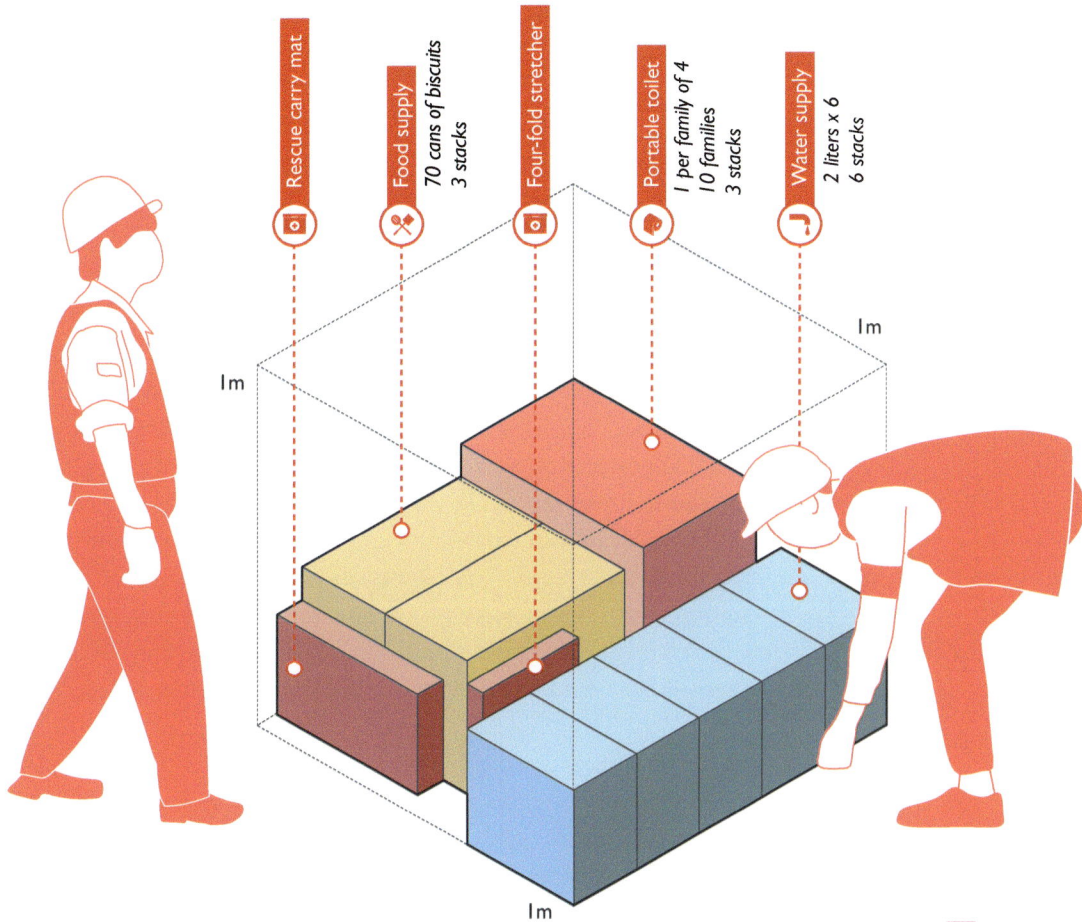

Rescue carry mat

Food supply
70 cans of biscuits
3 stacks

Four-fold stretcher

Portable toilet
1 per family of 4
10 families
3 stacks

Water supply
2 liters x 6
6 stacks

1m

1m

1m

+

ADDITIONAL SUPPLIES

Cleaning & sanitation supplies

First Aid supplies

Baby wipes, diapers

Milk powder, infant formula, baby food

Disinfecting tissues

Hearing aid battery

Canned foods

Stoves, fuel canister, ignition sticks

Non-allergenic foods, alpha rice

Water purification supplies

Adult diapers, denture cleaner

The grand staircase leading up to the third floor is intended as an obvious connection to the meeting rooms, which can convert into medical and other triage spaces after a disaster. A large portion of the ground floor is on piloti to allow for safe public gathering spaces, and the building has a bōsai storage area, generators, low-energy lighting systems, and stockpiles of food, temporary toilets, and blankets for seventy-two hours.

Mitsubishi Estate

Mitsubishi Estate, the largest real estate development and property management company in Japan, owns seventeen buildings in the 120-hectare district called Daimaruyū, home to the majority of Japanese business between Tokyo Station and the Imperial Palace. The former Marunouchi Building, owned by Mitsubishi, was the only building left near Tokyo Station after the 1923 earthquake. Employees distributed drinking water and meals to survivors and set up an emergency medical center. After the 2011 earthquake, the company accepted 3,500 people in ten of its buildings. Despite their own personal concerns, employees operated the buildings for twenty-four hours, providing power, toilets, and blankets. They also moved eighty large-scale television monitors to broadcast NHK news so that evacuees could receive information.[9]

In 2007, Mitsubishi Estate took a central role in the renovation of Gyōkō Avenue, the seventy-three-meter-wide historic passage at the center of Daimaruyū district. In addition to the avenue redesign, an underground pedestrian walkway was developed by renovating Japan's first city-planned parking lot (built in 1960). The company benefited from a policy called the "public contribution project outside the business building," which allowed it to overcome complicated regulations in its renovations. This policy also allowed an increase of the floor area ratio of its Shin-Marunouchi building—from the 1,300 percent floor area ratio to 1,760 percent—in exchange for developing this public space.[10] The space connects to rail, subway, streets, underground station plazas, and surrounding buildings. On a regular day, the underground walkway exhibits art, pop-up stores, and more than one hundred monitors screening local events and advertisements, which will no doubt be useful for sharing news when the space turns into a temporary overnight shelter after a disaster. Mitsubishi Estate also stores food, clothing, and bicycles to provide to employees and tenants who have difficulty returning home.

The area is governed by a Disaster-Resilient Machizukuri Council consisting of other corporations and agencies that signed an agreement with Chiyoda Ward in 2018 to accept a total of 21,400 stranded people. However, the number of commuters predicted to be stranded in this area from a 3:00 pm weekday earthquake is estimated at 330,000.[11]

Figure 84. Daimaruyū parking lot and evacuation space.

Toranomon Hills Complex

The Toranomon Hills complex is the second-highest building in Tokyo, with fifty-two floors aboveground and five floors below, and consists of a hotel, 172 residential units, offices, conference halls, and stores and restaurants. With three types of seismic damping devices, even a 2011 Tohoku-sized earthquake would not affect the building. Its generators can provide fifteen days of electricity and sixty-three hours of gas to operate off-grid. The complex is equipped with a stockpile of 250,000 meals, the largest private-sector food reserve in Japan, as well as blankets and other necessary emergency supplies. It has been called "a city you can escape to." It also set up sixteen wells to supply water for emergency use for its facilities and the surrounding neighborhood. To learn how to effectively accommodate thousands of stressed and emotionally fraught disaster survivors, its staff conducts emergency drills with the Hills neighborhood association, the fire department and the jishubō, shōbōdan, and elementary schools.[12]

Tokyo Dome City

Tokyo Dome City is the only large-scale leisure complex in central Tokyo, consisting of a baseball stadium, amusement park, hotel, and concert hall, with over 39 million annual visitors. As a designated emergency evacuation site, it also signed an agreement with Bunkyō Ward to accept stranded people who use Kōrakuen Station. It holds over 2,000 emergency drills annually across its various divisions in collaboration with local police and fire departments.[13]

Museums

The Edo-Tokyo Museum, the Museum of Contemporary Art Tokyo, the Tokyo Bunka Kaikan, and the Tokyo Metro Museum have all signed agreements with local wards to serve as temporary stay facilities. The Tokyo Metropolitan Art Museum and the Tokyo National Museum are assigned to accommodate visitors of Ueno Park, Ueno Zoo, and the shopping streets around Ueno's JR, Keisei, and subway stations. Given the high number of tourists, these places are among the few that hold multilingual emergency drills.[14]

Haneda Airport

Haneda Airport stockpiles a three-day supply of food and drinking water for 11,000 stranded people. The water is stored in a 175-ton yellow cypress tank, which not only gives the water a pleasing smell and taste for everyday use but also has natural antimicrobial properties for longer-term storage.[15] In a prolonged disaster situation, airport-managed stores and partner tenant stores would also provide products to these stranded people.

Convenience Stores

Convenience stores have become a staple in Japan, selling everything from full meals to clothing to emergency supplies. Open twenty-four hours, they illuminate dark streets and thus contribute to residents' safety, especially for women and the elderly. They house ATMs, copy machines, and restrooms, offer delivery options, and in some cases partner with laundry services. The meals range from fast food to healthy alternatives, including salads and fresh fruit; some even cater to vegetarians, vegans, and celiacs. After the 2011 Tohoku tsunami and the 2016 Kumamoto earthquakes, convenience stores were quick to respond by building and operating hubs for obtaining sustenance and meeting places for recovery planning.[16]

As these stores already play an important role as decentralized hubs within a city, on March 31, 2015, the TMG partnered with Seven & i Holdings Co. to procure and transport supplies for timely response. Seven & i Holdings will dispatch a liaison coordinator with specialized knowledge of supply chains and procurement to the TMG to quickly facilitate the process. Aggregated requests from the municipalities will guide the delivery of supplies to designated locations. In addition, NTT East Japan is installing special disaster public telephones at 7-Eleven convenience stores in Tokyo to prepare for a large-scale disaster. During an emergency, the telephones will be free for the public to use to connect with family members. A free Wi-Fi service called 00000JAPAN, provided through a consortium of network carriers, municipalities, universities, and companies, will help those who have difficulty returning home access up-to-date traffic and safety information. Convenience stores in Tokyo aim to become information stations and efficient distributors during a disaster.

SOCIO-SPATIAL CONNECTIONS

All of the aforementioned examples entail efforts of corporations, companies, institutions, and operators to prepare to assist in the event of a disaster and formally commit to aid through agreements with municipalities. These agreements open opportunities for new design interventions to consider dual-use spaces, such as museum/evacuation shelter or amusement park/evacuation shelter combinations.

As these types of projects increase, it will become even more important to connect spatial forms with social systems, such as education, awareness, traditions, and the everyday practices of caring for various demographics and meeting needs. The earlier section on schools details the adversity faced by teachers and principals in hosting crowds of potentially injured, panicked people and shows how their actions during these times of stress can affect survivors' recovery and future experiences of post-traumatic stress—as well as their own. It is vital, therefore, to consider both the operations of disaster programs as well as everyday uses during the design phase of dual-use spaces—and not view either one as an afterthought. This will lead to new inventions, including a new language to provide an identity for these dual-use buildings, making their roles explicit. In this way, design elements and social/everyday programming can engage and educate the public so that these structures can be used effectively by their constituents when the time comes. There is much to explore here, and with these new efforts to safely accommodate stranded people is a broadened potential for careful and innovative design.

The connection of social practices and spatial structures means not only understanding and working with existing social and cultural practices but also encouraging, facilitating, or making space for new cultural practices. Architects are called to embrace the disposition that disaster preparedness not only can, but should, be within their realm of design agency—and to consider disaster risk as a baseline for architectural design. Doing so will allow new types of projects to be born, which will in turn contribute to the creation of new bōsai cultures. Imagining how projects might be used in a disaster can create opportunities and open the way for ideas about how thoughtful design details can aid in making acute moments of fear and loss less painful for those who must endure them.

Countries around the world, including the United States, New Zealand, Canada, Peru, and India, have established designated emergency hubs in schools or community centers. Countries where those shelters themselves are likely unable to withstand the impacts of hazards are facing even larger issues. Perhaps surprisingly, these even include the United States, where Lori Peek, director of the Natural Hazards Center, has been advocating for school safety: "If we legally require children to attend school, then we should be held accountable for keeping them safe there. We need to see a real investment in our nation's school infrastructure and emergency planning efforts."[17] As disasters increase—and are compounded by factors such as pandemics, which limit the number of people who can safely gather in spaces—efforts to prepare networks of safe, hospitable spaces must exponentially increase. The social imaginary must include prioritization and creativity in endeavors that not only provide structure—shelter in existing buildings by default—but that welcome disaster survivors with care and dignity.

6

IT TAKES ALL OF US

The typologies in the previous chapters are all connected within their environments and populations. This book presents typological groupings—rather than regional or chronological groupings—to allow readers to retrieve information easily and to use *Design Before Disaster* as a reference. But it is important to emphasize how, in reality, disaster mitigation and preparation takes all of us, not just governments and emergency managers. Every person, every profession, every building, street, infrastructure, piece of furniture, and landscape: they all need to play a part in protecting our ecosystem and ensuring the safety of our people. This chapter highlights one prefecture and one town, focusing on their multisectoral efforts to enhance bōsai culture among all residents, in all infrastructures, and across all levels of society.

In anticipation of the Nankai disaster, the Act on Nankai Trough Earthquake Disaster Management and Special Tsunami Evacuation Regions have been prioritized for mitigation and preparedness activities for large-scale catastrophes.[1] Since the 2011 estimates were announced, residents and governments in all prefectures have been working on various countermeasures with accelerated goals. The 2014 estimate of casualties nationwide was 323,000 people, but through numerous mitigation and preparedness measures, some of which are outlined below, it was lowered to 231,000 in 2018. The goal is to further decrease the number to 65,000. Similarly, the 2014 estimate that 2.39 million buildings would collapse was lowered to 2.1 million in 2018, after many buildings were structurally reinforced. The aim is to further reduce the number to 1.2 million.[2] As of 2018, 87 percent of residential housing and 74 percent of nonresidential buildings nationwide are estimated to be seismically retrofitted through MLIT subsidies, and the retrofits are expected to be complete in 2030 and 2025, respectively.[3]

KOCHI PREFECTURAL PROJECTS

All across the coast of Kochi Prefecture, municipalities have been preparing by constructing TEBs. The head of the prefecture's Nankai Trough Earthquake Response Division stated that "because there is a tower prominently visible during ordinary days, it promotes residents' awareness of evacuation. I hope they will prepare through repeated evacuation drills."[4] As of September 2023, the city of Kochi, the capital of the prefecture, has designated 339 TEBs to accommodate approximately 282,663 evacuees in areas far from hills and high ground.[5] Many of the TEBs share similar characteristics, but the ones dotting the coastal farms near Kochi Airport are iconic, with ramps wrapping the reinforced raw concrete structure, almost like a collection of brutalist architectural monuments. Hanging from the top floor of each is a bronze bell, much like the ones found in Buddhist temples—an alternate, analog method for informing the public of a tsunami should all other systems fail. Resolute in their presence along the flat agricultural fields, the towers draw nearby residents to incorporate them in their exercise routines and enjoy the views.[6] The predicted disaster's overwhelming scale has inspired a multitude of new characters, typologies, and networks to step up and participate.

Education: Kōkatsu Project

In order to connect all the physical infrastructure improvements with the necessary social infrastructure, Kochi University students created a program offering bōsai instructor certificates to students who fulfilled designated courses, exams, and activities. They can then join a team of students and faculty who volunteer on weekends. About twenty members are working on planning and managing bōsai classes for elementary, middle, and high schools in Kochi, with the idea that children are the future of the community and should be the focal point for raising awareness.[7] The team also started a project to make use of abandoned fields with the local residents near their campus in 2014.[8] Kochi is located on Shikoku Island, which is connected to the Honshu main island by three bridges. If these were to be disrupted by a Nankai Trough earthquake, self-sufficiency in all aspects, including food, would be critical. The Kōkatsu Project addresses this need by using abandoned agricultural land to grow food reserves for emergencies; these include sweet yams, which are easy to grow, very nutritious, and can be dehydrated for long-term storage. The team also helps residents grow other vegetables on the weekends and plans cookouts with the harvested produce using the *kamado* benches. The elderly are encouraged to help in this work—a measure to actively decrease or delay dementia while building social networks in the neighborhood. Although this project is a small solution to a much larger problem, if the three bridges were to be damaged, the process involving the students, the elderly, and the community at large is nonetheless creating an indispensable social network.

Education and Evacuation: Dr. Trough

Another transformative project connecting the social and spatial aspects of tsunami evacuation was begun by the author of the famous superhero cartoon series *Anpanman*. Yanase Takashi, who grew up in Kochi, created more than fifty cartoon characters for the benefit of his native home. Among them are several who advise disaster preparedness for a Nankai Trough earthquake. (Yanase created this particular program in 2002 with the aim of increasing children's interest in bōsai topics.) One character, Dr. Trough, explains the earthquakes with the assistance of other characters, while lyrics to songs such as "Bokura-ga-mamoru" (we will protect), as well as *karuta* game cards and pamphlets, help families prepare for disasters.[9] Yanase retired in 2010 owing to his deteriorating physical health, but he emerged from retirement after the 2011 earthquake. He provided a tremendous amount of support to the survivors of the tsunami: his work included inspirational posters, and the *Anpanman* song became one of the theme songs for recovery. All of Kochi's pedestrian-level evacuation signs feature Dr. Trough characters giving guidance or indicating where to get help. This project is inscribed in physical structures across the region, increasing awareness and enhancing the bōsai culture of Kochi residents, young and old.[10]

KUROSHIO TOWN

Nested within Kochi Prefecture, the small fishing town of Kuroshio is celebrated for its proactive stance in bōsai infrastructure. Nearly half of the town's 11,500 residents are elderly. A jarring prediction came on March 31, 2012, when the Cabinet Office released a report stating that the Ogata district in Kuroshio should expect a tsunami of up to 34.4 meters within eleven minutes.[11] News of the predicted 34.4-meter tsunami height devastated the town: tourism plummeted and schools even canceled their field trips, as Kuroshio was rumored to be the most dangerous place in the country. The mayor, public officials, and residents alike all expressed that they felt helpless, had lost courage, and had considered giving up. Many worried about population decline.

Kuroshio considered using the Bōsai Collective Relocation Project but decided not to implement it for several reasons. Officials studied moving all fifty households of the Deguchi district to potential relocation sites—one nearby and another slightly farther away on higher ground. Including the development of the new site, the town concluded that relocating the fifty households would cost a total of ¥2.24 billion, and even though the national government subsidy would cover nearly one-third of the cost, due

KOCHI PREFECTURE

Kokatsu Project

Kuroshio Town

Saga District

Maehama TEB 1

Emergency communication bell

Maehama TEB 3

Dr. Trough

Nankai Trough

to a cap, the town would need to carry a ¥920 million burden. This was too large for such a small town.[12] Kuroshio is also prone to landslides, as its steep mountainous topography practically abuts the coast, creating challenges to collectively relocate to high ground unless mountains are drastically cut. Out of concerns over the financial burden, potential landslides, and fears that relocation might weaken the strong communal bonds, leaders instead decided to empower the residents by balancing a top-down and bottom-up approach.[13]

After analyzing the numerous options, the mayor, Onishi Katsuya, decided to publicly seize their challenge as an opportunity to persevere.[14] The residents decided that passing on their *furusato* (hometown) to the next generation was key to their future. This call for action energized everyone to become "Japan's best municipality in terms of coping with earthquakes and tsunamis."[15] They developed twenty guidelines for "not giving up" and achieving their goal of "zero casualties." These included relocating public facilities with key bōsai functions to high ground; securing large potable water tanks; assigning town officials to each of the fourteen shōbōdan to create evacuation paths in their respective districts; connecting to expressways for expedited logistics; and conducting evacuation drills at each school at least six times annually. (Some elementary schools conduct run-up-to-the-hill drills weekly.)[16] In order to increase communication among neighbors every day (and during disasters), they created voluntary committees to organize *tonarigumi* (the smallest unit of a neighborhood association, with five to ten families). The municipality created an evacuation chart for each of the 3,791 households in the expected tsunami inundation area, including their *tonarigumi* information, family information, possibility of self-evacuation, planned evacuation space, and method/time of evacuation. A total of over two hundred workshops were held in various districts of the town for developing evacuation infrastructure.[17] The multifaceted efforts include tsunami towers, evacuation routes, jishubō, new businesses, education, and new forms of signage.

The First Preemptive Relocation Project

Some of the first projects included relocating the Kuroshio Fire Department from the hazard zone to high ground in 2014. Four years later, the aging town hall was relocated to a site twenty-six meters above sea level. The new town hall serves as the disaster management headquarters, supporting a large evacuation space, a seismically resistant water tank, and two evacuation paths with direct access to the building.[18] Public housing and a bōsaikōen are under development in the same area. All the facilities around the new town hall are designated as part of an Integrated Tsunami Bōsai Cluster as the first preemptive project completed in Japan.[19] As of March 2021, the town has relocated nine public facilities to higher ground, and four others are under construction or planned.[20]

The town has also been relocating facilities used by its vulnerable population to

Figure 85. Kochi Prefecture demonstrates numerous tsunami evacuation strategies, ranging from education to the proliferation of TEBs.

higher ground, and residents have contributed to moving swiftly. A petition signed by 2,779 residents helped expedite relocating the nursery school in the Saga district to a tsunami-safe area in 2018.[21] The town also improved the evacuation path right behind the elementary and middle schools by paving the slope and evacuation space and adding railings, signage, and solar-generated lights for nighttime evacuation. The space is connected to a large network of evacuation paths along the mountain ridge connecting to multiple evacuation spaces in the wider area.[22] As of March 2021, 213 evacuation paths have been developed, including several shortcuts through agricultural flatlands; their white cement is in sharp contrast with the fields and visible from afar.

Ten districts are also creating a bōsai machizukuri hub[23] using the Comprehensive Urban Disaster Management Project subsidy. Overall, the town created 184 tsunami emergency evacuation spaces, 124 storage units, and 1,000 evacuation signs.[24] To reinforce the infrastructural efforts, residents in each district work together to organize their own jishubō activities to achieve the goal of zero tsunami casualties. This is paired with town officials assigned in each district to work with the jishubō on collaborative tsunami awareness activities, such as conducting nighttime drills to the district's tsunami evacuation tower. All two hundred town officials have a specific bōsai role in addition to their daily responsibilities.[25]

Saga District TET

The local jishubō in the Saga district worked to include input from residents for its 25-meter-high TET, famous for being the tallest in the country and designed by SUZUKi Design Office. At a height of 22 meters, the top evacuation floor can accommodate about 230 people in two rooms and is equipped with temporary toilets and a small room for breastfeeding. There is a space for a helicopter to hover to rescue evacuees from the rooftop. The site is expected to liquefy to a depth of 5 meters, so the main body of the tower is supported by twenty-six concrete piles that reach a depth of 30 meters to penetrate bedrock.[26] The tower cost ¥620 million to build, and it was completed in 2017. This project was covered by Kochi Prefecture's Special Subsidy Program for Accelerated Tsunami Evacuation Measures, so there was no fiscal burden for the town. Kuroshio borrowed the money in municipal bonds from the central government, and 70 percent of that amount was returned from the central government in subsequent years. The remaining 30 percent was paid by the prefecture.[27] Although the massive oblong structure is designed to withstand all forces, as an extra precaution, the structure is sited perpendicular to the coast and the direction of predicted incoming waves to reduce friction and erosion.

More compelling than the height or structural qualities of the building is how residents worked together to propose changes to the more standard towers in the area. They traveled to other districts that already had evacuation towers and took note of what needed to be different. A major change was to construct the ramp and stairs on the inside of the structure, protected by six buffer pillars, rather than the more common placement of stairs outside the structure. Residents were concerned about large objects, like boats and houses, hitting the structure as they climbed the stairs. They asked the town to lower the height of stair treads to accommodate the gait of elderly residents and to widen the slope for wheelchair accessibility. While some towns lock their towers for reasons of safety and liability, theirs remains unlocked, to be used for exercise or picnics.[28] The Kuroshio tower is Japan's highest open TET and is popular with tourists for its spectacular views.

Many of the residents like to exercise by climbing up and down the stairs, so they requested that the town add nonslip padding (which also helps muffle the sound of footsteps on the metal stairs so that people can avoid disturbing the neighbors). The stairs and ramps share landings on all seven floors, allowing for mutual assistance if someone needs help climbing to the top. Children were asked to design signs for each landing, depicting local fish and the height climbed. The top floor, with special round windows to the bay, displays paintings of the city, reminding people of the town they are working to save. The neighborhood jishubō group is run by women who organize an annual cookout to use the stored rice and other supplies and replenish it for the following year. Myojin Satoju, the vice president of the jishubō, noted that the gathering of residents is always a fun way to remind people to prepare. Next year's plan is to grill *yakiniku* (barbecued beef)![29]

TYPOLOGIES OF DUAL-USE EVACUATION STRUCTURES

Ōkata Akatsuki-Kan

Beyond the tower in Saga district, there are several other exciting typologies of dual-use evacuation structures in Kuroshio. Ōkata Akatsuki-Kan is a community space located in a pine forest 100 meters from the Irino Coast at a very popular beach, especially for surfers. The bright white sloped building, designed by Dan Norihiko, includes the public library, a museum celebrating the native Kuroshio novelist Kambayashi Akatsuki, a lecture hall with 210 seats, a community gallery space, and some meeting spaces, including a tatami room. The path from the beach leads to a prominent staircase that, as part of the building's façade, takes visitors directly to the rooftop. This large staircase was not originally intended for tsunami evacuation, but in 2014 the town built the Hamanomiya TET and connected it to the roofscape, designating both as an official tsunami evacuation space. The TET evacuation space has walls to protect evacuees from wind and rain; it is 115 square meters at TP+17.4 meters, and combined with the 400 square meters of the community building's open rooftop, it can accommodate 350 evacuees in total.[30] This Hamanomiya tower is one of six TETs managed by the

Figure 86 (*next page*). In the face of a 34.4-meter-high tsunami prediction, the town of Kuroshio and the Saga district have wide-ranging community-centered efforts to save all of the residents.

KUROSHIO TOWN

Integrated tsunami bosai cluster

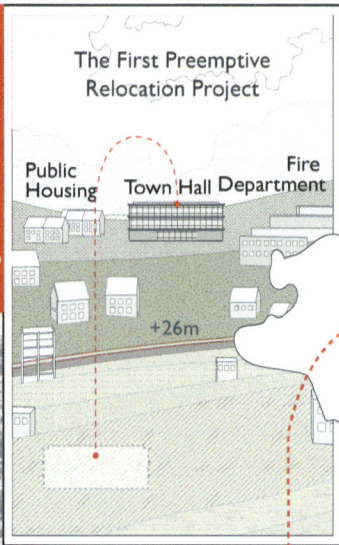

The First Preemptive Relocation Project

Public Housing | Town Hall | Fire Department

+26m

Relocation

Let's make jobs
Let's make friends
Let's make a dream
Just as people have dreams, so do towns
Let's make a dream for this town
Let's make the future of this town

黒潮町新産業創造プロジェクト
この町の未来を作ろう
この町の夢をつくろう
人に夢があるように、町にも夢がいる
夢をつくろう
仲間をつくろう
仕事をつくろう

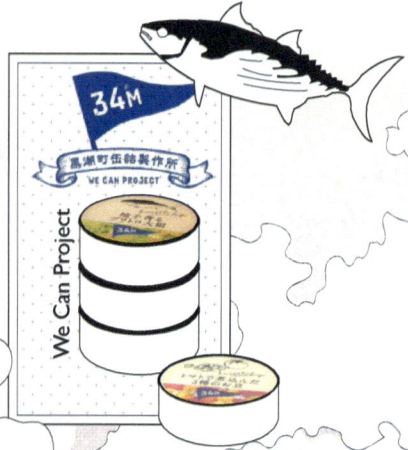

34M
黒潮町伍緒製作所
WE CAN PROJECT
We Can Project
一勝鰹宝島

Taisaku-kun

Jishinman

Tosa Seinan Park observation deck

Okata Akatsuki-Kan

Yudo-kun

SAGA DISTRICT

A *senryu* poem written in 2012 by an elderly woman captured her despair and futility, speaking of how her son offered to die with her should the big tsunami come.

In 2014, the same woman wrote another poem, this time of determination. "My legs weaken, but I will not die, evacuation drills." 2012

避難訓練
足萎えの我は行きたり
落としはせぬと
この命
2014

足萎え吾に
今日も息子が言う
共に死んでやる
大津波来たらば

Helper-chan

Evacuation radius

Saga tsunami evacuation tower

Evacuation routes

walking = 11min
r = 308m

Tsunaman

Ms. Satoju Myojin - VP Jishubo

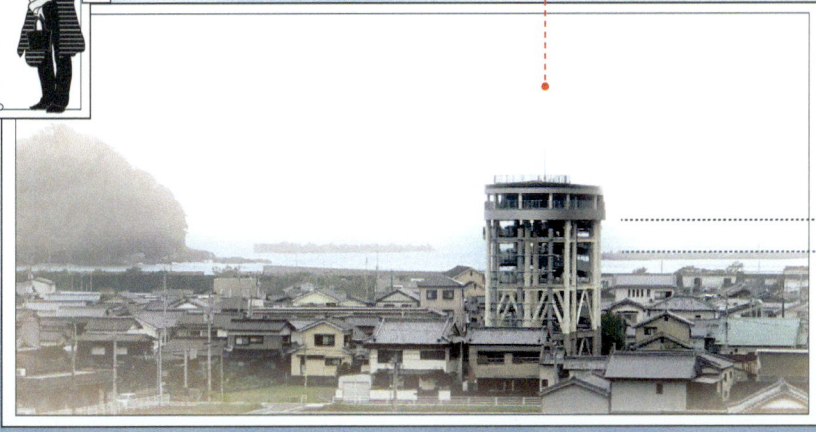

安金
8 階
もう大丈夫!!

Height to evacuation floor 22m
Estimated depth of flooding 18m max

危険
1 階
津波はすぐくる
急げ!

town. Both the design of this building (and connected tower) and the mixed programs demonstrate that such uses can not only coexist but can effectively support each other.

Tosa Seinan Park Observation Deck

Another nearby evacuation structure doubles as an observation deck overlooking the Irino Coast. This TET in Tosa Seinan Park is designed by the local firm Wakatake Machizukuri Design Firm, and it shares space with Nest West Garden Tosa, a hotel and wedding venue. The 250-square-meter observation deck is a reinforced concrete structure and can accommodate 450 evacuees. The coastal location is for park visitors, including surfers, to use for evacuation; residents have other assigned locations. The 4-meter-high deck is built on 3-meter landfill at TP+12-meter-high ground. The area is expected to be hit by a 13-meter tsunami as well as 2-meter land subsidence. This facility was built by Kochi Prefecture with MLIT's Urban Park Project subsidy, and the project cost of ¥181 million[31] was split between national and prefectural subsidies. (It is managed by the prefecture.)

Theoretically, the top floor of the tower could be used as a wedding venue, and there is even a plaque describing it as a sanctuary for "blissful marriages and raising a happy home." The breathtaking views could be used as a picturesque backdrop for photos. The gentle ramp encircling both the hill and structure could be used for a wedding procession and celebration. The railings and concrete structure conform with all safety requirements. The location, the form, and the construction all offer the potential for the tower's dual function to thrive.[32] Unfortunately, as the structure is owned by the prefecture, permission must be requested for each event use, and so it is not used for weddings. The hotel only uses the tower for evacuation drills and, should a tsunami occur, their employees, guests, and other beachgoers would use it for evacuation. This is a missed opportunity. If better used and appreciated in normal times, the tower would no doubt be better cared for and more people would know about its existence.

BUSINESS AND ENTREPRENEURSHIP

Kuroshio is also demonstrating its determination to establish bōsai businesses. Kochi created prefectural subsidies to encourage innovation and entrepreneurship in the bōsai companies. Kochi's system is categorized into *sonaeru* (readiness), *nigeru* (evacuation) and *ikiru* (survival), and products range from technology platforms to engineering and construction machinery, from vests that turn into flotation devices to super-long toilet paper rolls and straps for securing furniture. The product prototyping is subsidized up to 50 percent of the cost, up to ¥10 million, and products are promoted on the Kochi Bōsai website, kochi-bosai.com. The business strategy committee supports the company's mid- to long-term business plans. For overseas trade, the prefecture supports accompanied visits abroad to increase international sales among other disaster-prone countries.

We Can Project

One of Kuroshio's most successful public-private businesses was started by Mayor Onishi and the local university with a canned emergency food business called the We Can Project. The cans are adorned with a cute flag that reads "34M," embracing the tsunami height of 34.4 meters, which the Cabinet Office warned of hitting the Kuroshio coast within eleven minutes. The cans are filled with special local cuisine: most famously, grilled bonito. In Kochi, a popular delicacy is bonito flame-seared over a straw fire, with the center still rare, served with salt and myoga ginger or a citrusy ponzu sauce made from locally grown yuzu fruit. In addition, We Can also produces a variety of other low-priced staple canned goods, which include gluten-free and allergen-free items, but it is best known for the slightly higher-priced gourmet cans. Because post-disaster times are trying, the company hopes that people will share a little joy during such meals. These products have even entered the annual Japanese summer gift exchange culture, through which delicious food from local districts are shared across the country to business partners and teachers to show appreciation. The company motto is about residents of the town making their own future, and it has also successfully created many jobs for locals. As with many small towns in Japan, the shrinking economy and population present yet another slow disaster. New local businesses like We Can are vital to maintaining social and economic strength, preemptively supportive to recovery.

EDUCATION AND LEADERSHIP

Meanwhile, Kuroshio's educational efforts reach for international impact. In November 2016, five hundred high school students from thirty countries visited Kuroshio to participate in a United Nations–sponsored conference for future leaders from countries that suffer from disasters. Students shared personal stories, research, and fieldwork as well as recommendations. To conclude the inaugural gathering, the students created the Kuroshio Declaration, with an action plan to create a global network among high schools, promising to share their "knowledge and skills" to reduce risks from disasters. To close the ceremony, Nikai Toshihiro, who proposed Tsunami Awareness Day and was the secretary general of Japan's Liberal Democratic Party at the time, called on the private sector to support projects similar to the conference in Kochi, urging that "all stakeholders should take part."[33]

Two of the local Kochi high schools that participated in the 2016 conference started a new program shortly after, enthusiastic about contributing to disaster reduction. Susaki High School students created a team of volunteers and conducted an evacuation drill with elderly people from twenty households, accompanying them from their homes to their designated evacuation sites. They also used an app developed by Kyoto University's Disaster Prevention Research Institute to track their movement. Since then, the students have formalized their teams' weekend volunteer activities, which include securing furniture to walls in elderly people's homes. The forty-person student teams have been raising awareness, and elderly participants are joining for the pleasure of interacting with youth. The Susaki Technical High School started a project making regular objects into tools for use during disasters. For example, they have made tarps into partitions, steel oil drums into cooking pots, and even cut openings in school chairs for use as portable toilets.[34] No doubt many of these innovative ideas are feeding into the entrepreneurial businesses born out of Kochi.

DISCUSSION

A *senryū* poem written in 2012 by an elderly woman captured her despair and futility. It spoke of her son, who had offered to die with her should the big tsunami come. In 2014, the same woman wrote another poem, this time of determination: "My legs weaken, / but I will not die, / evacuation drills."[35]

The case of Kuroshio hints at a way of creating such a new, determined bōsai culture through the convergence of education, evacuation signage, innovation, entrepreneurship, relocation of public facilities, design of tsunami towers as markers in the landscape, evacuation routes illuminating paths to safety, and (most importantly) community participation. The commitment from both government and residents through individual family evacuation charts, neighborhood and district community groups, and connection between generations and across all ages through workshops creates the necessary matrix of social infrastructure fused with physical infrastructure. As everyone starts to participate in this dialogue, awareness rises along with new opportunities to invent ways to inscribe that knowledge into our urban environments. These opportunities are reinforced in the unique dual-use evacuation buildings in Kuroshio, which will hopefully prompt more innovative design that melds typologies.

Analysis of and response to Japan's numerous disasters have been central to creating a rigorous set of preparedness and mitigation policies, which have recently enabled a more integrated, proactive approach in many places across the country. Considering this case study as a modern day wajū with a multiscalar system and the full commitment of residents, Kuroshio deserves special attention for its ability to effectively use the top-down subsidies and to empower residents to make "zero casualties" their core philosophy. By applying this holistically across government, residents, and businesses and through visible infrastructure and educational projects, the multifaceted strategies from Kuroshio have invigorated the small yet mighty town—and its initiatives have inspired many other places across the globe.

7

ANTICIPATORY FUTURES

The United Nations University World Risk Index ranks Japan fourth in terms of exposure to natural hazards, but Japan also ranks among the highest in levels of "coping capacities" and "adaptive capacities"[1] thanks to citizens' collective efforts. From the bottom up, residents plan and build through learned and inventive methods, creating new programs and spaces. From the top down, Japanese laws and policies are agile and adaptive (and often used in combinatory ways to create projects that might otherwise not be feasible). This is evidenced by the fact that the Disaster Countermeasures Act has been amended at least once every two or three years since 1961, and even in some cases a few times a year, in order to adapt to lessons learned from major disasters as well as to changes in climate and society. This book has shared histories, stories, critiques, policies, and projects with the hope of inspiring dialogues around the world about how those narratives can relate to other countries' hazards, economies, environments, cultures, and people. The focus on details of how different locations have addressed, and been challenged by, disasters is intended to underscore that a disaster, much like design, is inherently local and often created. Designed environments have the potential to both expand and reduce disaster risk. For anyone who has a hand in shaping our physical environment—architects, urban designers, landscape architects, engineers, city planners, NGOs, public works officers, politicians, consultants—this book's intent is to extend aspirations and increase collaboration by outlining the principles of an anticipatory design framework.

OUR CLIMATE CRISIS

The principles in the anticipatory design framework—combining social/spatial, top-down/bottom-up, everyday/post-disaster, and ecology/engineering, along with designing with consideration for the entire disaster timeline—are critical for our disaster-prone futures, induced or enhanced by climate. The specter of our current climate crisis and the recent spate of disasters are harbingers of the future. The warming of our climate is a true global catastrophe, and radical strategies are required simply to slow its pace; scientists project that even if emissions were halted today, the planet would continue to warm.[2] Climate scientist Kerry Emanuel cautions that his tropical cyclone modeling, as well as several recent events, shows that hurricanes will become more intense and produce more rain.[3] Direct climate change mitigation, and the associated restructuring of economies and societies it would entail, is outside the scope of this book. Yet surviving the changes we have already wreaked on our planet—including the already intensifying typhoons, floods, droughts, and heat waves—will require transformations and adaptations to not only our architecture, landscapes, and cities but also to the ways we live and prepare.

Japan is preparing to face more dire effects of torrential rains, flash floods, stronger typhoons, landslides, and heat waves, all attributed to a warming planet, in addition to the seismic disasters mentioned earlier. In 2021, Japan's central government launched the National Resilience Project, a five-year, ¥15-trillion plan for 123 infrastructure, digitization, and education projects.[4] Starting from the third grade of elementary school, bōsai education is incorporated in various school subjects, including science, social studies, gym, history, and geology. The teaching guides even hint at collective relocation projects.[5] Designing holistically with various stakeholders (nation, prefecture, local government, private sector, NPO, and residents) at multiple scales throughout an entire region or watershed and across administrative boundaries will become more and more vital as the future holds more uncertainty and risk.

The UN Sendai Framework for Disaster Risk Reduction calls for an "all-of-society engagement" with an "all hazards approach."[6] This is becoming more important than ever, especially in meeting the unexpected challenges we face. It is important to consider root causes broadly and identify vulnerabilities, using projects to reduce the latter for those at highest risk, and create spaces to increase capacity to cope with and adapt to extreme weather disasters and other compounding hazards. Considered holistically, the concept of mitigation asks that we not only directly protect against climate-induced hazards but that we also consider how a project might reduce or avoid amplifying hazards outside its boundaries, including any contributions to greenhouse gases in our atmosphere during its construction and occupation. Climate change will generate a new order of hazards, resulting in cascading effects and disasters not yet seen. Bringing climate scientists, social scientists, ecologists, engineers, and disaster managers together with designers (architects, planners, and landscape architects) and local residents will be critical to approaching escalating climate challenges with proactive and unique solutions.

LOOKING BACK IN ORDER TO LOOK AHEAD

As Japan continues to plan and design visions for the future, learning from its existing knowledge and bōsai culture will be crucial. Watsuji Tetsuro wrote a book about climate and culture in the 1930s, describing characteristics of Japanese architecture that enhance sustainable living: traditional homes lifted off the ground allow for air circulation and protect against moisture; overhanging roofs provide shade and cooling; and the visible distinction between movable doors and load-bearing structures aids in maintenance and renovation of specific areas (as opposed to demolition). About the latter, he notes that "this distinction also makes the structure easy to dismantle and reconstruct in another location,"[7] which promotes material reuse and conservation.

The raised floors of the traditional home not only provide climatic comfort but also protect against less severe but more frequent flooding. They also uniquely tie into social habits, as raised floors provide a seat where neighbors can perch in the *genkan* (entranceway) or the *engawa* and chat without removing their shoes, thereby avoiding the imposition of entering the home itself. These small but valuable details increase social connections and enhance communal coping capacity during difficult times.

Similarly, traditional practices of landscape management illustrate a balance between humans and the natural environment. Iconic *satoyama* constitute "holistic management of cultural landscapes in agricultural communities that are marked by circular material flows and sustainable resource management."[8] In these spaces, sensitivity to nature allows culture to flourish. Murakami Akinobu, a professor at Tsukuba University, states, "The lowlands along the rivers and the coast had been used as rice fields and salt fields before WWII. However, advanced civil engineering inventions in the post-war period led people to think that they do not need to follow the natural features of the land, thereby erasing their ability to read the topography and geographical characteristics."[9]

With the related concept of *warichi,* joint ownership of arable land, shared ownership is tied to disaster risk. Under *warichi,* no one village family could stake a permanent claim over others to the most fertile ground, and no one would be stranded in a constantly flooded lot; instead, lotteries or other mechanisms redistributed land following a disaster or other transformation so that risks and rewards could be shared (creating "a risk-diversified portfolio of cultivation rights").[10] This was also the way ocean lots and bay management were allocated, emphasizing the reciprocal relationship between landscapes and their denizens.

These examples of Japanese vernacular typologies and social processes illustrate the extent to which these traditions, united with natural systems, still exist—but they are waning. We must learn from these traditions in order to evolve environmental-social-spatial thinking with the same attention to living with respect for the earth. All countries have Indigenous knowledge and traditional customs that have allowed a healthy coexistence on the planet for generations. Despite the past century's emphasis on infrastructural control and resistance, concrete walls and channelized rivers, the future belongs to those who learn, listen, and combine new inventions with long-held endemic knowledge.

TOWARD ANTICIPATORY DESIGN

The designer's skill set—assembling and overseeing diverse areas of expertise while also mediating the needs and desires of clients, stakeholders, and surrounding communities—is well suited for movement between the different forms of technical and experiential knowledge required for creating structures and spaces used during disasters. Designers have to negotiate between scientific and technical information (climate change models, hazard maps, safety standards) and the psychological experience of surviving a disaster to understand what types of spaces might best help people cope and respond. Designers are also used to working on multiple scales, from the detail of a door frame to the impact of a building on a surrounding city; this can mean thinking between issues like safe shelter details and evacuation routes as well as the way we navigate our built environments.

At the time of this writing, most national regulatory codes and flood maps do not consider sea-level rise. This includes Japan and the United States, although some well-funded municipalities have forged ahead with their own predictive modeling. This means that it is the designer's daunting responsibility to inform clients, developers, municipal leaders, and residents and, when necessary, advocate for taking precautions beyond what codes require. This is exceptionally difficult, especially when dry-floodproofing, wet-floodproofing, and lifting buildings are costly endeavors. In light of this, considerations of everyday/disaster dual-use design opportunities become especially significant, alongside understanding national subsidies and thinking through long and short timescales.

All five components of the anticipatory design framework ask designers to become conduits, negotiators, and collaborators—applying their skills to mediate between emergency management, policy, and communities and their physical places. The first three points of the anticipatory design framework have been discussed at length within the previous three chapters, so after a short reprise, this final chapter addresses in greater detail factors of ecology and engineering balance as well as considerations for the disaster timeline.

Social/Spatial Integration

This principle asks designers to consider both how preexisting social practices relate to spaces used during a disaster and what new social practices might help people effectively use a space before, during, and after a disaster. How can such knowledge be incorporated into the design of the space to facilitate or even inspire such uses? What knowledge and management structures are required to use it most effectively? As pre-disaster social networks are likely to be leveraged post-disaster,[11] these questions must be addressed on a case-by-case (place-by-place) basis.

As emergency physician Erik Auf der Heide has commented, "It is more effective to learn what people tend to do naturally in disasters and plan around that rather than design your plan and then expect people to conform to it."[12] Routines are often linked to spaces: the routine of accommodating guests at a hotel, the routine of exercising in a park every morning, the routine of using a neighborhood hand-pump well to water a community garden. Furthermore, spaces that facilitate strong social networks will create communities better able to help one another, which increases overall coping capacity during and after a disaster. While expanding such spaces is important, it is also critical to invest in and help existing ones thrive. Studying these links between place and practice, designers can imagine approaches that transform relationships between people and space.

Top-Down/Bottom-Up Placemaking

A common difficulty in all top-down planning is reconciling broader standards with specific locations and populations, not all of which conform to a policy's generalized approach to society. Political scientist James C. Scott terms this problem "seeing like a state" and argues that these "state simplifications" not only fail to see unique places and people as they are but can also be oppressive in their attempts to establish conformity.[13] However, in the realm of disasters, top-down policies, codes, subsidies, plans, communication, and drills can undeniably save countless lives and enable communities to recover more quickly and comprehensively. Collective, scaled approaches are necessary to mitigate the effects of disasters that cross social and political boundaries. Incorporating this top-down/bottom-up principle means understanding the policies fully, to creatively use and combine subsidies to make the most of an opportunity. Designers have the potential to address these policies (and the impact of laws and regulations) in local places: they can translate standards into site-specific designs and bring communities into the design process, providing opportunities specific to each culture, people, and place.

Communities themselves will be the best sources of information about a locale, and designers, planners, and community activists with backgrounds in participatory placemaking can serve as effective guides to render those ideas and processes into physical spaces. How can designers empower bottom-up community efforts to contribute local identities to design? How can designers be sensitive to power dynamics and promote equity in such contributions? One simple, straightforward way is to notice when project briefs leave out community participation and to advocate for an inclusive process on the grounds that it strengthens a project's capacity to succeed and meet the needs of all affected.

Active involvement in the creation of one's own environment also increases social capital.[14] Participatory processes introduce neighbors to one another, bringing them together around collective concerns and establishing shared goals for the futures of their communities. Such cooperation ensures a strong fit between projects and their stakeholders, increasing a sense of ownership and pride in the space.

Everyday/Disaster Dual Use

Many of the projects described in this book lean toward pragmatic and utilitarian design, but they are all intended to spark the imagination to consider how designers can creatively incorporate those types of programs to make better spaces, both for everyday use and for use during a crisis. Architects and landscape architects, working with emergency managers, can invent and integrate dual-use infrastructures into everyday places in ways that are locally specific, communicative, playful, and beautiful. While emergency managers are experts in life-saving strategies, they may be less knowledgeable about designing for the everyday: aspects like public space activation, participatory processes, and sustainable design are indirect but essential contributors to building social capacity.

Thriving public space design (which will manifest differently in different countries) encourages gathering and the creation of social networks, which in turn increases the capacity of those communities to cope with disasters. Developing social bonds in public spaces embedded with dual-use lifeline infrastructure only enhances the shared knowledge of how to cope during a disaster, reducing the learning curve and panic during the actual event. Strong community infrastructure in turn improves preparedness, particularly as neighbors often serve as a first response team following a disaster—as witnessed after many disasters, including the Kobe earthquake, when a majority of trapped survivors were rescued by fellow citizens.[15] A strong and diverse social fabric can also mitigate the alienation of minority groups that sometimes occurs after a disaster (e.g., violence against Koreans after the 1923 Tokyo earthquake) by increasing interaction across different communities. Designing spaces to increase social interactions, embedding them with dual-use infrastructure, and explicitly using them to prepare together all lend a hand in creating safer, more caring, and more equitable neighborhoods.

Ecology/Engineering Harmony

Japan's ample concrete shorelines and river corridors clearly show that the country spends vast amounts of funding on infrastructure projects. One recently constructed project, considered a heroic success, saved Tokyo from ¥26.4 billion of damage during the deadly Typhoon Hagibis in 2019.[16] The Metropolitan Outer Area Underground Discharge Channel is the world's largest underground system, consisting of 6.3 kilometers of tunnels, five shafts, a tank 30 meters in diameter (large enough to hold the Statue of Liberty), and a massive 177-by-78-meter "Underground Shrine" that can hold 670,000 cubic meters of floodwater before draining it into the Edo River.[17] The basin is surrounded by the Edo and Arakawa Rivers and has very low-lying topography. Historically, this flood-prone land was protected by small rice farming settlements, which used natural embankments and rice paddies as reservoirs.[18] However, rapid urbanization after World War II altered the ecosystem and *satoyama* lifestyle and left the region and economy vulnerable to disasters. The prodigious ¥230 billion discharge channel was built to protect Japan's capital.

As successful as it has been in preventing recent floods, this large engineering project ultimately renders the problems invisible by retaining the water underground and draining it out of sight. Similar enormous projects are planned for other rivers and urban centers around the country, but they should be considered in combination with other strategies that work with natural systems rather than against them. Anticipatory design has the potential to shift conversations away from purely technical solutions toward crucial considerations of how design can play a role in reducing vulnerability and increasing preparedness capacity. There is a danger inherent in solely engineered disaster mitigation strategies: too much faith in these systems can prevent people from also taking more localized adaptive actions. While engineered mitigation is an important component for adapting to climate risks, emergent discourses on creating "climate-proof" buildings, landscapes, and cities have a similar ring of false confidence,[19] particularly given the uncertainty regarding the impacts of global warming on our built environment. For example, when Typhoon Hagibis hit the east part of Japan on October 12 and 13, 2019, it broke through more than ninety embankments of 59 rivers in seven prefectures. This unexpected damage resulted in dozens of fatalities among those who failed to evacuate. Kawata Yoshiaki argues that even advanced flood-control engineering cannot guarantee human safety in this new era of climate change.[20] In order to design riverine infrastructure with nature in mind, landscape architect James Wescoat advocates for a greater understanding of how the morphological and physical features of a river shape habitats for flora and fauna during different times of the year, "all of which contribute to the health of the river ecosystem and its services and values for various human groups."[21] Planning and designing in these ways requires strengthening partnerships between ecologists, environmental engineers, civil

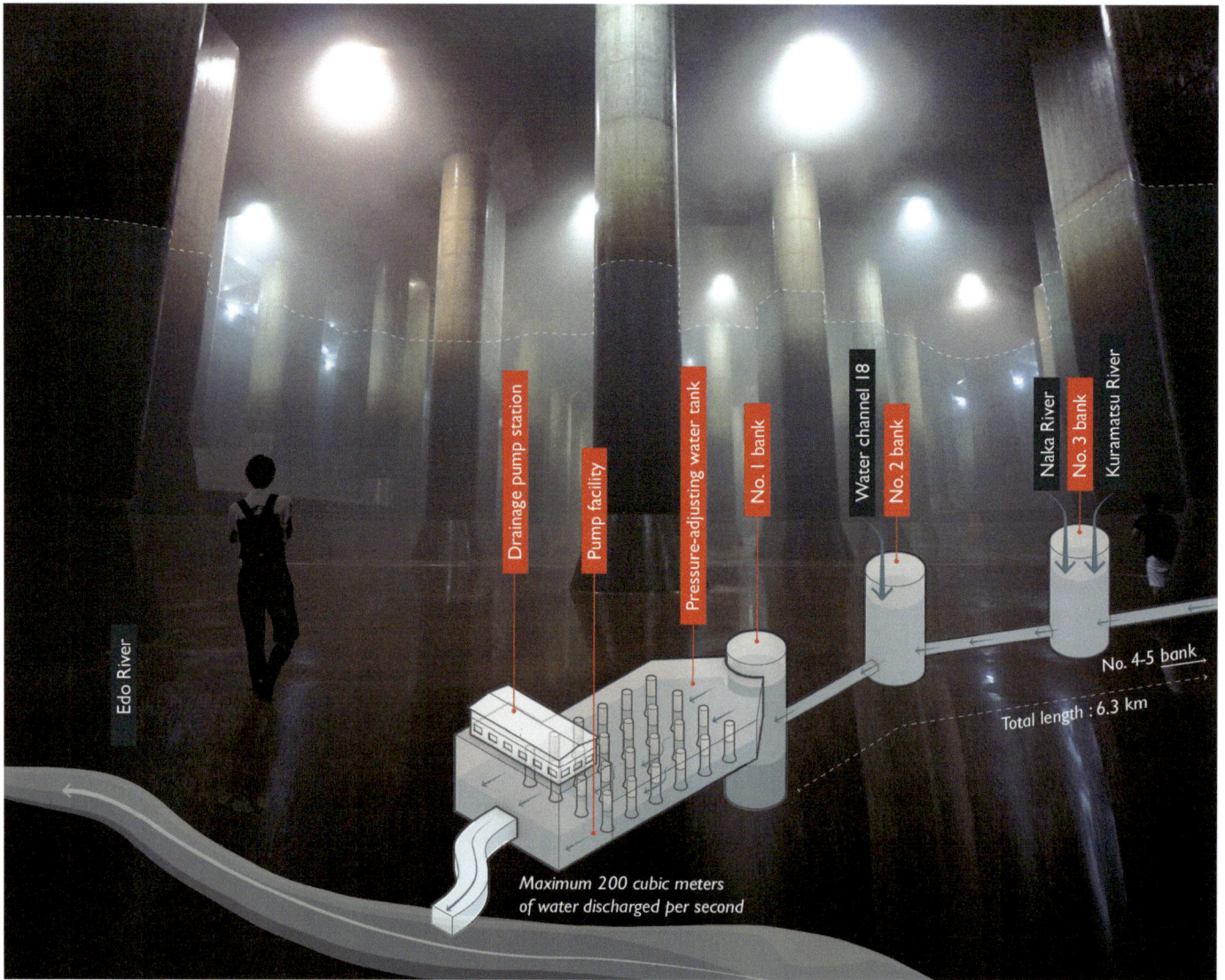

Figure 87. The Tokyo Metropolitan Discharge Channel.

engineers, landscape architects, and residents—similar to the strong collaborations formed between structural engineers and architects that have led to innovation and world-renowned projects.

These ideas are slowly starting to take hold across Japan, particularly in projects making flood mitigation infrastructure multifunctional. Fukakita Ryokuchi Park in Osaka serves as a flood basin of the Neya River, and the Kamisaigō River Flood Management Project promotes stewardship and education. For larger-scale projects, a new flood-control concept of "watershed flood control" is being planned for 121 rivers nationwide. The intention is for all stakeholders associated with the entire river basin to mitigate flood damage collaboratively by analyzing possible inundation areas. In addition to the river infrastructure improvements, such as dam and levee construction, planners are also considering reservoir and rice field activation, revisions of hazard zone designation, collective relocation, jishubō activities, and bōsai education in schools.[22] This holistic vision, including community and educational activities, is especially important as extreme climate fluctuations will bring both flooding and drought to regions. This means social, ecological, and engineering methods will need to further dovetail across entire watersheds in the decades to come.

Disaster Timeline

In order to consider the entire disaster timeline, it is important to start even before the point when cities have to contemplate building mitigation infrastructure. One question we should be asking ourselves is, Where should we live? Historical, economic, and political factors often greatly influence decisions about where to build in the first place. Such decisions are complex, but as many coastal communities now face difficult discussions about whether to relocate, it is critical to read the landscape before expanding new construction and sites. Especially in countries that are rapidly urbanizing, many existing and new cities are expanding into wetlands and coastal areas. This not only jeopardizes flora and fauna but also puts those new residents and properties at risk due to probable sea-level rise, storm surges, and (in some locations) tsunamis. The developments that can afford to raise the base floor level through infill or to create levees to protect just their property result in pushing more water, faster, to surrounding vulnerable regions. And yet, alarmingly, there is a constant flow of global development built even in designated hazard zones.

Although the 2011 tsunami also forewarned other tsunami risk areas, influencing them to revamp their own evacuation systems and planning—some as far away as the west coast of the United States[23]—many are weighing difficult land-use planning decisions. In the next fifty years, Oregon faces a one-in-three chance of experiencing a tsunami comparable to those that devastated Japan and Indonesia, and yet the governor of Oregon signed HB 3309 in June 2019, which allows municipalities to build schools, hospitals, and other public facilities within the tsunami inundation zone, claiming that the current economic "disaster" is a greater concern.[24] We, as a profession, need not only to design for but also to advocate for life safety. And if it is truly necessary to build in a floodplain or coastal tsunami zone, we need to ensure that it is done in a way that considers how the building or infrastructure will operate through the entire disaster timeline.

While resilient design projects sometimes frame climate change as a distant threat and often present mitigation strategies for sea-level rise, our anticipatory design framework proposes to see climate risk through the lens of the near-term disasters and to design for preparedness, response, and recovery in addition to mitigation and adaptation. Efforts to mitigate greenhouse-gas emissions in order to curb the heating of our planet are imperative and require government, institution, industry, and individual actions. It is equally critical to plan and design for potential impacts of extreme weather scenarios and prepare our communities in advance. Since most governments treat these phases of disaster-related work (mitigation, adaptation, preparedness, response, recovery, and reconstruction) in a siloed manner, opportunities for overlapping efforts are often overlooked. Putting climate-change adaptation within the disaster risk rubric asks designers and planners to consider not only long-term hazards, such as sea-level rise, but also immediate multi-hazard types, including more intense storms and flooding, and short-term responses to these events.

There is also often a gap between the work that emergency managers do in preparing for disaster response and the process toward recovery and reconstruction. Will municipal and community leaders be able to respond? What about electricians, carpenters, and plumbers? Where should temporary housing be located, and what type of housing? Once a disaster occurs and reconstruction becomes necessary, sometimes oppositional factors including cost, time, quality, and consensus building are all relevant and important. As of 2021, reconstruction costs for Tohoku reached ¥32.9 trillion.[25] Most countries cannot afford such exorbitant costs and can take steps now, before lives are lost, to have difficult discussions about mitigating, adapting, or resettling in less hazardous zones and start planning for recovery. Anticipating disaster scenarios and thinking through a recovery planning process may seem counterintuitive and fatalistic, but it is a critical step to reduce chaos and maximize the full transformative potential of recovery funds. It takes time to figure out how to use subsidies creatively, which ones to use, and how to combine them to achieve the ideal vision of the place. It takes time to engage diverse populations and build consensus. It takes time to create unique, innovative, and beautiful designs that also protect people from future disasters. As the climate crisis makes disasters even more unpredictable, accepting uncertainty as the new normal means anticipating hazards and their cascading effects in advance by encouraging the incorporation of holistic planning and preparedness into the development of all urban environments.

CALLING FOR A PARADIGM SHIFT TO CARE AND STEWARDSHIP BY ALL

The anticipatory design approach is intended to foster more multivalent strategies for increasing capacity across all built projects in order to mitigate risks associated with climate complacency. In this critical era, when the impacts of a century of polluting the earth are, inevitably, turning to ravage the natural environment, the challenge now is how behavior and expectations can be changed. Emphasizing holistic and long-term perspectives on our planet's health means looking beyond immediate conveniences and economic upturns. Building a society willing to allocate time and energy to being good stewards of our local environments requires commitment from all. We tend to maintain and care for what we love. In the ideal case, national policies and subsidies, public buildings and open spaces, private sector developments, new technologies, and education will all connect to the efforts of residents and community groups. The future calls for a change in the way we select our sites, advocate for equitable policies, design our built environment, and maintain and respect the planet bestowed to us.

The National Institute of Building Sciences in the United States released a summary report in 2020 that stated that mitigation grants before a disaster can save thirteen dollars for every one dollar spent rebuilding after a disaster. Beyond the financial savings, the report details ways of reducing deaths, injuries, and cases of post-traumatic stress disorders.[26] The report shares retrofitting and code requirements and mitigation strategies, but the thirteen-to-one ratio of reducing damage and saving lives elucidates how crucial it is for our design profession to more proactively engage with communities in advance to create locally specific strategies to accomplish these goals.

As the impact of climate change is already synonymous with disasters, it is urgent for designers to deeply engage with disaster management and social science research to develop practices rooted in the needs of communities living in hazard-prone areas and to design for them *before* disasters strike.

OPTIMISM

Design that always anticipates disasters can be a daunting task, with climate scientists producing increasingly dire reports on the future of our planet and the media cycling ceaseless images of unprecedented heat waves, fires, flooding, landslides, storms, volcanic eruptions, earthquakes, and tsunamis. Researching disasters, every day and for every project, can be distressing, and it is not what many designers want to spend their time thinking about. Yet the kindness and resilience of humanity emanate even during the worst calamities. An anticipatory design framework requires a certain optimism about the capacity of humanity in the face of these seemingly unending crises. While there are problems that design cannot solve, there are many others that architecture, landscape, urban design, and planning are complicit in intensifying and may be able to ameliorate in collaboration with other fields and areas of knowledge. As White et al. stated in 2001, "There is hope for a less hazardous environment, and its achievement will depend upon the linking and convergence, and the integration, of hazard studies into the larger consciousness of sustainability and equity."[27]

Writing this conclusion during a global pandemic reinforces the need for optimism and determination. Sociologist Zeynep Tufekci shared how virologist Edward Holmes

Coastal forest

Amusement park

Housing

School

Pocket park

Machizukuri

National bosai park

Education in parks

Mixed municipal bosai hub

Pedestrian bridge

Tsunami evacuation building

Museum

Parking

Convenience store

Temple

Mall

Community center

Fire reduction buffer

Train station

Initial evacuation park

Primary evacuation park

Shrine

Michi-no-eki

Resettlement

Floating tsunami shelter

Office building

Logistics hub

Coastal park

Hotel

Bosai living zone

Living shoreline

Initial pocket park
r = 250m

Initial neighborhood park
r = 500m

Airport

Evacuation route

Fish market

Breakwater

Municipal bosai
r = 1,000m

Resettlement

Municipal bosai
r = 1,000m

and others studying Covid-19 have faced the challenge with "open, rapid, collaborative, dynamic—and, yes, messy—scientific activity, which included ways of collaborating that would have been unthinkable even a few decades ago."[28]

There is much to learn from this collective effort, most urgently the interdisciplinary imperative to share methods, tools in research, and projects for the common good. There is plenty of work to do in the field of designing and preparing for disasters, and this collaborative work takes patience and effort. Understanding one another's vocabulary, models, and methods requires dedication, and we need to be assiduous in our pursuit of this collective goal.

In addition to the continuing pandemic, this year has brought racial violence, war, and countless and overwhelming deaths—but also astounding stories of exchange, aid, and care. We do not often have control over the dangers that threaten us (although we certainly have a hand in exacerbating them), but we have great control over where we live and how we plan, structure, design, and build our environments. By reminding ourselves of how our actions impact others, including other humans, flora, and fauna, and by grounding ourselves in the stewardship and care of the natural world, we can design and prepare for a range of possible futures. Our own agency and how we apply it will determine our ability to cope with the challenges that lie ahead and anticipate an optimistic future, together.

Figure 88. Anticipatory futures: imagining a city where everyone plays a role in preparing and adapting to hazards.

GLOSSARY

age-bune 揚船　A boat, stored under the eaves and ceilings of a house, that can be quickly accessed for rescuing people

age-butsudan 揚仏壇　An elaborate pulley system for hoisting the family altar to the attic during floods

age-dana 揚棚　Raised shelves under transom windows for the storage of goods

bōsai 防災　Disaster prevention, preparedness, and mitigation

bōsaikōen 防災公園　Disaster management park

bunka seikatsu 文化生活　Cultural lifestyle

doma 土間　Earth entryway

dondo bridge どんど橋　A covered evacuation corridor between the main house to the *mizuya*

dozō-zukuri 土蔵造り　Japanese traditional construction with thick plaster exterior walls to prevent the spread of fires

engawa 縁側　Living room porch

enkai-jō 宴会場　Banquet room

fukkō 復興　Reconstruction; incorporating long-term adaptation into the reconstruction process while considering the city as a whole, including households, businesses, and other spaces of daily life

fukkō-keikaku 復興計画　Reconstruction plan

fukkyū 復旧　Recovery, restoration; returning public infrastructures to their previous condition following a disaster

fureai ふれあい　Strong rapport

furoshiki 風呂敷　A square piece of rugged Japanese cloth traditionally used for wrapping and transporting goods

furusato 故郷　Hometown

fusuma 襖　Sliding doors used in traditional Japanese architecture to divide rooms

futon 布団　Traditional Japanese bedding

gasshō-style house 合掌造り　A vernacular Japanese home with a thatched roof; *gasshō* means "prayer with palms together"

genkan 玄関　Entranceway

gisō 義倉 Charitable granaries

"Gou ni itte wa gou ni shitagae" 郷に入っては郷に従え A traditional Japanese proverb: "When you go into the village, follow the villagers"

haiku A poem with seventeen syllables in three lines of five, seven, and five

hanami 花見 The Japanese tradition of cherry-blossom (*sakura*) viewing as a celebration of the changing seasons; the tradition arose out of a need for riverine flood mitigation

hinankeiro 避難経路 Evacuation routes

hinanro 避難路 Evacuation roads

hinomiyagura 火の見櫓 Fire lookout towers built by community firefighters during the Edo era

hirokōji 広小路 Widened streets intended to serve as firebreaks during the Edo era

hiyokechi 火除地 Plazas designed as evacuation spaces, intended to help stop the spread of fires during the Edo era

hiyoketsutsumi 火除堤 Seven-meter-tall berms that slowed the spread of flames during the Edo era

idobata kaigi 井戸端会議 "Gossiping at the well," referring to social and community assembly spaces used while doing chores

igune イグネ Small forest groves typically composed of Japanese cedar

inochi-yama 命山 An artificial hill, usually on a coastal or riverine plain, used for evacuation in the event of a tsunami or flood

jichikai 自治会 Neighborhood association

jiriki 自力 Self-reliance

jishubō 自主防災組織 An abbreviation for *jishu-bōsai-soshiki,* neighborhood disaster-preparedness organizations

jomeiboku 助命木 "Life rescue tree": a large tree on the raised property of shrines in *wajū* that could be climbed by people waiting to be rescued

jomeidan 助命壇 "Life rescue platform": high ground in the *wajū* used for community evacuation during a flood

kagura 神楽 Shinto ceremonial dance

kairanban 回覧板 Community clipboard

kamado bench かまどベンチ A bench that can be used as a cooking stove in the event of a disaster

kamishibai 紙芝居 Paper picture-story show, usually for children

karuta game かるた Japanese traditional card games

kawazukuri 多自然川づくり River making

keiyakukou 契約講 A community mutual support association, traditionally existing in each hamlet in the Tohoku region

kizuna 絆 Strength and bonding between people

kodokushi 孤独死 Solitary death, when a person dying alone and the body remains undiscovered for a long period of time

kou 講 Economic community organization of a hamlet, started during the Edo period

kura 蔵 Storage house

kyōdō tatekae 共同建て替え Joint rebuilding of housing; this method can solve various problems by jointly planning with neighboring properties, even if it is difficult to rebuild old buildings as a result of a site's shape, size, property rights, or financial problems

machibikeshi 町火消し Town firefighters in the Edo era

machizukuri まちづくり A community-planning process that includes physical design

matsuri 祭り Festival

michi-no-eki 道の駅 Rest area selling local produce and crafts *mikoshi* 神輿　A palanquin in which a Shinto deity is placed and carried by local residents

minashikasetsu みなし仮説　Vacancy rental or temporary housing lease program

miraizukuri 未来づくり　"Future creating," the name of the Onagawa community business council

mizuya 水屋　Water house; a grain warehouse built inside *wajū* that was used as an evacuation shelter during floods to protect property and lives

mokumitsu 木密:木造住宅密集地域　An abbreviation for *mokumitsu jūtakumisshū chiiki,* area of dense timber housing

"Mori wa umi no koibito" 森は海の恋人　"The forest is the ocean's love," a phrase made popular by Shigeatsu Hatakeyama in Kesennuma

nagaya 長屋　Tenement housing

O-Jizô-san 地蔵さん　Japanese bodhisattva who watches over children and travelers as well as the souls of the deceased

onsen 温泉　Hot-spring bath

osukui-goya 御救小屋　"Rescue shed," referring to a public shelter set up by the shogunate and clans to rescue victims of natural disasters such as earthquakes, fires, floods, and famines during the Edo era

roji 路地　Alleys

rojison 路地尊　Small gathering spaces with underground rainwater storage tanks in alleys to provide clean water and serve disaster-preparedness functions for the community in Sumida, Tokyo

ryokan 旅館　Traditional inns

satoyama 里山　An area between the natural environment and urban space, comprising rural villages, farmland, reservoirs, grasslands, and forest, where socioecologically productive landscape has been formed as a consequence of human habitation in harmony with the bounty of nature and various ecosystems

senryū 川柳　Japanese short poem similar to *haiku* but mainly about human nature

shōbōdan 消防団　Citizen fire corps, descendants of Edo-era *machibikeshi*

shoji 障子　A *washi* paper sliding door used in traditional Japanese architecture

shinbashira 心柱　The central pillar at the core of a structure (e.g., a pagoda)

shitamachi 下町　The areas in the low-lying lands of Tokyo; traditionally, these neighborhoods consist of working-class residents

suibōdan 水防団　Community-based flood-management groups

taiko 太鼓　Traditional Japanese drums

takadai-iten 高台移転　Relocating to high ground when existing property, residential or agricultural, is being rezoned as high risk in flood-prone or flood-inundated areas

tatami 畳　A woven rush flooring mat in vernacular Japanese rooms

terakoya 寺子屋　A facility (usually a temple) that provided elementary education in reading and writing to children; it was popularized in the Edo era

tochi kukaku-seiri 土地区画整理　Land readjustment, a process by which private land is pooled and parcel boundaries are adjusted. Owners relinquish a percentage of their property to become part of a collective project, such as a widened road or a new park. In some cases, private plots may be relocated entirely

tonarigumi 隣組　Neighborhood associations consisting of five to ten families in the same district; originated in 1507

torii 鳥居　The entrance gate at a Shinto shrine that represents the boundary separating the sacred area from the human world

toshi-keikaku 都市計画　City planning

tsubo 坪   A Japanese unit of spatial measure, roughly 3.3 square meters or 35.5 square feet, equivalent to the area of two tatami mats

tsunami-hi 津波碑   Tsunami stones, markers placed following tsunamis at the level of the inundation line in coastal regions across Japan

tsunami tendenko 津波てんでんこ   The importance of taking responsibility for one's own evacuation, with the expectation that one's family and loved ones will do the same

ujiko 氏子   Literally translated as "child of the guardian god," referring to shrine parishioners, residents who worship the local Shinto shrine deity

ukiyo-e 浮世絵   "Drawings of the floating world," Japanese woodblock prints and paintings popularized in the Edo era

wajū 輪中   "Inside the circle": an area, designed at many scales, reflecting social and environmental responses to living with floods during the Edo era

warichi 割地   Joint ownership of arable land

yamanote 山手   Uptown; high-end homes on a plateau with solid ground

NOTES

Many of the data points were updated during the production of this book. As of November 8, 2023, links to PDFs and websites are accurate, but some may be discontinued or have changed by the time of publication. To view the material posted as PDFs, and in full notation, please visit DesignBeforeDisaster.org.

When referring to individuals of Japanese descent, I have generally used traditional Japanese naming conventions, in which the family name appears first; however, for texts published in English, I have adopted Western-style naming conventions in the notes and bibliography.

INTRODUCTION

1. Yamori, "Disaster Culture."

2. Kawata, "Enriching Disaster Culture."

3. Nishi and Hozumi, *What Is Japanese Architecture?,* 53.

4. Wanouchi Tourist Committee, "Drainage Maintenance and Change of the Wajū" [in Japanese], accessed July 15, 2020, https://wajyu.jp/mania/change/.

5. Shimomoto Etsuko, "Now and Then: Community Bōsai in Wajū" [in Japanese], accessed April 29, 2021 (discontinued).

6. Fuji Clean Company, "Awareness of Flood Disaster."

7. Kurumado Shizuo, "Water Culture in Ōgaki, Series 3, Culture and Lifestyle in Wajū" [in Japanese], accessed April 21, 2021, http://www.jia-tokai.org/archive/sibu/architect/2012/09/mizu.html.

8. Kamabue, "Life in Wajū" [in Japanese], accessed April 2, 2020, http://machinokatachi.main.jp/21/21_kamabue.html.

9. Kurumado, "Water Culture."

10. "Jomeidan Evacuation Shelter" [in Japanese], accessed April 21, 2021, http://school.city.kaizu.lg.jp/~nishie-sho/03introduction/waju/dwelling/jomeidan.html.

11. Wanouchi Tourist Committee, "Daily Lives in the Past in Jūrenbō Wajū Embankment" [in Japanese], accessed July 15, 2020, https://wajyu.jp/column/story1/.

12. Kamabue, "Life in Wajū."

13. Fuji Clean Company, "Awareness of Flood Disaster."

14. Shimomoto, "Now and Then."

15. Latour, "Why Has Critique."

1. ANTICIPATORY DESIGN IN DISASTER PLANNING

1. Perry, "What Is a Disaster?," 12.

2. O'Keefe, Westgate, and Wisner, "Taking the Naturalness."

3. Kasperson et al., "Social Amplification," 177.

4. Beck, *Risk Society,* 21.

5. Wisner, Gaillard, and Kelman, "Framing Disaster," 24.

6. Another definition, commonly used by the United Nations, is Risk = Hazard × Exposure × Vulnerability.

7. Wescoat, "Gilbert Fowler White," 700.

8. Architecture 2030, "Why the Built Environment," accessed November 8, 2023, https://www.architecture2030.org/why-the-built-environment/.

9. Cuny, *Disasters and Development,* 200.

10. Adger, "Vulnerability," 268, 270.

11. Cutter, Boruff, and Shirley, "Social Vulnerability," 242, 243.

12. For more, see Blaikie et al., *At Risk;* Tierney, Lindell, and Perry, *Facing the Unexpected.*

13. Yarina, "Sea Wall."

14. Soja, *Seeking Spatial Justice.*

15. Morrow, "Community Vulnerability."

16. IPCC, *AR5 Climate Change 2014,* 2151.

17. Cuny, *Disasters and Development,* 80.

18. Aldrich, *Black Wave,* 14.

19. Klinenberg, *Palaces,* 5.

20. Klinenberg, *Palaces,* 7.

21. Mileti, *Disasters by Design,* 155.

22. Cuny also asserts that codes are often based on fully industrialized countries with regard only for engineered structures. Cuny, *Disasters and Development,* 208.

23. Wisner, Gaillard, and Kelman, "Framing Disaster," 28.

24. Mileti, *Disasters by Design,* 31–33.

25. Holling, "Engineering Resilience," 31.

26. Davoudi, "Resilience."

27. Tatsuki, "Natural Disaster."

28. Adger et al., "Social-Ecological Resilience," 1036.

29. Cutter et al., "Disaster Resilience."

30. Vale, "Politics of Resilient Cities," 191.

31. Orff, *Toward an Urban Ecology,* 16.

32. Wallace and De Balogh reference FEMA as the original source of the cycle. See Wallace and De Balogh, "Disaster Management." Singleton credits Bradford University researchers for the disaster cycle. See Singleton, *Since 1900,* 13. In Japan, Meguro and Murao are often credited with the concept. See Meguro and Murao, *City and Bōsai.*

33. Singleton, *Since 1900,* 13.

34. Nelson, Adger, and Brown, "Adaptation," 397.

35. Cuny, *Disasters and Development,* 206.

36. Matsuzaki et al., "Phase Free."

37. Quarantelli, *Sheltering and Housing.*

38. Murao, "Disaster Life Cycle," 1.

39. Tierney, *Social Roots,* 4.

40. Spokane, Mori, and Martinez, "Housing Arrays."

41. Morrish, "After the Storm."

42. Aldrich, *Building Resilience,* 4.

43. Perry, "Incident Management Systems," 406.

44. Richard Serino, former deputy administrator of FEMA and chief of Boston Emergency Medical Services, interview by author, May 15, 2017.

45. Nakano Akemi, "Interview with Prof. Shimatani Yukihiro, 'Integrating Flood Control Design with Environmental Design Is the Most Important Factor in Design'" [in Japanese], *Japan Dam Foundation,* accessed July 2020, http://damnet.or.jp/cgi-bin/binranB/TPage.cgi?id=595.

46. Schipper and Pelling, "Disaster Risk," 20.

47. Mileti, *Disasters by Design,* 21.

2. HAZARDS AND POLICIES

1. Kawasumi, "Seismic Activity." Magnitudes in this book are based on Japan Meteorological Agency (JMA) measurements.

2. Fraser, "Local Administration," 124.

3. NPO Real Japan' on, "Edo Fire Fighting Celebrating 300 Year Anniversary" [in Japanese], last modified March 2, 2018, https://www.on-japan.jp/2018/03/02/江戸町火消し-生誕300年/.

4. CAO, "Protecting Our Hometown."

5. CAO, "Special Edition: Tsunami Awareness Day."

6. Smits, *When the Earth Roars,* 49.

7. Rikkyō University Library, "Learnings from Disaster History: Hōjō-ki and Ansei Kenmon-shi" [in Japanese], accessed June 15, 2020, http://library.rikkyo.ac.jp/_asset/pdf/archives/exhibition/exhibition1/hojoki.pdf.

8. Britton, "National Planning."

9. Ohashi, "Structural Calculation Code."

10. CAO, "1896 Meiji Sanriku Earthquake Tsunami."

11. Okubo, "Temples and Shrines," 66–67.

12. CAO, "1923 Great Kantō Earthquake."

13. CAO, "Lessons Learned from 1923," first section, 180, 224–29.

14. CAO, "1923 Great Kantō Earthquake," 12.

15. CAO, "Lessons Learned from 1923," first section, 2.

16. Koshizawa, *Reconstruction Planning,* 41–42.

17. CAO, "1923 Great Kantō Earthquake."

18. Yasuda M., *Disaster Reconstructions,* 184.

19. Yasuda M., *Disaster Reconstructions,* 189.

20. Schencking, *Great Kanto Earthquake,* 62–63, 66–67.

21. Yasuda M., *Disaster Reconstructions,* 189–90.

22. Mitsubishi Estate, "Citizens—Community Disaster Drills," August 2023, https://www.mec.co.jp/news/detail/2023/08/16_mec230816_bosai.

23. Schencking, *Great Kanto Earthquake,* 68.

24. Weisenfeld, *Imaging Disaster,* 30.

25. Imaizumi, *Sacred Space,* 146.

26. Sato, "Social Metamorphoses."

27. Shuto and Fujima, "Short History," 269.

28. Okamura, "Disaster Reconstruction Policies," 129.

29. Maki, "Long-Term Recovery," 5.

30. CAO, *2015 Disaster Management in Japan* [in Japanese], March 2015, 5, http://www.bousai.go.jp/1info/pdf/saigaipamphlet_je.pdf.

31. CAO, "Lessons Learned from 1948," 151.

32. Among typhoon categories in Japan, class 5 represents the most severe level of typhoon. Class 5 wind speeds exceed 75 meters/second (168 mph). It is similar to a category 5 hurricane on the Saffir-Simpson scale, although the systems vary in measures of wind speed over time.

33. CAO, "Lessons Learned from 1959," 3, 7, 23.

34. Mizutani, "Typhoon Vera."

35. CAO, *2015 Disaster Management,* 6.

36. FDMA, "Guidelines for Jishubō Organizations" [in Japanese], March 2023, 8–9, https://www.fdma.go.jp/mission/bousai/ikusei/items/bousai_R5_3.pdf.

37. Okazaki and Pribadi, "Resilient Homes," 63.

38. CAO, *2005 White Paper on Disaster Management in Japan* [in Japanese], 2005, https://www.bousai.go.jp/kaigirep/hakusho/pdf/h17hakusho.pdf.

39. Kobe City, "Overview of the Great Hanshin-Awaji Earthquake and Reconstruction" [in Japanese], 2011, 15–24.

40. Kobe City, "Overview," 2.

41. CAO, "Earthquake Damage," in *2005 White Paper.*

42. Ozerdem and Jaco, *Disaster Management,* 3.

43. Hyogo Prefecture Medical Association, "1995 Great Hanshin-Awaji Earthquake, Statistics on Fatal Cases" [in Japanese], last modified 1996, https://www.hyogo.med.or.jp/jmat-hyogo/day-after/siryo/.

44. Comerio, *Disaster Hits Home,* 148.

45. Tierney and Goltz, "Emergency Response," 7.

46. Kobe City, *1995 Great Hanshin-Awaji Earthquake Reconstruction History* [in Japanese], January 2000, 28–29, https://www.dri.ne.jp/material/publication/hanshinawaji/.

47. Tierney and Goltz, "Emergency Response," 6.

48. Nakayama, *Kobe: 2 Step,* 12.

49. JMA, "Lessons Learned from the Great Hanshin-Awaji Earthquake" [in Japanese], accessed May 3, 2021, 1, https://www.data.jma.go.jp/svd/eqev/data/1995_01_17_hyogonanbu/sympo0117_kobayashi.pdf.

50. Kashihara, Ueno, and Morita, *Research on Shelters,* 7, 38, 69, 92.

51. Ministry of Construction, *Urban Disaster Management,* 61.

52. CAO, "The Hanshin-Awaji Earthquake Disaster Information Resource Book 03—Securing Firefighting Facilities and Equipment and Water Supply" [in Japanese], accessed June 15, 2020, http://www.bousai.go.jp/kyoiku/kyokun/hanshin_awaji/data/detail/1-5-3.html.

53. Nakayama, *Kobe: 2 Step,* 32.

54. General Administrative Agency of the Cabinet, *Great Hanshin-Awaji Earthquake Reconstruction Journal* [in Japanese], February 23, 2000, 7, https://www.bousai.go.jp/kyoiku/kyokun/hanshin_awaji .html.

55. Hyogo Prefecture, *Great Hanshin-Awaji Earthquake Reconstruction Records 1* [in Japanese], 1997, 113.

56. Ozerdem and Jaco, *Disaster Management,* 39.

57. Cabinet Secretariat, CAO, and MLIT, "Looking Back on the Great Hanshin-Awaji Earthquake" [in Japanese], March 29, 2002.

58. Homma, "National Disaster Medical System."

59. MIC (Ministry of Internal Affairs and Communications), "Promotion of ICT in the Field of Disaster Management" [in Japanese], *2005 White Paper on Information Communication,* 2005, https:// www.soumu.go.jp/johotsusintokei/whitepaper/ja/h17/html/H3502300.html.

60. CAO, *2015 Disaster Management,* 38.

61. S. Murakami, "Ready or Not."

62. MLIT, "The Fifth Comprehensive National Development Plan" [in Japanese], *Grand Design for the 21st Century,* March 1998, http://www.mlit.go.jp/kokudokeikaku/zs5-e/.

63. Hoshino, "Volunteer."

64. Ozerdem and Jaco, *Disaster Management,* 100.

65. FDMA, "Guidelines for Jishubō," 9.

66. Onouchi Nobuaki, general affairs officer of the Nakagyō Shōbōdan Hatsune Team, interview by author's team member Saeko Baird, December 6, 2015.

67. FDMA, "Guidelines for Jishubō," 10.

68. Good Design Award, "Activity [MUJI ITSUMO MOSHIMO]," September 1, 2020, https:// ryohin-keikaku.jp/eng/topics/034222.html.

69. Nagata Hirokazu, president of *+arts,* interview by author, June 18, 2019.

70. The acronym SI refers to "seismic intensity." Primarily used in Japan and Taiwan, it documents the severity of shaking at monitoring points on the earth's surface. SI values range from zero to seven. It is similar to the Modified Mercalli Intensity scale (MMI) used in the United States. The Richter scale measures the amount of energy released at the epicenter, ranging from zero to less than ten.

71. FDMA, "2011 Tohoku Region Pacific Coast Earthquake (Report No. 160)" [in Japanese], March 10, 2020, 1, 4, https://www.fdma.go.jp/disaster/higashinihon/items/160.pdf.

72. Iwate Prefecture, *Iwate Prefecture Record of the Great East-Japan Earthquake and Tsunami* [in Japanese], 2013, 22, https://www2.pref.iwate.jp/~bousai/shiryo/gakusyuu/kirokushi/allpage.pdf.

73. Iuchi, Maly, and Johnson, "Three Years After," 30.

74. Iwate Prefecture, *Great East-Japan Earthquake,* 24, 80.

75. Investigation Committee on the Accident at Fukushima Nuclear Plant, *Final Report,* July 23, 2012, https://www.cas.go.jp/jp/seisaku/icanps/eng/index.html.

76. Esteban et al., "Tsunami Culture," 700.

77. Ranghieri and Ishiwatari, *Learning from Megadisasters,* 125, 126.

78. MEXT, *Disaster-Resistant School Facilities—Tsunami Countermeasures and Preparedness Functions as Shelters* [in Japanese], March 7, 2014, 30, https://www.mext.go.jp/b_menu/shingi/chousa /shisetu/013/toushin/1344800.htm.

79. Cabinet Secretariat, "Proposals for Reconstruction: Hope in the Midst of Misery" [in Japanese], June 25, 2011, https://www.cas.go.jp/jp/fukkou/pdf/kousou12/teigen.pdf.

80. Officially called the Committee for Technical Investigation on Countermeasures for Earthquakes and Tsunamis Based on the Lessons Learned from the 2011 Off the Pacific Coast of Tohoku Earthquake. See CAO, "Report of the Committee for Technical Investigation on Countermeasures for Earthquakes and Tsunamis Based on the Lessons Learned from the '2011 off the Pacific Coast of Tohoku Earthquake,'" September 28, 2011, https://www.bousai.go.jp/kaigirep/chousakai/tohokukyokun/pdf/Report.pdf.

81. CAO, "Basic Measurements for Future Tsunamis" [in Japanese], June 6, 2011, http://www.bousai.go.jp/kaigirep/chousakai/tohokukyokun/pdf/teigen.pdf.

82. Reconstruction Agency, "Basic Policies for Reconstruction from the Great East-Japan Earthquake" [in Japanese], last modified August 11, 2011, https://www.reconstruction.go.jp/topics/000056.html.

83. Reconstruction Agency, "Reconstruction Grants Core Projects" [in Japanese], 2011, https://www.reconstruction.go.jp/topics/main-cat1/sub-cat1-14/sub-cat1-14-9/20160406_kohukin-1.pdf.

84. Onoda, Tsukuda, and Suzuki, "Complexities," 5.

85. MLIT, "Act on Development of Areas Resilient to Tsunami Disasters," accessed May 5, 2021, https://www.mlit.go.jp/sogoseisaku/point/tsunamibousai.html.

86. Akimoto, "Problems of Plan-Making," 28.

87. MLIT, "Recovery-Reconstruction Status" [in Japanese], last modified January 2020, https://www.mlit.go.jp/river/kaigan/main/fukkyufukko/pdf/fukkyufukko03_2002.pdf.

88. MLIT, "Seawall Heights" [in Japanese], 2019, https://www.mlit.go.jp/river/kaigan/main/fukkyufukko/pdf/fukkyufukko04_1908.pdf.

89. Miyagi Prefecture, Miyagi Prefecture Reconstruction and Machizukuri Archives [in Japanese], March 2021, 34–35, https://www.pref.miyagi.jp/soshiki/tosikei/ayumi.html.

90. Ubaura, "Land Use," 63.

91. Iuchi and Olshansky, "Tohoku's 5-Year Recovery," 99.

92. Ubaura, "Land Use," 63–64.

93. CAO, "Events at the 2021 Tsunami Preparedness Day" [in Japanese], October 2021, 3, http://www.bousai.go.jp/jishin/tsunami/tsunamibousai/pdf/r3_02.pdf.

94. CAO, "Strengthening Community Disaster Management through Mutual Support—Implementation of the Community Disaster Management Planning System" [in Japanese], June 2014, 19–21, https://www.bousai.go.jp/kyoiku/pdf/guidline_separate.pdf.

95. CAO, *2015 Disaster Management,* 41.

96. FDMA, "Guidelines for Jishubō," 9.

97. Ranghieri and Ishiwatari, *Learning from Megadisasters,* 128.

98. CAO, *2017 White Paper on Disaster Management in Japan* [in Japanese], 2017, 60–65, https://www.bousai.go.jp/kaigirep/hakusho/pdf/H29_honbun.pdf.

99. Chiba, Shaw, and Banba, "Mountain Disasters," 233.

100. MLIT, "2011 Great Kii Peninsula Flood" [in Japanese], 2013, 1, https://www.kkr.mlit.go.jp/bousai/kiroku/qgl8vlo000008lkt-att/kiihantou-kirokushi.pdf.

101. CAO, "Disaster by Typhoon Talas in 2011" [in Japanese], September 3, 2017, 2, https://www.bousai.go.jp/kaigirep/houkokusho/hukkousesaku/saigaitaiou/output_html_1/pdf/201102.pdf.

102. Wakayama Prefecture, "Damage and Restoration Report of the 2011 Kii Peninsula Flood" [in Japanese], August 2011, https://dwasteinfo.nies.go.jp/archive/past_doc/201108wakayama.pdf.

103. JSCE (Japan Society of Civil Engineers), "Typhoon Talas Sediment Damage Report" [in Japanese], last modified December 26, 2011, http://committees.jsce.or.jp/report/node/51.

104. MLIT, *2011 Great Kii Peninsula Flood—MLIT Kinki Regional Office Record of Disaster Response* [in Japanese], 2013, 30, https://www.kkr.mlit.go.jp/bousai/qgl8vl0000008ajd-att/kiihantou
-kirokushi.pdf.

105. Chiba, Shaw, and Banba, "Mountain Disasters," 228.

106. CAO, "Damage Caused by Torrential Rain in July 2018" [in Japanese], January 9, 2019, 4, http://www.bousai.go.jp/updates/h30typhoon7/pdf/310109_1700_h30typhoon7_01.pdf.

107. MLIT, "Flood Disaster Countermeasures in Response to Climate Change" [in Japanese], July 2020, https://www.mlit.go.jp/report/press/content/001352899.pdf.

108. SankeiBiz, "Seven Thousand Yen per Person to Develop Individual Evacuation Plans for the Elderly" [in Japanese], March 10, 2021, https://www.sankeibiz.jp/macro/news/210310/mca2103100631015
-n1.htm.

109. CAO, "Earthquake Disaster" [in Japanese], accessed May 5, 2021, http://www.bousai.go.jp
/kyoiku/hokenkyousai/jishin.html.

110. CAO, "Final Report: Tokyo Inland Earthquake's Estimated Overall Damage and Its Countermeasures" [in Japanese], accessed June 15, 2020.

111. CAO, "Basic Plan for Emergency Countermeasures for Tokyo Inland Earthquake" [in Japanese], March 31, 2015, 12–13 and 30, http://www.bousai.go.jp/jishin/syuto/pdf/syuto_keikaku_20150331.pdf.

112. Multilingual versions are available at https://nosigner.com/tokyo-bousai.

113. JMA, "What Is the Nankai Trough?" [in Japanese], accessed November 23, 2020, https://www
.data.jma.go.jp/svd/eqev/data/nteq/nteq.html.

114. CAO, "Earthquake," http://www.bousai.go.jp/kyoiku/hokenkyousai/jishin.html.

115. Ozawa Keiichi, "Nankai Quake Numbers Skewed to Prioritize Budgets over Science," *Japan Times,* July 10, 2020.

116. CAO, *2015 Disaster Management,* 17.

117. MLIT, "Comprehensive Social Infrastructure Development Subsidy and Bōsai Safety Subsidy" [in Japanese], accessed October 3, 2023, https://www.mlit.go.jp/page/content/001603555.pdf.

118. MLIT, "Ensuring Citizen Safety and Security" [in Japanese], Outline of Request for Budgetary Estimates, 2021, https://www.mlit.go.jp/page/kanbo05_hy_002080.html.

119. MLIT, "Comprehensive Urban Disaster Management Promotion Project," 2018, https://www
.mlit.go.jp/common/001231347.pdf.

120. MLIT, "Shift to Disaster Awareness Society," in *MLIT White Paper 2018* [in Japanese], 2018, 252, https://www.mlit.go.jp/hakusyo/mlit/h29/hakusho/h30/index.html.

3. URBAN SYSTEMS

1. Sorensen, "Changing Governance," 61.

2. Seidensticker, *Low City, High City,* 64.

3. Murao, *Architecture, Space, Disaster,* 99.

4. Kobayashi Ikuo, advisor of CO-PLAN, interview by author, July 2001.

5. Sorensen, *Making of Urban Japan,* 122–23.

6. Ishida, "Local Uniqueness."

7. Murakami A., "Why Doesn't Urban Planning Start," 196–97.

8. Nakamura, "Neighborhood Associations."

9. Hirakawa, "Reading the Guidelines."

10. Taniguchi and Marshall, "Formal Volunteering," 700.

11. Satoh, "Japanese Machizukuri," 28, 128.

12. Masuda, "Urban Autonomy."

13. Watanabe, "Toshi-keikaku vs Machizukuri," 40.

FIRE REDUCTION SYSTEMS

1. Rosen, *Limits of Power,* 4, 218, 248, 250, 280.

2. Frost and Jones, "Fire Gap."

3. Saito and Tabata, "Fire-Preventing Functions."

4. Horie, "Historical Research," 116.

5. Kayanoki and Ito, "Research."

6. Yasuda M., *Disaster Reconstructions,* 185.

7. CAO, "Lessons Learned from 1923," first section, 207.

8. CAO, "1923 Great Kantō Earthquake," 12.

9. Yasuda M., *Disaster Reconstructions,* 174.

10. Koshizawa, *Reconstruction Planning,* 62–63.

11. CAO, "Lessons Learned from 1923," third section, 8.

12. Japanese Institute of Landscape Architecture, *Reconstruction Landscape,* 22–23.

13. Ishikawa, "Landscape Planning," 833.

14. Yasuda M., *Disaster Reconstructions,* 194–95.

15. Koshizawa, *Reconstruction Planning,* 72.

16. Maejima, *Tokyo Park,* 219.

17. Sanada, "Green Belt."

18. CAO, "Lessons Learned from 1923," second section, 15.

19. FDMA, "Numerical Data on Shōbōdan Firefighters" [in Japanese], last modified April 2020, https://www.fdma.go.jp/relocation/syobodan/data/scale/.

20. Onouchi, interview, December 6, 2015.

21. CAO, "1923 Great Kantō Earthquake," 12.

22. CAO, "Lessons Learned from 1923," second section, 17.

23. Suzuki J., "Learning from Past Disasters."

24. TMG, "Greenbelt Concept," in *The Changing Face of Tokyo: From Edo to Today, and into the Future,* March 27, 2020, 58–59, https://www.toshiseibi.metro.tokyo.lg.jp/keikaku_chousa_singikai /pdf/tokyotoshizukuri/en_2_07.pdf.

25. MLIT, "Comprehensive Urban Disaster Management Promotion Project."

26. CAO, "Basic Plan," 4.

27. TMG Bureau of Urban Development, "Bōsai Living Zones" [in Japanese], 2018, https://www .toshiseibi.metro.tokyo.lg.jp/bosai/pdf/bosai4_kentou01_07.pdf.

28. TMG, *Bōsai City Planning Promotion Basic Policy (Revision)* [in Japanese], March 2020, 1-2, 2-1, 2-2, https://www.toshiseibi.metro.tokyo.lg.jp/bosai/bosai4.htm.

29. "No Progress in the Elimination of Dense Wooded Areas, Osaka Prefecture Has 60 Percent of the Whole Country" [in Japanese], *Nikkei Shimbun,* January 14, 2021.

30. TMG, "Subsidy for Rebuilding Condominiums, Residential Revitalization Project" [in Japanese], last modified March 20, 2019, https://www.mansion-tokyo.metro.tokyo.lg.jp/tatekae/33 joseiseido.html.

31. TMG, "Special Non-combustible Zones" [in Japanese], last modified April 4, 2021, https://www .toshiseibi.metro.tokyo.lg.jp/bosai/mokumitu/torikumi.html.

32. TMG, "10-Year Fireproofing Project" [in Japanese], last modified April 1, 2019, https://www.toshiseibi.metro.tokyo.lg.jp/bosai/mokumitu/.

33. In disaster management, the term "blue-sky days" often refers to regular day-to-day operations; "gray skies" means a disaster is unfolding.

34. Kyoto City, "Disaster Cooperative Well Registration System" [in Japanese], last modified April 8, 2021, https://www.bousai.city.kyoto.lg.jp/0000000186.html.

35. Kyoto City, "Development of Fire Suppression Models to Protect Cultural Properties" [in Japanese], 2012, https://www.city.kyoto.lg.jp/kensetu/cmsfiles/contents/0000275/275802/jigohyouka24tiyousiyo-2.pdf.

36. Cultural Heritage Department manager, Kyoto Fire Department Headquarters, interview by Saeko Baird, December 10, 2014.

37. Kyoto City, "Fire Suppression Models," 8.

38. Asada, Ochiai, and Kobayashi, "Shirakawa Village."

39. Shirakawa Village Office, "Shirakawa Village Community Firefighters" [in Japanese], last modified December 25, 2020, https://www.vill.shirakawa.lg.jp/2074.htm.

40. Kyodo, "Huts Burn Down Near World Heritage-Listed Thatched Farmhouses of Shirakawa-go," *Japan Times,* November 2019.

41. Hagihara, Hatayama, and Okada, "Historical Transition."

42. MLIT, "Status of Efforts in Model Districts: Creating Streams of Water" [in Japanese], (2008) 2-3-9-2-3–11, https://www.kkr.mlit.go.jp/plan/biwayodosaisei/cooperation/suishin/list_conf/200907/23.pdf.

43. Kyoto City, "The Horikawa Firefly (Revival) Project in Kyoto's Water Coexistence Plan" [in Japanese], last modified June 24, 2020, https://www.city.kyoto.lg.jp/kensetu/page/0000124464.html.

44. Onouchi, interview, December 6, 2015.

45. Kim and Okubo, "Horikawa River."

46. Murao, *Architecture, Space, Disaster,* 37.

47. Kojima, Yamasaki, and Kinugasa, "Façade Types," 1.

48. Tingey, "Machiya Design," 94, 98.

49. Fujisaki, Reyes, and Toyokawa, "Slum Clearance Redevelopment," 827.

50. URAJA, "Large-Scale Projects," 30.

51. URAJA, "Large-Scale Projects," 31.

52. Fujisaki, Reyes, and Toyokawa, "Slum Clearance Redevelopment," 825–33.

53. Murao and Kitazawa, "Verification."

54. TOKYO MX, "Tokyo Metropolitan Disaster Management: Sumida Ward; Latest Situation of the Shirahige-East Disaster Preparedness Apartment Complex" [in Japanese], YouTube, September 21, 2011, https://www.youtube.com/watch?v=kiH-1XiPgik&t=257s.

55. Murao and Kitazawa, "Verification."

56. Organization for Landscape and Urban Green Infrastructure, *Bōsaikōen Technical Handbook,* 2nd ed., 178.

57. CAO, "Shirahige-East Neighborhood Council 1" [in Japanese], accessed May 19, 2021, http://www.bousai.go.jp/kyoiku/minna/machidukuri/matidukuri/jirei/jireinew/syousai113.htm.

58. Flüchter, "Tokyo," 218.

59. Sumida Ward, "Subsidy for Installation of Rainwater Tanks" [in Japanese], last modified April 1, 2021, https://www.city.sumida.lg.jp/kuhou/sp/category/20200711/feature/article_05.html.

60. MLIT, "Report on Development of Disaster Management Evaluation and Countermeasure

Technology in Machizukuri" [in Japanese], 2001, C-19, https://www.nilim.go.jp/lab/jdg/soupuro/c
.pdf.

61. Hitokotokai Society website, last modified April 20, 2021, http://hitokotokai.com/.

62. Sumida Ward, "Rojison Types" [in Japanese], last modified April 17, 2008, https://www.city
.sumida.lg.jp.

63. Sumida Ward, "Fireproof Building Subsidy Project," last modified April 13, 2021, https://www
.city.sumida.lg.jp/kurashi/funenka_taishinka/funenka/joseikin/funenkasokushin.html.

64. Sumida Ward, *Sumida Ward Non-Combustibility Promotion Project Review* [in Japanese],
March 2007, 136, https://www.city.sumida.lg.jp/kuseijoho/sumida_info/houkokusyo/funenka1903
.files/gaiyo.pdf.

65. Sumida Ward, "Promoting a 10-Year Project to Make Dense Wooden Areas Noncombustible" [in
Japanese], last modified July 1, 2023, https://www.facebook.com/profile/100064495370029/search/?q
=%E3%81%B5%E3%82%8D%E3%81%97%E3%81%8D&locale=ja_JP.

66. Fujinokisan-chi, "Towards an Unburnable and Unbreakable Town—Disaster Prevention" [in
Japanese], accessed May 20, 2021, https://www.facebook.com/fujinokisanchi/.

67. Koto Ward, "Kōtō 5 District Hazard Maps of Large-Scale Flooding" [in Japanese], last modified
August 2018, https://www.city.koto.lg.jp/057101/bosai/bosai-top/topics/documents/haza-do.pdf.

68. Kajima Corporation, "Series 26 Kokugikan: A Sumo Hall of Fame Where Tradition and Technology Converge" [in Japanese], last modified July 28, 2009, https://www.kajima.co.jp/gallery/kiseki
/kiseki26/index-j.html.

69. Next Wisdom Foundation, "Spreading Rainwater Wisdom from Sumida Ward to the World:
'Turning the Kokugikan into a Rainwater Tank,'" last modified June 24, 2015, https://nextwisdom.org
/article/691/.

70. Tsukahara, "Tokyo Skytree Town."

71. Sumida Ward, "Rainwater Usage Facts," last modified June 22, 2018, https://www.city.sumida.lg
.jp/kurashi/kankyou_hozen/amamizu/riyou/dounyuu_sisetu/amamizu_riyouzisseki.html.

72. Erik de Castro, "Firefighting in Manila's Tinderbox Slums—a Picture Essay," *Guardian,* June 25,
2018.

MACHIZUKURI

1. Sorensen, *Making of Urban Japan,* 122–29.

2. Watanabe, "Toshi-keikaku vs Machizukuri," 48, 51.

3. Ministry of Construction, "Guidelines for City Planning Operations" [in Japanese], last modified
December 2000, https://www.mlit.go.jp/crd/city/singikai/sno105.htm.

4. Government of Japan, *Disaster Reduction,* 4.

5. Healey, "Neighbourhood Management Capacity," 8.

6. Matsubara E., "Machikyō Chart," 20.

7. Watanabe, "Toshi-keikaku vs Machizukuri," 44.

8. Watanabe, "Toshi-keikaku vs Machizukuri," 45.

9. Yasuda C., "Machizukuri Ordinances," 5.

10. Mouri, "Machizukuri."

11. President of the Mano machizukuri group, interview by author and Saeko Baird, Kobe, April 23,
2019.

12. Sorensen, "Changing Governance," 76.

13. Nakayama, *Kobe: 2 Step,* 92.

14. Kobayashi, "Eisuke Mizutani's Town Planning."

15. Coaffee and Lee, *Urban Resilience,* 195.

16. Olshansky et al., *Opportunity in Chaos,* 195.

17. Edgington, *Reconstructing Kobe,* 84.

18. Nakayama, "Enforcement Process," 48.

19. Kobe City, "Rokkōmichi Station South District Earthquake Reconstruction Type 2 Urban Redevelopment Project Record" [in Japanese], October 2005, 33.

20. Nakayama, *Kobe: 2 Step,* 70–71.

21. Ito, "Earthquake Reconstruction Machizukuri," 163.

22. Nakayama, *Kobe: 2 Step,* 73–74.

23. Olshansky et al., *Opportunity in Chaos,* 6–26.

24. Evans, "Machi-zukuri," 453.

25. Nakayama, *Kobe: 2 Step,* 129–32.

26. Sorensen, "Changing Governance," 78.

27. Edgington, *Reconstructing Kobe,* 112.

28. Mano District Machizukuri Deliberation Council, *Longest in Japan: Mano Machizukuri—Memorial Issue of the 10th Anniversary of the Kobe Earthquake* [in Japanese], November 2005, 137.

29. Olshansky et al., *Opportunity in Chaos,* 6–37.

30. Nakayama, "Kobe City Machizukuri Ordinance," 28.

31. Nishio Tatsuhiro, "Rokkōmichi Station North District Machizukuri" [in Japanese], Vigorous Kansai Regional Planning Meeting, December 16, 2005, 84–88, https://www.kkr.mlit.go.jp/plan/kansaigenki/symposium/051216_report/pdf/3-1.pdf.

32. Doi, "Projects in Reconstruction Machizukuri," 37.

33. Community member, Rokkōmichi North machizukuri parks group, interview by author and Taketani Maya, July 9, 2015.

34. Rokkōmichi North machizukuri parks group, interview.

35. Nakayama, *Kobe: 2 Step,* 70–71.

36. Arimitsu Yuko, "Rokkōmichi Station South District" [in Japanese], *Kinmokusei* 27 (April 29, 1996) and 47 (May 5, 1997), http://web.kyoto-inet.or.jp/org/gakugei/kobe/key/ni2030.htm.

37. Kobe City, "Rokkōmichi Station," 38.

38. Arimitsu, "Rokkōmichi Station South District."

39. Kurahashi Masami, "Summary of Rokkōmichi Station South District Redevelopment Project" [in Japanese], Urban Renewal Coordinator Association of Japan, 2003, https://www.urca.or.jp/chousa/mk_arc/07jireiken/02-2uerubu.pdf.

40. Tatani, "Urban Renewal," 3.

41. Olshansky et al., *Opportunity in Chaos,* 6–21.

42. URAJA, "Rokkōmichi Station South."

43. Arimitsu, "Rokkōmichi Station South District."

44. Matsumoto District Machizukuri Council, "Matsumoto District Reconstruction Memorandum" [in Japanese], 2003, 5–6.

45. Tsuji Nobukazu, director of Environmental Landscape Design Office, interview by author's team member Taketani Maya, July 8, 2015.

46. Tsuji, interview.

47. Kobayashi Ikuo, interview by author, April 23, 2019.

48. Onagawa Town, "Damages in Onagawa" [in Japanese], last modified March 2015, http://www.town.onagawa.miyagi.jp/ayumi.html.

49. Sue, "Reconstruction Machizukuri," 100.

50. Sue Yusuke, urban designer with Chuo Fukken Consultants, interview by author's team member Endo Kenya, September 18, 2019.

51. *Asahi Shimbun* DIALOG editorial, "Interview with Suda Yoshiaki, Mayor of Onagawa, Miyagi Prefecture, 8 years after 3/11, Our Mission Is to Show New Possibilities of Regional Areas" [in Japanese], *Asahi Shimbun,* March 22, 2019.

52. Tokyo Peil 東京湾中等潮位 is a measurement that uses the sea level of Tokyo Bay as the zero-meter reference surface. The height from the reference surface is elevation.

53. Onagawa, "Onagawa Revitalization Plan" [in Japanese], established on December 19, 2014; revised on February 9, 2016, https://www.reconstruction.go.jp/portal/sangyou_nariwai/onagawa keikaku-hontai.pdf.

54. Sue, "Reconstruction Machizukuri," 88.

55. Richard Vize, "'We Wanted a New Vibe': The Japanese Town That Outlawed Sprawl," *Guardian,* April 17, 2019.

56. Shigeru Ban Architects, "Onagawa Station + Yupo'po," last modified 2015, http://www.shigeru banarchitects.com/works/2015_onagawa/index.html.

57. VAN (Voluntary Architects' Network), "Disaster Relief Projects for East Japan Earthquake and Tsunami," accessed July 7, 2020, http://www.shigerubanarchitects.com/SBA_NEWS/SBA_van_p2 .htm.

58. Kobayashi, "Planner's View."

EVACUATION ROUTES

1. CAO, "Guidance on Designation of Emergency Evacuation Spaces" [in Japanese], March 2017, 44, http://www.bousai.go.jp/oukyu/hinankankoku/pdf/shiteitebiki.pdf.

2. NILIM (National Institute for Land and Infrastructure Management), *Guidelines for Planning, Design and Management of Disaster Prevention Parks,* 2nd rev. ed. [in Japanese], September 2017, 63.

3. Ando et al., "Fatality Rate," 411–12.

4. CAO, "Community Survey on Evacuation During the Great East Japan Earthquake," December 2012, 1, http://www.bousai.go.jp/jishin/tsunami/hinan/pdf/20121221_chousa3_1.pdf.

5. Murakami, Takimoto, and Pomonis, "Tsunami Evacuation Process."

6. Itabashi Ward City Planning Department staff, interview by author's team member Saeko Baird, Itabashi Ward, Tokyo, July 23, 2018.

7. Itabashi Ward City Planning Department staff, email interview by Saeko Baird, July 10, 2020.

8. Akasaki Mitsuo, member of the Kamaishi City Council, and the shōbōdan members, interview by author and team, Kamaishi, Miyagi Prefecture, July 6, 2015.

9. FDMA, "Summary of Evacuation Signs Investigation Report," June 21, 2013, https://www.fdma .go.jp/singi_kento/kento/items/130621hinan.PDF.

10. National Museum of Ethnology, "Cultural Heritage Sites Possessing Memories of Tsunamis: Database of Temples/Shrines and Stone Monuments" [in Japanese], last modified 2017, http://sekihi .minpaku.ac.jp/.

11. Good, "Disaster Heritage," 144.

12. Pescatore et al., *Memory across Generations,* 8.

13. The Megalithic Portal and Megalith Map, "Jōgan Tsunami Warning Tablet," The Megalithic Portal, last updated July 12, 2014, http://www.megalithic.co.uk/article.php?sid=35904.

14. Pescatore et al., *Memory across Generations,* 5–9.

15. Sato et al., "Recognition of Tsunami Stones."

16. Mark Weitzman, "First Japan Tsunami Monument Has QR Code Video and Advice," *Digital Journal,* December 23, 2011, http://www.digitaljournal.com/article/316636.

17. Boret and Shibayama, "Roles of Monuments," 58.

18. "Introducing the O-Jizô-san Project" [in Japanese], last modified March 11, 2018, http://www.o jizosan.net/en.

19. Kamaishi City, "Disaster Mitigation Measures in Kamaishi Port Area" [in Japanese], February 28, 2013, https://www.mlit.go.jp/common/000989415.pdf.

20. Kamaishi City, "Disaster Mitigation Measures."

21. Fukuroi City, "Ōno Life Hill / Nakashinden Life Hill" [in Japanese], March 20, 2007, https://www.city.fukuroi.shizuoka.jp.

22. MLIT, "Development of Inochi-yama during Heisei—Wisdom of Ancestors" [in Japanese], accessed May 20, 2021, https://www.mlit.go.jp/common/001275927.pdf.

23. Iwasaki Akiko, owner of Horaikan Hotel, interview by author and team, Kesennuma, Japan, June 2015.

24. Nikken Sekkei LTD, "Escape Map Project," accessed May 20, 2021, https://www.nikken.co.jp/ja /insights/benefits_of_the_escape_map.html.

25. Kinoshita, "Escape Maps," 53–55.

26. Hatori, "NIGECHIZU," 002–003.

27. Suppasri et al., "Lessons Learned," 993.

COASTAL STRATEGIES

1. Kawata Yoshiaki, "Disaster Information and Disaster Culture" [in Japanese], February 4, 2019, http://www.soumu.go.jp/main_content/000603366.pdf.

2. Ando et al., "Historical Study," 6.

3. Sugito, "Showa Sanriku Tsunami."

4. Shuto and Fujima, "Short History," 268–69.

5. Suppasri et al., "Lessons Learned," 999.

6. Shuto and Fujima, "Short History," 270.

7. MLIT, "Correspondence Summary by MLIT on the Great East Japan Earthquake" [in Japanese], May 2011, 8, http://www.mlit.go.jp/common/000147517.pdf.

8. Kamaishi City, "Kamaishi Port Bay Entrance Breakwater" [in Japanese], last modified April 30, 2018, https://www.city.kamaishi.iwate.jp/docs/2018043000022/.

9. Arikawa Taro, "Seawalls and Disaster Management: Damage Mechanism of Seawalls" [in Japanese], NHK Disaster Preparedness, last modified May 31, 2015, https://www.nhk.or.jp/sonae/column /20150534.html.

10. Shibuya Kazuhisa, "Breakwater at the Kamaishi Bay Had Certain Effects" [in Japanese], *Nikkei Shimbun,* March 3, 2011.

11. MLIT, "Kamaishi Port," in *MLIT White Paper 2011* [in Japanese], 2011, 27, https://www.mlit.go .jp/hakusyo/mlit/h22/hakusho/h23/index.html.

12. Tsuji Yoshinobu, "Learning from Sanriku Coast Tsunami Reconstruction Projects" [in Japanese], last modified September 6, 2017, http://www.city.shimanto.lg.jp/life/menu/topics/index.html.

13. Yamasaki Masayuki, Miyako City disaster preparedness department manager, interview by author and team, July 4, 2015.

14. Satake Kenji, "Tsunami off the Pacific Coast Tohoku Earthquake: Including Comparisons with

Past Tsunamis" [in Japanese], April 17, 2011, https://www.bosai.go.jp/sp/info/event/2011/pdf/20110417_03.pdf.

15. Deputy Director General of Home Ministry, Department of Urban Planning, "The Report on Reconstruction Plan in Damaged Municipalities by Sanriku Tsunami" [in Japanese], March 1934, 160, https://tsunami-dl.jp/document/019.

16. Shuto, "1933 Shōwa Sanriku," 54.

17. Yamashita, "Sanriku Coast, Taro," 167–68.

18. Yamashita, "Sanriku Coast, Taro," 165.

19. Muramatsu et al., "Tsunami Control," 90–91.

20. Ubaura and Akiyama, "Citizen Participation."

21. Miyako City, *Records of the Great East-Japan Earthquake in Miyako City 1, Tsunami History, Summary Edition* [in Japanese], September 2014, 1, 65, https://www.city.miyako.iwate.jp/kikaku/koho/higashinihondaishinsai_miyako-shi-no-kiroku/downoad_PDF_earthquake_tsunami_record.html.

22. Yamasaki, interview.

23. Miyako City, "Miyako-City Tarō Story" [in Japanese], November 22, 2015, 27, https://www.mlit.go.jp/common/001154345.pdf.

24. Mägdefrau, "Urban Resilience," 64.

25. MLIT, "Future Coastal Seawall Development" [in Japanese], May 28, 2012, 5–7, http://www.bousai.go.jp/jishin/nankai/taisaku_wg/2/pdf/1.pdf.

26. Kuwada, "Public Works," 19.

27. MLIT, "Guidelines for Setting Tsunami Inundation Assumptions Ver. 2.0" [in Japanese], October 2012, 13, https://www.mlit.go.jp/river/shishin_guideline/bousai/saigai/tsunami/shinsui_settei.pdf.

28. Yamazaki Masakatsu, "A Journalist's Insight — Consider the Seawalls — 6 Years after the Great East Japan Earthquake" [in Japanese], *Mainichi Shimbun,* March 23, 2017, https://mainichi.jp/articles/20170323/org/00m/070/003000c.

29. Kuwada, "Public Works," 18.

30. Onoda, Tsukuda, and Suzuki, "Complexities," 6.

31. Ubaura Michio, professor at the International Research Institute of Disaster Science, Tohoku University, interview by author and Saeko Baird, September 15, 2020.

32. MLIT, "Basic Approach to the Restoration of Coastal Seawalls Damaged by the 2011 Tohoku Region Pacific Ocean Earthquake and Tsunami" [in Japanese], November 16, 2011, 8–9, http://www.mlit.go.jp/river/shinngikai_blog/kaigantsunamitaisaku/kangaekata/kangaekata111116.pdf.

33. Ubaura, interview.

34. MLIT, "Guidelines for Landscape in Restoration of Rivers and Coastal Structures" [in Japanese], November 2011, https://www.mlit.go.jp/river/shinngikai_blog/hukkyuukeikan/tebiki/tebiki.pdf.

35. Kuwada, "Public Works," 13.

36. MOE (Ministry of Environment), "Response to Recovery and Restoration from the Great East Japan Earthquake" [in Japanese] October 16, 2013, 12, https://www.env.go.jp/council/02policy/y0212-01/mato4_2.pdf.

37. Akimoto, "Problems of Plan-Making," 28.

38. Miyagi Prefecture, "Landscape and Environment-Conscious Approaches to Disaster Recovery Works Following the Great East-Japan Earthquake" [in Japanese], March 2017, 16–24, https://www.pref.miyagi.jp/documents/13704/616110.pdf.

39. Kuwada, "Public Works," 17–18.

40. MLIT, "Review of the Height of Seawalls According to Local Conditions" [in Japanese], June 2020, https://www.mlit.go.jp/river/kaigan/main/fukkyufukko/pdf/fukkyufukko02_1706.pdf.

41. MLIT, "Approach to Tsunami Disaster Mitigation Measures Based on the Great East Japan Earthquake" [in Japanese], 2020, https://www.mlit.go.jp/river/kaigan/main/fukkyufukko/pdf/fukkyufukko04_1908.pdf.

42. Megumi Lim, "Seven Years after Tsunami, Japanese Live Uneasily with Seawalls," Reuters, March 10, 2018, https://www.reuters.com/article/us-japan-disaster-seawalls/seven-years-after-tsunami-japanese-live-uneasily-with-seawalls-idUSKCN1GL0DK.

43. Parady, Tran, and Gilmour, "Effect of Seawalls," 535–39.

44. NHK, "Super Currents which Seawalls Create—Ankle Depth Tsunami Can Sweep Away Humans" [in Japanese], March 2, 2020, https://www3.nhk.or.jp/news/special/saigai/select-news/20200302_01.html.

45. Residents in Yoriki and Niranohama, interview by author, July 2012.

46. Abe Mariko and Masuzawa Aruha, "Seawall and Environmental Assessment" [in Japanese], The Nature Conservation Society of Japan, last modified February 15, 2016, https://www.nacsj.or.jp/archive/2016/02/602/.

47. MOE, Biodiversity Center of Japan, "Tohoku Region Pacific Coastline Natural Environment Survey" [in Japanese], 2016, 16, http://www.shiokaze.biodic.go.jp/data/27pamphlet/digest.pdf.

48. Hatakeyama, *Forest Is Longing,* 96, 106.

49. Tanaka Katsumi, "Re-weaving 'Connections'" [in Japanese], Field Science Education and Research Center, Kyoto University, last updated April 13, 2020, https://fserc.kyoto-u.ac.jp/wp/social/2020/04/13/tanaka/3/.

50. Japan Society of Civil Engineers, "Technical Guidelines for Planning Coastal Protection Facilities against Tsunami" [in Japanese], June 2021, 4, https://coastal.jp/files/202106Technical_Guideline_for_Planning_of_Coastal_Protection_Facilities_against_Tsunami.pdf.

51. Kesennuma City, "Live with the Ocean" [in Japanese], special issue, *Kesennuma Magazine,* November 15, 2011, 1–4, https://www.kesennuma.miyagi.jp/sec/s019/010/050/010/hukko_keikaku_gaiyou.pdf.

52. Abe, "Consensus Building," 38, 40–41.

53. Abe Toshihiko, co-founder of SMDW and associate professor at Ritsumeikan University, email interview by author and Saeko Baird, August 17, 2020.

54. Kesennuma City, " Winners of 2019 Good Design Award" [in Japanese], December 13, 2019, https://www.kesennuma.miyagi.jp/sec/s002/020/030/050/020/080/0112/2019-12-13_toshikei.pdf.

55. Abe Toshihiko, interview by author's team member Endo Kenya, July 29, 2019.

56. MLIT, "About Super Levees" [in Japanese], accessed November 29, 2018, 1, http://www.mlit.go.jp/river/kasen/koukikaku/pdf/about.pdf.

57. Stein et al., "Hazard Assessment."

58. TMG, "Estimated Damage to Tokyo Due to the Nankai Trough Mega Earthquake" [in Japanese], May 26, 2013, 3, https://www.bousai.metro.tokyo.lg.jp/_res/projects/default_project/_page_/001/000/402/20130514gaiyou.pdf.

59. TMG, "River Facility Development Plan for Eastern Lowlands" [in Japanese], last modified December 27, 2012, https://www.kensetsu.metro.tokyo.lg.jp/jigyo/river/teichi_seibi/tobu_taishin/tobu_taishin.html.

60. Philip Brasor and Masako Tsubuku, "Flood Control: Destroying Neighborhoods to Save Them," *Japan Times,* October 24, 2010.

61. Kundzewicz and Takeuchi, "Flood Protection," 426.

62. MLIT, "About Super Levees," 4.

63. Kryspin-Watson et al., *Learning from Japan,* 140.

64. Tsuchiya and Mitsuhashi, "High Levee," 26–30.

65. Cameron Allan McKean, "Tokyo Building Enormous 'Super-Levees' to Hold Back Its River," Next City, December 4, 2013, https://nextcity.org/daily/entry/tokyo-is-building-enormous-super-levees-to-hold-back-its-river.

66. Hashiguchi, Hirabayashi, and Yamazaki, "High-Standard Levee," 76.

67. Miyagi Prefecture, *Survey Report on Tree Species Suitable for Coastal Disaster Mitigation Forests* [in Japanese], March 2012, 1, https://www.pref.miyagi.jp/documents/23707/113397.pdf.

68. Ranghieri and Ishiwatari, *Learning from Megadisasters,* 118.

69. Imamura and Suppasri, "Damage," 26.

70. MAFF, "Examination Based on Field Research" [in Japanese], Fifth Study Group on Rehabilitation of Coastal Disaster Management Forest after the Great East Japan Earthquake, January 25, 2014, 3–11, https://www.rinya.maff.go.jp/j/tisan/tisan/pdf/dai5kai-siryou1-4-1.pdf.

71. Shuto Nobuo, "Effects and Limits of Coastal Forests against Tsunami Attack" [in Japanese], in *Proceedings of the Coastal Engineering JSCE, no.* 32 (1985): 465–69.

72. Pasha et al., "Tsunami Mitigation."

73. PNV is used to evaluate the theoretical potential of the natural environment of an area, alongside the environmental and geographical consequences of the area's modification by human activities over time.

74. MLIT, "Resilient Structure of Seawalls" [in Japanese], accessed February 3, 2013, https://www.mlit.go.jp/river/shinngikai_blog/kaigan_hyouka/dai01/09-08.pdf.

75. Strusińska-Correia, "Tsunami Mitigation," 402.

76. Morino Project, "2018 Annual Report" [in Japanese], last modified January 2, 2019, https://tanokura.blog.jp/archives/77982204.html.

77. Watanabe, Mikami, and Shibayama, "Tsunami Attenuation," I_301–I_306.

78. Cabinet Secretariat, "Proposals for Reconstruction," 8–9.

79. Miyagi Prefecture, "Miyagi Coastal Forest Restoration Activities for Everyone" [in Japanese], last modified March 25, 2021, https://www.pref.miyagi.jp/soshiki/sinrin/minmori.html.

80. Suppasri et al., "Lessons Learned," 1002.

81. Nateghi et al., "Statistical Analysis," 17.

82. Harada and Imamura, "Effects of Coastal Forest."

83. Lunghino et al., "Tsunami Mitigation Parks."

84. White, "Flood Plain."

RESETTLEMENT

1. Shuto and Fujima, "Short History," 268–69.

2. Yamaguchi, *Tsunami and Villages.*

3. Sugito, "Showa Sanriku Tsunami," 118–20.

4. Maki, "Long-Term Recovery," 5.

5. Murao and Isoyama, "Transition of Housing."

6. Coaffee and Lee, *Urban Resilience,* 206.

7. Shimamura, "Environmental Impact Assessment," 61–62.

8. MLIT and MOE, "Technical Guide for Specific Environmental Impact Assessment Based on the

Great East-Japan Earthquake Special Area Act" [in Japanese], May 2012, 3–4, http://assess.env.go.jp/files/0_db/seika/0157_01/h23_02.pdf.

9. MOE, "Information for Environmental Impact Assessments" [in Japanese], accessed May 25, 2021, http://assess.env.go.jp/1_seido/1-1_guide/1-4.html.

10. Shimamura, "Environmental Impact Assessment," 61–62.

11. Miyagi Prefecture, "Landscape and Environment-Conscious Approaches," 26.

12. MLIT, "Land Readjustment Project" [in Japanese], accessed May 21, 2021, https://www.mlit.go.jp/crd/city/sigaiti/shuhou/kukakuseiri/kukakuseiri01.htm.

13. MLIT, "Guidance on Propagation of Land Readjustment Projects in the Affected Areas of the Great East-Japan Earthquake" [in Japanese], January 2012, 2–3, https://www.mlit.go.jp/toshi/city/sigaiti/toshi_urbanmainte_tk_000003.html.

14. Hirohara, "Rebuild Housing," 55.

15. Zakota Eiji and Tsusaka Naoki, "Disaster-Stricken Land to Be Purchased at High Prices, Promoting Relocation on the Assumption of Recovery" [in Japanese], *Asahi Shimbun,* November 24, 2011.

16. Reconstruction Agency, "Case Studies on Using Relocation Sites for Collective Relocations (Additional Edition)" [in Japanese], July 2017, https://www.reconstruction.go.jp/topics/m17/06/20170630_motochijireisyu_kisya.pdf.

17. MLIT, "Relocation of Hazardous Housing Near Cliffs and Other Risky Areas Project" [in Japanese], accessed May 21, 2021, https://www.mlit.go.jp/river/kasen/tokuteitoshikasen/pdf/7.pdf.

18. MLIT, "Summaries of the Disaster Preemptive Relocation Promotion Projects" [in Japanese], 2023, 11–12, https://www.mlit.go.jp/toshi/content/001609107.pdf.

19. Kondo, "Utilization and Expected Role," 2043–44.

20. MLIT, "List of Disaster Preparedness Collective Relocation Projects after the Great East Japan Earthquake" [in Japanese], last modified March 2023, https://www.mlit.go.jp/toshi/content/001610728.pdf.

21. MLIT, "Guidance for the Disaster Preparedness Collective Relocation Plan" [in Japanese], April 2023, 34–36, https://www.mlit.go.jp/toshi/content/001515251.pdf.

22. Imakawa Satoru, "Kesennuma Reconstruction Report 22: Trial and Error in Disaster Preparedness Collective Relocations" [in Japanese], December 12, 2015, 4, http://imakawa.net/wp/wp-content/uploads/8373d1c1e19cc3e19c87abd4a111ce0b.pdf.

23. Miyagi Citizens' Center for Great East Japan Earthquake Recovery and Restoration, "Great East Japan Earthquake after 5 Years: Overview of Miyagi's Reconstruction Status and Creative Initiatives" [in Japanese], June 19, 2016, 50–51, http://www.miyagikenmin-fukkoushien.com/pdf/material/6.19%205shuunensoukai%20pp.pdf.

24. Inamura, "Relocation Plan."

25. Imakawa Satoru, "Land Lease Fees of Kesennuma Disaster Preparedness Collective Relocation Plan" [in Japanese], last modified May 21, 2015, http://imakawa.net.

26. Reconstruction Agency, "Current Status and Challenges of Reconstruction" [in Japanese], July 2020, 4.

27. Ishibashi Hideaki, "Eight Years, Housing Reconstruction Almost Complete" [in Japanese], *Asahi Shimbun,* March 13, 2019.

28. Ishibashi, "Eight Years."

29. Iuchi and Olshansky, "Tohoku's 5-Year Recovery," 108.

30. Great East Japan Earthquake Reconstruction Support Miyagi Municipal Center, "5 Years," 51.

31. MLIT, "List of Disaster Preparedness Collective Relocation Projects."

32. Gusman and Tanioka, "Tsunami Inundation Forecasts," 158.

33. Rikuzentakata City, "Rikuzentakata Great East Japan Earthquake Investigation Report Summary" [in Japanese], August 2014, 2, https://www.city.rikuzentakata.iwate.jp/material/files/group/61/kensyouhoukokusyo_gaiyou.pdf.

34. Ogata Ryoichi, Rikuzentakata city officer, interview by author's team member Endo Kenya, August 7, 2019.

35. Rikuzentakata City, "Rikuzentakata Reconstruction Grant Program: Progress Report for FY2018" [in Japanese], March 2018, 1, https://www.pref.iwate.jp/_res/projects/default_project/_page_/001/022/442/30progress_rikutaka.pdf.

36. Rikuzentakata City, "Rikuzentakata Disaster Reconstruction Implementation Plan" [in Japanese], 2018, 15, https://www.city.rikuzentakata.iwate.jp/material/files/group/46/30-3.pdf.

37. Iwate Prefecture, "Exclusion Items from the Great East Earthquake and Tsunami Reconstruction Projects," 2019, https://www.pref.iwate.jp/kurashikankyou/kenchiku/tochi/riyou/1010191.html.

38. Nakamuta, Yamamoto, and Urabe, "Ground Raising."

39. Kotani Hiroshi, "Cost-Effectiveness of the Reconstruction Projects," *Nikkei XTECH,* March 11, 2015, https://xtech.nikkei.com/kn/article/knp/column/20150310/694269/.

40. Yokoyama Katsuhide, "Earthquake Reconstruction and Tidal Flat Restoration in Moune, Kesennuma" [in Japanese], July 29, 2012, https://www.pref.chiba.lg.jp/kansei/sanbanze/meeting/documents/01siryou1.pdf.

41. Fieldwork in Utatsu, 2011.

42. Matsubara H., "Municipal Merger," 65.

43. Matsubara H., "Municipal Merger," 60.

44. Matsubara H., "Municipal Merger," 59.

45. Miyasada, "Livelihood Rehabilitation."

46. Ishinomaki City, "Ishinomaki Disaster Preparedness Collective Relocation Plans" [in Japanese], 2020, https://www.city.ishinomaki.lg.jp/cont/10184000/100/8541/0001/02_ichizu_hanto_ogatu2.pdf.

47. "What Does the Massive Seawall Protect from Tsunami? Residents Leaving Their Hometowns. Ogatsu, Miyagi Prefecture" [in Japanese], *Asahi Shimbun,* January 31, 2016.

48. Miyagi Prefecture, "Current Status of Seawall Recovery and Reconstruction in Miyagi Prefecture" [in Japanese], last modified May 17, 2021, https://www.pref.miyagi.jp/soshiki/kasen/levee-1.html.

49. "Final Participants Start Reconstruction in Ogatsu District, Ishinomaki, Miyagi Prefecture" [in Japanese], *Nikkei Shimbun,* April 9, 2020, https://www.nikkei.com/article/DGXMZO57830100Y0A400C2L01000/.

50. Suzuki Kiyomi, "Returning Home and Returning to the Community! Utatsu Yoriki's New Leader" [in Japanese], *Minami Sanriku Now,* November 9, 2018, http://m-now.net/2018/11/kirameki.html.

51. MLIT, "Reconstruction Machizukuri Minamisanriku" [in Japanese], 2013, 3, http://www.thr.mlit.go.jp/bumon/b06111/kenseibup/pdf_tokai/h25.5_04jirei.pdf.

52. Suzuki K., "Returning Home."

53. MLIT, "Reconstruction Machizukuri," 4.

54. Yoriki resident, interview by Endo Kenya, 2019.

55. Minamisanriku Town, "Yoriki/Niranohama District Complex (40 Units) Completed" [in Japanese], October 30, 2016, https://www.town.minamisanriku.miyagi.jp/index.cfm/6,4215,81,316.html.

56. MLIT, "Status of Machizukuri Efforts to Improve Disaster Preparedness" [in Japanese], January 8, 2020, 27.

57. MLIT, "Machizukuri Efforts," 5.

58. MLIT, "Collection of Support Measures for the Formation of Compact Cities—Five Perspectives on Coexisting with Urban Agriculture" [in Japanese], accessed May 21, 2021, https://www.mlit.go.jp/toshi/city_plan/toshi_city_plan_tk_000026.html.

59. Ogawa Seiji, "Yamamoto: The Future of Rebuilding Homes and Communities" [in Japanese], in *Urgent Symposium: Reconstruction of Housing with Hope for Everyone,* November 8, 2015, 8, http://www.miyagikenmin-fukkoushien.com/pdf/material/11.8kinnkyuushinnpo%20yamamoto.pdf.

60. Tokyo Institute for Municipal Research, "Reconstruction and Self-Governance—General Research on Reconstruction and Regeneration of Municipalities" [in Japanese], 2017, 151–52, https://www.timr.or.jp/publish/200_all.pdf.

61. Hoshi, Akagawa, and Kanai, "Compact City," 612.

62. Ogawa, "Yamamoto," 2, 3–8.

63. Yamamoto Town, "Urban Reconstruction Efficiency Programs" [in Japanese], last modified July 11, 2019, https://www.town.yamamoto.miyagi.jp/site/fukkou/294.html.

64. Yamamoto Town, "Enforcement of Ordinance on Tsunami Disaster Hazard Zones" [in Japanese], last modified May 25, 2016, https://www.town.yamamoto.miyagi.jp/site/fukkou/318.html.

65. Yamamoto Town, "Notice about Purchase of Housing Lots" [in Japanese], last modified February 6, 2018, https://www.town.yamamoto.miyagi.jp/site/fukkou/3516.html.

66. Muroi Kenji, "Reconstruction Situation of Communities in the Sendai Plain Areas—Iwanuma City, Watari Town, and Yamamoto Town" [in Japanese], 2019, 10, http://www.waseda.jp/prj-sustain/Kaken2019-23/Kaken2019/2019_2-1%20muroi.pdf.

67. MLIT and Miyagi Prefecture, "Sendai Bay South Coastal Levee Complete—Major Step Forward in Tsunami Management and Mitigation Measures" [in Japanese], February 26, 2016, 4, https://www.thr.mlit.go.jp/sendai/kasen_kaigan/fukkou/pdf/160226.pdf.

68. Hoshi, Akagawa, and Kanai, "Compact City," 612–14.

69. Yamamoto Reconstruction Residential Association, *Strawberry Newspaper,* August 1, 2012, https://www.kahoku.co.jp/special/kawara/pdf/ichigo_03.pdf.

70. Ogawa, "Yamamoto," 11.

71. Yamamoto Town, "Residential Land Bōsai Construction Subsidy Guidelines" [in Japanese], *Yamamoto Town Magazine* 406 (September 2013): 4–5, https://www.town.yamamoto.miyagi.jp/uploaded/attachment/259.pdf.

72. Muroi, "Reconstruction Situation," 12.

73. Great East Japan Earthquake Reconstruction Support Miyagi Municipal Center, "5 Years," 20.

74. Yamamoto Town, "Yamamoto Regional Creation General Strategies" [in Japanese], March 2021, 12, https://www.town.yamamoto.miyagi.jp/uploaded/attachment/12729.pdf.

75. The additional 19 percent is covered through regional tax refunds. MLIT, "Preemptive Relocation Promotion Projects," 4.

76. National Governors Association, "Preparing for National Level Catastrophic Disasters" [in Japanese], May 2020, 9, http://www.nga.gr.jp/.

77. MLIT, "Preemptive Relocation Promotion Projects," 1–2.

78. MLIT, "Preemptive Relocation Promotion Projects," 5–7.

79. MLIT, "Preemptive Relocation Promotion Projects," 4.

80. MLIT, "Status of Machizukuri Efforts to Improve Bōsai Efforts" [in Japanese], January 8, 2020, 14, https://www.mlit.go.jp/common/001323942.pdf.

81. *Nikkei XTECH,* "MLIT Considers Whether to Regulate Housing Sites that Neglect Disaster Preparedness" [in Japanese], March 7, 2019, https://xtech.nikkei.com/atcl/nxt/column/18/00142/00365/.

82. Shimizu Yushi, "Increase of Collective Relocation in Areas Damaged by Torrential Rain around Gōno River, Shimane" [in Japanese], December 1, 2020, https://www.asahi.com/articles/ASNCZ725XNBFPTIB009.html.

83. Japan Agricultural News, "Hoping for a Disaster Resilient Region: Half Year Passed after Shimane/Gōnokawa River Flooding; Many Issues Arise after Deciding Relocation" [in Japanese], January 14, 2021, https://news.livedoor.com/article/detail/20825714/.

84. Sakakibara Orina, "Housing Lot Development Completed for Collective Relocation Site, River Flood Mitigation Measures: Misato Town, Shimane Prefecture" [in Japanese], *Asahi Shimbun,* March 1, 2023, https://www.asahi.com/articles/ASR3K6WV9R3KPTIB006.html.

85. NHK, "184 Municipalities Nationwide under Tsunami Inundation Risk According to NHK Research" [in Japanese], NHK, January 7, 2021.

86. "More than 40 Percent of Municipalities Implemented or Plan Relocation to Higher Ground to Avoid Tsunami" [in Japanese], *Asahi Shimbun,* December 21, 2020.

87. Sakamoto Yohei, "Relocating Public Facilities to Higher Ground in Preparation for the Nankai Trough Earthquake" [in Japanese], *Nikkei XTECH,* March 17, 2021, https://xtech.nikkei.com/atcl/nxt/column/18/01581/00012/.

88. Koyama Masahiko (city staff, Minamiise), email interview by author and Saeko Baird, August 11, 2020.

89. Minamiise Town, "Disaster Preparedness, such as Nankai Trough Earthquake" [in Japanese], *Minamiise Paper,* May 2020, 7.

90. Sakamoto Yohei, "Minami Ise's 'Preemptive Reconstruction,' Relocating Public Facilities to Higher Ground in Preparation for the Nankai Trough Earthquake" [in Japanese], *Nikkei XTECH,* March 17, 2021, https://xtech.nikkei.com/atcl/nxt/column/18/01581/00012/.

91. "Welcoming Young People to Minami-Ise: Aiming for Population Increase with Housing" [in Japanese], *Asahi Shimbun,* April 4, 2020, https://www.asahi.com/articles/ASN436W1TN2XONFB015.html.

92. Minamiise Town, "Subsidies for the Acquisition of New and Used Housing" [in Japanese], January 20, 2021, https://www.town.minamiise.lg.jp/iju/kurasisumai/1489.html.

93. Koyama, interview.

94. Minamiise Town, "New Kizuna Project" [in Japanese], September 2019, 10, https://www.town.minamiise.lg.jp/material/files/group/21/sougoukeikaku_gaiyou2019.pdf.

95. Maki, Norio, and Laurie Johnson, "How Will We Manage Recovery from a Catastrophic Disaster? Organization Structure for Recovery Management in the World," *Journal of Disaster Research* 11, no. 5 (2016): 895, https://doi.org/10.20965/jdr.2016.p0889.

URBAN SYSTEMS DISCUSSION

1. Roy, "Urban Informality."
2. Spirn, "Restoring Mill Creek."
3. Shatkin, "Bottom Line."
4. Nagamatsu, "Building Back," 38, 53.
5. TMG, "Disaster Reconstruction Grand Design" [in Japanese], May 2001, 2–4, https://www.toshiseibi.metro.tokyo.lg.jp/bosai/gd/honbun.htm.

6. TMG, "Grand Design for Urban Planning (Draft) Publication and Implementation of Public Comments" [in Japanese], last modified November 1, 2017, https://www.toshiseibi.metro.tokyo.lg.jp/kanko/toshi/public.html.

7. TMG, "Tokyo Metropolitan Earthquake Reconstruction Manual—Reconstruction Process Version" [in Japanese], March 2003, amended March 2016, https://www.bousai.metro.tokyo.lg.jp/_res/projects/default_project/_page_/001/000/404/purosesu.pdf.

8. TMG, "Tokyo Metropolitan Earthquake Reconstruction Manual," 9–19; TMG, "Handbook for Pre-Reconstruction of Urban Areas" [in Japanese], 2015, https://www.toshiseibi.metro.tokyo.lg.jp/bunyabetsu/bosai/pdf/shuto_01.pdf.

9. TMG, "Pre-Reconstruction Efforts for an Earthquake Directly Under the Tokyo Metropolitan Area" [in Japanese], last modified 2020, 12, https://www.toshiseibi.metro.tokyo.lg.jp/bunyabetsu/bosai/shuto.html.

10. TMG, "Tokyo Metropolitan Earthquake Reconstruction Manual," 49, 52–53.

11. TMG, "Outline of the Subsidy for the Promotion of Community Collaborative Reconstruction Projects" [in Japanese], April 26, 2019; modified May 18, 2020, https://www.toshiseibi.metro.tokyo.lg.jp/jouhou/pdf/hojyoshisyutsu_r1_03_01.pdf.

12. TMG, "Issues and Response Policies for Urban Reconstruction Procedures (Draft)" [in Japanese], September 7, 2018, https://www.toshiseibi.metro.tokyo.lg.jp/bunyabetsu/bosai/pdf/iinkai_05.pdf.

13. The Urban Risk Lab at MIT has been developing an online Preemptive Housing Recovery platform to run workshops with US localities since 2017, supported by FEMA and MIT Climate Grand Challenges. See https://urbanrisklab.org/work#/preemptive-recovery-platform/.

4. PARK NETWORKS

1. Sorensen, *Making of Urban Japan,* 43.

2. Tatsumi, *Park Culture,* 14.

3. Tokyo Metropolitan Archives, "First Grand Plan for Tokyo Remodeling" [in Japanese], accessed August 15, 2020, https://www.soumu.metro.tokyo.lg.jp/01soumu/archives/0701syoko_kara08.htm.

4. Shirahata, *History of Modern Urban Parks,* 186–91.

5. TMG, "Greenbelt Concept," 58–59, https://www.toshiseibi.metro.tokyo.lg.jp/jouhou/pdf/hojyoshisyutsu_r1_03_01.pdf.

6. Iinuma and Shirahata, *Park as Japanese Culture,* 6–8.

7. Tatsumi, *Park Culture,* 40, 55–56.

8. Schencking, *Great Kanto Earthquake,* 336.

9. Imaizumi, *Sacred Space,* 152.

10. CAO, "Lessons Learned from 1923," first section, 35–36.

11. Kawada and Yanagida, "Relationship."

12. Soma, "Study on the Fire Tornado," 16.

13. Saito Yohei, "Looking Back on the Great Hanshin-Awaji Earthquake 20 Years Later: Initiatives for Greening the Park and Park Development" [in Japanese], presentation at Kobe City Hall, June 25, 2015.

14. Sakamoto, *Parks in Japan,* 15–16.

15. Koshizawa, *Reconstruction Planning,* 40–41.

16. Yasuba, "Small Urban Parks," 429–32.

17. Nakajima, "Elementary Schools and Parks."

18. Koshizawa, *Reconstruction Planning,* 78–79.

19. Bunkyō Ward, "Motomachi Park" [in Japanese], last modified September 20, 2014, https://www.city.bunkyo.lg.jp/bosai/midori/kuritukouen/kouen/motomachi.html.

20. Seidensticker, *Tokyo Rising,* 11–12.

21. For example, the fire-shielding rate of *Ginkgo* is 99.99 percent; Chinese parasol tree, 98 percent; Japanese zelkova, 94.36 percent; and *Platanus,* 91.36 percent. Fire-resistant trees should have low oil content, high water ratio, and high shielding effect. See Organization for Landscape and Urban Green Infrastructure, *Bōsaikōen Technical Handbook,* 27–28, 289–310.

22. Isoya Shinji, "Preservation of Landscape Legacy" [in Japanese], *Gakujutsu no Dōkō,* March 2008, 76–79, https://www.jstage.jst.go.jp/article/tits1996/13/3/13_76/_pdf.

23. Imaizumi, *Sacred Space,* 144.

24. Hara et al., "Historic Consideration."

25. Kumagai, Gibson, and Filion, "Evaluating Long-Term Urban Resilience," 1026.

26. MLIT, "Current Situation and Issues of Green Policies" [in Japanese], 2006, 24, https://www.mlit.go.jp/singikai/infra/city_history/city_planning/park_green/h18_1/images/shiryou06.pdf.

27. Minomo, Takanashi, and Goto, "Park Governance," 179.

28. Luo et al., "Flood Control Policies."

29. Park et al., "Study on Water," 209.

30. POSA, "Summary on Disaster Management Parks after the Great Hanshin-Awaji Earthquake" [in Japanese], in *2006 Second Disaster Management Park Committee Material,* April 28, 2006, 2–3.

31. Kashihara, Ueno, and Morita, *Research on Shelters,* 142–43, 148.

32. Kashihara, Ueno, and Morita, *Research on Shelters,* 139–51.

33. POSA, "Summary on Disaster Management Parks," 4.

34. Kobe City, "Great Hanshin-Awaji Earthquake and Active Fault in Kobe" [in Japanese], July 1999.

35. Hyogo Earthquake Memorial 21st Century Research Institute, "Research Report on Financial Management of Affected Local Governments in the Great Hanshin-Awaji Earthquake" [in Japanese], 2006, 20.

36. MLIT, "Greening Priority Districts Planning Guideline" [in Japanese], April 1, 1997, https://www.mlit.go.jp/notice/noticedata/sgml/035/76000238/76000238.html.

37. Kobe City, "Green Kobe 21 Plan" [in Japanese], accessed May 21, 2021, https://www.city.kobe.lg.jp/a51321/shise/kekaku/kensetsukyoku/green/2010kaitei.html.

38. MLIT, "Urban Foothills Green Belt Development Project" [in Japanese], accessed May 21, 2021, https://www.mlit.go.jp/river/basic_info/yosan/gaiyou/yosan/h16budget/pdf/p34.pdf.

39. Tanaka, "Development of the Administration," 138, 139.

40. Kobe, "Revision of the Kobe Green Master Plan—Priority Issues to Be Reflected in the Kobe Green Master Plan—Summary of the Mid-Term Report (Draft)" [in Japanese], August 13, 2010, https://www.city.kobe.lg.jp/documents/8008/greenkobegaiyouban.pdf.

41. Park et al., "Study on Water," 219.

42. NILIM, *Guidelines for Planning,* 26.

43. CAO, "109: Parks and Green Spaces," in *Research on Summary and Validation of Survey of Great Hanshin-Awaji Earthquake* [in Japanese], 5, http://www.bousai.go.jp/kensho-hanshinawaji/chosa/index.htm.

44. CAO, "Maintenance Concept for Extensive Bōsai Hubs in Metropolitan Tokyo" [in Japanese], August 27, 2001, 2, https://www.bousai.go.jp/jishin/sonota/pdf/kihonkousou.pdf.

1. CAO, *2005 White Paper,* fig. 2-4-30.

2. Maekawa, "Disaster Medical Care Systems," 44.

3. CAO, *2010 White Paper on Disaster Management in Japan* [in Japanese], 2010, https://www.bousai.go.jp/kaigirep/hakusho/pdf/h20hakusyo.pdf, fig. 2-3-37.

4. The Tokyo Rinkai Disaster Prevention Park, "Flow of Disaster Response," accessed October 3, 2018, http://www.tokyorinkai-koen.jp/en/flow/.

5. The Tokyo Rinkai Disaster Prevention Park, "What Is This Base?," accessed May 20, 2021, http://www.tokyorinkai-koen.jp/en/what/.

6. MLIT, "Development of a Core Wide Area Disaster Prevention Center in the Tokyo Bay Waterfront Area" [in Japanese], January 29, 2014, http://www.ktr.mlit.go.jp/ktr_content/content/000098475.pdf.

7. Kawasaki City, "Kawasaki Tsunami Evacuation Plan" [in Japanese], April 24, 2013, 1 and 11, https://www.city.kawasaki.jp/601/cmsfiles/contents/0000047/47692/tsunamihinankeikaku.pdf.

8. Tokyo Rinkai Park, "General Introduction," http://www.tokyorinkai-koen.jp/en/.

9. Manager of Tokyo Rinkai Disaster Prevention Park, interview by author and Taketani Maya, July 17, 2015.

10. Director of Tokyo Rinkai Disaster Prevention Park, interview by author and Taketani Maya, July 17, 2015.

11. Tokyo Rinkai Park, "Park Facilities," http://www.tokyorinkai-koen.jp/en/park/.

12. CAO, "Concept for the Bōsai Hubs in the Keihanshin Metropolitan Area" [in Japanese], June 20, 2003, 2, http://www.bousai.go.jp/kohou/oshirase/h15/pdf/030620kousouo.pdf.

13. MLIT, "Sakai Senboku Port Sakai 2nd District Basic Disaster Management Base Development Project" [in Japanese], November 2015, 4, https://www.kkr.mlit.go.jp/plan/ippan/zigyohyoka/ol9a8voooooci17-att/5.pdf.

14. MLIT Kinki Regional Development Bureau, "Sakai Senboku Port Sakai 2nd District Multimodal Transport Project (Earthquake-Resistant)" [in Japanese], 2017, https://www.kkr.mlit.go.jp/plan/ippan/zigyohyoka/ol9a8voooooocg01-att/4.pdf.

15. MLIT, "Floating Disaster Management Base" [in Japanese], accessed September 16, 2018, http://www.pa.kkr.mlit.go.jp/kobeport/_know/p6/html/p-3-9.html.

16. MLIT, "Sakai Senboku Port 2 Ward National Disaster Prevention Bases" [in Japanese], March 7, 2013, 6, https://www.kkr.mlit.go.jp/plan/safety/bousai/bousairenraku/qgl8vloooooo7nmk-att/shiryou041_1.pdf.

17. MLIT, "Floating Disaster Management Base."

18. "Disaster Management Floats in Three Major Bays Unable to Move Due to Lack of Strength" [in Japanese], *Asahi Shimbun,* February 26, 2012, http://www.asahi.com/special/10005/OSK201202250041.html.

19. Organization for Landscape and Urban Green Infrastructure, *Bōsaikōen Technical Handbook,* 2nd ed., 167.

20. Hyogo Prefectural Emergency Management Training Center website, last modified May 12, 2021, https://www.fire-ac-hyogo.jp/.

21. E-Defense test observed by author, March 29, 2007.

22. MEXT, "Summary of the Proposed Budget for 2015: Promoting Science and Technology Innovation to Realize Growth Strategy" [in Japanese], January 2015, 13, https://www.mext.go.jp/b_menu/shingi/gijyutu/gijyutu2/067/shiryo/__icsFiles/afieldfile/2015/01/23/1354622_4.pdf.

23. Hyogo Prefecture, "Hyogo Prefectural Miki Emergency Management Base," 2005, https://www.fire-ac-hyogo.jp/downLoadFiles/pamphlet/hyogoPrefecturalMikiEmergensyManagementBase.pdf.

24. Pollock, "Beans Dome."

25. Endo Shuhei Architect Institute, "Slowtecture M," accessed May 21, 2021, http://www.paramodern.com/SM.html.

26. Organization for Landscape and Urban Green Infrastructure, *Bōsaikōen Technical Handbook,* 2nd ed., 168.

27. Miki City, "The 39th Disaster Management Festival" [in Japanese], September 29, 2019, https://www.city.miki.lg.jp/uploaded/attachment/14959.pdf.

28. Fieldwork, Miki Sōgō Bōsaikōen, April 5, 2007.

29. Fukuoka Prefectural Assembly, "Opinion Paper on the Development of a Core Regional Disaster Management Base in Kyushu" [in Japanese], June 27, 2012, http://www.gikai.pref.fukuoka.lg.jp/honkaigi/kaketsu-24062701.html.

30. Chūbu Region Strategy Meeting on Nankai Trough Earthquake Countermeasures, 2020, https://www.cbr.mlit.go.jp/senryaku/pdf/senryakukaigi_pamphlet2020.pdf.

MIXED BŌSAI HUBS

1. Tokyo Park Association, "Facilities in Bōsaikōen" [in Japanese], accessed May 21, 2021, https://www.tokyo-park.or.jp/special/bousai/sisetsu.html.

2. Oji Zoo Staff, "Zoo Director's Report 71: Thinking about Zoos II" [in Japanese], Kobe Oji Zoo, November 1, 2016, http://www.kobe-ojizoo.jp/blog/date/2016/11/01/.

3. CAO, "Research Report on Extensive Disaster Management Measures in the S.K.Y. Metropolitan Areas" [in Japanese], March 2005, 90, https://www.mlit.go.jp/kokudokeikaku/souhatu/h16seika/10bousai/10_sky2.pdf.

4. Kobe City, "List of Chūō Ward Emergency Evacuation Spaces and Shelters" [in Japanese], March 30, 2021, https://www.city.kobe.lg.jp/documents/20002/tyuuouhinannsyoo30330.pdf.

5. Kobe City, "Kobe Regional Disaster Management Plan (Common Edition)" [in Japanese], June 2023, https://www.city.kobe.lg.jp/documents/14602/01_kyoutuuhen2.pdf.

6. CAO, "Procurement and Distribution of Emergency Supplies in Kyoto Prefecture" [in Japanese], accessed September 15, 2020, https://www8.cao.go.jp/genshiryoku_bousai/pdf/02_fukui_0204l_4.pdf.

7. Kyoto Prefecture, "Kyoto Disaster Countermeasure Air Operations Coordination Manual, Appendix 5, Kyoto Gyoen Forward Base Layout" [in Japanese], April 2018, 7, https://www.pref.kyoto.jp/shingikai/shobo-01/documents/r1-siryou12_1.pdf.

8. Kyoto City, "Usage of Kyoto Imperial Palace During Large-Scale Disasters" [in Japanese], January 27, 2014, https://www.tomoko-kurata.jp/old/hibijoho14/gyoenkinkyu.pdf.

9. Hattori Ryokuchi Park, "Volunteer Activities" [in Japanese], accessed September 15, 2020, http://hattori.osaka-park.or.jp/parklife/minna_parklife/volunteer/.

10. Manager of BBQ Plaza, interview by author and Saeko Baird, April 22, 2019.

11. Park management director of Hattori Ryokuchi Park, interview by author and Saeko Baird, April 22, 2019.

12. Nishino, Himoto, and Tanaka, "Modeling of Destination Choice," 469–77.

13. CAO, "2016 Kumamoto Earthquake" [in Japanese], 2016, http://www.bousai.go.jp/kaigirep/houkokusho/hukkousesaku/saigaitaiou/output_html_1/pdf/201601.pdf.

14. Teshirogi and Okamura, "Evacuation by Vehicle," 59, 60, 62.

15. Organization for Landscape and Urban Green Infrastructure, "2016 Joint Investigation of Kumamoto Earthquake Park Usage" [in Japanese], December 2016, 21, https://urbangreen.or.jp/wp-content/uploads/2017/02/kumamoto-report.pdf.

16. Japanese Institute of Landscape Architecture Kumamoto Earthquake Reconstruction Support Committee, "Actual Use of City Parks in the Kumamoto Earthquake" [in Japanese], 2016, https://janet-dr.com/060_event/170415sympo/170415poster/P14.pdf.

17. Teshirogi and Okamura, "Evacuation by Vehicle," 60–61.

18. Organization for Landscape and Urban Green Infrastructure, "2016 Joint Investigation."

19. Initial evacuation space manager and community leader, interview by author, Kumamoto, August 25, 2018.

20. Organization for Landscape and Urban Green Infrastructure, "2016 Joint Investigation," 19.

21. Suzuki T., *Michi-no-eki.*

22. Ishinomaki City, "List of Collaboration Partners" [in Japanese], last modified May 13, 2020, https://www.city.ishinomaki.lg.jp/cont/10106000/kyotei/kyouteiichiran31.2.15.pdf.

23. MLIT, "Strengthening the Disaster Preparedness Functions of Michi-no-Eki" [in Japanese], accessed May 21, 2021, https://www.mlit.go.jp/road/ir/ir-council/michi-no-eki_third-stage/pdf01/09.pdf.

24. Newswitch, "Bōsai Michi-no-Eki, 1–2 Locations per Prefecture. MLIT Seeks Proposals" [in Japanese], February 26, 2020, https://newswitch.jp/p/21269.

25. MLIT, "39 Stations Selected as 'Roadside Stations for Disaster Prevention' for the First Time!," accessed September 20, 2023, https://www.mlit.go.jp/report/press/content/001408488.pdf.

26. Gifu Tourism Union, "Michi-no-Eki Palette Pier Ōno" [in Japanese], accessed September 15, 2020, https://www.kankou-gifu.jp/spot/6010/.

27. Gifu Prefecture, "New Regional Road Traffic Plan in Gifu Prefecture for Disaster Management Hubs" [in Japanese], March 2021, 3, https://www.pref.gifu.lg.jp/uploaded/attachment/235480.pdf.

28. Gifu Prefecture, "Regional Disaster Management Base" [in Japanese], last modified March 2023, https://www.pref.gifu.lg.jp/page/8447.html.

PRIMARY EVACUATION SPACES

1. MLIT, "Development of Disaster Management Parks" [in Japanese], accessed October 4, 2023, https://www.mlit.go.jp/toshi/park/toshi_parkgreen_tk_000134.html.

2. Sakamoto, *Parks in Japan,* 92.

3. Ema, "Minatogawa Park, Kobe" [in Japanese], *Japan 1000 Parks* (blog), last modified April 5, 2014, https://nippon1000parks.blogspot.com/2014/04/6361000.html.

4. Minatogawa Park, "Minatogawa Park Handcraft Mart" [in Japanese], last modified 2021, https://minatogawa-mart.net/about/.

5. Kobe City, "Hyōgo Prefecture New Office will Open on August 13th" [in Japanese], last modified June 27, 2019, https://www.city.kobe.lg.jp/a57337/shise/shichoshitsu/teireikaiken/h31/310627.html

6. Kobe City, "We Want to Tell You the Story of People Who Are Creating the New KOBE," accessed October 15, 2020, http://1995kobe20th.jp/2010/01/1641/.

7. Iwanuma City, "Millennium Hope Hills: English Home Page," accessed October 20, 2018, https://sennen-kibouno-oka.com/english/.

8. Fieldwork in Iwanuma, Japan, May 2015 and August 2019.

9. Miyagi Prefecture, "Millennium Hope Hills Master Plan" [in Japanese], July 12, 2013, https://www.pref.miyagi.jp/documents/9044/219839.pdf.

10. Nakano Ward, "Urban Planning of Former National Policy Academy" [in Japanese], last modified November 1, 2009, https://www.city.tokyo-nakano.lg.jp/dept/163000/d006792.html.

11. MLIT, "Report on New PPP Procedures for Machizukuri" [in Japanese], March 2017, I-2-20-21, https://www.mlit.go.jp/common/001184451.pdf.

12. Nakano Ward, "Machizukuri of Urban Nakano Shiki (Former Police Academy District)" [in Japanese], last modified November 1, 2009, https://www.city.tokyo-nakano.lg.jp/dept/163000/d006787.html.

13. Tokyo Tatemono, "Bōsai Measures to Maximize Operational Sustainability for Business Owners" [in Japanese], last modified October 2012, https://office.tatemono.com/nakano-centralpark/disaster.html.

14. MLIT, "New PPP Procedures," 5.

15. Kumagai, Gibson, and Filion, "Evaluating Long-Term Urban Resilience," 1036.

16. The AAA JHEP Certification for Futako Tamagawa Raizu, April 2019, https://www.ecosys.or.jp/certification/jhep/case/case73report.pdf.

17. One hundred landscapes in Setagaya Ward were selected by the residents in 1984. See Setagaya Ward, "100 Setagawa Ward Landscapes" [in Japanese], last modified March 23, 2018, https://www.city.setagaya.lg.jp/mokuji/sumai/005/003/d00158931.html.

18. Setagaya Trust & Community Design, "Survey on Kokubunji Gaisen Conservation" [in Japanese], accessed October 15, 2020, https://www.setagayatm.or.jp/trust/research/gaisen/aquatic/index.html.

19. Setagaya Ward, "Tentative Facility Plans" [in Japanese], Futakotamagawa Park Basic Design booklet, August 2011, 7, https://www.city.setagaya.lg.jp/mokuji/sumai/012/002/d00035487_d/fil/35487_1.pdf.

20. Setagaya Ward, Futakotamagawa Park Basic Design booklet, 12.

21. Setagaya Ward, "Residents Participatory Park Planning" [in Japanese], last modified June 19, 2014, https://www.city.setagaya.lg.jp/mokuji/sumai/012/002/d00021384.html.

22. Setagaya Ward, "Futakotamagawa Park Making Newsletters," no. 16, March 3, 2012, https://www.city.setagaya.lg.jp/mokuji/sumai/012/002/d00021384_d/fil/16.pdf.

23. Osaka Prefecture, "Neya River Reservoir" [in Japanese], 2004, https://www.pref.osaka.lg.jp/attach/469/00001460/Neyagawa%20Retarding%20Basin.pdf.

24. Osaka Prefecture, "Neya River Reservoir, Osaka Fukakita Park" [in Japanese], last modified April 9, 2020, https://www.pref.osaka.lg.jp/ne/sougoutisui/neyagawa.html.

25. Neyagawa Report, "Fukakita Ryokuchi Flooded by Heavy Rain Since Last Night" [in Japanese], May 21, 2021, https://www.neyagawa-np.jp/photo/fukakita-park-20210521.html.

26. Fukakita Ryokuchi official Twitter account (@eetoko_park), tweets related to the flood event, May 20, May 21, and June 2, 2021, https://twitter.com/eetoko_park.

27. Osaka Prefecture, "Fukakita Ryokuchi," last modified June 2023, https://www.pref.osaka.lg.jp/ne/sougoutisui/neyagawa.html.

28. CAO, "Guidance on Designation of Emergency Evacuation Spaces," 4.

29. Flüchter, "Tokyo," 234.

INITIAL EVACUATION PARKS AND POCKET PARKS

1. NILIM, *Guidelines for Planning*, 23–29.

2. TMG, "Evacuation Shelters and Evacuation Spaces" [in Japanese], July 2022, https://www.bousai.metro.tokyo.lg.jp/bousai/1000026/1000316.html.

3. Kobe, "Land Readjustment Project in the Built-up Urban Districts" [in Japanese], April 1, 2020, https://www.city.kobe.lg.jp/a13150/shise/kekaku/jutakutoshikyoku/adjustment/index1/index.html.

4. Enforcement Order of the Urban Planning Act, 1969, Article 25, item 6, https://elaws.e-gov.go.jp/search/elawsSearch/elaws_search/lsg0500/detail?lawId=344CO0000000158#272.

5. Kobayashi Ikuo, interview by author, May 29, 2020.

6. Fieldwork in Kamisawa, Kobe, July 2002.

7. Tsuji Nobukazu, interview.

8. Kobe, "Kamisawa Block 1 Park" (community handout), October 2000.

9. Kobe Machizukuri Workshop Kenkyukai, "Workshop Book," 52–53.

10. Kobayashi Ikuo and Yoshihara Makoto, "Park Planning and Management through Workshops among Residents" [in Japanese], 1998, http://web.kyoto-inet.or.jp/org/gakugei/judi/forum/forum8/zi024.htm.

11. Ito, "Earthquake Reconstruction Machizukuri," 166.

12. Resident, interview.

13. Resident, interview.

14. Great Hanshin Awaji Earthquake Reconstruction Foundation, "Aiming for Reconstruction: Reconstruction Foundation 5 Years Progress" [in Japanese], March 2000, 43, https://web.pref.hyogo.lg.jp/kk41/documents/000036471.pdf.

15. Ito, "Earthquake Reconstruction Machizukuri," 169.

16. Shirai Shintaro, "Creative Reconstruction to Create a Safe, Secure and Comfortable Community" [in Japanese], Urban Regeneration and Land Readjustment Association Forum, 2012.

17. Shirai, "Creative Reconstruction," 3.

18. Resident, interview.

19. Bryant and Allan, "Open Space," 192.

20. Shirai, "Creative Reconstruction," 3.

21. "House of Wind—Rokkōmichi Station North District Community House" [in Japanese], last modified May 31, 2021, https://w1.alpha-web.ne.jp/~kazenoie/index.htm.

22. Kobe, "Urban Bōsai Open Space Project" [in Japanese], last modified April 7, 2021, https://www.city.kobe.lg.jp/a96653/shise/kekaku/jutakutoshikyoku/misshu/matinakabousaikuuti.html.

23. Organization for Landscape and Urban Green Infrastructure, *Bōsaikōen Technical Handbook 2015*, 48–49.

24. Shinagawa Ward, "Hon-san Kujira Plaza in Nishi-Gotanda District 4 Opened" [in Japanese], last modified April 16, 2010, https://www.city.shinagawa.tokyo.jp/PC/shinagawaphotonews/shinagawaphotonews-2010/hpg000011148.html.

25. Organization for Landscape and Urban Green Infrastructure, *Bōsaikōen Technical Handbook 2015*, 48–49.

EDUCATION IN PARKS

1. National Institution for Youth Education, "Research on Youth Experience Activity Programs from the Perspective of Disaster Management Education" [in Japanese], March 2011, http://www.niye.go.jp/kenkyu_houkoku/contents/detail/i/68/.

2. NPO *+arts,* "Iza! Kaeru Caravan," accessed August 14, 2018, http://kaeru-caravan.jp/en.html.

3. Nagata, interview.

4. NPO *+arts,* "Red Bear Survival Camp," accessed August 14, 2018, http://red-bear.org/.

5. Organization for Landscape and Urban Green Infrastructure, *Bōsaikōen Technical Handbook,* 2nd ed., 149.

6. Kamakura Park, "Kamakura Central Park" [in Japanese], accessed September 7, 2018, http:// kamakura-park.com/go/central_park/index.html.

7. Kamakura Park, "Kamakura Central Park Festival" [in Japanese], October 27, 2019, http://www .kamakura-park.com/images/2019festival.pdf.

8. Yamazaki Yato Association website, last modified June 1, 2021, http://yato-yamasaki.sakura.ne.jp/.

9. Kamakura City, "Introduction to Kamakura Central Park" [in Japanese], last modified May 10, 2021, https://www.city.kamakura.kanagawa.jp/koen/p_cyuuou.html.

10. Kamakura City, "City Greening Promotion Program" [in Japanese], last modified December 23, 2020, https://www.city.kamakura.kanagawa.jp/midori/machinami.html.

11. Miyagi Prefecture, "Miyagi Coastal Forest Restoration and Everyone's Forest Development Activities" [in Japanese], March 25, 2021, https://www.pref.miyagi.jp/soshiki/sinrin/minmori.html.

12. Morino Project, "About Morino Project," accessed October 27, 2023, https://morinoproject.com /activities.

13. Morino Project, "About Morino Project," accessed May 22, 2021, https://morinoproject.com /activities#sec01.

14. Watari Green Belt Project, "Sapling Cultivation" [in Japanese], accessed May 22, 2021, http:// www.watari-grb.org/naegi/.

15. *Tohoku Fukkō Shimbun,* "Case Study: The Watari Green Belt Project in Miyagi," translated by Nate Hill, September 23, 2013, http://www.rise-tohoku.jp/?p=3158.

16. Kawasaki City, "School Watershed Project" [in Japanese], last modified August 2, 2019, http:// www.city.kawasaki.jp/takatsu/cmsfiles/contents/0000035/35881/p02.html.

17. Kawasaki City, "For Takatsu in 100 Years . . . Eco-City Takatsu: Protecting the Richness of the Earth from the Region" [in Japanese], accessed May 6, 2020, http://www.city.kawasaki.jp/takatsu/cms files/contents/0000035/35881/about_ectakatsu.html.

18. Hayashi, "Efforts for Small Nature Restoration," 2.

19. Hayashi, "River-Making," 3, 4.

20. MLIT, "Cases of Nature-Oriented River Planning 1" [in Japanese], accessed May 21, 2021, https://www.mlit.go.jp/river/shinngikai_blog/tashizen/daio1kai/pdf/5-3-1 gutairei1.pdf.

21. Kamisaigō River Association for the Best Sato River in Japan, *Kamisaigō River Illustrated Reference Book* [in Japanese], March 2020, https://drive.google.com/file/d/1aRn7Qj8pTN_7mCPFK g89oRJNgj2kctir/view?fbclid=IwAR0pwh-QCS3qXK28xYCkQ_ZHOzVNnMz_MVL-AsijyZ TvlSYMvlfy3TAytJ4.

22. Hayashi, "River-Making," 4–5.

23. Japan River Restoration Network, "Restore the Environment," 75.

24. "Flowing Water Functions" [in Japanese], *New Science 5* (Tokyo: Tokyo Shoseki, 2020), 91, https://ten.tokyo-shoseki.co.jp/text/shou/rika/introduction/page09.html#section2 (link discontinued).

25. JRRN, "Restore the Environment," 79.

26. Fieldwork in Minamisanriku, June–August 2011.

27. Sendai Broadcasting, "Broadcasting from the Disaster-Affected Area: The Great East Japan Earthquake" [in Japanese], DVD, Fusōsha, 2012.

28. Alexandra Lange, "A Journey to Isamu Noguchi's Last Work," *Curbed,* December 1, 2016.

29. Staempfli, "Reintroducing Adventure."

30. Kinoshita and Woolley, "Children's Play."

31. NPO Bōken Asobiba Sendai Miyagi Network, "Coastal Park Adventure Park" [in Japanese], last modified May 19, 2021, http://www.bouken-asobiba-net.com/bouhiro-top.

32. Park staff of NPO Bōken Asobiba Sendai Miyagi Network, interview by author and team, July 2, 2015.

PARK NETWORKS DISCUSSION

1. O'Connor et al., *San Francisco Relief Survey,* 14, 77–78.

2. Lindsey Hoshaw, "Transforming San Francisco Into a Model of Disaster Preparedness," KQED, November 20, 2013, https://www.kqed.org/quest/62076/transforming-san-francisco-into-a-model-of-disaster-preparedness.

3. Rung et al., "Escaping," 383.

4. Li, "Development of Disaster Prevention," 49.

5. See the PREPHubs at the MIT Urban Risk Lab website, risk.mit.edu.

6. European Environment Agency, "Trees Help Tackle Climate Change," January 6, 2012, https://www.eea.europa.eu/articles/forests-health-and-climate-change/key-facts/trees-help-tackle-climate-change.

7. CAO, "Damage Expectation of Tokyo Metropolitan Earthquake" [in Japanese], 2005, 11, http://www.bousai.go.jp/kaigirep/chuobou/senmon/shutohinan/1/pdf/shiryou_2.pdf.

8. MLIT, "Urban Renewal Safety Assurance Plan System" [in Japanese], April 2018, 3, https://www.mlit.go.jp/common/001231351.pdf.

9. MLIT, "Urban Renewal," 17–18.

10. Kyoto City, "Evacuation Guidance Plan for Stranded Sightseers" [in Japanese], December 2013, https://www.city.kyoto.lg.jp/gyozai/cmsfiles/contents/0000076/76886/keikaku_gaiyou.pdf.

11. Fieldwork in Kyoto, July 12, 2018.

5. ARCHITECTURAL TRANSFORMATIONS

1. Jilly Traganou and Kuroishi Izumi, *Design and Disaster: Kon Wajiro's Modernologio* (New York: Parsons and The New School for Design, 2014), 5.

2. CAO, "Lessons Learned from 1923," section 2, 28–44, and section 3, 65.

3. Kasetsu, *Recommendations!,* 43.

4. Aldrich, "Social, Not Physical, Infrastructure," 413.

5. Kaijima, Stalder, and Iseki, *Architectural Ethnography,* 9.

6. Kuroishi, "Urban Survey," 2016.

7. Kon, "Selected Writings," 197.

8. Unfortunately, architecture schools rarely required students to take Human Subject Training modules and apply for IRB approval before conducting research.

9. Matsuda, "Japan's Traditional Houses," 317.

10. Lazarin, "Temporal Architecture," 103.

11. Koolhaas et al., *Project Japan,* 307.

HOUSING: TEMPORARY TO PERMANENT

1. Reconstruction Agency, "Current Status," 3.

2. Imai, *Tokyo Roji,* 47.

3. Schulz, *Beyond Modernism,* 19–20.

4. Jinnai, *Tokyo,* 125.

5. CAO, "Lessons Learned from 1923," third section, 59–60.

6. Kasetsu, *Recommendations!,* 44.

7. Kasetsu, *Recommendations!,* 42.

8. CAO, "Lessons Learned from 1923," third section, 69–71, 76.

9. CAO, "Lessons Learned from 1923," third section, 75.

10. Otsuki, "Dōjunkai's Combined Development," 2.

11. Satoh et al., *Dōjunkai Apartment,* 13–14.

12. Imaizumi, *Sacred Space,* 153.

13. Kitahara, "Refugees," 159.

14. Tewari and Beynon, "Tokyo's Dōjunkai Experiment," 474.

15. Imaizumi, *Sacred Space,* 149.

16. Satoh et al., *Dōjunkai Apartment,* 15–18.

17. Hashimoto, Uchida, and Ōtsuki, *Disappearing Dōjunkai Apartment,* 16–19, 36–38, 125–51.

18. Hashimoto, Uchida, and Ōtsuki, *Disappearing Dōjunkai Apartment,* 23–24.

19. Fieldwork in Omotesandō, Tokyo, by author, 1997–99.

20. Sorensen, *Making of Urban Japan,* 132.

21. Tewari and Beynon, "Tokyo's Dōjunkai Experiment," 472–73.

22. After World War II, the building was converted into low-income women's public housing and stood until 2003.

23. Satoh et al., *Dōjunkai Apartment,* 21–23.

24. Imaizumi, *Sacred Space,* 147.

25. JPA, "Present Situation of Prefabricated Housing," accessed October 5, 2023, https://www.pure kyo.or.jp/about/prefab_building/present_situation/index.html.

26. For example, the All Japan Society of Wooden Construction has agreements with eight munici- palities and thirty-seven prefectures as of March 2020. See "Status of Bōsai Agreement" [in Japanese], https://www.zenmokkyo.jp/saigai/.

27. Executive trustee and director of the DASH project, Daiwa House Industry, Co., Ltd., interview by author's team member Saeko Baird, August 3, 2017.

28. CAO, "Survey of Emergency Temporary Housing" [in Japanese], December 2016, 2, 20, http:// www.bousai.go.jp/kaigirep/hisaishasumai/dai2kai/pdf/sanko.pdf.

29. Daiwa House Industry interview.

30. JPA, *2011 Great East-Japan Earthquake Emergency Temporary Housing Construction Record* [in Japanese], 2012, 21.

31. CAO, "Overview of Disaster Relief Act," 20.

32. JPA, *Housing Construction Record,* 29–34.

33. FDMA, "Confirmed Damages during Great Hanshin/Awaji Earthquake" [in Japanese], May 19, 2006, https://web.pref.hyogo.lg.jp/kk42/pa20_000000015.html.

34. CAO, "Progress in Construction of Temporary Housing after the Great Hanshin-Awaji Earth- quake" [in Japanese], 1995, 1, https://www.bousai.go.jp/kaigirep/kyuujorenkei/miyagi_hyogo_1/pdf /shiryo04_2.pdf.

35. JPA, "Great Hanshin-Awaji Earthquake" [in Japanese], accessed January 15, 2021, https://www .purekyo.or.jp/measures/saigai_hanshin.html.

36. Edgington, *Reconstructing Kobe,* 57.

37. Koshiyama, "Spatial Distribution," 30.

38. Miura, "Temporary Housing," 232.

39. Leckie, "Still Waiting," 25.

40. Shiozaki, "Disaster Recovery," 83.

41. Maly and Shiozaki, "Towards a Policy," 59.

42. Shiozaki, "Disaster Recovery," 83.

43. Leckie, "Still Waiting," 25.

44. Hirayama, "From Hanshin-Awaji to Tohoku."

45. Kako and Ikeda, "Volunteer Experiences."

46. Hirayama, "Collapse and Reconstruction," 122.

47. Leckie, "Still Waiting," 25, 26, 33.

48. Kashihara, Ueno, and Morita, *Research on Shelters,* 142–43.

49. Hirayama, "Collapse and Reconstruction," 121.

50. Kobe City, "Dense City Area Regeneration Policy" [in Japanese], March 2011, 17, https://www.city.kobe.lg.jp/documents/11677/misshu.pdf.

51. Supporters Network for Community Development Machizukuri, "Small Housing Site," in *Key Terminology in Restoration from Hanshin Earthquake Disaster,* accessed May 21, 2021, http://web.kyoto-inet.or.jp/org/gakugei/kobe/key_e/en1017.htm.

52. Olshansky et al., *Opportunity in Chaos,* 6–30.

53. Kobe City, "Dense City," 2.

54. CAO, "115 Projects in Dense Areas" [in Japanese], Research on Summary and Validation of Great Hanshin-Awaji Earthquake Research.

55. Yoshikawa, "Struggles," 248.

56. CAO, "The Hanshin-Awaji Earthquake Disaster Information Resource Book 02, Reconstruction and Supply of Private Housing" [in Japanese], accessed May 29, 2021, http://www.bousai.go.jp/kyoiku/kyokun/hanshin_awaji/data/detail/4-1-2.html.

57. Kobayashi Ikuo, "Completion of Kinmokusei Street Joint Housing," *Kinmokusei, no.* 42 (January 31, 1997).

58. Kobe City, "Overview," 116.

59. Ono Kōichirō, "Mikura District, Co-planning Citizen's Machizukuri" [in Japanese], 2000, http://web.kyoto-inet.or.jp/org/gakugei/kobe/kobe2000/kc006.htm.

60. Kawakami and Nakabayashi, "Study," 398.

61. Great Hanshin-Awaji Earthquake Timeline Mapping Project, "Mikura Street 5, 6, 7 District Machizukuri Council" [in Japanese], https://tm19950117.jp/interview/981/.

62. Machi-Communication, "Record of a Joint Reconstruction Project Mikura 5 up to Completion" [in Japanese], http://machi-comi.wjg.jp/m-comi/magazine/0408/0408-1.htm.

63. Miyasada Akira, "Creation of Communities by Residents and Volunteers in Mikura District," http://park15.wakwak.com/~m-comi/project/25/m-comi-his-Eng-ver.pdf.

64. Ono Kōichirō, "Joint Reconstruction Housing and 'Community Plaza' Initiative in Burnt Districts, Mikage Street, Districts 5 and 6 in Nagata" [in Japanese], *Kinmokusei, no.* 49 (July 3, 1997).

65. Machi-Communication, "Record."

66. Kobe City, "Project 11 HAT Kobe Wakinohama," 68–69, http://www.lib.kobe-u.ac.jp/directory/eqb/book/4-1009/pdf/12_chapter2_2_3.pdf.

67. Kobayashi Ikuo, email interview by author and Saeko Baird, December 26, 2019.

68. MLIT, "Summary of the Great East Japan Earthquake" [in Japanese], October 2011, https://www.mlit.go.jp/common/000170054.pdf.

69. Survivors in Minamisanriku, interviews by author, 2011–12.

70. Sendai City, "Response to Emergency Temporary Housing in Sendai after the Great East Japan Earthquake" [in Japanese], September 20, 2016, 13, http://www.bousai.go.jp/updates/h280414jishin/h28kumamoto/pdf/h280929shiryo09.pdf.

71. "251 Solitary Deaths in Disaster Public Housing Exceed Those in Temporary Housing" [in Japanese], *Kahoku Shimpō,* March 4, 2020.

72. JPA, interview by author and Saeko Baird, Tokyo, July 30, 2017.

73. Goda, "Construction," 25.

74. Murao, "Regional Comparison."

75. MLIT, "Completion and Construction of Emergency Temporary Housing Units" [in Japanese], last modified April 1, 2013, https://www.mlit.go.jp/common/000140307.pdf.

76. Reconstruction Agency, "Current Status and Challenges of Reconstruction" [in Japanese], August 2023, 4, https://www.reconstruction.go.jp/topics/main-cat1/sub-cat1-1/202308_genjoutorikumi.pdf.

77. MHLW, "Status of Temporary Housing Retrofitting" [in Japanese], March 7, 2012, https://www.mhlw.go.jp/stf/shingi/2r98520000024jyi.html.

78. CAO, "Summary of Emergency Temporary Housing," December 16, 2013, 3, http://www.bousai.go.jp/kaigirep/kentokai/hisaishashien2/wg/pdf/dai1kai/siryo4.pdf.

79. Kiwoikasu, Association for the Promotion of Wood-Conscious Architecture, "Case Studies of Wooden Temporary Housing" [In Japanese], March 2012, 1, https://www.bousai.go.jp/kaigirep/kentokai/hisaishashien2/wg/pdf/dai1kai/sankou6.pdf.

80. Forestry Agency, *2012 Forestry White Paper* [in Japanese], June 7, 2013, 53, https://www.rinya.maff.go.jp/j/kikaku/hakusyo/24hakusyo/190411_7.html.

81. Seike, Yoshiba, and Kim, "Research on Construction."

82. Kiwoikasu, "Case Studies," 1.

83. Iwata Tsukasa, "Fukushima Prefecture's Case on Temporary Housing Built by Local Construction Companies" [in Japanese], 28, dated July 20, 2011, https://www.mlit.go.jp/common/000162038.pdf.

84. All Japan Society of Wooden Construction, "Towards Disaster Agreements for Temporary Wooden Housing Construction" [in Japanese], 2014, 5, https://www.bousai.go.jp/kaigirep/kentokai/hisaishashien2/wg/pdf/dai2kai/siryo4.pdf.

85. Kiwoikasu, "Case Studies," 6–8, 108.

86. Good Design Award, "Wooden Temporary Houses" [in Japanese], 2012, https://www.g-mark.org/award/describe/38913?locale=ja.

87. Project architects from Haryū Wood Studio, interview by author's team member Lizzie Yarina, Aizu-Wakamatsu, March 2018.

88. Haryū Wood Studio, "Taishidō Housing Complex" [in Japanese], accessed May 21, 2021, http://www.haryu.jp/archives/project/taishido.

89. Fukushima Prefecture, "Reuse and Dismantling of Temporary Housing" [in Japanese], in *Fukushima Prefecture Temporary Housing Projects Record,* March 2020, 42, https://www.pref.fukushima.lg.jp/uploaded/attachment/425957.pdf.

90. Nakagawa Sugi Kyōhan Kumiai, "Report on the Reuse of Wood in the Conversion of Emergency Temporary Housing to Public Housing for Reconstruction" [in Japanese], March 2018.

91. Occupant interviews by Lizzie Yarina, Aizu-Wakamatsu, March 2018.

92. Tomiyasu et al., "Community-Care Temporary Housing."

93. Otsuki, "Community Design."

94. MIC, "2018 Housing and Land Survey" [in Japanese], April 26, 2018, 2, https://www.stat.go.jp/data/jyutaku/2018/pdf/g_gaiyou.pdf.

95. Miyagi Prefecture, "Basic Framework of Temporary Housing—Vacant Apartment Lease" [in Japanese], last modified April 1, 2023, https://www.pref.miyagi.jp/site/ej-earthquake/kasetsujutaku .html#minchin.

96. "Disappearing Temporary Housing and Raising Land . . . a Fixed Point of View from 9 Years after the Earthquake" [in Japanese], *Nikkei Shimbun,* March 10, 2020, https://www.nikkei.com/article /DGXMZO56364120U0A300C2000000/.

97. Meno, "Housing Lease."

98. MLIT and MHLW, "Use of Private Rental Housing for Disaster Victims" [in Japanese], November 2012, https://www.mlit.go.jp/common/000232197.pdf.

99. SAREX, "Problems," 1.

100. Meno, "Housing Lease."

101. SAREX, "Problems," 10.

102. SME Support Japan, "Temporary Shopping Centers Developed by SME Support Japan" [in Japanese], last modified December 2018, https://www.smrj.go.jp/reconstruction/eastjapan2011/support /temp/frr94k00000008hv-att/a1686618841420.pdf.

103. MLIT, "Schematic Study of Urban Reconstruction Patterns in Response to the Great East Japan Earthquake: Kesennuma Survey Summary" [in Japanese], accessed January 15, 2021, https://www .mlit.go.jp/common/000209538.pdf.

104. Abe Toshihiko, interview by author's team member Endo Kenya, July 29, 2019.

105. Abe Toshihiko, interview, 2019.

106. Kako and Ikeda, "Volunteer Experiences."

107. Maly and Shiozaki, "Towards a Policy," 60.

108. "251 Solitary Deaths."

109. Shichigahama Town, "Shichigahama Reconstruction Overview," June 1, 2018, https://www .shichigahama.com/town2/documents/gaikyo_e.pdf.

110. Shichigahama Town, "Reconstruction Overview," 1, 2.

111. Onoda, Tsukuda, and Suzuki, "Complexities," 14.

112. Shichigahama Town, "Newsletter of the Matsugahama District Public Housing Gathering 1–4" [in Japanese], 2014, https://www.shichigahama.com/town2/plan05_kjutaku.html.

113. Shichigahama Town, "Shichigahama Town Disaster Reconstruction Plan (2011–2020)" [in Japanese], December 2011, 14, https://www.shichigahama.com/town2/pdf/plan05_25_03a.pdf.

114. Shichigahama Town, "Shichigahama Evacuation Plan (Summary)," March 2013, https://www .shichigahama.com/town2/pdf/plan05_25_03a.pdf.

115. Onoda, Tsukuda, and Suzuki, "Complexities," 10.

116. Onoda, Tsukuda, and Suzuki, "Complexities," 15.

117. The living access typology was created in 1976. Kasai Clean Town Seishin-Kita Heights 4–9, one of the oldest living access housing typologies still in use in Japan, was built in 1983. The living rooms face the common corridor and flower bed, making the shared area a lively space for interaction. To maintain privacy, there is a sectional level difference of sixty centimeters between the housing unit and the common areas to prevent a direct line of sight. See Yatsuhashi Kana and Watanabe Yasushi, "Study of the Coexistence of Community Orientation and Privacy in Living Access Apartment Building" [in Japanese], 52nd Nihon University Industrial Engineering Academic Meeting, December 7, 2019, 459– 62, https://www.cit.nihon-u.ac.jp/laboratorydata/kenkyu/kouennkai/reference/No.52/pdf/5-15.pdf.

118. Tsukuda et al., "Co-Assisted Housing Complex."

119. "New Grammar," *Shinkenchiku,* 36.

120. Reconstruction Agency, "Shōbutahama District Disaster Public Housing" [in Japanese],

New Tohoku Housing Design Care Studies, 2013, https://www.reconstruction.go.jp/portal/juutaku
_koukyou/20131206171957.html.

121. "New Grammar," *Shinkenchiku,* 108.

122. Iwanuma City, "Reconstruction of Tamaura-nishi: Our Thoughts Are on the Future" [in Japanese], July 8, 2015, 17–18, https://www.city.iwanuma.miyagi.jp/bosai/fukko/seibi/documents /tamauranisi.pdf.

123. The Tamaura district was the first to close its shelter (on June 5, the day after evacuees moved into temporary housing on June 4, 2011). See Iwanuma, "Tamaura-nishi—Our Thoughts Are on the Future" [in Japanese], 2017, 4, https://www.city.iwanuma.miyagi.jp/kurashi/infrastructure/toshi-keikaku /sonota/documents/11.25-saisyuu-houkoku-honnpenn-1.pdf.

124. Iwanuma, "Tamaura-nishi—Our Thoughts Are on the Future," 13.

125. "New Grammar," *Shinkenchiku,* 35.

126. UAPP, "Iwanuma Tamaura-nishi Disaster Public Housing B-1 District" [in Japanese], accessed May 21, 2021, http://www.uapp.jp/works-koukyou-its.htm.

127. Iwanuma City, "Reconstruction of Tamaura-nishi," 13.

128. Kumamoto Prefecture, "Occupancy of Temporary Emergency Housing" [in Japanese], May 31, 2020, https://www.pref.kumamoto.jp/soshiki/27/51303.html.

129. "Three Years after the Kumamoto Earthquake: More Measures to Prevent Solitary Death Are Necessary," *Mainichi Shimbun,* April 16, 2019.

130. Philip Brasor and Masako Tsubuku, "Temporary Disaster Housing Has an Unforeseen Permanence," *Japan Times,* April 2, 2017.

131. TMG, "Agreement on the Provision of Private Rental Housing in the Event of an Earthquake, Conclusion" [in Japanese], December 22, 2020, https://www.metro.tokyo.lg.jp/tosei/hodohappyo/press /2020/12/22/11.html.

132. S. Murakami, "Support for Home Reconstruction," 265.

133. SAREX, "Problems."

134. See SEED Temporary Housing at the MIT Urban Risk Lab website (risk.mit.edu).

SHRINES AND TEMPLES

1. Kanaya, "Japan's Traditional Religion," 8.

2. Fujita and Kumagai, "Comparative Study," 19.

3. Endō and Mazereeuw, "Historical Study," 695.

4. Takada, Umetsu, and Kuwako, "Study on the Deity," I-173.

5. Sonoda, Takebayashi, and Tashiro, "Town-Festival."

6. Minai, "Role of the Shrines."

7. Kikigaki Project, "Utatsu Mishima Shrine Carrying the Omikoshi and Its Heritage" [in Japanese], April 2, 2012, http://kikigaki-pj-memokko.blogspot.com/2012/04/blog-post_2588.html (link discontinued).

8. Endō and Mazereeuw, "Historical Study," 696.

9. Aogawa Atsushi, "Evacuation at Togura Elementary School after the Great East-Japan Earthquake—Until Handing Children over to Their Caregivers" [in Japanese], Miyagi Prefecture, April 4, 2012, https://www.pref.miyagi.jp/documents/17564/12404.pdf.

10. Kamaishi City, "Kamaishi City Great East-Japan Earthquake Investigation Report [Evacuation Space Operation]" [in Japanese], March 2014, 15, https://www.city.kamaishi.iwate.jp/docs

/2015101400022/file_contents/2015101400022_www_city_kamaishi_iwate_jp_fukko_joho_torikumi
_shinsai_kensyo_detail___icsFiles_afieldfile_2015_10_21_26hinanjyouneihen.pdf.

11. The Protecting Life and Community Reporting Team, "Pitfalls in Preparation: (1) The Role of Shelters and the Spread of Misconceptions" [in Japanese], *Kahoku Shimpō,* April 29, 2013.

12. Inaba, "Religion's Response," 53.

13. Okubo, "Temples and Shrines," 66.

14. Schencking, *Great Kanto Earthquake,* 70.

15. Okubo, "Temples and Shrines," 67, 72.

16. Chiba, "What Temples Could Do," 232.

17. Kudo, *Tsunami Picture Book.*

18. McLaughlin, "What Have Religious Groups Done," 298.

19. Yamamoto Town, "Notice of Enforcement of Ordinance on Tsunami Disaster Hazard Zones" [in Japanese], last modified May 25, 2016, https://www.town.yamamoto.miyagi.jp/site/fukkou/318.html.

20. Teuchi and Hara, "Contemporary Significance," 8.

21. "Yamamoto Disaster Reconstruction, Saturday Meeting" [in Japanese], Facebook, last modified February 23, 2021, https://www.facebook.com/doyoubi.no.kai.

22. NPO KATARiBA, "All about KATARiBA," accessed February 24, 2021, https://www.katariba
.or.jp/english/.

23. Iwate Prefecture, "Collaboration School Project" [in Japanese], 2013, https://manabinet.pref.iwate
.jp/hp/sicyousonjiyou/24sicyousonjigyou/200otuchi.pdf.

24. "Ōtsuchi Campus (Iwate Prefecture), Collabo-School—After School Program in the Disaster Affected Areas" [in Japanese], last modified March 2020, https://www.katariba.or.jp/activity/project
/otsuchi/.

25. Okubo, "Temples and Shrines."

26. Breen and Teeuwen, *New History of Shinto,* 1.

27. Inaba, "Religion's Response," 55.

28. Kyoto City, "Evacuation Guidance Plan for Stranded Sightseers."

29. "Temples and Shrines Turning into Police Stations during Disasters; Extensive Sites for Temporary Hubs; Agreements between Kyoto and Tōji Temple" [in Japanese], *Mainichi Shimbun,* June 8, 2019.

30. Inaba and Kawabata, "Survey Report," 18.

31. Washimori Hiroshi, Satoh Ken, and Kitamoto Takumi, "27% of Dangerous Evacuation Sites across Japan at Risk of Flooding and Landslide—Limits to the Right Location, Cross-Municipality Cooperation Is the Key" [in Japanese], *Nikkei Shimbun,* August 2, 2020, https://www.nikkei.com
/article/DGXMZO62205030S0A800C2MM8000/.

32. Agency for Cultural Affairs, "Subsidy Guidelines for Bōsai Measures of the Cultural Heritage" [in Japanese], last modified April 1, 2015, https://www.bunka.go.jp/seisaku/bunkazai/joseishien/hojo
/pdf/juuyou_kenzoubutsu-bijutsukougei_ver03.pdf.

33. "Tokyo Metropolitan Area Network: Seven Years after the Earthquake, Making Religious Facilities into Disaster Management Bases" [in Japanese], NHK, March 9, 2018, http://altruism.blog56.fc2
.com/blog-entry-377.html?sp.

HOTELS

1. Drabek, *Disaster Evacuation Behavior,* 672.

2. Nguyen, Imamura, and Iuchi, "Barriers," 586.

3. Reitherman, "Frank Lloyd Wright's Imperial Hotel," 150–51.

4. Walker, *Earthquake,* 153–54.

5. Yoshimi Yoshiaki, "Seismic Design and Foundation of the Former Imperial Hotel" [in Japanese], October 14, 2019, http://yoshimi-yoshiaki.la.coocan.jp/teikoku.htm.

6. Reitherman, "Frank Lloyd Wright's Imperial Hotel," 147–48.

7. Maesaka Toshiyuki, "Japanese Leadership History (136) Learning from Decisions and Actions of Inumaru Tetsuzo of Imperial Hotel in the Great Kanto Earthquake" [in Japanese], Maesaka Toshiyuki official website, April 3, 2011, http://www.maesaka-toshiyuki.com/person/3241.html.

8. Maesaka, "Japanese Leadership."

9. Nagayama Kiyoko, "Why Did the Imperial Hotel Accept 2000 Stranded People Free of Charge?" [in Japanese], President Online, May 30, 2011, https://president.jp/articles/-/10280.

10. TMG, "Tokyo Metropolitan Government's Measures for People Having Difficulties Returning Home" [in Japanese], December 2, 2011, 6, https://www.chisou.go.jp/tiiki/toshisaisei/yuushikisya/anzenkakuho/231202/1.pdf.

11. TMG, "Support for Equipment in Private Temporary Accommodation Facilities" [in Japanese], 2023, https://www.bousai.metro.tokyo.lg.jp/kitaku_portal/1000048/1006430/1007875/index.html.

12. Abe Noriko, owner of Hotel Kanyō, Minamisanriku, interview by author, July 23, 2012.

13. Abe Noriko, interview.

14. Minamisanriku Hotel Kanyō, "Memories after 3.11," [in Japanese], February 2014, http://touhoku-ouendan.jp/archives/2493/.

15. "Keep the Light of Minamisanriku Alive—People Who Gather at the Hotel, People Who Don't Give Up—Minamisanriku Hotel Kanyō" [in Japanese], Nikkei Business Online, May 31, 2011.

16. Minamisanriku Hotel Kanyō, "Memories."

17. ¥5,000 per person. See MIC, "Q&A on Response to the Great East Japan Earthquake—Local Government Finance" [in Japanese], June 10, 2011, 4, https://www.soumu.go.jp/main_content/000117828.pdf.

18. Minamisanriku Hotel Kanyō, "Memories."

19. Fieldwork in Minamisanriku, 2011.

20. Kato Eiichi, Owner of Hotel Bōyō, interview by author and team, July 8, 2015.

21. Kato, interview.

22. "Hotel Bōyō Bankruptcy, Emergency Shelter after Disaster, Kesennuma/Miyagi" [in Japanese], *Mainichi Shimbun,* April 25, 2018.

23. Nguyen, Imamura, and Iuchi, "Barriers," 590.

24. Miyagi Prefecture, "Record of Secondary Evacuation during the Great East Japan Earthquake" [in Japanese], November 2011, 1, https://www.bousai.go.jp/updates/h280414jishin/h28kumamoto/pdf/h280929sanko02.pdf.

25. All Japan Ryokan-Hotel Association, "Disaster Response Manual for Ryokans and Hotels" [in Japanese], April 2018, http://www.yadonet.ne.jp/info/member/manual8/book.pdf.

26. Tokushima Prefecture, "Subsidy Program for Using Hotels and Ryokans as Emergency Shelters" [in Japanese], last modified July 3, 2020, https://www.pref.tokushima.lg.jp/file/attachment/575665.pdf.

27. Nguyen, Imamura, and Iuchi, "Public-Private Collaboration," 133, 136.

SCHOOLS

1. Yasuda M., *Disaster Reconstructions,* 188.

2. Yamakoshi, Nakai, and Numata, "Study on the Primary Schools," 531–36.

3. Otani Shunsuke, "Dawn of Earthquake Engineering," *Pacific Earthquake Engineering,* 2004, 5, https://peer.berkeley.edu/sites/default/files/0311_the_fifth_u.s.-japan_workshop_on_performance -based.pdf.

4. Architectural Institute of Japan, "Concrete School Buildings" [in Japanese], September 1950, 10.

5. Maeda, "Historical Changes."

6. MEXT, "Elementary School Maintenance" [in Japanese], August 2003, https://www.mext.go.jp /b_menu/shingi/chousa/shisetu/001/toushin/03082201.htm.

7. MEXT, "About National Subsidy Projects" [in Japanese], accessed February 26, 2021, http://www .mext.go.jp/a_menu/shotou/zyosei/zitumu.htm#a001.

8. MEXT, "Elementary School Facility" [in Japanese], March 2019, https://www.mext.go.jp/a_menu /shisetu/bousai/taishin/03071501.htm.

9. MEXT, "About Facilities Grant Division" [in Japanese], accessed May 21, 2021, https://www.mext .go.jp/a_menu/shotou/zyosei/nyuumon.htm.

10. MEXT, "Case Study of Bōsai Measures for Public School Facilities 1" [in Japanese], August 2013, 1, https://www.mext.go.jp/a_menu/shotou/zyosei/__icsFiles/afieldfile/2013/08/16/1312680_1.pdf.

11. MEXT, "Revision of the School Facility Maintenance Guidelines" [in Japanese], July 2014, https://www.mext.go.jp/b_menu/shingi/chousa/shisetu/013/toushin/1350224.htm.

12. MEXT, "Elementary School Facility."

13. MEXT, "Eco-School Activation Cases" [in Japanese], February 2020, 7–8, https://www.mext.go .jp/content/20200204-mxt_sisetuki-000006255_1.pdf.

14. MEXT, "About National Subsidy Projects."

15. Matsushima and Shen, "Study of the Transitions."

16. Nojima Naoki, "Designing Classrooms and Their Surroundings" [in Japanese], *Eye-span,* August 2011, https://www.iee-net.co.jp/24725.html.

17. Tokuyama, "Establishment and Operation," 144.

18. Kikuchi and Minami, "Study."

19. NHK, "Great East Japan Earthquake Archives: Protecting Students' Lives. Lessons from Ōkawa Elementary School" [in Japanese], last modified 2019, https://www9.nhk.or.jp/archives/311shogen /summary/evi/31/.

20. Hiroshi Suzuki, "Maintaining Remnants of Disaster for the Future," *Japan Times,* March 11, 2016.

21. Ishinomaki City, "Disaster Memorial—Ōkawa Elementary School Former Building" [in Japanese], Redevelopment Policy Plan, March 28, 2017, https://www.city.ishinomaki.lg.jp/cont/10051100 /9003/03_05_05_siryou2.pdf.

22. Kyodo, "Ishinomaki to Turn Okawa Elementary Ruins into 3/11 Monument," *Japan Times,* March 17, 2016.

23. CAO, *2012 White Paper on Children and Parenting* [in Japanese], 2012, chap. 5, https://www8 .cao.go.jp/shoushi/shoushika/whitepaper/measures/w-2012/24webhonpen/html/b2_s5_1.html.

24. Katada, "Behavior Disaster Preparedness Education," 38–40.

25. CAO, "Learning from Great East Japan Earthquake: How We Survived" [in Japanese], 2011, http:// www.bousai.go.jp/kohou/kouhoubousai/h23/64/special_01.html.

26. Okirai school principal, interview by author and team, July 6, 2015.

27. Okirai school principal, interview.

28. MEXT, "Survey of Bōsai Functions of Public Schools as Shelters" [in Japanese], July 12, 2023, https://www.mext.go.jp/content/20230712-mxt_bousai-000030611_1.pdf.

29. MEXT, "Survey of Bōsai Functions," 2.

30. Kashihara, Ueno, and Morita, *Research on Shelters,* 36–40.

31. Tokuyama, "Establishment and Operation," 116–29.

32. Tokuyama, "Establishment and Operation," 132.

33. Kashihara, Ueno, and Morita, *Research on Shelters,* 191–92.

34. MEXT, "Case Study of Bōsai," 7.

35. MEXT, *Disaster-Resistant School Facilities,* 30, 31–34, 35.

36. Ogatsu school vice principal, interview by author and Saeko Baird, June 27, 2019.

37. Shimizu and Tamamura, "Elderly People," 61.

38. MEXT, *Disaster-Resistant School Facilities,* 39.

39. Fieldwork in Minamisanriku, May–August 2011.

40. MEXT, *Disaster-Resistant School Facilities,* 40.

41. Shioiri Takeshi, architect and chairman, Tohoku Design Planning Research Studio, email interview by author, Taketani Maya, and Saeko Baird, May 20, 2016.

42. "Miyagi Prefecture, Yamamoto and Watari" [in Japanese], NHK, November 5, 2017, https://www.nhk.or.jp/sendai/hisaichikara/report/171105.html.

43. MEXT, *Disaster-Resistant School Facilities,* 42.

44. Yamashita schoolteacher, interview by author and team, July 13, 2015.

45. Yamashita schoolteacher, interview.

46. CAO, "Lessons Learned from 1923," section 3, 60.

47. Tokuyama, "Examination Theme," 72.

48. Oikawa, "City Level Response," 159.

49. Middle school teacher in Kesennuma, interview by author and team, July 9, 2015.

50. MLIT, "Disaster Education Portal" [in Japanese], last modified 2021, https://www.mlit.go.jp/river/bousai/education/precedent.html.

51. "Let's Learn Bōsai" [in Japanese], NHK, accessed June 2, 2021, http://www.nhk.or.jp/sougou/bosai/.

52. Johnson et al., "Evaluations of Disaster Education," 121.

53. MEXT, "Planning School Facilities, Learning from the Great Japan East Earthquake—Emergency Proposal" [in Japanese], July 2011, 35, https://www.mext.go.jp/component/b_menu/shingi/toushin/__icsFiles/afieldfile/2011/07/07/1308045_3.pdf.

54. Suginami Dai-ju school pamphlet and interview by author and Maya Taketani.

55. MEXT, *Disaster-Resistant School Facilities,* 105.

56. Edogawa School vice principal, interview by author and Taketani Maya, July 16, 2015.

57. Edogawa School vice principal, interview.

58. AXS SATOW Inc., "Yamamoto-cho Yamashita-daini Elementary School," last modified July 2016, https://www.axscom.co.jp/en/project/n003965/.

59. Yamashita Dai-ni School vice principal, interview by author and Saeko Baird, June 26, 2019.

60. Taniguchi Naohide, designer in AXS SATOW, email interview by author and Saeko Baird, June 17, 2019.

61. Watari Town, "Watari Great East Japan Earthquake Records" [in Japanese], March 2013, https://www.pref.miyagi.jp/documents/3689/watari2503.pdf.

62. Sato Kiwamu, project architect, Seki Kukan Sekkei, interview by author and Saeko Baird, June 27, 2019.

63. Arahama School principal, interview by author and Saeko Baird, June 28, 2019.

64. Ogatsu School vice principal, interview.

65. Fieldwork in Ishinomaki, 2019.

66. Eda Shinsuke, project architect, Seki Kukan Sekkei, interview by author and Saeko Baird, June 27, 2019.

67. Ronan, Crellin, and Johnston, "Correlates of Hazards Education."

68. Peek et al., "Children and Disasters," 253.

TSUNAMI EVACUATION BUILDINGS AND TOWERS

1. CAO, "Tonankai / Nankai Earthquake Measures Outlines" [in Japanese], December 2003, 1–2, https://www.bousai.go.jp/jishin/tonankai_nankai/pdf/shiryou_2.pdf.

2. CAO, "Guideline for Tsunami Evacuation Buildings (Plan)" [in Japanese], 2005, 2, https://www.bousai.go.jp/kohou/oshirase/h17/pdf/050323shiryou2.pdf.

3. CAO, "Ensuring Smooth Evacuation from Tsunami in the Shortest Possible Time" [in Japanese], March 26, 2012, 4, http://www.bousai.go.jp/jishin/tsunami/hinan/6/pdf/4.pdf.

4. CAO, "Amendment of the Disaster Countermeasures Act" [in Japanese], June 21, 2013, http://www.bousai.go.jp/kohou/kouhoubousai/h25/72/news_01.html.

5. CAO, "Number of Tsunami Evacuation Facilities" [in Japanese], August 2018, 2–3, http://www.bousai.go.jp/jishin/tsunami/hinan/pdf/3008gaiyou.pdf.

6. MLIT, "MLIT Nankai Trough Megathrust Earthquake Countermeasure Plan, FY 2017, Priority Measures" [in Japanese], 2017, 1, https://www.mlit.go.jp/river/bousai/earthquake/pdf/earthquake/7kai-ref02-06.pdf.

7. MLIT, "Outline of the Comprehensive Urban Disaster Preparedness Project" [in Japanese], last modified 2023, https://www.mlit.go.jp/toshi/toshi_tobou_tk_000008.html.

8. MLIT, "Guidelines for Tsunami Disaster Prevention Area Promotion Plan" [in Japanese], April 2018, 12, https://www.mlit.go.jp/common/001230612.pdf.

9. MLIT, "Design Guidelines for Tsunami Evacuation Facilities in Harbors (Draft)" [in Japanese], October 31, 2013, 20–24, https://www.mlit.go.jp/common/001008938.pdf.

10. CAO, "Number of Tsunami Evacuation Facilities" [in Japanese], April 2021, https://www.bousai.go.jp/jishin/tsunami/hinan/pdf/r304gaiyou.pdf.

11. Suppasri et al., "Lessons Learned," 1012.

12. Sendai City, "Evacuation Facilities," accessed September 17, 2018, http://sendai-resilience.jp/en/efforts/government/development/evacuation_facilities.html.

13. "Evacuation Towers above Roads: Yoshida Will Implement the First in the Nation" [in Japanese], Nikkei, October 9, 2013, https://www.nikkei.com/article/DGXNASFK0803E_Y3A001C1000000/.

14. Yoshida Town, *Yoshida Earthquake Disaster Preparedness Guidebook,* 2015, 7, http://www.town.yoshida.shizuoka.jp/secure/2303/download.pdf.

15. Velotti et al., "Beyond Vertical Evacuation," 67.

16. Yoshida Town, North Oasis Park website, accessed May 21, 2021, http://www.town.yoshida.shizuoka.jp/secure/4118/panfu1.pdf.

17. Fieldwork in Yoshida by Lizzie Yarina, 2018.

18. Yoshida Town, "Walking Map" [in Japanese], accessed May 21, 2021, http://www.town.yoshida.shizuoka.jp/3126.htm.

19. For example, Suzuka City provides subsidies of up to 10 million yen per facility at 50% of the cost of eligible construction. See: Suzuka City, "Tsunami Evacuation Facility Development Subsidy Program" [in Japanese], accessed October 6, 2024, https://www.city.suzuka.lg.jp/safe/taishin/index6.html.

20. Shimizu Corporation, "Frame Shelter" [in Japanese], accessed May 21, 2021, https://www.shimz.co.jp/solution/tech010/index.html.

21. Suzaki City staff, interview by author and Saeko Baird via email, November 26, 2019.

22. Hyūga City, "Zaikoji Temple North Public Housing, Outdoor Evacuation Stairs" [in Japanese], last modified June 11, 2020, http://www.hyugacity.jp/sp/tempimg/20170830110354.pdf.

23. Kushimoto Town, "Hazard Map," last modified July 2019, https://www.town.kushimoto.wakayama.jp/bousai/tsunami/files/tsunami-1920_201907.pdf.

24. "Tsunami Evacuation Tower at Kushimoto Fishing Port" [in Japanese], NHK, March 22, 2014.

25. Kushimoto Town, "Kushimoto Tsunami Disaster Management Regional Plan" [in Japanese], March 2015, 2–3, https://www.town.kushimoto.wakayama.jp/bousai/keikaku/files/tsunami_bousai.pdf.

26. "Kushimoto, Wakayama Prefecture Built a New Floating Shelter atop a Tsunami Evacuation Tower" [in Japanese], Sankei News, February 21, 2015, https://www.sankei.com/region/news/150221/rgn1502210033-n1.html.

27. Tajima Motor Corporation, "Main Features of the SAFE+ Floating Tsunami Shelter" [in Japanese], accessed May 21, 2021, https://www.tajima-motor.com/safeplus/shelter/feature.html.

28. Fire department staff of Kushimoto, interview by author's team member Saeko Baird, December 29, 2017.

29. "The Number of People Saved by Evacuating to Buildings in the Coastal Areas of the Great East Japan Earthquake" [in Japanese], Jiji.com, May 27, 2011, https://www.jiji.com/jc/graphics?p=ve_soc_jishin-higashinihon20110527j-02-w380.

30. Nagayama Satoru, Rikuzentakata Bureau of Construction, interview by author and team, July 7, 2015.

31. Onishi Kazumasa and Watanabe Yosuke, "Earthquake Remnants in Rikuzentakata Prepare to Open to the Public in 2021" [in Japanese], *Asahi Shimbun,* December 12, 2018, https://www.asahi.com/articles/ASLDC52SFLDCUJUB00S.html.

32. Rikuzentakata City, "Streets in the City Center and Park Design" [in Japanese], November 26, 2014, http://www.thr.mlit.go.jp/bumon/b06111/kenseibup/memorial_park/iwate/file/21_15_chushinshigaichi.pdf.

33. Taiki Town, "Nishiki Tower" [in Japanese], accessed May 21, 2021, http://www.town.taiki.mie.jp/files/bousaitower_doc_01.pdf.

34. Institute of Scientific Approaches for Fire and Disaster, "Firefighting Science Center Chairperson Prize: Tsunami Disaster Preparedness Community Planning (Nishiki Tower)" [in Japanese], 1998, https://www.bousaihaku.com/town/5882/.

35. FEMA, *Guidelines for Design of Structures for Vertical Evacuation from Tsunamis,* FEMA P-646 (Redwood City, CA: Applied Technology Council, 2012), 135.

36. Mie Prefecture, "Second-Class River, Okukawa River System Improvement Plan (Draft)" [in Japanese], February 2018, 14. https://www.pref.mie.lg.jp/common/content/000764515.pdf.

37. Nakaseko et al., "Tsunami Warning," 4.

38. Taiki Town, "Nishiki II" [in Japanese], 2012, http://www.town.taiki.mie.jp/files/bousaitower_doc_03.pdf.

39. CAO, "Tsunami Evacuation Towers as Symbols of the Town and Night Time Evacuation Drills" [in Japanese], (2015), 119–22, http://www.bousai.go.jp/jishin/tsunami/tsunamibousai/kunrenjireisyu/pdf/kunrenjireihonpen.pdf.

40. Nakaseko et al., "Tsunami Warning," 4.

41. Mie Prefecture, "Second-Class River," 15.

42. AEON, "Disaster Preparedness by AEON" [in Japanese], accessed May 21, 2021, https://www.aeon.info/bousai/.

43. AEON, "Towards Disaster Resilient Mall 1" [in Japanese], 2019, https://www.aeonmall.com/img/old/sustainability/assets/img/pdf/download/2019/8.pdf.

44. AEON, "Disaster Preparedness."

45. AEON, "AEON Mall Iwaki Onahama" [in Japanese] May 9, 2018, 18–19, https://www.aeon.info/news/2018_1/pdf/180509R_1_1.pdf.

46. AEON, "What We Can Do—Disaster Preparedness and Support" [in Japanese], *AEON Magazine* 62 (September 2018), https://www.aeon.info/company/message/magazine/pdf/vol62.pdf.

47. AEON, "Disaster Preparedness."

48. Kōrai Kenji and Endō Shūhei, "Study on Tsunami Evacuation Towers that Consider Harmony with the Landscape" [in Japanese], Kobe University, 2015, https://www.edu.kobe-u.ac.jp/eng-arch-sled/dat/research/korai-endo-1/1.pdf.

49. Sandi Doughton, "The New Gym at Ocosta Elementary Outside Westport Is Strong Enough to Withstand a Megaquake and Tsunami—and Can Shelter at Least 2,000 People on Its Roof," *Seattle Times,* June 10, 2016.

50. Sandi Doughton, "This Tiny Washington Town Has Little Hope of Escaping a Tsunami, so One Tribe Is Building Them All a Tower," *Seattle Times,* July 23, 2018.

ARCHITECTURAL TRANSFORMATIONS DISCUSSION

1. Lazarin, "Temporal Architecture," 108.

2. TMG, "TMG's Response to the Great East Japan Earthquake and Lessons Learned" [in Japanese], September 2011, 16–18, https://www.bousai.metro.tokyo.lg.jp/_res/projects/default_project/_page_/001/000/341/230914taiouhonsatu.pdf.

3. CAO, "Definition of Terms Related to Difficulty Returning Home," accessed May 21, 2021, http://www.bousai.go.jp/kaigirep/chuobou/senmon/shutohinan/6/pdf/shiryou_4.pdf.

4. TMG, "Emergency Project for Strengthening Disaster Hubs in Temporary Accommodations" [in Japanese], 2023, https://www.bousai.metro.tokyo.lg.jp/kitaku_portal/1000048/1006430/1007877/index.html.

5. "Mitsubishi Estate Training to Accept People with Difficulty Returning Home, Including Measures against Infectious Diseases" [in Japanese], *Nikkei Shimbun,* March 9, 2021, https://www.nikkei.com/article/DGXZQODZ0911T0Z00C21A3000000/.

6. TMG, "Subsidy for Charging Smartphones and Other Devices at Temporary Stay Facilities" [in Japanese], last modified 2021, https://www.bousai.metro.tokyo.lg.jp/mobile/kitaku_portal.

7. TMG, "Information on Temporary Evacuation Facilities" [in Japanese], last modified January 2023, https://www.bousai.metro.tokyo.lg.jp/kitaku_portal/1005196/index.html.

8. For example, as of July 2020 in Osaka, none of the private facilities around major stations have signed agreements with the city. The concern is liability, since the national government hasn't created rules regarding the responsibility of these facilities for injured evacuees. See Takahashi Sai and Funatsu Tatsuki, "No Progress in Securing Temporary Accommodation for 900,000 Stranded Commuters in Osaka" [in Japanese], *Nikkei Shimbun,* July 18, 2020, https://www.nikkei.com/article/DGXMZO61658220X10C20A7960E00/.

9. MEC and Daimaruyū District Regeneration Council, "Disaster Preparedness Projects in the Daimaruyū District" [in Japanese], November 2011, https://www.chisou.go.jp/tiiki/toshisaisei/yuushikisya/anzenkakuho/231107/2.pdf.

10. Okada, Arita, and Omura, "Study on Public Contribution," 320.

11. Tokyo Metropolitan and Seaside Area Urban Regeneration Development Council, "Ōtemachi/ Marunouchi/Yūrakuchō District Urban Regeneration Safety Assurance Plan" [in Japanese], March 29, 2023, 2, 10, https://www.city.chiyoda.lg.jp/documents/12004/toshianzenkeikaku-r5.pdf.

12. Mori Building, "From 'the City to Evacuate from to the City to Evacuate to' Comprehensive Earthquake Measurement of Mori Building" [in Japanese], 2017, 20, https://www.mori.co.jp/urban_design /img/safety_pamphlet.pdf.

13. Tokyo Dome City, "Participating Communities" [in Japanese], accessed May 21, 2021, https:// www.tokyo-dome.jp/csr/community/.

14. Taito Ward, "Measures for People with Difficulties Returning Home" [in Japanese], last modified February 19, 2020, https://www.city.taito.lg.jp/bosai/taisaku/kitakukonnan/kitaku.html.

15. Pamphlet at Haneda Airport, August 15, 2017.

16. Author's experience, Miyagi Prefecture, 2011, and Ben Lefebvre, "Food, Diapers, and Free Wifi: Japan Relies on 7–11 to Lead Earthquake Relief Efforts," *Quartz,* April 22, 2016, qz.com/667567/food -diapers-and-free-wi-fijapan-relies-on-7–11-to-lead-earthquake-relief-efforts/.

17. Lori Peek, "America's Deathtrap Schools," *New York Times,* April 7, 2018.

6. IT TAKES ALL OF US

1. CAO, "Concept for the Bōsai Hubs," 5, 21, 38.

2. "Nankai Trough Death Toll Decreased by 30 Percent, 'Preemptive Evacuation' is Specified" [in Japanese], *Nikkei Shimbun,* May 31, 2019, https://www.nikkei.com/article/DGXMZO45499510R30 C19A5MM0000/.

3. MLIT, "Estimation Method and Goals for Seismic Retrofitting Rate of Buildings" [in Japanese], December 2022, https://www.mlit.go.jp/jutakukentiku/house/content/001580488.pdf.

4. Kochi Prefecture Nankai Trough Earthquake Response Division, interview by author, August 2018.

5. Kochi City, "Tsunami Evacuation Buildings" [in Japanese], accessed September 30, 2023, https:// www.city.kochi.kochi.jp/soshiki/12/tunamihinannbiru.html#kohyou.

6. Fieldwork in Kochi City, August 2018.

7. Kochi University, Disaster Management Assistance Team, accessed February 5, 2021, http:// kochidisaster.web.fc2.com/kudt.html.

8. Kochi University, "Farming Activities Project" [in Japanese], last modified November 7, 2017, http://blog.livedoor.jp/koukatu_d_suketto/.

9. Kochi Prefecture, "To Survive."

10. Kochi Prefecture, "Earthquake and Tsunami Prediction for Your Neighborhood" [in Japanese], accessed June 8, 2021, https://www.pref.kochi.lg.jp/sonaetegood/.

11. Ozaki Masanao, "Kochi Prefecture's Challenge to Confront the Nankai Trough Earthquake" [in Japanese], 2017, 1, http://www.bousai.go.jp/jishin/nankai/taio_wg/pdf/h290131shiryo2-1.pdf.

12. Kochi Prefecture, "Enhancement of Subsidies to Promote the Use of the Pre-Disaster Group Relocation Project as a Tsunami Evacuation Measure" [in Japanese], 2017, https://www.pref.kochi.lg.jp /soshiki/111601/files/2015050900017/file_2017126484240_1.pdf.

13. Nishimura Takayuki, Kuroshio, Nankai Earthquake Countermeasures Section, email interview by author and Saeko Baird, January 6, 2020, and March 17–22, 2021.

14. Tokuhiro Seiji, director of Information Disaster Prevention Section, Kuroshio, interview by author, August 22, 2018.

15. Kuroshio Town, "Basic Concept of Kuroshio-cho's Second Disaster Management Plan for Nankai Earthquakes and Tsunami," January 31, 2013, https://www.town.kuroshio.lg.jp/img/files/pv/bousai/2013/11/06/jisintunamibousaikeikaku_kangaekata2_english.pdf.

16. Azechi, "Kuroshio," 53–55.

17. Hashitomi Masahiko, "The Challenge of Kuroshio, Kochi Prefecture, Where the Entire Town Must Overcome the Expected Shocking Tsunami Height of 34.4m" [in Japanese], Nikkei BP, March 11, 2020.

18. Kuroshio Town, "City Bōsai Project Plan (The Second Amendment)" [in Japanese], March 2019, 22, https://www.town.kuroshio.lg.jp/img/files/pv/sosiki/2019/08/cdpp_n_s.pdf.

19. Murakami and Ieda, "Area Cases," 894.

20. Nishimura, interview, 2021.

21. "Saga Nursery School—Play Freely and Safely—Opening Ceremony in Kuroshio, Kochi" [in Japanese], Mainichi Shimbun, last modified April 23, 2018, https://mainichi.jp/articles/20180423/ddl/k39/040/297000c (link discontinued); Azechi, "Kuroshio," 894.

22. MEXT, Disaster-Resistant School Facilities, 17, 19, 25.

23. Nishimura, interview, 2021.

24. Kuroshio Town, "Kuroshio Regional Disaster Preparedness Plan (Appendix)" [in Japanese], March 2022, 26–36 and 76–78, https://www.town.kuroshio.lg.jp/img/files/pv/sosiki/2022/05/tiiki bousaikeikaku_siryou202204.pdf.

25. MLIT, "Disaster Resilient Machizukuri Planning (Revision), Regional Model Kuroshio Town" [in Japanese], March 2018, 12, https://www.skr.mlit.go.jp/kensei/saigainituyoi/saigai_pdf/PDF20 kuroshioh26_03.pdf.

26. Japan Finance Organization for Municipalities, "Tsunami Hinan Tower in Saga District Kuroshio" [in Japanese], JFM Newsletter 30 (June 2019), 2–4, https://www.jfm.go.jp/book/u042mq00000 00aee-att/JFMdayori_vol30-2019.pdf.

27. Nishimura, interview, August 22, 2018.

28. Myojin Satoju, vice president of the jishubō, interview by author, August 22, 2018.

29. Myojin, interview.

30. Kuroshio Town, "Kuroshio Regional Disaster Preparedness Plan," 32.

31. Yamazaki Tomohiro, "Tsunami Evacuation Observation Deck at Seinan Park in Kuroshio, Kochi Prefecture, TP19" [in Japanese], Kochi Shimbun, March 3, 2018.

32. Fieldwork in Tosa Seinan Park, August 2018.

33. Kavi Chongkittavorn, "Young Leaders Vow to Raise Awareness of Natural Disasters: Regional Students Are Taking Disaster Response Lessons from Japan's 2011 Quake," Nikkei Asian Review, December 1, 2016.

34. Japan News—Yomiuri, "High School Students Becoming Regional Guardians" (third installment in the Disaster Education Series), Yomiuri Shimbun, March 30, 2017.

35. Hashitomi, "Challenge of Kuroshio," 2.

7. ANTICIPATORY FUTURES

1. UNU-EHS, "World Risk Report 2016."
2. Meehl et al., "How Much More."
3. Emanuel, What We Know, 39.
4. Cabinet Secretariat, "Five-Year Acceleration Measures for the National Resilience Project" [in Japanese], https://www.cas.go.jp/jp/seisaku/kokudo_kyoujinka/5kanenkasokuka/pdf/taisaku _gaiyou.pdf.

5. Cabinet Secretariat, "Learning Material 'Disaster Management Machizukuri and Nation Planning' Reference for Teachers" [in Japanese], November 2015, https://www.cas.go.jp/jp/seisaku/kokudo_kyoujinka/pdf/kyousi_sankou.pdf.

6. UNISDR, "Sendai Framework," 13, 15.

7. Nitschke, "Architecture and Aesthetic," 16.

8. Dimmer, "Place-Making," 213.

9. Murakami A., "Why Doesn't Urban Planning Start," 196.

10. Brown, "Constructing Nature," 99.

11. Dynes, "Community Emergency Planning," 142.

12. Auf der Heide, "Common Misconceptions," 364.

13. Scott, *Seeing Like a State*.

14. Jackson, "Relationship of Urban Design," 198.

15. Tierney and Goltz, "Emergency Response," 2–3.

16. MLIT, "Flood Control Effects of the Metropolitan Outer Area Underground Discharge Channel" [in Japanese], last modified 2019, https://www.ktr.mlit.go.jp/edogawa/edogawa00147.html.

17. MLIT, "Overview of Facilities," accessed June 8, 2021, https://www.ktr.mlit.go.jp/edogawa/edogawa_index045.html.

18. MLIT, "Nakagawa Ayasegawa Rivers' History" [in Japanese], last modified 2008, https://www.mlit.go.jp/river/toukei_chousa/kasen/jiten/nihon_kawa/0311_naka_ayase/0311_naka_ayase_01.html.

19. This language is particularly common in urban climate adaptation plans and related engineering projects. For example, see the Netherlands National Adaptation Strategy, *Adapting with Ambition: Rotterdam Climate Proof Adaptation Strategy,* December 2016, https://klimaatadaptatienederland.nl/publish/pages/125102/2016_12_02_nas_netherlands_4.pdf.

20. Kawata, "Disaster Information and Disaster Culture."

21. Wescoat and White, *Water for Life,* 140.

22. MLIT, "Watershed Flood Control Project" [in Japanese], last modified March 30, 2021, https://www.mlit.go.jp/river/kasen/ryuiki_pro/index.html.

23. Wood et al., "Tsunami Vertical-Evacuation Planning."

24. Kathryn Schulz, "Oregon's Tsunami Risk: Between the Devil and the Deep Blue Sea," *New Yorker,* July 1, 2019.

25. Reconstruction Agency, "Reconstruction Efforts and Related Programs" [in Japanese], February 27, 2023, 67, https://www.reconstruction.go.jp/topics/main-cat1/sub-cat1-1/20230227_torikumitokannrenshoseido.pdf.

26. National Institute of Building Sciences, "Mitigation Saves: Mitigation Saves up to $13 per $1 Invested" (Washington, DC: National Institute of Building Sciences, 2020), 1, https://www.nibs.org/files/pdfs/ms_v4_overview.pdf.

27. Wescoat, "Gilbert Fowler White," 700.

28. Zeynep Tufekci, "3 Ways the Pandemic Has Made the World Better," *Atlantic,* March 18, 2021, https://www.theatlantic.com/health/archive/2021/03/three-ways-pandemic-has-bettered-world/618320/.

SELECTED BIBLIOGRAPHY

Abe Toshihiko. "Consensus Building Process of the Seawall Plan in the Inner Port Area in Kesen-numa." [In Japanese.] *Journal of JSCE* [Japan Society of Civil Engineers] 73, no. 1 (2017): 37–51.

Adger, Neil W. "Vulnerability." *Global Environmental Change* 16, no. 3 (2006): 268–81.

Adger, Neil W., Terry P. Hughes, Carl Folke, Stephen R. Carpenter, and Johan Rockström. "Social-Ecological Resilience to Coastal Disasters." *Science* 309, no. 5737 (2005): 1036–39.

Akimoto, Fukuo. "The Problems of Plan-Making: Reconstruction Plans After the Great East-Japan Earthquake." In Santiago-Fandiño, Satō, Maki, and Iuchi, *2011 Japan Earthquake,* 21–36.

Aldrich, Daniel P. *Black Wave.* Chicago: University of Chicago Press, 2019.

Aldrich, Daniel P. *Building Resilience: Social Capital in Post-Disaster Recovery.* Chicago: University of Chicago Press, 2012.

Aldrich, Daniel P. "Social, Not Physical, Infrastructure: The Critical Role of Civil Society after the 1923 Tokyo Earthquake." *Disasters* 36, no. 3 (2012): 398–419.

Ando Akira, Sasaki Yoshihiro, Akatani Ryuichi, and Miura Tsuyoshi. "A Historical Study on Tsunami Disaster Prevention of the Coastal Area in Iwate." [In Japanese.] *Journal of JSCE,* no. 639-IV-46 (2000): 1–11.

Ando, Masataka, Mizuho Ishida, Yoshinori Hayashi, and Chiharu Mizuki. "Interviews with Survivors of Tōhoku Earthquake Provide Insights into Fatality Rate." *Eos, Transactions, American Geophysical Union* 92, no. 46 (2011): 411–12.

Asada Makiko, Ochiai Chiho, and Kobayashi Masami. "Research on Activity of Community Disaster Management in Shirakawa Village, Gifu Prefecture: Community Patrol for Fire Prevention and Maintenance of Disaster Prevention Water Supply System." [In Japanese.] *Reports of the City Planning Institute of Japan,* no. 8 (May 2009): 42–45.

Auf der Heide, Erik. "Common Misconceptions about Disaster: Panic, the Disaster Syndrome, and Looting." In *The First 72 Hours,* edited by Margaret O'Leary. Lincoln, NE: iUniverse, 2004.

Azechi Kazuya. "Kuroshio Town Board of Education Initiatives." [In Japanese.] In *Proceedings of the Disaster Management Education Promotion Meeting 1,* 53–55. Maebashi: Gunma University Metropolitan Area Disaster Prevention Research Center, March 2015. https://www.katada-lab.jp/bousai/doc/a1-all.pdf.

Beck, Ulrich. *Risk Society: Towards a New Modernity.* London: Sage, 1992.

Blaikie, Piers, Terry Cannon, Ian Davis, and Ben Wisner. *At Risk: Natural Hazards, People's Vulnerability and Disasters.* New York: Routledge, 1994.

Boret, Sébastien Penmellen, and Akihiro Shibayama. "The Roles of Monuments for the Dead during the Aftermath of the Great East-Japan Earthquake." *International Journal of Disaster Risk Reduction* 29 (2018): 55–62.

Breen, John, and Mark Teeuwen. *A New History of Shinto.* Chichester: John Wiley & Sons, 2010.

Britton, Neil R. "National Planning and Response: National Systems." In *Handbook of Disaster Research,* edited by Havidán Rodríguez, Russell R. Dynes, and Enrico L. Quarantelli, 347–67. New York: Springer Science+Business Media, 2007.

Brown, Philip C. "Constructing Nature." In *Japan at Nature's Edge,* edited by Ian Jared Miller, Julia Adeney Thomas, and Brett L. Walker, 90–114. Honolulu: University of Hawai'i Press, 2013.

Bryant, Martin, and Penny Allan. "Open Space Innovation in Earthquake Affected Cities." In *Approaches to Disaster Management—Examining the Implications of Hazards, Emergencies and Disasters,* edited by John Tiefenbacher, 183–204. N.p.: IntechOpen, 2013.

CAO (Cabinet Office, Government of Japan). "1896 Meiji Sanriku Earthquake Tsunami." [In Japanese.] *Bōsai* 28 (July 2005): 18–19.

CAO. "Master Plan for the Development of Tokyo Bay Waterfront, Principal Extensive Bōsai Hubs." [In Japanese.] January 8, 2004. Modified August 2, 2004. https://www.bousai.go.jp/jishin/sonota/pdf/kihonkeikaku.pdf.

CAO. "1923 Great Kantō Earthquake—Overview and Characteristics on Fire Damage." [In Japanese.] *Bōsai* 40 (July 2007): 12–13.

CAO. "Overview of Disaster Relief Act." [In Japanese.] May 2023. https://www.bousai.go.jp/oyakudachi/pdf/kyuujo_a7.pdf.

CAO. "Protecting Our Hometown 1000 Years from Now—Inamura's Fire Returns to Japanese Textbook after 64 Years." [In Japanese.] *Bōsai* 62 (March 2011): 17.

CAO. "Report of the Expert Committee on the Lessons Learned from 1959 Typhoon Vera." [In Japanese.] March 2008. https://www.bousai.go.jp/kyoiku/kyokun/kyoukunnokeishou/rep/1959_isewan_typhoon/index.html.

CAO. "Report of the Expert Committee on the Lessons Learned from the 1923 Great Kanto Earthquake." [In Japanese.] July 2006 (first section); March 2008 (second and third sections). https://www.bousai.go.jp/kyoiku/kyokun/kyoukunnokeishou/rep/1923_kanto_daishinsai/index.html; https://www.bousai.go.jp/kyoiku/kyokun/kyoukunnokeishou/rep/1923_kanto_daishinsai_2/index.html; https://www.bousai.go.jp/kyoiku/kyokun/kyoukunnokeishou/rep/1923_kanto_daishinsai_3/index.html.

CAO. "Report of the Expert Committee on the Lessons Learned from the 1948 Fukui Earthquake." [In Japanese.] March 2011. https://www.bousai.go.jp/kyoiku/kyokun/kyoukunnokeishou/rep/1948_fukui_jishin/index.html.

CAO. "Special Edition: Tsunami Awareness Day." [In Japanese.] *Bōsai* 76 (Autumn 2014): 4–7.

Chiba Nozomi. "What Temples Could Do in the Aftermath of a Major Disaster—The Actions and Attempts of Temples that Became Shelters." [In Japanese.] *Modern Religion,* 2017, 221–36.

Chiba, Yohei, Rajib Shaw, and Michiko Banba. "Japan's Experiences of Catastrophic Mountain Disasters in Wakayama." In *Land Use Management in Disaster Risk Reduction,* edited by Michiko Banba and Rajib Shaw, 215–36. Tokyo: Springer, 2016.

Coaffee, Jon, and Peter Lee. *Urban Resilience: Planning for Risk, Crisis and Uncertainty.* London: Palgrave, 2016.

Comerio, Mary C. *Disaster Hits Home: New Policy and Urban Housing Recovery.* Berkeley: University of California Press, 1998.

Cuny, Frederick C. *Disasters and Development.* New York: Oxford University Press, 1983.

Cutter, Susan L., et al. "Disaster Resilience: A National Imperative." *Environment: Science and Policy for Sustainable Development* 55, no. 2 (2013): 25–29.

Cutter, Susan L., Bryan Boruff, and W. Lynn Shirley. "Social Vulnerability to Environmental Hazards." *Social Science Quarterly* 84, no. 2 (June 2003): 242–60.

Davoudi, Simin. "Resilience: A Bridging Concept or a Dead End?" *Planning Theory & Practice* 13, no. 2 (2012): 299–307.

Dimmer, Christian. "Place-Making before and after 3.11: The Emergence of Social Design in Post-Disaster, Post-Growth Japan." *Review of Japanese Culture and Society* 28 (2016): 198–226.

Doi Kohei. "Projects in Reconstruction Machizukuri." [In Japanese.] In *Hyogo Prefecture: 10 Years of Reconstruction Reviews and Proposals,* 10–62. March 2005. https://web.pref.hyogo.lg.jp/kk41/documents/000039315.pdf.

Drabek, Thomas E. *Disaster Evacuation Behavior: Tourists and Other Transients.* Boulder: University of Colorado, Institute of Behavioral Science, 1996.

Dynes, Russell R. "Community Emergency Planning: False Assumptions and Inappropriate Analogies." *International Journal of Mass Emergencies and Disasters* 12, no. 2 (August 1994): 141–58.

Edgington, David W. *Reconstructing Kobe: The Geography of Crisis and Opportunity.* Vancouver: UBC Press, 2011.

Emanuel, Kerry. *What We Know about Climate Change.* Cambridge, MA: MIT Press, 2018.

Endo Kenya and Mazereeuw Miho. "Historical Study on Geographical Features of Shrines in the Town of Minamisanriku, Miyagi Prefecture." [In Japanese.] *Journal of the Japanese Institute of Landscape Architecture* 78, no. 5 (2015): 693–96.

Esteban, Miguel, Vana Tsimopoulou, Tomoya Shibayama, Takahito Mikami, and Koichiro Ohira. "Analysis of Tsunami Culture in Countries Affected by Recent Tsunamis." *Procedia Environmental Sciences* 17 (2013): 693–702.

Evans, Neil. "Machi-zukuri as a New Paradigm in Japanese Urban Planning: Reality or Myth?" *Japan Forum* 14, no. 3 (2002): 443–64.

Flüchter, Winfried. "Tokyo before the Next Earthquake: Agglomeration-Related Risks, Town Planning and Disaster Prevention." *Town Planning Review* 74, no. 2 (2003): 213–38.

Fraser, Andrew. "Local Administration: The Example of Awa-Tokushima." In *Japan in Transition: From Tokugawa to Meiji,* edited by Marius B. Jansen and Gilbert Rozman, 111–30. Princeton, NJ: Princeton University Press, 2014.

Frost, Lionel E., and Eric L. Jones. "The Fire Gap and the Greater Durability of Nineteenth Century Cities." *Planning Perspective* 4, no. 3 (1989): 333–47.

Fuji Clean Company. "Awareness of Flood Disaster Management Born out of Life in Wajū." [In Japanese.] *Mizu no Hanashi* 177 (October 1, 2012): 2–8.

Fujita Naoko and Kumagai Yoichi. "Comparative Study between Distributions of Shrine, Temple and Park in Urban Areas Analyzed by GIS." [In Japanese.] *Journal of Japan Association for Landscape Ecology* 12, no. 1 (2007): 9–21.

Goda Junichi. "Construction of Temporary Emergency Housing in Times of Disasters by JPA." [In Japanese.] *Urban Housing Sciences* 98 (Summer 2017): 21–27.

Good, Megan. "Shaping Japan's Disaster Heritage." In *Reconsidering Cultural Heritage in East Asia,* edited by Akira Matsuda and Luisa Elena Mengoni, 139–61. London: Ubiquity Press, 2016.

Government of Japan. *National Report of Japan on Disaster Reduction for the World Conference on Disaster Reduction.* Geneva: International Strategy for Disaster Reduction, 2005.

Gusman, Aditya Riadi, and Yuichiro Tanioka. "Effectiveness of Real-Time Near-Field Tsunami Inundation Forecasts for Tsunami Evacuation in Kushiro City, Hokkaido, Japan." In *Post-Tsunami Hazard,* edited by V. Santiago-Fandiño, Y. A. Kontar, and Y. Kaneda, 157–77. Cham: Springer, 2015.

Hagihara Yoshimi, Hatayama Michinori, and Okada Yusuke. "Historical Transition of the Waterside, Influence on Urban Disaster Prevention in Kyoto City." [In Japanese.] *Annals of the Disaster Prevention Research Institute, Kyoto University,* no. 47 B (2004): 1–14.

Hara Yasuyuki, Ono Ryohei, Ito Hiromu, and Shimomura Akio. "Historic Consideration about Positioning of Scenic Zone before WWII." [In Japanese.] *Journal of the Japanese Institute of Landscape Architecture* 69, no. 5 (2006): 813–16.

Harada, Kenji, and Fumihiko Imamura. "Effects of Coastal Forest on Tsunami Hazard Mitigation—a Preliminary Investigation." In *Tsunamis,* 279–92. Dordrecht: Springer, 2005.

Hashiguchi, Yumi, Rika Hirabayashi, and Motoya Yamazaki. "High-Standard Levee from the Viewpoint of City Planning." *Reports of the City Planning Institute of Japan,* no. 7 (February 2009): 73–76.

Hashimoto Fumitaka, Uchida Seizo, Otsuki Toshio, and Kanehira Yuki. *Disappearing Dōjunkai Apartment.* [In Japanese.] Tokyo: Kawadeshobōshinsha, 2003.

Hatakeyama Shigeatsu. *The Forest Is Longing for the Sea, the Sea Is Longing for the Forest.* [In Japanese.] Tokyo: Bunshun Bunko, 2006.

Hatori Tatsuya. "From Evacuation Maps to Platforms for Machizukuri: The Potential of NIGECHIZU." [In Japanese.] *Kenchikuzasshi* 127, no. 1638 (2012): 2–3.

Hayashi Hironori. "Efforts for Small Nature Restoration in Kamisaigō River." [In Japanese.] *RIVER FRONT* 80 (March 2015): 2–5.

Hayashi Hironori. "River-Making at Kamisaigō River." [In Japanese.] *Public Research Institute* (2017): 1–5. https://www.pwri.go.jp/team/kyousei/jpn/events/link/03_hayashi2017.pdf.

Healey, Patsy. "Developing Neighbourhood Management Capacity in Kobe, Japan: Interactions between Civil Society and Formal Planning Institutions." *Case Study Prepared for the Global Report on Human Settlements* (2009). https://staging.unhabitat.org/downloads/docs/GRHS2009CaseStudyChapter04Kobe.pdf.

Hirakawa Takehiko. "Reading the Guidelines for the Development of Burakumin Associations and Neighborhood Associations (Ministry of Home Affairs Instruction No. 17, September 11, 1940)—Understanding the Negative Legacy of Local Communities." [In Japanese.] *Niigata Seirryō Gakkaishi* 3, no. 2 (2011): 11–15.

Hirayama, Yōsuke. "Collapse and Reconstruction: Housing Recovery Policy in Kobe after the Hanshin Great Earthquake." *Housing Studies* 15, no. 1 (2000): 111–28.

Hirayama Yōsuke. "From Hanshin-Awaji to Tohoku—Rebuilding Homes." [In Japanese.] *Toshijūtakugaku* 88 (Winter 2015): 9–13.

Hirohara Kouichi. "Efforts to Rebuild Housing after the Great East-Japan Earthquake." [In Japanese.] *Rippō to Chōsa,* no. 341 (June 2013): 51–60.

Holling, Crawford Stanley. "Engineering Resilience Versus Ecological Resilience." In *Engineering within Ecological Constraints,* edited by P. C. Schulze, 31–44. Washington, DC: National Academies Press, 1996.

Homma, Masato. "Development of the Japanese National Disaster Medical System and Experiences during the Great East-Japan Earthquake." *Yonago Acta Medica* 58, no. 2 (2015): 53–61.

Horie Koh. "Historical Research of Arterial Road Planning and Implementation in Tokyo by Rear-rangement Ordinance (Meiji Era)." [In Japanese.] *Journal of JSCE,* no. 327 (November 11, 1982): 115–27.

Hoshi Takashi, Akagawa Toshiya, and Kanai Hiroki. "Situation of Compact City Formation by Earthquake Recovery Project in Yamamoto Town, Miyagi Prefecture." [In Japanese.] *Journal of Architecture and Planning* 84, no. 757 (2019): 611–19.

Hoshino, Masako. "Who Wants to Be a Volunteer." *Look Japan,* August 2000, 14–16.

Iinuma Jiro and Shirahata Yozaburo. *Parks as a Japanese Culture.* [In Japanese.] Tokyo: Yasaka Shobō, 1993.

Imai, Heide. *Tokyo Roji: The Diversity and Versatility of Alleys in a City in Transition.* New York: Routledge, 2018.

Imaizumi, Yoshiko. *Sacred Space in the Modern City: The Fractured Pasts of Meiji Shrine, 1912–1958.* Leiden: Brill, 2013.

Imamura, Fumihiko, and Anawat Suppasri. "Damage Due to the 2011 Tōhoku Earthquake Tsunami and Its Lessons for Future Mitigation." In *Proceedings of the International Symposium on Engineering Lessons Learned from the 2011 Great East-Japan Earthquake,* March 2012, 21–31.

Inaba, Keishin. "Religion's Response to the Earthquake and Tsunami in Northeastern Japan." *Proceedings of Osaka University Graduate School of Human Sciences* 42 (February 2016): 43–59.

Inaba Keishin and Kawabata Akira. "Survey Report on Disaster Cooperation between Municipalities and Religious Organizations." [In Japanese.] *Shūkyō to Shakai Kōken* 10, no. 1 (2020): 17–29.

Inamura Hajime. "Why Did the Small-Scale Isolated High-Rise Disaster Preparedness Relocation Plan Occur? An Analysis of the Policy Making Process." [In Japanese.] *Proceedings of Infrastructure Planning,* no. 50 (2014): 1–8.

IPCC (Intergovernmental Panel on Climate Change). *AR5 Climate Change 2014: Mitigation of Climate Change.* New York: Cambridge University Press, 2014.

Ishida Yorifusa. "Local Uniqueness and Decentralization in Japan's Urban Regional Policy." [In Japanese.] *Sōgō Toshi Kenkyū* 74 (2001): 23–45.

Ishikawa, Mikiko. "Landscape Planning for a Safe City." *Annals of Geophysics* 45, no. 6 (2002): 833–45.

Ito, Atsuko. "Earthquake Reconstruction Machizukuri and Citizen Participation." In *Living Cities in Japan,* edited by André Sorensen and Carolin Funck, 157–71. New York: Routledge, 2007.

Iuchi, Kanako, Elizabeth Maly, and Laurie Johnson. "Three Years after a Mega-Disaster: Recovery Policies, Programs and Implementation after the Great East-Japan Earthquake." In *Post-Tsunami Hazard,* edited by V. Santiago-Fandiño, Y. A. Kontar, and Y. Kaneda, 29–46. Cham: Springer, 2015.

Iuchi, Kanako, and Robert Olshansky. "Revisiting Tohoku's 5-Year Recovery: Community Rebuilding Policies, Programs and Implementation." In Santiago-Fandiño, Satō, Maki, and Iuchi, *2011 Japan Earthquake,* 29–46.

Jackson, Laura E. "The Relationship of Urban Design to Human Health and Condition." *Landscape and Urban Planning* 64, no. 4 (2003): 191–200.

Japanese Institute of Landscape Architecture. *Reconstruction Landscape—A Concept Book for Supporting Reconstruction through Landscape Revitalization.* [In Japanese.] Tokyo: Marumo, 2012.

Japan River Restoration Network. "Elementary School and College Students Join Forces to Restore the Environment of a River." [In Japanese.] *Case Studies of Small Nature Restoration in Waterfront Areas* (March 2015): 72–79. http://jp.a-rr.net/jp/activity/publication/files/2015/03/JRRNcollaboriver2015case13.pdf.

Jinnai, Hidenobu. *Tokyo: A Spatial Anthropology.* Translated by Kimiko Nakamura. Berkeley: University of California Press, 1995.

Johnson, Victoria A., Kevin R. Ronan, David M. Johnston, and Robin Peace. "Evaluations of Disaster Education Programs for Children: A Methodological Review." *International Journal of Disaster Risk Reduction* 9 (2014): 107–23.

Kaijima, Momoyo, Laurent Stalder, and Yu Iseki. *Architectural Ethnography.* Tokyo: TOTO, 2018.

Kako, Mayumi, and Sugako Ikeda. "Volunteer Experiences in Community Housing during the Great Hanshin-Awaji Earthquake, Japan." *Nursing & Health Sciences* 11, no. 4 (2009): 357–59.

Kanaya Nobuko. "Japan's Traditional Religion and Social Capital: A Case of Shinto Shrines." [In Japanese.] *Religion and Social Contribution* 3, no. 2 (2013): 1–25.

Kasetsu Shigaichi Kenkyūkai. *Recommendations! Temporary Urban District—Preparing for a Large Earthquake.* [In Japanese.] Kyoto: Gakugei Shuppansha, 2008.

Kashihara Shiro, Ueno Jun, and Morita Takao. *Research on Shelters during the Great Hanshin-Awaji Earthquake.* [In Japanese.] Osaka: Osaka University Press, 1998.

Kasperson, Roger E., et al. "The Social Amplification of Risk: A Conceptual Framework." *Risk Analysis* 8, no. 2 (1988): 177–87.

Katada Toshitaka. "Disaster Preparedness Behavioral Education: Lessons Learned from the Autonomous Behaviors of Students in Kamaishi City—Survivors of the Massive Tsunami." [In Japanese.] *Saigaijōhō,* no. 10 (2011): 37–42.

Kawada Masaru and Yanagida Yūzō. "The Relationship among Fires, Woods, and Trees." [In Japanese.] *JSCE Magazine* 10, no. 2 (1924): 403–24.

Kawakami Makiko and Nakabayashi Itsuki. "A Study on Nonprofessional Volunteer Activities for Supporting Reconstruction Machizukuri—A Case of Mikura 5 and 6 Districts in Nagata Ward of Kobe City." [In Japanese.] *CPIJ Journal* 36 (2001): 397–402.

Kawasumi, Hiroshi. "Measures of Earthquake Danger and Expectancy of Maximum Intensity Throughout Japan as Inferred from the Seismic Activity in Historical Times." *Bulletin of the Earthquake Research Institute, University of Tokyo,* 1951, 469–82.

Kawata Yoshiaki. "Enriching Disaster Culture." [In Japanese.] *FESC Monthly* 463 (May 2020): 2–9.

Kayanoki Madoka and Ito Hirohisa. "Research on the Modern History of the Fireproof District and Communal Buildings after the Great Kanto Earthquake in Tokyo." [In Japanese.] *Journal of the City Planning Institute of Japan* 43, no. 2 (2008): 11–18.

Kikuchi Yoshihiro and Minami Masaaki. "Study on the Tsunami Evacuation Behavior of the School in the Great East-Japan Earthquake—A Case of the Elementary and Junior High School in the Iwate Coast." [In Japanese.] *Journal of the City Planning Institute of Japan* 49, no. 3 (2014): 333–38.

Kim Dowon and Okubo Takeyuki. "Research of Disaster Mitigating Abilities on the Horikawa River in Kyoto." [In Japanese.] *Disaster Mitigation for Urban Cultural Heritage* 8 (2014): 303–10.

Kinoshita Isami. "Promoting Intergenerational and Intercommunity Cooperation through the Creation of Escape Maps for Various Disasters." [In Japanese.] *Research Report for the Japan Science and Technology Agency* (2015): 53–55. https://www.jst.go.jp/ristex/pdf/anzenanshin/JST_1115080_14532671_2015_kinoshita_YR.pdf.

Kinoshita, Isami, and Helen Woolley. "Children's Play Environment after a Disaster: The Great East-Japan Earthquake." *Children* 2, no. 1 (2015): 39–62.

Kitahara Itoko. "Refugees from the Great Kanto Earthquake—from the Administrative Data." [In Japanese.] *Disaster Reconstruction Research,* no. 3 (2011): 141–65.

Klinenberg, Eric. *Palaces for the People.* New York: Broadway Books, 2018.

Kobayashi Ikuo. "Examination by the City Planner's View." [In Japanese.] *Journal of the Japanese Institute of Landscape Architecture* 68, no. 3 (2005): 216–20.

Kobayashi Ikuo. "Look Back at City Planner Mizutani Eisuke's Town Planning." [In Japanese.] *Ie to Machinami,* November 2018, 14–22.

Kobe Machizukuri Workshop Kenkyukai, ed. "Workshop Book—Kobe Machizukuri Participation Recipe." [In Japanese.] *SORA 2.* Kobe: Kobe Machizukuri Center, April 2005.

Kochi Prefecture. "To Survive: Prepare for the Nankai Trough Earthquake." [In Japanese.] December 2013. https://anzenkyouiku.mext.go.jp/todoufuken/data/39kochi/39-04/39-04-1.pdf.

Kodama, Satoshi. "Tsunami-Tendenko and Morality in Disasters." *Journal of Medical Ethics* 41 (2015): 361–63.

Kojima Ayano, Yamasaki Masafumi, and Kinugasa Satoshi. "A Study on the Façade Types of Fireproofing Traditional Houses (Nuriya-zukuri) and Their Distribution." [In Japanese.] *Historic Urban Disaster Management* 4 (July 2010): 1–4.

Kon, Wajiro. "Selected Writings on Design and Modernology." Translated by Izumi Kuroishi. *West 86th: A Journal of Decorative Arts, Design History, and Material Culture* 22, no. 2 (2015): 197.

Kondo Tamiyo. "The Utilization and Expected Role of the 'Relocation of Dangerous Buildings in the Near-Cliff Area Project' in Post–Great East-Japan Earthquake Recovery." [In Japanese.] *Journal of Architecture and Planning* 80, no. 715 (2015): 2043–49.

Koolhaas, Rem, Hans Ulrich Obrist, Kayoko Ota, et al. *Project Japan: Metabolism Talks. . . .* Cologne: Taschen, 2011.

Koshiyama Kenji. "The Spatial Distribution of Temporary Construction Housing Sites in the Damaged Area in the Great Hanshin-Awaji Earthquake." [In Japanese.] *Institute of Social Safety Science,* no. 31 (2017): 29–36.

Koshizawa Akira. *Reconstruction Planning: From the Great Fires of the Late Edo and Meiji Periods to the Great Hanshin-Awaji Earthquake.* [In Japanese.] Tokyo: Chuō Kōronsha, 2005.

Kryspin-Watson, Jolanta, Shoko Takemoto, Zuzana Stanton-Geddes, Kenya Endo, and Masatsugu Takamatsu. *Learning from Japan's Experience in Integrated Urban Flood Risk Management: A Series of Knowledge Notes.* Washington, DC: World Bank, 2020.

Kudō Mayumi. *Tsunami Picture Book—My Hometown.* [In Japanese.] Tokyo: Shiseisha, 2012.

Kumagai, Yoichi, Robert B. Gibson, and Pierre Filion. "Evaluating Long-Term Urban Resilience through an Examination of the History of Green Spaces in Tokyo." *Local Environment* 20, no. 9 (2015): 1018–39.

Kundzewicz, Zbigniew W., and Kuniyoshi Takeuchi. "Flood Protection and Management: Quo Vadimus?" *Hydrological Sciences Journal* 44, no. 3 (1999): 417–32.

Kuroishi, Izumi. "Urban Survey and Planning in Twentieth-Century Japan: Wajiro Kon's Modernology and Its Descendants." *Journal of Urban History* 42, no. 3 (2016): 557–81.

Kuwada Tajima. "Lessons Learned from Large Public Works Projects in the Recovery from the Great East-Japan Earthquake: Focusing on the Seawall Developing Projects." [In Japanese.] *Regional Economic Studies* 35 (2008): 11–30.

Latour, Bruno. "Why Has Critique Run out of Steam? From Matters of Fact to Matters of Concern." *Critical Inquiry* 30, no. 2 (2004): 225–48.

Lazarin, Michael. "Temporal Architecture: Poetic Dwelling in Japanese Buildings." *Footprint* 2 (2008): 97–112.

Leckie, Scott. *Still Waiting: Housing Rights Violations in a Land of Plenty; The Kobe Earthquake and Beyond.* Mexico City: Habitat International Coalition, 1996.

Li, Shuhua. "The Development of Disaster Prevention Green Space in China." *Landscape Architecture Frontiers* 2, no. 4 (2014): 44–52.

Lunghino, Brent, Adrian F. Santiago Tate, Jenny Suckale, Simone Marras, Francis X. Giraldo, Miho Mazereeuw, and Abdul Muari. "The Protective Benefits of Tsunami Mitigation Parks and Ramifications for Their Strategic Design." *Proceedings of the National Academy of Sciences of the United States of America* 117, no. 20 (2020): 10740–45.

Luo, Pingping, Yousuke Yamashiki, Kaoru Takara, Daniel Nover, and Bin He. "Assessment of Japanese and Chinese Flood Control Policies." *Annals of the Disaster Prevention Research Institute, Kyoto University,* no. 53 B (2010): 61–70.

Maeda Sae. "Historical Changes in School Building Standards." [In Japanese.] *School Crisis and Mental Care* 5 (2013): 18–27.

Maejima Yasuhiko. *Tokyo Park Historical Story.* [In Japanese.] Tokyo: Tokyo Metropolitan Park Association, 1989.

Maekawa Kazuhiko. "Disaster Medical Care Systems." In *Hyogo Prefectural Government Committee for Global Assessment of Earthquake Countermeasures 2.* Kobe: Disaster Management Division, Hyogo Prefectural Government, 2000.

Mägdefrau, Nadine. "Creating Urban Resilience Using Spatial Planning: The Case of Miyako City during the First Five Years after the Great East-Japan Earthquake." In Santiago-Fandiño, Satō, Maki, and Iuchi, *2011 Japan Earthquake,* 55–66.

Maki, Norio. "Long-Term Recovery from the 2011 Great East-Japan Earthquake and Tsunami Disaster." In *Post-Tsunami Hazard,* edited by V. Santiago-Fandiño, Y. A. Kontar, and Y. Kaneda, 1–13. Cham: Springer, 2015.

Maly, Elizabeth, and Yoshimitsu Shiozaki. "Towards a Policy that Supports People-Centered Housing Recovery—Learning from Housing Reconstruction after the Hanshin-Awaji Earthquake in Kobe, Japan." *International Journal of Disaster Risk Science* 3, no. 1 (2012): 56–65.

Masuda Shiro. "A Crucial Issue in Urban Autonomy." [In Japanese.] *Toshi Mondai* 43, no. 2 (1952): 49–59.

Matsubara Eiki. "Characteristics of Community Development Councils as Seen in the Machikyō Chart." [In Japanese.] *Toshi Seisaku* 147 (2012): 18–26.

Matsubara Hisashi. "The Problems and Features of Disaster Recovery Process in the Region Experienced Municipal Merger in Heisei: Case Study of Ogatsu Town in Ishinomaki City." [In Japanese.] *Shakaigaku Nenpō* 46 (2017): 57–67.

Matsuda, Naonori. "Japan's Traditional Houses: The Significance of Spatial Conceptions." In *Asia's Old Dwellings: Tradition, Resilience, and Change,* edited by Roland G. Knapp, 285–318. Oxford: Oxford University Press, 2003.

Matsuhara, Ichiro. "Care for Most Vulnerable to Disaster." In *Hyogo Prefectural Government Committee for Global Assessment of Earthquake Countermeasures 3.* 2000.

Matsushima, Yukiko, and Yue Shen. "The Study of the Transitions of Japanese Elementary School Playgrounds, since the Meiji-Era." *Journal of the Japanese Institute of Landscape Architecture* 66, no. 5 (2003): 427–32.

Matsuzaki Gen, Satō Tadayuki, Hada Yasunori, Nishihara Toshihito, and Meguro Kimiro. "Phase Free Concept and Its Expansion for Design." [In Japanese.] *Bulletin of JSSD,* 2018, 114–15.

McLaughlin, Levi. "What Have Religious Groups Done After 3.11? Part 1: A Brief Survey of Religious Mobilization after the Great East-Japan Earthquake Disasters." *Religion Compass* 7, no. 8 (2013): 294–308.

Meehl, Gerald A., Warren M. Washington, William D. Collins, Julie M. Arblaster, Aixue Hu, Lawrence E. Buja, Warren G. Strand, and Haiyan Teng. "How Much More Global Warming and Sea Level Rise?" *Science* 307, no. 5716 (2005): 1769–72.

Meguro Kimiro and Murao Osamu. *City and Bōsai*. [In Japanese.] Tokyo: Foundation for the Promotion of the Open University of Japan, 2008.

Meno Fumitake. "Actual Situations of the Housing Lease Program for Disaster Victims in Sendai City." [In Japanese.] *Journal of Architecture and Planning* 78, no. 689 (2013): 1589–96.

Mileti, Dennis. *Disasters by Design: A Reassessment of Natural Hazards in the United States.* Washington, DC: Joseph Henry Press, 1999.

Minai Namiko. "Role of the Shrines in Villages: As Evacuation Sites from Tsunami Disaster of the 2011 Earthquake in Japan." [In Japanese.] *Architectural Institute of Japan, Summaries of Technical Papers of Annual Meeting* E–2 (September 2012): 103–4.

Ministry of Construction, City Bureau. *Urban Disaster Management Handbook: Earthquake Edition.* [In Japanese.] Tokyo: Gyōsei, 1997.

Minomo Toshitaro, Takanashi Masaaki, and Goto Kazuo. "Current Situation and Future of the City Park Governance." [In Japanese.] *Landscape Magazine* 53, no. 4 (1990): 178–83.

Miura Fumio. "Temporary Housing Policies, Great Hanshin-Awaji Earthquake." In *Hyogo Prefectural Government Committee for Global Assessment of Earthquake Countermeasures 2,* 53–61. Kobe: Disaster Management Division, Hyogo Prefectural Government, 2000.

Miyasada Akira. "Livelihood Rehabilitation in City Reconstruction Planning in a Stricken Area." [In Japanese.] In *Proceedings of the 12th Symposium on Urban Flooding Disaster,* November 2013, 1–3.

Mizutani Takeshi. "Impacts of the Typhoon Vera Disaster and Secular Changes in a Postwar Typhoon Disaster." [In Japanese.] *Bōsai Kagaku Gijutsu Kenkyūjo Kenkyū Hōkoku* 75 (September 2009): 11–32.

Mori Suguru. "Exploring the Possibility of Collective Relocation to Higher Ground as Prevention— Uchiura-Omosu District, Numazu City." [In Japanese.] *Shintoshi* 67, no. 1 (2013): 1–5.

Morrish, William R. "After the Storm: Rebuilding Cities upon Reflexive Infrastructure." *Social Research: An International Quarterly* 75, no. 3 (2008): 993–1014.

Morrow, Betty Hearn. "Identifying and Mapping Community Vulnerability." *Disasters* 23, no. 1 (1999): 1–18.

Motoki, Fujisaki, Joseph Thomas Reyes, and Saikaku Toyokawa. "A Study on the Slum Clearance Redevelopment Project and the Community Design Project for Disaster in Koto-Delta." *International Planning History Society Proceedings* 18, no. 1 (2018): 825–33.

Mouri Yoshizō. "Machizukuri Is Building a Nation: Residents Are the Protagonists, Let's Build a City of Residents." [In Japanese.] *Jūmin Katsudō* 41 (1984): 32–35.

Murakami Akinobu. "Why Doesn't Urban Planning Start from Considering the Relationship between Human and Nature?" [In Japanese.] In *Heated Lecture: Is Urban Planning Necessary for the Future of Japan?,* 194–211. Kyoto: Gakugei, 2014.

Murakami, Hiromi, Koichi Takimoto, and Antonios Pomonis. "Tsunami Evacuation Process and Human Loss Distribution in the 2011 Great East Japan Earthquake—A Case Study of Natori City, Miyagi Prefecture." In *Proceedings of the 15th World Conference on Earthquake Engineering, Lisbon, Portugal, 2012,* 1–10. https://www.iitk.ac.in/nicee/wcee/article/WCEE2012_1587.pdf.

Murakami Ryo and Ieda Hitoshi. "The Area Cases of Efforts and Challenges: 'Pre-disaster Planning for Post-disaster Recovery' in the Tsunami-Prone Area along the Nankai Trough." [In Japanese.] *Journal of the City Planning Institute of Japan* 53, no. 3 (2018): 889–96.

Murakami, Suminao. "Ready or Not: How Prepared Is Japan for the Next Major Quake?" *Look Japan,* February 1996, 32.

Murakami, Suminao. "Support for Home Reconstruction." *Hyogo Prefectural Government Committee for Global Assessment of Earthquake Countermeasures 4.* Kobe: Disaster Management Division, Hyogo Prefectural Government, 2000.

Muramatsu Hirohisa, Ando Akira, Igarashi Hideo, and Aakatani Ryuichi. "The Construction of Tsunami Control Embankments and the Enlargement of an Urban Area—In the Case of Tarō Town Located on Sanriku Coast at Iwate Prefecture." [In Japanese.] *Dobokushikenkyū* 11 (1991): 85–94.

Murao Osamu. *Architecture, Space, Disaster.* [In Japanese.] Tokyo: Corona Publishing, 2013.

Murao, Osamu. "Case Study of Architecture and Urban Design on the Disaster Life Cycle in Japan." *Proceedings of the 14th World Conference on Earthquake Engineering,* 2008, 1.

Murao, Osamu. "Regional Comparison of Temporary Housing Construction Processes after the 2011 Great East-Japan Earthquake and Tsunami." In *Tōhoku Recovery,* 37–50. Tokyo: Springer, 2015.

Murao Osamu and Isoyama Sei. "Transition of Housing Location in Tsunami-Prone Coasts in Iwate Prefecture—A Case Study of Damaged Areas Due to the Sanriku Tsunamis in 1896 and 1933." [In Japanese.] *Journal of Architecture and Planning* 77, no. 671 (2012): 57–65.

Murao Osamu and Kitazawa Gaku. "Verification of the Shirahige East Area Disaster Prevention Base Redevelopment Project Considering Changes in Surrounding Urban Environment." [In Japanese.] *Journal of the City Planning Institute of Japan* 57, no. 3 (2022): 964–71.

Murosaki Yoshiteru. "Encouragement on Neighborhood Disaster Preparedness." [In Japanese.] *Chiiki Bōsai,* 2015, 6–7.

Nagamatsu, Shingo. "Building Back a Better Tōhoku after the March 2011 Tsunami: Contradicting Evidence." In Santiago-Fandiño, Satō, Maki, and Iuchi, *2011 Japan Earthquake,* 37–54.

Nakajima Shin. "Elementary Schools and Parks in Imperial Reconstruction Project." [In Japanese.] *Journal of Architecture and Building Science* 131, no. 1683 (April 2016): 58–59.

Nakamura Hachirō. "Neighborhood Associations in Prewar Tokyo." [In Japanese.] In *Human and Social Development Research Japanese Experience.* HSDRJE-3J / UN University Press-23. Tokyo: UN University Press, 1979. https://d-arch.ide.go.jp/je_archive/pdf/workingpaper/unu_jpn3.pdf.

Nakamuta Tadaaki, Yamamoto Shuichi, and Urabe Shohei. "Ground Raising Construction for Residential Development in Rikuzentakata City Center." [In Japanese.] *Concrete Engineering Journal* 53, no. 1 (2014): 32–36.

Nakaseko, Tsugio, Fumiaki Kimata, Shigeyoshi Tanaka, and Makoto Takahashi. "Tsunami Warning and Evacuation System in Nishiki of Central Japan." *Proceedings of International Conference on Tsunami Warning, Bali, Indonesia* (2008): 1–6.

Nakayama Hisanori. *Disaster Reconstruction Project in Kobe: 2 Step City Planning and Machizukuri Proposal.* [In Japanese.] Kyoto: Gakugei Shuppan, 2011.

Nakayama Hisanori. "Earthquake Reconstruction Projects and the Kobe City Machizukuri Ordinance." [In Japanese.] *Toshi Seisaku* 147 (December 2012): 27–34.

Nakayama Hisanori. "The Implementation Process and Evaluation of the 'Two-Stage City Planning' Policy under Weak Disaster Legislation of Crisis Management Philosophy." [In Japanese.] *Kobe Gakuin Journal of Contemporary Social Studies* 2 (2016): 46–60.

Nateghi, Roshanak, Jeremy D. Bricker, Seth D. Guikema, and Akane Bessho. "Statistical Analysis of the Effectiveness of Seawalls and Coastal Forests in Mitigating Tsunami Impacts in Iwate and Miyagi Prefectures." *PLoS ONE,* August 10, 2016. https://journals.plos.org/plosone/article?id=10.1371/journal.pone.0158375.

Nelson, Donald R., W. Neil Adger, and Katrina Brown. "Adaptation to Environmental Change: Contributions of a Resilience Framework." *Annual Review of Environment and Resources* 32 (2007): 394–419.

Nguyen, David N., Fumihiko Imamura, and Kanako Iuchi. "Barriers towards Hotel Disaster Preparedness: Case Studies of Post 2011 Tsunami, Japan." *International Journal of Disaster Risk Reduction* 28 (2018): 585–94.

Nguyen, David N., Fumihiko Imamura, and Kanako Iuchi. "Public-Private Collaboration for Disaster Risk Management: A Case Study of Hotels in Matsushima, Japan." *Tourism Management* 61 (2017): 129–40.

Nishi, Kazuo, and Kazuo Hozumi. *What Is Japanese Architecture? A Survey of Traditional Japanese Architecture.* Translated by H. Mack Horton. Tokyo: Kodansha International, 1985.

Nishino Tomoaki, Himoto Keisuke, and Tanaka Takeyoshi. "Modeling of Destination Choice for Evacuation by Residents in a Post-Earthquake Fire Event." [In Japanese.] *Journal of Environmental Engineering* 76, no. 663 (2011): 469–77.

Nitschke, Günter. "Architecture and Aesthetic of an Island People." In *In Detail: Japan—Architects, Constructions, Ambiance,* edited by Christian Schittich, 15–55. Basel: Birkhauser, 2002.

O'Connor, Charles James, Francis H. McLean, Helen Swett Artieda, James Marvin Motley, Jessica Peixotto, and Mary Roberts Coolidge, comps. *San Francisco Relief Survey: The Organization and Methods of Relief Used after the Earthquake and Fire of April 18, 1906.* New York: Survey Associates, 1913.

Ohashi Yuji. "The Process of the Formation of the Structural Calculation Code of the Building Standards Law, Loads Combination, Sustained and Temporary Concepts." [In Japanese.] *Journal of Structural and Construction Engineering* 424 (June 1991): 1–10.

Oikawa, Yukihiko. "City Level Response: Linking ESD and DRR in Kesennuma." In *Education for Sustainable Development and Disaster Risk Reduction,* edited by Rajib Shaw and Yukihiko Oikawa, 155–76. Tokyo: Springer, 2014.

Okada Tadao, Arita Tomokazu, and Omura Kenjiro. "A Study on Public Contribution in Urban Development through Public-Private-Partnership—A Case Study of an Urban Development Project in the Marunouchi Area." [In Japanese.] *Journal of the City Planning Institute of Japan* 45, no. 3 (2010): 319–24.

Okamura Kentaro. "A Comparative Study of Disaster Reconstruction Policies of the Meiji Sanriku Tsunami and Showa Sanriku Tsunami." [In Japanese.] *Rekishi Jishin* 31 (2016): 125–38.

Okazaki, Kenji, and Krishna S. Pribadi. "Resilient Homes Make Cities Resilient." In *Urban Disasters and Resilience in Asia,* edited by Rajib Shaw, Atta-Ur-Rahman, Akhilesh Surjan, and Gulsan Parvin, 49–68. Oxford: Butterworth-Heinemann, 2016.

O'Keefe, Phil, Ken Westgate, and Ben Wisner. "Taking the Naturalness out of Natural Disasters." *Nature* 260 (1976): 566–67.

Okubo, Takeyuki. "Temples and Shrines as Temporary Shelters that Support Evacuees." In *Tōhoku Recovery,* edited by Rajib Shaw, 65–78. Tokyo: Springer, 2015.

Olshansky, Robert B., Laurie A. Johnson, Kenneth C. Topping, Yoshiteru Murosaki, Kazuyoshi Ohnishi, Hisako Koura, and Ikuo Kobayashi. *Opportunity in Chaos: Rebuilding after the 1994 Northridge and 1995 Kobe Earthquakes.* Urbana: Department of Urban and Regional Planning, University of Illinois at Urbana-Champaign, 2005.

Onoda, Yasuaki, Haruka Tsukuda, and Sachi Suzuki. "Complexities and Difficulties behind the Implementation of Reconstruction Plans after the Great East-Japan Earthquake and Tsunami of March 2011." In Santiago-Fandiño, Satō, Maki, and Iuchi, *2011 Japan Earthquake,* 3–20.

Orff, Kate. *Toward an Urban Ecology.* New York: Monacelli Press, 2015.

Organization for Landscape and Urban Green Infrastructure. *Bōsaikōen Technical Handbook: Bōsaikōen and Facilities 2015—Bōsaikōen and Park Facilities that Can Be Activated During Disaster.* [In Japanese.] Tokyo: Environmental Communications, 2015.

Organization for Landscape and Urban Green Infrastructure. *Bōsaikōen Technical Handbook, 2nd Edition—Bōsaikōen for Safe and Reliable Community Building.* [In Japanese.] Tokyo: Kankyo Communications, 2005.

Otsuki, Toshio. "Community Design to Prevent Dying Alone in Super-Aged Japanese Cities." In *Creative Ageing Cities: Place Design with Older People in Asian Cities,* edited by Keng Hua Chong and Mihye Cho, 185–204. New York: Routledge, 2018.

Otsuki Toshio. "Dōjunkai's Combined Development and Disaster Recovery Housing." [In Japanese.] *Kansai University Re-Danchi Leaflet* 12 (March 2012): 1–4.

Ozerdem, Alpaslan, and Tim Jaco. *Disaster Management and Civil Society: Earthquake Relief in Japan, Turkey and India.* London: I. B. Tauris, 2005.

Parady, Giancarlos Troncoso, Bryan Tran, and Stuart Gilmour. "The Effect of Seawalls on Tsunami Evacuation Departure Time: A Case Study of the 2011 Great East-Japan Earthquake." In *Proceedings of Transportation Research Board 97th Annual Meeting,* 2018, 535–39.

Park, Suil, Shigeaki Takeda, Hiroyuki Kaga, and Noboru Masuda. "Study on Water and Greenery Networks in the 'Green Master Plan and Master Plan for Parks and Open Spaces' of Kobe City." *Urban and Regional Planning Review* 3 (2016): 203–21.

Pasha, Ghufran Ahmed, Norio Tanaka, Junji Yagisawa, and Fuadi Noor Achmad. "Tsunami Mitigation by Combination of Coastal Vegetation and a Backward-Facing Step." *Coastal Engineering Journal* 60, no. 1 (2018): 104–25.

Peek, Lori, David Abramson, Robin Cox, Alice Fothergill, and Jennifer Tobin. "Children and Disasters." In *Handbook of Disaster Research,* edited by Havidán Rodríguez, William Donner, and Joseph E. Trainor, 243–62. Cham: Springer, 2017.

Perry, Ronald W. "Incident Management Systems in Disaster Management." *Disaster Prevention and Management: An International Journal* 12, no. 5 (2003): 405–12.

Perry, Ronald W. "What Is a Disaster?" In *Handbook of Disaster Research,* edited by Havidán Rodríguez, Russell R. Dynes, and Enrico L. Quarantelli, 1–15. New York: Springer Science+Business Media, 2007.

Pescatore, Claudio, Radu Botezvan, Abe Luik, Cornelius Holtorf, and Peter C. Van Wyck. *Preservation of Records, Knowledge and Memory across Generations (RK and M): Markers-Reflections on Intergenerational Warnings in the Form of Japanese Tsunami Stones.* No. NEA-RWM-R–2014–4. Paris: Organisation for Economic Co-operation and Development, 2014.

Pollock, Naomi R. "Miki Disaster Management Park Beans Dome." *Architectural Record,* June 19, 2008.

Quarantelli, Enrico. *Sheltering and Housing after Major Community Disasters: Case Studies and General Observations.* Washington, DC: FEMA, 1982.

Ranghieri, Federica, and Mikio Ishiwatari, eds. *Learning from Megadisasters: Lessons from the Great East-Japan Earthquake.* Washington, DC: World Bank, 2014.

Reitherman, Robert. "Frank Lloyd Wright's Imperial Hotel: A Seismic Re-evaluation." In *Proceedings of the Seventh World Conference on Earthquake Engineering,* 1980, 145–52.

Ronan, Kevin R., Kylie Crellin, and David Johnston. "Correlates of Hazards Education for Youth: A Replication Study." *Natural Hazards* 53, no. 3 (2010): 503–26.

Rosen, Christine Meisner. *The Limits of Power: Great Fires and the Process of City Growth in America.* Cambridge: Cambridge University Press, 2003.

Roy, Ananya. "Urban Informality: Toward an Epistemology of Planning." *Journal of the American Planning Association* 71, no. 2 (2005): 147–58.

Rung, Ariane L., Stephanie T. Broyles, Andrew J. Mowen, Jeanette Gustat, and Melinda S. Sothern. "Escaping to and Being Active in Neighbourhood Parks: Park Use in a Post-disaster Setting." *Disasters* 35, no. 2 (2011): 383–403.

Saito Yohei and Tabata Sadatoshi. "A Study on the Fire-Preventing Functions of Open Space in the Urban Area of Edo." [In Japanese.] *Zōen Zasshi* 55, no. 5 (1992): 355–60.

Sakamoto Shintaro. *Urban Parks in Japan: A History of Their Development.* [In Japanese.] Edited by the Publication Committee of Japanese City Parks. Tokyo: Interaction, 2005.

Sanada Junko. "A Study on the Green Belt Ring Plan of the Tokyo Park System." [In Japanese.] *Toshikeikaku Ronbunshū* 38 (2003): 601–6.

Santiago-Fandiño, Vicente, Shinji Satō, Norio Maki, and Kanako Iuchi, eds. *The 2011 Japan Earthquake and Tsunami: Reconstruction and Restoration.* Cham: Springer, 2018.

SAREX Japan. "Problems with Leased Temporary Housing." [In Japanese.] *SAREX News,* no. 7 (May 31, 2016).

Sato Kenji. "Social Metamorphoses after the Great Kanto Earthquake." [In Japanese.] In *Historic Disasters and Cities—Focusing on Kyoto and Tokyo,* 85–87. Kyoto: Ritsumeikan University 21st Century COE Program, 2007.

Sato Shosuke, Hirakawa Yuta, Shirahata Katsumi, and Imamura Fumihiko. "Residents' Recognition of Tsunami Stones in Rikuzentakata City, Iwate Prefecture, before the Great East-Japan Earthquake." [In Japanese.] *Journal of Japan Society of Civil Engineers, Ocean Engineering* 73, no. 2 (2017): I_1537–I_1542.

Satoh, Shigeru. "Evolution and Methodology of Japanese Machizukuri for the Improvement of Living Environments." *Japan Architectural Review* 2, no. 2 (2019): 127–42.

Satoh Shigeru, Takamizawa Kunio, Ito Hirohisa, Ōtsuki Shigeo, and Mano Yōsuke. *Dōjunkai Apartment and Its Era.* [In Japanese.] Tokyo: Kashima Shuppankai, 1998.

Schencking, J. Charles. *The Great Kanto Earthquake and the Chimera of National Reconstruction in Japan.* New York: Columbia University Press, 2013.

Schipper, Lisa, and Mark Pelling. "Disaster Risk, Climate Change and International Development: Scope for, and Challenges to, Integration." *Disasters* 30, no. 1 (2006): 19–38.

Schulz, Evelyn. "Beyond Modernism." In *Future Living: Collective Housing in Japan,* edited by Claudia Hildner, 11–28. Basel: Birkhauser, 2014.

Scott, James C. *Seeing Like a State: How Certain Schemes to Improve the Human Condition Have Failed.* New Haven, CT: Yale University Press, 1998.

Seidensticker, Edward. *Low City, High City: Tokyo from Edo to the Earthquake, 1867–1923.* Middlesex: Penguin, 1985.

Seidensticker, Edward. *Tokyo Rising: The City since the Great Earthquake.* Cambridge, MA: Harvard University Press, 1991.

Seike Tsuyoshi, Yoshiba Haruka, and Kim Yongsun. "Research on Construction of Temporary Houses in Fukushima." [In Japanese.] *AIJ Journal of Technology and Design* 20, no. 45 (2014): 503–8.

Shatkin, Gavin. "The City and the Bottom Line: Urban Megaprojects and the Privatization of Planning in Southeast Asia." *Environment and Planning A* 40, no. 2 (2008): 383–401.

Shimamura Takeshi. "Post-disaster Reconstruction and Environmental Impact Assessment." [In Japanese.] *Japan Association for Real Estate Sciences* 26, no. 3 (2012): 58–64.

Shimizu Sadao and Tamamura Kunihiko. "Elderly People and the Great East-Japan Earthquake." [In Japanese.] *Bulletin of Nara University of Education* 62, no. 1 (2013): 59–70.

Shinkenchiku. "New Grammar of Collective Housing: Disaster Public Housing after the Great East-Japan Earthquake." [In Japanese.] August 2016.

Shiozaki Yoshimitsu. "Disaster Recovery with Emphasis on Housing and Community." [In Japanese.] *Toshimondai* 100, no. 12 (2009): 79–85.

Shirahata Yōzaburō. *History of Modern Urban Parks: A Genealogy of Europeanization.* [In Japanese.] Kyoto: Shibunkaku Shuppan, 1995.

Shuto Nobuo. "1933 Shōwa Sanriku Earthquake and Tsunami." [In Japanese.] In *Learning from the Di-*

saster History, edited by the Central Disaster Management Council, 49–57. Tokyo: Central Disaster Management Council, March 2011.

Shuto, Nobuo, and Koji Fujima. "A Short History of Tsunami Research and Countermeasures in Japan." *Proceedings of the Japan Academy,* ser. B, 85, no. 8 (2009): 267–75.

Singleton, John. *Economic and Natural Disasters since 1900: A Comparative History.* Cheltenham: Edward Elgar Publishing, 2016.

Smits, Gregory. *When the Earth Roars: Lessons from the History of Earthquakes in Japan.* Lanham, MD: Rowman & Littlefield, 2014.

Soja, Edward W. *Seeking Spatial Justice.* Minneapolis: University of Minnesota Press, 2010.

Soma Seiji. "Study on the Fire Tornado at the Former Site of the Army Clothing Depot." [In Japanese.] *Chigaku Zasshi* 84, no. 4 (1975): 12–25.

Sonoda Minoru, Takebayashi Seizō, and Tashiro Yoritaka. "Town-Festival, Market, and Community." [In Japanese.] *KikanYūkyū* 83 (October 2000).

Sorensen, André. "Changing Governance of Shared Spaces: Machizukuri as Institutional Innovation." In *Living Cities in Japan,* edited by André Sorensen and Carolin Funck, 56–90. New York: Routledge, 2007.

Sorensen, André. *The Making of Urban Japan: Cities and Planning from Edo to the Twenty-First Century.* New York: Routledge, 2002.

Spirn, Anne Whiston. "Restoring Mill Creek: Landscape Literacy, Environmental Justice and City Planning and Design." *Landscape Research* 30, no. 3 (2005): 395–413.

Spokane, Arnold, Yoko Mori, and Frank Martinez. "Housing Arrays Following Disasters: Social Vulnerability Considerations in Designing Transitional Communities." *Environment and Behavior* 45 (October 2013): 887–911.

Staempfli, Marianne B. "Reintroducing Adventure into Children's Outdoor Play Environments." *Environment and Behavior* 41, no. 2 (2009): 268–80.

Stein, Ross S., Shinji Toda, Tom Parsons, and Elliot Grunewald. "A New Probabilistic Seismic Hazard Assessment for Greater Tokyo." *Philosophical Transactions of the Royal Society of London A: Mathematical, Physical and Engineering Sciences* 364, no. 1845 (2006): 1965–88.

Strusińska-Correia, Agnieszka. "Tsunami Mitigation in Japan after the 2011 Tōhoku Tsunami." *International Journal of Disaster Risk Reduction* 22 (2017): 397–411.

Sue Yusuke. "Coordination of Reconstruction Machizukuri: Based on the Experience of Onagawa Reconstruction Machizukuri Coordination." [In Japanese.] *Chuo Fukken Consultants Technical Report* 48 (January 2018): 87–106.

Suganuma, Katsutoshi. "3-D Full-Scale Earthquake Testing Facility (E-Defense)." *Science & Technology Trends Quarterly Review,* no. 14 (January 2005): 83–91. https://core.ac.uk/download/pdf/236667252.pdf.

Sugito Katsuhiro. "Showa Sanriku Tsunami." [In Japanese.] In *Implications for the Reconstruction from the Great East-Japan Earthquake by Analyzing Past Reconstruction Cases: Toward the Reorganization of Agriculture and Fisheries and the Revitalization of Village Communities,* 115–26. Tokyo: PRIMAFF (Policy Research Institute, Ministry of Agriculture, Forestry and Fisheries), September 2012. https://dl.ndl.go.jp/view/download/digidepo_10199083_po_zirei.pdf?contentNo=1&alternativeNo=.

Suppasri, Anawat, Nobuo Shuto, Fumihiko Imamura, Shunichi Koshimura, Erick Mas, and Ahmet Cevdet Yalciner. "Lessons Learned from the 2011 Great East-Japan Tsunami: Performance of Tsunami Countermeasures, Coastal Buildings, and Tsunami Evacuation in Japan." *Pure and Applied Geophysics* 170, no. 6–8 (2013): 993–1018.

Suzuki Jun. "Learning from Past Disasters 22 — Great Kanto Earthquake on September 1, 1923, Part 1." [In Japanese.] *Bōsai* 51 (May 2009): 28–29.

Suzuki Takaya. *Michi-no-eki Roadside Station Consolidating Support.* [In Japanese.] Ishinomaki: Sanriku Kahoku Shimpōsha, 2014.

Takada Tomoki, Umetsu Kimio, and Kuwako Toshio. "A Study on the Deity and Spatial Arrangement of Shrines in Tsunami Disaster Caused by the Tohoku Earthquake." [In Japanese.] *Journal of JSCE* F6 68, no. 2 (2012): I_167–I_174.

Tanaka Mitsuru. "The Development of the Administration of the Park and Greenery Concerned with the Revival of the Disaster Areas in Kobe City." [In Japanese.] *Landscape Research* 60, no. 2 (1996): 138–40.

Taniguchi, Hiromi, and Gul Aldikacti Marshall. "Neighborhood Association Participation and Formal Volunteering in Japan." *Voluntas: International Journal of Voluntary and Nonprofit Organizations* 27, no. 2 (2016): 695–723.

Tatani Takahisa. "Urban Renewal in Rokkōmichieki-South District by the Recovery from the Hanshin-Awaji Earthquake Disaster." [In Japanese.] *Seisan to Gijutsu* 59, no. 4 (2007): 1–4.

Tatsuki Shigeo. "Natural Disaster and Resilience — Lessons Learned from the Experiences of the Great Hanshin-Awaji Earthquake and Great East-Japan Earthquake." [In Japanese.] *Chihogikaijin,* August 2016, 16–20.

Tatsumi Shinya. *Park Culture from Kobe: Parks in Hyogo Prefecture 1868–2000.* [In Japanese.] Tokyo: Brain Center, 2000.

Teshirogi Jun and Okamura Atsushi. "Evacuation by Vehicle to Urban Parks in Disasters, Based on the Situation of the Kumamoto Earthquakes." [In Japanese.] *Landscape Research* 11 (2018): 59–62.

Teuchi Akitoshi and Hara Sayuri. "Contemporary Significance of Temples as the Base of Residents' Activities: The Role of the Temples in Regional Reconstruction after the Great East-Japan Earthquake." [In Japanese.] *Meikei Social Education Research* 5 (2014): 2–17.

Tewari, Shilpi, and David Beynon. "Tokyo's Dōjunkai Experiment: Courtyard Apartment Blocks 1926–1932." *Planning Perspectives* 31, no. 3 (2016): 469–83.

Tierney, Kathleen. *The Social Roots of Risk: Producing Disasters, Promoting Resilience.* Stanford, CA: Stanford University Press, 2014.

Tierney, Kathleen, and James D. Goltz. "Emergency Response: Lessons Learned from the Kobe Earthquake." Disaster Research Center, University of Delaware, 1997. http://udspace.udel.edu/handle/19716/202.

Tierney, Kathleen, M. K. Lindell, and R. W. Perry. *Facing the Unexpected: Disaster Preparedness and Response in the United States.* Washington, DC: Joseph Henry Press, 2001.

Tingey, William R. "The Principal Elements of Machiya Design." In *Process Architecture 25, Japan: Climate, Space and Concept,* edited by Yagi Koji, 83–102. Tokyo: Process Architecture, 1981.

Tokuyama Akira. "Establishment and Operation of Shelters." [In Japanese.] In *The Great Hanshin-Awaji Earthquake International Comprehensive Verification Project Report 2.* Hyogo Prefectural Government, 2000.

Tokuyama Akira. "Examination Theme: New Disaster Education and School Disaster Management System." [In Japanese.] *Great Hanshin-Awaji Earthquake Forum,* 2010, 49–92.

Tomiyasu Ryosuke, Imoto Saori, Otsuki Toshio, Nishide Kazuhiro, Cho Sung-eun, Okamoto Kazuhiko, Koizumi Hideki, Goto Jun, and Kano Toru. "Proposal and Practice of 'Community-Care Temporary Housing.'" [In Japanese.] *Architectural Institute of Japan Journal of Technology and Design* 19, no. 42 (June 2013): 671–76. https://www.jstage.jst.go.jp/article/aijt/19/42/19_671/_pdf.

Tsuchiya Nobuyuki and Mitsuhashi Hisashi. "Interview with Residents Living along the River with a High Levee." [In Japanese.] *RIVER FRONT* 86 (February 2018): 26–30. http://www.rfc.or.jp/pdf/vol_86/p026.pdf.

Tsukahara Keiji. "Tokyo Skytree Town—Rainwater Harvesting, Inheriting Edo Culture, Sumida Ward's Inspiring Project." [In Japanese.] *Institute for Built Environment and Carbon Neutral for SDGs* 36, no. 2 (2015): 16–20.

Tsukuda Haruka, Ishii Satoshi, Yang Shuan, and Onoda Yasuaki. "Study on Co-assisted Housing Complex for Continuing the Autonomous Life of the Elderly—Case Study on the Co-assisted Housing Complex in the Affected Area from the Great East Japan Earthquake.'" [In Japanese.] *Jusoken Research Institute Research Papers—Practical Research Reports* 49 (2022): 249–59. https://www.jstage.jst.go.jp/article/jusokenronbunjisen/49/0/49_1914/_pdf.

Ubaura Michio. "Land Use Regulation and the Great East-Japan Earthquake." [In Japanese.] *Toshi-keikaku* 291 (2011): 62–65.

Ubaura Michio. "The Pre-reconstruction from the Perspective of the Great East-Japan Earthquake." [In Japanese.] *21st Century Hyogo* 22 (2017): 42–43.

Ubaura, Michio, and Sei Akiyama. "Planning Processes for Reconstruction with Citizen Participation after Large-Scale Disasters: A Case Study of Reconstruction Study Meetings in Miyako City after the Great East-Japan Earthquake." *Journal of Disaster Research* 11, no. 3 (2016): 486–95.

UNISDR (United Nations International Strategy for Disaster Reduction). *Hyogo Framework for Action 2005–2015: Building the Resilience of Nations and Communities to Disasters; Extract from the Final Report of the World Conference on Disaster Reduction (A/CONF.206/6)*. Geneva: UN/ISDR, 2007. https://www.unisdr.org/files/1037_hyogoframeworkforactionenglish.pdf.

UNU (United Nations University). *World Risk Report 2016*. Berlin: Bündnis Entwicklung Hilft, 2016. http://collections.unu.edu/eserv/UNU:5763/WorldRiskReport2016_small_meta.pdf.

URAJA (Urban Renewal Association of Japan). "Large-Scale Disaster Management Projects Based on the Master Plan for Disaster Preparedness Bases." [In Japanese.] *The 50th Anniversary Magazine of the Urban Redevelopment Law,* 2012, 30–35.

URAJA. "Rokkōmichi Station South, Shin Nagata Station South." [In Japanese.] *The 50th Anniversary Magazine of the Urban Redevelopment Law,* 2012, 88–89.

Vale, Lawrence J. "The Politics of Resilient Cities: Whose Resilience and Whose City?" *Building Research & Information* 42, no. 2 (2014): 191–201.

Velasco, Erik, Matthias Roth, Leslie Norford, and Luisa Molina. "Does Urban Vegetation Enhance Carbon Sequestration?" *Landscape and Urban Planning* 148 (2016): 99–107.

Velotti, Lucia, Joseph E. Trainor, Karen Engel, Manuel Torres, and Takumi Myamoto. "Beyond Vertical Evacuation: Research Considerations for a Comprehensive Vertical Protection Strategy." *International Journal of Mass Emergencies & Disasters* 31, no. 1 (2013): 60–77.

Walker, Bryce. *Earthquake (Planet Earth)*. Amsterdam: Time-Life Books, 1982.

Wallace, William A., and Frank De Balogh. "Decision Support Systems for Disaster Management." *Public Administration Review* 45 (1985): 134–46. https://doi.org/10.2307/3135008.

Watanabe, Shun-ichi J. "Toshi-keikaku vs Machizukuri: Emerging Paradigm of Civil Society in Japan, 1950–1980." In *Living Cities in Japan,* edited by André Sorensen and Carolin Funck, 39–55. New York: Routledge, 2007.

Watanabe Shun, Mikami Takahito, and Shibayama Tomoya. "Experimental Study on the Tsunami Attenuation Effect of Sadayama Canal." [In Japanese.] *Journal of Japan Society of Civil Engineers* 71, no. 2 (2015): I_301–I_306.

Weisenfeld, Gennifer. *Imaging Disaster: Tokyo and the Visual Culture of Japan's Great Earthquake of 1923.* Berkeley: University of California Press, 2012.

Wescoat, James L. Jr. "Gilbert Fowler White, 'Wisdom in Environmental Geography.'" *Geographical Review* 96, no. 4 (2006): 700–710.

Wescoat, James L. Jr., and Gilbert F. White. *Water for Life: Water Management and Environmental Policy.* Cambridge: Cambridge University Press, 2003.

White, Gilbert F. "Strategic Aspects of Urban Flood Plain Occupance." *Journal of the Hydraulics Division, Proceedings of the American Society of Civil Engineers* 86, no. 2 (1960): 89–102.

Wisner, Ben, Jean-Christophe Gaillard, and Ilan Kelman. "Framing Disaster: Theories and Stories Seeking to Understand Hazards, Vulnerability and Risk." In *Handbook of Hazards and Disaster Risk Reduction,* 18–33. New York: Routledge, 2012.

Wood, Nathan, Jeanne Jones, John Schelling, and Mathew Schmidtlein. "Tsunami Vertical-Evacuation Planning in the US Pacific Northwest as a Geospatial, Multi-Criteria Decision Problem." *International Journal of Disaster Risk Reduction* 9 (2014): 68–83.

Yamaguchi Yaichiro. *Tsunami and Villages.* [In Japanese.] Tokyo: Kōshunkaku Shobō, 1943.

Yamakoshi Rei, Nakai Norihiro, and Numata Mamiko. "Study on the Primary Schools Built after the Kanto-Great Earthquake Focusing on Their Function as an Evacuation Center." [In Japanese.] *Journal of the City Planning Institute of Japan* 49, no. 3 (2014): 531–36.

Yamashita Fumio. "Sanriku Coast, Taro—Declaration of a Tsunami Bōsai Town; History of Large Seawalls." [In Japanese.] *Rekishi Jishin* 19 (2003): 165–71.

Yamori Kazuya. "Disaster Culture." [In Japanese.] In *Applied Psychology Encyclopedia,* edited by Kazunari Okamura, 588–89. Tokyo: Maruzen, 2007.

Yarina, Lizzie. "Your Sea Wall Won't Save You." *Places Journal,* March 2018.

Yasuba Kouichiro. "A Study on the Concept of Planning and Design for Small Urban Parks during the Reconstruction Period after Great Kantō Earthquake." [In Japanese.] *Journal of the Japanese Institute of Landscape Architecture* 61, no. 5 (1998): 429–32.

Yasuda Chusaku. "Kobe's Regional Machizukuri and Machizukuri Ordinances: Their Place in Urban Policy." [In Japanese.] *Toshi Seisaku* 147 (2012): 4–17.

Yasuda Masahiko. *Japanese History in Disaster Reconstructions.* [In Japanese.] Tokyo: Yoshikawa Kōbunkan, 2013.

Yoshikawa Tadahiro. "Struggles in the Joint Housing Projects." [In Japanese.] In *Social Study in the Great Hanshin-Awaji Earthquake,* vol. 3, edited by Iwasaki Nobuhiko, Ukai Kozo, Urano Masaki, Tsuji Katsuji, Nitagai Kamon, Noda Takashi, and Yamamoto Takeo, 247–62. Kyoto: Shōwadō, 1999.

INDEX

Page numbers in italics refer to illustrations.

construction Fukushima, 107, 111, 113–14. *See also under* Iwate Prefecture: Miyako, Taro district

community-based typologies: shift toward engaging the public in, 52; *suibōdan* (citizen flood-management groups), 28. See also *machizukuri* (community-planning processes) movement; shōbōdan (citizen fire corps)

—, permanent housing: defined, 20; HAT Kobe Fureai Public Housing, 245–46; living access housing typology, 256, *257*, 395n117; as part of the disaster timeline, 261; post-earthquake permanent housing in Dōjunkai, 233, *234–35*, 236; protection of social ties in public housing, 255; Shobutahama Public Housing, 256, *257*, 258, 395n117; Tamaura-nishi public housing project, 258, *259*, 260. *See also* community-based typologies: temporary housing transformed into permanent housing

—, temporary housing: defined, 19–20; after the 1923 earthquake, 231–32; after the 1995 Kobe earthquake, 237, 240–42; housing barracks constructed in open spaces after the 1923 Tokyo earthquake, 231–32; housing complexes constructed for tsunami survivors in Ogatsu (2011), 136; *jiriki* (self-built/initiated) temporary housing, 150, 240; *minashikasetsu* (emergency rental housing), 251–52, 262; open spaces used for temporary housing in Chuo, 240; *osukui-goya* (rescue-sheds) during the Edo era, 229, *230*, 324; shopping complexes, 252–53; temporary social structures and housing assembled after the 1923 Tokyo earthquake, 225

—, temporary housing transformed into permanent housing: Aizu-Matsunaga Danchi transitional housing, 248–49; Haryū Wood Studio units, 249, 324; Itakura wooden panel system, 249–50, 261

—, temporary shelters: defined, 19; in the disaster response phase, 19; museums as, 221, 330; tatami mats and tatami rooms in, 231, 266, 270, 271, 276, 339

Comprehensive Urban Disaster Management Project, 311, 338

coping capacity: as addressed by Cuny and Aldrich, 14–15; bōsai planning, 91; collective housing projects, 229; community, 147; as it relates to disaster risk, 12; traditional home, 347

culture of preparedness: in Japan's history, 59–60;

Kuroshio's proactive stance in bōsai infra-structure, 335, 337–38, *340*, 344; recognition as integral to disaster-related plans across the globe, 1–2. *See also* bōsai education; *jishubō* (or *jishu-bōsai-soshiki,* neighborhood disaster-preparedness organizations); *machizukuri* (community-planning processes) movement; *michi-no-eki* (rest areas with a local produce market); stockpiles of emergency supplies

Cuny, Frederick C.: on building codes, 15, 364n22; on coping and adapting, 14; on disaster preparedness, 19

Cutter, Susan L.: community resilience defined by, 16; vulnerability defined by, 13

Davoudi, Simin, 16

De Balogh, Frank, and William A. Wallace, 364n32

De Urbanisten, 17

Disaster Countermeasures Act (1961): as the backbone of Japan's bōsai policy, 35, 48; bōsai machizukuri movement fostered in the context of earthquake reconstruction, 78; designation of AEON as a "lifeline" during a disaster, 320; en-actment following Typhoon Vera, *26*, 34; regular amending of, 345; revision in 2013 for developing signs based on the Hazard Specific Evacuation Guidance Sign System, 196; revision in 2013 including new article, 311; revisions following the 2011 earthquake, 44, 45, 47; revisions to issue evacuation orders rather than advisories, 49; September 1 established as National Bōsai Day, 33; support of *jishubō* made more official with the 1995 amendment, 39

disaster management laws and standards: Landslide Countermeasures Act (2011), *27*, 48; Livelihood Support Act (1998), 38, 141; national standards established by the JMA (1952), 26; New Seismic Design Act (1979), 281; Nonprofit Organization Law established (1998), 39; postwar era prolif-eration of, 34; Seismic Design Standards (1981), 310; Tsunami Bōsai Regional Development Law (2011), 44–45, 127–28, 311. *See also* Building Standards Law (1950); Disaster Countermea-sures Act (1961); Disaster Relief Act (1947); Great East Japan Earthquake Reconstruction Special Area Act (2011); Nankai Trough Earth-quake Disaster Management Act (2013)

Disaster Medical Assistance Team (DMAT), 38, 43

Bōsaikōen; parks; tsunami evacuation buildings (TEBs); tsunami evacuation towers (TETs)

Federal Emergency Management Agency's (FEMA): city parks used as sites for temporary housing during Hurricane Katrina, 217; culture of preparedness recognized by, 1; disaster cycle concept attributed to, 364n32; tsunami evacuation building constructed in Washington State, 322

Fire and Disaster Management Agency (FDMA): base camps in logistics hubs, 160; evacuation sign guidelines, 96; hub in the Imperial Park, 175

firefighting and fire prevention: bōsai living zones, *53, 63, 64,* 149, 157; education at Kamakura Central Park on planting trees, 209; fire and flood risk reduction projects in Sumida Ward, 68–69, *70–71,* 72–74, 76; Fireproofing and Greenbelt Plan (1943), 62; fire resistance managed as a collective project, 76; *furoshiki* water maps, *71, 74, 75; gasshō*-style houses protected in Shirakawa-gō, 66–67, *67;* Greening Kobe 21 Plan, 157; Higashiyama Fire Fighting Project in Kyoto, 65–66; *hinomiyagura* (fire lookout towers), 59, *60; hiyokechi* evacuation spaces, 59, 152, 154, 156, 229; *machibikeshi* (town firefighters), 28, *29,* 59; municipal firefighters established in Japan (1873), 61; during the 1923 Tokyo earthquake, 62; water collection for firefighters from the Horikawa River, 68, *69.* See also *shōbōdan* (citizen fire corps)

flood control and mitigation: climate change as a challenge to, 351–53; Fukakita Ryokuchi Park, 194, *195,* 196, 352; *hanami* (*sakura* viewing) associated with, 1, 21; modern flood controls introduced by Johannnis de Rijke, 2. *See also* Kamisaigō River project; *kawazukuri* (river-planning) method; *wajū* ("inside the circle")

"forest is the ocean's love": The Forest Is the Ocean's Love (nonprofit organization), 135; "*Mori wa umi no koibito*" (The forest is the ocean's love), made popular by Hatakeyama Shigeatsu, 115

Fukakita Ryokuchi Park, 194, *195,* 196, 352

Fukuoka: location in Fukuoka, *6. See also* Kamisaigō River project

Fukushima Prefecture: AEON Mall Iwaki Onahama, 321–22; Aizu-Matsunaga Danchi transitional housing, 248–49; impact of the 2011 Tohoku disaster on, 40, 45, 107, 283; Itakura

wooden panel system used in housing projects, 249–50, 261; JPA prefab housing in, 247; location of, *6;* Miharumachi wooden recovery housing, 248; PNV method followed in, 123; seawall construction in the Tohoku recovery, 107, 111, 113–14; temporary housing projects following the 2011 Tohoku disasters, 248

gasshō-style houses in Shirakawa-gō, 66–67, *67*

Gifu Prefecture: Palette Pier Ōno, 182, *183;* Shirakawa-gō, 66–67, *67;* Takasu Wajū, 2

Goryō, Hamaguchi, 29–30

Great East Japan Earthquake (2011). *See* 2011 Tohoku disaster

Great East Japan Earthquake Reconstruction Special Area Act (2011): damaged housing included, 131; methods for land readjustment projects specified to speed up recovery, 128; municipalities designated as Special Reconstruction Areas (2011), 33

Great Kanto Earthquake (September 1, 1923): Dōjunkai's recovery from, 232–33, *234–35,* 236; evacuation of victims, *31,* 32; firefighting during, 62; impact on the reconstruction of schools, 294, *297;* the Imperial Reconstruction Plan led by Gotō Shimpei (1924–30), *26,* 33, 55, 60–61, 77, 155; location of, *6;* loss of relationships and social environments during reconstruction, 230; magnitude of, 31, 60; National Bōsai Day established to commemorate, 33, 169; rebuilding of schools from reinforced concrete following, 280; role in reshaping Tokyo, 33; survival of the Marunouchi Building, 328; temporary housing barracks constructed in open spaces, 231–32; temporary social structures and housing assembled after, 225; Tokyo's Imperial Hotel during, 272, 274; violence against Koreans after, 350

greenbelt plans: European urban plans, 61; Fireproofing and Greenbelt Plan (1943), 62, 155; greenbelt buffer as apart of Sendai's layered defense system, 123–24; greenbelt evacuation path in the Tōbu district of Kamaishi, 99; in Japanese coastal regions, 131; in response to concerns about air defense during the Japan-China War (1930s), 61; Tokyo City Planning Green Space designated by the MLIT (1948), 62; Tokyo Green Space Plan (or Tokyo Circular Greenbelt Project) (1939), 61. *See also* coastal protection

Kobe earthquake (1995) (*continued*)
evacuation spaces, 156–57, 162; solitary deaths
in permanent housing in Kobe (2020), 255;
temporary housing challenges, 237, 240–42. *See
also* land readjustment (*tochi kukaku-seiri*) and
joint housing typologies in Kobe

Kochi Prefecture: emergency communication bells,
334, *336;* evacuation staircase for Suzaki city
hall, *309,* 314; Hakuhō Nankai earthquake and
tsunami (684), 25; innovation ideas of Susaki
Technical High School students, 343–44;
Kōkatsu Project, 334, *336;* location on Shikoku
Island, *6,* 334; Special Subsidy Program for
Accelerated Tsunami Evacuation Measures, 338;
tsunami evacuation strategies in, 334, *336. See also*
Kuroshio Town

Kon, Wajiro, 225

Kumamoto Earthquakes (2016): location, *6;* park
infrastructure examined following, 180–81

Kumamoto Prefecture: location of, *6*

Kuroshio Town: bōsai machizukuri hub in, 338;
global impact of their educational efforts, 343–
44; Kambayashi Akatsuki from, 339; location
of, *336;* Ōkata Akatsuki-Kan in Saga district of,
309, 339, *340;* proactive stance in bōsai infrastructure, 335, 337–38, *340,* 344; Saga District as
a tsunami-safe area, *336,* 338, *341;* Saga District
TET in, 338–39; Tosa Seinan Park Observation
Deck, *340,* 342; We Can Project, *340,* 342

Kyoto: Higashiyama Fire Fighting Project, 65–66;
Horikawa River, 67–68, *69;* Imperial Palace, *159,*
175, *176*

land readjustment (*tochi kukaku-seiri*): in the
City Planning Law (1919), 55; Cliff Relocation
Project, 129, 131; households asked to reduce
their lot sizes, 52, 54, 81; Kamisawa pocket parks
developed in tandem with, 198, *199;* Minamimachi Murasaki Market in Kesennuma, 253, *254;*
performed in the name of disaster mitigation,
55; Special Reconstruction Areas designated by
the Basic Policy for Reconstruction (2011), 44;
strategies introduced in the City Planning Law
and the Urban Building Law (1919), 30; subsidies
for rehabilitating damaged parks, 157. *See also*
Imperial Reconstruction Plan led by Gotō
Shimpei (1924–30)

land readjustment (*tochi kukaku-seiri*) and joint

housing typologies in Kobe: Bōsai Blocks Act
for Dense Urban Areas, 242–43; experiments
in collective *kyōdō tatekae,* 242, *244;* impact of
the Building Standards Law (1950) on, 80, 81,
242; Mikura 5 in Nagata Ward, 243–45, *244;*
Rokkōmichi Kaze-no-Sato bōsaikōen developed
as part of, 82, 200–201

Landslide Countermeasures Act (2011), *27,* 48

large-scale reconstruction projects: compact
city projects, 139–40, 299; fragmentation of
communities and loss of local culture, 252; guidelines of the Tokyo Metropolitan Earthquake
Countermeasures Ordinance of 2001, 149–50;
Matsumoto stream project, 84–85, *86–87,* 91,
148; out-migration and population decline
associated with, 149; project in Rikuzentakata,
128, 132–33, *134,* 135, 146, 149, 252; reframing as a
process informed by anticipatory design, 151

Latour, Bruno, 10

Lazarin, Michael, 324

logistics hubs: Fire and Disaster Management
Agency base camps in, 160; Higashi-ōgishima
Park, 161, 162, 163–64, *164;* location selection,
161; Sakai Senboku Port, *159,* 161, 165–66; SDF
base camps in, 160, 161, 162, 172; Tokyo Bay
national logistics hub, 162, 163; varying types
of, 158, *159,* 160. *See also* Miki Sōgō Bōsaikōen;
Tokyo Rinkai Park

machizukuri (community-planning processes)
movement: bōsai machizukuri facilitated by
the Disaster Countermeasures Act, 78; bōsai
machizukuri hub in Kuroshio, 338; challenges
faced as Japan ages and changes, 151; City
Planning Law Amendment for (1992), *27;*
collective housing in *mokumitsu* district
facilitated through, 65; future bōsai machizukuri,
210, *356;* impact of the 1995 Kobe earthquake on
its growth, 39; initiation as a common planning
process (1989), *27;* integration of the bottom-up
into larger planning processes, 57, 77–81, 91,
147; Kobe Machizukuri Ordinance (1981), *27,*
78, 79; *machizukuri* as a term, 56–57; Murasaki
Market machizukuri process, 253, *254;* Nonprofit
Organization Law established (1998), *27;* origins
of, 56; as a paradigm in community-led planning,
79, 91; in Rokkōmichi, 82–84, *83,* 201; Taro's
reconstruction planning compared with, 109

Nankai Trough plate subsequent to the Ansei-Tokai earthquake (1954), 310; location of, *6, 50*; preemptive action in anticipation of a disaster caused by, 142–44; projected tsunami height of an earthquake from, 119; TEBs and TETs in special disaster-preparedness areas of, 312

National Bōsai Day: annual drills focusing on response activities for residents, 33, 169; September 1 established to commemorate the 1923 Tokyo earthquake, 33

National Institute of Building Sciences, 355

Nelson, D., N. W. Adger, and K. Brown, 18

NIGECHIZU (evacuation map) workshops: description of, 101; national presentations of, 101–2

1923 Tokyo earthquake: Kiyosumi Garden used as an evacuation space, 155. *See also* Great Kanto Earthquake (September 1, 1923)

Okirai Elementary School: evacuation bridge, 104, 285; *karuta* game developed by sixth graders at, 285–86, *286*

Onishi Takashi, 44

Onoda, Yasuaki: criticism of planning by municipalities, 111–12; help in drafting public housing guidelines, 256

Orff, Kate, 17

Osaka Prefecture: Hattori Ryokuchi Park, *159,* 175, *177, 178–79,* 180, 183; Sakai Senboku National Bōsai Hub, *159,* 161, 165–66

Otsuka Joshi (Otsuka women's apartment building), *235, 236*

Otsuki Toshio, 251

Ozerdem, Alpaslan, and Tim Jaco, 39

parks: city parks used as sites for temporary housing during Hurricane Katrina, 217; as dual-function bōsai infrastructures, 197; in the 1888 Tokyo City Code, 154; Fukakita Ryokuchi Park, 194, *195,* 196, 352; Futakotamagawa Park in Setagaya Ward, 191, *192–93,* 194; Higashi-ōgishima Park, 161, 162, 163–64, *164;* Kaigan Kōen Bōken Hiroba (Coastal Park Adventure Plaza), *214,* 214–15; Kaze-no-Sato bōsaikōen, 200–201, *202;* Minatogawa Park, 184–85, *188,* 196; Motomachi Park, 155–56; Nakano-Shiki-no-Mori Park, 189–90, *190;* National Park Law (1931), 154; park infrastructure examined following the Kumamoto Earthquakes (2016), 180–81; parks

identified as safe in the Regional Disaster Management Plan, 220–21; parks used as evacuation spaces following the Kobe earthquake (1995), 156–57; Rokkōmichi North and South, 82–84, *83,* 201; role of park networks in disasters, *153,* 158–60, *159;* stockpiles of emergency supplies in designated Tokyo parks, 220; Suginami Dai-ju Elementary School paired with an evacuation park, *296–97;* Takata Matsubara Tsunami Reconstruction Park, 316, *317;* Urban Parks Law (1956), 156. *See also bōsaikōen* (disaster-prevention parks); Kaigan Kōen Bōken Hiroba (Coastal Park Adventure Plaza); Miki Sōgō Bōsaikōen; Millennium Hope Hills; Tokyo Rinkai Park

—, pocket: Kamisawa Pocket Parks, *159,* 198, *199,* 201; role in anticipatory design, *153, 159,* 160, 172, 197, 204–5, *356;* role of machizukuri groups in the planning of, 81; Shinagawa Pocket Park Network, *159,* 201–3, *204*

Peek, Lori, 306, 332

permanent housing. *See under* community-based typologies

phase free, 19

potential of natural vegetation (PNV), 121–23, 378n73

preemptive action: in anticipation of a disaster caused by the Nankai Trough plate, 142–44; Bōsai Collective Relocation Project, 142–44, 145; the Integrated Tsunami Bōsai Cluster, 337, *340;* pre-disaster agreements made at multiple levels, 237, 247, 260–61; Preemptive Group Relocation Planning in Misato, 143–44; relocation of public buildings in Kushimoto, 314; We Can Project, *340,* 342. *See also bōsaikōen* (disaster-prevention parks); stockpiles of emergency supplies

Reconstruction Design Council (2011), *27,* 44

reconstruction laws. *See* Basic Policy for Reconstruction (2011); Great East Japan Earthquake Reconstruction Special Area Act (2011)

Regional Disaster Management Plan: ad hoc parks not identified as evacuation sites in, 157; parks identified as safe in, 220–21

resilience: as a concept in landscape architecture, 16–17; coping capacity, 14–15, 24, 91, 147, 229, 345, 347, 349; Disaster-Resilient Machizukuri Council in Tokyo's Chiyoda Ward, 328; hybrid types of, 16. *See also* anticipatory design

pagodas constructed of wood, 223; *satoyama,* 191, 347, 351; traditional homes lifted off the ground, 347; *warichi,* 347. *See also* community-based typologies

Ubaura Michio, 113
Uchida Yoshikazu, 68, 233
Urban Architectural Design Group/UAPP Tamaura-nishi public housing project, 258, *259,* 260
Urban Renaissance: Kamisaigō River *kawazukuri* project aligned with their ongoing work, 211; management of the Bōsaikōen Block Development Project, 158; operation of Happy Active Town (HAT), 245; rezoning and land readjustment for a super levee in Edogawa Ward, 120
Urban Risk Lab. *See* MIT Urban Risk Lab

Vale, Lawrence J., 16
Venice Biennale: Ito Toyo, Home-for-All Community center at (2012), 225; Kajima Momoyo, "Architectural Ethnography" at (2018), 226
Vulnerability: as defined by Adger, Cutter and others, 13; disaster risk and, 12; machizukuri, 78; relationship between design and, 13–14, 351

wajū ("inside the circle"): anticipatory design exemplified by, 2; bōsai culture express in, 4–5; destruction during the Great Kii Peninsula flood (2011), 48; Edo era construction of, 2; Kuroshio

as a modern-day example of, 344; multiscalar strategies of, 2, *3,* 4; Takasu Wajū, 2
Wakatake Machizukuri Design Firm Include, 342
Wakayama Prefecture: evacuation tower of the Wakayama East Fishermen's Association, *309,* 314; Kushimoto Tower (floating unit), *309,* 315; relocation of public buildings in Kushimoto, 314
Wallace, William A., and Frank De Balogh, 364n32
Watsuji Tetsuro, 347
We Can Project Okay, *340, 342*
Weisenfeld, Gennifer, 33
Wescoat, James L., Jr., 351
White, Gilbert F., 13, 23, 124–25
windows. *See under* anticipatory design
Wisner, Ben, Jean-Christophe Gaillard, and Ilan Kelman, 12
World War II: air raids during, 34, 55, 156; evacuation and air defense green spaces, 156, 175; Fireproofing and Greenbelt Plan (1943) launched following, 62, 155; Kobe's neighborhoods spared during, 36, 80, 84, 197; machizukuri during, 56; rapid urbanization following, 351; relationships and social environments lost during reconstruction, 230; shortage of housing in the aftermath of, 236
Wright, Frank Lloyd: Imperial Hotel, Tokyo designed by, 272, *273,* 274

Yamamoto Toshiya laboratory NIGECHIZU workshop, 101
Yorifuji Bunpe, 40